PRESCRIPTION AND LIMITATION

AUSTRALIA
LBC Information Services
Sydney

CANADA and USA
Carswell
Toronto

NEW ZEALAND
Brooker's
Auckland

SINGAPORE and MALAYSIA
Thomson Information (S.E. Asia)
Singapore

PRESCRIPTION AND LIMITATION

by

David Johnston
Advocate

Published under the auspices of
SCOTTISH UNIVERSITIES LAW INSTITUTE LTD

EDINBURGH
W. GREEN
1999

First published 1999

Published in 1999 by W. Green & Son Limited
21 Alva Street
Edinburgh EH2 4PS

Computerset by LBJ Typesetting Ltd
of Kingsclere

Printed in Great Britain by
MPG Books Ltd, Bodmin, Cornwall

No natural forests were destroyed to make this product; only farmed
timber was used and replanted

A CIP catalogue record of this book is available from the British Library

ISBN 0 414 01315 8

For Sarah and Peter Milligan

Problems in prescription and limitation arise in virtually the whole of the law. As a result, while starting to write a book on prescription and limitation is bad enough, managing to stop is even harder. It is possible only by recognising that some areas must remain untreated and in those that are treated imperfections necessarily remain.

I have attempted to state the law as at March 1, 1999. The following are the main limits and limitations of the book, so far as I am aware of them. Nothing is said about criminal law. The book is largely confined to the general rules on prescription and limitation contained in the Prescription and Limitation (Scotland) Act 1973. There is no detailed discussion of other special statutory regimes, although the principal ones are at least referred to in Appendix 2. By far the greater part of the book is concerned with negative prescription. This is mainly because on positive prescription there already exist valuable discussions in W. M. Gordon, *Scottish Land Law* (1989) and K. G. C. Reid, *The Law of Property* (1996). With the likely abolition of the feudal system by the Scottish Parliament, some of the details of positive prescription will soon need to be rewritten; and with the extension of registration of title to the whole of Scotland in 2003, the role of positive prescription is destined to become less important.

In writing the book, I have been helped by many people. It is more than five years since Lord Rodger of Earlsferry suggested to me that I should write it, and during those years he has been generous with his time in discussing its (lack of) progress. Lord Eassie, George Gretton, Peter Milligan and Stephen Woolman each read all or part of the text. I am extremely grateful to them for taking the time to do so: their helpful comments have much improved the text and saved me from various errors. I also thank everyone from whose suggestions I have learned, or whose criticisms or questions have caused me to rethink my views or think of some in the first place. They are too many to name here, but perhaps it is not too invidious to single out Neil Brailsford, Paul Farlam, Jonathan Lake, Laurent Mayali, Louise Milligan, Horatia Muir Watt, Kenneth Reid, Joe Thomson and Reinhard Zimmermann. For pointing me towards the discussions of prescription in the classical economists I am grateful to my father, Tom Johnston. For their help I also thank the staff of the libraries where the book was written: the Advocates' Library, Edinburgh; the Squire Law Library, Cambridge; and the Robbins Collection, School of Law, University of California at Berkeley. I am glad to be able to dedicate the book to my great friends Sarah and Peter Milligan, in acknowledgment not least of the many welcome interruptions to prescription which they have provided over the years.

David Johnston
March 1999

CONTENTS

x   *Contents*

APPENDICES

ABGB	*Allgemeines Bürgerliches Gesetzbuch* (Austrian Civil Code)
A.L.R.	*Australian Law Reports*
BGB	*Bürgerliches Gesetzbuch* (German Civil Code)
C.L.J.	*Cambridge Law Journal*
C.L.R.	*Commonwealth Law Reports* (Australia)
E.C.R.	*European Court Reports*
E.L.R.	*Edinburgh Law Review*
F.C.	*Faculty Collection*
L.Q.R.	*Law Quarterly Review*
N.Z.L.R.	*New Zealand Law Reports*
OR	*Obligationenrecht* (Switzerland)
P.N.	*Professional Negligence*
S.A.	*South African Law Reports*
S.J.	*Solicitors Journal*
SLC	Scottish Law Commission
S.L.P.Q.	*Scottish Law and Practice Quarterly*
V.R.	*Victorian Reports* (Australia)

Abschlussbericht	*Abschlussbericht der Kommission zur Überarbeitung des Schuldrechts* (1992)
Armour	*Armour on Valuation for Rating* (5th ed. by J. J. Clyde and J. A. D. Hope, Edinburgh, 1985)
Bankton	Bankton, *An Institute of the Laws of Scotland* (3 Vols, Edinburgh 1751–53, reprinted 1993–95)
Bell, *Comm.*	G. J. Bell, *Commentaries on the Law of Scotland and on the Principles of Mercantile Jurisprudence* (7th ed. by J. Maclaren, 2 Vols, Edinburgh, 1870)
Bell, *Prin.*	G. J. Bell, *Principles of the Law of Scotland* (10th ed. by W. Guthrie, Edinburgh, 1899)
Carey Miller, *Corporeal Moveables*	D. Carey Miller, *Corporeal Moveables in Scots Law* (Edinburgh, 1991)
Chitty, *Contracts*	*Chitty on Contracts* (27th ed. by A. G. Guest, London, 1994)
Clerk and Lindsell, *Torts*	*Clerk and Lindsell on Torts* (17th ed. by M. Brazier, London, 1995)
Cusine and Paisley, *Servitudes and Rights of Way*	D. J. Cusine and R. R. M. Paisley, *Servitudes and Rights of Way* (Edinburgh, 1998)
Dicey and Morris, *Conflict of Laws*	*Dicey and Morris on the Conflict of Laws* (12th ed. by L. Collins, London, 1993)
Erskine	J. Erskine, *An Institute of the Law of Scotland* (8th ed. by J. B. Nicolson, 2 Vols, Edinburgh, 1871)
Gloag, *Contract*	W. M. Gloag, *The Law of Contract* (2nd ed., Edinburgh, 1929)
Gloag and Henderson	W. M. Gloag and R. C. Henderson, *The Law of Scotland* (10th ed. by W. A. Wilson and A. D. M. Forte, Edinburgh, 1995)
Gloag and Irvine, *Rights in Security*	W. M. Gloag and J. M. Irvine, *Law of Rights in Security* (Edinburgh, 1897)
Gordon, *Land Law*	W. M. Gordon, *Scottish Land Law* (Edinburgh, 1989)
Gore-Brown, *Companies*	*Gore-Brown on Companies* (44th ed. by A. J. Boyle, London, 1986)
Graham Stewart, *Diligence*	J. Graham Stewart, *The Law of Diligence* (Edinburgh, 1898)
Gretton, *Inhibition and Adjudication*	G. Gretton, *The Law of Inhibition and Adjudication* (2nd ed., Edinburgh, 1996)

Spiro, *Die Begrenzung*

K. Spiro, *Die Begrenzung privater Rechte durch Verjährungs-, Verwirkungs- und Fatalfristen* (2 Vols, Bern, 1975)

Stair Memorial Encyclopaedia

Stair Memorial Encyclopaedia of the Laws of Scotland (25 Vols, Edinburgh, 1987 and subsequently updated)

Walker

D. M. Walker, *Prescription and Limitation of Actions* (5th ed., Edinburgh, 1996)

Walker, *Contract*

D. M. Walker, *The Law of Contract and Related Obligations* (3rd ed., Edinburgh, 1995)

Walker, *Judicial Factors*

N. M. L. Walker, *Judicial Factors* (Edinburgh, 1974)

Walkers, *Evidence*

A. G. Walker and N. M. L. Walker, *The Law of Evidence in Scotland* (Edinburgh, 1964)

Wilson, *Debt*

W. A. Wilson, *The Law of Debt in Scotland* (2nd ed., Edinburgh, 1991)

Wilson and Duncan, *Trusts, Trustees and Executors*

W. A. Wilson and A. G. M.Duncan, *Trusts, Trustees and Executors* (2nd ed., Edinburgh, 1995)

TABLE OF CASES

Location references are to paragraph numbers. Paragraph numbers in bold show where a case is mentioned in the text.

TABLE OF STATUTES

References are to paragraph numbers. Paragraph numbers in bold refer to detailed discussion of the section within the text. Page numbers refer to the Appendices. Appendix I reproduces the Prescription and Limitation (Scotland) Act 1973 in full.

Statutes – Non UK

CHAPTER 1

HISTORY AND THE JUSTIFICATION FOR PRESCRIPTION

I. INTRODUCTION

When the poet Ovid spoke of time as the devourer of things, he might **1.01** have been speaking of prescription.[1] Negative prescription consumes rights and obligations; positive prescription fortifies doubtful titles, in a sense by consuming existing ones. In fact, Ovid was reporting Pythagoras's views on the virtues of vegetarianism: while it is unnatural that one animal should consume another, what is perfectly in accord with nature is that all things should be consumed by time.

This book is concerned with the consumption, extinction and barring **1.02** of rights by time; in other words, with the doctrines of prescription and limitation. These are doctrines which require some justification: why is it that time should grant rights? And why should it take them away?

It may be useful to begin with definitions: "Prescription is the **1.03** common extinction and abolishing of all rights", according to Stair.[2] Erskine is more precise in defining positive prescription as "the establishing or securing to the possessor his right against all future challenge" and negative prescription as "the loss or forfeiture of a right, by the proprietor's neglecting to exercise or prosecute it during that whole period which the law hath declared to infer the loss of it".[3] Limitation, about which neither Stair or Erskine has anything to say, does not involve the loss of any substantive right but is the procedural barring of an action after the lapse of a period during which the law insists that it must, if at all, be brought.

The book is divided into four main parts. The first two are concerned **1.04** with the loss of or barring of rights of action, by negative prescription or limitation. The third deals with the fortification of rights by positive prescription. The final part discusses points common to prescription and limitation, such as procedure and international private law. The remainder of this chapter is an introduction to the whole book. Most of the historical matter in the book is confined to this chapter, and it concentrates in particular on the justification for prescription.

II. THE BASIS OF THE MODERN SCOTS LAW OF PRESCRIPTION AND LIMITATION

Nearly all of the modern Scots law on prescription and limitation is **1.05** contained in the Prescription and Limitation (Scotland) Act 1973 ("the

---

[1] *Metamorphoses*, 15. 234: "*tempus edax rerum, tuque invidiosa vetustas/omnia destruis vitiataque dentibus aevi/paulatim lenta consumitis omnia morte.*"

[2] 2.12.1.

[3] III, vii, 2 and III, vii, 8.

[4] *cf.* Bell, *Prin.*, s. 586.

1973 Act"). It is not too much of an exaggeration to say that the Act amounts in essence to a code of prescription and limitation for Scotland. The long title of the Act reads:

> "An Act to replace the Prescription Acts of 1469, 1474 and 1617 and make new provision in the law of Scotland with respect to the establishment and definition by positive prescription of title to interests in land and of positive servitudes and public rights of way, and with respect to the extinction of rights and obligations by negative prescription; to repeal certain enactments relating to limitation of proof; to re-enact with modifications certain enactments relating to the time-limits for bringing legal proceedings where damages are claimed which consist of or include damages or solatium in respect of personal injuries or in respect of a person's death and the time-limit for claiming contribution between wrong-doers; and for purposes connected with the matters aforesaid."

1.06   It can be seen that the 1973 Act swept away a good deal of elderly legislation. Its aim was essentially to simplify and rationalise the existing law. This was less necessary for positive than for negative prescription: to a great extent the Act simply restates the broad principles which applied to positive prescription in the past. The treatment of negative prescription is far more radical. The Act abolished an extraordinary accretion of different prescriptive periods: three, five, six, seven, 10 and 20 years. These various periods applied in various different circumstances; there was no unitary order. The 1973 Act replaced this multiplicity with a relatively simple regime composed of positive prescription (two periods only), negative prescription (two periods only) and limitation.

1.07   Nonetheless, many and diverse statutes still make provision for different prescriptive periods in specific circumstances: to give just one example, carriage by air. Appendix 2 lists some of the more important of these periods. Equally, the signs are that the simple regime introduced in 1973 is not destined to last. Already amendments to the Act have introduced new complexity. Now there is talk of alteration of some of the statutory periods. But this is not necessarily a bad thing. To impose a uniform prescriptive period, attractively straightforward though that may seem, may risk distorting other aspects of the law.[5] This question is considered further in the course of the book.

1.08   The 1973 Act contains provisions not just for prescription but also for the limitation of actions. Scots law is relatively unusual in making use of the twin concepts of prescription, by which a right is extinguished, and limitation, where the right subsists but no action may be brought into court to enforce it. Several of the early Scottish Acts were in this sense statutes of limitation rather than prescription, a number of them in fact doing no more than limiting the mode of proof which was admissible, after the limitation period had run, to proof by writ or oath. The modern Scots law of limitation has, however, nothing to do with this but is

---

[5] Some other jurisdictions have a wide range of prescriptive periods: in Germany the standard period is 30 years, but there are other periods for particular cases, *e.g.* six months, two years, three years and four years (BGB, Arts 195–197, 477 and 852). In France 30 years is also standard, but there are again special cases, *e.g.* six months, two years and five years (*Code Civil,* Arts 2262, 2271–2273 and 2277).

essentially an import from England. The first Scottish statute on this matter, the Law Reform (Limitation of Actions etc.) Act 1954, in many respects followed the English statute, the Limitation Act 1939. The Scottish provisions have since been substantially amended.[6]

Recent changes in the law of prescription and limitation, starting with **1.09** the enactment of the 1973 Act, result from work carried on, and recommendations made, by the Scottish Law Commission. Its first programme of law reform included prescription and limitation of actions as a subject for examination, and in due course this resulted in a memorandum, followed by a report, whose recommendations were for the most part enacted in the 1973 Act.[7]

Further legislative change has followed. The Law Reform (Mis- **1.10** cellaneous Provisions) Act 1980 amended the 1973 Act with respect to limitation.[8] After a report published in 1983,[9] the Prescription and Limitation (Scotland) Act 1984 substituted entirely new sections for the original and much-criticised sections of the 1973 Act dealing with limitation.[10] It also introduced new provisions on conflicts of law, and on the treatment of obligations to make contribution between wrongdoers. The Prescription (Scotland) Act 1987 made amendments concerned with company liquidation and the interruption of negative prescription, while the Consumer Protection Act 1987 inserted into the 1973 Act a new Part IIA dealing with product liability.

The Scottish Law Commission has continued its work by publishing a **1.11** consultative memorandum and then a report on prescription and limitation of actions dealing in particular with latent damage and a few other areas which had caused concern.[11] So far this has not led to any legislation.

All this legislative activity may suggest that to understand the law **1.12** there is little reason to look back beyond 1973. In some areas that may be true. But the earlier law can be important, for example, in interpreting the likely intention of Parliament at points of doubt or difficulty in the Act, of which there are many. Apart from this, in general there is much to be gained from placing these institutions of the law in historical perspective. Those who disagree should move on to Chapter 2, since the rest of this chapter is concerned with doing precisely that.

III. THE HISTORICAL BACKGROUND

Scots law uses the terms "positive" and "negative" prescription to **1.13** denote respectively a prescription which fortifies a title in the possessor,

---

[6] Prescription and Limitation (Scotland) Act 1984.

[7] SLC Memo no. 9 (1968); Report no. 15 (1970).

[8] s. 23 of the 1980 Act introduced a new s. 19A into the 1973 Act, conferring a judicial discretion to override the limitation period. See below, para. 12.02.

[9] SLC Report no. 74 (1983), *Prescription and the Limitation of Actions: Report on Personal Injuries Actions and Private International Law Questions*. This followed upon SLC Memo no. 45 (1980), *Time Limits in Actions for Personal Injuries*; and *Consultation Paper on Prescription and Limitation in Private International Law* (1980).

[10] It also excluded personal injury claims from the long negative prescription: amendment to s. 7(2) of the 1973 Act.

[11] SLC Memo no. 74 (1987), *Prescription and Limitation of Actions (Latent Damage)*; Report no. 122 (1989), *Report on Prescription and Limitation of Actions (Latent Damage and Other Related Issues)*.

and a prescription which extinguishes a right or obligation, at the end of the prescriptive period.[12] The origins of both of these types of prescription are to be found in Roman law, the difference being that Roman law had (at least initially) reserved the term *"usucapio"* for acquisitive prescription and employed the term *"praescriptio"* for negative prescription.

1.14 A brief glance at the three Roman legal institutions of a prescriptive nature is in order.[13] The first is *usucapio*, the only one of the three which existed in classical law. By this means ownership of property was acquired with the passage of time under certain circumstances, notably that the acquirer had begun to possess in good faith and for good cause. In classical law the prescriptive periods were one year for moveables and two years for land; under Justinian a uniform period of three years for *usucapio* of any kind of property was introduced.

1.15 The second institution is *longi temporis praescriptio*, a later innovation, initially developed for provincial circumstances and for the particular case of land. This too required good faith and a good cause in the possessor. It did not create a title in the possessor but generated only a defence against the owner's claim; in other words, it was a form of negative prescription. The prescriptive periods here were 10 years if the parties were present in the same province, and 20 years if they were not.[14]

1.16 The post-classical history of this institution is tortuous. In relation to actions for recovery of property only, legislation by the emperor Constantine in the early fourth century A.D. provided a new negative prescription of 40 years.[15] A possessor could therefore not be challenged after that time had run; in this instance (alone) good faith in acquiring the property in question was immaterial. The 10- and 20-year periods seem to have fallen into disuse, although the 40-year period appears later to have been reduced to 30 years.

1.17 The third institution was a negative prescription of 30 years for actions, which was introduced by the emperor Theodosius II in A.D. 424[16]; some actions, however, prescribed only after 40 years.

1.18 Under Justinian the two institutions of classical law came closer together, the term *"usucapio"* being reserved for a three-year prescrip-

---

[12] The same distinction is found in other legal systems, although the terms used are sometimes "acquisitive" and "extinctive". "Acquisitive" and "positive" are not necessarily synonymous: *cf.* below, para. 14.04.

[13] For an outline of these, see W. W. Buckland, *A Textbook of Roman Law* (3rd ed., 1963), pp. 241 *et seq.*; more recently, M. Kaser, *Das römische Privatrecht*, Vol. 2 (2nd ed., 1975), pp. 71 and 285 *et seq.*

[14] It may be noted that Art. 2265 of the French *Code Civil* continues to apply, to prescription of land, periods of 10 or 20 years according to whether parties are domiciled within the jurisdiction of the same *cour d'appel* as or a different one from the land in question.

[15] The legislation is mentioned in C. 7.39.2 (A.D. 365), although it is probably to be dated to between A.D. 325 and 333: it is referred to in a papyrus of A.D. 339 (P. Col. VII 175 (lines 26–28 and 39–40)); applicability to actions *in rem* is mentioned in C. Th. 4.11.2 (A.D. 349).

[16] C. 7.39.3; *cf.* Nov. Val. 27 (A.D. 449).

tion of moveables and *"longi temporis praescriptio"* for a 10-year prescription of land.[17] In principle both were now treated as forms of acquisitive prescription. In addition there was now a 30- or 40-year *longissimi temporis praescriptio* which applied where the possessor did not have good cause for being in possession. Negative prescription of actions remained, but which actions were subject to prescription of 30, and which to prescription of 40, years is left in Justinian's *Code* remarkably unclear.[18]

In sum, at the end of its historical development in antiquity, Roman **1.19** law operated with two types of acquisitive prescription, with periods of three and 10 or 20 years; and two types of negative prescription, with periods of 30 and 40 years. These two strands, of acquisitive and negative prescription, the central concepts of the modern law, can therefore be traced back to Roman law. Explicit reference to the Roman law has died out. It is, however, not uninteresting to note the reference to the civil law in the preamble to the principal early Scottish statute on prescription, James VI's Act 1617, c. 12[19]: the Act notes the prevailing uncertainty of the lieges about their heritable rights as "divers pleas and actions are moved against them, after the expiry of 30 or 40 years, which nevertheless by the Civil Law, and by the laws of all nations, are declared void and ineffectual".[20]

From Rome to Scotland
It is not possible to trace here in any detail the line of development **1.20** from the Roman sources to the Scottish ones. Instead, the approach taken in the next section is to examine just one topic in historical perspective. The topic is the justification for prescription, which provides an illustration of how the Roman materials were employed over the centuries to elaborate workable doctrines of prescription.

The historical perspective adopted here is itself rather selective: most **1.21** attention is paid to the sixteenth- and seventeenth-century sources which appear substantially to have influenced Stair. That means in particular Hugo Grotius (1583–1645), the leading light of the school of natural lawyers, and the late Spanish scholastics, such as Covarruvias, Lessius and Suarez, who greatly influenced him. In connection with the justification for prescription, the contribution made by the Spanish scholastics in reconciling the sometimes conflicting tenets of canon law with those developed in the civil law is clear. In doing this, of course, they were able to draw on a tradition of scholarship on the Roman texts which went back to about 1100, when the study of Roman law appears to have revived in Bologna.

Although it is not really permissible to account for 500 years of legal **1.22** history in a single paragraph, for present purposes the following are the key moments in the historical development. From 1100 onwards there was a great variety in the approaches adopted to the *Digest* and the other

---

[17] C. 7.31.1 (A.D. 531).
[18] See, *e.g.*, C. 7.39.9 (A.D. 529); C. 7.40.1 (A.D. 530).
[19] Repealed only by the 1973 Act, s. 16 and Sched. 5.
[20] The confusion sown in Justinian's *Code* between prescriptive periods of 30 and 40 years had left its mark.

sources of Roman law by successive schools of civil law jurists: beginning in the twelfth century, the Glossators wrote marginal comments ("glosses"), explaining the texts by means of scholastic and logical methods and without regard to their practical application. It is from the twelfth century that Rogerius's *Tractatus de praescriptionibus* dates, the earliest monograph on prescription.[21] At much the same time, and for the next couple of centuries, a parallel process of writing glosses on the canon law material, the *Decretum* of Gratian of about A.D. 1140 and the later decretals, was taking place. The Glossators were followed by the Commentators, so called because of their more sustained commentaries on the *Digest* and *Code*, which began to appear in the course of the fourteenth century. They attempted to accommodate the Roman texts to the demands of legal practice, even although this naturally involved construing the texts in a way quite different from what their ancient authors had intended. As early as the fourteenth and fifteenth centuries the first signs of a purist backlash against this practical approach appeared in the shape of the Humanist school. The result was that Grotius and his predecessors had a vast, disparate and highly sophisticated range of scholarly material from which to fashion their own approach to the question of prescription, and in doing so they combined elements drawn from the civil law and the canon law.

1.23   In the next section, some of these civilian legal materials and the Scottish institutional writings are examined in the context of the justification for prescription. Before that it is convenient simply to set out the early history of Scottish legislation dealing with prescription and limitation.

Early Scottish statutes

1.24   The history of prescription in Scots law is a history of statutes, all now repealed. That prescription is a matter of statute rather than common law is a point which goes back as far as Hope's *Major Practicks*.[22] Craig gives extensive references to prescription in feudal law, but when he comes to deal with the law of Scotland says that prescription is little recognised.[23] Hume takes the same view. In speaking of prescription, he says: "Considering the weight of the reasons, and the authority, also of the Roman law, the wonder rather is, that it did not engraft itself through the judgments of Courts upon our Common Law, and was established only by Statute."[24]

1.25   Here it must suffice to note the main statutes, which fall into three groups.[25] Rather than take up time with explaining the old conveyancing terminology, this discussion simply summarises the contents of the statutes but then attempts to state their main effects in plain terms.

1.26   The first group deals with positive prescription.[26] The Act 1594, c. 218 introduced protection for a possessor who had possessed for 40 years

---

[21] See H. Lange, *Römisches Recht im Mittelalter* I (1997), p. 198.

[22] 6.43.3 "Found *quod in regno Scotiae non currit praescriptio nisi in obligationibus ex actu parliamenti*: 13 Maii 1575, C. 394".

[23] Craig, *Jus Feudale* (trans. J. A. Clyde, 1934), 2.1.8; *cf.* 2.2.1. In 2.4.12 Craig does refer to the Act 1594, c. 218.

[24] Hume, *Lectures*, 3.63.

[25] For further details, see *Encyclopedia of the Laws of Scotland*, (1931) Vol. 12, paras 41–166.

[26] See Napier, pp. 43–51.

and whose charter and instrument of sasine were extant. It provided that there was no obligation on such a possessor to produce procuratories or instruments of resignation or precepts of sasine or *clare constat*; and that the lack of these was not a cause for reduction of the title. In short, the effect of the Act was the limited one of restricting the right to call on a possessor to produce his full progress of titles.

This statute was replaced by the Act 1617, c. 12, which ameliorated the **1.27** possessor's position. Now he was required only to show a charter followed by 40 years' possession, together with the instrument of sasine following on the charter, or else instruments of sasine standing together for 40 years following on retours or precepts of *clare constat*. From this point onwards it was settled that a possessor need show only part of his progress of titles, namely the title that immediately preceded possession and those falling within the prescriptive period. The same principle applied when the prescriptive period was shortened to 20 years and subsequently (for most cases) to 10 years.[27]

The second group is made up of statutes which provided that on the **1.28** expiry of the prescriptive period the subsistence of the obligation in question should be unaffected but that the creditor should be restricted to proving it by writ or oath. This is true of:

(1) the three-year prescription of debts, house mails (that is, rents), mens ordinars (that is, board), servants' wages, merchants' accounts, and other similar debts not founded on written obligations[28]; (2) the five-year prescription of bargains concerning moveables, and of stipends, multures, and rents[29]; (3) the 20-year prescription of holograph writings[30]; and (4) the six-year prescription of bills and notes.[31]

The third group is of statutes which extinguished the right to bring **1.29** particular types of action. This group is made up of:

(1) the three-year prescription of spuilzies and ejections[32]; (2) the three-year prescription of removings[33]; (3) the seven-year prescription of cautionary obligations[34]; (4) the 10-year prescription of tutors' and curators' accounts[35]; and (5) the 20-year prescription of retours.[36]

In addition to these specific types of negative prescription, a general **1.30** negative prescription of obligations was first introduced in 1469: this provided that all obligations which were more than 40 years old should be of no strength and that all obligations not followed within 40 years

---

[27] Conveyancing (Scotland) Acts 1874, s. 34 and 1924, s. 16; Conveyancing and Feudal Reform (Scotland) Act 1970, s. 8.
[28] Act 1579, c. 83; Napier, pp. 714–813.
[29] Act 1669, c. 9; Napier, pp. 813–822.
[30] Act 1669, c. 9; Napier, pp. 866–867.
[31] Bills of Exchange Act 1772; Napier, pp. 822–850.
[32] Act 1579, c. 81; Napier, pp. 710–712.
[33] Act 1579, c. 82; Napier, pp. 712–713.
[34] Act 1695, c. 5; Napier, pp. 850–854.
[35] Act 1696, c. 9; Napier, pp. 854–857.
[36] Act 1617, c. 13; Napier, pp. 857–866.

should prescribe and be of no avail.[37] The Act 1617, c. 12, at the same time as placing positive prescription on a firm footing, extended a general negative prescription of 40 years to heritable as well as moveable rights and obligations. The prescriptive period was reduced in 1924 to 20 years.[38]

IV. THE JUSTIFICATION FOR PRESCRIPTION

Positive prescription

1.31   The civil law tradition contains a good deal of discussion about the proper basis of *usucapio* or acquisitive prescription; to a lesser extent, so does Roman law. There are good reasons for this: it is not self-evident why time alone should have the effect of extinguishing rights or obligations. As a rule it does not, after all, impose them.[39] So it is that in the European tradition writers consistently maintain that prescription is an institution not of natural law but of positive law.[40] Equally, in various authors we read that prescription is a matter of utility and not of equity. Even if it is not just, it satisfies practical demands. And it seems to be this that Stair (and later authorities) have in mind in describing negative prescription as "odious". These two strands of natural law and equity come together in well-known and much-cited dicta in the *Digest* to the effect that "by the law of nature it is fair that nobody should be enriched at the expense and cost of another".[41] Precisely these dicta suggested to certain authors that prescription was objectionable, since it did benefit the new proprietor at the cost of the old, and appeared therefore to infringe this basic principle of natural justice.

1.32   Discussions about the propriety of prescription surface in particular in relation to the question of good faith. Roman law, for example, had required for *usucapio* no more than that the possessor should be in good faith at the time of acquisition. His opportunity to prescribe title was unaffected by the fact that he might in the course of the prescriptive period become aware that the property in fact belonged to somebody else. In the civil-law tradition this line, for which there was much good Roman authority, continued to be followed. But there was a strong contrary tendency to be found in the canon law writers, for whom it was unconscionable that anyone should acquire title unless he had been in good faith throughout the prescriptive period.[42]

---

[37] Act 1469, c. 28, as explained by Act 1474, c. 54; Napier, pp. 34–39 and 57–58.

[38] Conveyancing (Scotland) Act 1924, s. 17.

[39] Gothofredus on D. 41.10.5, Neratius 5 *membranarum*. Later, Sir Henry Maine, *Ancient Law* (7th ed., London, 1878), p. 286, spoke of a "disrelish for prescription" and of the notion that, whatever turn legislation might take, "a right, how long soever neglected, was in point of fact indestructible".

[40] Donellus, *Commentarii*, 5.30; H. Grotius, *Inleiding tot de Hollandsche Rechts-geleertheyd* (transl. by R. W. Lee as *The jurisprudence of Holland*, (Oxford, 1926)), 2.7.4; A. Vinnius, *In quattuor libros Institutionum commentarius* (ed. used: Venice, 1783) on Inst. 2.6, pr. init.; *cf.* Stair, II, xii, 9, clearly influenced by H. Grotius, *de iure belli ac pacis* (ed. used: Amsterdam, 1646), 2.4.1 and 2.4.11; Erskine, III, vii, 1.

[41] D. 50.17.206, Pomponius 9 *ex variis lectionibus: iure naturae aequum est neminem cum alterius detrimento et iniuria fieri locupletiorem* (also D. 12 6.14, Pomponius 21 *ad Sabinum*: *nam hoc natura aequum est neminem cum alterius detrimento fieri locupletiorem*); *cf.* the note by D. Gothofredus on D. 41.10.5, Neratius 5 *membranarum* (ed. used: *Corpus iuris civilis cum notis Gothofredi*; Amsterdam, J. Blaeu and D. Elzevier, and Leiden, F. Hackius, 1663); D. Covarruvias, *Relectio regulae possessor malae fidei de regul. iur. libro sexto* (ed. used: Relectionum tomi II; Lyon, 1568, *apud haeredes Iacobi Iunctae*) Pt 3, init. para. 1 (p. 629 in ed. cited).

[42] *cf.* Stair, II, xii, 5.

Indeed some of the canonists went further, maintaining that, even had **1.33**
the possessor completed the whole prescriptive period in good faith, he
was nonetheless obliged in conscience—as they put it, *in foro interno*—to
restore the property to its true owner if at any time thereafter he
discovered the truth. Clearly a doctrine of this sort rendered the whole
institution of acquisitive prescription pointless (at least as a matter of
conscience). It also led to the inconvenient result that a judge applying
civil law and one applying canon law would arrive at contradictory
judgments. Covarruvias, a leading figure in late Spanish scholastic
jurisprudence, pointed out that this was unacceptable.[43] His view was
that, although a law might from time to time work injustice, if it was on
the whole productive of justice, it was a just law, and a just law was to be
observed even in conscience. It followed that even the judge at canon
law ought to have regard to the civil law rules of prescription.[44]
Accordingly, the debate seems to have come to an end with an
acceptance that positive laws which introduced prescription were just
and were to be observed.[45]

That still left the question what the justification for prescription was. **1.34**
Here two of the most popular explanations went back to the Roman
jurists of the second century A.D. The first of these (to be found in the
Institutes of Gaius) is that *usucapio* was introduced "so that ownership of
property should not be uncertain for too long", and the periods
applicable in classical Roman law were regarded as sufficient for the
owner to discover his property and so to vindicate it.[46] Elsewhere, Gaius
is recorded as saying that *usucapio* was introduced for the public good,
this being supported on much the same grounds as are set out in his
Institutes.[47] The second explanation (advanced by the early second-
century jurist Neratius) is that *usucapio* exists "so that there should be
some end to litigation."[48]

It has already been mentioned that under the emperor Justinian, the **1.35**
period for *usucapio* was increased to three years. The motivation for this

---

[43] D. Covarruvias, *op. cit.*, Pt 3, scct. 2, paras 1–2 (at 635–636). (This is a commentary on
the rule *"possessor malae fidei ullo tempore non praescribit"*, to be found in Boniface VIII's
Liber Sextus decretalium, Bk 5, title 12, rule 2.)

[44] Still having regard, however, to the fact that the canon law requirements for good
faith were more exacting than those of the civil law: *cf.* Bankton, II, xii, 79.

[45] In fact this is very much the position found already in the *Decretum* of Gratian
(c. A.D. 1140): D. 1 c. 2 gloss *ius* notes that "it is equitable and just that nobody should
become richer through another's loss [Liber Extra 5.37.9 and D. 12.6.14 are cited].
Nevertheless, *usucapio* and prescription have been constituted contrary to this equity. . . .
But you may say that in all of these cases a right contrary to natural equity has been
instituted for a purpose and for the sake of peace or society." The civil law Glossators on
D. 50.17.206 (above, n. 41) had arrived at the same result: that the general rule against
enrichment did not apply in the cases of usucapion and prescription; similarly on
D. 12.6.14 (above, n. 41) the Commentators noted that the reason for this was that
prescription is rigour in a particular case as opposed to general equity. For further detail
on the canon law, see R. H. Helmholz, The *Spirit of Classical Canon Law* (Athens,
Georgia, 1996), pp. 174–199, as well as his essay in W. Krauwietz, N. MacCormick and
G. H. von Wright (eds), *Prescriptive Formality and Normative Rationality in Modern Law*
(Berlin, 1994), pp. 265–283; on the Glossators and Commentators see J. Hallebeek in
E. Schrage (ed.), *Unjust Enrichment* (Berlin, 1995), pp. 112–117.

[46] Gaius, Inst. 2.44.

[47] D. 41.3.1, Gaius 21 *ad edictum provinciale*.

[48] D. 41.10.5, Neratius 5 *membranarum*.

change is set out both in Justinian's *Code* and in his *Institutes*: "that owners should not be too quickly deprived of their property".[49] The *Code* provides a fuller account of "poor" owners being excluded from their property even without their knowledge, and observes that there can be nothing more inhumane than that a man in his absence and ignorance should lose his property in such a short time. More interesting than the rhetoric is the clear notion that there must be a proportion between the length of the prescriptive period and the original owner's prospects of recovering his property. It follows that the short periods of *usucapio* which had been quite acceptable within the small agricultural community of Rome in its early days were quite inappropriate in a world empire; they had remained unchanged, doubtless owing to inertia, awaiting only the attention of a determined legislator. The same consideration under-lies the 10- or 20-year period for *longi temporis praescriptio*: a person in the same province is in a much better position to look after his interests than a person based in a different one.

1.36   Later writers elaborated these Roman ideas. In the seventeenth century, Grotius still defended prescription on the basis of certainty of title.[50] Rather earlier Hugo Donellus had relied on ease of proof of title.[51] His point was that without prescription there would be an infinite regress, each successive owner having to prove the validity of the title of each of his predecessors, so that nobody could ever be sure about the validity of his own title. (Earlier jurists had referred to this as the problem of the *probatio diabolica*.) To these were added various other considerations: that there was a public interest in prescription, based on the certainty to which it led and its discouragement of litigation, and this offset the private losses which it inflicted.[52] Or that there was a presumed alienation[53] or abandonment[54] by an owner who did not vindicate his property within the prescriptive period; and prescription was a sanction for the negligence of an owner who failed to vindicate his property, and an encouragement to owners to look after their property and keep their land in good heart.[55] To this it was added that they could not complain of loss which they had by their own fault brought on themselves.[56]

1.37   That last argument was of course itself a hostage to fortune; and it was indeed argued by some that, since prescription was a penalty for the negligent owner, it could not operate where he was able to show that he had not been negligent. Again, the late Spanish scholastics rebutted this argument: fault or negligence of the original owner was not the sole

---

[49] C. 7.31.1, pr. (A.D. 531); Inst. 2.6, pr.

[50] Grotius, *Inleiding*, 2.7.4.

[51] Donellus, *Commentarii*, 5.30; *contra*, A. Alciatus in his commentary on C. 3.39.5, *De quinque pedum praescriptione liber* (ed. used: appendix to his *Ad rescripta principum commentarii* (Lyon, 1537)).

[52] Vinnius, *Commentarii*. on Inst. 2.6, pr., *ne rerum dominia in incerto essent*.

[53] Gothofredus on D. 41.10.5, Neratius 5 *membranarum*; Donellus, *loc. cit.*

[54] Heineccius, note on Vinnius, *Comm.*, Inst. 2.6, pr. *ne rerum dominia in incerto essent*—in the case of land, he observes, they can hardly say they did not know where it was. See also Grotius, *de iure belli ac pacis* 2.4.5; (criticised by S. de Coccei in his commentary on that chapter, printed, *e.g.*, in the Lausanne, 1758–59 ed. of *de iure belli ac pacis*) on the ground that silence is no basis for presuming the intention to abandon).

[55] This rationale goes back to Cicero, *pro Caecina* 73–74; de Coccei, *loc. cit.*; Grotius, *Inleiding* 2.7.4; Vinnius, *loc. cit.*; Donellus, *loc. cit.*

[56] Donellus, *loc. cit.*

rationale of prescription[57]; the prescription statutes never invoked negligence as their rationale, but instead the public good, and it was open to the emperor to deprive his subjects of their property even without their fault in the interest of the common good.[58] Accordingly, after much debate and the expenditure of much ingenuity, in the end what it came down to was this: prescription was adjudged as valid both at civil and at canon law; and its justification, just as it had been in the second century A.D., was the public interest. In support of the public interest any or all of this range of possible reasons might be prayed in aid.

Interruption and suspension of prescription
The doctrine of interruption and suspension of prescription illustrates **1.38** the same question—of justifying prescription—from a different perspective. The late Spanish scholastics provide a three-part categorisation, most conveniently summarised by Lessius[59]:

> (1) Prescription cannot proceed when for some reason it cannot begin, namely, where there is no possession, no title, no good faith or the subject-matter in question is inalienable. (2) Prescription is said to sleep when it has been begun but for some reason ceases and is later continued cumulatively with the initial period. This applies in time of war or plague; in relation to Church property when a church is without a rector; and finally, when the person against whom prescription is pled cannot sue, that is, the person is a minor or pupil or a wife during her marriage. (3) Prescription is said to be interrupted when, if it is interrupted after it has begun, the time is not cumulated with what has preceded but must begin again. Interruption can be natural, such as loss of possession (or, in canon law, of good faith); or it may be civil, by a juridical act, *litis contestatio* or citation. Lessius goes on to explain that *litis contestatio* does not interrupt *usucapio*, although it does interrupt the longer prescriptions; and that there is deemed to be no interruption if the pursuer fails in the action or abandons it or, more surprisingly, if his only reason for raising it was to interrupt prescription.

The second of these categories, "dormant" prescription, suggests that **1.39** the basis of prescription is acquiescence in the loss of a right. For the period that a person is unable to enforce any right, he or she cannot be said to have acquiesced in its prescription, and the time does not run. This appears to be the basis of the plea, known for short as *non valens agere cum effectu* (loosely translated, that "the pursuer is unable effectively to pursue his claim"), which was commonplace in Scots law in earlier centuries and may or may not still survive.[60]

Negative prescription
In the *jus commune* positive and negative prescription tended to be **1.40** treated as a unitary institution of *praescriptio*, which covered both loss of rights by non-use and acquisition of rights by use or possession.

---

[57] Covarruvias, *op. cit.*, Pt 3, sect. 2, para. 3 (p. 637 in ed. cited).

[58] L. Lessius, *De iustitia et iure* (ed. used: (Lyon, 1653)), Bk 2., ch. 6. dub. 17, citing D. 41.3.3, Modestinus 5, *pandectarum*; D. 41.10.5, Neratius 5, *membranarum*.

[59] (Lessius was from the Netherlands, at this time a Spanish posession.) Lessius, *op. cit.*, Bk 2, ch. 6, dub. 16; *cf.* Covarruvias, *op. cit.*, Pt 2, sect. 12.

[60] See below, para. 7.18; the notion of "dormant" prescription persists in relation to the five-year negative prescription: s. 6(4) and (5).

Although this inclusive doctrine would not survive the strictures of the Pandectist movement,[61] it is the reason why until the nineteenth century very little is said specifically about negative prescription or limitation: everything is dealt with under a single heading.[62] Most authors dealt with the justification for prescription by using examples from positive prescription. No doubt the apparent infringement of principles of natural law was more striking, and the need for justification more pressing, in the case where what was lost was property in an object as opposed to the right or ability to pursue an action.

1.41 Donellus founds the loss of a right of action on the pursuer's silence: if maintained throughout the prescriptive period, this silence does not extinguish an obligation automatically but brings about the result that the action is barred by the defence of prescription.[63] Here, as elsewhere, silence seems to lead to a presumption of abandonment.

1.42 Roman law had been quite clear that prescription runs against a claim only from the time the obligation on which it is founded is enforceable.[64] The same view appears to have been adopted among the late Spanish scholastics.[65] Among them the corollary was also put forward: where rights are lost because of failure to exercise them, they begin to prescribe from the date when the person entitled to them did not exercise them, provided that he was at that time able to do so. Clearly this fits with the notion of abandonment. One can only abandon what one either has or is entitled to have.

1.43 Much of the discussion in this area is preoccupied with the question of good faith or the lack of it. Lessius again provides a conveniently brief account.[66] According to him, good faith is needed in order for prescription to run against a money debt or an action for such a debt. This means that it is not enough for the creditor to fail to exact the debt or to mention it for the entire prescriptive period. What is required is that the debtor should believe that he owes nothing, either because he thinks the creditor has made him a gift, or because the debtor thinks he has discharged the debt, or has simply forgotten about it. But in the absence of such good faith the debtor is not regarded as possessing the right not to pay. Lessius observes, however, that in practice it can happen that prescription proceeds even where the debtor is in bad faith: he would be condemned to pay if he were shown to be in bad faith. But this can scarcely happen except by his own admission.

1.44 It is essentially this practical consideration, as well as the generally accepted rule that good faith is presumed until bad is proved, that meant

---

[61] B. Windscheid, *Lehrbuch des Pandektenrechts* (8th ed., 1900), Vol. 1, § 105; H. Dernburg, *Pandekten* (7th ed, 1902), Vol. 2, para. 336, both authors referring to the discussion in Savigny, *System des heutigen römischen Rechts* (1841), Vol. 4, paras 315 *et seq*. These authors took exception to the extension of a doctrine of acquisitive prescription beyond the *usucapio* of ownership of property which Roman law had allowed. See H. Coing, *Europäisches Privatrecht*, II (1989), pp. 280–283 and 389–392.

[62] This also accounts for the unitary treatment found in some of the earlier civil codes, *e.g.* French *Code Civil*, Art. 2219: "La prescription est un moyen d'acquérir ou de se libérer par un certain laps de temps, et sous les conditions déterminées par la loi."

[63] Donellus, *Commentarii*, 22.2.

[64] C. 7.39.7.4 (A.D. 525).

[65] Molina, *disp.* 78, citing C. 7.39.7.4.

[66] Lessius, *op. cit.*, Bk 2, ch. 6, dub. 6; see also Covarruvias, *op. cit.*, Pt 2, sect. 11; Molina, *disp.* 66.

that good faith and these anxious discussions about it had such a minor role to play in the later law. Much more significant, curiously enough, was the characterisation of negative prescription as "odious".

A note on odiousness

The older Scottish sources contain many references to the odiousness **1.45** of prescription. What is its significance, and what is its origin? The origin appears to be the use of the term in one of Justinian's laws, dealing with negative prescription. There he is concerned with the question, when a creditor sues for a sum without specification as to which of his claims against the debtor he is bringing into issue, whether the action suffices to interrupt all claims, none, or, if some, which.[67] Justinian provides that the action interrupts the prescription of all claims "since odious defences are advanced against slothful men and those contemptuous of their own right". What appears to be meant is that, since prescription is intended to strike at those who do not take proper care of their affairs, it is not to be construed strictly against those who have taken the trouble to raise an action. It seems that "odious" is not much more than a rhetorical way of referring to the fact that prescription is in a sense a legal technicality.

The Spanish scholastics refer to the same question. Covarruvias notes **1.46** that Justinian's law does not insist on good faith but is aimed purely at the detriment of the careless (*in odium negligentis*)[68]; much the same is said by Molina.[69] Covarruvias identifies three types of prescription: the 30-year prescription, which is directed purely against careless people; the purely favourable prescription, which benefits the possessor, such as *usucapio*; and the mixed prescription of 10 or 20 years, which is both in favour of the possessor and hostile to the careless.[70] Covarruvias extends this to apply to the sort of act which will suffice to interrupt the prescription. So *usucapio* is not interrupted even by *litis contestatio*, whereas the 10- or 20-year prescription is. But the 30-year prescription is interrupted merely by citation.[71] It can therefore be seen that the less "worthy" the prescription is regarded as being, the more readily it can be interrupted.

Odiousness surfaces in Stair. Dealing with negative prescription, he **1.47** says "prescription being odious, the forty years are accounted *de momento in momentum*".[72] In a similar context, that of giving the creditor the benefit of the doubt when suing on an unclearly dated deed, Bankton asserts that "the negative prescription is odious, and every equitable interpretation is admitted to exclude it".[73] But, as will be clear from the above, this does not mean that Stair or the other writers regarded prescription as being unfair.[74] The older cases produce quite a

---

[67] C. 7.40.3.3 (A.D. 531).

[68] Covarruvias, *op. cit.*, Pt 2, sect. 12, para. 4.

[69] L. Molina, *De iustitia et iure* (ed. used: (Venice, 1611)), tract. 2, disp. 78.

[70] The same distinction between positive prescription *in favorem possidentis* and negative prescription *in odium negligentis* is found in Dirleton's *Doubts, s.v.* Prescription, and in Kames, *Elucidations*, 264.

[71] This view is said to be approved by Bartolus and other doctors commenting on D. 41.3.5, Gaius 21 *ad edictum provinciale.*

[72] Stair, II, xii, 14; *cf.* also II, i, 23, justifying the *bona fide* possessor's acquisition of fruits in part as being "in hatred of the negligence of the other party not pursuing his right."

[73] Bankton, II, xii, 48.

[74] *cf.* Napier, pp. 15–18.

crop of references to odiousness, all directed at the same point: that the negative prescription ought to be interpreted strictly rather than liberally.[75] It is not at all clear that in the modern law this principle of strict construction still applies. Nor, if prescription is really directed at the common good, is it very clear why it should.

Institutional writers

1.48 To the reader of the institutional writers' chapters on prescription, the outline of the civil law tradition sketched above provides the necessary background. To a great extent their general remarks on prescription are directed at both the positive and negative forms.

1.49 Stair begins with the distinction between *usucapio* and *praescriptio*. He deals with the rival views on the question of good faith, and how to determine whether or not a possessor is in good faith. He mentions (in a clear reminiscence of Grotius) that prescription is "founded more upon utility than upon equity". He explains its grounds as being "public utility . . . and also because the law accounteth it as a dereliction of the owner's right, if he own it not, neither pursue it within such a time".[76] And he then turns to give an account of the positive law of prescription in Scotland.

1.50 Bankton, similarly, speaking of both positive and negative prescription, states "that one who ceases to make use of his right, for a long term of years, has renounced it; or that there was nothing truly due to him: and the law has rendred this *Praesumptio juris et de jure*, and thereupon transfers the right from the former owner, or creditor, to the prescriber". He too asserts that prescription is founded in the nature of things and is conducive to the peace of mankind, but that no certain time for completing it is fixed by the law of nature, and this must therefore be done by positive law.[77] Turning to the negative prescription, Bankton also notes, in an echo of Covarruvias, that the new proprietor may take the benefit of prescription "without impeaching his conscience . . . because the right is discharged and extinguished by the public law, to which all our rights are subject. And therefore it is absurd to term prescription an impious defence, since it is equally just and reasonable, as the other laws instituted for the good of the common-wealth".[78] It follows, he says, that a party who has acquired a right or liberation from an obligation can in conscience hold the property against the owner or plead immunity from the debt. Bankton goes on to refer to the conflict between the civil and canon laws, observing that by requiring good faith throughout the period of possession, canon law has improved on civil law. As for Scots law, "[w]e make no enquiry into the party's *bona fides*, but only require a just title, and the course of 40 years' possession. But that does not hinder one from being guilty before God and, in point of conscience, if he detains from the owner what is his after he knew that to be the case, and before the law transfers the right to him the prescriber, which is not done till the whole time limited is passed".[79]

---

[75] See esp. *Nicolson v. Philorth* (1667) M. 11233; also *Lord Lawers v. Dunbars* (1637) M. 10719 at 10720; *Earl of Argyle v. McNaughton* (1671) M. 10791 at 10794; *Home v. Home* (1683) M. 11247. Contrast recently *Richardson v. Quercus Ltd* 1999 S.C. 278, 290, IH.

[76] Stair, II, xii, 1–II, xii, 10.

[77] Bankton, II, xii, 76.

[78] *ibid.* II, xii, 77.

[79] *ibid.* II, xii, 79.

The focus of Erskine's discussion is somewhat different: he begins by **1.51** noting that "[t]he presumption is, that one, who possesses for a long course of time, possesses by a just right; and that the old proprietor was duly denuded".[80] He also notes the rationale of prescription as being first "for fixing and ascertaining property", a tradition which stretches back through Grotius and Donellus to the Roman jurists; and secondly "for preventing forgeries", a proposition which he supports by reference to the concern expressed about this in the Act 1617, c. 12. Erskine goes on to explain that prescription is profitable to society and that the sovereign is entitled "to punish by forfeiture itself the negligence of proprietors when the great purposes of government demand it". Here, again, the utilitarian argument is pressed into service: the public good outweighs private loss resulting from prescription. The same was found in Vinnius's commentary on Justinian's *Institutes*. Erskine concludes with the remark that prescription is grounded on the proprietor's relinquishing or abandoning his right, again a view with a respectable pedigree in the civil law tradition. So far as negative prescription is concerned, Erskine focuses on negligence by the creditor, asserting that "prescription is the penalty of negligence".[81]

Hume is less enthusiastic about the notion of presumed abandonment. **1.52** He prefers to rest prescription on the notion of equity and the recognition of the hardship of disturbing a man's peace and injuring his fortune with a claim which had been long forgotten.[82]

Bell takes the view that 40 years' inaction is a fair ground to presume **1.53** that a claim has been abandoned or satisfied, and supports this by referring to the danger of false evidence, the probability that payment had been made, loss of documents, the equity of discouraging forgotten debts, and disfavour to a person guilty of negligence in pressing a claim. So far as positive prescription is concerned, he notes that this was introduced on grounds of policy "for the settling of men's minds and the encouragement of improvement".[83]

This rapid paraphrase of the main accounts given by the institutional **1.54** writers serves to confirm, as indeed appears from references they cite from time to time, that they wrote with awareness of the civil law background to the subject of prescription. The views which they chose to adopt from that tradition range widely and sometimes appear to have been the subject of a rather random process of selection. That makes it difficult to assert that any uniform notion of the basis of prescription underlies the institutional works.

Early Scottish statutes

Some of the early Acts give reasons for the institution of negative **1.55** prescription. Two of the more notable are worth citing. The Act 1594, c. 24 refers to the problem that procuratories of resignation, instruments

---

[80] Erskine, III, vii, 1.
[81] III, vii, 36. Kames, *Elucidations*, 255 speaks of the role of negligence but emphasises that it is not the whole point: the negative prescription is "to quiet the minds of people who have acquired a conviction of freedom, from being left undisturbed forty years".
[82] *Lectures*, 3.64.
[83] Bell, *Prin.*, s. 606.

of resignation, precepts of *clare constat* or other precepts of sasine are
lost

> "pairtlie be Iniquitie of tyme, pairtlie be perisching of prothogollis
> and scrollis of notaris, pairtlie for nocht delivering of the samyn be
> the personis sellaris and disponeris thairof, pairtlie becaus the
> evidentis of Comprysit landis usis to be abstractit and withhaldin
> upoun malice of pairties, and pairtlie as evidentis nocht thocht
> necessar to have bene kepit efter sa lang tyme Be ressone that the
> charteris makis mentioun of the procuratories and instrumentis of
> resignationis and instrumentis of sasing makis mentioun of the
> preceptis of sasing".

1.56   The Act 1617, c. 12 refers to

> "the gryit preiudice whiche his Maiesties liegis sustenis in thair
> landis and heretages not onlie by the abstracting corrupting and
> conceilling of thair trew evidentis in thair minoritie and les aige and
> by the amissioun thairof by the Iniurie of tyme throche warre,
> plague, fyir or suche lyik occasiounes bot also by the Counterfutte-
> ing and forgeing of fals evidentis and wreatis and Concealling of the
> same to suche a tyme that all meanis of Improving thairof is takin
> away".

1.57   Both of these Acts are much concerned, as is the modern law, with the
question of loss of evidence, and in particular with the role played by
prescription in preventing people's rights or titles being impugned when
with the passage of time they no longer have the evidence to support or
defend them. The 1617 Act is also much preoccupied with forgery, again
a problem which may become harder to detect with the passage of time.

Modern rationales for prescription
1.58   The rationales for prescription which emerge from the modern cases
are mentioned where they arise in later chapters. It is therefore
unnecessary to discuss them here in any detail. But a few paragraphs will
bring the present discussion more or less up to date.

1.59   Friedrich Carl von Savigny (1779–1861) identified the following
rationales for prescription.[84] First, to bring an end to uncertainty, which
was as important for prescription of actions as for positive prescription.
Second, the presumption after the passage of time that a right was
extinguished. Third, to penalise negligence, although he regarded this
not as a substantial ground in itself but as providing justification for what
might (otherwise) appear to be unfair. Fourth, to safeguard the rights of
defenders, since if there were no prescription it would be up to a pursuer
when to proceed, and through long delay he might make the defender's
defence more difficult, for example owing to loss of evidence. Fifth, to
reduce litigation, a point which overlaps with the points about legal
certainty and loss of evidence. There is the same concern as in the
earlier literature with balancing the interests of the parties on the one
hand and with securing the public interest on the other. Savigny was
writing half a century before the German Civil Code came into force.

---

[84] Savigny, *System des heutigen römischen Rechts* (1841), Vol. 5, paras 267–273.

But the modern commentaries on the Code still refer to the public interest, legal certainty, and quiet enjoyment of rights.[85]

Closer to home, it is difficult to improve upon the words of John **1.60** Stuart Mill in his discussion of positive prescription[86]:

"Possession which has not been legally questioned within a moder- **1.61** ate number of years ought to be, as by the laws of all nations it is, a complete title. Even when the acquisition was wrongful, the dis- possession, after a generation has elapsed, of the probably *bona fide* possessors, by the revival of a claim which has been long dormant, would generally be a greater injustice, and almost always a greater private and public mischief, than leaving the original wrong without atonement. It may seem hard that a claim, originally just, should be defeated by mere lapse of time; but there is a time after which, (even looking at the individual case, and without regard to the general effect on the security of possessors) the balance of hardship turns the other way."

This is in essence the modern concept of prescription: punishment for **1.62** the negligence of dilatory proprietors or creditors has disappeared and survives only in the notion that the competing interests of the parties must be weighed. And the weighing of interests surely lies behind the perennial concern about the risk of loss of evidence. In an English case it was noted that "when a period of limitation has expired, a potential defendant should be able to assume that he is no longer at risk from a stale claim. He should be able to part with his papers if they exist and discard any proofs of witnesses which have been taken, discharge his solicitor if he has been retained, and order his affairs on the basis that his potential liability has gone".[87]

But it would be wrong to suppose that there is no more to prescription **1.63** than justice between the parties. Although little overt consideration tends to be given to the idea that prescription serves the public interest, that must remain one of its main justifications. Legal certainty is one of the primary goals of prescription, and it goes beyond the question of the interests of individuals in a particular dispute. It is perhaps this consideration too which points to the relatively limited role played by the doctrine of acquiescence in the modern law. Nowadays positive prescrip- tion and the 20-year negative prescription run even against those who are not of age. They cannot be said to have acquiesced in the loss of their rights, since it was not in their power to defend them. But the policy reflected in the Act is that the public interest in legal certainty demands that entitlement to the benefit of rights and obligations be clear after a period of 10 or 20 years has run. To allow this clear rule to become blurred by considerations of acquiescence might well be to do justice in an individual case. But it would be against the public interest as a whole.

---

[85] See, *e.g., Münchener Kommentar zum BGB*, preliminary comments on Art. 194.

[86] *Principles of political economy* (4th ed., 1857), 2.2.2. See also Adam Smith, *Lectures on Jurisprudence* (Glasgow ed., 1978), pp. 32 and 461 (positive prescription) and 135–136 (negative).

[87] *Yew Bon Tew v. Kenderaan Bas Maria* [1982] 3 All E.R. 833 at 839, *per* Lord Brightman.

PART I

NEGATIVE PRESCRIPTION

The 1973 Act contains the following provisions on negative prescription: a five-year prescription of certain obligations (s. 6); a 20-year prescription of obligations (s. 7); a 20-year prescription of rights relating to property (s. 8); a two-year prescription of obligations to make contribution (s. 8A); and a 10-year prescription of obligations arising under the Consumer Protection Act 1987 (s. 22A).

Each of these prescriptive regimes has its own peculiarities, and to some extent each therefore has to be discussed separately. But there is much common ground, and the approach adopted here is therefore to cover the common ground first, and then to discuss the special points which arise in relation to the different regimes. In particular, it will be clear that sections 6, 7 and (to a lesser extent) 8A have a good deal in common. Section 8, on the other hand, is concerned with property rights, while section 22A derives from different legislation, and its provisions are structured differently.

The next two chapters are concerned with defining the scope of the prescription of obligations. The first of them deals with obligations which do prescribe, the second with rights and obligations which do not. There then follow two more chapters on general issues: the beginning and end of prescriptive periods; and the interruption of prescription. After that attention turns to the specific different types of prescription.

CHAPTER 2

OBLIGATIONS AND THEIR CORRELATIVE RIGHTS

Sections 6, 7 and 8A speak of "obligations", about their subsistence or **2.01**
extinction, and about relevant claims or acknowledgments made in
relation to them. None of these sections speaks of contracts or delicts or
of the sources of obligations, but only of the obligations which arise from
them or in some other way.

Accordingly, the first question in any case will be to identify what the
obligation in question is. Broadly, there might be said to be three
reasons for doing this: first, to see whether the section is applicable at all
to that sort of obligation; then, where this is relevant, to see precisely
what obligation has been the subject of a relevant claim or acknowledgment; and finally, in the light of those considerations, to see what it is
exactly that has or has not prescribed.[1]

"Obligation"

A necessary preliminary is to define "obligation", the key term for the **2.02**
purposes of section 6, 7 and 8A. The 1973 Act provides only that "In this
Part of this Act, unless the context otherwise requires, any reference to
an obligation includes a reference to the right or, as the case may be, to
the obligation (if any), correlative thereto".[2]

For present purposes, however, it is more important that, in the **2.03**
absence of a statutory definition, "obligation" must be given its ordinary
meaning. Stair says "obligation is that which is correspondent to a
personal right . . . and it is nothing more but a legal tie, whereby the
debtor may be compelled to pay or perform something, to which he is
bound by obedience to God, or by his own consent and engagement".[3]
There is a clear resonance here of the—admittedly more secular—
definition in Justinian's *Institutes*.[4] An obligation is (as the etymology
suggests) something which binds one person to another.

From section 15(2) it also emerges that "obligation" in the Act is to **2.04**
be taken to cover not only bilateral obligations but unilateral ones too:
otherwise the reference to a correlative "obligation (if any)" would be
redundant.

---

[1] There also arise questions as to the meaning of more specific terms used in the Act,
such as "obligation relating to land" (Sched. 1, para. 2(e)).

[2] s. 15(2). Walker, p. 51 takes this to refer to the analysis of rights by W. N. Hohfeld,
Fundamental Legal Conceptions as Applied in Judicial Reasoning (ed. W. W. Cook, New
Haven, 1923), esp. pp. 35 *et seq.* and 65 *et seq.* on "jural correlatives".

[3] Stair, I, i, 22; *cf.* Erskine, III, i, 2.

[4] Inst. 3.13, pr.: "an obligation is a legal bond, by which we are constrained by the
necessity of making some performance according to the laws of our state" (*obligatio est
iuris vinculum, quo necessitate adstringimur alicuius solvendae rei secundum nostrae civitatis
iura*).

Identifying which obligation prescribes

2.05　　There are various reasons, as suggested already, why it is essential to be able to identify which obligation (if any) has been extinguished, or claimed upon, or acknowledged, but these questions have not been explored very fully by the courts.

2.06　　The fundamental question is whether a particular legal relationship comprises a single obligation or several different obligations. The remainder of this chapter attempts to explore this question in a general way, although it will be necessary to return to it in various later chapters.[5]

2.07　　The answer to the question is straightforward in some cases. For example, an obligation to pay for construction works and an obligation to submit to arbitration in the event of dispute about the construction works are different obligations. Matters are much less clear in delict, and for that reason this is discussed at greater length.

2.08　　An example is provided by the case of *Dunlop v. McGowans*.[6] The case was concerned with the date when an obligation to make reparation arises. The Act provides that the appropriate date for the start of prescription is when loss, injury or damage has been caused by an act, neglect or default.[7] In this case the defenders were a firm of solicitors who had acted for the pursuers. They failed timeously to serve on a tenant a notice to quit, with the result that the tenant was able to continue in occupation of the leased premises for a further year. Some years later the pursuers raised an action seeking damages from their solicitors. They founded on negligence and breach of contract.

2.09　　While the pursuers accepted that by prescription they had lost any right to sue for loss sustained more than five years earlier, they argued that they could still sue for losses more recent than that. This required them to contend that on these facts there was not just a single obligation but a series of different obligations to make reparation. If there was a single obligation to make reparation, which merely had consequences in damages extending over a number of years, the pursuers' entire claim had prescribed. But if each item of loss rendered enforceable a separate obligation to make reparation for that particular item of loss, only part of their claim would have prescribed. The pursuers' argument was rejected. In the House of Lords, Lord Keith said:

> "The language of section 11(1) affords no warrant for splitting up, in the manner and to the effect contended for, the loss, injury or damage caused by an act, neglect or default. An obligation to make reparation for such loss, injury and damage is a single and indivisible obligation, and one action only may be prosecuted for enforcing it. The right to raise such an action accrues when *injuria* concurs with *damnum*. Some interval of time may elapse between the two, and it appears to me that section 11(1) does no more than recognize

---

[5] See, *e.g.*, in connection with relevant claims, below, paras 5.13–15, and minutes of amendment; below, para. 20.21.

[6] 1979 S.C. 22; 1980 S.C. (H.L.) 73.

[7] ss. 6(3) and 11(1). For detail, see below paras 4.18 *et seq.*

this possibility and make it clear that in such circumstances time is to run from the date when *damnum* results, not from the earlier date of *injuria*."[8]

Accordingly the proper approach is to raise the action within five years of the loss—or for those who prefer it in Latin, the *damnum*—, even although it will not necessarily be possible to quantify loss fully at that point.[9]

The conclusion that there was a single indivisible obligation was not **2.10** too extravagant in *Dunlop*. There was a single breach of duty—in Latin, *injuria*—consisting in the solicitors' failure to serve a notice by a particular date. The consequence of that breach of duty was loss which increased daily.

In other cases it is far less clear that there is only a single obligation, **2.11** and it would be inappropriate to treat *Dunlop* as authority for any such general proposition.

(1) Where, for example, there is a continuing wrong, the analysis has to be quite different. An example of this would be nuisance, which a defender is under a continuing obligation to abate. If the right analysis is that a fresh nuisance is committed every day, it follows that there are many points at which the wrong (*injuria*) and the loss (*damnum*) concur.[10] So it would be open to the pursuer at any time to sue for interdict and damages, but the obligation on the defender to make reparation would prescribe, so far as damages were attributable to a time which preceded the relevant prescriptive period.

(2) In a complex building dispute it is clearly possible for there to be a number of different faults in the process of construction— design or construction faults, failure to use the correct or adequate materials, lack of supervision, failure to inspect, and so forth—and a number of different defects in the building. It would be odd to maintain that these give rise to a single indivisible obligation and to suppose that the discovery of the first defect necessarily starts the running of the prescriptive period in relation. to any other defects which may later be discovered.[11] It follows that in order to apply section 6 or 7 it will be necessary to identify precisely which obligation is in question; and that, where there is a series of defects, it will be necessary to relate individual defects to individual obligations. In other words, the matter of causation will have to be considered.

---

[8] At 81.

[9] *cf. City of Glasgow D.C. v. Excess Insurance Co. Ltd*, 1986 S.L.T. 585. *cf. Gray v. Braer Corporation*, Lord Gill, December 29, 1998, unreported, on s. 9 of the Merchant Shipping (Oil Pollution) Act 1971.

[10] See *Stevenson v. Pontifex and Wood* (1887) 15 R. 125 at 129, *per* L.P. Inglis; and below, para. 7.14. *cf.* in South Africa *Oslo Land Co. Ltd v. Union Government*, 1938 A.D. 584 at 589, *per* Watermeyer J.A.: "there is a distinction between what may be regarded as a single wrongful act giving rise to one cause of action and a continuing injury causing damage from day to day which may give rise to a series of rights of action arising from moment to moment". This was followed recently in *Mbuyisa v. Minister of Police, Transkei*, 1995 (2) S.A. 362.

[11] An argument of this sort was advanced in *Greater Glasgow Health Board v. Baxter Clark & Paul*, 1990 S.C. 237 at 248–249, but since it was not foreshadowed in the pleadings, it was not adjudicated on by the court.

(3) The five-year prescription of section 6 applies only to obligations listed in paragraphs (a)–(g) of Schedule 1 to the Act. It has been held that these paragraphs set out "separate categories of obligations", so that to make a claim under one paragraph for a sum of money is in no way to make a relevant claim under a different paragraph.[12] The context of that remark was the difference between obligations based on contract and those based on unjustified enrichment.[13] But the question is more complicated than this. Would a creditor's claim for interest not be a relevant claim with respect to the debtor's (other) obligations in contract?[14] The answer is surely that it depends on the contractual obligation in issue.

(4) The question exactly what it is that prescribes may also arise in a rather different context: the case of infringement of an obligation not to do something. An important practical instance is the case where a person is subject to a real burden and breaches its terms. The question arises what the effect of the breach is. The Scottish Law Commission has recently posed the question in relation to a burden which prohibits all building on a certain area of land. The burden is breached by the construction of a garden shed. "If the breach continues for the prescriptive period, the right to object to the shed is lost. But is the burden wholly extinguished, leaving the owner free to build a house alongside the shed? Or does the burden survive except insofar as it relates to that particular shed?"[15] To conclude that the burden is wholly extinguished would be odd. That conclusion might be avoided by insisting that there has been no acquiescence in non-observance of the real burden except to the extent of the particular breach, and that the particular breach of the real burden ought to be identified and the effect of prescription confined to it alone. But there appears to be no authority on the question. The Scottish Law Commission recommends that legislation should clarify that the burden is extinguished only to the extent of the particular breach.

2.12   In short, the question of identifying the particular obligation in issue is of general importance: not just to determine when a prescriptive period began to run and whether it has therefore been completed, but also to determine whether the prescriptive period has been interrupted by a relevant claim in relation to the obligation, and what precisely it is that has prescribed.[16]

2.13   In general it is breach of obligations which seems to be most problematic from this point of view. Performance of an obligation may be possible in only one way; but breach of an obligation will frequently be possible in many. Complication may be introduced by the fact that in some cases a pursuer will be able to elect between seeking payment

---

[12] *Alexander Hall & Son (Builders) Ltd v. Strathclyde R.C.*, Lord Morton of Shuna, Feb. 9, 1989, unreported.

[13] Sched. 1, para. 1(b) and (g).

[14] *i.e.* claims under Sched. 1, para. 1 (a)(i) and (g) respectively.

[15] SLC Discussion Paper no. 106 (1998), *Real Burdens*, para. 5.46.

[16] Some points which arise in connection with the making of a "relevant claim" are necessarily anticipated here.

in terms of the contract and seeking damages for breach.[17] It is necessary to deal with the main categories of obligation separately.

Delict

In *British Railways Board v. Strathclyde Regional Council*[18] a writ simply **2.14** set out that a tunnel had collapsed, and that the collapse was due to the fault of the defenders or one of them. It did not identify the act, neglect or default which was contended for as the basis of the obligation. It did not indicate what the defenders had done wrong, who the wrongdoer was, how the obligation on the defenders arose, or even who owned the tunnel. In spite of these defects in specification, the writ in question was in the proper form. It was held to be a relevant claim in terms of section 9 of the Act and to have interrupted prescription. Similarly, in *Macleod v. Sinclair*,[19] a case which concerned amendment of a summons after the expiry of the five-year prescriptive period of section 6, the court allowed detailed averments of fault to be added to the case of negligence and averments of breach of contract to be added for the first time, the original summons having contained (in relation to contract) only a plea-in-law referring to breach of contract. Lord Jauncey held that "if as a result of a certain set of circumstances there arises an obligation to make reparation on the ground of negligence, an action raised within five years which relies on one ground of negligence will prevent the extinction of the obligation albeit different grounds of negligence are added to or substituted for the original grounds after the expiry of the five-year period. There is, for the purposes of s. 6, one obligation to make reparation on the ground of negligence and not a number of different obligations based on different grounds of negligence".[20] It may therefore be possible to plead very generally a case based on negligence.

These issues tend to crop up when a pursuer seeks to amend an action **2.15** after the prescriptive period has run. It is true to say that in most cases the degree of latitude requested has been much less than in *Macleod v. Sinclair*, so it has not actually been necessary to apply Lord Jauncey's dictum *in extremis*. For example, in a solicitors' negligence case it was held that a new case sought to be added by amendment was based on the same obligation arising from professional negligence. Both cases turned essentially on the solicitors' having attached the wrong schedule to an offer.[21]

But in any event it may well be thought that the *Macleod v. Sinclair* **2.16** approach is too broad. For instance, it is very hard to see why a delictual claim against "design and build" contractors based on negligent design should be thought to arise from the same obligation as a claim based on negligent construction. If that is right, there seems to be no good reason why the raising of an action based on the one obligation should have any effect on the prescription of the other. On the other hand, it may be that a new case, based for example on breach of statutory duty, proceeds on

---

[17] *ERDC Construction Ltd v. H. M. Love & Co.*, 1995 S.L.T. 254.
[18] 1981 S.C. 90.
[19] 1981 S.L.T. (Notes) 38.
[20] At 39.
[21] *Safdar v. Devlin*, 1995 S.L.T. 530 (following *McLeod v. Sinclair*, 1981 S.L.T. (Notes) 38 and *N.V. Devos Gebroeder v. Sunderland Sportswear*, 1990 S.C. 291).

precisely the same facts and is directed at precisely the same act or omission as an existing common law case founded on fault and negligence. Here it would make little sense to insist that the two obligations were entirely separate.[22] A practical approach is therefore needed to assessing whether two obligations are the same or different.

2.17　　Recent decisions have taken a more rigorous approach to identifying particular obligations. So a claim in delict has been held not to constitute a relevant claim for breach of contract, and the fact that the contractual claim was said to be implicit in the pleadings founding on delict was held to make no difference.[23] The Inner House has also refused to allow an amendment where the claim remained based in delict and breach of contract but the basis for it was different. The action as originally raised was based on the allegation that the defenders had negligently and without instructions loosed an arrestment; the proposed amendment alleged that the defenders had negligently failed to check the proper designation of a company before raising proceedings and instructing diligence against it.[24]

Contract

2.18　　In contract a narrower approach is clearly preferred. The view has been put forward (*obiter*) that for contractual obligations it is necessary to consider whether a claim founded on one clause of a contract can be a relevant claim in relation to another clause; and the opinion has been expressed that what matters is whether the clauses contain different obligations or are different aspects of a single obligation.[25] This approach to contractual obligations is surely the right one. It does, however, have its drawbacks, since the need to specify every particular clause which is breached can lead in a complex case to vast pleadings.[26] So an action based on one clause of the contract would not prevent the operation of prescription against a quite different obligation contained elsewhere in the contract. The same approach seems to be appropriate where the obligations in question are implied rather than express. The question will again be whether the obligations based on the implied terms are different or are different aspects of the same obligation.[27]

2.19　　If that line is favoured, then it must follow that a completely general assertion of breach of contract (*a fortiori* pleadings—as in *Macleod v. Sinclair*—which fail to condescend on the breach at all) would not necessarily serve to interrupt the prescription of a particular obligation. From this in turn it follows that, where a summons or writ contains no more than a simple plea that money is due and resting owing, it may sometimes be (just) arguable that no relevant claim is made, since it is

---

[22] *cf. Matusczyk v. NCB*, 1955 S.C. 418 (although in terms of the 1973 Act this case would fall under limitation of actions rather than prescription of obligations, so different considerations would apply).

[23] *Middleton v. Douglass*, 1991 S.L.T. 726.

[24] *J. G. Martin Plant Hire v. Bannatyne Kirkwood France & Co.*, 1996 S.C. 105.

[25] *GA Estates Ltd v. Caviapen Trustees Ltd*, 1993 S.L.T. 1045 at 1049. *cf.* also *Gibson v. Carson*, 1980 S.C. 356; *Wylie v. Avon Insurance Co.*, 1988 S.C.L.R. 570.

[26] The recent case in which the summons in a complex building contract extended to several thousand pages comes to mind.

[27] *Ductform Ventilation Ltd v. Andrews-Weatherfoil Ltd*, 1995 S.L.T. 88, where this point was conceded.

unclear what contractual obligation (if any) is founded upon or whether, for example, the action is based in unjustified enrichment. But an argument of this sort would probably be convincing only on particular and unusual facts and not, for instance, where the action arose out of a straightforward debtor and creditor relationship between the parties.

This kind of question—identifying the particular contractual obliga- **2.20** tion in question, determining when prescription began to run and whether it has been interrupted—is of particular importance in complex contracts. In simple contracts, the question of analysing the different obligations contained within the contract can scarcely arise. This would be the case, for example, where a creditor lends the debtor £100 to be repaid in three months with 10 per cent interest. Here there is essentially just one obligation on the borrower: to repay the loan with interest. There is no real scope for considering whether, when the creditor raises an action in relation to the loan, the claim is a relevant one or not. Whether the creditor sues for repayment of the whole or only part of the principal or for interest alone, any claim is likely to be a relevant claim.

Sale, on the other hand, is already a more complex case. Although the **2.21** primary duty on the buyer is to pay the price and on the seller to deliver, there are other standard terms of contract: the seller, for example, impliedly warrants title and quality.[28] If the buyer sues for breach of the warranty of title, can one say that this is the same obligation as the warranty of quality, and that it therefore interrupts the prescriptive period? The answer to this question ought surely to be "no". These are different obligations, and neither one is simply a different aspect of the other; a claim in respect of one should interrupt the prescription of that one but no other. All this is the simple corollary of the fact that the concern of the 1973 Act is with the prescription not of the contract as a whole but of the particular obligation.

In more complex cases still, such as building contracts, there is no **2.22** reason why a claim under a warranty as to suitability of a site should affect the prescription of obligations relating to performance or time for completion. These are neither the same obligation nor are they merely different aspects of a single obligation.

What is required therefore, for example in a building case, is to **2.23** identify the specific obligation which is in question, and to plead not that there has been a breach of a general duty in contract to construct in accordance with the contract, but that there have been specific failures. These failures give rise to particular obligations arising from breach rather than to a single and indivisible breach of contract writ large.

In turn this raises the question of causation of the particular defects **2.24** complained of. Each will have to be related to the breach of a particular contractual obligation. In cases in which defects may emerge over a lengthy period—building contracts are the prime example—for the purposes of prescription it will be particularly important to examine the question of causation and whether any given defect is an exacerbation of

---

[28] Sale of Goods Act 1979, ss. 12 and 14.

a defect which has already come to light, or is unrelated. So, for example, in *Sinclair v. MacDougall Estates Ltd*,[29] it was observed that it would be unjust if a minor failure to design or construct were held sufficient to constitute a breach of duty in relation to a major and different failure of design or construction discovered later, and if it were therefore to start the prescriptive period running at an early stage.[30] It was found in that case after a preliminary proof that there was no causal link between the damage discovered earlier and the major defect complained of by the pursuer. The obligation to make reparation for the major defect had therefore not prescribed.

2.25 There will continue to be difficulties at the borderline. To hope for absolute clarity is unrealistic. For example, it has been observed that there is very little difference between a claim for costs arising from delay in a building contract and a claim for damages for breach of contract for failing to give access to the site, with consequent delay.[31] This is of course true. But it seems difficult in principle to treat a claim for payment in terms of a contract as amounting to, or arising from, the same obligation as a claim for damages for breach of a contract. The same constraint might not, however, apply where both obligations were directed either at performance or at damages. In the interests of avoiding artificiality, probably the best that can be done is again to say that what matters is whether the contractual clauses contain different obligations or are different aspects of the same one.

2.26 The conclusion seems to be that what is required is to take a pragmatic approach to considering whether two obligations are different or merely different aspects of the same one.[32] There is another reason for this: plainly, unfairness might result if some contractual obligations were extinguished by prescription while others remained alive. While this problem is contained to some degree by the doctrine of mutuality of contractual obligations, there may be cases which can only be fairly resolved by the courts' adoption of a pragmatic approach to identifying the obligations in question. In carrying out this exercise, it may be that some guidance can be derived from the considerations which apply to *res judicata*. If a later action (for example on the basis of a breach of a warranty of title to goods) would not be barred *re judicata* by the fact that there had been an earlier one (for example on warranty as to the quality of those goods), that is a fair indication that the obligations which are the foundation of the two actions are different.[33] So far as prescription is concerned, a claim under one ought therefore to have no effect on a claim under the other.

Unjustified enrichment

2.27 In *NV Devos Gebroeder v. Sunderland Sportswear*[34] the question arose whether the pursuers' claim for recompense for the value of goods which they had supplied to the defenders had prescribed. Owing to the

---

[29] 1994 S.L.T. 76.

[30] At 82.

[31] *Ductform Ventilation Ltd v. Andrews-Weatherfoil Ltd*, above.

[32] In passing, it may be noted that the test the South African courts apply is whether the pursuer seeks to enforce the same or substantially the same claim or right: *Mokoena v. SA Eagle Insurance Co. Ltd*, 1982 (1) S.A. 780 at 786D; *Neon & Cold Cathode Illuminations (Pty) Ltd v. Ephron*, 1978 (1) S.A. 463; Loubser, *Extinctive Prescription*, pp. 127 *et seq.*

[33] *cf. Matusczyk v. NCB*, above; see also below, paras 5.13–15 on interruption of prescription in this context.

[34] 1990 S.C. 291.

pursuers' material breach of contract—the fact that the goods supplied were disconform to contract—the pursuers' action in contract failed. They then proceeded with a claim based on recompense.[35] Was the contractual action a relevant claim with respect to the obligation to make recompense? In the Inner House a majority found that if the essential basis of an obligation is different in fact and law, then the obligation must be a different one for the purposes of the Act, even if the surrounding circumstances are the same.[36] These two obligations were constituted at different times and in different ways: the obligation to pay the contract price by agreement at the time the contract was made; the obligation to make recompense on principles of equity at the time of enrichment of the defenders at the pursuers' expense.[37]

Lord Coulsfield, dissenting, thought it artificial to say that, until they **2.28** pleaded recompense, the pursuers made no claim on the defenders for payment of the value of the goods. He did not question that contract and recompense were different grounds of claim but thought that the fact that the pursuers' claim was originally based in contract should not require that claim "to be read so narrowly as to exclude another legal ground derived from exactly those facts and circumstances which have always formed the subject matter of the action".[38] Although this approach is in many ways attractive, it is difficult to square with the words of the Act. A relevant claim must be made upon an obligation; and, if contract and unjustified enrichment are different sources of obligation, it is hard in logic to see how a contractual claim can affect an obligation arising in unjustified enrichment or delict.

Concluding comments

There may be some force in the view that a stricter approach should **2.29** be taken to the case of contract than other obligations. Where contractual obligations are concerned, it is true to say that each could readily have been included in a separate agreement. Their inclusion in one and the same document, although far from fortuitous, need not mean that they give rise to only one single and indivisible obligation. In the case of delict and the various kinds of unjustified enrichment—what Stair calls obediential obligations[39]—it makes more sense to say that (as it were, in retrospect) there is one obligation of that nature in the circumstances which have actually arisen. For that reason, it may be appropriate to allow slightly more latitude in such areas.[40]

But it is far from clear, when the same statutory provisions are being **2.30** applied, on what satisfactory basis the adoption of a general approach in delict and a particular one in contract can be justified. This point is all

---

[35] They were allowed to amend their contractual action to plead recompense, and the question of prescription of that claim was debated on procedure roll.

[36] At 303.

[37] At 304.

[38] At 310.

[39] Stair, I, i, 19 and I, iii, 3–I, iii, 4.

[40] In *GA Estates Ltd v. Caviapen Trustees Ltd*, above, in order to distinguish the case from *British Railways Board v. Strathclyde R.C.*, above, Lord Coulsfield suggested at 1049 J–K that: "The obligation to refrain from causing damage by fault is general and permanent. Obligations which arise from contracts are quite different: they are particular and may be temporary."

the more important since concurrent cases of negligence and breach of contract may be pleaded against the same defenders arising from the same facts. This is more or less routine in professional negligence cases. While some latitude may be appropriate in the case of extra-contractual obligations, there is therefore no good reason to allow very much more. The stricter approach taken in more recent cases (as opposed to the liberal line followed in *Macleod v. Sinclair*) is therefore to be welcomed.[41]

2.31   There is another reason for this view. Concurrence of actions is, broadly speaking, of limited importance in this area of Scots law. The reason is that the causes of action in breach of contract and in delict arise, in terms of section 11 of the Act, at the same time. By contrast, in England the limitation periods in respect of those two different causes of action begin at different times.[42] That has led to some distortion of the underlying substantive law.[43] While this has been avoided in Scotland, unwelcome confusion may nonetheless arise if the pleadings required in order to interrupt prescription are significantly different.

---

[41] There is more to say on this question later in connection with adjustment and amendment of pleadings: see below, para. 20.21.

[42] Limitation Act 1980, ss. 2 and 5: both sections provide that the limitation period runs from the date of accrual of the cause of action. In breach of contract this is taken to occur at the date of breach; in tort only when loss is sustained. See McGee, *Limitation Periods*, pp. 65 *et seq.* and 165 *et seq.*

[43] *Société Commerciale de Réassurance v. Eras (International) Ltd* [1992] 2 All E.R. 82 at 85, *per* Mustill L.J. See also J. A. Weir, "Prescription, classification and concurrence" (1962) 36 Tulane L.R. 556–571.

CHAPTER 3

IMPRESCRIPTIBLE RIGHTS AND OBLIGATIONS

Schedule 3 sets out a list of rights and obligations which are not subject **3.01** to negative prescription. It is probably right to suppose that the Schedule should be interpreted narrowly, since it is a list of exceptions to the rule that rights and obligations should prescribe; and in the law before the 1973 Act the long negative prescription was applied liberally. As Bell noted, "abandonment is presumed in respect to all absolute rights and obligations whatever, mutual or unilateral, heritable or moveable, if not insisted on within the term".[1]

"SCHEDULE 3

Rights and Obligations which are Imprescriptible for the Purposes of Sections 7 and 8 and Schedule 1

The following are imprescriptible rights and obligations for the purposes of sections 7(2) and 8(2) of, and paragraph 2(h) of schedule 1 to, this Act, namely—

(a) any real right of ownership in land;
(b) the right in land of the lessee under a recorded lease;
(c) any right exercisable as a *res merae facultatis*;
(d) any right to recover property *extra commercium*;
(e) any obligation of a trustee—

(i) to produce accounts of the trustee's intromissions with any property of the trust;
(ii) to make reparation or restitution in respect of any fraudulent breach of trust to which the trustee was a party or was privy;
(iii) to make furthcoming to any person entitled thereto any trust property, or the proceeds of any such property, in the possession of the trustee, or to make good the value of any such property previously received by the trustee and appropriated to his own use;

(f) any obligation of a third party to make furthcoming to any person entitled thereto any trust property received by the third party otherwise than in good faith and in his possession;
(g) any right to recover stolen property from the person by whom it was stolen or from any person privy to the stealing thereof;
(h) any right to be served as heir to an ancestor or to take any steps necessary for making up or completing title to any interest in land."

---

[1] Bell, *Prin.*, s. 608. *Cf.* Stair, IV, xl, 20, noting that prescription "excludes all title and action upon rights".

Schedule 3: the details

(a) "real right of ownership in land"

3.02   A real right of ownership in land is constituted by recording the deed granting the title in the General Register of Sasines or registering the "interest in land" in the Land Register of Scotland, as appropriate. Accordingly, a person who is owner of land by reason of recording or registering the disposition granting him title to it is secure against the 20-year prescription.[2] The point is that real rights of ownership in land are lost not by negative prescription but when, by the operation of positive prescription, the title of another person to the land in question becomes exempt from challenge.[3] That depends on that person satisfying the requirements of positive prescription, which are discussed in Chapters 14–16. Here it is enough to say that it is essential to a system of land ownership which depends on the faith of the registers that only positive prescription should apply in this context, since it will run only upon a sufficient recorded or registered title,[4] and the faith of the registers will therefore be unaffected. If, on the other hand, negative prescription were allowed to extinguish rights of ownership in land, the standing of the property registers would soon become very dubious.

3.03   While positive prescription will prevent challenge to a possessor who has possessed on a sufficient title for the prescriptive period, that will not apply where the deed on which he founds was *ex facie* invalid or forged. In that case the true owner's right must subsist, since it cannot be excluded by negative prescription either. It follows that the true owner's right to bring an action of reduction in such circumstances will never prescribe.[5]

3.04   Matters are different where rectification under section 9 of the Land Registration (Scotland) Act 1979 is concerned. This is because registration, even when it is erroneous, makes the person named in the register the owner of the "interest in land" registered. A person who challenges the registered owner cannot therefore claim that it is he who is currently the owner—by definition he is not, since the registered owner is. Instead, a person seeking rectification is claiming that ownership of the land ought, by rectification, to be made over to him. The right to seek rectification will prescribe under the 20-year negative prescription.[6] (It may be barred earlier, if the registered owner satisfies the requirements for positive prescription before then.)

3.05   In a conveyancing transaction, until his or her title is recorded or registered, the grantee has no real right (*jus in re*).[7] The grantee's right is

---

[2] It may be noted that this sort of right is not one which can be treated as correlative of any obligation; accordingly, it may be assumed that this paragraph of Sched. 3 is directed at the scope of s. 8 rather than s. 7.

[3] There is an elaborate debate on this question in Napier, pp. 80 and 98, criticising Erskine, III, vii, 8. But the essential point is as stated in the text.

[4] Apart from the special cases dealt with in s. 2 of the Act.

[5] Bell, *Prin.*, s. 610; Napier, p. 551; *Cubbison v. Hyslop* (1837) 16 S. 112, *per* Lord Corehouse.

[6] *cf.* also para. 7.14; *Short's Tr. v. Keepers of the Registers of Scotland*, 1996 S.C. (H.L.) 14; *MRS Hamilton Ltd v. Baxter*, 1998 S.L.T. 1075.

[7] I give the traditional Latin term in each instance, since this appears in many of the older texts and cases.

capable of prescribing, so long as it is no more than a right against the granter based on missives of sale (a contractual right or right *in personam*) and the disposition has yet to be delivered. It remains at that stage a right correlative to the granter's contractual obligation which is capable of prescribing under section 7.[8] Once the disposition has been delivered but before it has been recorded or the title has been registered, the grantee has a personal right to the subjects (*jus ad rem*).[9] This is not a real right and therefore does not fall within paragraph (a) of Schedule 3, but it does fall within paragraph (h), which is discussed later.[10]

(b) "right in land of the lessee under a recorded lease"
This applies to leases for a term in excess of 20 years, which can be **3.06** recorded under the Registration of Leases (Scotland) Act 1857 Act.[11] In terms of section 2 of that Act, on registration the grantee's right is effectual against any singular successor of the granter. The same applies here as to the case of ownership of land: negative prescription has no place, but the tenant's right could nonetheless be excluded if another person completed positive prescription in relation to the subjects of the lease.

(c) "res merae facultatis"[12]
This Latin expression is sometimes—not very helpfully, perhaps— **3.07** glossed in English as "a mere faculty". Its meaning is explored in the following pages, but the essence is that it is a right which a person is at liberty to exercise or not. Although the term does not appear in the *Digest*, it has an extremely fine pedigree in the civil law tradition.[13] There are also plenty of old cases. Morison's *Dictionary* devotes a section to *res merae facultatis*.[14] But the term can hardly be said to be in common usage, and the use of a deeply obscure term within the scheme of the 1973 Act causes some problems.

The description of *res merae facultatis* given by the Scottish Law **3.08** Commission in its memorandum preceding the 1973 Act is not accurate: "rights of such a character that their exercise would be expected only periodically or irregularly."[15] Better is the statement made to the House of Lords by the Minister of State when commenting on this provision in

---

[8] Not under s. 6, because it is an "obligation relating to land".

[9] *Sharp v. Thomson*, 1997 S.C. (H.L.) 66, depending on how extensively it is interpreted, may suggest that the holder of the delivered disposition has greater rights than had been thought hitherto. But for present purposes it makes no difference, since the right in question is clearly imprescriptible.

[10] Again, a *jus ad rem* appears to fall within s. 8 rather than s. 7, it not being an obligation in the normal sense nor the correlative of one.

[11] In areas operational for registration of title, in order to constitute a real right in the land the lease must be registered in the Land Register: Land Registration (Scotland) Act 1979, s. 3(3).

[12] For discussion see Napier, pp. 645–647; Millar, pp. 86–87; A. Brett, *Liberty, Right and Nature* (Cambridge, 1997), pp. 192 *et seq.*

[13] See, *e.g.* in the 16th century: A. Cravetta, *Tractatus de antiquitate temporis* (Venice, 1549), Pt 4, n. 214; J. F. Balbus, *Tractatus de praescriptione* (Cologne, 1573), Pt. 5, n. 1; M. Wesembecius, *Paratitla in pandectas iuris civilis* (Basel, 1568); in the 17th century: Grotius, *de iure belli ac pacis* (Amsterdam, 1646), 2.4.15 (only in the rubric); Voet, *Commentarius* 13.7.7.

[14] M. 10724–10732.

[15] SLC Memo. no. 9 (1968), p. 12.

the Bill: "the right to exercise the ordinary uses of property, which the proprietor may assert or not as he pleases, without the risk of losing the right by failure to assert it."[16]

3.09 The essence of the matter is that things which a person has a free choice or *facultas* to do or not do not prescribe; a typical example given in the sixteenth-century works is the right of walking along a public road. Even if a person never makes use of that faculty, no lapse of time, however long, will ever bar him or her from exercising the faculty at some later date.

3.10 But some caution is required in employing the old authorities, since the law in certain cases is now different. So far as public rights of way are concerned, in the *Digest* it is said that they do not prescribe through non-use,[17] and for this reason the early authorities took them as a typical illustration of a *facultas*. But this is not the whole truth: Johannes Voet in his *Commentary on the Digest* (1698–1704) points out that a public right of way does prescribe if somebody has obstructed it for the prescriptive period so that it cannot be used.[18] Certainly, public rights of way can prescribe in Scots law nowadays.[19] Equally, another common illustration of the *res merae facultatis* has now to be viewed with circumspection. This is the right to redeem a pledge. Again, the old authorities take the view that the passage of time should not prevent the debtor from discharging the debt and asserting his property right to the pledge; and that he can be displaced only by the acquisition of a positive title to the pledge by somebody else. But it seems clear that under the 1973 Act the right of ownership of moveable property can prescribe.[20] If that is so, it is hard to see how the debtor's right of redemption can now be imprescriptible. The old authorities probably no longer state the law.[21] They do, however, bring out an important point: that a critical question is the distinction between non-use of the right and acquisition of an adverse right by some other person.

3.11 This point is developed in the main institutional discussion, which is by Bankton. According to him, "a mere faculty, or power of using a thing, cannot prescribe. A faculty is either a Liberty granted by the public law . . . or private, competent to one in the exercise of his right, as to build on his ground at pleasure; to redeem a wadset; to take seisin on a charter; or the like. . . . But when one has a faculty to exercise a right, which is competent by way of action, if the same is not sued within 40 years, it prescribes . . . every right in law or equity is excluded by the long prescription . . . ."[22] The key point which emerges from this account is that the person who enjoys the right has the option whether or not to exercise it. That, however, is of little help in identifying the rights which are properly so described, since in a weak sense it is true of virtually all rights.[23]

---

[16] *Hansard*, H.L. Vol. 341, col. 422.
[17] D. 43.11.2, Iavolenus 10 *ex Cassio*.
[18] *Commentarius*, 13.7.7.
[19] Erskine, III, vii, 10 (and note (a)); *Macfarlane v. Morrison* (1865) 4 M. 257; 1973 Act, s. 3(3); Cusine and Paisley, *Servitudes and Rights of Way*, para. 24.04.
[20] s. 8; see below, para. 3.18.
[21] *Drum v. Coltness* (1684) M. 10726; *Chalmers v. Oliphant* (1766) M. 5178; *cf. Thomson v. Stewart* (1840) 2 D. 564; Bankton, III, ii, 75; Napier, p. 136; Millar, p. 21.
[22] Bankton, II, xii, 22–23.
[23] *cf.* Gloag, *Contract*, p. 738.

Bankton distinguishes between the faculty to exercise a right which is, **3.12**
and that which is not, competent by way of action. In the second case,
the right prescribes; in the first it does not. The notion is essentially that
all rights and uses of property which imply no claim against another may
be exercised at any time. This is certainly how the matter was understood
by the leading sixteenth-century authors. A faculty must involve no right,
no action and no defence but simply the free choice of the person who
exercises it.[24] This of course is not to say that exercise of the right will
have no effect on others. But it does not amount to an assertion of any
right against them.

So *res merae facultatis* will cover things which are a part of ownership **3.13**
proper[25] or, in more modern terminology, the normal incidents of
ownership. An instance is the landowner's right to put up gates on a
servitude right of way, provided the gates do not obstruct the use of the
servitude by the dominant tenement.[26] Such rights can be exercised or
not at any time, at the pleasure of the party who has them, if they are
not inconsistent with the rights of another party.[27] Accordingly, where
there is or can be no adverse right, the landowner's right to do
something is not susceptible of being extinguished by prescription. These
considerations apply to such matters as "choosing a spot for a kitchen
garden, planting a tree, or building a house at my march",[28] filling in
drainage ditches or opening up a doorway in a wall.[29] Of course there is
something slightly odd and probably not very helpful in speaking of these
as "rights". They are certainly not rights in the Hohfeldian sense of
having correlative duties. It is perhaps better simply to describe them as
being incidents of ownership.[30]

There is a second sense in which the term "*res merae facultatis*" is **3.14**
used: the case where it is possible for an adverse right to arise, but only
by positive prescription. An illustration is provided by the case of *Leck v.
Chalmers*.[31] In that case for the prescriptive period one *pro indiviso*
proprietor of land made no use of an access stairway built on the
common land. It was held that his right to do so was *res merae facultatis*
and could not be lost by non-use. A right of property of that sort was not
affected by negative prescription. But it might be affected by positive
prescription if, through possession on a sufficient title, the adverse right
of another party became fortified by positive prescription.[32]

---

[24] Cravetta, above, Pt 5, n. 1; Balbus, above, Pt 5, n. 4.

[25] Wesembecius, above: *quae absolutae sunt facultatis et iure dominii competunt nec ab alio debentur sed insunt propriis dominiis.*

[26] *Sutherland v. Thomson* (1876) 3 R. 485.

[27] *ibid.* at 490.

[28] These examples are from Kames, *Elucidations*, 248.

[29] *Haigues v. Halyburton* (1704–07) M. 10726 (building a mill); *Anderson v. Robertson*, 1958 S.C. 367 (drainage ditch); *Smith v. Stewart* (1884) 11 R. 921 (right to obtain access when occasion arises); *Gellatly v. Arrol* (1863) 1 M. 592 (right to open up a doorway into a common stair).

[30] In *Sutherland v. Thomson*, above, at 490 Lord Neaves describes the right as a function of the permanent right of property.

[31] (1859) 21 D. 408 at 417. A similar example was given by Lord Neaves in *Gellatly v. Arrol*, above at 602.

[32] It must be emphasised that servitudes prescribe under the 20-year prescription of s. 8, and that they are accordingly not *res merae facultatis*. In this case, the reason use of the access stairway was not a servitude is that it was over land owned *pro indiviso* by the user.

3.15   Accordingly, rights of this sort will be unaffected by negative prescription and affected only as a consequence of some other party obtaining an unchallengeable right by positive prescription. That, however, will in the ordinary way proceed only through possession upon a sufficient title. These considerations apply in much the same way to cases of working mineral rights and enjoying fishings. It is only where another acquires an unchallengeable adverse right by the necessary possession on a sufficient title that the right to such enjoyment is lost.[33]

3.16   It seems reasonable therefore to conclude that a *res merae facultatis* is a property right which cannot be lost by negative prescription either (1) because it is a right whose exercise implies no claim on anyone else or against their rights or (2) because it is a (normal) incident of ownership which can be lost only as a consequence of the fortification in some other person of a right inconsistent with it. The common ground between these two categories is that they are rights which are lost only by the establishment of an adverse right, and that can happen, if at all, only by positive prescription. But so long as there is no adverse right there is no question of their prescribing.

3.17   In passing, it may be noted that the establishment of an adverse right or interest is inevitably more problematic in cases of property than obligations. In obligations, by definition there is another party to an obligation; in property cases this will depend on the assertion of an adverse claim. In each case it will be reasonable, when nothing is done in the face of that adverse right or claim, to speak of abandonment or acquiescence by the person whose right has prescribed. But until that point a failure to exercise or assert a right involves neither acquiescence nor abandonment and has for prescription precisely no significance.

3.18   **Rights which are not** *merae facultatis*. Various other rights have sometimes been described as *res merae facultatis* and therefore ought to be mentioned here:

> (1) "Rights to exact payments of feu-duty, rent, interest and similar periodical payments; the rights to particular terms' payments are extinguished by the short negative prescription, but the continuing right to exact payments as they fall due is not extinguished."[34] It is clear that these rights, which do involve correlative rights or obligations on the part of the payee, are quite different in character from those discussed above.
>
> The inclusion of this class of right under *res merae facultatis* appears to be based on a misunderstanding.[35] It is true that a right to exact rent in the future does not prescribe in the present, but that is not because it is imprescriptible but because the obligation is not yet enforceable and time has not therefore begun to run. Rights such as annuities consist on the creditor's part in a series

---

[33] *Crawfurd v. Bethune* (1821) 1 S. 110 (working minerals below land held on a prescriptive title); *Agnew v. Mags of Stranraer* (1822) 2 S. 36 (at 42) (fishings); *Warrand's Trs v. Mackintosh* (1890) 17 R. (H.L.) 13 at 19 (fishings).

[34] Walker, p. 78.

[35] The right to exact feu duty does not prescribe, but this is because it is regarded as inherent in the feudal relationship: Erskine, III, vii, 12; *Duke of Argyll v. Campbell*, 1912 S.C. 458 at 480. (Claims for arrears of feu duty prescribe in the normal way.)

of rights to payment of instalments for particular periods. These prescribe individually. Because there is no entitlement to any annual instalment until the particular year in which it falls due, it follows that there is, so far as that instalment is concerned, no enforceable obligation and no prescription of the right to payment. Every year's payment is a separate obligation.[36] Similarly, in a lease it does not make any real sense to speak of a tenant's general obligation to pay rent for the term of the lease, as opposed to the tenant's obligation to pay rent for specific periods. The corollary is that the obligation to make payment cannot prescribe until the payment is due. For these reasons, although the right to exact periodical payments does not prescribe in the ordinary way, this is not because it is *res merae facultatis*. It has been seen already that the term *"res merae facultatis"* properly applies to rights which do not involve any claim against another party. Rights to periodical payments clearly do not fall within that class.

Indeed, it is sometimes possible for the underlying or "principal" obligation itself to be extinguished by prescription. This shows that such an obligation is not *merae facultatis*. Authority on this point is elderly and not quite consistent. But the position seems to be this: in some cases it may be possible to analyse the obligation as being a single principal obligation, with individual periodical obligations of payment which are accessories to it. In such a case if no periodical payment was made for the whole prescriptive period, then the principal obligation to make payments would be extinguished; the individual annual obligations of payment would also fall, being extinguished as accessories of the principal.[37]

(2) Ownership of moveables. It has been pointed out that the argument that ownership of moveables is lost by prescription assumes that their ownership is not *res merae facultatis*.[38] It seems unlikely that it is, because the assertion of ownership is of a character rather different from the assertion of the various rights which the authorities establish as being *res merae facultatis*.[39] Secondly, and perhaps more importantly, if it is, then paragraph (g) of Schedule 3 to the 1973 Act is redundant: it provides that the right to recover stolen property from the thief or one privy to the theft is imprescriptible. If the right to recover moveable property never prescribed anyway, under Schedule 3(c), this provision would not be required.

The expression *"res merae facultatis"* is used in the old cases in a wide range of contexts, and not invariably with precision.[40]

---

[36] Erskine, III, vii, 13; *Lockhart v. Duke of Gordon* (1730) M. 10736.

[37] Bankton, II, xii, 19; Napier, pp. 647–650; Kames, *Elucidations*, 250.

[38] *Stair Memorial Encyclopaedia*, Vol. 18, para. 567.

[39] But see *Turnbull v. Husband* (1697) M. 10726, where the husband's right to recover a gift from his wife is described as *res merae facultatis*: this, however, is because such gifts are revocable and are confirmed only by the death of the donor.

[40] See preceding note. For further illustrations, see *Encyclopedia of the Laws of Scotland*, Vol. 12, para. 73; Napier, pp. 645 *et seq.*; see, *e.g.*, vassal's right to enter with over-superior: *Cheyne v. Smith* (1832) 10 S. 622; right to surrender teinds: *Chisholm-Batten v. Cameron* (1873) 11 M. 292; *Earl of Minto v. Pennell* (1874) 1 R. 156; right of holder of decree of sale of teinds to call on titular to denude: *Cardross v. Graham* (1710) M. 10657; right of redemption of burdens imposed on land: *Reid's Trs v. Duchess of Sutherland* (1881) 8 R. 509.

Although it is suggested that the core meaning of the term is as explained above, nonetheless it may be that not all cases fit readily. In these circumstances it is rather to be regretted that the draftsman of the 1973 Act thought it appropriate to employ the term at all, let alone without any clarification.[41]

(3) Servitudes. These clearly prescribe and so cannot be *res merae facultatis*,[42] although sometimes the borderline between a servitude right and a right *merae facultatis* may be difficult to draw.[43]

(4) Miscellaneous decided cases. Some old decisions have determined that certain obscure rights are not *res merae facultatis*.[44]

(d) right to recover property extra commercium

3.19   A *res extra commercium* is a thing which is not susceptible of private ownership. The term *"res extra commercium"* does not appear to have any technical meaning in Scots law. There is a modest amount of authority in the cases for particular types of *res extra commercium*. Erskine, in a discussion of classes of things which is heavily dependent on Roman law, includes among *res extra commercium* (1) *res communes*, things common to all, such as air and running water; (2) *res publicae*, state property, such as highways, harbours, and navigable rivers; (3) *res universitatis*, property destined to special uses, such as that of boroughs, hospitals, or lawful corporations and societies; (4) *res divini juris*, such as churches.[45]

3.20   There is a certain amount of (slightly) more recent authority. Erskine's third category has been held not to prevent the sale of municipal buildings.[46] The basis for that decision was that the purpose of the restriction was to ensure that the municipality had a place in which it could carry on its administrative functions; since in that case it did, there was no reason to prevent it selling its previous administrative premises. Accordingly, there is some reason to suppose that the courts will take a narrow, functional approach to determining what property is to be treated as *extra commercium*.

3.21   It has been held that records of a presbytery are *extra commercium*, on the basis that, as records of one of the established courts of the country, they are held inalienably for the benefit of the public and are altogether unsuitable to be acquired by commerce.[47] It was the example of court records and other public documents which was used by the Minister of State in explaining to the House of Lords why this provision was needed in the Act: it must be possible for the proper legal custodians of such

---

[41] "Why cannot we put these things in English?", as was said of this Act in another context in the House of Lords: *Hansard* H.L. Vol. 341, cols 423–425.

[42] *Pace* Walker, p. 78; see, *e.g.*, Erskine, II, ix, 37.

[43] *Smith v. Stewart* (1884) 11 R. 921, better regarded as a servitude since it relates to another's property. In *Gellatly v. Arrol* (1863) 1 M. 592 the decision that the right to open up a doorway into a common stair was not a servitude but *res merae facultatis* seems to have been influenced by the fact that there was an existing doorway, which had for some reason been blocked up.

[44] A right of constabulary: *Dun v. Montrose* (1731) M. 10732; a right to assume a penal jurisdiction ("repledgiation"): *Mags of Ayrshire v. Irvine* (1712) M. 10731 (reported by Fountainhall under the name *Boswell v. Gray*, Jan. 29, 1712).

[45] Erskine, II, i, 5–II, i, 8.

[46] *Mags of Kirkcaldy v. Marks & Spencer Ltd*, 1937 S.L.T. 574.

[47] *Presbytery of Edinburgh v. University of Edinburgh* (1890) 28 S.L.R. 567.

things to recover them regardless of the lapse of time.[48] It seems not unlikely that this is the area in which the restriction will retain some significance.

The discussions of the institutional writers mention *res extra commer-* **3.22** *cium* in the context of positive prescription.[49] They observe that the fact that such a *res* cannot be privately owned means that, even if it were possessed by a private individual in circumstances in which positive prescription would normally take place, no title to it could be acquired by prescription.[50] That proposition is self-evident and justifies the silence of the Act on this question. Positive prescription, however, is only one side of the coin. Here the Act is concerned with negative prescription. Although a practical instance of this is hard to imagine, without provision of the sort made here, it would theoretically be possible for the person enjoying rights in a *res extra commercium* to lose them by negative prescription. If that occurred, but it was impossible for anybody else to prescribe title positively to the *res*, then it would presumably become *res nullius* and fall into the ownership of the Crown.

(e) any obligation of a trustee—(i) to produce accounts of the trustee's intromissions with any property of the trust; (ii) to make reparation or restitution in respect of any fraudulent breach of trust to which the trustee was a party or was privy; (iii) to make furthcoming to any person entitled thereto any trust property, or the proceeds of any such property, in the possession of the trustee, or to make good the value of any such property previously received by the trustee and appropriated to his own use

These questions arise in the law of trusts in the narrow sense: for **3.23** example, trustees are under a duty to account; trust beneficiaries can claim from trustees trust property or its surrogatum. But the Act gives a much broader definition of "trustee" and of "trust", capable of extending well beyond the law of trusts. This causes some problems. The definition given in the Act is this: "'trustee' includes any person holding property in a fiduciary capacity for another and, without prejudice to that generality, includes a trustee within the meaning of the Trusts (Scotland) Act 1921; and 'trust' shall be construed accordingly".[51] The definition in the 1921 Act is that "'trustee' shall mean and include any trustee under any trust whether nominated, appointed, judicially or otherwise, or assumed, whether sole or joint, and whether entitled or not to receive any benefit under the trust or any remuneration as trustee for his services, and shall include any trustee *ex officio*, executor nominate, tutor, curator, guardian (including a father or mother acting as guardian of a child under the age of 16 years) and judicial factor".

It is important to be clear that owing to the broad definition of "trust" **3.24** and "trustee" in the 1973 Act—"any person holding property in a fiduciary capacity for another"—, the question of an obligation being imprescriptible can arise well outside the context of trusts proper, and may cover all or many cases in which there is no trust but the debtor in the obligation owes a fiduciary duty to the creditor. There is, however,

---

[48] *Hansard*, H.L. Vol. 342, col. 257.
[49] *cf.* Stair, II, ii, 10; Bankton, II, xii, 13; Erskine, III, vii, 13.
[50] *cf. Code Civil*, Art. 2226.
[51] s. 15(1).

little certainty about the precise scope of this category. Solicitors seem clearly to fall within it, since (in England) the solicitor–client relationship has been described as "one of the most important fiduciary relationships known to our law".[52] It has been held that Schedule 3(e) can extend to company directors, as they are in fiduciary positions with respect to their companies.[53] Liquidators too may be said to be fiduciaries.[54] But it is not possible here to attempt to define "fiduciary capacity" for the purposes of the 1973 Act.

3.25   A leading account suggests that the core content of the fiduciary position is that "a fiduciary (a) cannot misuse his position, or knowledge or opportunity resulting from it, to his own or to a third party's advantage; and (b) cannot in any manner falling within the scope of his service have a personal interest or an inconsistent engagement with a third party—unless this is freely and informedly consented to by the ben-eficiary or is authorized by law."[55] This seems to suggest that the characteristic remedy for breach of fiduciary duty will either be restitu-tionary in nature or else an accounting. Nonetheless, damages can be given at least for certain breaches of fiduciary duty, although the award of damages threatens to blur the borderline between breach of fiduciary duty and the ordinary breach of duty in delict.[56] There will be a little more to say on this below.

3.26   Nothing is said either in the consultative memorandum or in the report of the Scottish Law Commission which preceded the 1973 Act to explain why the Act adopts such a broad definition of trust and trustee.[57] The English legislation adopts no such definition.[58] This difference is the more surprising since the Scottish provisions follow the English, more or less word for word.[59]

3.27   **(i) The obligation to produce accounts.** A trustee (in the strict sense) will never be relieved of his obligation to produce accounts. It is sometimes assumed that this provision is dealing with the trustee's general obligation to account.[60] But the wording—the obligation to produce accounts—is narrower than this, and a narrower interpretation of it is supported by the following considerations. The very next sub-paragraph in this Schedule makes the trustee's liability for fraudulent

---

[52] *Re van Laun* [1907] 2 K.B. 23 at 29, *per* Cozens Hardy M.R.
[53] *Ross v. Davy*, 1996 S.C.L.R. 369 at 374.
[54] Gore Brown, *Companies*, para. 34.6.
[55] P. D. Finn, "Fiduciary law in the modern world" in E. McKendrick (ed.), *Commercial aspects of trusts and fiduciary obligations* (1992), pp. 7 and 9. For further discussion see R. P. Austin, "Moulding the content of fiduciary duties" in A. J. Oakley (ed.), *Trends in contemporary trust law* (1996), p. 153.
[56] See *Nocton v. Ashburton* [1914] A.C. 932, with the comments of Lord Browne-Wilkinson in *Henderson v. Merrett Syndicates Ltd* [1995] 2 A.C. 145 at 205–206.
[57] SLC Memo. no. 9 (1968), paras 85–90; Report no. 15 (1970), paras 125–132.
[58] Limitation Act 1980, ss. 21 and 38(1) referring to s. 68(17) of the Trustee Act 1925 which, in brief, extends trusts to cover implied and constructive trusts.
[59] The 1973 Act follows the Limitation Act 1939, s. 19 (now 1980 Act, s. 21), the only difference being that where the 1973 Act in Sched. 3(e)(iii) has "the proceeds of any such property", the 1980 Act has "the proceeds of trust property". There remains, of course, the fundamental difference that the Scottish legislation is concerned with prescription of obligations, and the English with the limitation of actions in respect of trust property.
[60] Walker, p. 79; *Stair Memorial Encyclopaedia*, Vol. 24, para. 221.

breach of trust imprescriptible.[61] Nothing is said there about liability for negligent breach of trust, which docs prescribe. If, however, owing to the present provision the trustee's obligation to account were imprescriptible, it would follow that no liability to make a payment which the accounts disclosed would prescribe, whether it arose from a fraudulent or negligent breach of trust. In short, there is a conflict between sub-paragraphs 3(e)(i) and (ii) unless the former is interpreted more restrictively.

Accordingly, the preferable view is to take this provision to apply to an **3.28** obligation to produce accounts only. That liability is enforceable by means of an action of count, reckoning and payment. It makes sense to insist that the obligation to produce accounts should not prescribe, since this may well be the only way of uncovering a fraudulent breach of trust on the part of the trustee; and liability in respect of that would not prescribe either. But if the production of the accounts were to disclose only a liability to make a payment because of a negligent breach of trust more than 20 years earlier, then there would be no obligation to make payment, since that obligation would itself have prescribed. This conclusion is in accordance with the established law under which the obligation of a trustee to make payment to the trust in respect of a particular transaction which is challenged as being in breach of trust can prescribe, unless it is fraudulent.[62]

Owing, however, to the fact that the Act defines "trustee" so broadly, **3.29** this question can also arise outside the law of trusts. For example, an agent is in a fiduciary position with respect to his principal, and may hold property in a fiduciary capacity for him. That means, in terms of Schedule 3(e)(i), that the agent's obligation to produce accounts to his principal is imprescriptible. The same will be true of partnerships. Indeed the effect of this sub-paragraph, combined with the Act's definition of "trustee" and "trust", is that in any case where property is held by one person who owes a fiduciary duty to another, the obligation to produce accounts is imprescriptible. It does not appear that, prior to the 1973 Act, there was any question of the duty to produce accounts of agents or fiduciaries in general being imprescriptible. It may therefore be doubted whether this consequence of the Act's broad definition of "trustee" was intended.

(ii) The obligation to make reparation or restitution in respect of **3.30** **fraudulent breach of trust to which the trustee is party or privy.**[63] As mentioned already, the trustee can be relieved of liability in respect of an individual transaction, although not of the obligation to produce accounts. This provision, however, makes imprescriptible certain obligations arising from a fraudulent breach of trust. Clearly, these are obligations owed by the trustee to the trust beneficiaries.

The present provision appears to be concerned not with the trust **3.31** beneficiary's right to claim the trust property or its *surrogatum* (that is

---

[61] Sched. 3(e)(ii); see below, paras 3.30 *et seq.*
[62] *Barns v. Barns's Trs* (1857) 19 D. 626 at 638; *Hastie's J.F. v. Morham's Exrs*, 1951 S.C. 668 at 676.
[63] *cf.* in England 1980 Act, s. 21(1)(a).

covered in paragraph (e)(iii)) but with the claim against a trustee for loss
arising from breach of trust. In the law of trusts that claim will regularly
be for the loss which the trustee has caused to the trust estate by his
breach, which is a claim for restitution in the broad sense,[64] rather than a
claim for reparation, its aim being not damages but the restoring to the
trust estate of the losses arising from the breach.[65] There may, however,
be cases in which damages can be awarded for particular breaches of
trust.[66] Those claims appear to arise from obligations "to make reparation", and so would prescribe in five years.[67]

3.32   The breach of trust may of course cause no loss to the trust but only
result in a gain on the part of the trustee. On general principle, the
trustee is liable to surrender the gain; and it is his gain (rather than
the extent of any loss by the beneficiary) which is the measure of his
liability.[68] There is room for argument about whether this situation is
best treated as falling within this sub-paragraph as a claim for restitution
arising from fraudulent breach of duty, or under the next sub-paragraph
as an instance of claiming the proceeds of trust property. It will be
obvious that the only cases in which this question will matter are those in
which this sub-paragraph cannot apply because the breach of trust is not
fraudulent or the next sub-paragraph cannot apply because the trustee is
not in possession of the proceeds. In any event, these are claims for
restitution which do not prescribe in the normal manner in five years
but, provided the conditions of the sub-paragraphs are met, are
imprescriptible.

3.33   The question arises what the reference to "reparation" is intended to
cover. The answer appears to be that it extends to (i) such claims for
breach of trust as are capable of giving rise to liability in damages; and
(ii) claims for damages not against trustees proper but against those who
are assimilated to them owing to the broad definition employed by the
Act.[69] Such persons, by breach of their fiduciary duties, can become
liable in damages to those to whom they owe their duties. That
obligation to make reparation is imprescriptible, provided always that
the breach is fraudulent, and they are party or privy to it. As already
indicated, the precise rules on damages for breach of fiduciary duty
remain a matter of some controversy.[70]

3.34   It is sometimes said that a trustee cannot by prescription acquire
a right to perpetuate a breach of trust.[71] No doubt that is true. But as a

---

[64] Rather than in the narrow sense of a claim for delivery of corporeal property other
than money, which would anyway appear to fall within Sched. 3(e)(iii) and to be
imprescriptible whether or not there is fraud.

[65] *cf. Hobday v. Kirkpatrick's Trs*, 1985 S.L.T. 197.

[66] *Hood v. Macdonald's Trs*, 1949 S.C. 24, 27: here damages were awarded for breach of
trust in making over assets otherwise than in accordance with the testator's will. In a case
of this sort, where the value of the trust estate has not been in any way diminished, clearly
a claim for restitution would not meet the pursuer's complaint. But the categories in which
damages claims should be admitted remain unclear; there was no real discussion of the
point in *Hood*.

[67] Sched. 1, para. 1(d).

[68] *Ronaldson v. Drummond & Reid* (1881) 8 R. 956.

[69] *cf. Ross v. Davy*, 1996 S.C.L.R. 369 at 381 and 384.

[70] See for comments from an Anglo–Australian perspective W. M. C. Gummow,
"Compensation for breach of fiduciary duty" in T. G. Youdan (ed.), *Equity Fiduciaries and
Trusts* (1989).

[71] Walker, p. 79. See *Thain v. Thain* (1891) 18 R. 1196 at 1202; *University of Aberdeen v.
Mags of Aberdeen* (1876) 3 R. 1087 at 1094.

matter of negative prescription the question is whether an obligation to make redress for breach of trust can prescribe. And the answer to this is that it can, unless the breach is fraudulent and the trustee a party or privy to it. The trustee will not cease to be in breach of trust, but in the absence of fraud or complicity he will cease to be liable for the consequences of the breach.

Accordingly, this provision protects the trust beneficiary's claim to **3.35** have the value of the trust restored, and the claim of a person to whom fiduciary duties are owed to obtain damages for its breach. But in each case the obligation is made imprescriptible only if the breach of trust is fraudulent.

The word "fraudulent" is not defined.[72] The corresponding provisions **3.36** of the English legislation have been said to be designed to relieve the trustee in due course from responsibility for innocent or negligent breaches.[73] It has also been held in England that "fraud" should be interpreted in the broad sense of conduct which would make it inequitable for the defendant to avail himself of the lapse of time.[74] It is not clear that Scots law would take exactly the same line, although it has been held that for the purposes of the 1973 Act the conduct need not be fraudulent in the criminal law sense of being a false pretence procuring a practical result, and that it is enough if there is conduct which is dishonest or from which dishonesty can be inferred.[75] It seems clear, therefore, that negligent breach of duty will not go far enough,[76] but that the definition of fraud for these purposes may be a rather broad one. It also seems likely that, to be relevant, the fraud would have to be perpetrated on the beneficiary. Proof of fraud in civil litigation would normally be on a balance of probabilities; particularly where the acts complained of do not amount to fraud in the criminal sense, this seems appropriate.[77]

If the breach is not fraudulent, this provision does not apply. But some **3.37** claims will anyway fall under the next sub-paragraph, which is discussed immediately below. For example, a claim for restitution of trust assets or their value would plainly do so, and a claim for the profits made from trust property would presumably do so too. But that provision itself does not apply to such claims unless the trustee is in possession of the property or proceeds derived from it,[78] and if he is not it may be that the 20-year prescription will extinguish the trustee's obligation. The five-year prescription will apply if there is an obligation arising from enrichment, contract or breach of contract, or where what is sought is

---

[72] It may be worth comparing the interpretation given to fraud in s. 6(4), below, paras 6.116 *et seq.*, although it is not self-evident that exactly the same considerations apply in deciding that a trustee's fraudulent act should render his liability imprescriptible and that any debtor's fraudulent act should be capable of suspending the running of prescription.

[73] *Re Sale Hotel & Botanical Gardens Co.* (1897) 77 L.T. 681 at 682.

[74] *cf. Tito v. Waddell (No. 2)* [1977] Ch. 106 at 245; *King v. Victor Parsons & Co.* [1973] 1 W.L.R. 29 at 33.

[75] *Ross v. Davy*, above, at 388.

[76] It is not clear why Walker, p. 79 supposes that this may include even negligent breach of trust; this was not followed in *Ross v. Davy*, above, nor does it accord with the proposals of the SLC Report no. 15 (1970), para. 132.

[77] Walkers, *Evidence*, p. 80.

[78] For comment on the requirement of possession, see below, para. 3.44.

reparation. But in a claim for restitution of trust assets there is not necessarily enrichment, what is sought is not reparation,[79] and a claim based on breach of trust would not normally be categorised as arising from contract or breach of contract.[80] This is not the place to enter into such questions in detail; it must suffice to say that it is at least arguable that a claim of this sort would prescribe, but only under the 20-year prescription. In passing, it may be noted that this is one of a number of problems which arise from the fact that the 1973 Act is drafted in terms of rights and correlative obligations, without any apparent recognition that some legal relationships—in particular fiduciary relationships—do not fit neatly into that sort of analysis.

3.38   In the event that such a claim does prescribe, it will do so from the date when it became enforceable. Clearly this may be subject to postponement where the beneficiary's right does not vest at once. That postponement is achieved by virtue of prescription's running from the date an obligation becomes enforceable.[81]

3.39   (iii) The obligation to make furthcoming trust property, the proceeds of trust property, or its value.[82] This provision is concerned with the trust beneficiary's right to claim the trust property or its surrogatum, or the proceeds of trust property, in the hands of the trustee. Before the 1973 Act it was already well established that the beneficiary's right to claim trust property remaining entire in the hands of the trustee could not be barred by lapse of time.[83]

3.40   An important qualification has to be read into this sub-paragraph. It cannot be supposed to extend to all claims directed at trust property in the hands of a trustee but only at those directed at him in a fiduciary capacity. Otherwise it has the effect of extending to a drastic extent the range of imprescriptible obligations. Suppose that the deceased failed to pay his milkman's bill. His executor would be liable to pay it. But could a claim for payment raised by a dilatory milkman be argued to be imprescriptible, since directed at payment of trust property by an executor, a trustee? There is no reason why the deceased's death should turn a prescriptible obligation into an imprescriptible one; and any argument that it should would be hard to reconcile with the principle that an executor is the same legal person as the deceased (*eadem persona cum defuncto*). The essential point is that, although the executor may pay the debt with trust property, the claim is one of debt rather than one arising from trust.

---

[79] So ruling out Sched. 1, paras 1(b) and (d).

[80] In *Allen v. McCombie's Trs*, 1909 S.C. 710 at 716 it was said that a breach of trust was not merely a breach of contract or a quasi-delict but a breach of duty. Unfortunately, the nature of the duty was not explained. Wilson and Duncan, *Trusts, Trustees and Executors* (2nd ed.), para. 28.15 say claims for breach of trust arise in delict or quasi-delict.

[81] s. 6(3). Specific provision for postponed vesting as made in s. 21(3) of the Limitation Act 1980 is therefore unnecessary.

[82] *cf.* in England Limitation Act 1980, s. 21(1)(b); some useful examples of retention and conversion of trust property are given in the *Current Law Statutes* commentary on that section.

[83] *Thain v. Thain* (1891) 18 R. 1196 at 1201; *United Collieries v. Lord Advocate*, 1950 S.C. 458 at 467 with further references. Note that in *Murray v. Mackenzie* (1897) 4 S.L.T. 231 the claim was directed at the heir of a trustee: he had never stood in any fiduciary relationship to the pursuer or owed any duty to him; at best the relationship was that of debtor and creditor: hence prescription did apply.

Similarly, it has been held that a legatee's claim against the executor **3.41**
for payment of a legacy is nothing more than a claim by a creditor
against a debtor and therefore subject to 20-year prescription. It is
claims against a party in his or her fiduciary character which are
imprescriptible.[84] Again, the same has to be said for claims of legal rights
from the executor: these are regarded as debts due by the deceased's
estate and therefore prescribe from the date of death.[85] This may seem
odd, but it is an interpretation which is confirmed by the fact that legal
rights are expressly excluded from the five-year prescription.[86] If they
were anyway imprescriptible in terms of Schedule 3(e), clearly that
exclusion would be redundant.

The same question arises in other contexts, such as bankruptcy. It will **3.42**
be sufficient to deal first with the case of judicial factors and then briefly
with that of trustees in bankruptcy.

(1) *Judicial factors*. Claims made against judicial factors might be
thought to be imprescriptible, because a judicial factor falls within
the definition of "trustee" in the Trusts (Scotland) Act 1921.[87] But
it seems unlikely that this can be so. Take the case of a judicial
factor on the estates of an insolvent partnership. There is no
obvious reason why creditors' claims for payment should suddenly
become imprescriptible when a judicial factor is appointed. Until
that time they would have prescribed in the normal way under
section 6 or 7. Nor, if claims made against executors—who are
also assimilated by statute to trustees[88]—for payment of legacies
can prescribe, is it clear why claims for payment of debts should
not. Equally, it has never been suggested that the obligations of
liquidators or trustees in bankruptcy are imprescriptible, and it is
far from clear why judicial factors should be treated in any way
differently.

(2) *Liquidators and trustees in bankruptcy*. An answer to this last point
might be that actually the obligations of liquidators and trustees
in bankruptcy are imprescriptible, presumably so long as the
liquidation or sequestration lasts. But this too would be odd, for
much the same reasons. It would also fit poorly with section 9 of
the Act, which deals with interrupting prescription by making a
relevant claim. Claims in a liquidation and a sequestration are
included in the definition of "relevant claim", so that they
interrupt negative prescription. But there would be something
rather strange about describing them as interruptions if their

---

[84] *Jamieson v. Clark* (1872) 10 M. 399 at 405 and 406. But see more recently *Sinclair v. Sinclair*, Lord McCluskey, September 24, 1985, unreported, where it was held that a claim for a share of residue from an executor was a claim not just for payment but for an accounting and so was preserved by sub-paragraph (e)(i).

[85] Or the date when the estate falls into intestacy: *Sanderson v. Lockhart-Mure*, 1946 S.C. 298; *Campbell's Trs v. Campbell's Trs*, 1950 S.C. 48; *Mill's Trs v. Mill's Trs*, 1965 S.C. 384.

[86] Sched. 1, para. 2(f).

[87] s. 2. It is true that not all judicial factors are vested in the estate, some merely superseding its management by the "ward'" *e.g.* the *curator bonis*: see *Inland Revenue v. McMillan's CB*, 1956 S.C. 142. But others are vested in it. See *Stair Memorial Encyclopaedia*, Vol. 24, para. 246; Walker, *Judicial Factors*, pp. 4, 31 and 49. A petition for directions was recently raised on the question of prescription in relation to estate vested in a judicial factor, in effect by the Accountant of Court, but the court unfortunately shed no light on the matter.

[88] 1921 Act, s. 2.

effect was immediately to make the obligation in question imprescriptible.

3.43   For these reasons, it seems right to conclude that the question of imprescriptibility in relation to trustees and the like has to be read rather narrowly. Although the Act does define trusts and trustees broadly, so that in principle a wide range of obligations is covered by Schedule 3 and is imprescriptible, to focus purely on the definition of "trustee" and "trust" is misleading. A reading of the Act as a whole reveals that only obligations actually having a fiduciary quality are imprescriptible; those that arise between a "trustee" in the broad sense and a person entitled to "trust" property can prescribe if they are merely "debtor and creditor" cases.[88a]

3.44   To fall within this paragraph, the property (or its proceeds) must either be in the possession of the trustee or have been in his possession and appropriated to his own use. It is clear that these provisions are modelled on the English legislation,[89] which refers to actions by which the beneficiary seeks to recover trust property in the possession of the trustee, the proceeds of trust property, or trust property previously converted to the trustee's own use. But the insistence on possession has the rather odd consequence that trust assets which are incorporeal and therefore cannot be possessed apparently cannot fall within this provision. There is no obvious reason of principle why this should be so, and the matter would merit reconsideration if the Scottish Law Commission or parliament were to consider amendments to the 1973 Act.

3.45   Where the trustee is no longer in possession of the trust property, questions about its recoverability from third-party acquirers will arise.[90] So will questions about the trustee's liability to make good the loss to the trust estate: this has been discussed under sub-paragraph (e)(ii). To the extent that a trustee has benefited from possession of the trust estate, he comes under a liability to disgorge the amount of his enrichment: it is fundamental that a trustee should not profit at the expense of the trust beneficiary. This applies as much to profits made in breach of fiduciary duty as it does to trusts in the strict sense.[91]

3.46   Where trust property is no longer held by the trustee *in specie*, it cannot be claimed in the normal manner. But here the provisions about appropriation to the trustee's own use may apply. One instance would be where there had been *specificatio* of trust property, so that ownership in the original goods no longer subsisted. The new species created would be trust property.

(f) any obligation of a third party to make furthcoming to any person entitled thereto any trust property received by the third party otherwise than in good faith and in his possession

3.47   In the general law of trusts the trust beneficiary can trace trust property into the hands of third parties, provided only that they are not bona fide purchasers for value without notice of the trust.[92] This regime

---

[88a] *cf. Coulthard v. Disco Mix Club Ltd* [1999] 2 All E.R. 457.

[89] Limitation Act 1939, s. 19 (now s. 21 of the 1980 Act).

[90] See below, paras 3.47 *et seq.*

[91] See, *e.g.*, *Dale v. Inland Revenue Commissioners* [1954] A.C. 11 at 26–27; *Black v. Brown*, 1982 S.L.T. (Sh.Ct) 50.

[92] *Hastie's J.F. v. Morham's Exrs*, 1951 S.C. 668 at 676. Wilson and Duncan, *Trusts, Trustees and Executors* (2nd ed.), paras 1.04 *et seq.*

also extends to a certain degree to those who are not trust beneficiaries but merely the beneficiaries of fiduciary duties.[93]

Under this provision the third party's obligation to restore the trust **3.48** property is imprescriptible only if he was not in good faith and still has possession.[94] What is surprising, since the general law of trusts emphasises the protection of those who have given value for trust property, is that no distinction is taken here between purchasers for value and recipients of gifts. Apparently, even if the third party paid nothing for the trust property, his obligation to restore it will still prescribe. It is not very clear why prescription should run against the beneficiary's claim, to the benefit of a third-party gratuitous acquirer.[95]

This imprescriptible obligation to restore arises only where the third **3.49** party is in possession of the trust property. Presumably, therefore, when he loses possession he ceases to be under any such obligation. In principle, one would expect the former possessor in such cases to remain under a liability in enrichment, to the extent that he had profited by his possession of the trust property. That obligation would prescribe under the five-year prescription.[96]

In the case of those, such as agents, who are not trustees in the strict **3.50** sense, it used to be said that their claims involved principles of both trust and contract: while the liability of the agent was measured by his gain rather than the principal's loss (a trust-like feature), in the bankruptcy of the agent the principal ranked as a creditor rather than as a trust beneficiary.[97] Such statements were founded on English authority which has since been disapproved by the Privy Council in *Attorney-General of Hong Kong v. Reid.*[98] There it was held that property received as bribes by a Crown servant in breach of his fiduciary duty to the Crown was held in a constructive trust for the Crown. If this were to be followed in Scotland, which is far from certain,[99] then it could at least be said that there has been an assimilation of trust and fiduciary duty such that it is reasonable to apply the same rules on prescription to both. In each case therefore the third-party recipient who was not in good faith would be under an imprescriptible obligation to restore trust property in his possession.

(g) any right to recover stolen property from the person by whom it was stolen or from any person privy to the stealing thereof
The owner's right to recover property from its thief or a person privy **3.51** to its theft will never prescribe. This paragraph implies that the owner's right to recover from others can prescribe, since only the real right of

---

[93] See *Southern Cross Commodities Ltd v. Martin*, 1991 S.L.T. 83; *Att.-Gen. of Hong Kong v. Reid* [1994] A.C. 324.
[94] Note too that, owing to the terms of s. 2(1) of the Trusts (Scotland) Act 1961, the third party will not in any case be under an obligation to restore where he acquired as a result of the trustees' purported exercise of powers conferred on them by s. 4 of the Trusts (Scotland) Act 1921.
[95] Unless it is argued that a gratuitous acquirer from a trustee cannot be in any better position than the trustee himself, whose obligation to restore the property is in any event imprescriptible: *Thain v. Thain* (1891) 18 R. 1196 at 1201.
[96] Sched. 1, para. 1(b).
[97] Gloag, *Contract*, p. 521; *cf.* also Gloag and Henderson, para. 22.6.
[98] above.
[99] See Gretton, "Constructive Trusts" (1997) 1 E. L.R. 281 at 408.

ownership in land is said elsewhere in schedule 3 to be imprescriptible.[1] It is clear that *nemo dat quod non habet*, and that an acquirer in good faith from the thief does not obtain good title. Nonetheless, after 20 years the owner's right to recover the property from a possessor who neither stole nor was privy to the theft would be lost by negative prescription.[2]

(h) any right to be served as heir to an ancestor or to take any steps necessary for making up or completing title to any interest in land

3.52   Service as heir is a procedure which is available only in relation to deaths before the Succession (Scotland) Act 1964 came into force.[3] It is well established that a right of this sort does not prescribe. Both Stair and Erskine note that *juri sanguinis numquam praescribitur*: a person may serve heir to his ancestor at any time if no other has been served already.[4] Much as with *res merae facultatis*, the point is that there is no reason why a right of this sort, which does not necessarily involve any adverse claim against anyone, should prescribe negatively. But it can of course be excluded by a better right established by someone else.[5]

3.53   Much more important in the modern law is the question of completion of title. The title to be completed must be to an "interest in land". The definition in the Act is unhelpful: "'interest in land' does not include a servitude."[6] It is clear that what is being protected here from prescription is something short of the real right which is acquired by recording a deed or registering a title. But the courts have held that the right protected must go beyond a purely contractual right. So a right to demand a disposition is a *jus crediti* and not a right to take any steps for completing title to any interest in land: until delivery of the disposition, the pursuer has no title to complete but only a contractual right to delivery, which could not have been recorded.[7]

3.54   It appears that once a disposition has been delivered to the disponee—and, to use the old terminology, he or she has acquired a *jus ad rem*—his or her right to register it is imprescriptible. This requires some explanation. In a schedule that lists, by and large, property rights, why is it that the right to complete title is listed as imprescriptible, since by definition it is not a real right? The explanation is surely this: an uninfeft proprietor is at liberty to record or register his title as he wishes. There is no obligation to do so. And so long as nobody else claims the same land there is no adverse claim against him. There is no reason why his personal right of property should begin to prescribe the moment he receives the disposition. After all, if it did, the odd result would presumably be to leave the last infeft proprietor—quite likely to be the

---

[1] Sched. 3(a).

[2] s. 8. *Cf.* Erskine, III, vii, 14; Carey Miller, *Corporeal Moveables*, p. 100.

[3] *i.e.* September 10, 1964.

[4] Stair, II, xii, 15; Erskine, III, vii, 12; *Officers of State v. Alexander* (1866) 4 M. 741.

[5] Stair, II, xii, 15; Erskine, III, vii, 12.

[6] s. 15(1); *cf.* below, paras 15.07 *et seq*. The expression "interest in land" will be replaced by the term "real right in land" if the draft Bill annexed to the SLC Report no. 168, *Report on Abolition of the Feudal System* (1999) is enacted: see paras 9.5–9.6 of that report.

[7] *Macdonald v. Scott*, 1981 S.C. 75; 1981 S.L.T. 128. See also *Stewart's Exrs v. Stewart*, 1993 S.L.T. 440 at 450 (in the Inner House, reported at 1994 S.L.T. 466, prescription was not in issue).

same person as disponed the land to him in the first place—with a clear title, now unaffected by any personal rights granted to the disponee. So the personal right will subsist until an adverse right is established against it. Since the Act makes the personal right imprescriptible, it will only be possible for the adverse right to be established either by positive prescription or on the basis of a disposition in favour of another party which that party records or registers.[8]

This is precisely the position described above for the case of *res merae* **3.55** *facultatis*: the right is lost only in the face of the establishment of an adverse right. Indeed there is some authority for holding the right to complete title as itself being *res merae facultatis*.[9] Its isolation from that category and the creation of a separate paragraph 3(h) may have done little but cause confusion about the basis on which such rights do not prescribe. This suggestion may gain some support from the case of *Porteous's Executors v. Ferguson*[10]: "In terms of the law current in . . . 1972, the deceased's right to make up title to the heritage left to her in her mother's will prescribed. . . . What has, however, puzzled me is that the change in the law provided by Schedule 3 para. (h) has passed virtually without comment. No commentator, it appears, has emphasised that the kind of personal right to property which was held to have prescribed in *Pettigrew v. Harton* is now imprescriptible." It was not suggested either in *Porteous's Executors* or in *Pettigrew v. Harton* that the right to complete title was a *res merae facultatis*. For the reasons given above it is suggested that it was, and that the right was therefore imprescriptible before the 1973 Act.

There is, however, a change in the law, as an examination of *Pettigrew v.* **3.56** *Harton* will show. In that case, more than 20 years after an heir had obtained a decree of general service to a woman who was thought to have died intestate, the pursuers raised an action of reduction of that decree founding on a will purporting to bequeath the property to them. The Second Division held that their claim was merely a personal right which was subject to negative prescription, and that with the passage of 20 years that personal right had been extinguished. "The authorities are clear that a right to heritage, not completed by infeftment and being therefore only a personal right, is not a right of property in land and is subject to the long negative prescription: *Paul v. Reid*; Hume's *Lectures*, vol. iv. pp. 535–6; and the case of *Robertson v. Robertson*, there referred to."[11]

---

[8] A difficult question, which cannot be answered here, is what happens if the disponer remains in possession and the disponee does not complete title. What is clear is that the disponee's right cannot be extinguished by negative prescription. But can it be cut out by the operation of positive prescription running in favour of the disponer in possession? That conclusion would seem odd, since it would mean that after 10 years the disponee would effectively be deprived of a property right. On the other hand, it may be said that (1) that is the penalty for permitting the disponer to remain in possession for so long; and (2) that, if the disponee had completed title but had not taken possession of the whole subjects, and the disponer had remained in possession of part, the effect of the running of the prescriptive period would apparently be to revest the disponer in that part of the subjects (*cf.* below, para. 15.50).

[9] Bankton, II, xii, 22–23; *Johnston v. Johnston* (1730) M. 10732: it is *res merae facultatis* for the obtainer of the precept of sasine to take infeftment thereon; *Cheyne v. Smith* (1832) 10 S. 622, vassal's right to enter with over-superior; *Bain v. Bain*, Lord MacLean, January 17, 1994, (1994 G.W.D. 410), the right to serve as heir is imprescriptible.

[10] 1995 S.L.T. 649 at 651, *per* Lord Maclean.

[11] *Pettigrew v. Harton*, 1956 S.C. 67 at 74, *per* Lord Patrick and 77, *per* Lord Mackintosh.

3.57   But this is not quite accurate. The authorities referred to and the decision in *Pettigrew v. Harton* itself[12] depended on the terms of the Act 1617, c. 12: "all actions competent of the law . . . shall be pursued within the space of forty years." Accordingly, what was cut off by the negative prescription of the Act 1617 was not a (substantive) right to heritage but an action.[13] This makes a difference. Not in the case where an uninfeft proprietor remains in possession, for then he will generally have no need to bring an action. But in the case that he is out of possession, and (for example) a subsequent disponee of the same property has entered into possession of it, he does need an action to recover possession or perhaps to reduce the rival disposition. It is precisely such a right of action which is cut off by the Act 1617.

3.58   *Pettigrew v. Harton* depended heavily on a passage from Hume's *Lectures* and three examples given in it.[14] A few words on each of those must suffice:

> (1) A, a disponee from B, is uninfeft but in possession. After 40 years C takes general service as heir to B and challenges A's right on the grounds of fraud or minority and lesion. Hume rightly remarks that A, being uninfeft, has no defence based on positive prescription. But C's right of heritable action is cut off by the lapse of 40 years: Hume explains that C, having acquiesced for so long in the deed of B, the common author of his and A's right, cannot now challenge it. These are essentially the facts of the case of *Paul v. Reid*.[15] (2) A, who is uninfeft proprietor, dispones to B. B takes neither infeftment nor possession. A remains in possession. Again, there is no scope for positive prescription since there is no recorded title. According to Hume, B loses the benefit of the conveyance by negative prescription.[16] The reason is that he is unable to bring an action, since that is cut off by the passing of 40 years. (3) Two disponees derive title from the same author. Neither of them is infeft. Each relies on a deed more than 40 years old. The right of action of the disponee who is out of possession is extinguished after the prescriptive period of 40 years. These are the facts of *Robertson v. Robertson*.[17]

3.59   In all of these cases it is clear that what prescribed was a right of action. Because the right of action was susceptible of prescription, the uninfeft proprietor who was out of possession lost his chance of regaining it. But the position is quite different in the law after 1973, since Schedule 3 is concerned to make not actions but "rights" imprescriptible. If the right is imprescriptible, it cannot matter whether the uninfeft proprietor retains possession or not. His right to the property subsists until it can be excluded by a better right, and that can

---

[12] In its case, as extended by the Conveyancing (Scotland) Act 1924, s. 17, so as to reduce the prescriptive period to 20 years.

[13] For the distinction, *cf. Cardross v. Buchlivie* (1710) M. 10657 at 10658; *Cubbison v. Hyslop* (1837) 16 S. 112 at 120, *per* Lord Corehouse: "although you cannot plead the negative prescription directly against a right of ownership, yet it may be pleaded against an action necessary to reduce a right *ex facie* valid".

[14] Hume, *Lectures*, 4.535–4.536.

[15] February 8, 1814, F.C. *Cf. Thomson v. Stewart* (1840) 2 D. 564 at 571.

[16] *cf.* below, para. 15.50.

[17] (1770) M. 10694.

happen only by positive prescription or else by completion of title by some other person. Accordingly, the modern law is more generous to the uninfeft proprietor who is out of possession. The reason it is is not that it has introduced a new category of cases of imprescriptibility but that it focuses on extinction of rights rather than remedies.

CHAPTER 4

THE BEGINNING AND END OF THE PRESCRIPTIVE PERIOD

The general rule is that prescription runs on an obligation from the date **4.01** when it became enforceable.[1] This is an invariable rule for the 20-year prescription. There is a list of exceptions to the rule in the case of the five-year prescription,[2] which are discussed together with other questions specific to that prescription in Chapter 6. The two-year prescription runs from "the date on which the right to recover contribution became enforceable by the creditor in the obligation".[3]

This chapter deals with three points: (1) the dates on which the main **4.02** types of obligation become enforceable and prescription therefore begins to run; (2) the computation of a continuous prescriptive period; and (3) the effect of completion of the prescriptive period.

There are two preliminary points of some importance. The first concerns European law; the second the construction of section 13 of the 1973 Act.

European Community law

It is a general rule of European Community law that national rules of **4.03** prescription and limitation should not discriminate between national and European law rights. Nor should they make it excessively difficult to enforce European law rights.[4] So far as prescription and limitation are concerned, this raises just one point, but it may sometimes be of practical significance. This is that the European Court of Justice has held that a prescription or limitation period laid down by national law does not begin to run until the Directive in question has been properly transposed, and legal certainty as to the full extent of the rights of individuals has been achieved.[5]

Accordingly, when a pursuer seeks for example to enforce an obliga- **4.04** tion which arises under a European Directive, and is met with the plea of prescription, it may be open to the pursuer to argue that the prescriptive period has not yet begun or been completed. This argument was successful in an English case in which an applicant relied on the EEC Directives on sex discrimination, to support her claim against a local authority for a redundancy payment calculated in the same way as

---

[1] 1973 Act, ss. 6(3) and 7(1).
[2] *ibid.* s. 6(3) and Sched. 2.
[3] *ibid.* s. 8A(1).
[4] *Rewe-Zentralfinanzamt AG & Rewe-Zentral AG v. Landwirtschaftskammer für das Saarland* [1976] E.C.R. 1989 at 1998; *Peterbroeck, van Campenhout & Cie SCS v. Belgium; Jeroen van Schijndel v. Stichting Pensionenfonds voor Fysiotherapeuten* [1995] 1 E.C.R. 4705 at 4712, 4715 and 4736–4737.
[5] *Emmott v. Minister of Social Welfare and Att.-Gen.* [1991] E.C.R. 4269 at 4299; *Swan v. Secretary of State for Scotland*, 1st Div., February 24, 1998, unreported.

it would have been for a man.[6] Since the directives were only properly transposed into United Kingdom law by the Employment Act 1989, the employment appeal tribunal held that the local authority could not rely on time prior to the date on which the Act came into force in support of its argument that the claim was out of time.

Section 13

4.05   **"Prohibition of contracting out**
13.—Any provision in any agreement purporting to provide in relation to any right or obligation that section 6, 7, 8 or 8A of this Act shall not have effect shall be null."

The general effect of this provision must be that an agreement that, at the end of a prescriptive period, a right or obligation shall not have prescribed is to have no effect. Unfortunately, the precise scope of the provision is unclear. The following considerations arise:

(1) An agreement that an obligation is not to be enforceable until a certain date does not fall foul of section 13. Prescription is concerned only with what happens after an obligation becomes enforceable. For that reason, suspensive conditions which have the effect that an obligation does not even become enforceable for a significant period are not affected.[7]

(2) An agreement that a period longer than the relevant statutory prescriptive period should apply in its place is prejudicial to the debtor in the obligation, undermines the whole rationale of prescription and must be regarded as the principal mischief at which section 13 is directed. Other jurisdictions have rules similarly prohibiting agreements lengthening the statutory prescriptive period.[8]

(3) An agreement that a shorter prescriptive period should apply is not clearly an infringement of section 13, although it may be said to have the effect of disapplying the relevant statutory prescriptive periods by extinguishing the obligation in question at an earlier date. Other jurisdictions differ on the admissibility of such agreements.[9] Since the rationale for prescription is essentially that obligations should cease to be enforceable after an excessively long period, it is by no means clear that agreements which shorten the prescriptive period should be struck at by section 13. In conveyancing, it is common for what is in effect a two-year contractual prescription to be agreed to in missives. It is, of course, possible that some terms in consumer contracts providing that obligations should cease to be enforceable after a very short period might be regarded as unfair, and that relief might therefore be available under other legislation.[10]

---

[6] *Cannon v. Barnsley MBC* [1992] 2 C.M.L.R. 795, EAT.

[7] See, *McPhail v. Cunninghame D.C.*, 1983 S.C. 246; *Ferguson v. McIntyre*, 1993 S.L.T. 1269.

[8] See Hondius, *Extinctive Prescription*: Belgium, at p. 55; France, at pp. 156–157; Quebec, at p. 314; Germany, at pp. 204–205 on Art. 225 I BGB (although such agreements are permissible for the shorter prescriptive periods: Arts 477 I and 638 II); *cf.* also Peters and Zimmermann, *Gutachten*, pp. 267 and 311.

[9] For: France, Germany (Art. 225 II BGB); against: Quebec (references as in the previous note).

[10] Notably the Unfair Terms in Consumer Contracts Regulations 1994 (S.I. 1994 No. 3159) implementing Council Directive 93/13; *cf.* Chitty, *Contracts*, paras 14.088–14.104.

(4) An agreement that a relevant claim or acknowledgment should not interrupt prescription is an agreement which makes prescription more difficult to achieve, and may be thought to be struck at by section 13.[11]

(5) An agreement that, under the five-year prescription of section 6, prescription should not be suspended during a period of minority or legal disability ought surely to be regarded as contrary to the public interest.[12] Accordingly, it would appear to be within the proper scope of section 13 and so void.

If nothing else, this brief discussion suggests that the drafting of section 13 is excessively vague. The question which agreements affecting prescription are void is too important to be left so uncertain.

I. WHEN OBLIGATIONS BECOME ENFORCEABLE

In some cases identification of the date when an obligation became **4.06** enforceable is straightforward. The following paragraphs attempt to deal with the main points which arise. The question of enforceability is assessed objectively. A person therefore cannot delay the start of the prescriptive period because of his or her personal circumstances.[13]

Contract

In contract, the essential point is to establish when the obligation in **4.07** question became enforceable. Everything will turn on a proper construction of the terms of the contract. When an obligation becomes enforceable may depend on the other contracting party first satisfying an obligation on his or her part, on the satisfaction of a condition, or on the passing of a time-limit. Equally, not all obligations in a contract will become enforceable at the same time. An obligation to perform will become enforceable before an obligation to make good defects in performance; obligations of payment or performance will become enforceable before obligations relating to resolution of disputes about payment or performance.[14] It will also be necessary to distinguish when an obligation arose from when it can be quantified.[15]

Conditions

(1) The time at which the obligation became enforceable may be **4.08** affected by conditions or other modalities in the contract. Where an obligation is subject to a suspensive condition (or "condition precedent"), it is not enforceable until the condition has been purified, and for that reason time cannot begin to run until purification of the condition.[16] It will therefore be important to

---

[11] It would be valid in France, but probably not in Germany or Belgium (references as above).

[12] So in France: see J.C.P. 1980 19311 (describing the suspension provisions of *Code Civil* Art. 2252 as rules of *"ordre public"*).

[13] Unless they fall within the scope of s. 6(4): see below, paras 6.105 *et seq.* See also *Stewart's Exrs v. Stewart*, 1993 S.L.T. 440 at 445.

[14] See, *e.g. Douglas Milne Ltd v. Borders R.C.*, 1990 S.L.T. 558 (reference to contract engineer).

[15] *McPhail v. Cunninghame D.C.*, 1985 S.L.T. 149.

[16] *cf.* in France *Code Civil* Art. 2257 al. 1.

determine whether the proper construction of a clause is that it is a condition suspensive of the obligation in question. For example, in *Scott Lithgow v. Secretary of State for Defence*[17] a clause provided that the pursuers, in the event that they sustained loss owing to defective materials which might result in their claiming under an indemnity, should report the loss and should submit a priced claim "as soon as possible". This was found in the House of Lords (although not before the arbiter or the Inner House) to be insufficiently precise to amount to a condition suspensive of the defender's obligation to indemnify. Since it did not suspend the moment at which the obligation became enforceable, the normal rules about when obligations to indemnify became enforceable applied. The result was that the obligation to indemnify was held to have arisen when the defect was discovered.[18] On the other hand, an arbitration clause in a contract will not normally— subject, of course, to construction of the particular contract in question—prevent a contractual obligation from becoming enforceable and so will not suspend the date from which prescription runs.[19]

(2) Often rules about mutuality of obligation will clarify the point, since one obligation will become enforceable only when another has been performed.[20]

(3) In the case of resolutive conditions, in principle the obligation is immediately enforceable but subject to defeasance in the event that the resolutive condition materialises. The prescriptive period therefore begins at once.

(4) Where potestative conditions are concerned, on general principle it would seem that where one of the parties to the contract has prevented a condition from materialising, it should be held as having been satisfied.[21] On the same basis the date at which the obligation became enforceable should be taken to be the date at which fulfilment of the condition was obstructed by the contracting party.[22]

(5) In an obligation subject to a term (or *dies*), whether the term is a future date certain to arrive (*dies certus*) or a future date which may never arrive (*dies incertus*), in either case the obligation is not yet enforceable. Accordingly, prescription does not run against the obligation until the term arrives.[23]

Specialities relating to parties

4.09   Specialities regarding the date of enforceability arise in the case of particular debtors. In particular, a debt has to be constituted against a firm before its partners can be charged on it.[24] Accordingly, the date on

---

[17] 1989 S.C. (H.L.) 9.

[18] Other cases where enforceability of the obligation is postponed: *Royal Bank of Scotland v. Brown*, 1989 S.C. 89 (demand); but not *City of Glasgow D.C. v. Excess Insurance Co. Ltd*, 1986 S.L.T. 585 or *Flynn v. UNUM*, 1996 S.L.T. 1067.

[19] *Lowland Glazing Co. Ltd (in receivership) v. GA Group Ltd*, 1997 S.L.T. 257.

[20] See recently *Bank of East Asia v. Scottish Enterprise*, 1997 S.L.T. 1213, HL; McBryde, *Contract*, paras 14.25 *et seq.*; *e.g.* Sale of Goods Act 1979, s. 28: the obligation to deliver and the obligation to accept and pay the price are concurrent conditions.

[21] Gloag, *Contract*, p. 277; D. Daube, "Condition prevented from materializing" (1960) 28 *Tijdschrift voor rechtsgeschiedenis* 271–296; *Paterson v. McEwan's Trs* (1881) 8 R. 646 at 654; Erskine, III, iii, 85.

[22] *cf. Gibson v. Carson*, 1980 S.C. 356.

[23] *cf.* in France *Code Civil* Art 2257 al. 3.

[24] Partnership Act 1890, s. 4(2).

which such an obligation becomes enforceable against a partner is the date of constitution against the firm. That is the appropriate date for prescription.[25]

Contractual obligations in general

4.10 Since in contract everything turns on construction of the terms of the particular contract, there is little point in going into any detail about when contractual obligations become enforceable. Only a few general points concerning the commonest types of contract are made here.

4.11 First, for obligations arising from breach of contract, the party in breach comes under an obligation to the "innocent" party at the date of breach. From that date the innocent party has a right to claim damages and may have a right to rescind. Where the question of rescission arises, it seems likely that the date of the repudiation (which justifies the rescission) will be the appropriate date for the start of prescription.[26]

4.12 Second, in anticipatory breach the innocent party can elect to treat the contract as at an end or can seek to hold the other party to it when performance is due. Prescription will therefore run either from the date performance is due and the obligation is enforceable or, if this is earlier, the date on which the innocent party elected to treat the contract as being at an end.[27]

4.13 Third, in certain circumstances a pursuer will be able to elect between, on the one hand, affirming a contract and seeking damages and, on the other, rescinding a contract and claiming damages or *quantum meruit*.[28] If the pursuer affirms the contract, the date on which any claim for damages for breach begins to prescribe will be the date when the loss was sustained,[29] while the appropriate date for any claim for payment under the contract will depend on the terms of the contract. On the other hand, if the pursuer chooses to rescind the contract, he will be able to choose between a claim for damages (which again will prescribe from the date the loss arose) and a claim *quantum meruit*, which will prescribe from the date the defender was enriched by the work done.[30] The difference between the appropriate dates for prescription is a factor which a pursuer will have to bear in mind when making the election which remedy to pursue.

4.14 Fourth, obligations to pay damages for breach of contract are, like obligations to pay damages in delict, covered by the expression "obligation to make reparation" and by the same statutory provisions in section 11 of the 1973 Act. Essentially the same issues arise for both damages in delict and in breach of contract, and the two subjects are discussed together, under the heading of delict. There are of course

---

[25] *Highland Engineering Ltd v. Anderson*, 1979 S.L.T. 122. *cf.* Wilson, *Debt*, para. 30.9.

[26] *cf.*, in another context, *Moschi v. Lep Air Services* [1973] A.C. 331.

[27] *cf.* in England Chitty, *Contracts*, para. 28.022; *Reeves v. Butcher* [1891] 2 Q.B. 509 (although here the decision turns mainly on construction of the contract rather than general principle).

[28] *ERDC Construction Ltd v. H. M. Love & Co.*, 1995 S.L.T. 254, with Wolffe (1997) 1 E.L.R. 469.

[29] s. 11; see further below, paras 4.16 *et seq.*

[30] See below, para. 4.92.

differences arising from the substantive law; for example, economic loss which may be irrecoverable in delict may be recoverable in contract.

Particular contracts

4.15   It may be helpful to add a few comments on particular contracts:

(1) *Sale of goods*.[31] The Sale of Goods Act 1979 enables the seller to sue for the price of goods either when property has passed to the buyer or when the price is due in terms of the contract.[32] Accordingly, where a contract specifies a date for payment of the price, that will be the date from which prescription runs. Where it does not do so, the question will arise when property passed. This is determined under the Sale of Goods Act 1979.[33]

Where the goods are claimed to be disconform to contract and the buyer refuses to pay the price, the seller will have a claim to the price only if the buyer's assertion of disconformity is unwarranted. In that event the seller's right to claim the price will prescribe from the date when it was due. If the buyer wrongfully refuses to accept the goods, the seller may bring an action for damages for non-acceptance.[34] In this case, prescription must run from the date when the goods ought to have been accepted.

If the goods are defective the buyer can seek damages, and, if this amounts to a material breach of contract, may also treat the contract as repudiated.[35] The buyer's claim for damages will prescribe from the date of delivery or attempted delivery of the defective goods. Where the seller wrongfully neglects or refuses to deliver the goods,[36] the buyer's claim will prescribe from the date delivery was due.

(2) *Sale of heritage*. Here the obligation to pay the price becomes enforceable when a validly executed disposition is delivered by the seller.[37] This is simply an illustration of the mutuality rule.[38] The disposition does not now as a matter of course supersede unimplemented obligations in the missives.[39]

(3) *Building contracts*. The contractor's liability for not completing the works in accordance with the contract will normally arise not on the date when the particular defective part of the works was carried out but on the date of completion or purported completion.[40] A claim for failure to comply with defects liability obligations will normally arise at the date after completion on or by which the contract specifies that those obligations should be

---

[31] Note that the law set out here is applicable to contracts made on or after January 3, 1995, the date on which certain amendments made in the Sale and Supply of Goods Act 1994 came into force.

[32] s. 49.

[33] ss. 17 and 18.

[34] s. 50.

[35] ss. 15B(1)(a), (b). It should be noted that in certain circumstances the seller may also be liable under the Consumer Protection Act 1987 where a defect in a product has caused death, personal injury or property damage: see s. 2(3) and Chaps 17 and 21 below.

[36] ss. 51 and 15B(1).

[37] *Muir & Black v. Nee*, 1981 S.L.T. (Sh.Ct) 68.

[38] On this see recently *Bank of East Asia Ltd v. Scottish Enterpise*, 1997 S.L.T. 1213, HL.

[39] Contract (Scotland) Act 1997, s. 2.

[40] Keating, *Building Contracts*, pp. 268 *et seq.*; Hudson, *Building and Engineering Contracts*, paras 4.030 and 4.292; *Strathclyde R.C. v. Border Engineering Contractors Ltd*, 1997 S.C.L.R. 100 at 105.

carried out.[41] So far as breaches by the employer are concerned, such as failure to give access or to provide instructions or drawings, the obligation will arise at the date the access or instructions should have been given.[42]

In a contract where payment is by instalments, provided the contractor's obligation is to complete the whole works for a lump sum, again it seems that prescription should run from the date of practical completion.[43] But, where the proper construction of the contract is that it is to carry out each instalment of work against payment for that particular instalment, clearly it may be arguable that prescription in relation to that instalment runs from the date on which it was completed.

Furthermore, so far as the five-year prescription is concerned, special provision is made for instalment contracts: prescription runs from the date the last instalment of work was due to be executed. That date, it seems, must be the date on which completion is due rather than the date on which practical completion is certified to have been achieved.[44] It is therefore clear that, at least so far as five-year prescription is concerned, it is necessary to distinguish between unitary and instalment contracts.

Building contracts commonly include conditions precedent to payment, such as the approval of an architect or the certification or measurement of claims. Obligations affected by such conditions are not enforceable until the conditions have been purified.[45]

(4) *Indemnities.*[46] The general rule is that an obligation to indemnify against loss arises on the date of loss, unless a proper construction of the contract indicates another date.[47] The most common contingencies are: (a) the person seeking to be indemnified must take certain steps to notify his loss. This raises the question whether those steps relate merely to quantification or are conditions suspensive of the obligation to indemnify. In the second case, clearly the obligation will begin to prescribe only from the date the condition is purified; (b) the person seeking to be indemnified must first have liability judicially established against him. In that event the obligation to indemnify him will start to prescribe not from the date of the loss but only from the date the liability is constituted by the court.[48]

The short point is that the date on which the obligation becomes enforceable turns on construction of the contract.

(5) *Insurance contracts.* In a contract of insurance the insured becomes entitled to payment on the occurrence of the event

---

[41] Keating, *op cit.*, pp. 268 *et seq.*; Hudson, *op cit.*, para. 4.292; *Bellway (South East) v. Holley* (1984) 28 B.L.R. 139.

[42] Keating, *op cit.*, p. 404.

[43] *ibid.* pp. 268 *et seq.*

[44] Sched. 2, para. 4(2); see below, paras 6.81 *et seq.*

[45] Keating, *Building Contracts*, pp. 109 *et seq.*; *McPhail v. Cunninghame D.C.*; *W. Loudon & Son Ltd v. Cunninghame D.C.*, 1985 S.L.T. 149; *Douglas Milne Ltd v. Borders R.C.*, 1990 S.L.T. 558 (reference to contract engineer a condition precedent to right to go to arbitration). *Cf. Costain Building and Civil Engineering Ltd v. Scottish Rugby Union plc*, 1994 S.L.T. 573 at 579 (on suspensive condition on payment under the ICE conditions of contract).

[46] Note that there is special provision for the case of prescription of obligations to make contribution between wrongdoers: s. 8A, and see below, paras 8.01 *et seq.*

[47] *Scott Lithgow Ltd v. Secretary of State for Defence*, 1989 S.L.T. 236.

[48] *cf.* for English law, *Telfair Shipping Corp. v. Intersea Carriers SA* [1985] 1 W.L.R. 553.

insured against. That is therefore the starting date for prescription. There is no general or implied duty on the insured to give notice to the insurer or provide details of the event or of the loss.[49] Nonetheless, insurance contracts typically contain provisions on the steps the insured must take after the occurrence of an insured peril. It will be a question of construction of the contract whether those provisions amount to conditions suspensive of the insurer's obligation to make payment under the policy. If they do, clearly the obligation to make payment will begin to prescribe not from the date of the loss but from the date the conditions are purified.[50] For the case of repudiation of liability by the insurer, see below.[51]

In the case of life assurance, prima facie the obligation to make payment becomes enforceable on the death of the life assured or other event on the occurrence of which the policy is payable. Where payment depends on proof of the death of the life assured, if such proof is a condition suspensive of the right to demand payment, in principle it would seem to postpone the start of the prescriptive period until it has been satisfied. This seems to be correct in principle, although the contrary view has been expressed for English law.[52] It is true that this will leave it in the hands of the beneficiary to determine when the obligation under the policy becomes enforceable and therefore begins to prescribe; on the other hand, that is something which can readily be corrected by appropriate drafting of the policy.

(6) *Cautionary obligations.* Here the question when prescription begins to run is the ordinary one of when the cautioner's obligation becomes enforceable.[53] Again, this is simply a question of construction of the contract. So, where a guarantee provides that a demand must be made on the cautioner, a demand is a condition suspensive of the obligation's becoming enforceable,[54] and the date on which the obligation becomes enforceable is the date of demand against the cautioner. If no provision for demand is made in the contract, typically the cautioner's obligation will become enforceable immediately on the default of the principal debtor.[55] Sequestration of the principal debtor may itself amount to default; but this will depend on the terms of the cautionary obligation. Similarly, with performance bonds, unless there is a suspensive condition which postpones enforcement (for example) to the making of a demand or to certification by an architect, the

---

[49] Except under s. 62(3) of the Marine Insurance Act 1906.

[50] In England it has been held that, if something is to be a condition precedent, the insurers must say so quite clearly; if that is done, they are entitled to rely on it being so: *Jones & James v. Provincial Insurance Co. Ltd* (1929) T.L.R. 71 at 73.

[51] para. 4.45.

[52] McGillivray and Parkington, *Insurance Law* (8th ed.), para. 1235 (at pp. 593–594), taking the view that proof of death is a matter of procedure rather than of substantive entitlement.

[53] A demand on a guarantor does not fall within the special provisions of Sched. 2, para. 2 for the purposes of the five-year prescription: see below, para. 6.75; *Royal Bank of Scotland v. Brown*, 1982 S.C. 89.

[54] *Royal Bank of Scotland v. Brown*, above, at 100.

[55] Gloag and Irvine, *Rights in Security*, p. 789; *City of Glasgow D.C. v. Excess Insurance Co. Ltd*, 1986 S.L.T. 585; *City of Glasgow D.C. (No. 2) v. Excess Insurance Co. Ltd*, 1990 S.L.T. 225; *Moschi v. Lep Air Services* [1973] A.C. 331.

date when the obligation becomes enforceable will be the date on which there is default in performance giving the creditor in the bond the right to sue for enforcement.[56]

If there is more than one default by the principal debtor, then, subject to the terms of the contract, it seems likely that a separate obligation will be incurred by the cautioner each time, and will be subject to a separate prescriptive period.

In passing it may be noted that the old cases are particularly unhelpful in this area. This is because cautionary obligations were formerly subject to a seven-year limitation under the Cautioners Act 1695, and time ran under that Act from the date of the deed, rather than, as now, from the date the obligation became enforceable.[57]

In general, the principal debtor's own obligation to repay his cautioner becomes enforceable when payment is made to the creditor by the cautioner.[58] At that point it is open to the cautioner to raise an action, based on his mandate, against his principal. The same should apply where one cautioner has paid more than his proportionate share and seeks relief from his co-cautioners.[59]

(7) *Bills of exchange*. Prescription should run from the date when the bill is payable. The rules about this are set out in the Bills of Exchange Act 1882. A bill may be payable on demand or at a fixed or determinable future time.[60] The principles on which the time of payment is computed are set out in section 14 of the 1882 Act: a bill is due and payable on the last day of the time of payment as fixed by the bill or, if that is a non-business day, the succeeding business day. Where a bill is payable at a fixed period after its date or after an event, in reckoning the period, the day from which time begins to run is excluded but the date of payment is included.

Where the bill is payable at a fixed period after sight, time runs from the date of acceptance. If acceptance is refused, time runs from the date of noting or of protest.[61]

These provisions allow the date when payment is due to be calculated. That will also be the date on which the obligation to make payment begins to prescribe.

Delict

Special provision is made in section 11 of the Act for the date on **4.16** which obligations to make reparation become enforceable, and this of course extends to all actions in delict in which damages are sought. No special provision is made for obligations arising from delict other than payment of damages, and these will therefore prescribe from the date on

---

[56] *City of Glasgow D.C.*, above; on the effect of special clauses in the contract see, *City of Glasgow D.C. (No. 2)*, above; *cf. Moschi v. Lep Air Services*, above.

[57] See, *e.g.*, Bell, *Commentaries*, 1.374 *et seq.*; Napier, pp. 850 *et seq.*

[58] *Smithy's Place Ltd v. Blackadder & McMonagle*, 1991 S.L.T. 790.

[59] Provided each cautioner has not separately assumed liability for a separate sum. The obligation of relief in such cases may be regarded as arising from unjustified enrichment rather than contract, but the starting date for prescription is unaffected.

[60] 1882 Act, s. 3(1). See s. 10(1) and (2) for the circumstances in which a bill is regarded as payable on demand; Chitty, *Contracts*, paras 33.012–33.014.

[61] s. 14(3).

which they became enforceable.[62] This will apply, for example, to obligations which are the basis of actions of specific implement, or declarator, or reduction.

Obligations to make reparation: section 11

4.17 **"Obligations to make reparation**

11.—(1) Subject to subsections (2) and (3) below, any obligation (whether arising from any enactment, or from any rule of law or from, or by reason of any breach of, a contract or promise) to make reparation for loss, injury or damage caused by an act, neglect or default shall be regarded for the purposes of section 6 of this Act as having become enforceable on the date when the loss, injury or damage occurred.

(2) Where as a result of a continuing act, neglect or default loss, injury or damage has occurred before the cessation of the act, neglect or default the loss, injury or damage shall be deemed for the purposes of subsection (1) above to have occurred on the date when the act, neglect or default ceased.

(3) In relation to a case where on the date referred to in subsection (1) above (or, as the case may be, that subsection as modified by subsection (2) above) the creditor was not aware, and could not with reasonable diligence have been aware, that loss, injury or damage caused as aforesaid had occurred, the said subsection (1) shall have effect as if for the reference therein to that date there were substituted a reference to the date when the creditor first became, or could with reasonable diligence have become, so aware.

(4) Subsections (1) and (2) above (with the omission of any reference therein to subsection (3) above) shall have effect for the purposes of section 7 of this Act as they have effect for the purposes of section 6 of this Act."

General

4.18 Section 11 is concerned only with obligations to make reparation. It makes clear that this extends not just to reparation in the sense of liability in damages for delict but also to liability (for example) to pay damages for breach of contract. The appropriate date is when the loss, injury and damage occurred, except that special provision is made for continuing acts, neglects or defaults and for cases where the victim of the loss was not, and could not with reasonable diligence have been, aware of the loss, injury or damage at the date when it occurred.

Contract and delict

4.19 While there have been swings of fashion so far as allowing concurrent liability in contract and delict is concerned, the present law appears to find it unobjectionable.[63] The same facts can give rise to causes of action in both contract and delict. In contract there can in principle be an

---

[62] ss. 6(3) and 7(1).

[63] *Henderson v. Merrett Syndicates Ltd* [1995] 2 A.C. 145; for earlier reluctance, *Tai Hing Cotton Mill Ltd v. Liu Chong Hing Bank* [1986] A.C. 80. There is much to be said against the now-prevailing view: see J. A. Weir, *International Encyclopaedia of Comparative Law* Vol. 11, Chap. 12, para. 55. In Germany, reform of the law of prescription is proposed such that where there is concurrence of contractual and delictual claims the contractual claim should take precedence: *Abschlussbericht*, p. 36.

action for breach even where there is no loss[64]; in delict there cannot. In each case prescription runs from the same date, namely the date on which loss flows from the wrong, whether it is a breach of contract or a delict. The significance of the fact that the date on which prescription begins to run is the same, whether the cause of action is based on breach of contract or delict, can hardly be exaggerated. While this is not an easy area of the law, the difficulties which English law encounters owing to employing different dates for the commencement of prescription in contract and tort are at least avoided.[65]

"Act, neglect or default" and "loss, injury or damage"
The section requires that loss, injury or damage be caused by an act, **4.20** neglect or default. Neither expression is defined. Both seem apt for broad construction. The Scottish Law Commission has proposed that "act or omission" might be a formula preferable to "act, neglect or default", but this proposal has yet to be enacted.[66] This section comes into play only where there is an act, neglect or default, so where what is sought is really payment or performance in terms of a contract, it has no application and the ordinary rules apply.[67]

The expression "loss, injury or damage" has been said to be "a phrase **4.21** of style commonly used to comprehend the various types of loss which may be sustained as a result of breach of a legal duty or obligation. It covers all kinds of *damnum*".[68]

In any event, it is clear that the act, neglect or default must either **4.22** precede, or be contemporaneous with, the loss, injury or damage. It has become conventional to speak of the moment at which the act, neglect or default results in loss, injury or damage as the concurrence of *injuria* (act, neglect or default) and *damnum* (loss, injury or damage).[69] Since the Latin appears to add nothing but the possibility of confusion, it would be better discarded.

Delict in particular
In terms of the general law of delict, "the right to reparation requires **4.23** the presence of two elements, *injuria* and *damnum*. Unless a pursuer can prove loss resulting from an invasion of his rights he is not entitled to damages".[70] This is not the place to go into the substantive requirements of the law of delict; it is enough to say that to be relevant, the loss injury or damage must be caused by the act, neglect or default. There is no obligation to make reparation until there is loss, and for the purposes of prescription the appropriate date is the date on which the loss injury or damage was sustained. Establishing what that date is is the major problem which arises in applying section 11. It makes no difference

---

[64] McBryde, *Contract*, paras 20.04 and 20.87–20.88.
[65] Limitation Act 1980, ss. 2 and 5; see, *Société Commerciale de Réassurance v. Eras (International) Ltd* [1992] 2 All E.R. 82 at 85, *per* Mustill L.J.
[66] SLC Report no. 122 (1989), paras 2.14–2.15 and rec. 1.
[67] ss. 6(3) and 7(1); *McPhail v. Cunninghame D.C.; W. Loudon & Sons Ltd v. Cunninghame D.C.*, 1985 S.L.T. 149.
[68] *Dunlop v. McGowans*, 1979 S.C. 22 at 33.
[69] *ibid.* at 30 and 40; 1980 S.C. (H.L.) 73 at 80.
[70] *Kenyon v. Bell*, 1953 S.C. 125 at 128; *cf. Watson v. Fram Reinforced Concrete Co. and Winget Ltd*, 1960 S.C. (H.L.) 92; *Brownlie & Son v. Mags of Barrhead*, 1923 S.C. 915.

whether the loss can be fully quantified at the time it is sustained: what matters for prescription is that there is loss and that an obligation to make reparation for loss is enforceable.

Materiality of loss

4.24 How serious must the loss be in order to start the prescriptive period running? This question is specifically addressed in the sections of the 1973 Act dealing with limitation of actions for personal injuries, where it is provided that time will not start to run until (among other things) the injuries are "sufficiently serious" to justify raising an action.[71] But nothing is said about this question in the context of negative prescription.

4.25 It does seem, however, that some threshold of seriousness must exist, so that an entirely trivial loss, albeit arising from the same act, neglect or default, should not be held to start prescription running against an obligation to make reparation for significant loss incurred later. In some cases the question can be resolved in terms of causation: the trivial loss might be related to a different act or default from the later, serious loss. But plainly this will not work on the facts of all cases. A general view therefore has to be taken.

4.26 There is solid authority in Scots law to the effect that all losses must be recovered in a single action, and this has been the view taken in the specific context of prescription.[72] A rule of this nature is not (or at least not equitably) consonant with a notion that even the most trivial loss will start prescription running. If it did, it would result in the courts having to enter into potentially long-term projections of future loss, running a serious risk of undercompensating a pursuer, instead of being able at least to quantify accurately the first loss of some significance.

4.27 Although for these reasons it seems likely that the law is that loss should trigger the running of the prescriptive period only when it is of some materiality, and there are some hints in the cases to this effect,[73] it would be helpful if this could be clarified. The Scottish Law Commission has proposed that this should be done.[74]

Types of loss

4.28 In order to fix the date for the running of prescription it will be necessary to consider precisely what interest of the pursuer has been infringed, that is, whether the loss is to be characterised as physical or economic.[75] These are discussed separately in what follows.

Damage to property

4.29 In simple cases, such as road accidents, there is no difficulty in determining the date on which the loss, injury or damage occurred: it will be the date of the accident.[76] Loss consisting in damage to property

---

[71] s. 17(2)(b); see below, para. 10.44.

[72] *Dunlop v. McGowans*, 1980 S.C. (H.L.) 73; *Stevenson v. Pontifex & Wood* (1887) 15 R. 125; *Balfour v. Baird & Sons*, 1959 S.C. 64.

[73] *Strathclyde R.C. v. W.A. Fairhurst & Ptrs*, 1997 S.L.T. 658. In England the view has been expressed that the damage must be "relevant and significant" before a cause of action arises: *London Borough of Bromley v. Rush & Tompkins Ltd* (1985) 4 Con. L.R. 44, QBD.

[74] SLC Memo. no. 74 (1987), para. 4.11; Report no. 122 (1989), paras 2.18–2.24.

[75] *Hawkins v. Clayton* (1988) 164 C.L.R. 539 at 600–601, High Ct of Australia.

[76] This applies to property damage resulting from the accident; personal injuries are excluded from s. 6: see Sched. 1, para. 2(g).

is often reasonably easy to identify, and so therefore is the date on which it occurred. This is, however, not always true, and difficulties may well arise in identifying, for example, when mining subsidence occurred.[77]

Loss of property

Loss of property is a slightly more awkward case. Take the facts of **4.30** *East Hook Purchasing Corporation v. Ben Nevis Distillery Ltd.*[78] The pursuers' whisky was held on deposit by the defenders in a bonded warehouse. The defenders altered the books, so as to show that title to the whisky was in another party. It was held that this caused no loss to the pursuers, and that the date when loss occurred was when the defenders parted with the possession of some part of the goods to a third party. This view can be defended, since altering the books did not create any property right adverse to the pursuers; the defenders had merely interfered with evidence as to the pursuers' title to the whisky.[79] Although in altering the books the defenders had plainly committed a breach of duty, it would be hard to say that the pursuers were tied in to any loss at that stage. All they had was less evidence of their title to the whisky.

In general, therefore, in determining the date on which an obligation became enforceable in relation to lost property, it will be important to focus on the moment the property or right was lost.

Economic loss

As usual, economic loss is much more problematic. Loss may not **4.31** always be quite what it seems. Damage to a building arising from its own physical defects used to be regarded as physical loss. The House of Lords has now held that it is economic loss.[80] Not only can this make a difference to the question whether the loss is recoverable; it can also affect the question when the loss arises, and therefore when the prescriptive period begins.

It is important to keep in mind the fact that the concern here is not **4.32** with the possibility of quantifying the loss but with the fact that a loss, which may be presently unquantifiable, has been sustained. The moment when a loss—whether quantifiable or not—is sustained is the moment at which the prescriptive period begins to run. But the issue is not straightforward.

Two different situations can usefully be distinguished, according to **4.33** whether the act complained of causes the pursuer to enter into a transaction or not. Transaction cases involve additional complexities, so it will be simpler to start with the others:

(1) *No-transaction cases.* Take an example. If a solicitor offered negligent advice to a client not to pursue litigation, the date of the act, neglect or default would be the date of the advice. But it could not be said that the client would certainly sustain any loss

---

[77] For further discussion, and for the point that some such loss is properly characterised as economic, see below, paras 4.31, 4.78 *et seq.*
[78] 1985 S.L.T. 442.
[79] *cf.* on the nature of book entries, *Smith v. Allan & Poynter* (1859) 22 D. 208.
[80] *Murphy v. Brentwood D.C.* [1991] 1 A.C. 398.

until the client relied to his or her detriment on the advice. It seems therefore to follow that, while it may be later, the date of the loss cannot be earlier than the date of reliance. In this sort of situation, reliance upon the advice does not bind the client to anything, in the way that concluding a contract would do. The negligent advice has a decisive effect only when the litigation is time-barred. But is the date for prescription of the obligation arising from solicitors' negligence the date of reliance or the date of time-bar? Something may be said for each, depending on the facts of a given case. Many imponderables may intervene between the advice and the date of time-bar which may make it difficult to suppose that there was any certainty of loss before the date of time-bar arrived. But on the other hand the loss may be bound to occur unless some extraneous factor intervenes, and in that case the date of reliance would seem to be the appropriate date.

So, for example, in an English case accountants gave negligent advice on the taxation consequences of ceasing to trade as a partnership. This involved the partners in an increased charge to tax. The date on which the cause of action in tort arose was held to be the date when the increased charge to tax became inevitable: that was the date of cessation rather than the date on which the accounts were signed.[81] For prescription to start to run, the loss had to be certain rather than simply potential or prospective.

Or take the case where, owing to someone's negligence, a tenant's lease is irritated for non-payment of rent. Here the tenant is not tied in to loss of the right to occupy until the landlord has served notice on him, and that notice still gives him not less than 14 days to remedy his breach.[82] It does not seem that there is any certain loss until the period of notice has expired without payment.

The same seems likely to be true where the loss arises from the act of a third party consequential upon the defender's wrong. For example, in one case of misrepresentation, the pursuer alleged that he had lost his job owing to misrepresentation by the defender. It was agreed that the appropriate date was the date of the pursuer's dismissal from his employment. The wrong was the alleged misrepresentation; the loss concurred with it at that date.[83] Here it probably would be far-fetched to say that the pursuer sustained any loss at the time of the misrepresentation, since at that point it was unclear that anyone was likely to pay any attention to the defender's representations. For the pursuer actually to be tied in to a loss, it was necessary for an act prejudicial to him (dismissal) to follow upon the defender's wrong.

In all these instances, therefore, what is crucial is to pinpoint a moment at which it can be said that loss was certain or bound to occur, leaving extraneous factors aside.

---

[81] *Moon v. Franklin*, Ct of Appeal, December 19, 1991, unreported.

[82] Law Reform (Miscellaneous Provisions) (Scotland) Act 1985, s. 4.

[83] *Lamont v. Thomson*, Lord Coulsfield, October 26, 1989, unreported. The question may well then arise—as it did in this case—when the pursuer came to know of the statement complained of (in this case a medical report): in principle, postponement of the date on which prescription starts to run in terms of s. 11(3) will apply (in this case on the facts it did not). For another example, *Esso Petroleum Co. v. Mardon* [1976] Q.B. 801.

(2) *Transaction cases.* Here too an example may assist. Take the case of a negligent valuation by the surveyor of a house. Relying on the survey, a purchaser sustains loss by purchasing a property at an excessive price. When is the loss sustained? It does not seem probable that the purchaser can be said to sustain loss until irrevocably committed to the purchase. Until formation of a contract which binds the purchaser—that is, the conclusion of missives of sale—it is not clear that the purchaser will ever act on the valuation and sustain loss as a consequence. Accordingly, there must be a step taken in reliance on the negligent advice which ties the purchaser in to the transaction and to the loss. For the delict to be completed and for the prescriptive period to begin to run, it is necessary not just for the negligent advice to be tendered but for it to be relied upon.[84] The date of conclusion of missives therefore appears to be the earliest date from which prescription can run.

But that is not the only possible date. On one view, the purchaser sustains loss immediately, because he is contractually bound to acquire an asset which is worth less than the agreed price; but on another view, since he may succeed in obtaining an adequate price when he sells the asset, he therefore in fact sustains no loss at all until he realises an inadequate price. If the purchaser keeps the property for a significant period, whether loss will or will not eventuate from the surveyor's negligence will turn on the state of the property market at the time of sale. The law's dilemma is therefore whether the loss must be actualised before prescription begins to run. Other legal systems have been confronted with the same question.[85]

For prescription to start running there must be loss, injury or damage. If the appropriate date for prescription is held to be the date when a pursuer came to be bound by a transaction, it is essential that at that date it can be said that loss was clearly sustained. It is not enough that there may be a risk or a possibility of future loss arising from a transaction from which the pursuer cannot (freely) extricate himself.

The examples mentioned so far indicate that on particular facts it may be possible to argue more strongly for one date than the other, but that often more than one possible date will come into consideration as the operative date for prescription. A few more words about the possibilities seem to be required.

View 1: Loss at the date of realisation
Take the example of house purchase and surveyors' negligence. On **4.34** the view that loss is incurred only on resale, there will be actual loss, which will be quantifiable. On resale, the original purchaser will have obtained an inadequate price, at least some part of the diminution in value being attributable to the negligent valuation. This approach has the

---

[84] *cf. Caparo Industries plc v. Dickman* [1990] 2 A.C. 605; *Beard v. Beveridge, Herd & Sandilands, W.S.*, 1990 S.L.T. 609. For negligence post-dating the missives, see below, para. 4.51.

[85] For English law, see Jackson and Powell, *Professional Negligence*, paras 1.130 *et seq.*, with many examples. The issue is also raised in the Australian cases cited in the following pages.

advantage that, if the property market rises and as a result no actual loss results from the negligent valuation (except on the view that there is still the loss of a chance to make a greater gain), the assessment of damages takes account of the facts and the fate of the transaction.[86] Equally, it is not unreasonable for the pursuer to wait until sustaining actual loss before raising proceedings. But it has to be borne in mind that to allow prescription to begin at such a late date may be prejudicial to the debtor, and so defeat a primary objective of prescription, which is to cut off stale claims. Suppose in this example that the property is not sold for 20 years and the loss accrues only then? To say that prescription begins to run only then is highly unsatisfactory, even if in practice the longer the delay, the less probable it is either that the negligent valuation will have any continuing significance or (perhaps) that loss will eventually be realised. So this consideration can be tempered by reasons of practicality.

4.35 There remains the difficulty that, if actual loss is required to start the prescriptive period running, a number of arbitrary factors may intervene. What if, in the surveyor's negligence case, the property market rises? (The short answer may be that there will be no litigation.) Or if it falls and then rises, but the purchaser does not resell at the optimal moment?

4.36 Such considerations may make it exceptionally difficult—in some cases—to establish the date at which any loss accrues and so may lead to great uncertainty. And what if the purchaser might have a way out of the defective transaction, such as rectification or reduction? Does this mean that there is no loss until that means has been tried and failed? Again this leads to great uncertainty.

View 2: Loss at the date of transaction

4.37 The alternative view is that loss is sustained already at the time of contracting, following upon negligent advice: the focus is on the value of the right acquired (or lost) by the purchaser at the time of contracting. Where there is no continuing breach of duty but one which consists purely in giving negligent advice which commits a client to entering into an ill-advised transaction, in principle it ought to be possible even at the time of entering the transaction to assess damages based on the difference between a transaction advised upon with ordinary competence and one which is ill-advised. Although quantification of the loss may be difficult, nonetheless the purchaser sustains an immediate loss which is measured by the difference between what he would, properly advised, have paid and what he actually paid; or the right which he would, properly advised, have acquired or surrendered and what he actually acquired or surrendered.[87] So, for example, in *Secretary of State for the*

---

[86] In favour of this view, see (*e.g.*) *UBAF Ltd v. European American Banking Corp.* [1984] 1 Q.B. 713; *Wardley Australia Ltd v. Western Australia* (1992) 66 A.L.R. 839.

[87] In favour of this view, see (*e.g.*) *Forster v. Outred & Co.* [1982] 1 W.L.R. 86; *Baker v. Ollard & Bentley* (1982) 126 S.J. 593; *Costa v. Georghiou* (1984) 1 P.N. 201 (defective rent review clause: date of loss was the date of entering into the lease, not the date when the review was intended to operate); *D. W. Moore & Co. Ltd v. Ferrier* [1988] 1 W.L.R. 267 (invalid restrictive covenant: the claim against the solicitors for their negligent drafting accrued at the time of the drafting of the contract, not when the covenant was found not to be enforceable); *Lee v. Thompson* [1989] 2 E.G.L.R. 151; (1990) 6 P.N. 91 (solicitor failed to acquire freehold of property as instructed); *Iron Trades Mutual Insurance Co. Ltd v. J. K. Buckenham Ltd* [1990] 1 All E.R. 808; *Islander Trucking Ltd v. Hogg Robinson & Gardner Mountain (Marine) Ltd* [1990] 1 All E.R. 826 (in both of these insurance contract cases the cause of action was held to accrue when the contract was made, not when the insurers avoided it).

Environment v. Essex, Goodman & Suggitt,[88] it was held that the cause of action accrued when the pursuers acted in reliance upon a negligent survey and became committed to a lease on particular terms of a particular property. Equally, in *Forster v. Outred & Co.*, an action against solicitors whose negligence had led to the plaintiff's signing a mortgage deed and so encumbering her house with a security, it was held that her loss accrued when she signed the deed and not when a demand for payment in terms of the mortgage was subsequently made.[89] In each of these cases, once the defenders had assumed responsibility towards the pursuer or the pursuer had reasonably relied upon the defenders, and once the pursuer was tied into a disadvantageous transaction, he had no real control over what loss might materialise from it. Although there is nothing very radical about saying that there is loss which is not (yet) susceptible of immediate and full quantification, it has to be conceded that to insist on assessing damages at this early date may have an air of unreality about it,[90] and more importantly may risk allowing the pursuer a less than full recovery.

For these reasons, it is vital to insist that the loss sustained by the **4.38** pursuer at the date of the transaction can be said to be material. It is unfair to put pressure on a pursuer to raise an action before the extent of the loss arising from the act or default can be clearly appreciated. This is the more important owing to the rule that all losses must be sued for in one action. That rule would prevent a pursuer who had sued for damages which had to be assessed on the basis of future projections from suing further if he later realised quantifiable loss far in excess of the damages he had been awarded.

So far as the five-year prescription is concerned, it seems that the **4.39** worst injustices in such circumstances may be righted by section 11(3) of the 1973 Act, which allows the pursuer postponement of the start of the prescriptive period where he had neither actual nor constructive knowledge that loss, injury or damage had occurred.[91]

On this approach to loss, once the purchaser has been tied into the **4.40** transaction, he or she sustains a loss, a diminution in the value of his or her rights; there is a completed cause of action in delict or breach of contract. That in itself constitutes loss. A clear distinction is drawn between loss and the assessment of damages. Various contingencies may arise which will affect the measure of any loss, but they do not in any way affect the question whether, as a matter of applying section 11 of the 1973 Act, a loss has followed upon a delict or breach of contract. The date on which prescription begins to run is therefore unaffected by the movement of (for example) the property market in relation to a surveyor's negligent valuation. That is a question solely for the quantum of loss.[92] For the same reason, it cannot be maintained that there is no

---

[88] [1986] 1 W.L.R. 1432.

[89] [1982] 1 W.L.R. 86 at 98 and 99.

[90] But the courts are of course used to making projections of future loss. *E.g* in *Costa v. Georghiou*, above, it was held that loss arising from a defective rent review clause was sustained at the time the lease was entered into and could be valued at that time, having regard to the future projected diminished rental value.

[91] See below, paras 6.87 *et seq.*

[92] On this, see recently *South Australia Asset Management Corp. v. York Montague Ltd* [1996] 3 All E.R. 365, HL, (successful) appeal from the Court of Appeal in *Banque Bruxelles Lambert SA v. Eagle Star Insurance Co. Ltd* [1995] 2 All E.R. 769, noted by O'Sullivan (1997) 56 C.L.J. 19.

loss simply because possible future court proceedings to reduce or rectify the problematic transaction may allow the loss to be mitigated or avoided.[93] Equally, this approach fits better with a duty to mitigate loss: on the "realisation of loss" approach it is hard to justify any duty to mitigate what has not yet occurred; by contrast, on this view all circumstances arising since the date of the transaction will be relevant to the question of mitigation.

Which approach is preferable?

4.41   Everything turns on the facts of the case. In many cases it will be difficult to take the view that the relevant date for prescription is the date of transacting. That view is now mostly associated with the English cases of *Forster v. Outred & Co.* and *D. W. Moore & Co. Ltd v. Ferrier.*[94] But outside England those cases have not invariably been followed with enthusiasm or indeed at all. In particular, a series of Australian cases expresses doubts about them. The most significant criticism amounts essentially to this: that there is no certainty of loss at the date of the transaction.

4.42   In *Forster* there was said to be loss because the pursuer, by entering into the mortgage, had reduced the value of her interest in the property.[95] That might be justified in England, although not in Scotland, on the basis that the pursuer parted with a chose in action, which is regarded as a form of property.[96] But, viewed—as Scots law would have to view it—in terms of obligations, it can be strongly objected that at that stage the pursuer had not sustained loss at all. The mortgage was entered into in order to secure a loan made to her son. It was only when he defaulted that the pursuer became bound to repay his indebtedness. There was therefore no certainty that she would sustain loss until the date of his default.[97] So long as a pursuer is merely exposed to a contingent loss or liability, he or she sustains no loss or damage until the contingency is fulfilled and the loss becomes actual.[98]

4.43   In short, the court must always be satisfied that loss was sustained at the date of entering into the transaction rather than at some later time. For this reason it may be necessary for there to be inquiry into the facts before the starting date for prescription can be ascertained. It certainly seems undesirable that in anything other than the clearest cases decisions about prescription should be made solely on the pleadings.[99]

4.44   An illustration may be helpful. In a case where lenders have lent in reliance on a negligent valuation, it will be necessary to consider, had the

---

[93] See Jackson and Powell, *Professional Negligence*, paras 1.153.

[94] See above, n. 87.

[95] at 98 and 100.

[96] *Islander Trucking Ltd v. Hogg Robinson & Gardner Mountain (Marine) Ltd*, above, at 831.

[97] *Magman International Pty Ltd v. Westpac Banking Corp.* (1991) 100 A.L.R. 575 at 581, Fed. Ct. These views of the judge were approved in *Western Australia v. Wardley Australia Ltd* (1991) 102 A.L.R. 213 at 232, Fed. Ct.

[98] See *Wardley Australia Ltd v. Western Australia* (1992) 109 A.L.R. 247 at 258, High Ct. of Australia.

[99] *cf. Wardley Australia Ltd*, above, n. 98, 259–260; *cf. Magman International Pty Ltd v. Westpac Banking Corp.* (1991) 104 A.L.R. 575, Fed. Ct. on appeal, where the court refused to determine the limitation point without hearing evidence.

valuation not been negligent, whether they would have lent at all or would have lent less. But in either case a critical question will be whether the amount lent actually was more than the value of the property secured at the date of the loan. Clearly, if the security was adequate at the date of the loan then, while there was a negligent valuation, since no loss had yet flowed from it, the cause of action had not yet arisen and prescription would not begin to run. So in *First National Commercial Bank plc v. Humberts*,[1] the court held that on the facts the bank had had security in respect of the advance it made adequate to cover its outlay and notional costs and profits until a date which was within the limitation period.[2] By contrast, in *Nykredit Mortgage Bank plc v. Edward Erdman Group Ltd*,[3] the amount of the loan had at all times exceeded the true value of the property, the borrower had defaulted immediately, and the House of Lords found that the date at which the lenders had suffered loss was the date of the loan and not the date when they realised their security. Matters will become even more complicated factually where the transaction in question is not a "one-off"—a simple loan—but there is a continuing relationship—for instance, the loan is periodically rolled over.[4]

Scots authority

Both of the views outlined above have been followed in Scotland. A **4.45** few words about the cases follow:

(1) *Loss at the date of realisation.* It has been held that where loss arises owing to the repudiation by insurers of an insurance contract, and that loss is alleged to flow from the negligence of the brokers who placed the insurance, the act, neglect or default must have taken place at the time the contract was concluded, and the loss at the time of the repudiation. Accordingly prescription begins to run against a claim by the insured against his brokers five years from the date of repudiation.[5] This can be justified on the basis that it is not certain at the date of conclusion of contract that the loss will ever occur. There is no certainty that an insured peril will occur within the period of the policy or that, if it does, the insurers will repudiate liability.

In *Riddick v. Shaughnessy, Quigley & McColl*,[6] the pursuer sustained loss owing to the negligence of his solicitor in concluding the purchase of a business in the name not of the pursuer but of his agent. When relations between the pursuer and his agent became strained, the pursuer was ejected from the business premises. He then sought to interdict his agent from them. Since even the date of the interdict was more than five years before the action was raised against the solicitors, the court did not require to decide on precisely what date loss, injury or damage had occurred. But it held that on any view it had done so when the

---

[1] [1995] 2 All E.R. 673 at 678–679, CA.
[2] *cf. Sasfin (Pty) Ltd v. Jessop*, 1997 (1) S.A. 675 at 693.
[3] [1998] 1 All E.R. 305. *Cf. Byrne v. Hall Pain & Foster* [1999] 2 All E.R. 400, CA: loss arose at the date of exchange of contracts.
[4] *cf. Magman International Pty Ltd v. Westpac Banking Corp.*, above, at 591.
[5] *Arif v. Levy & McRae*, Lord Couslfield, December 17, 1991, unreported. The English authorities (see above, n. 87) are contrary to this.
[6] 1981 S.L.T. (Notes) 89.

pursuer was ejected from the premises and obtained interdict
against his agent. Counsel for the defenders had argued that
prescription ran from the date entry was taken to the premises.
Even this summary of the facts indicates that several contingencies intervened between the contract and the pursuer's loss, so
there would seem to be little to be said for the view that the date
on which loss occurred was the date of transaction, that is the
date on which the pursuer, owing to his solicitor's negligence,
became bound by the missives. Instead, it is necessary to focus on
the later date on which the first event caused the pursuer to
realise loss.

(2) *Loss at the date of transaction.* In an action for professional
negligence by a solicitor, the basis of the claim was that a
disposition failed to carry the whole subjects contracted for in
missives.[7] This is a case in which in principle it ought to be
possible to seek rectification of the disposition on the basis that it
fails to express the intention of the parties as manifested by the
missives.[8] Nonetheless, it seems clear that here there is an
immediate loss: the purchaser has acquired less land than he
contracted for. It is true that it may be possible to avoid or reduce
this loss in the future, but that cannot alter the fact that loss has
been sustained and that the prescriptive period therefore begins
to run. The loss presumably arises at the date when the purchaser
acquires a right worth less than he bargained for. On these facts,
since the disposition failed to carry the full subjects, the purchaser
could not have been sued to implement his part of the contract in
exchange for the disposition. The earliest date for the start of
prescription would therefore be the date on which the disposition
was delivered and accepted.[9] It is not clear that it should be
necessary to insist on the purchaser's acquiring a real right to only
part of the subjects rather than a personal one, and therefore the
running of prescription need not await the recording or registration of the disposition.[10]

A less clear case is *Beard v. Beveridge, Herd & Sandilands*,[11]
where the clients were tied in by the defenders, their solicitors, to
a lease with a defective rent review clause. Did loss arise only at
the date at which the rent might have been reviewed upwards? Or
did it arise already at the date of execution, the loss simply being
at that stage unquantifiable? The court held that it arose at the
date of execution. From that date the clients could have sued for
damages for the difference between a lease with a valid and one
with an invalid rent review clause.[12]

---

[7] *Stewart v. J. M. Hodge & Sons*, Lord Couslfield, December 17, 1995, unreported.

[8] Law Reform (Miscellaneous Provisions) (Scotland) Act 1985, s. 8.

[9] In *Stewart v. J. M. Hodge & Sons*, above, it was observed *obiter* that the earliest possible
date for prescription was the date of granting of the disposition. In *Roulston v. Boyds*,
Sh.Ct, unreported (1990 G.W.D. 633), the date of recording the standard security
complained of was held to be the latest date for the start of prescription.

[10] In *Glasper v. Rodger*, 1996 S.L.T. 44 it was conceded that the appropriate date was the
date of recording, but nothing turned on this, since even it was more than five years
earlier.

[11] 1990 S.L.T. 609.

[12] The decision is criticised by Walker at p. 64 on the basis that there was no certainty
that there would ever be loss (a point sufficiently discussed above) and that there was no
injuria until the clause was declared void. But that must be wrong, since *injuria* must have
taken place at the time of the negligent advice or drafting, after which the solicitors had no
further part to play. The English case *Costa v. Georghiou*, above, was not cited.

Here it can be said that, although loss was not certain at the date of execution of the lease, it was bound to occur unless the tenants decided not to take advantage of a defective rent review clause. In this case it seems reasonable to say that the loss arose at the date of the lease because, for it to be avoided, an extraneous factor—loosely, a *novus actus interveniens*—would have to intervene. It does not seem reasonable to postpone the start of prescription in order to see whether such a factor does actually materialise.

In *Osborne & Hunter Ltd v. Hardie Caldwell & others*,[13] the pursuers sued a firm of accountants in connection with advice on a loan made to a debtor who had defaulted. The question was whether loss had been sustained at the date of the loan or only at the date of default in repaying it. The Second Division found that, while as a rule there may be no loss until there is default, each case turns on its own facts. In the present case the borrower's position was such that to make any loan to it at all was inadvisable. On those facts it could be said that the pursuers sustained loss as soon as they parted with their money to the borrower.[14]

In another case the question arose when a claim for breach of contract and negligence against solicitors had begun to prescribe. The basis of the claim was that they should have checked the correct designation of a defender company before raising proceedings. The court held that it was not necessary to wait until the fate of the defective action was known before it could be said that there was loss: at the date of raising the defective action there was "at least potential loss" to the pursuers, and that was sufficient.[15] The use of the term "potential loss" may be misleading, if it means that there was just a prospect that loss would be sustained in the future. The decision may, however, be justifiable on the facts, on the basis that at the date of raising the defective action there was a certainty that the pursuers would sustain at least loss consisting in the expenses of curing the defect by amendment. Such a view would seem to be justifiable provided it can be said that that loss was material, in the sense of exceeding a minimal threshold. Otherwise it would be preferable to take prescription to run from a later date.

Conclusions

The following general conclusions emerge. There are two possible **4.46** views: that prescription runs from the date when loss is realised, and that it runs from the earlier date of entry into the transaction complained of. Which is appropriate depends on when loss can be said to be sustained. The view that loss is sustained at the date of the transaction may be justifiable on the facts, provided that (1) the loss is material; (2) the loss is certain or only to be avoided if some extraneous factor intervenes; and

---

[13] 1999 S.L.T. 153, reversing the Lord Ordinary (reported 1998 S.L.T. 420).
[14] The action was not dismissed since a case under s. 11(3) remained; see below, paras 6.87 *et seq.* A similar case is *Nykredit Mortgage Bank plc v. Edward Erdman Group Ltd* [1998] 1 All E.R. 305.
[15] *J. G. Martin Plant Hire v. Bannatyne, Kirkwood France & Co.*, 1996 S.C. 105 at 109 and 110E (where the word "defenders" must be a misprint for "pursuers").

(3) the loss is not speculative, prospective, contingent or deferred. If these conditions are not met, the loss must arise at a later stage.

Omissions and continuing breach of duty

4.47   The phrase "act, neglect or default" is plainly broad enough to include omissions, for which liability may of course arise in either delict or breach of contract. Omissions cause difficulty because they are not events but continuing states of affairs. In each case, a preliminary question will be whether there is a continuing duty to act, so that an omission to do so is a continuing breach of that duty. For instance, the surveyor's duty is to carry out a survey and report on the state of the property in question at the date of the survey. If this is done negligently, there is a breach of duty. But it is not a continuing breach, since there is no continuing duty to act (to keep surveying).

4.48   By contrast, builders, architects and engineers will regularly be subject to continuing duties: to build in conformity with the contract or, during the course of construction, to supervise or review the suitability of designs. These are continuing duties. The obligation to design is not "one-off", but the architect is under a duty, if he discovers it is inappropriate or defective, to correct it.[16] Omission to perform such duties is therefore a continuing breach of duty.

When does loss accrue as a result of the omission? Two different cases must be distinguished: cases where there is a duty to act before a certain date and cases where there is not.

4.49 The case of a duty to act before a certain date. Where there is a duty to act before a certain date, and the negligence consists in failing to do so, it seems correct in principle to say that, whatever the date of the neglect or default, there is no concurrence of that neglect or default with loss, injury or damage until the date on which the act ought to have been performed.

4.50   The point is that there is no omission to act until the due date has arrived. An example would be the duty to register a deed or document or lodge it in court before a certain date. In such cases it makes no sense to attempt to pinpoint a particular date before the deadline on which the document should have been registered or lodged, and to say that that is the date the loss occurred. The reason is quite simple. In cases of this sort there is no breach of the duty to register or lodge timeously until the deadline has passed, so until then there is no act, neglect or default from which loss, injury or damage can flow.[17]

4.51   Here are three examples. Take the case where in a conveyancing transaction a solicitor fails properly to satisfy himself as to the usual property searches which the missives require and nonetheless proceeds to settle the transaction. His duty is to obtain the searches before the transaction is settled, so only at the date of settlement will it be clear that there has been negligence and loss resulting from it. Second, take the facts of *Dunlop v. McGowans*,[18] in which a landlord's solicitors

---

[16] Hudson, *Building and Engineering Contracts,* paras 2.083, 2.108 and 2.222.
[17] For this reason too the provisions of s. 11(2) are not relevant here.
[18] 1979 S.C. 22; 1980 S.C. (H.L.) 73.

negligently failed to serve a notice to quit on tenants, with the result that they were able to retain possession against the landlord. Here the solicitors were under a duty to their client to serve the notice so as to comply with the contractual requirements, that is, that notice of termination must be given 40 days before Whitsunday in any year. Their default accordingly took place at the moment they missed that deadline. And at that date loss was bound to occur, unless an extraneous factor—a *novus actus interveniens*—intervened in the shape of the happy chance that the tenants decided to move out anyway.[19]

Third, suppose a negligent omission by a solicitor to advise the raising **4.52** of proceedings, or to raise them, before the prescriptive period has expired. In such cases the neglect or default may continue throughout the period from which the client first seeks advice[20] until the claim is extinguished by prescription, but the breach and the loss arise only when the deadline is missed and the possible claim (on the primary obligation) is extinguished by prescription. It follows that it is at that date that an obligation to make reparation arises in the solicitors (a secondary obligation). Accordingly, any claim against the solicitors must be made within five years from that date, before that (secondary) obligation is itself extinguished by prescription.[21]

Matters will be slightly more difficult in personal injuries cases, since **4.53** there the solicitors' failure will result only in limitation of the client's claim, and there will remain the possibility that the court will allow the late claim to be pursued, so that there may be no eventual loss.[22] Nonetheless, on the argument outlined above, it would seem that the missing of the deadline is the breach and that loss is sustained when the right to proceed as of right is lost, so that prescription of the claim in negligence against the solicitors runs from that date. The fact that, on application to the court under section 19A of the 1973 Act, the claim was ultimately allowed to proceed would go to quantification of loss, but it would not affect the fact that a loss had been sustained sufficient to trigger the running of the prescriptive period.

Suppose an action is raised timeously but dismissed owing to solici- **4.54** tors' negligence. When does their clients' action in negligence against them arise? It is arguable that loss follows upon the default only when the action is dismissed; it is also arguable that it arises at the earlier date of the default which precipitated the dismissal, such (for example) as failure to lodge the closed record.[23] In England, the first of these views has been preferred, the cause of action arising when the writ is struck out.[24] This is of course a possible approach. But on the general view

---

[19] Lord Kissen at 36 and Lord Thomson at 39 took the view that the relevant date was that when vacant possession would otherwise have been obtained; the opinion of the Lord Justice-Clerk (Wheatley) is less clear but may be to the same effect (at 34).

[20] Here and throughout complications of substantive law are left aside: for example, it is clear that liability in this sort of case will depend among other things on the quality of information the solicitor was given, and when.

[21] *Arif v. Levy & McRae*, Lord Coulsfield, December 17, 1991, unreported. It will be for the pursuer in such a case to aver when the (primary) obligation prescribed: *Keddie v. Digby Brown & Co.*, Lord Osborne, November 11, 1997, unreported.

[22] s. 19A; see below, Chap. 12.

[23] RCS, r. 22.3(3).

[24] *Hopkins v. Mackenzie*, Times L.R., Nov. 3, 1994 (delay).

set out above, it seems preferable to say that, where the negligence consists in a failure to perform a particular act before a deadline, the breach and the loss should be taken to arise at the point when the deadline is missed. At that stage there is at least nominal loss, even if for some reason the court ultimately decides not to dismiss the action and substantial loss is not therefore sustained.[25]

4.55   There is some difficulty, however, in knowing exactly how far to extend this category. It does seem that the same principles should apply *mutatis mutandis* to the case of obligations which must be performed not by a certain date but within a reasonable time.

4.56   It may also be that this should be said of obligations which do not have to be performed by a certain fixed date but which must be performed before a certain event whose date is uncertain. An example is provided by the case of *Porteous v. Dollar Rae*.[26] The pursuers were the proprietors of a property on which the defenders were carrying out building works. The defenders (it was averred) had undertaken to obtain planning permission. They failed to so so before constructing the building, and permission was refused. The planning authority served an enforcement notice requiring destruction of the work. It was held that the pursuers sustained loss, injury or damage when the enforcement notice was served on them, so prescription ran from that date. In this case it was impossible to say, until the planning authority had exercised its statutory discretion, that the pursuers would sustain any loss at all.

4.57   It might, however, be possible to figure a case in which for some reason objection by a statutory authority was absolutely certain. On such facts it could be said that the pursuers would be bound to suffer some loss—at least expenses—as soon as unauthorised construction began. Accordingly, unless those expenses were not material, prescription would run from the date construction began, the defenders on these facts being under an obligation to obtain the necessary consents before the date of starting construction. In any event, in each of these cases it is clear that prescription starts to run well before the date of demolition of the building.[27]

4.58   Omissions where there is no duty to act before a certain date. Two lines of authority can be distinguished in the English cases. First, that where there is a continuing obligation to act and an omission to do so, there is no loss until it becomes impossible to act in order to remedy the omission. Secondly, that there is loss at the initial moment of failure to act, even though the loss may only be nominal, and may in the event be sustained, if at all, only in part.

4.59   The choice between these two lines of reasoning is precisely the same choice as was outlined in the previous section, between taking loss to

---

[25] Presumably it might in some cases be plausible to argue for a later date on the basis that at the date of the deadline no material loss had yet occurred.

[26] 1979 S.L.T. (Sh.Ct) 51.

[27] *cf. Steel v. CRGP Bute Ltd*, Sh.Ct, unreported (1996 G.W.D. 1069), where loss ran not from the date the pursuer was told a building would have to be demolished but (at latest, in terms of s. 11(3)) from the date the pursuer received a report detailing substantial defects in it.

arise at the date of realisation and taking it to arise at the earlier date of the act or transaction which led to it. The prevailing view in England has been that it is a matter of complete indifference to the pursuer when a duty is performed by the defender, so long as it is indeed performed, and it can therefore be said that the duty to perform has not been breached until performance becomes impossible. This was the line followed in a leading case, *Midland Bank Trust Co Ltd v. Hett Stubbs & Kemp*,[28] in which the defendant solicitors' obligation to register an option to purchase land was held to be a continuing duty on them, and their failure to register it was held to have caused loss only when, owing to sale of the land, it became impossible to do so.[29] This view clearly corresponds to the "realisation of loss" view outlined earlier.

The English courts have on occasion favoured a different view, so that **4.60** loss is held to be sustained when the defendants ought to have performed rather than at the last opportunity on which they might have done so.[30] So in *Bell v. Peter Browne & Co.*,[31] solicitors failed to execute a declaration of trust or make the appropriate entries in the Land Register in order to protect their client's interest in a house which was transferred to his wife as part of a divorce settlement. The Court of Appeal accepted that the solicitors continued to be under an obligation to take steps to protect their client's interest, and that such protection continued to be possible until the client's wife sold the house. But it did not accept that there was no loss before then, and identified loss at the time of the transfer to the client's wife or at least shortly thereafter.[32] It will be clear that this decision applies the *Forster v. Outred & Co.*[33] and *D. W. Moore & Co. Ltd v. Ferrier*[34] decisions mentioned in the previous section. It introduces consistency between the cases on acts and the cases on omissions, but it is affected by the same criticism which applies to those decisions.

The Scottish courts have tended to follow the *Midland Bank* line, **4.61** which, as mentioned, is consistent with the "realisation of loss" approach adopted in economic loss cases. For example, in *Duncan v. Aitken, Malone & Mackay*,[35] the pursuer's complaint was that solicitors had failed to transfer her husband's reversionary interest in heritage to her; loss was held to accrue only when the transfer became impossible owing to his sequestration. The case was argued without the citation of any authority other than *Dunlop v. McGowans*, but the line pursued is clearly the *Midland Bank* line. In *Fergus v. MacLennan*,[36] solicitors negligently failed to secure the transfer to their client of heritable property. The property was transferred to another party whose title by positive prescription became exempt from challenge after 10 years. The question

---

[28] [1979] Ch. 384 at 435.
[29] *Midland Bank*, above, at 435 and 438.
[30] *Lee v. Thompson* [1989] 2 E.G.L.R. 151 at 153; (1990) 6 P.N. 91.
[31] [1990] 2 Q.B. 495.
[32] At 509, *per* Beldam L.J. (For example, if expenses had been incurred in seeking the advice of other solicitors about the conduct of the original solicitors, those would have been recoverable loss: 503.)
[33] [1982] 1 W.L.R. 86.
[34] [1988] 1 W.L.R. 267.
[35] 1989 S.C.L.R. 1.
[36] 1991 S.L.T. 321.

arose when the loss had been sustained. The court was not satisfied on the pleadings that the pursuer had necessarily sustained loss until the third party's title became unchallengeable. The question of prescription was left to be considered after proof.[37]

4.62   The same approach was adopted in *Fitzpatrick v. Kenneth Pendreigh & Co.*[38] The pursuer's solicitors failed to advise him to have an informal agreement executed in legally binding form, with the result that he was unable to enforce his (informal) entitlement to acquire his siblings' shares of a house at the executry valuation. The claim was therefore one of a continuing breach of duty in contract and delict to take reasonable care to secure the agreed position in legally enforceable terms. Here the court rejected the pursuer's submission that there was no loss while it remained possible for the pursuer's siblings voluntarily to honour the (non-binding) agreement. This was held to be a matter which went only to quantification of loss: if some of them did indeed agree to sell to him at the executry valuation, this would reduce the quantum of damages. On the facts it was unnecessary for the purposes of prescription to go further than saying that prescription ran from the date when the pursuer lost the opportunity to secure a formal agreement with his siblings. This is surely right. A loss was sustained at that date, and the fact that it might for extraneous reasons be mitigated subsequently cannot affect the date for the running of prescription.

4.63   There is no need to multiply examples. The Scottish cases have invariably favoured the line that the loss arises when remedying the omission becomes impossible, a line which is consistent with the "realisation of loss" approach to cases of acts rather than omissions. Nonetheless, it was seen earlier that, where positive acts are concerned, there are cases in which the date of transaction is the appropriate date for the running of prescription. The corollary is that there are likely to be cases of omissions where on the facts it is preferable to take prescription to run from the date when the duty ought to have been performed, rather than the date when remedying the omission became impossible.

Intended but disappointed beneficiaries

4.64   In this case different rules apply. Where a solicitor's failure consists in omitting to draft a valid will in which legacies are made to intended beneficiaries, the beneficiaries are now able to sue for that loss, at least in England, although existing Scottish authority is adverse to such a claim.[39] But one can hardly say that their loss arises—as it would in the

---

[37] At 324 L.

[38] Lord Clyde, June 19, 1986, unreported.

[39] *White v. Jones* [1995] 2 A.C. 207. The House of Lords decision in the Scottish case of *Robertson v. Fleming* (1861) 4 Macq. 167 at 177 is to the opposite effect, although the House declined to follow it in *White v. Jones*: see 258–259. See also in Scotland *MacDougall v. MacDougall's Exrs*, 1994 S.L.T. 1178; in England *Ross v. Caunters* [1980] Ch. 297. The view expressed in McGee, *Limitation Periods*, pp. 82–83 that these cases cannot be distinguished from the principle applied in *Forster v. Outred & Co.*, above, and *D. W. Moore & Co. Ltd v. Ferrier*, above, seems odd. The point is surely that in those cases there was a breach of duty to identified persons at the time of the negligent drafting, whereas it is clear that for the disappointed beneficiary to have a claim he must survive the testator, the testator must die without altering the will, and the will must be invalid as a direct result of the negligent drafting (as opposed, for example, to the testator's incapacity).

normal case—at the time the solicitors ought to have done the necessary drafting. This is because there is no prospective entitlement to anything and therefore until the death of the deceased there is neither any wrong done to the prospective beneficiaries nor any recoverable loss.[40] This is consistent with the line pursued in *Lawrence v. McIntosh & Hamilton*,[41] where a solicitor failed to obey instructions on drafting a will, as a result of which his client's estate passed on intestacy. In this case it is hard to tell exactly what weight was placed on this point, but it appears that it was held that the appropriate date for prescription was the date of the deceased's death. At that point it became impossible for the solicitor to remedy the omission, and loss to the testamentary beneficiaries became unavoidable.

The provisions of section 11(2)

> "Where as a result of a continuing act, neglect or default loss, injury **4.65** or damage has occurred before the cessation of the act, neglect or default the loss, injury or damage shall be deemed for the purposes of subsection (1) above to have occurred on the date when the act, neglect or default ceased."

Section 11(2) presents another aspect to consider. Curiously enough, it does not appear to have been pled in any of the cases discussed above. It provides that where an act, neglect or default is a continuing one, and loss, injury or damage has occurred before the date on which the default ceased, the date of cessation is the appropriate date for prescription. The provision is apt to cover continuing wrongs, for example nuisances such as the emission of noxious substances, and economic delicts, such as breach of competition law. Under section 11(2) the liability in delict will not begin to prescribe so long as the nuisance or other wrongful act continues.

A good instance of where this subsection can usefully be called into **4.66** service is provided by the case of *Richardson v. Quercus Ltd*.[42] This appears to be founded on section 11(2), although the case was decided on another ground and the subsection is not mentioned in the opinion. Here building works interfered with a right of support. The defenders argued that prescription began to run when the wrong which caused the damage stopped, even though the damage might continue thereafter more or less indefinitely.

Section 11(2) is to the advantage of the creditor in postponing the **4.67** date on which prescription begins to run: not from the (first) date on which loss was sustained but from the later date of cessation of the act, neglect or default.[43]

In the preceding sections a distinction has been drawn between cases **4.68** where there is a duty to act before a certain date and cases where there

---

[40] This case cannot be explained in terms of assumption of responsibility, because then one would not be able to grant the beneficiaries, to whom the solicitors assumed no responsibility, a claim. (Perhaps one should not: Weir (1995) 111 L.Q.R. 357.)

[41] 1981 S.L.T. (Sh.Ct) 73.

[42] J. F. Wheatley, Q.C. March 25, 1997, unreported; 1999 S.C. 278, I.H.

[43] In many cases of continuing default, there will be no loss until after the default has ceased, and so no need for any variation of the ordinary rule of s. 11(1).

is simply a continuing duty to act. In cases where there is a duty to act before a certain date, section 11(2) does not apply, since there is no continuing duty to act and no breach of duty until the deadline has passed. It is reasonably easy to say that, when the deadline is missed, the wrong and the loss flowing from it come into being.

4.69   On the other hand, where there is a continuing duty to act, the two views outlined above were respectively (1) that there is loss only when it becomes impossible to remedy the default (the *Midland Bank* line); and (2) that there is loss at the initial moment of default. In each case the breach of duty is a continuing one and subsists after the date on which the loss occurs.[44] Section 11(2), however, provides that in a case of continuing default loss is deemed to have occurred on the date when the default ceased. Which, if either, of these two options does this represent? Plainly it is not option (2), loss at the initial moment of default. In fact it appears to be option (1), provided that the date the default ceased can be equated with the date it became irremediable.

4.70   Four more general comments may be made, all of them concerned with possible reform or clarification of the law. First, it might be preferable if the section were worded to refer to when a default became irremediable rather than when it ceased. This is because it is not always plain when a default, especially an omission, ceases. Take the case of the failure of a solicitor to record a title, his client losing out irrevocably when someone else recorded a title to the same land and completed positive prescription upon it. The solicitor's omission is a continuing one. It is obvious that it becomes irremediable once title has been perfected in the name of the acquirer by positive prescription. Clearly there is a loss then. It is not quite so clear, although it still may be correct to say, that this means that the default has ceased.

4.71   Second, the whole object of negative prescription is to contain the defender's exposure to risk and to introduce certainty about when obligations are no longer enforceable. Section 11(2) is rather generous in postponing the start not just of the five-year but also of the 20-year prescriptive period in the case of continuing wrongs. Since the 20-year prescription is conceived as a long stop, it might be more satisfactory if it were to run from an earlier date, such as the date of the initial act or default, and the five-year prescription were to run from the date of the loss (or at latest the date on which it was discoverable).[45]

4.72   Third, at least for the five-year prescription, it may be thought that postponement of the start of prescription until the act, neglect or default ceases is unnecessary. This is because section 11(3) corrects injustice which would arise if the prescriptive period were to run against the pursuer while he was in ignorance of his rights.[46] If the pursuer can show that he was in justifiable ignorance that he had a claim, he can argue that

---

[44] In case (1) this assumes that a breach of duty continues even after, owing to the passing of some deadline, it has become impossible to remedy: this seems likely to be correct in principle.

[45] As in Germany, BGB Art. 852; and as now proposed for England by the Law Commission: Consultation Paper no. 151 (1998), paras 15.3 and 15.16–17.

[46] See below, paras 6.87 *et seq.*

prescription should run from a later date. This possibility means that it is not excessively harsh to hold that in principle prescription should start to run not from the date when a default ceased but from the date of the default.

Fourth, in general it is difficult to see precisely what the rationale is **4.73** for a provision of this nature. Why should claims for damages relating to early periods not prescribe, and only those lying within the prescriptive period remain recoverable? That result might be reached if the courts were to interpret a continuing wrong (for example, nuisance) as a series of independent causes of action, each causally related to a particular quantum of harm. But this approach does not sit well with some of the existing authorities.[47] If the law on prescription and continuing wrongs is ever reconsidered, it may be worth considering whether it would be appropriate to treat a continuing wrong as a series of independent wrongs.[48]

Defects in and damage to buildings[49]
There has been major change in this area in recent years, and a series **4.74** of judgments which are not at all easy to reconcile. Much turns on how damage to property is categorised—whether as physical or economic loss—and whether any distinction is to be drawn between defects and damage.

The earlier law up to 1991 was reasonably clear. So, for example, in **4.75** *Renfrew Golf Club v. Ravenstone Securities Ltd*,[50] a case based on a failure in design (a golf course whose greens flooded), the court distinguished between defects which might never give rise to any damage and damage itself. The existence of defects did not in itself constitute damage (*damnum*); and it was held that there was no loss, and therefore the prescriptive period did not begin, until damage to the golf course had been sustained: physical damage was a prerequisite.[51]

The distinction applied in this case was drawn from the decision of the **4.76** House of Lords in *Pirelli General Cable Works Ltd v. Oscar Faber & Partners Ltd*,[52] which (dealing with the English Limitation Acts) held that a cause of action in tort, in this case for negligent advice given by an engineer on the design of a chimney, accrued when physical damage came into being, even though that was before the date on which

---

[47] Notably *Dunlop v. McGowans*, 1980 S.C. (H.L.) 73.

[48] As is proposed in Israel by the Law Reform Committee in relation to reform of s. 89 of the Civil Wrong Ordinance 1968: see I. Gilead in Hondius (ed.), *Extinctive Prescription*, p. 212.

[49] See generally MacQueen, 1991 S.L.T. (News) 77 and 91 and 99; Clerk and Lindsell, *Torts*, paras 31.05 *et seq.*; Jackson and Powell, *Professional Negligence*, paras 1.137 *et seq.*; McGee, *Limitation Periods*, pp. 67 *et seq.*; J. Stapleton, "The gist of negligence" (1988) 104 L.Q.R. 213–238; I.N.D. Wallace, "Negligence and defective buildings: confusion confounded?" (1989) 105 L.Q.R. 46–78; E. McKendrick, "Pirelli re-examined" (1991) 11 *Legal Studies* 326; N. J. Mullany, "Limitation of actions and latent damage—an Australian perspective" (1991) 54 M.L.R. 216–243; "Reform of the law of latent damage", *ibid.*, 349–384; "Limitation of actions—where are we now?" (1993) L.M.C.L.Q. 34–59

[50] 1984 S.C. 22.

[51] Followed in *Greater Glasgow Health Board v. Baxter Clark & Paul*, 1990 S.C. 237; *Sinclair v. MacDougall Estates*, 1994 S.L.T. 76.

[52] [1983] 2 A.C. 1, esp. at 16, *per* Lord Fraser.

damage was actually discovered or could, with reasonable diligence, have been discovered. The Latent Damage Act 1986 (which applies only in England) was subsequently passed in order to deal with cases in which plaintiffs' claims became time-barred before they knew of them.[53] *Pirelli* also established that generally time would start to run on the date damage occurred rather than the date of construction, although there was a possible class of exceptions to this rule where it was inevitable that damage would occur eventually, so the building was "doomed from the start".[54]

4.77　　Accordingly, on this line of authority it is possible to distinguish three different periods: (1) when a defect is latent[55]; (2) when physical consequences have arisen from the defect, but have not been discovered and could not with reasonable diligence have been discovered; (3) when the physical consequences are discovered or could with reasonable diligence have been discovered. Under this categorisation, it may make some sense to say in period (1) that there is no obligation on which prescription can run, because there is as yet no loss; in period (2) that there is loss, but its non-discoverability may allow the creditor to rely on provisions delaying the start of the prescriptive period[56]; and in period (3) that there is loss, and provisions delaying the running of prescription have no further application.

4.78　　But the categorisation may require reconsideration. In England, following the decision of the House of Lords in *Murphy v. Brentwood District Council*,[57] loss, injury or damage to a building (rather than to persons or other property) arising from defects in that building is now to be characterised as economic. Although in this section most attention is directed at buildings, because that is the focus of most litigation, it is important to be clear that the same principle applies to anything in which there is a defect which may cause damage to the thing itself but not to persons or to any other property.

4.79　　Matters may be different in Scotland owing to the decision in *Junior Books Ltd v. Veitchi Co. Ltd*,[58] which is discussed below. But if *Murphy* is followed in Scotland, two main consequences follow: first, loss of this kind, since it is purely economic, will in general be irrecoverable in delict; second, it is not clear that it can still be right to insist on physical damage to determine the date when the loss injury or damage arises.[59] Instead, it would appear that periods (1) and (2) become condensed into one and the same: throughout that period there is "loss, injury or

---

[53] This Act inserted a new s. 14A(6)–(8) into the 1980 Act.

[54] At 18; discussed in *Ketteman v. Hansel Properties Ltd* [1987] 1 A.C. 189; *London Borough of Bromley v. Rush & Tompkins Ltd* (1985) 4 Con. L.R. 44, QBD.

[55] This, as suggested in *Pirelli* at 16 F–H, is analogous to a predisposition or natural weakness in a human body which may never develop into disease or injury. The analogy seems attractive enough so long as the damage to the building is regarded as physical rather than economic loss.

[56] That is, in Scotland, for purposes of the five-year prescription, 1973 Act, s. 11(3). This is subject to considerations about reasonable diligence: below, paras 6.101 *et seq. cf.* D. 21.1.55, Papinian 12 *responsorum*.

[57] [1991] A.C. 398 at 466.

[58] 1982 S.C. (H.L.) 244.

[59] *cf.* McKendrick (1991) 11 *Legal Studies* 326; *contra*, *Strathclyde R.C. v. Border Engineering Contractors Ltd*, 1997 S.C.L.R. 100 at 107.

damage" of an economic nature caused by an act, neglect or default. Although there may be no physical manifestation of the loss, injury or damage, it is constituted by the object's being inherently defective.[60] At least as a rule this loss will not be discoverable until some physical consequences have flowed from it.

To this, however, the following objection might be made: "If the **4.80** interest infringed is the value of property, it may be appropriate to speak of a cause of action in negligence for economic loss sustained by reason of latent defect as accruing when the resultant physical damage is known or manifest, for . . . it is only then the actual diminution in market value occurs. . . . If, on the other hand, the interest infringed is the physical integrity of property then there is a certain logic in looking at the time when physical damage occurs, as was done in *Pirelli*."[61]

The question is therefore whether, although the loss is economic, it **4.81** should be held to occur only when it is known to exist. The suggestion seems paradoxical, although on particular facts—where a property with a latent defect has been sold on for an undiminished price to another purchaser—it is clearly true that the market value is not affected by the unknown defect. But if this were the law in Scotland, it would be hard to imagine a case in which section 11(3) of the 1973 Act could apply, that is, a case in which the starting date of the five-year prescription should be postponed until the loss was discoverable. For, on this basis, the loss only arises and reduces the value of the property when it is known about. And, if that is the ordinary starting date for prescription, that will be the date from which the 20-year prescription runs, a result that makes nonsense of any notion that it is a long-stop prescription. These reasons alone seem to suggest that, whatever the merit of the argument in principle, it does not accord with the framework of the 1973 Act.

Accordingly, if a defect is itself regarded as amounting to loss, time **4.82** should run from the moment the defect came into being. As with other economic loss cases, this date will have to be on or after the date of the pursuer's reliance on the defender or the defender's assumption of responsibility. On the same reasoning as set out earlier, this rule would seem to need qualification only if the defect itself was so trivial as not to amount to material economic loss. In that event, time would not start to run until material economic loss in the shape of a material defect, latent or other, had been sustained.

It should, however, be emphasised that it is not certain that *Murphy* **4.83** will be applied in Scotland in precisely the way outlined; if not, then in principle the *Pirelli* approach will still apply, and time will start to run from the date of physical damage, subject to the possibility of its starting at the date of construction for buildings which are "doomed from the start".

This is not the place for detailed discussion of the question of **4.84** recovering damages for pure economic loss. But the following points are

---

[60] *cf.* perhaps D. 39.2.18.11, Paul 48 *ad edictum.*
[61] *Hawkins v. Clayton* (1988) 164 C.L.R. 539 at 601; followed in *Western Australia v. Wardley Australia Ltd* (1991) 102 A.L.R. 213 at 229–230.

material to the question of prescription. Now that loss or damage to a building itself arising from its defective design or construction is characterised as purely economic, it will in general be irrecoverable in delict.[62] But that is not invariably so and, in cases where it is not, it is therefore still important to identify when prescription starts to run.

(1) There can be liability for latent damage arising from the breach of a contract, such as a collateral warranty, and in Scotland the prescriptive period will start to run against such contractual claims for loss when the loss is sustained.

(2) There can in principle still be recovery in delict for pure economic loss, at least where the proximity between the parties is very great, and the defenders know (or ought to know) that the pursuers are relying on them and would be likely to suffer loss as a consequence of their negligence.[63] Indeed, in *Murphy* itself Lord Keith said that in cases in which the tortious liability arose out of a contractual relationship with professional people, the duty of the professional people extended to taking reasonable care not to cause economic loss to the client by the advice given. Lord Keith regarded both *Pirelli* and *Junior Books Ltd v. Veitchi Co. Ltd* as falling within that principle.[64] While that is certainly not how the House of Lords in *Pirelli* seems to have regarded it, nonetheless it indicates that in certain circumstances recovery of pure economic loss may be possible.[65]

(3) These circumstances are particularly likely to include cases in which the pursuer seeks to recover from professionals, since the claim to proximity is likely to be facilitated by the reasonableness of relying on professional advice.[66] Accordingly, it seems likely that the considerations set out above would extend to builders, engineers, and architects.

(4) Successors in title. It seems right to take it that prescription will run not just against the first owner (for example) of a new property, so far as claims against the builder or professional adviser are concerned, but also against his or her successors in title.[67] In the course of consultation the Scottish Law Commission raised the question whether this should be clarified by legislation, but in their eventual report took the view, following the decision of the House of Lords in *D. & F. Estates Ltd v. Church Commissioners for England and Wales*,[68] that it was now very

---

[62] To this extent *Dynamco Ltd v. Holland & Hannen & Cubitts (Scotland) Ltd*, 1971 S.C. 257 still stands; *cf.* recently *Coleridge v. Miller Contruction Ltd*, 1997 S.L.T. 485.

[63] *Junior Books Ltd v. Veitchi Co. Ltd*, above, admittedly more often distinguished than followed. See, *e.g.*, *Nitrigin Eireann v. Inco Alloys Ltd* [1992] 1 W.L.R. 498 at 505; also below, para. 4.85.

[64] *i.e.* the principle of *Hedley Byrne & Co. v. Heller & Partners Ltd* [1964] A.C. 465.

[65] In *Pirelli*, above, however, at 16 F–G Lord Fraser drew a distinction between non-actionable defect and actionable damage. The following comment by Lord Keith in *Murphy*, above, at 466 E–F about the *Pirelli* case does not sit at all well with this distinction: "If the plaintiffs had happened to discover the defect before any damage had occurred there would seem to be no good reason for holding that they would not have had a cause of action in tort at that stage, without having to wait until some damage had occurred. They would have suffered economic loss through having a defective chimney upon which they required to expend money for the purpose of removing the defect."

[66] Clerk and Lindsell, *Torts*, paras 7.83 and 7.90.

[67] So *Jones & Anor v. Stroud D.C.* [1986] 1 W.L.R. 1141 at 1149, CA; *Investors in Industry Commercial Properties Ltd v. S. Bedfordshire D.C.* [1986] 2 W.L.R. 937, CA.

[68] [1989] A.C. 177.

unlikely that a successor in title could have a claim in delict against the builder.[69] Clearly there would be no claim in contract (apart from assignation of any claim available to the first owner). Following *Murphy*, in normal circumstances it seems improbable that such claims could arise, since they would be for economic loss in circumstances in which the necessary proximity would be unlikely to be present.

(5) As a consequence of *Murphy*, cases in which defects have physical consequences such as cracking and cases where the problem is that the materials used, although intrinsically sound, are of the wrong quality or colour[70] can now be treated in the same manner. In each instance the question will be when the economic loss was sustained.

Where economic loss is recoverable, there seem to be two possible **4.85** starting dates for the running of prescription: either (a) the date on which some material economic loss was sustained or (b) the date on which the defender assumed responsibility towards the pursuer or the pursuer acted irrevocably to his detriment in reliance on (for example) the defender's design.[71] The first of these possible dates can be justified on the basis that in principle it will be necessary to repair the defective object or, alternatively, on the basis that its value is less than the pursuers paid for it. This is essentially the principle underlying *Junior Books Ltd v. Veitchi Co. Ltd*,[72] in which the pursuers, owners of a factory, were able to recover damages for the cost of replacing a defective floor from the defenders, the nominated sub-contractors who had laid it. The case was one of pure economic loss, because there was no physical damage to persons or to any property other than the floor itself. Accordingly, the measure of damages was the cost of repairing the defective object. It would therefore seem reasonable to say that the cause of action accrued when the pursuers sustained economic loss. That would probably be on their acceptance of or payment for the defective floor.[73]

The second of these possible dates—of assumption of responsibility or **4.86** of reliance—can be justified on the basis discussed above for other cases of economic loss. Once there has been an act of reliance upon the defenders—in the present context likely also to be acceptance of or payment for the defective property—time should start to run. But, as in the cases discussed earlier, this will require that actual and material rather than merely potential loss can be identified at that date.

It has been suggested in the House of Lords that a general principle of **4.87** assumption of responsibility underlies the categories both of providing negligent information and of performing negligent services.[74] If this

---

[69] SLC Memo. no. 74 (1987), paras 4.89 *et seq.*; Report no. 122 (1989), para. 2.86.

[70] *Simaan General Contracting Co. v. Pilkington Glass Ltd (No. 2)* [1988] Q.B. 758; *Department of Environment v. Bates* [1991] 1 A.C. 499.

[71] *cf. Murphy* at 466 F–G (Lord Keith), noting that cases such as *Pirelli* would fall within the *Hedley Byrne* principle.

[72] 1982 S.C. (H.L.) 244.

[73] *cf. Council of Shire of Sutherland v. Heyman* (1985) 157 C.L.R. 424 at 505.

[74] *Henderson v. Merrett Syndicates* [1995] 2 A.C. 145 at 180–1; *cf. Spring v. Guardian Royal Exchange Assurance* [1995] 2 A.C. 296 at 316, *per* Lord Goff.

unitary approach finds more general favour, it certainly supports the treatment of the building cases along the same lines as the economic loss cases already discussed. But, for the purpose of starting prescription running, it would remain essential that there was material loss at the date of assumption of responsibility.

Summary of economic loss issues

4.88   The upshot of this discussion of the economic loss cases in general can be summarised in these propositions:

(1) When, at the date on which the defender assumed responsibility or the pursuer reasonably relied upon her, there was no certainty that loss would occur, prescription can run only from the date loss either becomes certain or is realised.

(2) When, at the date of reliance or assumption of responsibility, loss was inevitable or bound to happen failing the intervention of an extraneous factor, prescription should run from that date.

(3) In principle these points are capable of applying to latent defect cases.

(4) This is so, however, only if a latent defect is not itself treated as loss but as something which may or may not give rise to actual loss.

(5) On the view that a material latent defect itself constitutes economic loss, prescription must run from the date the material latent defect arose.

(6) That date will be at earliest the date when the pursuer placed reliance on the defender or the defender assumed responsibility towards the pursuer.

(7) Damage to an object arising from a defect in itself is properly categorised as economic loss, which is rarely recoverable in delict.

(8) The loss, since it is economic, need leave no visible traces; the victim may have no idea that his object is unsound or his contract defective.

(9) It follows that the prescriptive period may well have run before there is any discoverable loss at all.

(10) The saving provision in section 11(3), which applies only to the five-year prescription,[75] in which the question of the creditor's knowledge is raised, therefore becomes of the greatest importance.

(11) This is true both in cases of defective property and in other cases where loss accrues at the date of reliance or assumption of responsibility.

(12) In defective property cases it is worth adding simply this: physical damage is important now not as triggering the start of the prescriptive period but so that the court can determine whether the pursuer could with reasonable diligence have known of his loss injury and damage.

Unjustified enrichment

4.89   In principle the cause of action in unjustified enrichment must accrue when the enrichment results in the defender's hands. So in repetition it is at the moment of receipt (for example) of the undue transfer that the

---

[75] See below, paras 6.87 *et seq.*

obligation towards the creditor arises. Similarly, in a building case, the obligation to make recompense was found to be enforceable at latest when the building work was completed.[76] The same ought presumably to apply in cases where the builder diverges so far from the contract as to lose his right to sue upon it. To the extent that the defender is enriched by the builder's part performance, there must be a liability in recompense, and that must arise when the work is done so as to accede to the defender's property.[77]

So too, in *NV Devos Gebroeder v. Sunderland Sportswear Ltd,*[78] a claim **4.90** for recompense was held to arise when the defenders were enriched. Their enrichment took place when they received goods from the pursuers. In that case the pursuers' claim was brought in recompense because the goods were found to be disconform to contract and the pursuers' action in contract was dismissed owing to their material breach of contract. The pursuers' argument was that a right to sue in contract is generally thought to exclude a right to claim recompense, so that the defenders' obligation to make recompense to the pursuers arose only when the pursuers' contractual action was dismissed. This argument was rejected: the pursuers' inability to sue successfully in contract arose from their material breach of contract rather than the dismissal of their action so far as founded in contract. If the existence of a contract was a bar to recompense it ceased to be so before the dismissal of the action.

In the present state of the law it may in any event be going too far to **4.91** say that contract always excludes recompense.[79] Why might there not be concurrent remedies in contract and recompense, provided the remedy in recompense is not inconsistent with the terms of the contract? Any claim in recompense would come into being at the moment enrichment arose in the hands of the defenders, whether or not they were under any contractual obligation.

Where a claim is made for payment *quantum meruit* it will be exigible **4.92** on that basis only where the contract has been rescinded or discharged so that the parties' obligations under it have ceased to exist.[80] It seems to make sense to say that any obligation to make payment on the part of the recipient of goods or services arises at the time the goods or services are rendered, those being valued in such cases not under the contract but according to ordinary or market rates.[81] The alternative would be to say that the claim *quantum meruit* was suspensively conditional on the rescission or discharge of the contract, but it is difficult to see why that should be so.

---

[76] *Alexander Hall & Sons (Builders) Ltd v. Strathclyde R.C.*, Lord Morton of Shuna, February 9, 1989, unreported.

[77] *Ramsay v. Brand* (1898) 25 R. 1212.

[78] 1990 S.C. 291; 1989 S.L.T. 382 and 1990 S.L.T. 473.

[79] *cf. Henderson v. Merrett Syndicates* [1995] 2 A.C. 145. In general, if there can be concurrent remedies in contract and tort, it is not clear why there should not be in contract and unjustified enrichment. But in an earlier case, *Pan Ocean Shipping Ltd v. Creditcorp Ltd* [1994] 1 W.L.R. 161 at 166 Lord Goff referred to the fact that "serious difficulties arise if the law seeks to expand the law of restitution to redistribute risks for which provision has been made under an applicable contract".

[80] *ERDC Construction Ltd v. H. M. Love & Co.*, 1995 S.L.T. 254.

[81] Gloag, *Contract*, p. 358.

II.   COMPUTATION OF A CONTINUOUS PRESCRIPTIVE PERIOD

4.93 The basic principles for calculating the prescriptive period are the same for positive prescription and negative prescription.[82] Section 14 of the Act sets them out. Only a few comments on these provisions seem to be needed.

"Computation of prescriptive periods

14.—(1) In the computation of a prescriptive period for the purposes of any provision of this Part of this Act—

(a) time occurring before the commencement of this Part of this Act shall be reckonable towards the prescriptive period in like manner as time occurring thereafter, but subject to the restriction that any time reckoned under this paragraph shall be less than the prescriptive period;

(b) any time during which any person against whom the provision is pled was under legal disability shall (except so far as otherwise provided by subsection (4) of section 6 of this Act including that subsection as applied by section 8A of this Act) be reckoned as if the person were free from that disability;

(c) if the commencement of the prescriptive period would, apart from this paragraph, fall at a time in any day other than the beginning of the day, the period shall be deemed to have commenced at the beginning of the next following day;

(d) if the last day of the prescriptive period would, apart from this paragraph, be a holiday, the period shall, notwithstanding anything in the said provision, be extended to include any immediately succeeding day which is a holiday, any further immediately succeeding days which are holidays, and the next succeeding day which is not a holiday;

(e) save as otherwise provided in this Part of this Act regard shall be had to the like principles as immediately before the commencement of this Part of this Act were applicable to the computation of periods of prescription for the purposes of the Prescription Act 1617.

(2) In this section "holiday" means a day of any of the following descriptions, namely, a Saturday, a Sunday and a day which, in Scotland, is a bank holiday under the Banking and Financial Dealings Act 1971."

4.94 Section 14(1)(a) is a transitional provision, whose effect is that, where prescription was in the course of running, time which had run towards prescription before the commencement of the 1973 Act (July 25, 1976) is counted towards the relevant prescriptive period, but at least some part of the prescriptive period must occur after the commencement of the Act. Clearly this does not mean that, where prescription had already been completed before July 25, 1976, obligations had to prescribe all over again after that date.[83]

---

[82] See below, paras 16.42 *et seq.* for further comments.
[83] *Porteous's Exrs v. Ferguson*, 1995 S.L.T. 649.

So far as negative prescription is concerned, it seems unlikely that this **4.95** provision can now be of any significance. The only exception might be where prescription had been suspended, either on the basis of the statutory provisions applying to the five-year prescription or as a matter of common law in the case of the 20-year prescription.[84] In either case it would be conceivable that some part of the prescriptive period had run before July 25, 1976 and that this fell to be added to a prescriptive period which resumed running after that date once the reason for suspending prescription had been removed.

Legal disability does not have any effect to interrupt or suspend the **4.96** prescriptive period, except as specially provided for the five-year prescription.[85]

Prescription begins to run at the beginning of the day, that is, at the **4.97** instant after midnight.[86] If the obligation becomes enforceable at a later point in the day, prescription will begin to run at the instant after midnight the following day. So if an obligation becomes enforceable at 1530 on a Tuesday, it will begin to prescribe not on Tuesday but on the first instant of the following day, that is just after 0000 on Wednesday.

The prescriptive period will not end on a holiday (as defined) but will **4.98** be extended so as to end on the next succeeding day which is not a holiday.[87] It follows from the fact that prescription begins at the start of the day that it will be completed at the end of the day. Accordingly, if the last day of the prescriptive period is in fact the day after a holiday, prescription will be completed at midnight on that day.

The "like principles" which applied to computation of the prescriptive **4.99** period under the previous legislation, the Act 1617, are applicable except so far as is otherwise provided in Part I of the 1973 Act.[88] In fact, the principles set out in section 14 seem to mirror the earlier regime, so this provision is probably just for the avoidance of doubt. So, for example, the cases on the 1617 Act say that "the time runs from midnight to midnight, or, in other words, the day which forms the *terminus a quo* is thrown out of calculation"; or "the day itself is a *dies non* in the computation".[89] An example is given: a 30-year prescription began "to run at midnight on 7 May 1868 and did not expire until midnight on 7 May 1898".[90] Although this example is not as clear as the formulation in section 14, the intent is plainly the same: that the prescriptive period should begin with the first complete day.[91]

The old books speak of negative prescription running *de momento in* **4.100** *momentum*,[92] by which they mean that it is not complete until the very

---

[84] s. 6(4); see below, paras 6.105 *et seq.*, and 7.18 *et seq.*
[85] s. 14(1)(b); s. 6(4).
[86] s. 14(1)(c).
[87] s. 14(1)(d); "holiday" is defined in s. 14(2).
[88] s. 14(1)(e).
[89] *Simpson v. Melville* (1899) 6 S.L.T. 355, and the reclaiming motion in the same case: *Simpson v. Marshall* (1900) 2 F. 447 at 457; *cf. Parish Council of Cavers v. Parish Council of Smailholm*, 1909 S.C. 195.
[90] *Simpson v. Marshall*, above, at 459.
[91] The formulation in Walker at p. 73 is wrong, since it suggests that the same date (*e.g.* May 7) will end up being counted once at the beginning and once at the end of the prescriptive period.
[92] Stair, II, xii, 14; Bankton, II, xii, 43; Erskine, III, vii, 30; Napier, p. 658.

last moment of the period has expired, and in particular that the period has not been completed if only part of the last day has run: the whole day must be completed.[93]

III. THE EFFECT OF COMPLETION OF THE PRESCRIPTIVE PERIOD

4.101 The effect of completing a continuous and uninterrupted prescriptive period, whether it be of two, five or 20 years,[94] is that the obligation in question is extinguished. This is not merely a procedural bar to initiating proceedings based on the obligation. The obligation simply does not exist.[95] Various points follow from this:

(1) *Set-off*. There can be no question of setting off a prescribed obligation against a live obligation. Regardless whether set-off would have been admissible had the creditor (in the prescribed obligation) been sued before his claim was extinguished, after prescription there is no basis on which set-off can operate since the obligation no longer subsists.

(2) *Absolvitor*. Where the obligation is found to have prescribed, the defender will be entitled to absolvitor (rather than dismissal) as there is no foundation for an action based on a prescribed obligation. Generally a court will be willing to grant absolvitor only after proof.

(3) *Accessory obligations*. Any obligations which are accessory to a principal obligation which has prescribed must be extinguished with it.[96]

---

[93] The maxim *dies inceptus pro completo habetur* does not apply in this context: see, *Simpson v. Melville*, above. *cf.* in France *Code Civil* Arts 2260–2261.

[94] ss. 8A, 6, and 7 respectively.

[95] Contrast the position in England, where there is simply a procedural bar on suing: Limitation Act 1980, s. 1 refers to "time limits for bringing actions", with McGee, *Limitation Periods*, pp. 28–29; or in Germany, BGB, Art. 222I, where once prescription has run the debtor is entitled to refuse performance.

[96] Erskine, III, iii, 66.

CHAPTER 5

INTERRUPTIONS OF THE PRESCRIPTIVE PERIOD

The rules about interruption are the same for the five-, 20- and two-year **5.01** negative prescriptions. In each case an obligation which has subsisted continuously for the appropriate period will not be extinguished if (1) a relevant claim has been made in relation to the obligation or (2) relevant acknowledgment has been made of it. These terms are defined in sections 9 and 10 of the Act.

Position before the 1973 Act

For reasons which will appear in the next paragraph, before looking in **5.02** more detail at the 1973 Act it is worth glancing at the position prior to it. The running of negative prescription could then be interrupted (1) by any declaration signed by the debtor acknowledging the debt or promising payment; (2) by part payment; (3) by citation or action by the creditor against the debtor; or (4) by diligence.[1] The first and second of these amount in modern terminology to relevant acknowledgments; and the third and fourth to relevant claims. But, while most of these categories exist in essentially the same form under the 1973 Act, the effect of section 9 of the Act is to cut down the circumstances which amount to a relevant claim. For example, citation (which was formerly effective, subject to being renewed at seven-year intervals) is no longer effective to interrupt prescription; an extrajudicial demand for payment is not now a relevant claim (previously in some circumstances it was). Other instances will be mentioned later.

The previous law therefore took a more relaxed view about what **5.03** constituted an interruption of the prescriptive period. Accordingly, the intention of Parliament in 1973 appears to have been to restrict the circumstances which amount to interruption.

I. RELEVANT CLAIM

"Definition of 'relevant claim' for purposes of sections 6, 7 and 8 **5.04** **9.**—(1) In sections 6, 7 and 8A of this Act the expression 'relevant claim,' in relation to an obligation, means a claim made by or on behalf of the creditor for implement or part-implement of the obligation, being a claim made—

(a) in appropriate proceedings; or
(b) by the presentation of, or the concurring in, a petition for sequestration or by the submission of a claim under section 22 or 48 of the Bankruptcy (Scotland) Act 1985; or

---

[1] Erskine, III, vii, 39; *Yuill's Trs v. Maclachlan's Trs*, 1939 S.C. (H.L.) 40 at 51; Napier, pp. 660 *et seq.*

    (c) by a creditor to the trustee acting under a trust deed as defined in section 5(2)(c) of the Bankruptcy (Scotland) Act 1985;

    (d) by the presentation of, or the concurring in, a petition for the winding up of a company or by the submission of a claim in a liquidation in accordance with rules made under section 411 of the Insolvency Act 1986;

and for the purposes of the said sections 6, 7 and 8A the execution by or on behalf of the creditor in an obligation of any form of diligence directed to the enforcement of the obligation shall be deemed to be a relevant claim in relation to the obligation.

(2) In section 8 of this Act the expression 'relevant claim,' in relation to a right, means a claim made in appropriate proceedings by or on behalf of the creditor to establish the right or to contest any claim to a right inconsistent therewith.

(3) Where a claim which, in accordance with the foregoing provisions of this section, is a relevant claim for the purposes of section 6, 7, 8 or 8A of this Act is made in an arbitration, and the nature of the claim has been stated in a preliminary notice relating to that arbitration, the date when the notice was served shall be taken for those purposes to be the date of the making of the claim.

(4) In this section the expression 'appropriate proceedings' and, in relation to an arbitration, the expression 'preliminary notice' have the same meanings as in section 4 of this Act."

For an obligation to be extinguished under any of the five-, 20- or two-year negative prescriptions,[2] it must have subsisted continuously for the relevant prescriptive period. But this will not be the case if the prescriptive period has been interrupted by the making of a relevant claim in relation to the obligation. "Relevant claim" is defined in section 9. It must be a claim "in relation to the obligation", so the question of identifying the relevant obligation again arises.[3]

The various types of relevant claim fall into three broad categories: (1) claims made in litigation, in appropriate proceedings; (2) claims made in the debtor's insolvency or bankruptcy; (3) diligence. These will be considered in turn.

(1)   Claims made in appropriate proceedings[4]

5.05 The term "appropriate proceedings" is defined in section 4 of the Act, in connection with the provisions for judicial interruption of positive prescription, and the same definition is applied for relevant claims under section 9[5]:

"In this section 'appropriate proceedings' means—

    (a) any proceedings in a court of competent jurisdiction in Scotland or elsewhere, except proceedings in the Court of Session initiated by a summons which is not subsequently called;

---

  [2] ss. 6, 7 or 8A.
  [3] For this see above, paras 2.05 *et seq.*
  [4] See also the comments on s. 4 in connection with positive prescription, below, paras 16.19 *et seq.*
  [5] s. 9(1) and 4(2).

(b) any arbitration in Scotland;

(c) any arbitration in a country other than Scotland, being an arbitration an award in which would be enforceable in Scotland."

Provided the claim is made in appropriate proceedings as defined it has effect to interrupt prescription of the obligation in any forum having jurisdiction.[6] From the fact that the Act makes express provision in section 9(1)(b)–(d) for claims made in bankruptcy or company winding-up proceedings, it must follow that claims of that sort are not claims made in "appropriate proceedings", otherwise the express provisions made for them in the Act would be redundant. The expression "appropriate proceedings" in section 9 has therefore to be read in a sense narrowly restricted to court or arbitration proceedings.

But does "court" mean court in the narrow sense, or might it include **5.06** tribunals? The answer to this question might be important, for instance, where a claim for unfair dismissal was made in an employment tribunal. It might later be necessary to decide whether that had been a "relevant claim" under the contract of employment. There appears to be no authority on this question in Scotland. But the balance is probably against such a claim being a "relevant claim", first, because this section of the Act refers specifically to other types of proceedings, such as arbitrations, and might have done the same for tribunals had this been intended, and second, because elsewhere the Act does mention tribunals, in speaking of "any obligation to recognise or obtemper a decree of court, an arbitration award or an order of a tribunal or authority exercising jurisdiction under any enactment".[7] This makes it difficult to argue that the draftsman of the Act overlooked the jurisdiction of tribunals. The better view therefore appears to be that tribunal proceedings are not "appropriate proceedings" within the meaning of the 1973 Act.

Arbitration proceedings

A claim which is made in any arbitration in Scotland or in any **5.07** arbitration an award in which would be enforceable in Scotland can be a relevant claim. Special provision is made for determining the date of such a claim; this is discussed below. Presumably any arbitration in Scotland to which the parties have validly submitted will be covered by this provision.

So far as foreign arbitrations are concerned, the precise significance of **5.08** the provision—especially the force of the word "would"—is not clear: does it mean only that the arbitration proceedings are in principle capable of generating an award which would be enforceable in Scotland? Or that the particular award would itself be enforceable in Scotland? Or simply that there is a relevant claim even without any attempt to enforce it in Scotland?

(1) It seems likely enough that the last of these was intended: in saying that the award "would" be enforceable in Scotland, the Act

---

[6] *British Railways Board v. Strathclyde R.C.*, 1981 S.C. 90; *Kinnaird v. Donaldson*, 1992 S.C.L.R. 694.

[7] Sched. 1, para. 2(a).

indicates that, in order to be a "relevant claim", a claim in a foreign arbitration need not actually have been followed up by any registration or enforcement proceedings in Scotland. But other considerations also arise.

(2) There exist various mechanisms by which foreign arbitration awards can be enforced in Scotland. Arbitration awards which are enforceable in the same way as judgments in the country in which they were pronounced are, in the case of a number of countries, enforceable in Scotland under special statutory provisions.[8] There also exists the possibility at common law of seeking decree conform in relation to a foreign arbitration award: this, if granted, would make the award enforceable in Scotland.[9]

That the section is referring to the general question whether an arbitration award would in principle be enforceable in Scotland therefore seems improbable. It is hard to think of any foreign arbitration award which, as a matter of principle, would not be enforceable in Scotland, at least by means of decree conform.

(3) It therefore seems more likely that the Act should be taken to refer to the individual case. Whether any given award is actually enforced depends on such questions as whether the submission to arbitration was valid; whether the award is valid and final under the law governing the arbitration proceedings; whether the common law or statutory procedure for enforcement of the award in Scotland has been followed correctly; and whether there are reasons of public policy why a court might decide not to enforce the award. It would be strange if, in order that it could be known whether an award was enforceable in Scotland or not, and whether therefore there was a "relevant claim", the Act required that the statutory or common law process for determining whether an award was to be enforced had already taken place. Nonetheless, it might be reasonable for a defender who argued that there had been no relevant claim to rely on factors relating to the particular arbitration which pointed to the fact that a Scottish court would not enforce the arbiter's award. For instance, just as an incompetent summons would (it is suggested below) have no effect on the running of prescription, so it might just be arguable that an arbiter's award which (for example) exceeded his powers could be said to have none.

Date of the claim

5.09   It is well established that an action is commenced on the date of citation of the defender.[10] That is accordingly the date on which prescription is interrupted. Court of Session proceedings fall within the

---

[8] England: Civil Jurisdiction and Judgments Act 1982, s. 18(2)(e); most commonwealth countries and a number of European countries: Administration of Justice Act 1920, Pt II; Foreign Judgments (Reciprocal Enforcement) Act 1933, Pt I and s. 10A; for the details see Dicey and Morris, *Conflict of Laws* (12th ed.), pp. 601–633. In addition, the Arbitration Act 1950 provides for arbitration proceedings between subjects of different states; the Arbitration Act 1975 for enforcement of foreign arbitral awards; and the Law Reform (Miscellaneous Provisions) (Scotland) Act 1985 s. 66 and Sched. 7 for the UNCITRAL model law on international commercial arbitration to have effect in Scotland. For a summary of the main statutory provisions, see *Stair Memorial Encyclopaedia*, Vol. 2, para. 507.

[9] Anton, *Private International Law*, pp. 366–367.

[10] Erskine, III, vi, 3; *Smith v. Stewart & Co. Ltd*, 1960 S.C. 329 at 334; *Barclay v. Chief Constable Northern Constabulary*, 1986 S.L.T. 562.

definition of "appropriate proceedings" only when the summons has called.[11] It does not follow that the action commences on the date of calling.[12] The vital point is that a summons which is served but not called will not interrupt prescription. But, provided it is called, the date of interruption will be the date of citation. Calling must take place within a year and a day of citation or any shorter period fixed by protestation for not calling.[13] It seems likely that the calling procedure in the Court of Session will soon be abolished.

If it were not for this provision about calling in the Court of Session, **5.10** there would surely have been room for argument about whether a claim was made at all in appropriate proceedings if nothing more happened than that a writ was served. But if it had been intended that anything more was required in sheriff court proceedings,[14] presumably that would have been stated.

So far as petition proceedings are concerned, the date of commence- **5.11** ment has been held to be the date when the petition is lodged in court (rather than the date of the order for intimation and service or the date of service itself).[15]

The date of a claim in arbitration is the date of service of a **5.12** preliminary notice which states the nature of the claim.[16] A preliminary notice which does not meet this requirement does not constitute a claim capable of interrupting prescription. For interruption to take place it appears that the arbitration must proceed: this is so because the requirements of section 9(3) appear to be cumulative: the date of the notice is the date of the claim "where a claim . . . is made in an arbitration, and the nature of the claim has been stated in a preliminary notice relating to that arbitration". It does not seem that these requirements are met if nothing happens after the preliminary notice is served. The significance of the preliminary notice provision is therefore that the commencement of proceedings is backdated once they actually take place. But if they do not, the notice itself has no significance.[17]

Relevance of the claim

The claim must relate to the obligation. The question how **5.13** specifically the claim must refer to a particular obligation has been discussed already.[18] It is clear that "relevant" in terms of the Act has nothing to do with relevance as a matter of pleading, so that a claim which is irrelevant might nonetheless interrupt prescription, provided that it brought the obligation in question into issue.[19] This is in accord

---

[11] For interruption of prescription calling was not a requirement of the old law, so the old cases need to be used here with some caution *e.g. Lord Leslie* (1630) M. 11320; *McKie v. Lag* (1637) M. 11320.

[12] Contrary to Walker, p. 24.

[13] *McKidd v. Manson* (1892) 9 R. 790; *Barclay v. Chief Constable Northern Constabulary*, above.

[14] *e.g.* tabling, under the old rules (OCR, r. 35); there is no obvious equivalent under the 1993 rules.

[15] *Secretary of State for Trade and Industry v. Normand*, 1994 S.C.L.R. 930.

[16] s. 9(3).

[17] *John O'Connor (Plant Hire) Ltd v. Kier Construction Ltd*, 1990 S.C.L.R. 761.

[18] See above, paras 2.05 *et seq.*

[19] *British Railways Board v. Strathclyde R.C.*, 1981 S.C. 90.

with the old law; as Bankton said, "Tho' an executed summons, or a decree, labour under considerable defects, it will be sufficient for interruption."[20]

5.14   But what if the claim is so inadequately focused as to give rise to doubt whether a claim was actually made in relation to a particular obligation?[21] If that is so, there seems to be no good reason why a court should not take the view that there was no claim on that obligation, and that prescription had therefore not been interrupted. Such cases would no doubt be extreme, and would be likely to turn on the particular circumstances and the particular relationship or course of dealings between the parties to the obligation. But it is at least justifiable in principle that, where a claim wholly misses the point and completely fails to identify the obligation on which it proceeds, it should not be held to be a relevant claim with respect to that obligation.[22]

5.15   Provided that the claim can be connected with the obligation, it need not be relevant in the pleading sense. Accordingly, where the defect in the summons or writ is curable by amendment, it would seem appropriate that interruption of prescription should proceed as normal and should date from the date the action was raised.[23] As Lord McLaren once said, "the moment we reach the stage of allowing the amendment, it must be conceded that there was the substance of an action in court at the time when the summons was called".[24] If there was the substance of an action, there will in most cases[25] have been the substance of a relevant claim.

Title to sue
5.16   A relevant claim has to be made "by or on behalf of the creditor". If the pursuer had no title to sue, probably he would not be the creditor or suing on the creditor's behalf and his claim would not therefore interrupt prescription. Although this is less clear than the provisions of the 1973 Act on positive prescription, which specify that the action has to be raised by a "person having a proper interest to do so",[26] nonetheless it appears that it arrives at the same result. An action raised by a person with no title to sue would not interrupt prescription.

---

[20] Bankton, II, xii, 57.
[21] *cf.* Bankton, II, xii, 56: "a blank summons can have no effect since it does not relate to any particular claim."
[22] *cf. Lawrence v. McIntosh & Hamilton*, 1981 S.L.T. (Sh.Ct) 73 at 75–76 (*obiter*).
[23] *cf. Bank of Scotland v. W. & G. Fergusson* (1898) 1 F. 96: an action sued upon a bill of exchange failed to set out the terms of the bill in the conclusion (as required by the Rules of Court) but did so in the condescendence: it was held that the action was plainly a judicial demand against the acceptor of the bill, that the action was not null, and that the conclusion could be amended.
[24] at 103.
[25] Subject to what is said in the preceding paragraph.
[26] s. 4(1).

Competence of the claim

Although the point has not been determined expressly, it is likely that **5.17** an action which is incompetent and consequently null will not have the effect of interrupting prescription.[27] The question of competence has to be judged at the time the action is commenced.[28] Matters are straightforward where the claim is made in a court which does not have jurisdiction: in that event the claim does not meet the statutory definition of "relevant claim", since it is not raised in a court of "competent jurisdiction", and is therefore not made in "appropriate proceedings".[29]

But, even where the court does have jurisdiction, and the pursuer does **5.18** have title to sue, if there is a fatal defect in the summons or writ, it is not obvious why this should interrupt prescription. If there is nothing in court which can be amended, it cannot be said that there is a claim at all.[30] On the other hand, the court is sometimes prepared to allow incompetent actions to be amended; in a leading case it was said only that "the court will not in general allow a pursuer by amendment . . . to cure a radical incompetence in his action".[31] In such cases, by definition there is a claim and prescription will have been interrupted.

It is difficult to say which cases of incompetence fall on the right side **5.19** of the line.[32] Questions of that sort are best left to the books on procedure. There is a danger of a circular argument here, but the conclusion can only be this: if the court takes the view that the summons is incurably incompetent, it cannot have interrupted prescription; if the defect is curable, then there will be both the substance of an action in court and an interruption of prescription. To put the same point in another way, if the court would have no option but to dismiss the action as incompetent, then it would be fundamentally null. But if, in the absence of a plea to the competency by the defender, the action might have proceeded, the defect is likely to be a curable one.[33]

In *Thomas Menzies (Builders) Ltd v. Anderson*,[34] two pursuers con- **5.20** joined in a single action for breach of contract, although each was suing

---

[27] See *Shanks v. Central R.C.*, 1987 S.L.T. 410 at 411 (*obiter*): the Lord Ordinary was not satisfied that an action at the instance of a company to which a receiver had been appointed pursued without the consent of the receiver was necessarily null. The Inner House opinion is reported at 1988 S.L.T. 212: it was held that the Lord Ordinary was under no obligation to determine the question of competency before exercising his discretion whether or not to allow the minute of amendment. See also *Stewart v. J.M. Hodge & Ptrs.*, Lord Coulsfield, February 17, 1995, unreported (one partner in a firm raised an action which was later amended to include other partners as pursuers). In France citation even before a judge who is not competent interrupts prescription: *Code Civil* Art. 2246.

[28] *Thomas Menzies (Builders) Ltd v. Anderson*, 1998 S.L.T. 794.

[29] ss. 9(1)(a) and (4) and 4(2)(a).

[30] *Boslem v. Paterson*, 1982 S.L.T. 216 (the defender had died before citation); *Tennent Caledonian Breweries Ltd v. Gearty*, 1980 S.L.T. (Sh.Ct) 71; *Rutherford v. Virtue*, 1993 S.C.L.R. 886 (in both the action was raised under the wrong type of sheriff court procedure).

[31] *Pompa's Trs v. Edinburgh Mags*, 1942 S.C. 119 at 125 *per* L.J.-C. Cooper.

[32] The following have been held to be curable: *Wilson v. Lothian R.C.*, 1995 S.L.T. 991 at 994 L (the summons contained no conclusions); *cf. Bank of Scotland v. W. & G. Fergusson* (1898) 1 F. 96 (the conclusions of the summons were not in proper form).

[33] An objection to competency of that sort would have to be taken *in limine*, or else it would come too late: Maxwell, *The Practice of the Court of Session*, p. 194, with references.

[34] 1998 S.L.T. 794.

in respect of a separate ground of obligation. On procedure roll this was held to be incompetent.[35] Thereafter one pursuer raised a new action and deleted his claim in the original action. The new action was raised more than five years after the obligation to make reparation had come into being. The question was whether the pursuer's incompetent claim in the original action had served to interrupt prescription. The court held that it had. A distinction was drawn between fundamental nullities and curable defects; and it was suggested that a practical rather than technical approach should be taken to applying this distinction.

Content of the claim

5.21   Section 9 speaks of a relevant claim being for "implement or part-implement" of the obligation. The question arises which actions this includes.

5.22   It is clear that actions of payment or of damages are capable of amounting to relevant claims. An action seeking specific implement of an obligation will also be such a claim, and this should also apply where an action of reduction is used in effect to obtain implement of an obligation, by concluding for reduction of the correlative right.[36]

5.23   In a multiplepoinding, if the action is raised by a person seeking payment from the fund, since this is directed at implement or part-implement of an obligation, it would appear to satisfy the requirements of "relevant claim". (On the other hand, raising of the action by a pursuer and real raiser who seeks only to dispose of the fund to the various claimants upon it would appear not to amount to a relevant claim, since it would not seek implement, but be directed only at obtaining a discharge.) Submission of a claim in a multiplepoinding would be a claim made in appropriate proceedings, and would therefore amount to a relevant claim and an interruption of prescription.

5.24   Certain petition proceedings also seem apt to fall under the definition of "relevant claim". For instance, if a defender is under an obligation to deliver documents to a pursuer, it can be argued that that obligation is capable of prescribing,[37] but that its prescription could be interrupted by a petition for commission and diligence to recover the documents in question. It seems therefore to be arguable that a petition under section 1 of the Administration of Justice (Scotland) Act 1972 would be capable of amounting to a relevant claim, which would interrupt prescription of the obligation to deliver the items in question. The critical point, as ever, is that the nature of the procedure is not what matters. Instead it is the fact that the procedure seeks implement of an obligation.

5.25   Such procedures as sequestration for rent, actions of maills and duties and poinding of the ground are all directed at the enforcement of an obligation and therefore interrupt prescription whether viewed under the head of "appropriate proceedings" or—as may be preferable—as forms of diligence.[38]

---

[35] 1996 S.L.T. 587.
[36] s. 15(2).
[37] Under s. 7; under s. 6 only if it arose from a contract: Sched. 1, para. 1(g).
[38] See below, para. 5.62.

The position with respect to other actions is less clear. An action of **5.26** declarator of contractual rights may be thought not to be a claim in the necessary sense, since it does not seek implement but is at best merely a preliminary to payment or implement.[39] This would appear also to apply to actions for declarator that a defender, if liable, has a claim of contribution or relief against another party.[40] Certainly an action which contains only declaratory conclusions cannot clearly be said to amount to a claim for "implement or part-implement" of an obligation.

This raises the general question whether the notion of a claim "for **5.27** implement" is to be construed strictly as covering only conclusions for payment or performance or can be read more broadly to cover the raising of proceedings which may ultimately have the result of obtaining payment or performance. For instance, in England a petition for winding up a company has been held to be an action to recover a sum of money, on the basis that, although the immediate effect of the proceedings would be to obtain a winding-up order, the ultimate effect would be to obtain money.[41] Although in Scotland a winding-up petition may, in the same way, result in the creditor obtaining money and so (partial) implement of an obligation, it is not a natural interpretation of section 9 to say that a winding-up petition is a claim "for implement or part-implement of the obligation" in question. And the point is put beyond all doubt by the fact that such proceedings are specifically mentioned elsewhere in section 9. This therefore seems to point to a relatively narrow reading of the expressions "implement or part-implement" and "relevant claim".

Counterclaims

There is no reason why the claim should be made by way of a principal **5.28** action. A counterclaim is merely a procedural device, which enables a defender to raise his own claim in the principal proceedings. It must therefore be capable of being a relevant claim.[42]

Against whom must the claim be made?

A relevant claim must be brought against the debtor in that obligation **5.29** and not against somebody else. In one case the pursuers contended that, because they had pursued a claim against the manufacturer of a chimney, their claim against those who gave professional advice about it had not prescribed. This contention was described by the judge as absurd.[43] That is plainly right. An obligation is a legal bond which binds

---

[39] *Wylie v. Avon Insurance Co.*, 1988 S.C.L.R. 570. Contrast *Cape Town Municipality v. Allianz Insurance Co. Ltd*, 1990 (1) S.A. 311, where the declaratory order was held to interrupt prescription, being a process whereby the pursuers claimed payment of a debt.

[40] *i.e.* a claim such as that made in *Central SMT Co. v. Lanarkshire County Council*, 1949 S.C. 450, now subject to prescription in terms of s. 8A of the 1973 Act. (Walker, p. 89 takes a different view.) It would appear that, although a claim of this sort would not interrupt prescription, once constituted in terms of a declaratory decree, the obligation would no longer be subject to the five-year but only to the 20-year prescription: see Sched. 1, para. 2(a).

[41] *Re Karnos Property Co. Ltd* (1989) 5 B.C.C. 14; *cf. Re a Debtor* [1997] 2 All E.R. 789.

[42] *Beveridge & Kellas, WS v. Abercromby*, 1996 S.C.L.R. 177 (Sh.Ct), 558, Sh.Pr.; 1997 S.C. 88, I.H. There is no provision in Scots law for prescription to run against obligations sought to be enforced in counterclaims from the same date as that on which the principal action is based; that, however, is the position in England: Limitation Act 1980, s. 35; *Ernst & Young v. Butte Mining plc (No. 2)* [1997] 2 All E.R. 471.

[43] *Kirkcaldy D.C. v. Household Manufacturing Ltd*, 1987 S.L.T. 617 at 620.

only the parties to it; clearly, an action of one nature founded on one obligation cannot have any effect on the question of prescription of another obligation owed by a different party.[44]

5.30   The earlier legislation, in particular the Act 1469, was interpreted rather broadly, so as to allow any creditor to rely on an interruption made by an action which had been raised to "promote the common interest of the creditors"[45] But there is no reason why this liberal interpretation should extend to the terms of the 1973 Act, which expressly require the claim to be brought "by or on behalf of the creditor".

5.31   The question is more complicated where there are several parties to an obligation.[46] Where there are several creditors in an obligation, their entitlement may be either *pro rata* or *pro indiviso*. In the first case, a claim by the creditor could amount to a relevant claim only in respect of his own proportionate share. In the second case, a relevant claim by any creditor would have the effect of interrupting prescription in respect of all creditors.[47]

5.32   Conversely, where there are several debtors in an obligation, if each debtor is liable only *pro rata*, then a relevant claim directed against a debtor could interrupt prescription only so far as that debtor's own personal liability was concerned. But if the debtors were each liable for the whole, because the notion of joint and several liability is that there is a single obligation undertaken by more than one person, a relevant claim directed against any debtor would have the effect of interrupting prescription as against all.[48] The same would apply to cases in which there is joint and several liability of cautioner and principal debtor, that is, where on the face of the deed they appear to be co-obligants ("improper cautionry").[49]

Who can make a relevant claim?
5.33   Section 9 says the claim must be made "by or on behalf of the creditor". This clearly covers the creditor's agents as well as certain statutory agents. It will also cover certain others:

(1) *Executor*. An executor is treated in law as the same legal person as the person whose estate he administers (as some of the older cases say, *eadem persona cum defuncto*). For that reason a claim by an executor is as apt to interrupt prescription as one by the deceased creditor.

It should, however, be noted that the same person may have claims in two different capacities, such as a claim in person and a claim as executor. These claims are subject to different prescrip-

---

[44] The outcome of the one action might, however, affect such things as the state of the pursuer's knowledge with respect to the prescription of any claim based on the other obligation: s. 11(3), on which see below, paras 6.87 *et seq.*

[45] Erskine, III, vii, 41; Napier, p. 660. But see Bankton, II, xii, 54 for a narrower view.

[46] *cf.* Gloag, *Contract*, pp. 198 *et seq.*; McBryde, *Contract*, paras 16.01 *et seq.*

[47] *Grindall v. John Mitchell (Grangemouth) Ltd*, 1987 S.L.T. 137; *cf. Cole-Hamilton v. Boyd*, 1963 S.C. (H.L.) 1 at 12.

[48] *Gordon v. Bogle* (1784) M. 11127.

[49] Contrast "proper" cautionry, where each cautioner undertakes liability only *pro rata*.

tive regimes, so a claim made in one capacity will not serve to interrupt prescription of a claim in the other.[50]

(2) *Administrator of a company.* By statute an administrator acts as the agent of the company, and is empowered to carry on litigation on its behalf.[51]

(3) *Receiver.* The receiver too is by statute made the agent of the company "in relation to such property of the company as is attached by the floating charge by virtue of which he was appointed". He is also empowered to carry on litigation in relation to such property on behalf of the company.[52]

(4) *Liquidator.* The management of the company becomes vested in the liquidator for the purpose of winding it up and distributing the assets among the creditors (and contributories, if there is a balance). But the company property does not vest in the liquidator, unless he seeks a vesting order from the court.[53] Before a winding-up order has been made it is the function of the directors to decide what the company should do. After the order only the liquidator can decide that, in order to secure the beneficial winding-up of the company.[54] The liquidator is given powers for the general purpose of getting in, realising and distributing the company assets.[55]

Although the liquidator is not expressly stated in statute to be the agent of the company nor is he vested in the company property, given that he supersedes the directors of the company, it is hard to see that he can be anything but its agent; and, owing to his functions of management, he must be able to make a relevant claim. To do so in a winding-up by the court, he will require the sanction of the court or liquidation committee.[56]

(5) *Trustee in sequestration.* The bankrupt's estate does not vest in the interim trustee. But the court can "make such other order to safeguard the debtor's estate as it thinks appropriate".[57] It therefore seems likely that an interim trustee could make a relevant claim if granted authority to do so by the court. One good ground for such a grant would be the fact that an obligation was in danger of being extinguished by prescription.

It is clear that the permanent trustee can make a relevant claim. The bankrupt's estate vests in him.[58] He is entitled to sist himself in place of the bankrupt even in proceedings which he could not himself have initiated.[59]

(6) *Judicial factor.* A judicial factor has the powers granted to him on appointment to preserve the estate. Since the judicial factor falls

---

[50] *Robertson v. Robertson* (1776) M. App. "Prescription" No. 2; *Robertson v. Watt & Co.,* 2nd Div., July 4, 1995, unreported.

[51] Insolvency Act 1986, s. 14(5) and Sched. 1, power 5.

[52] 1986 Act, s. 57(1) and Sched. 2, power 5.

[53] *ibid.* s. 145.

[54] Gore Brown, *Companies,* para. 34.1; *Smith v. Lord Advocate,* 1978 S.C. 259 at 271.

[55] 1986 Act, ss. 143(1) and 165 (voluntary winding-up), and 167 (winding-up by the court) and Sched. 4. Note also that s. 169(2) gives the liquidator the same powers as a trustee on a bankrupt estate, subject to the Insolvency Rules.

[56] *ibid.* Sched. 4, power 4.

[57] Bankruptcy (Scotland) Act 1985, s. 18(3)(c).

[58] *ibid.* s. 31 (with exceptions).

[59] *Watson v. Thompson,* 1990 S.C. 38. The bankrupt's own title to sue is restricted accordingly: *Dickson v. United Dominions Trust,* 1988 S.L.T. 19.

within the definition of "trustee" for the purposes of the Trusts (Scotland) Act 1921, he will also have the general powers which trustees have under that Act.[60] There is no doubt that the factor is empowered to pursue claims which fall within the terms of his appointment,[61] and there can be no real doubt that making such a claim would amount to a relevant claim for the purposes of the 1973 Act.

The nature of a depending process

5.34   When a relevant claim is made, the action will remain in court until it is abandoned or finally disposed of by the court. The question therefore arises when and for how long a claim is made. There are two main possibilities: (1) that a claim is a continuing process, and is made so long as the action in question is before the court; (2) that a claim is an instantaneous event, and is made on the date when the action is raised. Both views have been supported.[62] In *GA Estates Ltd v. Caviapen Trustees Ltd* it was observed that the choice between these two constructions of relevant claim was not an easy one.[63] If anything, that is an understatement. All that it is possible to say with complete confidence is that the Act seems to be unsatisfactorily unclear. The two options will be considered in turn.

A continuing process?

5.35   In *George A. Hood & Co. v. Dumbarton District Council,*[64] claims had been advanced in one action but subsequently abandoned. More than five years after the commencement of that action, the same claims were raised in a second action. The court was faced with the question when the relevant claim represented by the first action had been made. The defenders argued that it was the single event of raising an action which operated to interrupt the five-year prescription (that had occurred more than five years before the raising of the second action). The pursuers maintained that the action once raised constituted a continuing relevant claim against the obligation in question. The pursuers succeeded. Lord Kincraig held that the five-year period must be one during which no claim was insisted in. If a claim was being insisted in, then section 6 had no application, the date upon which the claim was first insisted in being immaterial. He pointed out that, on the defenders' view, the obligation which was the basis of the action would be extinguished before judgment if the litigation was not concluded within five years: this seemed improbable.[65]

5.36   Similarly, in *GA Estates Ltd v. Caviapen Trustees Ltd,*[66] it was held that as long as an action seeking to enforce an obligation was in court, a relevant claim in respect of that obligation was being made. In that case averments in relation to one claim had been deleted by amendment. From the date of amendment of the record, the relevant claim was no

---

[60] 1921 Act, s. 4; for the same reason he can seek additional powers from the court: s. 5.
[61] Walker, *Judicial Factors*, pp. 90 *et seq.*
[62] See in particular *British Railways Board v. Strathclyde R.C.*, 1981 S.C. 90; *George A. Hood & Co. v. Dumbarton D.C.*, 1983 S.L.T. 238.
[63] 1993 S.L.T. 1045, at 1049.
[64] 1983 S.L.T. 238.
[65] At 240.
[66] 1993 S.L.T. 1045, O.H. and 1051, I.H.

longer being made and the new prescriptive period began to run. In the Inner House the remarks made on prescription were *obiter dicta*, but a litigation in respect of an obligation was treated as a continuing making and asserting of the claim: "If a person makes a relevant claim in proceedings and then takes any step in the process, such as lodging an open record or a closed record or an amended record or enrolling a motion to cause the case to proceed further, he is of new positively asserting and reasserting his claim. In my view, the only realistic way to look at a litigation in court is to regard it as a continuous making and asserting of the claim which the pursuer seeks to enforce in the proceedings".[67] The question was raised but left open whether in the event of dismissal, abandonment or material change of scope the new period of prescription would run again from the date of the original interrupting act.[68]

This interpretation seems to be generous to the pursuer since its effect **5.37** appears to be that, once he has raised an action, prescription does not run until the action is in one way or another disposed of.[69] Suppose the pursuer raises his action and then immediately moves to sist it: even then, on this view, his action would be a continuing relevant claim and prescription would not run against the obligation. This may seem unfair, and further comment is made on it below.[70]

An alternative view: interruption as a single event

There are nonetheless arguments in favour of the view that a relevant **5.38** claim is a single event which interrupts prescription at the date it is made, and which, for the purposes of the 1973 Act, has no continuing subsistence. Of the three arguments noted here, the last seems powerful.

(1) "Without any relevant claim having been made". These words in section 6(1)(a) may be thought more apt to describe an instant, an event, rather than a process.

(2) Sections 6(4) and (5) provide for the suspension of the prescriptive period. It might be thought that, had a relevant claim been intended to be viewed as a continuing period during which prescription was in suspense, it would have been dealt with there rather than in section 6(1)(a).

(3) The other types of relevant claim mentioned in section 9 are events rather than processes.

    (a) *Sequestration*.[71] It is reasonably clear that the presentation or concurring in a petition for sequestration and the submission of a claim are single events rather than processes. So far as presentation of a petition is concerned, it is of no significance whether sequestration ultimately follows on the petition, or even if it is recalled. There remains an interruption which took place at the date of presentation. (The same applies to petitions for winding up a company.) Equally, submission of a claim is much more readily taken to refer to

---

[67] At 1051 and 1059 H–I, *per* Lord McCluskey.
[68] At 1065 J.
[69] See below, paras 5.42, 5.96.
[70] para. 5.41.
[71] See below, paras 5.46 *et seq.*

an event rather than to the continuing state of having been submitted as a claim.

(b) *Diligence.*[72] It is the event of execution of diligence which is the relevant claim, rather than the continuing fact (for example) of an inhibition being on the Register of Inhibitions and Adjudications or a schedule of arrestment remaining in the hands of the arrestee.

(c) *Arbitration.*[73] Section 9(3) provides that "the date when the notice was served shall be taken for those purposes[74] to be the date of making of the claim". It is clear that here the relevant claim is made on a specific date: the date of the notice. If it had been intended that the arbitration proceedings themselves should be viewed as a continuing relevant claim, it seems more likely that the Act would have referred to the date when the claim was "first made" or "commenced". This interpretation also accords better with the approach adopted in the Act towards judicial interruption of positive prescription: there the date of the interruption is the date of the notice.[75]

Excursus: The law before the 1973 Act

5.39   The 1973 Act does not say anything about the duration of an interruption. The question therefore arises how far the 1973 Act has displaced the previous law. Various scarcely consistent views can be found in the old authorities, and unfortunately it seems necessary to review them here. Matters are obscured by the fact that it is often said that prescription begins to run again from the date of the interruption, without any explanation being given as to whether the date of the interruption really does mean simply the date the action was raised or the date on which it was finally disposed of.[76]

The following four views are found. Most of them also appear in one modern legal system or another, to which reference is made in passing in the notes:

(1) Prescription once interrupted does not run while an action is in dependence.[77] Support for this view can be derived from Stair,[78] who says "prescription is ordinarily interrupted and excluded by the dependence of any action, whereupon the right might have been taken away or excluded".

(2) Prescription once interrupted runs again from the date the action falls asleep. Once the action has fallen asleep, there is nothing to interrupt prescription.[79]

(3) Prescription once interrupted runs again from the date of the last step taken in the process.[80] Since the action falls asleep a year

---

[72] s. 9(1); see below, paras 5.55 *et seq.*

[73] s. 9(3); see above, paras 5.07 *et seq.*

[74] That is, for the purposes of ss. 6, 7 or 8A.

[75] s. 4; see below, para. 16.20.

[76] Hume, *Lectures*, 4.517 "interruption . . . has effect of making the forty years begin to run anew"; Erskine, III, vii, 45; Millar, p. 107.

[77] *cf.* in France *Code Civil*, Art. 2244; Italy, *Codice Civile*, Art. 2945. But both jurisdictions have special rules for the case of abandonment.

[78] Stair, II, xii, 26.

[79] *Pillans & Co. v. Sibbald's Trs* (1897) 5 S.L.T. 186.

[80] This is the rule applied in Switzerland OR, Art. 138, and in Germany, BGB, Art. 211. In Austria a claim only interrupts if it is "duly pursued" (*gehörig fortgesetzt*): ABGB, Art. 1497.

after the last step taken in the process, it follows that this allows a year less than view (2) does. One of the cases supporting this view is decided expressly on the wording of the Act 1685, c. 14 which is concerned only with prescription of diligence.[81] But Bankton seems to favour this view in general. He notes that, after an action is raised, the debtor in the obligation "cannot thereafter regularly perfect prescription, but must begin from the last step of the procedure in the action, and 40 years silence thereafter will give the benefit of prescription anew".[82] Later he adds this: "Tho' regularly an action or suit interrupts for 40 years, yet, in some cases, it must be wakened or insisted in within a certain limited time, as was already remarked, which, if omitted, the case is the same, as if action had not been sued, the same being prescribed".[83]

(4) Prescription once interrupted runs for 40 years after the date of interruption.[84] Erskine says this: "if, upon the citation, there shall follow the appearance of parties, or any judicial act, it is no longer accounted a bare citation, but an action, which subsists, though not renewed, for forty years: *Creditors of Liberton*".[85] And later he says: "Interruption has the effect to cut off the course of pre-scription; so that the person prescribing cannot avail himself of any part of the former time, but must begin a new course, commencing from the date of the interruption in the negative prescription".[86] The reference to "the" date of interruption seems to suggest that what Erskine has in mind is that prescription is interrupted at the date when an action is raised; and that, since a new 40-year course of prescription has to run from that date, prescription will extinguish the obligation in question only after 40 years from the date the action was raised. Although the reports of the old cases leave much unclear, they do appear to be capable of supporting this view.[87]

The alternative seems to be this: that an action is treated as a continuing interruption, but one which itself prescribes after 40 years. Some of the old cases seem to support this view.[88] But it would have the

---

[81] *Graham v. McFarlane*, May 30, 1811, F.C.

[82] Bankton, II, xii, 53, citing *Montgomery v. Home* (1664) M. 10627; *Lord Philorth v. Lord Fraser* (1666) M. 11320.

[83] Bankton, II, xii, 56.

[84] The first clause of the passage of Bankton just quoted, II, xii, 56, seems to support this view. *cf.* also *Herring v. Ramsay* (1622) M. 11319; *McKie v. Lag* (1637) M. 11320; *Lord Leslie* (1630) M. 11320.

[85] Erskine, III, vii, 43; the reference is to (1731) M. 11321. *cf.* also Bell, *Prin.* s. 2007.

[86] Erskine, III, vii, 45.

[87] *Lord Philorth v. Lord Fraser*, above; *Creditors of Liberton v. His Tutors and Curators* (1731) M. 11321; *Wilson v. Innes* (1705) M. 10974 and 11330.

[88] Two unclear cases may be mentioned: (1) *Wallace v. Earl of Eglinton* (1830) 8 S. 1018: in 1776 by declarator of non-entry a pursuer challenged a defender's title, which dated from 1742. This therefore interrupted the 40-year prescription. The process repeatedly fell asleep but was wakened in 1825 and was still subsisting at the time the present action of reduction was raised in 1829. It therefore looks as if the 1776 action was still regarded as an interruption 53 years later, in 1829. In the pursuer's case (in *Session Papers* at 19), it is certainly argued that the process was kept alive by subsequent wakenings although the point is not discussed by the judges. It is, however, also made clear in the same passage of the pursuer's case that one of the pursuer's predecessors was in minority between 1806 and 1823, so that the prescriptive period would anyway not have run completely before 1830

curious consequence that, if an interruption itself lasts 40 years, and a new 40-year period of prescription has to begin once the interruption is over, the raising of an action will in effect prevent an obligation being extinguished for twice the prescriptive period, that is, 80 years.

Both views (3) and (4) seem to owe something to the rules of Roman law, under which the prescriptive period of 40 years ran from the last step in process.[89] It may be that the odd consequence just outlined derives from a misunderstanding of the Roman law. The Roman law is absolutely clear on the point that the 40-year period runs from the last step in process.[90] Each step in process therefore amounts to an interruption, from which a new prescriptive period must begin.[91] It follows from this that interruption is being regarded as a single event. It would be entirely inconsistent with this view to say that an action is automatically a continuing interruption of prescription for 40 years.

Of these four views, the third seems to have the strongest support. Indeed, it is possible that views (1) and (4) are no more than slightly incomplete or inaccurate accounts of precisely that view. The attractive feature of view (3) is that it preserves the creditor's claim by construing an interruption of prescription each time he takes a step in pursuit of his claim. The corollary is that the creditor who raises an action and then does nothing ceases to be protected by the interruption, but the debtor does not need to wait until the action is dismissed or otherwise disposed of for this happy result to arrive.

In general (and subject to different rules applied by special statutes), the better view seems to be this. The raising of an action is a single event. Prescription is interrupted by that event, so a new prescriptive period will begin. Each successive step in process also constitutes a fresh interruption of prescription. A new prescriptive period must run from the date of each such interruption.

Conclusions

5.40　　Why does this matter? First, enough has been said to suggest that the 1973 Act did not clearly alter the law applying to the effect of relevant claims. This argument therefore provides some support for the view that a relevant claim ought properly to be regarded as an event rather than a continuing process, and that a new interrupting event occurs each time the creditor takes a new step in process. Second, the 1973 Act states that, except where otherwise provided, regard is to be had to the "like principles" as were applied to computation of periods of prescription for the purposes of the Prescription Act 1617.[92] How narrowly is "computation" to be construed? It must be at least arguable that it would cover the questions for how long and at what points a prescriptive period was interrupted by a litigation. If this is right, it provides further support for the view of litigation as a series of interrupting events.[93]

(only the years 1776–1806 and 1823–29 could be counted). (2) *Wilson v. Innes*, above may also support this interpretation, depending whether (which is unclear in the reports) the second action of reduction was raised more than 40 years after the first action was raised in 1662.

[89] C. 7.39.9 (A.D. 529); C. 7.40.1.1e (A.D. 530). *Cf.* Savigny, *System des heutigen römischen Rechts* (1841), 5.322–5.323.

[90] C. 7.39.9.3 (*novissima cognitio*); C. 7.40.1.1e (*ex quo novissimum litigatores tacuerunt*).

[91] The similarity between this and the position suggested in *GA Estates Ltd v. Caviapen Trustees Ltd* 1993 S.L.T. 1045, at 1059 H–I *per* Lord McCluskey is striking.

[92] s. 14(1)(e).

[93] Each interruption would start a fresh period of negative prescription, which is now generally a period of 20 years: s. 7.

That in turn seems the fairest and most satisfactory way of dealing **5.41** with the recurrent practical problem that actions are frequently raised and then sisted for long periods. If a pursuer in a sisted action had for many years done precisely nothing to press his claim, there would be something slightly disquieting about the conclusion that for all those years prescription did not run against his claim.

Procedural questions

So long as a relevant claim is viewed as an event which takes place in **5.42** the instant the claim is raised and which interrupts prescription on that date, there is little need to consider many of the finer points about adjustment and amendment of pleadings. But, on the currently prevailing view that a claim is being made continuously so long as an action founded on the relevant obligation is before the court, these matters assume critical importance. More detail is given about these questions in Chapter 20.[94]

Reform and clarification

It seems perfectly clear—and the Scottish Law Commission has **5.43** recognised as much—that the law in this area is uncertain. Clarification is required.

There is a further point. There is something odd in the very idea that a claim on an obligation should interrupt—as opposed to suspend— prescription of that obligation. This is for the following reasons. Suppose that a claim is made, and the court decides that it is of merit and it therefore succeeds. Frequently, the making of the claim will mean that any further claim in relation to the same obligation is now *res judicata*. The fact that the claim interrupted prescription is therefore of no possible interest, since no further claim is now possible. On the other hand, if the claim is decided to be without merit, the fact that it interrupted prescription of the obligation will often be of no interest, since any future claim on the same obligation might suffer from the same demerits.[95]

There are of course cases in which this dilemma does not represent **5.44** the whole truth, for example where an action has been dismissed rather than absolvitor granted. But the fact remains that much more coherent reasons can be given for ordering the law so that the dependence of a claim suspends prescription until the claim has been disposed of. It is interesting, therefore, that this approach comes close to the reform suggested by the Scottish Law Commission, albeit for quite different reasons.

The Scottish Law Commission advanced a number of different options **5.45** which the law might adopt in the future, and in its (as yet unimplemented) report favoured the adoption of a regime essentially the same as that introduced by the Consumer Protection Act 1987. The provisions of that Act are discussed later.[96] Here it is enough to say that the new

---

[94] Below, para. 20.21.

[95] *cf.* for this point in German law, Peters and Zimmermann, *Gutachten*, pp. 260 *et seq.*; *Abschlussbericht*, pp. 84 *et seq.*

[96] The 1987 Act inserted new ss. 22A–22D into the 1973 Act. See below, paras 9.17 *et seq.*

proposal is that the making of a relevant claim should neither interrupt nor suspend the running of prescription. Instead, it should extend the prescriptive period, if a claim is raised in the course of it, until the date when the claim is finally disposed of or abandoned.[97] New provisions are also proposed for claims made in arbitration or insolvency proceedings where, before the claim has been adjudicated upon, those proceedings have come to an end (or, where the claim was lodged under a voluntary trust deed, it has been superseded by an award of sequestration). Here the proposal is that the obligation should not be extinguished until six months after the end of proceedings or the award of sequestration.[98]

(2) CLAIMS MADE IN SEQUESTRATION, UNDER TRUST DEED OR ON INSOLVENCY

Sequestration

5.46   The 1973 Act denotes as relevant claims the presentation of a petition for sequestration[99]; concurring in a petition for sequestration; submission of a claim to an interim trustee in sequestration with prima facie evidence to support it[1]; and submission of a claim to a permanent trustee for adjudication.[2]

Petition for sequestration

5.47   In order to effect an interruption what is required is presentation of a petition (or concurrence in its presentation). For prescription to be interrupted, there is no need for sequestration actually to be awarded. Nor does it affect the interruption that the award of sequestration may be recalled.[3]

Submission of a claim

5.48   The 1985 Act sets out the requirements for submission of a claim in a sequestration. The claim must be supported by an account or voucher constituting prima facie evidence of the debt.[4] It is reasonable to take it that a claim which satisfies the statutory requirements, or satisfies them so far as the trustee has not dispensed it from satisfying them (as he is empowered under the Act to do) will amount to a relevant claim.[5]

5.49   Section 9(1)(b) itself makes it reasonably clear that there is a relevant claim—and prescription is therefore interrupted—when one of the steps mentioned—petition, concurrence, submission—is taken by or on behalf of the creditor. In other words, the fact that one creditor (for example) presents a petition has no effect on the prescription of the claims of other creditors. Prescription of their own claims will be interrupted, if at all, only if they concur in the petition or submit their own claims in the seqestration.

Trust deeds

5.50   A claim made to a trustee acting under a trust deed is also a relevant claim. "Trust deed" is said in the 1973 Act to be defined in section 5(2)(c) of the 1985 Act. In fact the definition of trustee acting under a

---

[97] SLC Report no. 122 (1989), paras 4.41–4.55 and rec. 24 and draft Bill, cll. 11B and 11C.
[98] *ibid.*
[99] Bankruptcy (Scotland) Act 1985, s. 5.
[1] *ibid.* s. 22.
[2] *ibid.* s. 48.
[3] *ibid.* s. 17(5)(a).
[4] s. 22(2)(b).
[5] ss. 22(2) and 48(3).

trust deed now appears in section 5(4A) of the 1985 Act (as amended): "a trustee acting under a voluntary trust deed granted by or on behalf of the debtor whereby his estate (other than such of his estate as would not, under section 33(1) of this Act, vest in the permanent trustee if his estate were sequestrated) is conveyed to the trustee for the benefit of his creditors generally".[6] It seems likely that a claim made under a trust deed which does not meet this statutory definition will not interrupt prescription.[7]

Provisions in the Bankruptcy (Scotland) Act 1985

The 1985 Act (as amended) contains a number of provisions relevant **5.51** to prescription, although they do little to introduce clarity. It provides that presentation of and concurrence in a petition for sequestration, and the submission of a claim "bar the effect of any enactment or rule of law relating to the limitation of actions in any part of the United Kingdom".[8] The same is said about claims submitted to trustees acting under trust deeds[9] and about the equivalent provisions in company insolvency.[10] The interpretation section of the 1985 Act goes on to provide that any reference to the presentation of or concurrence in a petition, and the submission of a claim, is to be "construed as a reference to that act having the same effect, for the purposes of any such enactment or rule of law, as an effective acknowledgment of the creditor's claim".[11] This applies to all enactments except one which "implements or gives effect to any international agreement or obligation".[12]

These provisions have the effect of giving sequestration proceedings in **5.52** Scotland effect to interrupt prescription or limitation elsewhere in the United Kingdom,[13] for example under the (English) Limitation Act 1980. But this is subject always to the requirement that there should be no effect on enactments which implement or give effect to any international agreement or obligation. That would apply, for example, to such things as the Carriage by Air Act 1961 (Warsaw Convention), Carriage of Goods by Road Act 1965, Carriage of Goods by Sea Act 1971 and the Merchant Shipping Act 1995. In such cases sequestration proceedings will not interrupt the limitation period.

These provisions do not seem to be at all well drafted:

(1) There is no reference to prescription but only to limitation. This is comprehensible so far as the provisions are dealing with other parts of the United Kingdom but not in relation to Scotland.[14]

(2) The reference to "effective acknowledgment" does not square with the treatment of these matters as "relevant claims" under the 1973 Act, but seems to fit better with the acknowledgment provisions of the (English) Limitation Act 1980.[15]

---

[6] The definition in s. 5(2)(c) of the 1985 Act before these provisions were amended was the same, with the omission of the words which appear in s. 5(4A) in brackets.
[7] McBryde, *Bankruptcy* (2nd ed.), para. 20.23.
[8] ss. 8(5), 22(8) and 48(7).
[9] Sched. 5, para. 3.
[10] Insolvency (Scotland) Rules 1986, r. 4.76.
[11] s. 73(5).
[12] *ibid.*
[13] s. 78(6).
[14] Although certain obligations are subject to prescription rather than limitation even in England: *e.g.* Consumer Protection Act 1987, s. 2.
[15] 1980 Act, ss. 29–31.

(3) In the 1973 Act it is reasonably clear that interruption by presentation of a petition (etc.) is a single event. It is the event rather than the currency of sequestration proceedings which interrupts prescription. That is confirmed by the fact that whether sequestration ultimately proceeds upon the petition does not matter. But the conception underlying the provisions in the 1985 Act seems to be different, since the words "bar the effect" do not seem to be apt to describe a single event or interruption but rather to denote the continuing state of being barred. In principle these words, if they do not refer to interruption, might refer to suspension of prescription or even (although this is less likely) to making the obligation in question imprescriptible.

(4) Section 8(5) of the 1985 Act provides that "The presentation of, or the concurring in, a petition for sequestration shall bar the effect of any enactment or rule of law relating to the limitation of actions in any part of the United Kingdom". This too introduces some doubt about the proper construction of section 9(1)(b), since it is at least capable of being read so as to mean that the presentation of or concurrence in a petition interrupts prescription so far as all creditors are concerned rather than merely prescription of the obligation of the individual petitioning or concurring creditor.[16]

The lack of clarity in these provisions is unfortunate. It is suggested that where the 1973 and 1985 Acts appear to be inconsistent, and in particular in relation to points (3) and (4) above, the provisions of the 1973 Act should be preferred. This can be supported by the principle that an Act which makes special provision for a subject should be taken to be displaced by a subsequent general enactment only where the intention to displace it is manifest.[17] Where the question at issue is the scope of prescription (rather than simply the prescriptive period),[18] it seems not unreasonable to treat the Bankruptcy (Scotland) Act 1985 as a general statute with respect to the 1973 Act.

Liquidation: section 9(1)(d)

5.53   This provision was added by the Prescription (Scotland) Act 1987, which came into force on May 1, 1987, but it applies to any claim whenever submitted, provided it is made in a liquidation where the winding-up commenced on or after December 29, 1986.[19] The 1987 Act was enacted in order to cure a problem which had arisen from the insolvency legislation of the mid-1980s, which had made an unintended change in the law to the effect of excluding petitions for winding-up from interrupting prescription.[20] Accordingly, for windings-up commencing after

---

[16] *cf.* McBride, *Bankruptcy* (2nd ed.), para. 10.37, n. 67.

[17] The rule is more concise in Latin: *generalia specialibus non derogant*. See Craies, *Statute Law* (7th ed., 1971), p. 377; *Seward v. Vera Cruz* (1884) 10 App. Cas. 59 at 68; Maxwell, *Interpretation of Statutes* (12th ed., 1969), pp. 196 *et seq.*

[18] So far as other statutes impose their own prescriptive or limitation periods, these must of course take precedence over the 1973 Act; this must be so on general principle, even though there is no Scottish equivalent to the English s. 39 of the Limitation Act 1980, which displaces the 1980 Act where an alternative statutory limitation period is provided.

[19] This is the date on which the Insolvency Act 1986 and the Insolvency (Scotland) Rules came into force: 1987 Act, s. 1(3).

[20] Hansard, H.L. Vol. 487, col. 709; *cf.* Palmer, *Company Law*, para. 15.673; 1987 J.L.S.S. 5.

December 29, 1986, the presentation or concurrence in a winding-up petition or the submission of a claim will interrupt prescription.

The claim must be made in accordance with rules made under section **5.54** 411 of the Insolvency Act 1986. The relevant rules are the Insolvency (Scotland) Rules. What this amounts to in practice is that a claim must be made in Form 4.7(Scot.) or must be any less formal claim which the liquidator has accepted.[21]

(3) DILIGENCE

Execution by or on behalf of the creditor in an obligation of any form of **5.55** diligence directed to the enforcement of the obligation will interrupt prescription. This will extend to arrestment and inhibition or adjudication in security, sequestration for rent, and summary diligence on bill or bond.

(a) Arrestment or inhibition on the dependence

These forms of diligence proceed upon a warrant in the summons or **5.56** writ (or, in inhibition in sheriff court proceedings, on letters of inhibition), which requires for support only that there be a pecuniary conclusion or crave. Clearly, where there is diligence on the dependence of an action, there will also be an action, and so in the normal case there will be a relevant claim made in appropriate proceedings. This is, however, not invariable, for example if the action is never served. In *Hogg v. Prentice*[22] it was held that service of letters of inhibition on the dependence of an action constituted a relevant claim; and that, since it is competent to serve an inhibition without serving the action, there was a relevant claim at the date of registration of the inhibition in the Register of Inhibitions and Adjudications, even although the defender might be entitled to have the Register cleared if no action proceeded.[23]

Diligence on the dependence of the action will fall if the summons **5.57** falls, for example, for want of jurisdiction.[24]

(b) Arrestment or inhibition in execution; poinding

Forms of diligence in execution will mostly (see below) be preceded by **5.58** a court decree, so that the action on which the decree proceeded is itself a relevant claim.

Obligations to satisfy decrees are not subject to the five-year prescrip- **5.59** tion but do fall under the 20-year prescription.[25] It follows that interruption of prescription of the obligation to satisfy the decree can itself be made by carrying out diligence in execution at any time before the obligation under the decree itself prescribes.

---

[21] r. 4.15.

[22] 1994 S.C.L.R. 426.

[23] *cf.* also *Allied Irish Banks plc v. GPT Sales and Service Ltd*, 1993 S.C.L.R. 778, in which it was held that the signeting of letters of inhibition (a Court of Session procedure) was a different proceeding from the raising of a sheriff court action, and its validity could therefore be judged separately.

[24] Graham Stewart, *Diligence*, pp. 19 and 574.

[25] Sched. 1, para. 2(a); see below, paras 6.39 *et seq.*

5.60   Arrestment in execution may also proceed on a warrant inserted in an extract from the Books of Council and Session containing a clause consenting to registration for execution. In such cases there will be no prior proceedings, so that only the diligence is available to interrupt prescription. The reason for this is that an extract of the warrant is itself regarded as a decree of registration. Owing to the repeal of the provisions which excepted probative writs from prescription, this provision comes to be of particular importance.[26]

5.61   Arrestment in execution can also proceed (1) where the debtor has consented in a deed to summary diligence, that is to registration of the deed in the Books of Council and Session for preservation and execution[27]; (2) upon a protest by a notary public of a bill for non-payment, provided that the protest has been registered in the Books of Council and Session[28]; or (3) upon a summary warrant for recovery of rates or taxes.[29] In the first two of these categories, the key is again the fact that owing to the registration an extract can be treated as a decree of registration.

(c) Other forms of diligence

5.62   The following forms of diligence are clearly directed at the enforcement of the creditor's right, whether they are best regarded as forms of diligence or as claims made in appropriate proceedings. They will therefore amount to relevant claims.

(1) *Poinding of the ground*. This is in form an action and has been said to be not so much a diligence as a declaratory action that the pursuer's real right in the land carries the moveables thereon as accessories.[30]

(2) *Action of maills and duties*. This seeks recovery of rents due by tenants.[31]

(3) *Sequestration for rent*. This gives effect to the real right which the landlord has over moveable property of the tenant by virtue of his hypothec.[32] It may be either in execution of rent arrears or in security for rent not yet payable.[33]

Prescription of diligence

5.63   A relevant claim by way of diligence is made at the date of execution of the diligence. A new prescriptive period therefore begins to run the day following the execution of the diligence.

5.64   Diligence, however, is itself subject to prescription:

(1) Arrestments on the dependence prescribe under special statutory provisions, on the expiry of three years from the date of final

---

[26] Sched. 1, para. 2(c), repealed by 1995 Act; see below, paras 6.47 *et seq.*
[27] *Stair Memorial Encyclopaedia*, Vol. 8, para. 122.
[28] Gloag and Henderson, para. 53.5.
[29] Debtors (Scotland) Act 1987, s. 87; Taxes Management Act 1970 s. 63; Gloag and Henderson, para. 53.5.
[30] Gloag and Henderson, para. 53.27; Graham Stewart, *Diligence*, p. 491.
[31] Gloag and Henderson, para. 53.31.
[32] *Stair Memorial Encyclopaedia*, Vol. 18, para. 386; Erskine, II, vi, 56; Bell, Comm., 2.33. An alternative view, that it is sequestration itself which first creates a real right over the property, has the support of Graham Stewart, *Diligence*, p. 460.
[33] Gloag and Henderson, para. 41.15; Graham Stewart, *Diligence*, p. 460.

decree,[34] unless followed through, for example, by an action of furthcoming.[35] Arrestments in execution prescribe three years from the date of service, except that where the debt concerned is due only contingently, prescription runs only from the date of purification of the contingency.[36]

(2) Inhibitions, whether on the dependence or in execution, prescribe five years after they take effect, except in the event of sequestration, where they require to be renewed every three years.[37] The date when an inhibition takes effect is the date it is registered in the Register of Inhibitions and Adjudications, although if a notice of inhibition has been registered and the inhibition itself then registered within the following 21 days, the effective date is the date of the notice.

Given that an inhibition prescribes in five years, the question arises from what date the right to challenge a transaction as being in breach of an inhibition itself prescribes. Different views are held on this point: some favour the view that the right to challenge is extinguished at the same moment as the inhibition[38]; others take the view that prescription runs from the date of the breach.[39] Although the matter is not free from doubt, the second appears to be the better view: (a) a breach of inhibition cannot be characterised in the same way as an inhibition itself, so it is not obvious why it should fall under the special prescriptive regime of the Conveyancing (Scotland) Act 1924; (b) the 1924 Act does not speak of prescription of the right to reduce a breach of inhibition but only of prescription of the inhibition: there is no reason therefore why the right of reduction should not prescribe under the ordinary rules of prescription; (c) it would be odd if the length of time for which the right to reduce subsisted depended on when in the five-year term of an inhibition the breach had taken place, a day before the beginning or a day before the end.[40] It would seem altogether more rational that time should run from the date of the breach. The breach would therefore have to lie within the five-year term of the inhibition, but the right to reduce the offending transaction would thereafter prescribe under the ordinary rules of prescription.

So far as those ordinary rules are concerned, there is room for argument about whether the 20-year negative prescription of section 7 or section 8 of the 1973 Act should apply. Section 8 may be thought more likely, since what is asserted in an action of reduction is not an obligation owed by a particular person but a right to a specific property. In any event, where the person in

---

[34] This does not apply to an earnings, current maintenance or conjoined arrestment order: Debtors (Scotland) Act 1838, s. 22(3).

[35] 1838 Act, s. 22; Graham Stewart, *Diligence*, p. 223; *Paterson v. Cowan* (1826) 4 S. 477; *Jamieson v. Sharp* (1887) 14 R. 643.

[36] 1838 Act, s. 22; Graham Stewart, *ibid.*; *Paterson v. Cowan*, above.

[37] 1924, s. 44(3)(a). (Adjudications prescribe from their date, rather than the date of expiry of the legal: Gretton, 1983 J.R. 187, n. 3; *cf.* SLC Discussion Paper no. 78, *Adjudication for Debt* (1988), para. 3.103.)

[38] Graham Stewart, *Diligence*, p. 575; Macdonald, *Conveyancing Manual* (6th ed.), para. 33.35.

[39] Gretton, *Inhibition and Adjudication*, pp. 68–69; Cusine, 1987 J.L.S.S. 66; SLC Discussion Paper no. 107, *Diligence against Land* (1998), paras 3.137–3.140.

[40] *cf.* Gretton, above, p. 68.

possession under a sasine title (or a Land Register title in which indemnity had been excluded)[41] has possessed for ten years, his title would become unchallengeable by the operation of positive prescription, so cutting off any right of challenge on the part of the inhibitor.[42]

Claims which are not relevant

5.65　　(1)　An extrajudicial demand for payment is not a relevant claim and will have no effect on prescription[43]: a demand is only relevant if made in court proceedings or in one of the other ways set out in section 9.

(2)　To draw a cheque on an account with a bank is not to make a relevant claim on the bank's obligation to repay its debt.[44]

(3)　A letter calling for the appointment of an arbiter to determine a dispute is not a relevant claim. It cannot be a preliminary notice either, unless it meets the terms of section 4 by setting out the nature of the claim (it would of course often do this).[45]

(4)　Claims intimated to a person acting in relation to a company voluntary arrangement or to an administrator or receiver are not included in section 9 and so are not relevant claims.[46] They therefore do not interrupt prescription. But the fact that the prescriptive period for a particular claim was about to expire would seem to be a relevant factor for the court to consider when deciding whether to grant leave for an action to be raised against a company in administration or liquidation.[47] It seems harsh nonetheless that creditors who may be able to obtain only very modest dividends on their debts have no option, in order to preserve their claims, but to embark on litigation, unless the administrator or receiver is prepared to make a relevant acknowledgment.

(5)　The question has arisen (but has not been decided) what the status is of a claim submitted in a judicial factory. Such claims are not within the narrow reading of "appropriate proceedings", nor are they expressly provided for in the Act. It follows that they do not appear to constitute relevant claims for the purposes of section 9.[48]

These various considerations indicate that it is not enough that something is done which shows that the creditor is aware of or is insisting in his rights or intends to press a claim. What matters is that what is done falls within the strict confines of the statutory definition.

---

[41] This would be likely to be the case if the Keeper knew of the inhibition.

[42] Gretton, above, pp. 68–69; SLC Discussion Paper no. 107, above, para. 3.140.

[43] Even under the law before 1973 an extrajudicial demand of debt amounted to an interruption only if it was accompanied by some acknowledgment of the debt by the debtor: Erskine, III, vii, 3.7.39, so that a claim pure and simple would not be relevant.

[44] Walker, p. 67 takes a different view. This did interrupt prescription before the 1973 Act: *Macdonald v. North of Scotland Bank*, 1942 S.C. 369 at 372–373.

[45] *Douglas Milne Ltd v. Borders R.C.*, 1990 S.L.T. 558.

[46] Insolvency Act 1986, ss. 1, 8 and 50.

[47] *ibid.* ss. 10, 11 and 130(2).

[48] On the question whether such claims may be imprescriptible, see above para. 3.42.

II. RELEVANT ACKNOWLEDGMENT

"Relevant acknowledgment for purposes of sections 6, 7 and 8A 5.66
10.—(1) The subsistence of an obligation shall be regarded for the purposes of sections 6, 7 and 8A of this Act as having been relevantly acknowledged if, and only if, either of the following conditions is satisfied, namely—

> (a) that there has been such performance by or on behalf of the debtor towards implement of the obligation as clearly indicates that the obligation still subsists;
> (b) that there has been made by or on behalf of the debtor to the creditor or his agent an unequivocal written admission clearly acknowledging that the obligation still subsists.

(2) Subject to subsection (3) below, where two or more persons are bound jointly by an obligation so that each is liable for the whole, and the subsistence of the obligation has been relevantly acknowledged by or on behalf of one of those persons then—

> (a) if the acknowledgment is made in the manner specified in paragraph (a) of the foregoing subsection it shall have effect for the purposes of the said sections 6, 7 and 8A as respects the liability of each of those persons, and
> (b) if it is made in the manner specified in paragraph (b) of that subsection it shall have effect for those purposes only as respects the liability of the person who makes it.

(3) Where the subsistence of an obligation affecting a trust estate has been relevantly acknowledged by or on behalf of one of two or more co-trustees in the manner specified in paragraph (a) or (b) of subsection (1) of this section, the acknowledgment shall have effect for the purposes of the said sections 6, 7 and 8A as respects the liability of the trust estate and any liability of each of the trustees.

(4) In this section references to performance in relation to an obligation include, where the nature of the obligation so requires, references to refraining from doing something and to permitting or suffering something to be done or maintained."

This is the second of the two ways of interrupting prescription. It does not apply to bills of exchange or promissory notes.[49] It does not apply to prescription of rights relating to property either.[50]

"Relevant acknowledgment" requires that one or other of two condi- 5.67
tions be satisfied: either such performance by or on behalf of the debtor towards implement of the obligation as clearly indicates that the obligation still subsists or else an unequivocal written admission by or on behalf of the debtor to the creditor or his agent clearly acknowledging that the obligation still subsists. Each of the two branches of section 10(1) requires that the performance or admission be made "by or on behalf of the debtor". It is clear that nothing else will amount to a

---

[49] Proviso to ss. 6(1) and 7(1). This preserves the same rules as applied under the Bills of Exchange (Scotland) Act 1772, under which only action or diligence would interrupt prescription of a bill or note; *cf.* Napier, pp. 846 *et seq.*
[50] s. 8.

relevant acknowledgment, since section 10(1) expressly provides that there is relevant acknowledgment "if and only if" one of these two conditions has been satisfied.

(a) Performance

What amounts to performance?

5.68   The test must be a fairly high one, since the performance has clearly to indicate that the obligation still subsists.

5.69   Payment of money—for example, interest[51]—on a particular debt may well be such as clearly to indicate that the obligation still subsists and so constitute a relevant acknowledgment. Continuing to make payments in terms of an agreement has been held to amount to performance.[52] Similarly, if a bank honours a cheque drawn on it by its customer, that will clearly indicate that the bank's obligation to pay still subsists, that is, that the account is either in credit or the cheque does not exceed any limit agreed between the customer and the bank.

5.70   Since the point for present purposes is that there should be clear acknowledgment that the obligation still subsists, the amount of the payment does not matter. Clearly, it will be difficult to say whether a payment of £10 acknowledges the subsistence of a debt of £100 or £1,000; but all that matters here is that, if the payment can clearly be connected with the debt, then the debt has not prescribed.[53] Plainly this is a different question from proving what the extent of the debt actually is.

5.71   The question of ascription of payments will arise where the same debtor is subject to more than one obligation in favour of the same creditor. The general rule is that the debtor is entitled to ascribe his payment to a particular debt and that, if he does not do so, the creditor may do so.[54] This is subject to presumptions, such as the so-called rule in *Clayton's Case*,[55] that in a current account the earliest credit is applied to extinguish the earliest debit.

5.72   In the event that the debtor ascribes his payment to a particular debt, it is of course in his own hands to make or omit to make performance which will amount to relevant acknowledgment of a particular obligation. Matters are less clear where the debtor makes no ascription. Given that the performance must clearly indicate that the obligation still subsists, it seems doubtful whether the creditor can rely on an unascribed payment as interrupting prescription of any obligation he chooses.[56] Even if the creditor were to intimate to the debtor the fact that he had ascribed payment to a particular debt (as he would be entitled to do), it would still be difficult to say that the debtor's performance had been such as clearly to indicate that any of his obligations in particular still subsisted.

---

[51] *Kermack v. Kermack* (1874) 2 R. 156 at 158.
[52] *Inverlochy Castle Ltd v. Lochaber Power Co.*, 1987 S.L.T. 466.
[53] *Garden v. Rigg* (1743) M. 11274.
[54] Wilson, *Debt* (2nd ed.), para. 12.5.
[55] *Devaynes v. Noble* (1816) 1 Merivale 529 at 572.
[56] *Contra*, Walker, p. 70.

Accordingly, if it is unsafe for the creditor to rely on payment as relevant acknowledgment in these circumstances, his best course will be to require a written admission of the obligation (or in the last resort to institute a relevant claim).

Performance need not, of course, consist in payment. For example, the **5.73** grant of security in relation to performance of an obligation would seem clearly to acknowledge its existence. Other clear examples of relevant acknowledgments would be carrying out repairs to work which had been done or goods which had been supplied. In a recent case the whole series of events and writings passing between the parties were examined in reaching the conclusion that there had been a relevant acknowledgment.[57]

Performance need not consist in doing a positive act. It is expressly **5.74** provided that performance can consist in refraining from doing something or permitting or suffering something to be done or maintained.[58] So, for example, a failure to recover possession of subjects let might be regarded as a relevant acknowledgment of an obligation to allow a tenant to possess them.

In one case it was argued that where a landlord and tenant had **5.75** entered into an informal agreement for the tenant to purchase the subjects of let, the fact that the landlord gave possession of the house to the tenant without demanding rent was a relevant acknowledgment of his obligation to grant a conveyance of it to the tenant.[59] It was held that in the circumstances this was not a relevant acknowledgment of that particular obligation, although it might be a relevant acknowledgment of an obligation to grant possession of the subjects. This case makes clear that it is important to be able to identify the particular obligation which has been acknowledged. Whether the performance is such as to amount to a relevant acknowledgment was said in the same case to be a question of fact and degree.[60]

Performance by whom?
For performance to amount to a relevant acknowledgment it must be **5.76** made "by or on behalf of the debtor".

Where parties are jointly and severally liable, performance by one will **5.77** have effect "as respects the liability of each of those persons".[61] Presumably this means that each is taken to have given a relevant acknowledgment, so that none can rely on any prescriptive period prior to the date of the acknowledgment. So, for example, a payment by either a cautioner or the principal debtor, where they were bound jointly and severally, would amount to a relevant acknowledgment not just by the one but also by the other.[62]

---

[57] Clearly it would be necessary to be able to relate the work done to the particular obligation; *cf.* above, paras 2.05 *et seq.; Richardson v. Quercus Ltd*, 1999 S.C. 278, I.H.
[58] s. 10(4).
[59] *Gibson v. Carson*, 1980 S.C. 356.
[60] at 360. *cf. Richardson v. Quercus*, above.
[61] s. 10(2)(a).
[62] *Smithy's Place Ltd* v. *Blackadder & McMonagle*, 1991 S.L.T. 790 at 793 D.

5.78   Specific provision is made for obligations affecting trust estates: here relevant acknowledgment by one trustee affects not only that trustee but also has effect "as respects the liability of the trust estate and any liability of each of the trustees".[63]

5.79   (1) *Persons other than the individual debtor* who can make a relevant acknowledgment by performance will be those, such as executors, who stand in the same right as the debtor, as well as agents of the debtor. Where the performance relied on was made by the debtor's agent, it will be necessary to consider whether the agent had actual or ostensible authority to make the performance in question. If not, it will be difficult to impute acknowledgment of the obligation to the principal.

(2) *Statutory agents* such as administrators and receivers have the powers granted to them under the Insolvency Act 1986, and these are likely to cover most forms in which a relevant acknowledgment by performance might be made.[64] Although the liquidator is not expressly constituted the agent of the company by statute, nor is its property vested in him,[65] his management functions mean that he must be able to make a relevant acknowledgment of an obligation. Such a thing would, after all, have been done prior to the winding-up order by the directors in whose place the liquidator now effectively stands. Acknowledgment in the form of payment could only be made with sanction, regardless of the sort of liquidation in question.[66]

(3) *Trustee in sequestration*. In this case matters are less clear. On the face of it, the ordinary provisions about trusts might apply, since sequestration is no more than a statutory trust. The trustee would therefore be capable of making acknowledgment.[67] But the particular provisions of the 1985 Act cast some doubt on this. It may be that an interim trustee cannot make a relevant acknowledgment, since he neither acts as agent of the bankrupt nor is the bankrupt's estate vested in him. The fact that the 1985 Act makes provision for the interim trustee to give directions to the bankrupt or require him to implement transactions he has entered into seems to suggest that the power to make performance amounting to relevant acknowledgment remains for the time being with the bankrupt.[68]

On the other hand, the bankrupt's estate does vest in the permanent trustee. As a result the bankrupt certainly cannot make a relevant acknowledgment which would bind the trustee. Conversely, the fact that the bankrupt's rights and obligations vest in the trustee suggest that the trustee should be able to make relevant acknowledgment of the bankrupt's obligations. It would after all be strange if neither he nor the bankrupt could do so, since this would mean that after an award of sequestration prescription could be interrupted only if the creditor sued for

---

[63] s. 10(3).
[64] 1986 Act, ss. 14(5) and 57(1) and Sched. 1, powers 13–14; Sched. 2, powers 13–14.
[65] Unless an order under s. 145 of the Insolvency Act 1986 has been made by the court.
[66] 1986 Act, Sched. 4, powers 1–3.
[67] See s. 10(3).
[68] 1985 Act, s. 18(1) and (2)(e).

implement, a consequence which would seem impractical and counter-productive to the good management of the sequestration.

Of course it is true that questions of this sort will in practice be unlikely to arise: the trustee will be mainly concerned not with acknowledging indebtedness but with discovering its extent and ultimately, if possible, paying a dividend to creditors. The question of relevant acknowledgment may therefore arise only when the trustee finally settles the distribution of the estate. And by then it does not really matter.

(4) *Judicial factor*. It is clear that performance by a judicial factor would also suffice. This follows from the fact that trustees are able to make relevant acknowledgment binding the trust estate, and a judicial factor is a trustee for the purposes of the 1973 Act.[69]

(b) Unequivocal written admission

In what terms must the admission be made?

What is needed is "an unequivocal written admission clearly acknowl- **5.80** edging that the obligation still subsists". It would be inadvisable to attempt to state any kind of general rule in the abstract, but it is clear enough that this test is a high one. So, for example, a letter stating that "we regret that we are unable to deliver the letter [of obligation] to you" was not regarded as an unequivocal admission.[70] On the other hand, a somewhat more liberal view was adopted in *Fortunato's Judicial Factor v. Fortunato*.[71] In that case the draft minutes of a meeting of trustees were circulated for revisal, to the pursuer among others. The minutes included reference to the fact that a majority of trustees accepted the pursuer's claim. The minutes were held to be a record of a final and unequivocal decision and the circulation of the minutes was held to be a communication made to the agents of the creditor in terms of section 10(1)(b). Several points discussed below suggest, however, that it may be necessary to consider the circumstances in, and the purpose for, which the admission was made. It may be thought that in *Fortunato's Judicial Factor v. Fortunato* insufficient weight was placed on this issue.

The terms of the Act indicate that the acknowledgment must be **5.81** clearly referable to the particular obligation. Otherwise it cannot be said that it is in any way unequivocal. What is required is acknowledgment that the obligation still subsists. This is different, for instance, from acknowledging the fact that the obligation was once incurred.[72] So it seems that the acknowledgment itself, if unequivocal, interrupts prescription, although in order to measure the surviving obligation other circumstances and evidence would need to be taken into account. A credit note has been held to constitute an unequivocal written admission that a debt had not been discharged and that the obligation to which it related therefore subsisted at the time it was issued.[73] Whether an admission is unequivocal or makes clear acknowledgment is a question

---

[69] s. 10(3) and 15(1); Trusts (Scotland) Act 1921, s. 2.
[70] *Lieberman v. G. W. Tait & Sons SSC*, 1987 S.L.T. 585.
[71] 1981 S.L.T. 277.
[72] *Steel v. Dundaff Ltd*, 1st Div., January 13, 1995, unreported.
[73] *Steel v. Dundaff Ltd*, above: the terms were "for VAT charged on invoices dated May 27, 1984".

of interpretation in particular circumstances. A recent case has held (*obiter*) that even a letter written "without prejudice to liability" might be capable of amounting to a relevant acknowledgment when viewed against the background of other writings and the conduct of the parties.[74]

Who can make an unequivocal written admission?

5.82   To amount to a relevant acknowledgment the admission must be "by or on behalf of the debtor":

(1) Again, this will cover the case of an admission made by a *person*, such as an executor, *standing in the same right as the debtor*. Again, it will cover authorised agents; and once again the question will arise whether the agent had actual or ostensible authority to make the performance in question. If not, it will be difficult to impute acknowledgment of the obligation to the principal.[75]

(2) The statutory powers of *administrators* and *receivers* appear to cover the granting of admissions, so that they too would be capable of making relevant acknowledgment of this kind.[76] So far as liquidators are concerned, there is little to add to what was said earlier about acknowledgment by performance. For the same reasons, a liquidator will be able to make the necessary admission, although it will require sanction if it commits the company to a compromise or arrangement.[77]

(3) *Trustee in sequestration.* There is not much to add here either to what was said about performance. The likelihood is that an admission which amounted to a relevant acknowledgment could be made by the permanent trustee but not by the interim trustee. A further reason for doubting the interim trustee's capacity to make an acknowledgment is this. The interim and permanent trustees must accept or reject creditors' claims.[78] In the case of an interim trustee, acceptance or rejection determines the entitlement of the creditor to vote at the statutory meeting. In the case of the permanent trustee it also determines the creditor's right to a dividend from the sequestrated estate.[79] Given the purpose of the interim trustee's acceptance, and the fact that it is based only on submission by the creditor of evidence prima facie supporting his claim,[80] it seems unlikely that such acceptance would amount to a relevant acknowledgment. But for the avoidance of doubt the trustee might wish to qualify his acceptance accordingly.

(4) *Judicial factor.* It is clear that performance by a judicial factor would also suffice. This follows from the fact that trustees are able to make acknowledgment binding the trust estate, and a judicial factor is a trustee for the purposes of the 1973 Act.[81] It seems likely that a judicial factor can make an admission of the

---

[74] *Briggs v. Swan's Exr* (1854) 16 D. 385 at 394; *cf. Greater Glasgow Health Board v. Baxter Clark & Paul*, 1990 S.C. 237; *Richardson v. Quercus Ltd*, 1999 S.C. 278, I.H.

[75] So, *e.g.*, accountants have been held not to have authority to acknowledge debts in the company accounts, as they merely certify that the accounts meet the statutory requirements: *Re Transplanters (Holding Co.) Ltd* [1958] 1 W.L.R. 822.

[76] 1986 Act, ss. 14(5) and 57(1), Sched. 1, power 9; Sched. 2, power 9.

[77] *ibid.* Sched. 4, powers 1–3, 7.

[78] 1985 Act, ss. 23 and 49.

[79] ss. 23(2) and 49(2).

[80] s. 22(2)(b).

[81] ss.10(3) and 15(1), Trusts (Scotland) Act 1921, s. 2.

necessary sort. Where he is appointed to wind up estates, it would be odd if he was not entitled to grant any acknowledgment of due debts such as could be founded on to interrupt the running of prescription.[82] It is true that any such admission would be provisional, as the Accountant of Court has to approve any scheme of division before the judicial factor obtains a discharge, so that no adjudication by the judicial factor on a debt is of itself final. But it seems implausible that this means that no admission can be made, and more likely that it is simply open to being disturbed.

On arguments similar to those made in relation to an interim trustee in bankruptcy, something will turn on the stage at which the admission is made. The judicial factor is unlikely to be in a position to make a relevant acknowledgment of a claim until he has received from the creditor sufficient details and documentation supporting the claim to allow him to adjudicate on the validity of the claim and thereafter to make an unequivocal admission that it falls to be paid. An acknowledgment by the judicial factor—especially at an early stage—that he has received a claim is unlikely to be more than an administrative exercise. A bare acknowledgment of receipt of a claim would not go far enough.

Where parties are bound jointly and severally, an admission by one is expressly provided to have effect only against that party.[83] Accordingly, the admission will not prevent others bound by the obligation from pleading prescription of their own obligations to the creditor. So, for example, if B, C and D are jointly and severally liable to A, and B makes an admission to A, prescription is interrupted as against B alone. If five years pass uninterrupted from the date the obligation became enforceable, C and D will no longer be bound, their obligations having prescribed. B alone will remain liable to A, since fewer than five uninterrupted years have passed. This, however, should have no effect on B's right of relief against C and D, since that is based on a separate obligation, and one which became enforceable only when B satisfied the obligation to A.

To whom must the admission be made?

The Act requires that it be made to the "creditor or his agent". The **5.83** question therefore has to be considered to whom the admission is addressed. Two examples may help to clarify the point. First, when real burdens are repeated in a new disposition or charter, this does not appear to amount to an unequivocal admission that they subsist. One good reason for this is that such an admission is not made to the creditor in the real burden.[84]

Second, in England several cases have concerned company accounts in **5.84** which either in the balance sheet or in the notes to the accounts reference was made to indebtedness to a particular creditor.[85] Company

---

[82] *Briggs v. Swan's Exrs* (1854) 16 D. 385 at 389.
[83] s. 10(2)(b); but in the case of trustees, the admission will have effect as respects "the liability of the trust estate and any liability of each of the trustees": s. 10(3).
[84] Reid, *Property* paras 396 and 431; Napier, p. 590.
[85] *Jones v. Bellgrove Properties* [1949] 1 All E.R. 498; *Ledingham v. Bermejo Estancia* [1949] 1 All E.R. 749; *Re Transplanters (Holding Co.) Ltd* [1958] 1 W.L.R. 822.

accounts are not addressed to the company's creditors, and even a creditor who requested a copy of the accounts and had it sent to him might still not be able to rely on this as an admission within section 10(1). If this is right, this must be because the reason for sending the accounts was not to make any admission but (presumably) to give information. On the other hand, if the creditor has been sent a copy of the accounts in his capacity as a shareholder, it might just be arguable that a relevant acknowledgment has been made to him, since accounts are addressed to shareholders. But even this is far from being a clear case: what seems really to be needed is an acknowledgment made to a person in his capacity as creditor and not in some other capacity.

5.85   Accordingly, it will be necessary to consider whether an admission can properly be said to be made to the creditor or his agent.

5.86   The same questions about the meaning of "creditor" and "agent" arise in this context too:

(1) Once again, the case of the *executor*, who stands in the same right as the deceased, and the cases of *agents*, whether contractual or, like *administrators* and *receivers*, statutory, are straightforward. Admissions made to them will be capable of amounting to relevant acknowledgments. Since a liquidator is empowered, for example, to take security for the discharge of indebtedness to the company, *a fortiori* he must be able to receive acknowledgment of such obligations.[86]

(2) *Trustee in sequestration.* Here essentially the same points arise as have been discussed in connection with making relevant acknowledgment of an obligation.[87] Since the bankrupt's estate is vested in the permanent trustee, and he therefore stands in effect in the bankrupt's place as creditor in relation to third parties, admissions directed to the permanent trustee should amount to relevant acknowledgment within section 10(1)(b). But this is not clear for the interim trustee, precisely because the bankrupt's estate is not vested in him, and probably the better view is that the admission would still need to be made to the bankrupt. (This might be a case for the interim trustee to give the bankrupt directions.[88])

   If, where a permanent trustee has been appointed, he is the proper person to receive admissions, in theory—odd though it may seem—it should follow that an admission made to the bankrupt would not meet the terms of section 10(1)(b) and would not interrupt prescription.

(3) *Judicial factor.* In terms of the Trusts (Scotland) Act 1921, a judicial factor will automatically have power "to uplift, discharge, or assign debts due to the trust estate".[89] This would cover the case of receiving acknowledgment of a debt to the trust estate.

The date of relevant acknowledgment

5.87   The question arises whether interruption by relevant acknowledgment is taken to be the date of the writing by the debtor or of its receipt by the creditor. It is hardly possible to suppose that it can be anything other

---

[86] 1986 Act Sched. 4, power 3.
[87] Above, para. 5.82.
[88] 1985 Act, s. 18(1).
[89] 1921 Act, ss. 2 and 4(1)(h).

than the second: an undelivered acknowledgment could hardly be thought to interrupt prescription.

Continuing acknowledgments

It might be supposed that an acknowledgment would be a single event **5.88** rather than a continuing state of affairs, so that a letter from the debtor acknowledging the debt in appropriately unequivocal terms would interrupt prescription at the date the acknowledgment was made. This view seems to makes good sense. But it is not the only sort of acknowledgment.

Take the case that in litigation the debtor's pleadings admit the **5.89** obligation. This appears to fall within the statutory definition of "relevant acknowledgment". But is the acknowledgment made at the instant it enters the pleadings or does it subsist as long as it remains in the pleadings? It does not seem that the Scottish Law Commission considered this question in its consultation prior to the 1973 Act. Its concern was principally with the sort of written acknowledgment which would be adequate to interrupt prescription without any action being raised.[90] In cases of this sort, it would seem more appropriate to say that in general the acknowledgment continues as long as the admission remains on record.[91] But it is not sufficient to treat this as a purely formal question about what is or is not in the pleadings. For example, in one case the relevant acknowledgment relied upon by the pursuers was an earlier action raised by the defender in which he had sought implement of the contract. It was held that an acknowledgment subsisted as long as it represented the position of the party making it. Here the pursuers could not rely on the defender's pleadings in the earlier action when, although the action had not formally been disposed of, the defender—who was the pursuer in the earlier action—had intimated to the pursuers that he did not intend to insist in it.[92]

The effect of interruption by a relevant claim or acknowledgment

The Act does not state expressly what the effect of a relevant claim or **5.90** acknowledgment is. The natural reading of the section is, however, that an obligation will be extinguished only if it has subsisted for any continuous period of the necessary length after the appropriate date without claim or acknowledgment. If it has not, then it is not extinguished.

It has been contended that a prescriptive period is capable of **5.91** beginning only on the appropriate date for the particular obligation, and that it is not possible for it to begin to run on any later date.[93] If correct, this would mean that after a relevant claim or acknowledgment no prescription was possible,[94] since by definition it would be beginning at a

---

[90] SLC Consultative Memo. no. 9 (1968), para. 83 and Report no. 15 (1970) para. 101.

[91] *Safdar v. Devlin*, 1995 S.L.T. 530. In England the contrary view has been adopted in the Court of Appeal, and an admission held to be effective on the day it is communicated but not to persist for the whole period the action is in being: *Horner v. Cartwright*, July 11, 1989, unreported.

[92] *Barratt (Scotland) Ltd v. Keith*, 1994 S.L.T. 1337 at 1341–1342.

[93] *British Railways Board v. Strathclyde R.C.*, 1981 S.C. 90 at 98; *R. Peter & Co. Ltd v. The Pancake Place Ltd*, 1993 S.L.T. 322.

[94] Under s. 6, 7 or 8A.

date later than the appropriate date. But there is nothing in the Act to suggest that a prescriptive period for the purposes of the Act must commence on the appropriate date and cannot commence at any later date if, for example, there has been interruption of that period. The language of the Act speaks against that proposition: "if, after the appropriate date, an obligation to which this section applies has subsisted for a continuous period of five years". Here the only apparent requirements are that the period be (1) after (not "from and after") the appropriate date and (2) continuous. There is no indication that the continuous period must begin on the appropriate date. Furthermore, if that were so, since section 7 is phrased in the same way as section 6, the 20-year prescription would also be excluded if prescription had once been interrupted, so that the long stop would disappear and in such circumstances obligations would become imprescriptible.

5.92   Accordingly, a period of two, five or 20 years which, owing to interruption, begins at some time later than the appropriate date prima facie falls within the terms of the section. There is no reason why a prescriptive period should not begin immediately after a relevant claim (or acknowledgment) has been made and be completed the appropriate number of years after the date on which the relevant claim ceased to be made.[95]

5.93   It is of course possible for the prescriptive period to be interrupted more than once. Suppose, in a case concerning the five-year prescription, that a relevant acknowledgment is made three years after the obligation becomes enforceable and a relevant claim is made four years after that. The relevant acknowledgment interrupts prescription, and a new five-year period begins to run. The relevant claim then interrupts that period before it has been completed. It makes no difference that the relevant claim itself comes seven years after the obligation became enforceable. The reason is that, for prescription to be completed, the five-year (or other) period must be continuous and uninterrupted. In this example it has not been.

5.94   For the same reason, it is not possible to carry forward (say) three years' worth of prescription in one prescriptive period and add it to another course of prescription when prescription resumes after an interruption. Here the prescriptive period has not been continuous, and it therefore does not meet the statutory requirements.[96]

5.95   Under the old law on computation of the prescriptive period, a new prescriptive period started to run again on the day of the interruption.[97] It would follow from what was said above about the computation of the prescriptive period that the date of interruption itself should not be included in the new prescriptive period, but that it should start to run at the first instant of the next day.[98]

---

[95] *cf. British Railways Board v. Strathclyde R.C.*, above; *R. Peter & Co. Ltd v. The Pancake Place Ltd*, above, 325; on the same point in earlier statutes, Erskine, III, vii, 39; Bell, *Prin.*, s. 615.

[96] s. 6, 7 or 8A. The only circumstances in which such cumulation of prescriptive periods is allowed are set out in section 6(4) and (5) (fraud, induced error, legal disability under the five-year prescription); see below, paras 6.105 *et seq.*

[97] Erskine, III, vii, 45; Millar, p. 107.

[98] s. 14(1)(c); and see above, para. 4.97.

Application of these principles is simple if relevant claim and relevant **5.96** acknowledgment are regarded as "events" which take place on a given day. Prescription then starts to run on the day after the making of the claim or acknowledgment. On the view that relevant claim and acknowledgment continue as interruptions until they cease to be made, prescription should begin again on the day following their cessation.

CHAPTER 6

FIVE-YEAR PRESCRIPTION

Introduction

"Extinction of obligations by prescriptive periods of five years   **6.01**
6.—(1) If, after the appropriate date, an obligation to which this section applies has subsisted for a continuous period of five years—

    (a) without any relevant claim having been made in relation to the obligation, and

    (b) without the subsistence of the obligation having been relevantly acknowledged,

then as from the expiration of that period the obligation shall be extinguished:
Provided that in its application to an obligation under a bill of exchange or a promissory note this subsection shall have effect as if paragraph (b) thereof were omitted.

(2) Schedule 1 to this Act shall have effect for defining the obligations to which this section applies.

(3) In subsection (1) above the reference to the appropriate date, in relation to an obligation of any kind specified in Schedule 2 to this Act is a reference to the date specified in that Schedule in relation to obligations of that kind, and in relation to an obligation of any other kind is a reference to the date when the obligation became enforceable.

(4) In the computation of a prescriptive period in relation to any obligation for the purposes of this section—

    (a) any period during which by reason of—

        (i) fraud on the part of the debtor or any person acting on his behalf, or

        (ii) error induced by words or conduct of the debtor or any person acting on his behalf,

    the creditor was induced to refrain from making a relevant claim in relation to the obligation, and

    (b) any period during which the original creditor (while he is the creditor) was under legal disability,

shall not be reckoned as, or as part of, the prescriptive period:
Provided that any period such as is mentioned in paragraph (a) of this subsection shall not include any time occurring after the creditor could with reasonable diligence have discovered the fraud or error, as the case may be, referred to in that paragraph.

(5) Any period such as is mentioned in paragraph (a) or (b) of subsection (4) of this section shall not be regarded as separating the time immediately before it from the time immediately after it."

This chapter deals with four topics which are specific to the five-year **6.02** prescription introduced by section 6 of the 1973 Act. They are:

(1) the obligations subject to the prescription; (2) special provisions relating to the commencement of prescription of some of those obligations; (3) postponement of the starting date of prescription of obligations to make reparation; and (4) suspension of the running of prescription.

6.03 This five-year prescription was entirely new to the 1973 Act, which repealed a number of special prescriptions of various lengths, some of them extinctive and others affecting only the mode of proof admissible. Before the 1973 Act came into force these obligations were mostly subject to the general 40-year negative prescription of the Act 1617, although some were subject to special periods of prescription or limitation under other legislation.[1] Since no five-year prescription existed before the 1973 Act, it is not possible to draw from the earlier law any conclusions about whether or not the five-year prescription should now apply to any given obligation.[2]

6.04 The five-year prescription runs against the Crown.[3]

I. THE OBLIGATIONS AFFECTED

6.05 This prescription applies to most obligations. But it does not apply to all, and it is important to keep that restriction in mind. Section 6(2) provides that "Schedule 1 to this Act shall have effect for defining the obligations to which this section applies". That Schedule is made up of two paragraphs, the first of which sets out the obligations to which section 6 applies; the second paragraph sets out a number of obligations to which the section does not apply.

6.06 Since the Schedule is said to "define" the obligations to which section 6 applies, the courts have taken the list in Schedule 1 to be exhaustive.[4] Accordingly, if an obligation is not included in that list, the five-year prescription will not apply to it. This does not mean it is an imprescriptible obligation, since most obligations are caught by the 20–year prescription of section 7.[5]

"SCHEDULE 1[6]

OBLIGATIONS AFFECTED BY PRESCRIPTIVE PERIODS OF FIVE YEARS
UNDER SECTION 6

1. Subject to paragraph 2 below, section 6 of this Act applies—

    (a) to any obligation to pay a sum of money due in respect of a particular period—

---

[1] See Napier, pp. 706 *et seq.*

[2] So, *e.g.*, it is of no significance for the question whether the five-year prescription applies that an obligation was previously subject only to the 20-year prescription; but see *Barratt (Scotland) Ltd v. Keith*, 1994 S.L.T. 1343 at 1346L.

[3] s. 24.

[4] *e.g. Lord Advocate v. Butt*, 1992 S.C. 140.

[5] Imprescriptible obligations are listed in Sched. 3 to the Act; see above, Chap. 3.

[6] The words printed in square brackets were repealed with effect from August 1, 1995 by the Requirements of Writing (Scotland) Act 1995, s. 14(2) and Sched. 5. The effect of the repeals is discussed below.

    (i) by way of interest;
   (ii) by way of an instalment of an annuity;
  (iii) by way of feuduty or other periodical payment under a feu grant;
  (iv) by way of ground annual or other periodical payment under a contract of ground annual;
   (v) by way of rent or other periodical payment under a lease;
  (vi) by way of a periodical payment in respect of the occupancy or use of land, not being an obligation falling within any other provision of this sub-paragraph;
 (vii) by way of a periodical payment under a land obligation, not being an obligation falling within any other provision of this sub-paragraph;

(b) to any obligation based on redress of unjustified enrichment, including without prejudice to that generality any obligation of restitution, repetition or recompense;

(c) to any obligation arising from *negotiorum gestio*;

(d) to any obligation arising from liability (whether arising from any enactment or from any rule of law) to make reparation;

(e) to any obligation under a bill of exchange or a promissory note;

(f) to any obligation of accounting, other than accounting for trust funds;

(g) to any obligation arising from, or by reason of any breach of, a contract or promise, not being an obligation falling within any other provision of this paragraph.

2. Notwithstanding anything in the foregoing paragraph, section 6 of this Act does not apply—

(a) to any obligation to recognise or obtemper a decree of court, an arbitration award or an order of a tribunal or authority exercising jurisdiction under any enactment;

(b) to any obligation arising from the issue of a bank note;

[(c) to any obligation constituted or evidenced by a probative writ, not being a cautionary obligation nor being an obligation falling within paragraph 1(a) of this Schedule;]

(d) to any obligation under a contract of partnership or of agency, not being an obligation remaining, or becoming prestable on or after the termination of the relationship between the parties under the contract;

(e) except as provided in paragraph 1(a) of this Schedule, to any obligation relating to land (including an obligation to recognise a servitude);

(f) to any obligation to satisfy any claim to terce, courtesy, legitim, *jus relicti* or *jus relictae*, or to any prior right of a surviving spouse under section 8 or 9 of the Succession (Scotland) Act 1964;

(g) to any obligation to make reparation in respect of personal injuries within the meaning of Part II of this Act or in respect of the death of any person as a result of such injuries;

(gg) to any obligation to make reparation or otherwise make good in respect of defamation within the meaning of section 18A of this Act;

(ggg) to any obligation arising from liability under section 2 of the Consumer Protection Act 1987 (to make reparation for damage caused wholly or partly by a defect in a product);

(h) to any obligation specified in Schedule 3 to this Act as an imprescriptible obligation.

[3.—(1) Subject to sub-paragraph (2) below, where by virtue of a probative writ two or more persons (in this paragraph referred to as 'the co-obligants') are bound jointly and severally by an obligation to pay money to another party the obligation shall, as respects the liability of each of the co-obligants, be regarded for the purposes of sub-paragraph (c) of the last foregoing paragraph as if it were a cautionary obligation.

(2) Nothing in the foregoing sub-paragraph shall affect any obligation as respects the liability of any of the co-obligants with respect to whom the creditor establishes—

(a) that that co-obligant is truly a principal debtor, or

(b) if that co-obligant is not truly a principal debtor, that the original creditor was not aware of that fact at the time when the writ was delivered to him.]

4. In this Schedule—

(a) 'land obligation' has the same meaning as it has for the purposes of the Conveyancing and Feudal Reform (Scotland) Act 1970;

[(b) 'probative writ' means a writ which is authenticated by attestation or in any such other manner as, in relation to writs of the particular class in question, may be provided by or under any enactment as having an effect equivalent to attestation.]"

Taxonomy of Schedule 1

6.07   The Schedule does not present any great coherence. The first paragraph sets out the list of obligations to which it applies; the second a list of those to which it does not apply. Since the first is exhaustive, the second might be thought, strictly speaking, to be redundant. Its purpose appears to be to qualify some of the obligations included in paragraph 1 and for the avoidance of doubt to remove certain others from the scope of the five-year prescription.

6.08   The Schedule does refer, in addition to a few special cases, to the three categories of obligations: contract, delict and unjustified enrichment. But there is an oddity about the drafting. Most of the references in the Schedule are to the source of the obligation in question (unjustified enrichment, contract, breach of contract and so forth), but there is no reference to delict as a source of obligation. Instead, sub-paragraph (d) refers not to the source of the obligation but to a remedy—reparation— which is typically available in respect of such an obligation. This means that obligations arising from delict other than obligations to pay damages are not included within the Schedule,[7] and are therefore not subject to the five-year prescription.[8]

---

[7] *e.g.* an obligation to make specific implement of a statutory obligation: *Miller v. Glasgow D.C.*, 1989 S.L.T. 44; an obligation to abate a nuisance.

[8] Less importantly, this formulation means that, because obligations to make reparation arise not just from delict but also from breach of contract, there is an overlap between Sched. 1, paras 1(d) and (g).

Schedule 1 paragraph 1: the details

(a) Sums of money due in respect of particular periods

Nearly all of the seven instances mentioned here relate to payments in **6.09** respect of occupancy of land. The exceptions are (i) interest and (ii) instalments of annuity. It is clear, therefore, that this provision is concerned only with a selected range of periodical payments and not with all payments of that sort. Accordingly, obligations to make payment in respect of periodical services are not covered[9]; neither are obligations to pay sick pay,[10] even if they can be said to arise in respect of particular periods. What the seven instances in this sub-paragraph have in common is that they are payments due in respect of a particular period: for example, an annuity for a given year, rent for a given quarter, or interest for a particular month. Since it is part of the definition of these obligations that they arise "in respect of a particular period", it follows that each is a separate obligation on which prescription may operate separately. With the expiry of the five-year period from the date on which payment in respect of one particular period was due, the obligation in relation to that period is extinguished. But there is no effect on the continuing obligation to pay further instalments in respect of any later periods.[11]

The question arises whether "a particular period" must be a definite **6.10** period. It has been held that this provision does not apply to interest which accrues indefinitely during a period of non-payment of a principal sum, but only to obligations to pay interest falling due for payment on a particular day.[12] This seems right, since, where all that happens is that a single sum of interest due becomes greater by the day, it is hard to see that any question of its being in respect of "a particular period" arises; and if this were all that the statute meant, it would be hard to understand why it did not simply say "interest". Similarly, a payment which becomes due from time to time, such as a casualty payable when new assignees take over a lease, is not a periodical payment.[13]

The Scottish Law Commission has recently proposed that leasehold **6.11** casualties should be abolished.[14] It is also proposed that compensation for the loss of the casualty should be payable to the landlord by the tenant if demanded within one year of the date the Act is passed, and that the five-year prescription should apply to the obligation to pay compensation.[15] The result would be that a maximum of six years could elapse from the date of the Act until all obligations to pay compensation thereunder had been extinguished.

Furthermore, as a consequence of the proposals for abolition of **6.12** the feudal system, the Scottish Law Commission also propose that the

---

[9] *Reid v. Beaton*, 1995 S.C.L.R. 382.

[10] *Flynn v. UNUM Ltd*, 1996 S.L.T. 1067.

[11] *cf.* Sched. 3(c) and above, para. 3.18. For an early illustration of this principle, *Elliot v. Marquis of Lothian* (1808) Hume 465.

[12] *Lord Advocate v. Butt*, 1992 S.C. 140, IH; this view was not, however, adopted in *Zani v. Martone*, 1997 S.L.T. 1269.

[13] *MRS Hamilton Ltd v. Arlott*, Extra Div., May 24, 1995, unreported; *MRS Hamilton Ltd v. Keeper of the Registers of Scotland*, Lands Tribunal, May 19, 1998, unreported.

[14] SLC Report no. 165, *Report on Leasehold Casualties* (1998).

[15] cl. 4 of the draft Bill annexed to the report inserts a new sub-para. (aa) in Sched. 1, para. 1.

references in this paragraph to feuduty and ground annuals should cease to have effect.[16] Two further changes are proposed in the same report: that obligations to pay feuduty redemption money should come under the five-year negative prescription, and that obligations on the part of former vassals to make compensatory payments to their former superiors for the extinction of their feuduty should do so too.[17]

6.13   Some comment is perhaps required in relation to the two residual categories, (vi) and (vii). So far as (vi) is concerned, "a periodical payment in respect of the occupancy or use of land, not being an obligation falling within any other provision of this sub-paragraph" might include such things as the obligation to pay rates. Since they are levied on the person in rateable occupation of lands or heritages, it appears that the obligation to pay rates is an obligation to make periodical payment in respect of the occupancy of land.[18]

6.14   Paragraph 1(a)(vii) is concerned with "a periodical payment under a land obligation, not being an obligation falling within any other provision of this sub-paragraph". The definition of "land obligation" in section 1(2) of the Conveyancing and Feudal Reform (Scotland) Act 1970 is applied[19]: "a land obligation is an obligation relating to land which is enforceable by a proprietor of an interest in land, by virtue of his being such proprietor, and which is binding upon a proprietor of another interest in that land, or of an interest in other land, by virtue of his being such proprietor". In general, the term "land obligation" is therefore capable of including such things as real burdens and conditions and obligations contained in registered leases.[20] Periodical payments under leases are excluded from head (vii), since it is a residual head, and they are already covered by head (v). But periodical payments under real burdens and conditions, other than feu duty or ground annuals which are themselves set out in heads (iii) and (iv), would seem to fall within head (vii).

(b) Redress of unjustified enrichment, including without prejudice to that generality any obligation of restitution, repetition or recompense

6.15   It is reasonably clear that this sub-paragraph is intended comprehensively to bring obligations arising from unjustified enrichment within the scope of the five-year prescription.[21] In fact, the Scottish Law Commission raised the question whether obligations arising from unjustified enrichment should fall within the scope of this prescription. It concluded that they must. Otherwise the purpose of the prescription might be defeated if (for example), on prescription of their contractual claims, pursuers were able to resort to restitutionary ones.[22]

---

[16] Sched. 1, para. 1(a)(iii) and (iv). See SLC Report no. 168 (1999): in the draft Abolition of Feudal Tenure etc. (Scotland) Bill annexed to the report, the relevant provisions are cl. 70(1) and Sched. 8, Pt I, para. 35(5). Para. 36 makes transitional arrangements for the prescription of these obligations if they fall due before the appointed day.

[17] See cll. 12 and 51 of the draft Abolition of Feudal Tenure etc. (Scotland) Bill.

[18] See Armour, *Valuation for Rating* (5th ed., 1985), Chap. 14.

[19] 1973 Act, Sched. 1, para. 4(a).

[20] Halliday, *Conveyancing*, paras 19.13 *et seq.*; Reid, *Property*, paras 344 *et seq.*

[21] It may be noted in passing that real rights which redress unjustified enrichment are not within the scope of the sub-paragraph, not being obligations nor the correlatives of obligations (s. 15(2)).

[22] SLC Memo. no. 9 (1968), para. 46; Report no. 15 (1970), para. 63.

It is not necessary here to give an account of restitution, repetition **6.16** and recompense. But one point about the meaning of "restitution" should be noted, since in principle it might refer either to the owner's proprietary claim to his property or to his personal right against the defender in possession of it. It has been suggested that this provision extends to the owner's right to delivery of moveable property, which would therefore prescribe in five years. But this can apply to the right to delivery only so far as it is correlative to an obligation on the part of some person to make delivery.[23] Accordingly, it appears to be correct to restrict the application of the five-year prescription to the personal obligation on an individual to make restitution to the pursuer, and not to suppose that it extends to the real right of ownership.[24] For the purposes of this Act, therefore, "restitution" is to be taken to mean the remedy in the law of obligations directed at redress of unjustified enrichment by transferring ownership of a thing to the pursuer.

This provision brings in a wide range of obligations whose source is **6.17** unjustified enrichment. It is made clear that it is not confined purely to obligations which are redressed by repetition, restitution or recompense. It follows that it will cover any obligations not listed within the sub-paragraph which are founded on redress of unjustified enrichment. The obligation of relief is a possible instance.[25]

The critical point, however, is that what matters is not the remedy but **6.18** the source from which it arises, namely the unjustified enrichment of the defender. This means that less obvious remedies such as reduction are capable of falling within this provision, provided they are called into play in order to redress unjustified enrichment. One example would be a case in which a disposition of heritable property has conveyed too much land to the purchaser.[26] Here the seller's remedy of reduction of the disposition must be founded on the purchaser's unjustified enrichment at his expense. It follows that the obligation on which such a claim proceeds could in principle be extinguished by the five-year prescription.[27]

So this provision is capable of covering a wide range of obligations **6.19** based on unjustified enrichment. Nonetheless, it has to be said that the use in the Act of the general term "unjustified enrichment" is surprising, since Scots law has not traditionally relied on any such general concept. Furthermore, the provision is not well expressed: not only is terminology relating to the substance (unjustified enrichment) mixed with that relating to the remedy (restitution, repetition, recompense),[28] but the remedies

---

[23] s. 15(2).

[24] See SLC Memo. no. 30 (1976), *Corporeal Moveables: Usucapion or Acquisitive Prescription*, para. 3 with the criticisms of D. Carey Miller, *Corporeal Moveables*, paras 7.05 and 10.13.

[25] See Stair, I, viii, 9; and recently *Moss v. Penman*, 1994 S.L.T. 19; *Christie's Exr v. Armstrong*, 1996 S.L.T. 948. Note that obligations of relief between joint wrongdoers are subject to a two-year prescription under s. 8A; see below, para. 8.02. They also fall within both s. 6 and s. 7.

[26] *Anderson v. Lambie*, 1954 S.C. (H.L.) 43; this is the equivalent for heritable property of "restitution" in the sense described above.

[27] It seems likely, however, that it would in fact be excluded from the five-year negative prescription as an obligation relating to land: Sched. 1, para. 2(e).

[28] *cf.* P. Birks, *Introduction to the Law of Restitution* (Oxford, revd. ed. 1989), p. 9, who uses the terms "event" and response rather than substance and remedy.

listed are described as "obligations", which they are not; and the debtor's obligation to pay unjustified enrichment arising in his hands to his creditor is not very felicitously described as an "obligation based on redress of unjustified enrichment".

6.20   If "unjustified enrichment" is the key, there remain nonetheless some awkward borderline cases to which the provision does not clearly apply. Here it is possible only to give a few examples of difficult cases:

(1) One is *negotiorum gestio*, but doubts about it are dispelled since it is dealt with expressly in the next sub-paragraph.

(2) Another doubtful case is salvage, which is not clearly restitution-ary: the award to the salvor does not necessarily correspond to the enrichment of the owner of the saved property.[29]

(3) Yet another is general average (or liability under the principle of the *lex Rhodia*): this is not within the normal scope of recompense.[30]

(4) A final example is so-called Melville Monument liability,[31] that is, pre-contractual liability where the pursuer acts in reliance on an implied assurance by the defender that there is a binding contract between the parties. Although this is sometimes regarded as a restitutionary liability, it does not plainly fall within the scope of this provision, since it turns not on enrichment of the defender but on loss by the pursuer.

6.21   What all this points to is this: that there are some categories of obligation which do not appear to fall within section 6 at all, because they are neither contractual nor delictual nor, because they do not necessarily turn on enrichment by the defender, are they (clearly) founded upon unjustified enrichment.

(c) Negotiorum gestio[32]

6.22   It might be thought that this category would in any event have been included in the general category (b) as arising from unjustified enrich-ment. But clarification that such obligations are within the five-year prescription is useful, since it might otherwise be argued that the basis of *negotiorum gestio* is not necessarily unjustified enrichment. The liability can exist even where no enrichment arises from the *gestor*'s actions.

(d) Liability (whether arising from any enactment or from any rule of law) to make reparation

6.23   It appears from the reference to any enactment or any rule of law that this provision is not intended to cover liability arising from contract or other agreement. The point is of little materiality since liability of that sort is in any event covered by sub-paragraph (g). The term "reparation" accordingly has a different sense here from that in section 11, where it expressly includes obligations arising from breach of contract or promise.

---

[29] P. Birks, "Six questions in search of a subject: unjust enrichment in a crisis of identity", 1985 J.R. 227 at 248–249; Birks, *op. cit.*, pp. 304 *et seq.*; Gloag and Henderson, para. 30.14.
[30] Gloag and Henderson, paras 30.1 *et seq.*; Rose (1997) 113 L.Q.R. 569.
[31] *Walker v. Milne* (1823) 2 S. 379; recently *Dawson International plc v. Coats Patons plc*, 1988 S.L.T. 854 at 865–866.
[32] Gloag and Henderson, para. 22.31.

Here it appears to be confined to the obligation to pay damages arising from delictual liability whether at common law or under statute, and this is how the courts have interpreted the provision.[33]

The scope of this provision is much cut down by exclusions set out in **6.24** paragraph 2 of this Schedule: obligations to make reparation for personal injuries, death resulting from personal injuries, defamation, and liability under the Consumer Protection Act 1987 are all excluded.[34] There remain under this heading other delictual causes of action arising for example from damage to property or to economic interests.

The fact that this provision is expressed in terms of "reparation" **6.25** rather than "delict" means that remedies in delict which are not directed at damages are excluded. On this basis it has been held that a claim for specific implement of a statutory obligation is not within the sub-paragraph, since it is not a claim for reparation[35]; the same must apply to claims for implement of common law obligations. The fact that damages can be claimed in the alternative for the event that specific implement is not granted does not make a claim for specific implement into a claim for reparation.[36]

This is true also of a claim for indemnity under section 12 of the Land **6.26** Registration (Scotland) Act 1979. Since there is nothing wrongful about the events which may give rise to a claim for indemnification, and nothing at all about wrongdoing is said in section 12, this obligation to indemnify does not fall within the scope of the term "obligation to make reparation".[37]

Equally, a claim for compensation under the Town and Country **6.27** Planning Acts has been held not to be a claim arising from the planning authority's obligation to make reparation, on the basis that it is essential to reparation that it should be made for a wrong, and that there is no legal wrong when an authority acts within its statutory powers, even though this may give rise to a statutory obligation on its part to pay compensation.[38] The central point is therefore that the object of these actions is not damages. The same is true of another case, where trustees wrongly alienated trust property and had therefore come under an obligation to restore its value to the trust estate. This was held not to be a claim for reparation but a claim for restoration of the value of property wrongly parted with.[39]

Just as a claim for specific implement falls outside this paragraph since **6.28** it is not a claim for reparation, so does an action of reduction. For that

---

[33] *Hobday v. Kirkpatrick's Trs*, 1985 S.L.T. 197, relying on Stair, I, ix, 6 and Bankton, I, x, 13.

[34] Sched. 1, para. 2 (g), (gg) and (ggg). See below, Chaps 10, 11 and 13.

[35] *Miller v. Glasgow D.C.*, 1989 S.L.T. 44. On the other hand, if the claim were for specific implement of a contractual obligation it would fall within sub-paragraph (g).

[36] *Miller v. Glasgow D.C.*, above. The obligation to pay damages is presumably a separate one which is suspensively conditional on refusal of specific implement.

[37] *MRS Hamilton Ltd v. Keeper of the Registers of Scotland*, Lands Tribunal, May 19, 1998, unreported; Lord Hamilton, June 18, 1998, unreported. It was observed that, had Parliament intended this case to fall within s. 6, it could have amended Sched. 1, para. 1 accordingly, just as it did in the case of s. 1 of the 1973 Act.

[38] *Holt v. City of Dundee D.C.*, 1990 S.L.T. (Lands Tr.) 30.

[39] *Hobday v. Kirkpatrick's Trs*, 1985 S.L.T. 197.

reason, in the case of a delict such as fraud, the defrauded pursuer's right to seek damages will prescribe in five years, but his right to seek reduction of any deed which he has been fraudulently induced to grant will prescribe only under the 20-year prescription of section 7.

6.29 So too the phrasing of paragraph 1(d) in terms of "reparation" has the consequence that a right to claim damages for a civil wrong will prescribe in five years, but the right to restrain the same wrong by interdict will not. What this amounts to in practice is that where a wrong continues it will remain possible to seek to interdict it; but it will not be possible to seek damages for any harm done more than five years before the raising of the action.[40]

6.30 Other actions may be directed partly at reparation and partly at other redress. This is true, for example, of the case of spuilzie,[41] a remedy which is admittedly rare in practice. It is the possessory remedy by which a possessor recovers possession of moveable property with which the defender has wrongfully interfered. It was previously governed by the Act 1579, c. 21. It has been suggested that spuilzie falls within this subparagraph of Schedule 1 as an obligation to make reparation.[42] But the action is directed not merely at reparation (in this case of so-called "violent profits") but also at the recovery of the object of which the pursuer has been dispossessed. So far as directed at recovery, the action cannot be said to be directed at enforcement of an obligation to make reparation. It would appear therefore that it will prescribe only under the 20-year prescription.[43]

(e) Obligation under a bill of exchange or promissory note
6.31 Banknotes are expressly excluded by paragraph 2(b) of this Schedule. Bills of exchange and promissory notes are as defined in the Bills of Exchange Act 1882.[44] They were formerly subject to a six-year limitation.[45] The underlying notion in subjecting them to the five-year prescription is that obligations of this nature ought to be promptly enforced, and the drawer of the bill or note not exposed to claims after a long interval.[46]

(f) Obligation of accounting other than accounting for trust funds
6.32 An obligation of accounting depends on the existence of a particular kind of relationship.[47] Typical examples are the relationship between partners, agent and principal, pupils and their tutors, trustees and

---

[40] s. 11(2) of the Act makes provision for postponing the starting date for prescription of obligations to make reparation for continuing wrongs. But note the criticisms of this subsection made above, paras 4.70 *et seq.*

[41] See Carey Miller, *Corporeal Moveables*, paras 10.23 and 28; *Stair Memorial Encyclopaedia*, Vol. 18, paras 161–166.

[42] Walker, p. 55.

[43] s. 7; *cf.* below, para. 7.14.

[44] See 1973 Act, s. 15(1). Bills of exchange are defined in s. 3 of the 1882 Act and promissory notes in s. 83.

[45] Bills of Exchange (Scotland) Act 1772, ss. 37, 39 and 40.

[46] Napier, pp. 822 *et seq.*

[47] *Unigate Food v. Scottish Milk Marketing Board*, 1975 S.C. (H.L.) 75 (the point on accounting was argued only in the Outer House); in *Sinclair v. Sinclair*, Lord McCluskey, September 24, 1985, unreported, it was held that a former partner in a firm was entitled to an accounting up to the date of his retirement from the firm, but not afterwards, there being then no appropriate relationship.

beneficiaries. Some relationships are not capable of giving rise to an obligation of accounting. An example is that between a taxpayer and the Crown, which has been held to be purely an obligation to pay the amount of the tax assessment.[48] Obligations of accounting between the parties to contracts of partnership and agency remain or become prestable when those contracts have come to an end. They are therefore covered by this provision and not excluded under paragraph 2 of the Schedule.[49] A trustee's obligation to account is subject to prescription, but owing to the terms of this provision it is not subject to the five-year prescription and will prescribe only under the 20-year prescription.[50] The same seems to be true of the accounts of a tutor or curator, who are within the definition of "trustee" given in the Trusts (Scotland) Act 1921.[51]

(g) Obligation arising from, or by reason of any breach of, a contract or promise, not being an obligation falling within any other provision of this paragraph

This is a general category which covers obligations to perform or pay **6.33** in terms of a contract or promise as well as obligations arising from its breach. It seems appropriate that the length of the prescriptive period is the same for obligations to perform and obligations arising from breach; different prescriptive periods might make it more attractive for a party to breach the contract than perform it. This provision is not restricted, as is the case with the provision relating to delict,[52] to specific types of remedy arising from contract or breach of contract. Accordingly, it will extend beyond damages to the obligation to make specific implement of a contract. It will also cover obligations which have no pecuniary content. Examples are the obligation to appoint an arbiter[53]; or to refer a dispute to a contract engineer, which has been held to fall within this provision since it arose by reason of breach of contract.[54] It must also cover a contracting party's right to rescind a contract owing to repudiation by the other party. The remedy of rescission, whether accompanied or not by a claim in damages, is merely a remedy for enforcement of an obligation arising out of breach of contract. Equally, it should cover the sort of contractual obligations which are the subject of proceedings seeking "positive interdict", notably where landlords seek to have their tenants ordered to continue in occupation of leased premises.[55]

The range of contractual obligations affected by this provision is **6.34** somewhat cut down by the exclusion from the five-year prescription of obligations relating to land.[56] But the exclusion from the five-year

---

[48] *Lord Advocate v. Hepburn*, 1990 S.L.T. 530.

[49] Sched. 1, para. 2(d); see below for comments on this sub-paragraph. On the question whether these obligations are in fact imprescriptible, see above, paras 3.27 *et seq.*

[50] See above, paras 3.23 *et seq.* on Sched. 3(e) and the various obligations of trustees which are imprescriptible.

[51] 1921 Act, s. 2. Previously their obligations to account were subject to a 10–year prescription: Prescription Act 1696, c. 9.

[52] Sched. 1, para. 1(d).

[53] *MRS Hamilton Ltd v. Arlott*, Extra Div., May 24, 1995, unreported.

[54] *Douglas Milne Ltd v. Borders R.C.*, 1990 S.L.T. 558.

[55] *Church Commissioners for England v. Abbey National plc*, 1994 S.C. 651; *Retail Parks Investments Ltd v. Royal Bank of Scotland plc (No. 2)*, 1996 S.C. 227; *Co-operative Wholesale Society Ltd v. Saxone Ltd*, 1997 S.L.T. 1052; *Co-operative Insurance Society Ltd v. Argyll Stores (Holdings) Ltd* [1997] 3 All E.R. 297 (HL).

[56] Sched. 1, para. 2(e); several of the examples given by Walker at p. 56, n. 25 are for this reason inapposite.

prescription of obligations constituted or evidenced by probative writings has now been repealed by the Requirements of Writing (Scotland) Act 1995.[57] There are now no specialities of prescription which turn on the formality with which a deed was executed.

Obligations not included

6.35   It would be unwise to attempt to list exhaustively the obligations which are not included in Schedule 1 and to which the five-year prescription therefore does not apply. The point is rather that unless an obligation can be brought within Schedule 1, paragraph 1 it is not subject to the five-year prescription. There are, however, a few cases worth commenting on.

Statutory obligations

6.36   Some statutes impose on public authorities obligations which are actionable at private law and sound in damages.[58] Such obligations will prescribe as obligations to make reparation.[59] But Scots law does not establish any general prescriptive regime for sums which are due under statute.[60] Whether such obligations prescribe under section 6 therefore depends entirely on whether they can be brought within one of the headings of Schedule 1. Many cannot. Here are some examples:

(1) Compensation under planning legislation cannot be said to be due as a matter of contract, nor does it amount to damages or fall within any category in Schedule 1. It is therefore not subject to five-year prescription.[61] The only hesitation must be whether such compensation could be said to be due as a matter of unjustified enrichment. On some facts a case could perhaps be made for this. But the fact that the planning legislation itself contains time limits applicable to claims made under it would suggest that such claims are not within Schedule 1 to the 1973 Act.[62]

(2) Specific implement. Obligations to make specific implement which arise from a statutory duty do not fall within Schedule 1. It has been argued that an obligation of this sort is an obligation to make reparation within paragraph 1(d), but the courts have rejected this view.[63]

(3) Liabilities to taxes or to social security contributions are obligations to make payment. They are also obligations to pay money due in respect of a particular period, but they do not fall within any of the sub-headings of paragraph 1(a). An argument that the obligation to pay tax under Schedule D was an obligation of accounting[64] has been rejected. By the time a tax assessment has been issued, the taxpayer's obligation is quite simply an obligation to make payment.[65] The same appears to apply to the employer's

---

[57] Sched. 1, para. 2(c) of the 1973 Act has been repealed. See below, paras 6.47–52.

[58] For recent discussion, *O'Rourke v. Camden LBC* [1997] 3 All E.R. 23 (HL).

[59] Sched. 1 para. 1(d).

[60] Contrast English law: s. 9 of the Limitation Act 1980 deals generally with "sums due under an enactment".

[61] *Holt v. Dundee D.C.*, 1990 S.L.T. (Lands Tr.) 30; contrast in England, *Hillingdon LBC v. ARC Ltd, The Times*, June 25, 1997, Ch.

[62] *Holt v. Dundee D.C.*, above.

[63] *Miller v. City of Glasgow D.C.*, 1989 S.L.T. 44 at 47.

[64] *i.e.* within Sched. 1, para. 1(d).

[65] *Lord Advocate v. Butt*, 1991 S.L.T. 248 at 252; affirmed in the Inner House 1992 S.C. 140, where it was also held that interest on unpaid tax falls to be treated as tax and not as interest, and therefore does not prescribe under Sched. 1, para. 1(a). *cf.* also *Lord Advocate v. Hepburn*, 1990 S.L.T. 530.

obligation to make payment to the Revenue of the amounts which he was required to deduct under the PAYE scheme.[66] This is true also of payment of VAT: the tax stated on the tax return is a payment which is due and recoverable as a debt due to the Crown.[67]

The important point to note is that the reason such matters do not prescribe under section 6 is not because of any special treatment of the Crown (which is of course bound by the Act)[68] but because they are not obligations of the sort set out in Schedule 1.

There is a risk of labouring the point but it remains important to insist upon it: what matters for the question whether an obligation is subject to the five-year prescription is purely whether it can be accommodated within Schedule 1. For that reason, obligations arising under statutes or (for example) under European Union legislation are as susceptible of prescribing in this way as are those that derive from private agreements.

Fiduciary obligations

This subject has been discussed more fully in connection with Sched- **6.37** ule 3.[69] Here it is sufficient to say that it appears that debtor–creditor claims arising from trusts or fiduciary relationships are prescriptible. But it is not clear that they can prescribe under section 6, as they do not clearly arise from breach of contract or from unjustified enrichment; nor are they necessarily directed at reparation.

Cases excluded by Schedule 1, paragraph 2

The cases which are expressly excluded from the operation of the five- **6.38** year prescription are listed in paragraph 2 of Schedule 1. These obligations will prescribe under the 20-year prescription of section 7.

(a) obligation to recognise or obtemper a decree of court, arbitration award or order of a tribunal or authority exercising jurisdiction under any enactment

This provision is difficult to understand. It seems likely that what it is **6.39** intended to do is exclude decrees from the five-year prescription. They would accordingly prescribe in 20 years. The effect would be that after 20 years no charge or diligence could be done on the prescribed decree.

Four main points may be made. First, the provision is limited in terms **6.40** to court decrees, decrees arbitral, and orders of statutory tribunals. The decrees of tribunals whose jurisdiction is purely consensual would therefore not fall within this provision. The decrees of foreign courts, once registered or followed by decree conform, would presumably fall within the scope of this provision.

Second, the words "recognise or obtemper" are unclear. Although to **6.41** "obtemper" a decree is presumably to do what it says (pay, make specific implement of an obligation), to "recognise" a decree is much less clear. It seems likely that it is supposed to cover compliance with a decree

---

[66] Income and Corporation Taxes Act 1988, s. 203 and regulations made thereunder.
[67] Value Added Tax Act 1994, ss. 1(2) and 25(1) and Sched. 11, para. 5(1).
[68] s. 24.
[69] Above, paras 3.24–25, 37.

which does not consist in doing a positive act; an example would be not infringing an interdict. But the language is excessively vague.

6.42   Third, a significant effect of this provision is that, regardless whether an obligation was itself subject to five-year prescription, it ceases to be so once a decree has been pronounced. For instance, a decree of declarator of a contractual right would mean that the right subsisted and was enforceable for 20 years, although it would as a contractual right have been subject to the five-year prescription. Other jurisdictions have rules to this effect.[70]

6.43   Fourth, this last point raises a much more difficult question, which is what the effect is on an obligation of raising an action, whether it is pursued as far as final decree or not. In Roman law, to which some reference is made in the older Scottish authorities, joinder of issue or *litis contestatio* substituted for the obligation on which the action was founded an obligation to satisfy the eventual judgment debt (if any). So, by raising an action for payment in terms of a contract, the pursuer brought about the novation of the contractual obligation and its replacement by an obligation on the part of the defender to satisfy the terms of the judgment in the action.

6.44   The effect of *litis contestatio* in Scots law is much less clear, and the textbooks have consistently avoided dealing with the matter in any depth.

(1) It is clear that the lodging of defences, which in Scotland is generally said to be the moment of *litis contestatio*,[71] cannot have the effect of novating the original obligation. The main reason for this is that it still remains possible for the pursuer to abandon the action and, subject to prescription, it remains open to him to raise a new action founding on the same obligation. If a relevant claim transformed the original obligation into an obligation to satisfy the judgment, then a pursuer who abandoned and later raised a fresh action would be suing on a non-existent obligation. But this is not the law.

(2) It is clear too that the raising of an action based on the same obligation is impossible once the matter in the first action is *res judicata*. Therefore once a decree *in foro* has been pronounced, the pursuer will be unable to raise another action based on the original obligation, unless the decree was of dismissal, in which case he is free to proceed again.[72]

(3) From this it seems to follow that there is no effect on the original obligation until a decree has been pronounced *in foro*. To state a conclusion positively is more difficult. But the fact that, when a decree has been pronounced *in foro*, a pursuer can no longer found on the same obligation may suggest that the decree itself takes the place of the original obligation. Once there is a decree,

---

[70] Germany: BGB, Art. 218 I; Switzerland: OR 137 II.

[71] Mackay, *Manual of Practice*, p. 228; Maclaren, *Court of Session Practice*, p. 403; Maxwell, *The Practice of the Court of Session*, p. 186; *Argyllshire Weavers Ltd v. A. Macaulay (Tweeds) Ltd*, 1962 S.C. 388 at 402.

[72] Or if the decree was in absence, in which case it can become *res judicata* between the parties only on certain conditions, including the expiry of 60 days: RCS, r. 19.1(7).

prescription can run upon it, with the result that the right to execute the judgment prescribes.[73] It will prescribe only after 20 years.

(4) It therefore appears that references ancient and modern to the effect of *litis contestatio* as constituting a *nova causa obligationis*[74] or a quasi-contract to refer the cause to the decision of the judge[75] should be treated with extreme caution.[76] Whatever this means, it cannot in the modern law mean that the original obligation between the parties has been novated and replaced by a quasi-contractual one.[77]

In a recent consultation exercise the Scottish Law Commission raised **6.45** the question whether obligations to satisfy decrees should be made imprescriptible, or whether some provision should be made to extend the prescriptive period applicable to them in the event that the holder of the decree is unable to enforce it, for example owing to the defender's absence abroad.[78] The question has also been raised whether "decree" is to be taken to cover decrees of registration, such as extracts of deeds registered for execution in the Books of Council and Session.[79] In its Report following upon consultation the Scottish Law Commission did not advance these proposals any further, other than to propose a statutory definition of "decree", and no legislation has yet followed on these proposals.[80]

(b) Obligation arising from the issue of a bank note

It is not necessary to say much about this. While policy demands that **6.46** in the normal case creditors should present their bills or notes promptly, such a requirement in the case of banknotes would be not only unnecessary but highly impracticable.

(c) Obligations constituted or evidenced by a probative writ

This exclusion from the five-year prescription, which applied to all **6.47** obligations within this category other than cautionary obligations and obligations listed in paragraph 1(a) of this Schedule, was repealed with effect from August 1, 1995 by the Requirements of Writing (Scotland) Act 1995.[81]

Prior to the 1973 Act, the Scottish Law Commission suggested that all **6.48** obligations constituted by attested writing should be exempt from the

---

[73] *cf.* for South Africa, Loubser, *Extinctive Prescription*, p. 39.

[74] Erskine, IV, i, 70.

[75] Stair, IV, xl, viii–IV, xl, ix; Erskine, IV, i, 69; *Argyllshire Weavers Ltd v. A. Macaulay (Tweeds) Ltd*, above at 402.

[76] See now *Coutts's Tr v. Coutts*, 1998 S.C.L.R. 729; and for earlier doubts on the matter *Dick v. Burgh of Falkirk*, 1976 S.C. (H.L.) 1 at 20–21, *per* Lord Wilberforce, 26–27, *per* Lord Kilbrandon.

[77] It is true that a trustee in sequestration, who could not have raised an action for solatium in respect of the bankrupt's personal injuries, can sist himself as pursuer once an action is raised by the bankrupt. But the reason for this, as explained in *Coutts's Tr. v. Coutts*, above, is simply that until the action is raised there is no asset which can vest in the trustee; once it is raised, there is. See also *Watson v. Thompson*, 1991 S.C. 447.

[78] SLC Memo. no. 74 (1987), para. 6.101.

[79] *ibid.* para. 6.105. Wilson, *Debt* (2nd ed), para. 19.5 uses the term "constructive decree" for these cases.

[80] SLC Report no. 122 (1989) para. 1.19; cl. 11 of the draft Bill.

[81] 1995 Act, s. 14(2) and Sched. 5, s. 15(2). The definition of "probative writ" in Sched. 1, para. 4(b) of the 1973 Act was also repealed by the 1995 Act. For details of the previous regime see Walker, pp. 56 and 57.

five-year prescription, and also pointed out that, while rights relating to land would in most cases be excluded from this prescription owing to their being constituted by attested writs, nonetheless there should be a general exclusion of rights relating to land in order to cover those created in some other way, for example by holograph writing.[82] Essentially this proposal appears to have been enacted.

6.49 Until the 1995 Act came into force there were therefore obligations which were excluded from the five-year prescription on two grounds: the manner in which they were constituted and the fact that they related to land. To these obligations the repeal of paragraph 2(c) of Schedule 1 makes no practical difference. Similarly, obligations to make periodical payments and cautionary obligations were never covered by paragraph 2(c), and so the law relating to them remains unchanged. Furthermore, the law was interpreted by the courts in such a way that obligations (for example) to pay damages for breach of an obligation constituted in a probative writ were not regarded as constituted or evidenced by that writ, and so did not fall within the terms of paragraph 2(c). These obligations too are unaffected by the repeal.[83]

6.50 Other obligations are in principle affected. But section 14(3) of the 1995 Act provides that "nothing in this Act shall (a) apply to any document executed or anything done before the commencement of this Act or (b) affect the operation, in relation to any documents executed before such commencement, of any procedure for establishing the authenticity of such a document". While the exclusion of probative writs from the five-year prescription has now been abolished, it would seem that documents executed before August 1, 1995, the commencement date of the Act, must remain excluded from it: to hold otherwise would be to hold, contrary to the express terms of the Act, that something in the 1995 Act did apply to a document executed before its commencement or did affect the procedure for establishing its authenticity.

6.51 The effect of the repeal of paragraph 2(c) is therefore qualified in two important respects. First, because it does not touch documents executed before August 1, 1995. Secondly, because obligations relating to land—a substantial sub-set of probative writs—remain excluded from five-year prescription.

6.52 There are, however, obligations formerly constituted or evidenced by probative writs which are not obligations relating to land. For such obligations, the enactment of the 1995 Act means that all obligations contained in documents executed after August 1, 1995 now prescribe in five years rather than 20. This applies, for example, to deeds of trust and

---

[82] SLC Memo. no. 9 (1968), para. 47; Report no. 15 (1970), para. 65.
[83] *Hobday v. Kirkpatrick's Trs*, 1985 S.L.T. 197, 199 (breach of trust); *cf. Lord Advocate v. Shipbreaking Industries Ltd*, 1991 S.L.T. 838. In *James Howden & Co. Ltd v. Taylor Woodrow Property Co. Ltd*, Extra Div., July 1, 1998, unreported, the question was raised (but not answered) whether the right to resile from a probative deed might, owing to the terms of Sched. 1, para. 2(c), be extinguished only by the 20-year prescription. Clearly, this could apply only to a deed executed before August 1, 1995. It does seem to be arguable that this might be so if the right was itself constituted within the probative deed; but a right to resile simply (*e.g.*) on grounds of contractual mutuality would not seem to fall within the scope of an obligation "constituted or evidenced by a probative writ".

to certain bonds. It is true that cautionary obligations, even though contained in probative writs, were subject to five-year prescription, the idea being that the liability of cautioners should be cut off within a reasonable number of years.[84] The same was true where a probative writ bound two or more people jointly and severally to pay money to another person, since the Act provided that that obligation was to be regarded as a cautionary obligation.[85] But if the creditor could establish that the obligant in question was in fact a principal debtor rather than a cautioner or that he had not been aware at the time of taking delivery of the writ that the obligant was not the principal debtor, this was not regarded as a cautionary obligation. So, if it was contained in a probative writ, it would not previously have been subject to five-year prescription.[86] With the enactment of the 1995 Act, those cases, formerly excluded from the five-year prescription, now fall within it.[87]

(d) Obligation under a contract of partnership or agency which does not remain or become prestable on or after the termination of the relationship between the parties to the contract

This provision is less clear than it might be: it says only that the **6.53** obligation must arise under a contract of partnership or agency. On a literal reading it would be possible to take the view that this covers not only obligations owed by the parties to that relationship *inter se* but also obligations owed by way of *jus quaesitum tertio* to strangers to the contract. But, given that the provision is concerned only with obligations which are prestable during the currency of the agency or partnership relationship, it seems likely that the purpose of the exclusion is simply to ensure that obligations owed to the parties to such a relationship *inter se* do not prescribe during its currency simply because the relationship has continued for more than five years. (They will, however, unless imprescriptible or relevantly claimed upon or acknowledged, prescribe after 20 years in terms of section 7.) There is no need for any special protection to be given to these obligations once the relationship has terminated, and they are therefore then subject to the ordinary five-year prescription.[88]

Although the wording of the provision leaves something to be desired, **6.54** the intention appears to be to exclude from the five-year prescription not any obligation which is capable of remaining or becoming prestable on termination of the agency or partnership, but any obligation which actually does then remain or become prestable. If this is right, then an obligation (for example) to account in respect of a subsisting partnership could not, simply because it is capable of arising at termination, be said

---

[84] Sched. 1, para. 2(c); SLC Report no. 15 (1970), para. 53; Memo. no. 9 (1968), para. 39. The Act does not provided a definition of "cautionary obligation", and this is not entirely straightforward: the line between cautionary obligations for performance by a debtor and insurance contracts for the same performance may be difficult to draw: Gloag and Henderson, para. 20.7. Nonetheless, in the Outer House a performance bond—that is, a bond undertaken by one person together with insurers to guarantee performance by a third person—has been held to be a cautionary obligation; *Glasgow D.C. v. Excess Insurance Co.*, 1986 S.L.T. 585.

[85] Sched. 1, para. 3(1), repealed by the 1995 Act, as above.

[86] Sched. 1, para. 3(2), repealed by the 1995 Act, as above.

[87] Sched. 1, para. 1(g).

[88] See below on Sched. 2, para. 3 for specialities regarding the date on which prescription commences.

to be subject to the five-year prescription. In short, the essential point is that all such obligations become prescriptible under section 6 once the relationship has ended. It is only during its currency that they do not prescribe.[89]

(e) Obligation in relation to land (including an obligation to recognise a servitude), except as provided in paragraph 1(a)

6.55   Paragraph 1(a) of the Schedule deals only with periodical payments. They are subject to the five-year prescription, but in terms of this provision all other obligations in relation to land are excluded. Accordingly, if prescriptible at all, they will be subject only to the 20-year prescription.

6.56   What is an "obligation in relation to land"? The broadness of the expression causes some difficulty. The present provision gives only two hints. The first is that obligations to recognise servitudes are such obligations. This does not take us very far, since it is not at all clear what it means. Nothing is said about what amounts to recognition or whose recognition is in question. It may be that it is intended to refer to the obligation on the proprietor of the servient tenement to tolerate exercise by the proprietor of the dominant tenement of his servitude right.

6.57   The second hint in the sub-paragraph is that the obligations mentioned in paragraph 1(a) are capable of being obligations in relation to land. Otherwise they need not have been excluded. These are obligations to pay feuduty, ground annuals, rent or other periodical payment under a lease, and periodical payments in respect of occupancy or use of land or under a "land obligation". The example of payment of rent under a lease indicates that it is possible for the obligation to be no more than a personal obligation to make payment and yet still amount to an "obligation in relation to land". Accordingly, certain personal obligations will fall within this category.

6.58   A prime instance of such an obligation is the seller's obligation under missives to deliver a disposition of heritable property to a purchaser.[90] To approach the question for a moment from the point of view of the purchaser's right correlative to the seller's obligation.[91] If the purchaser had a real right in the heritable property (a *jus in re*), it would be imprescriptible[92]; equally, a right to make up title by registering a (delivered) disposition (a *jus ad rem*) would be imprescriptible.[93] Accordingly, in paragraph 2(e) the purchaser's right in relation to land cannot be any higher right in the land than a purely personal right against the seller, which is correlative to the seller's personal obligation. This interpretation accords with the literal meaning of the expression "obligation in relation to land".[94] It has been suggested that the obligation

---

[89] Subject to Sched. 3 and its catalogue of imprescriptible obligations.

[90] *Barratt Scotland Ltd v. Keith*, 1994 S.L.T. 1337; 1994 S.L.T. 1343, IH. *Cf.* also *Wright v. Frame*, Sh.Ct, unreported (1992 G.W.D. 447).

[91] s. 15(2).

[92] Sched. 3(a).

[93] Sched. 3(h); see above, para. 3.54.

[94] Although *Sharp v. Thomson*, 1997 S.C. (H.L.) 66 has introduced great uncertainty about the position of the holder of an unrecorded disposition, it appears not to affect this point, since in any event the right of such a person will be imprescriptible.

undertaken in a letter of obligation to deliver a clear search in the General Register of Sasines may be an obligation in relation to land.[95] This is a more doubtful case, because it is less closely connected with the land than the obligation to deliver a disposition, and because the obligation is undertaken by a person (the seller's agent) who has himself no rights in the land.

If the right to demand a disposition is a right in relation to land, **6.59** conversely, the right to reduce a disposition (or missives) would appear also to be a right in relation to land. In cases where the action of reduction is based on a claim of ownership (for example, because the deed is invalid), since it anyway amounts only to a procedure for asserting a real right of ownership, it would be imprescriptible.[96] But where it is a procedure for obtaining implement of an obligation (based, for example, on unjustified enrichment) it would in principle be subject to the five-year prescription, were it not excluded from it by virtue of being a right correlative to an obligation in relation to land.[97]

The question arises how much further than these cases the category **6.60** extends. In general, obligations relating to the use of land will fall within the category. In particular, real burdens, which confer rights on the proprietor of one interest in land by imposing correlative obligations on the proprietor of another, clearly fall within the category, since it is part of the definition of a real burden that it must "relate to the use or employment of the land or of buildings erected upon it".[98] Obligations arising under warrandice seem clearly to fall within paragraph 2(e); so do obligations not merely to transfer but also to create, vary or extinguish interests in land. But it is not clear that the paragraph would extend to other or collateral obligations undertaken in missives. Equally, it seems unlikely that the expression "obligation in relation to land" extends to every contract to do work on land.[99] If it did, it would exempt from the five-year prescription a large number of cases concerning building on land which are routinely assumed to be subject to it, including all building and construction contracts. That this interpretation might be correct is inconceivable. Accordingly, a test, such as the courts have suggested, to the effect that land must be the main object of the obligation seems likely to be necessary.[1]

Yet to provide an elegant dividing line is difficult. The gardener's **6.61** entitlement to remuneration for work done may seem clearly to be an obligation having services rather than land as its main object.[2] But, although a stronger case, it is not self-evident that the tenant's obligation to pay rent should be said to have land as its main object.[3] Certainly, not

---

[95] Gretton and Reid, *Conveyancing*, p. 145.
[96] Sched. 3(a); see above, para. 3.02.
[97] s. 15(2); *cf.* above on Sched. 1, para. 1(b).
[98] *Earl of Zetland v. Hislop* (1882) 9 R. (H.L.) 40, 43. An obligation to create a real burden would presumably fall within this category too: see, *e.g. Pearson v. Malachi* (1892) 20 R. 167.
[99] *Lord Advocate v. Shipbreaking Industries Ltd*, 1991 S.L.T. 838 at 840 (*obiter*).
[1] *Barratt Scotland v. Keith*, above.
[2] *ibid.*
[3] Although this seems to be implied by the exclusion from para. 2(e) of obligations falling within para. 1(a).

all obligations undertaken by the parties to a lease will be obligations in relation to land, so that the conclusion must be that it is necessary to focus on the particular obligation in question (rather than the contract as a whole) and to ask whether it has land as its main object. Furthermore, an obligation to pay damages for breach of an obligation in relation to land would probably not itself be an obligation in relation to land.[4]

6.62   A question about nuisance also arises: the obligation to pay damages arising out of a nuisance is an "obligation to make reparation" and so would appear to be covered by the five-year prescription.[5] But the question arises whether it is in fact excluded from that prescription by the present sub-paragraph, as being an obligation relating to land. It can probably be said to be an obligation having land as its main object. The pursuer's complaint is that, *qua* landowner, he has been exposed to something which goes beyond what is tolerable.[6] If that were an end of the matter, there would be the curious consequence that, while other obligations to pay damages arising from delict prescribe five years after they become enforceable, such obligations when based on nuisance would prescribe only after 20 years.[7] The rationale of such a distinction is far from plain.

6.63   This conclusion, however, may not be necessary. The obligation to pay damages arising from nuisance may not itself be an obligation in relation to land, even though the obligation to abate the nuisance would probably be such an obligation.[8] The distinction can be justified on the basis that, so far as abatement of the nuisance is concerned, there is no require-ment for the pursuer to prove fault since liability is founded on the pursuer's exposure to something which goes beyond what is tolerable. By contrast the obligation to pay damages for nuisance depends on fault.[9] Even if this interpretation seems forced, it is perhaps more rational than the alternative.

(f) Obligation to satisfy a claim to terce, courtesy, legitim, jus relicti or relictae or prior right of surviving spouse under section 8 of the Succession (Scotland) Act 1964

6.64   These obligations prescribe under the 20–year prescription, as they did prior to the 1973 Act.[10] The references to terce and courtesy will cease to have effect on implementation of the Scottish Law Commission's proposals for abolition of the feudal system.[11]

---

[4] *cf. Lord Advocate v. Shipbreaking Industries Ltd*, above, at 840; also *Hobday v. Kirkpatrick's Trs*, 1985 S.L.T. 197 at 199.
[5] Sched. 1, para. 1(d).
[6] *Watt v. Jamieson*, 1954 S.C. 56.
[7] s. 7.
[8] That obligation itself, not being an obligation to make reparation, would not fall within Sched. 1, para. 1(d).
[9] *RHM Bakeries (Scotland) Ltd v. Strathclyde R.C.*, 1985 S.C. (H.L.) 17; *Logan v. Wang (UK) Ltd*, 1991 S.L.T. 580; *Kennedy v. Glenbelle*, 1996 S.C. 95.
[10] See s. 7 and below, para. 7.06.
[11] SLC Report no. 168 (1999), with draft Bill cl. 70(1) and Sched. 8, Pt I, para. 33(5)(b).

(g)   Obligation to make reparation in respect of personal injuries

(gg)   Obligation to make reparation in respect of defamation

(ggg)   Obligation arising under section 2 of the Consumer Protection Act 1987

(h) Obligation specified in Schedule 3 as imprescriptible

These last four categories of Schedule 1, paragraph 2 are dealt with **6.65** elsewhere in the Act. These obligations are unaffected by the five-year prescription either because they are imprescriptible or because they are subject to different provisions of prescription or limitation. Obligations in relation to personal injuries are subject to a three-year period of limitation[12]; obligations in relation to defamation to a three-year limitation period and to prescription[13]; and obligations under the Consumer Protection Act 1987 to a 10-year prescription and a three-year limitation period.[14]

II.   WHEN PRESCRIPTION BEGINS TO RUN: THE SPECIAL CASES IN SCHEDULE 2

Section 6(1) sets out the basic rule that an obligation to which the **6.66** section applies is extinguished if, subject to certain provisos, it has subsisted for a continuous period of five years "after the appropriate date". Section 6(3) provides that in general the "appropriate date" is the date when an obligation becomes enforceable. When an obligation becomes enforceable has been discussed already.[15] But section 6(3) also sets out a list of exceptions to the general rule: for certain obligations specified in Schedule 2 the appropriate date is the date specified in that Schedule for that kind of obligation.

"SCHEDULE 2

APPROPRIATE DATES FOR CERTAIN OBLIGATIONS FOR PURPOSES OF SECTION 6

1.—(1) This paragraph applies to any obligation, not being part of a banking transaction, to pay money in respect of—

(a) goods supplied on sale or hire, or
(b) services rendered,

in a series of transactions between the same parties (whether under a single contract or under several contracts) and charged on continuing account.

(2) In the foregoing sub-paragraph—

(a) any reference to the supply of goods on sale includes a reference to the supply of goods under a hire-purchase

---

[12] ss. 17 and 18; see below, Chap. 10.
[13] ss. 18A and 7; see below, Chap. 11.
[14] ss. 22A–22D; see below, Chaps 9 and 13.
[15] See above, paras 4.06 *et seq.*

agreement, a credit-sale agreement or a conditional sale agreement as defined (in each case) by section 1 of the Hire Purchase (Scotland) Act 1965; and

(b) any reference to services rendered does not include the work of keeping the account in question.

(3) Where there is a series of transactions between a partnership and another party, the series shall be regarded for the purposes of this paragraph as terminated (without prejudice to any other mode of termination) if the partnership or any partner therein becomes bankrupt; but, subject to that, if the partnership (in the further provisions of this sub-paragraph referred to as "the old partnership") is dissolved and is replaced by a single new partnership having among its partners any person who was a partner in the old partnership, then, for the purposes of this paragraph, the new partnership shall be regarded as if it were identical with the old partnership.

(4) The appropriate date in relation to an obligation to which this paragraph applies is the date on which payment for the goods last supplied, or, as the case may be, the services last rendered, became due.

2.—(1) This paragraph applies to any obligation to repay the whole, or any part of, a sum of money lent to, or deposited with, the debtor under a contract of loan or, as the case may be, deposit.

(2) The appropriate date in relation to an obligation to which this paragraph applies is—

(a) if the contract contains a stipulation which makes provision with respect to the date on or before which repayment of the sum or, as the case may be, the part thereof is to be made, the date on or before which, in terms of that stipulation, the sum or part thereof is to be repaid; and

(b) if the contract contains no such stipulation, but a written demand for repayment of the sum or, as the case may be, the part thereof, is made by or on behalf of the creditor to the debtor, the date when such demand is made or first made.

3.—(1) This paragraph applies to any obligation under a contract of partnership or of agency, being an obligation remaining, or becoming, prestable on or after the termination of the relationship between the parties under the contract.

(2) The appropriate date in relation to an obligation to which this paragraph applies is—

(a) if the contract contains a stipulation which makes provision with respect to the date on or before which performance of the obligation is to be due, the date on or before which, in terms of that stipulation, the obligation is to be performed; and

(b) in any other case the date when the said relationship terminated.

4.—(1) This paragraph applies to any obligation—

(a) to pay an instalment of a sum of money payable by instalments, or

    (b) to execute any instalment of work due to be executed by instalments,

not being an obligation to which any of the foregoing paragraphs applies.

(2) The appropriate date in relation to an obligation to which this paragraph applies is the date on which the last of the instalments is due to be paid or, as the case may be, to be executed."

Schedule 2: the details

1. A series of transactions between the same parties charged on continuing account

The point of this provision[16] is to postpone the starting date for the **6.67** running of prescription beyond the date which would apply to payment for each separate transaction. The starting date becomes that on which payment became due for the last supply of goods or services,[17] provided that they were supplied in a series of transactions and charged on continuing account. This has been said to be intended to cover the case of parties who repeatedly transact with one another but do not bother to render specific accounts for each transaction.[18]

The existence of the series of transactions gives the creditor an **6.68** advantage, in that earlier transactions do not begin to prescribe until the series of transactions has come to an end and payment for the last one has fallen due. Nothing is said in the Act about the date on which the series of transactions terminates or is deemed to terminate, except to provide that this is so where a partnership or any of its partners becomes insolvent.[19] Apart from the case of bankruptcy, if the partnership is succeeded by a partnership at least one of whose partners was a partner in the dissolved firm, the new firm takes the place of the old, and the dissolution of the firm has no effect on prescription.

Since what is required is a "continuing account", it seems likely that **6.69** any substantial change in the manner of keeping the account or of rendering invoices under it would be capable of bringing the continuity to an end and so making the creditor rely on the ordinary rules on commencement of the prescriptive period. Certainly this was so under the earlier law.[20]

But "a continuing account" does not seem to demand that the goods **6.70** or services supplied should be of the same character or value. All that appears to matter is the manner in which they are accounted for. Support for this view is provided by the fact that the work of keeping the account in question is expressly excluded from the definition of "services rendered".[21] If goods or services supplied always had to be of the same character this would be unnecessary.

---

[16] It appears to go back to the triennial prescription under the Prescription Act 1579, c. 21.

[17] para. 1(4).

[18] *H. G. Robertson v. Murray International Metals Ltd*, 1988 S.L.T. 747 at 749; *cf. R. Peter & Co. Ltd v. The Pancake Place Ltd*, 1993 S.L.T. 322 at 324.

[19] para. 1(3).

[20] *Christison v. Knowles* (1901) 3 F. 480.

[21] para. 1(2)(b).

6.71   The exclusion of the work of keeping the account makes it clear too that the creditor cannot postpone the running of prescription until whatever day he chooses to make up the account. Instead prescription runs from the date when payment for the last supply was due (for example, depending on the terms of contract, 30 days after the last supply).

6.72   The paragraph expressly excludes banking transactions (which are dealt with in paragraph 2) and is confined to "goods supplied on sale or hire" and "services rendered".[22] "Services rendered" has been held not to apply to the case of employer and employee, so that an employee who was paid weekly could not rely on this paragraph to claim that earlier weekly payments had not prescribed; instead in the normal way payments prescribed week by week as each became enforceable.[23]

6.73   Clearly, where dealings between debtor and creditor have continued over a period of more than five years, it may be of considerable importance to the creditor to be able to rely on this postponement of the running of prescription. The question arises whether the onus is on the creditor to show that the transactions fall within the terms of Schedule 2. In practice this seems likely to be so, since, where a pursuer is faced with a plea of prescription by a defender, it will be a matter for him to counter the plea by pleading this paragraph and averring facts to support such a plea.

2. Repayment of money lent or deposited with a debtor under a contract of loan or deposit

6.74   Here the Act distinguishes between two cases. First, where the contract fixes a date on or before which repayment of the sum or part of it is to be made, the appropriate date is that date.[24] Second, where the contract makes no such provision, but a written demand for repayment of the sum or part of it is made to the debtor by or on behalf of the creditor, the appropriate date is when the demand is made or first made.[25]

6.75   Little requires to be said about the first case, which will turn on construction of the contract. The second requires more consideration. The demand must be made to "the debtor". In *Royal Bank of Scotland v. Brown*[26] it was held that the word "debtor" must apply to the principal debtor and not to a guarantor of the debt. The main reason for this view was that the word 'debtor' in paragraph 2(1) referred to the original debtor to whom money was lent or with whom it was deposited, and it was thought that "debtor" in paragraph 2(2) ought to have the same meaning. In *Bank of Scotland v. Laverock*,[27] however, a majority of the court took the view that a demand made to the debtor's judicial factor was a demand made to the "debtor". In that case the original debtor had no control over the estate, so there would have been no point in making

---

[22] Further defined in para. 1(2).
[23] *Reid v. Beaton*, 1995 S.C.L.R. 382 (Sh.Ct).
[24] para. 2(2)(a).
[25] para. 2(2)(b).
[26] 1982 S.C. 89 at 98 and 101.
[27] 1991 S.C. 117 at 125–126 and 130–131.

a demand to him, and the only method of making a demand would be by making it to the judicial factor. Certainly it would be curious if, when a judicial factor had been appointed, a loan obligation which contained no set date for repayment became subject only to the 20-year prescription because it was now impossible to trigger the mechanism set out in paragraph 2(2)(b).

These considerations apply equally, for example, to liquidators and to **6.76** trustees in sequestration. Clearly, a claim could also be made to the debtor's executor, since the executor is regarded as being the same legal person as the deceased. It therefore seems reasonable to take it that demand can be made within the terms of the paragraph either to the debtor or to a person who represents the same interest, such as a person charged with managing or winding up his estate, but not to one having a different interest, such as a cautioner.[28]

The paragraph requires the creditor to make a "written demand for **6.77** repayment", and this has been construed narrowly by the courts. In *Bank of Scotland v. Laverock*[29] it was held that a demand involved "a peremptory request or claim". In that case, in response to an advertisement placed by the defender's judicial factor asking for claims against the defender to be notified to him, the bank sent a note of its claim. The Second Division found that the bank's letter was no more than an assertion by the bank of its rights and found it significant that nothing whatsoever was said in the letter about repayment of the sums.[30] It was not a "written demand for repayment" within the meaning of the Schedule; accordingly the prescriptive period had not even started to run against the bank's claim. This is a very narrow reading of the Schedule, since it may be wondered what the bank's purpose in notifying its claim was, if not to have it paid. Clearly it is important to be able to distinguish between a bank statement indicating that an account is overdrawn and a demand for payment. But it may be thought that the present law goes too far in protecting banks against prescription of their claims. On the other hand, the same would presumably apply to loans made to banks, that is, to the accounts of customers with credit balances.

A general difficulty with this provision is that it allows a creditor, by **6.78** refraining from making a demand, to postpone the start of prescription indefinitely and so to rely upon his own inaction. The position is essentially the same in England.[31] This problem is dealt with in some jurisdictions by interpreting the date of demand to be the date when the demand could first be made,[32] or by requiring a demand to be made

---

[28] See above, paras 5.33, 79, 82 for more detailed discussion of these questions in connection with relevant claims and acknowledgments.

[29] 1991 S.C. 117 at 125.

[30] at 125.

[31] Limitation Act 1980, s. 6.

[32] In Switzerland OR, Art. 130 II, and in Germany, BGB, Art. 199, provide that prescription runs from the date the demand can be made. Furthermore, the proposed revisions to the German civil code, the BGB, are to the effect that, in order to prevent the creditor delaying the issue of an invoice so as to affect the running of prescription to his own advantage, where a claim arises only once an invoice has been rendered, prescription should run from the date when the creditor could have rendered the invoice: *Abschlussbericht*, p. 59 and proposed Art. 196 II.

within a reasonable time, prescription then running from that date.[33] In South Africa, on the other hand, the courts require a clear indication that the parties intended a demand to be a condition suspensive of the debt's becoming due; if it is such a condition, prescription runs from the date of demand.[34] Any of these approaches might be worth considering in Scots law. But apart from the question how soon the demand must be made, much turns on the meaning of "demand". It does seem unfortunate and contrary to principle that in *Bank of Scotland v. Laverock* the meaning of "demand" was construed so strictly. The result is to extend the scope of an exception to the normal rule about when prescription begins to run, as well as to amplify the circumstances in which a creditor can postpone the start of prescription and rely on his own inactivity.

3. Obligation between the parties to a contract of partnership or agency becoming prestable on or after the termination of the relationship between the parties under the contract

6.79   The Act provides that the five-year prescription does not run against the obligations of principal and agent or partners *inter se* during the currency of their relationship,[35] but that provision does not affect obligations which arise on or survive termination of the relationship. The present paragraph fixes the date on which prescription is to start running against any obligation surviving or arising after that relationship has been terminated. If the contract provides for a date on or before which performance of the obligation is to be made, that is the appropriate date. In other cases, the date of termination of the relationship is the appropriate date.

6.80   Accordingly, this paragraph is essentially concerned with the partners' (or agent's and principal's) agreement as to dissolution of their relationship: in the event that they have agreed that obligations are to be performed on or before a certain date after termination, that is the operative date for prescription; otherwise the Act deems prescription to run on their obligations from the date of termination.[36]

4. Obligation to pay an instalment of a sum of money payable by instalments or execute any instalment of work due to be executed by instalments

6.81   This paragraph covers the obligation to pay an instalment of a sum payable by instalments and the obligation to execute any instalment of work to be executed by instalments, where such obligations do not fall within any of the previous paragraphs of the Schedule. In such cases the appropriate date is the date on which the last of the instalments is due to be paid or the last instalment of work is to be executed.

6.82   Since the paragraph deals only with cases not dealt with elsewhere in Schedule 2, it is clear that it does not apply (for example) to services rendered on continuing account or loans repaid in instalments.[37]

---

[33] See for discussion of various U.S. jurisdictions (1950) 63 Harvard L.R. 1177 at 1211. What is a reasonable time depends on the nature of the transaction and the intentions of the parties.

[34] Loubser, *Extinctive Prescription*, p. 63.

[35] Sched. 1, para. 2(d); above, para. 6.53.

[36] *cf.* SLC Report no. 15 (1970), para. 73.

[37] paras 1 and 2, respectively.

A question arises about the relationship of this paragraph to the **6.83** provision for periodical payments elsewhere in the Act which states that "any obligation to pay a sum of money due in respect of a particular period . . . by way of an instalment of an annuity" is subject to the five-year prescription.[38] This means that each instalment itself prescribes without there being any effect on the principal obligation to pay the annuity. But, if the present paragraph applied in such a case, then no instalment of the annuity would begin to prescribe until the date on which the last instalment was due for payment.

The answer to the difficulty appears to be that an annuity is not a sum **6.84** of money payable by instalments. It is not a fixed amount of capital which will be fully paid over a terms of years; it is instead a continuing liability to pay a fixed sum, regardless what the total sum paid over the years may be. The same is true of the payment of rent, or of sick pay. Accordingly, this paragraph covers only cases where the total liability is fixed and is gradually discharged.[39] The same should apply to instalments of work. A standing arrangement to do certain work at certain intervals would not fall within the paragraph, since the total liability to do work would not be fixed, but a fixed amount of work to be done gradually would fall within this paragraph.

It seems likely that this paragraph is the embodiment of the Scottish **6.85** Law Commission's recommendation on long-term contracts, including building and engineering contracts: "As regards long-term contracts we suggest that the prescription should run from the date when the last item of the contract becomes due for payment".[40] Nonetheless, it has to be said that so far as execution of work, rather than payment of money, is concerned, the wording leaves something to be desired. While there is certainly no need for each instalment of work to be of the same amount, the phrasing of the paragraph—"the date on which the last of the instalments is due . . . to be executed"—seems to suggest that at least the last instalment is the work of a single day. But to construe this provision so as to apply only where the last instalment takes only a single day to carry out seems to come close to absurdity. Accordingly, it seems best to take it that prescription will run from the due date for completion, regardless of the nature or extent of the last instalment of work.

Furthermore, the provision as enacted makes prescription run not **6.86** from the date when payment for the last instalment is due (as the Scottish Law Commission proposed) but from the date when the last instalment is due to be executed. Accordingly, it seems that the paragraph cannot apply unless there is a fixed date for completion of the contract. In building contracts, there will of course almost always be a fixed date for completion, subject to extensions of time. But it seems possible that other long-term contracts, which have no fixed completion date, will not fall within the paragraph, and therefore prescription will run from the date when the relevant obligation became enforceable.

---

[38] Sched. 1, para 1(a).
[39] *Flynn v. UNUM*, 1996 S.L.T. 1067.
[40] SLC Report (1970), para. 71.

III. POSTPONEMENT OF THE STARTING DATE FOR PRESCRIPTION: SECTION 11(3)

6.87   "**11.**–(3) In relation to a case where on the date referred to in subsection (1) above (or, as the case may be, that subsection as modified by subsection (2) above) the creditor was not aware, and could not with reasonable diligence have been aware that loss, injury or damage caused as aforesaid had occurred, the said subsection (1) shall have effect as if for the reference therein to that date there were substituted a reference to the date when the creditor first became, or could with reasonable diligence have become, so aware."

6.88   Broadly speaking, the point of section 11(3) is to make sure that the creditor in an obligation does not lose his claim owing to the operation of section 6 before he knows of its existence. The injustice of that was pointed out for English law in the *Pirelli* case.[41] Although this subsection remains of potential importance in building cases of the *Pirelli* sort, as discussed above,[42] the fact that such loss is now classified as economic means that it may well be irrecoverable in delict. In any event, section 11(3) remains of great importance in other cases of latent damage, such as that resulting from negligent professional advice by solicitors and accountants.[43]

6.89   Under this provision it is open to a creditor to seek to postpone the appropriate date to that on which he or she first became aware, or could with reasonable diligence have done so, of "loss, injury or damage caused as aforesaid". The subsection says nothing about the burden of proof in such cases, but it has generally been accepted that the onus is on the creditor to contend for a particular later starting date by demonstrating that he was not and could not have been aware of the material facts until that date.[44] The facts on which such a demonstration would have to be based are after all peculiarly within his knowledge.[45] Equally, this accords with the ordinary rules of statutory interpretation: the party relying upon an exception to the general statutory rule must bring himself within it.[46]

6.90   There is nothing in the subsection to suggest that the knowledge of the pursuer's agent, guardian or legal representative should be imputed to him or her. Given the use elsewhere in the Act of expressions such as "by or on behalf of the creditor" and "by or on behalf of the debtor to the creditor or his agent",[47] it seems likely that the knowledge here has to be the personal knowledge of the creditor and not that of his agent.

---

[41] *Pirelli General Cable Works Ltd v. Oscar Faber & Partners Ltd* [1983] 2 A.C. 1 at 19 *per* Lords Fraser and Scarman; the Act in question was the Limitation Act 1939.

[42] Above, paras 4.74 *et seq.*

[43] See, *e.g. Curran v. Docherty*, Lord Osborne, November 11, 1994, unreported on this point (1994 G.W.D. 2321): solicitors' failure to obtain discharge of a standard security; but the pursuer had not known of this until a date within the prescriptive period.

[44] *Kirk Care Housing Association Ltd v. Crerar & Ptrs*, 1996 S.L.T. 150; *Greater Glasgow Health Board v. Baxter, Clark & Paul*, 1990 S.C. 237; *Glasper v. Rodger*, 1996 S.L.T. 44; *Strathclyde R.C. v. W. A. Fairhurst & Ptrs*, 1997 S.L.T. 658; *Peco Arts Inc. v. Hazlitt Gallery Ltd* [1983] 1 W.L.R. 1315.

[45] *cf. Fitzpatrick v. Kenneth Pendreich & Co.*, Lord Clyde, June 19, 1986, unreported.

[46] Walkers, *Evidence*, pp. 68 and 78.

[47] ss. 9(1) and 10(1)(b).

Lack of awareness of what?

Several cases have raised the question exactly what the creditor **6.91** requires not to know in order to bring himself within the subsection. The difficulty is caused by the fact that section 11(3) requires that the creditor should neither, before the date contended for, have been aware "that loss, injury or damage caused as aforesaid had occurred" nor with reasonable diligence have been able to be so aware. The words "caused as aforesaid" plainly point back to section 11(1)—the only reference to causation in section 11—which speaks of "loss, injury or damage caused by an act, neglect or default". But they leave room for argument about what exactly it is that the creditor must not be aware of. In other words, does the time begin to run as soon as he is aware of loss? Or must he also be aware that it was caused by act, neglect or default? The Scottish Law Commission report says only that "the period should run from the date when the damage is, or could reasonably have been, ascertained by the aggrieved party".[48]

In *Dunfermline District Council v. Blyth & Blyth Associates*[49] it was held **6.92** that the creditor has the knowledge referred to by the section, and so the prescriptive period begins to run, when he knows that he has suffered loss in circumstances giving rise to an obligation upon someone to make reparation to him. From that date he has five years to identify the person concerned and bring his claim.[50] This amounts to interpreting section 11(3) to mean that before time begins to run the creditor must be aware both of the loss and that it was caused by an act neglect or default giving rise to an obligation to make reparation.

In *Greater Glasgow Health Board v. Baxter Clark & Paul*[51] the pursuers **6.93** sued their architects for various defects in a hospital designed by them. The pursuers' pleadings indicated that they were aware that they had sustained loss, and that it was attributable to an act neglect or default. But until the starting date for which they contended, they believed the loss was due to a construction fault rather than a design fault. It was held that section 11(3) did not cover this case. In other words it did not require that the debtor in the obligation should be identified before time could begin to run against the creditor's claim. Accordingly, knowledge that a right of action exists is prior to the obligation being deemed to be enforceable, and the reasonable diligence consists in the steps to be taken to discover the cause of the loss sustained, including the identity of the proper defender.[52]

The same line was followed (by the same judge, Lord Clyde) in *Kirk* **6.94** *Care Housing Association Ltd v. Crerar & Partners*,[53] another case concerning building defects. After a preliminary proof the court found

---

[48] SLC Report no. 15 (1970), para. 97; cf. Memo. no. 9 (1968), para. 80. In SLC Memo. no. 74 (1987), paras 2.9 and 4.6, it has since been explained that what the Scottish Law Commission intended was that time should run from when the loss or damage, as opposed to all the facts, became ascertainable by the pursuer.

[49] 1985 S.L.T. 345.

[50] at 345.

[51] 1990 S.C. 237.

[52] at 251–252.

[53] 1996 S.L.T. 150 (reported in note form only). In the full transcript of July 28, 1995 see esp. pp. 24, 25 and 27.

that the pursuers had been aware more than five years before raising the action that they had sustained loss injury or damage and that it had been caused by some wrongfulness. If they were not actually aware of this, in any event it was found that with reasonable diligence they could have been before the critical date. Since these facts were found, it was not necessary to decide whether the defenders' submission—that section 11(3) deals only with lack of awareness of the fact of loss injury or damage having occurred—was correct. The defenders' argument was that awareness went only to questions of fact (not law) so that it was enough that the pursuers knew the loss injury or damage had occurred. There will be more to say about this shortly.

6.95   This line was also approved (*obiter*) by the First Division in *Glasper v. Rodger.*[54] Section 11(3), it was held, is concerned not just with the fact of loss but of its being caused by negligence; the lack of awareness is a lack of awareness that a loss has occurred caused by an act, neglect or default which gives rise to an obligation to make reparation for it.

Conclusions and queries

6.96   It can therefore be seen that the courts in Scotland have adopted a consistent approach to the meaning of section 11(3), in treating it as postponing the start of the prescriptive period until the creditor is aware both that he has sustained loss and that it was caused by act neglect or default.

6.97   But this interpretation has been adopted in the face of cogent argument to the contrary. This is only one of three possible options: (1) to read section 11(3) more favourably to the creditor, as requiring that the creditor also be aware of the identity of the debtor before time begins to run; (2) to read it more favourably to the debtor, as requiring only that the creditor be aware of the fact of loss before time begins to run; or (3) to read it in line with the interpretation set out above, and so far followed by the courts, in effect as a middle way between these courses. A few comments can be offered on each of these options:

(1)   What becomes enforceable on the date of loss is an obligation to make reparation. There is something odd about saying that an obligation is enforceable when the person bound by it is not known. After all, the whole section is directed to establishing the date on which an obligation to make reparation became enforceable, and it is difficult to see how this can be so if the debtor in the obligation is unidentified, given that an obligation is a bond which binds the parties to it.

Although this view may seem liberal, it has to be borne in mind that there is a long stop (the 20-year prescription of section 7) and that the reference to constructive knowledge may well mean that the date the court finds to be relevant under this section is considerably earlier than the date on which the creditor actually identified the debtor in the obligation.[55]

This, for example, is the approach adopted in German law, in which, subject to a long stop of 30 years running from the date of

---

[54] 1996 S.L.T. 44.
[55] Below, paras 6.101 *et seq.*

the delict, a three-year prescriptive period runs from the date when the injured party knows of the loss and the identity of the person liable in damages for it.[56] Similarly, in South Africa the running of prescription is postponed until the debtor has (*inter alia*) "knowledge of the identity of the debtor", but the Act qualifies this "Provided that a creditor shall be deemed to have such knowledge if he could have acquired it by exercising reasonable care".[57] Similarly, the definition of "relevant knowledge" introduced into English law by the Latent Damage Act 1986 provides (in short) that such knowledge must extend to the seriousness of the damage, its attributability to a negligent act or omission, and the identity of the defendant.[58]

In Scotland, however, this approach is not possible on the words of section 11(3).

(2) Non-awareness of facts is an intelligible basis for postponing the start of the prescriptive period, but questions of legal liability are not matters of fact but matters (at least in part) of law. There is, as the defenders argued in *Kirk Care*, something unsatisfactory about saying that the creditor must have knowledge of something which is a matter of law before time can start to run; and it can be strongly argued (as in *Kirk Care*) that the words "caused as aforesaid" need not import an additional element which must be known by the creditor before time begins to run, but might simply refer back to section 11(1) so as to exclude loss injury or damage which is not caused by the act neglect or default relied upon by the creditor.

In South Africa time begins to run as soon as the creditor has knowledge of "the facts from which the debt arises". Here the wording of the statute is commendably clear, and the courts have not extended it beyond questions of fact into the legal implications of facts or the fact that they may support a legal remedy.[59]

It may well be that approach (2) is what the Scottish Law Commission had in mind in speaking of the date "when the damage is, or could reasonably have been, ascertained by the aggrieved party".[60]

(3) This is the approach currently in favour in Scotland, and enough has been said about it already.

Reform?

The Scottish Law Commission has proposed reform in this area of the **6.98** law. In brief, what is proposed is that the "discoverability formula" in the Act should provide that before time starts to run (a) the damage must be material; (b) the pursuer must know the cause of the damage; and (c) the pursuer must know the identity of the defender.[61] This is approach

---

[56] BGB, Art. 852 I. In France, Art. 2270–1 provides that a 10-year prescription runs from the date of manifestation or aggravation of the loss; if, however, the plaintiff can establish that he could not have had knowledge of the loss at that date, the starting date is postponed: *Bulletin des arrêts de la cour de cassation, chambres civiles*, 1991, V, no. 598.
[57] Prescription Act 68 of 1969, s. 12(3); on reasonable care, see *Gericke v. Sack* (1978) 1 S.A. 821 (A).
[58] Limitation Act 1980, s. 14A(6)–(8); see McGee, *Limitation Periods*, pp. 95 *et seq.*
[59] *ibid.*; *cf.* Loubser, *Extinctive Prescription*, p. 104.
[60] SLC Report no. 15 (1970), para. 97.
[61] SLC Memo. no. 74 (1987), paras 4.11–4.26; Report no. 122 (1989), paras 2.17–2.73 and cl. 6(3) of the draft Bill; MacQueen, 1991 S.L.T. (News) 77 and 91 and esp. 99.

(1), outlined above. Support for this view is derived from the fact that the Scottish limitation provisions, the Consumer Protection Act 1987 as applied in the 1973 Act, and the (English) Latent Damage Act 1986 all insist on the pursuer's having knowledge of (b) and (c) before time starts to run. As mentioned already, other jurisdictions have taken this approach.

6.99   If this area of the law is to be reformed, it may be worth considering why postponement of the starting date for prescription is allowed only for actions of damages. A claim in unjustified enrichment may well arise before the pursuer is aware of it, and this is particularly so now that it is clear that there is no bar to seeking recovery of payments made under error of law.[62] It may be that in claims based on unjustified enrichment it would be appropriate to postpone the start of the prescriptive period until the pursuer was aware of the ground for seeking recovery.[63] At present, however, it is possible to disregard periods of time only where the pursuer's reason for delay was legal disability or fraud or error induced by the defender in the obligation.[64]

Constructive knowledge

6.100   As already noted, it will be for the party relying on section 11(3), that is the creditor in the obligation, to bring himself within it. There are two elements to this: (1) he must show that he was not and could not with reasonable diligence have been aware that "loss, injury or damage caused as aforesaid had occurred" on the date on which it did occur; (2) he must establish some later date on which he "first became, or could with reasonable diligence, have become so aware". Obviously, section 11(3) will benefit him only if the date which he does establish is within the five years before the raising of his claim. Equally obviously, if he succeeds in demonstrating (2), then he will *ipso facto* have demonstrated (1).

Reasonable diligence

6.101   "Reasonable diligence" indicates that the creditor is not held to some absolute or extreme criterion in assessing whether he has carried out the necessary inquiries. The views expressed in a leading case on the equivalent English limitation provisions have been cited in Scotland with approval.[65] There the question was whether the purchaser of a valuable work of art ought to have had it authenticated by an expert. The court held that the buyer was not obliged to do so: "reasonable diligence means not the doing of everything possible, not necessarily the using of any means at the plaintiff's disposal, not even necessarily the doing of anything at all; but that it means the doing of that which an ordinarily prudent buyer and possessor of a valuable work of art would do having regard to all the circumstances, including the circumstances of the purchase".[66]

---

[62] *Morgan Guaranty Trust Co. of New York v. Lothian R.C.*, 1995 S.C. 151.
[63] *cf.* for English law, McLean, "Limitation of actions in restitution" (1989) 48 C.L.J. 472–506.
[64] s. 6(4); see next section.
[65] *Peco Arts Inc. v. Hazlitt* [1983] 1 W.L.R. 1315, applied in *Glasper v. Rodger*, 1996 S.L.T. 44; *cf. Greater Glasgow Health Board v. Baxter, Clark & Paul*, 1990 S.C. 237.
[66] at 1323.

Accordingly the creditor will have done enough if he does what an **6.102** ordinary prudent person would do having regard to all the circumstances. It follows that the test as developed by the courts is neither purely subjective nor purely objective. It takes account of the circumstances of the individual creditor, but it assesses the reasonable diligence of the individual by reference to an objective standard, that of the ordinarily prudent person. It is true that this approach to the section is not self-evident on the face of the section. The Scottish Law Commission has proposed that a clearer formulation should be adopted, which avoids any implication that the creditor is under a duty to search for damage even where there may be no reasonable grounds for suspecting it. The proposed rewording of the statutory wording is essentially that of the limitation provisions of the 1973 Act[67]: the relevant date would be the date on which the creditor became, or on which it was first reasonably practicable for him to become, aware of the relevant facts.[68] Since this test may raise questions of fact and degree, it may be necessary to hear evidence before determining the issue.[69]

Since the answer to the question depends on considering all the **6.103** circumstances, the inquiries incumbent on the creditor will vary. In some cases it may be enough simply to aver that a party was unaware that he had suffered loss through fault on the part of the other, and that there were no circumstances which should have led a reasonably diligent person to make inquiries to become aware of loss or of fault. *Glasper v. Rodger* seems to be such a case.[70] There the defender, a solicitor, had failed to take the title to a house in the pursuers' names as (allegedly) instructed but in the name of their son; it was accepted that the actual date of loss injury or damage was the date of recording of the disposition in the General Register of Sasines. The pursuers argued for a later date under section 11(3) as they had not known of the title problem until later. Here the pursuers' lack of awareness related not to causation but to the fact of loss, so the question arose whether the pursuers had any reason to exercise reasonable diligence to discover that a loss had occurred. It was held that there was no general practice of inquiring into the acts of solicitors in conveyancing transactions and no reason to suspect that anything had gone wrong with the purchase.

In other cases the particular circumstances may make it necessary for **6.104** a party to make specific averments about why he made no inquiries. This will certainly be so if the pleadings suggest that a person exercising reasonable diligence would have made inquiries and leave it unclear why the creditor did not.[71] The particular circumstances will also determine

---

[67] ss. 17 and 18; below, paras 10.29 *et seq.*
[68] SLC Memo. no. 74 (1987), paras 4.47 *et seq.*; Report no. 122 (1989), paras 2.56 *et seq.*
[69] *Southside Housing Association Ltd v. David Harvey & Ors*, 1st Div., July 2, 1992, unreported. So, for example, in *Dumfries Labour and Social Club and Institute Ltd v. Sutherland Dickie and Copland*, Lord Abernethy, April 28, 1993, unreported (1993 G.W.D. 1314) after proof it was concluded that there were doubts about how closely the pursuers had checked the building, and they were found to have had constructive knowledge of the defects more than five years before raising the action. *cf.* also *Jones v. Kippen Campbell & Burt*, Lord Johnston, May 10, 1996, unreported (1996 G.W.D. 1290; a brief opinion allowing proof before answer on the s. 11(3) point).
[70] 1996 S.L.T. 44.
[71] *Beveridge & Kellas, WS v. Abercromby*, 1997 S.C.L.R. 399.

whether it is reasonable for a pursuer to rely purely on his advisers to exercise reaonable diligence, or whether he must do so himself.[72]

IV. SUSPENSION OF THE RUNNING OF PRESCRIPTION

6.105 Suspension of the prescriptive period may arise in two ways. By far the more common and more important is suspension in terms of section 6(4) of the 1973 Act, which is discussed immediately below. But for completeness it ought also to be noted that in terms of section 1 of the Limitation (Enemies and War Prisoners) Act 1945, the five-year prescription does not run against a creditor while he is an enemy or detained in enemy territory; and the five-year prescriptive period will in no case expire until 12 months after he ceased to be an enemy or to be detained.

6.106   It is convenient to repeat the text of the relevant subsections, section 6(4) and (5), here:

> "(4) In the computation of a prescriptive period in relation to any obligation for the purposes of this section—
>
> > (a) any period during which by reason of—
> >
> > > (i) fraud on the part of the debtor or any person acting on his behalf, or
> > > (ii) error induced by words or conduct of the debtor or any person acting on his behalf,
> >
> > > the creditor was induced to refrain from making a relevant claim in relation to the obligation, and
> >
> > (b) any period during which the original creditor (while he is the creditor) was under legal disability,
> >
> > > shall not be reckoned as, or as part of, the prescriptive period:
>
> Provided that any period such as is mentioned in paragraph (a) of this subsection shall not include any time occurring after the creditor could with reasonable diligence have discovered the fraud or error, as the case may be, referred to in that paragraph.
> (5) Any period such as is mentioned in paragraph (a) or (b) of subsection (4) of this section shall not be regarded as separating the time immediately before it from the time immediately after it."

6.107   Section 6(4) excludes from the reckoning of the prescriptive period periods during which the creditor in the obligation was under legal disability or was induced to refrain from making a relevant claim by fraud or error induced by or on behalf of the creditor. The effect of section 6(5) is that the running of prescription is suspended for the period while the creditor is affected in terms of section 6(4).

Burden of proof
6.108   In this context it must be for the creditor (the pursuer, or in a counterclaim the defender) to demonstrate why prescription should not run against the obligation during a certain period.[73] It will be incumbent

---

[72] *Dumfries Labour and Social Club and Institute Ltd*, above, at 40.
[73] See below, para. 20.18.

upon the creditor to make specific averments to support a case under section 6(4),[74] and ultimately to prove the whole extent of the period during which he was induced to refrain from claiming.[75] That follows from the fact that it is for him to establish that "any period" during which he was affected by error or fraud "shall not be reckoned as, or as part of, the prescriptive period". To establish this about "any period" he will have to establish its beginning and end.

If he relies on fraud or error, the creditor must also prove that during **6.109** that period he was induced to refrain from raising his claim. But it is not necessary for the creditor to aver (for example) that he had every intention of raising a claim until deterred, by fraud or error induced by the debtor, from doing so. If that were so, it would leave the creditor without a remedy in cases where, because the fraud or error had left him entirely unaware that he might have a claim, he had never so much as considered claiming.[76] Accordingly, all that the creditor need aver is the fraud or error and the basis on which it has induced him to refrain from making a claim. There is no need to say anything about his intention had he not been the victim of fraud or error.

In turn, with respect to the proviso to section 6(4)—that prescription **6.110** will not be suspended for any period after the creditor could with reasonable diligence have discovered the fraud or error—on normal principles of statutory construction the onus would be upon the debtor.[77] This seems right, since it is a qualification placed on the effect either of the debtor's own fraud or of error induced by him. It seems appropriate to suppose that the debtor will have to aver how and when the creditor could with reasonable diligence have discovered the fraud or error. If the debtor is able to establish the proviso, the end of the period will be the date on which it is proved that the creditor could with reasonable diligence have discovered the fraud or error. Although in practice this seems less likely to occur, the same principles ought to apply to establishing the date on which the period began: so, for example, the debtor might seek to show that the creditor's error could not have occurred before a certain date.

It may not be possible to determine these questions without proof; so **6.111** sometimes a preliminary proof on the matters raised in section 6(4) may be appropriate.[78]

Fraud and error

Fraud and error are relevant to suspend the running of prescription **6.112** only if they induce the creditor to refrain from making a relevant claim in relation to the obligation. That is a substantial restriction: so, for example, the creditor's error is relevant only if it was both induced by words or conduct of the debtor and induced the specific result of his refraining from making a claim in relation to the particular obligation.

---

[74] *Arif v. Levy & McRae*, Lord Coulsfield, December 17, 1991, unreported.
[75] *BP Exploration Operating Co. Ltd v. Chevron Shipping Co.*, Lord Dawson, January 26, 1999, unreported.
[76] *Thorn EMI Ltd v. Taylor Woodrow Industrial Estates Ltd*, Lord Murray, October 29, 1982, unreported.
[77] *ibid.*
[78] *Robertson v. Watt & Co.*, 2nd Div., July 4, 1995, unreported.

Timing

6.113   To be relevant, fraud or error need not occur before the prescriptive period begins to run. This is because the effect of section 6(5) is that any period within the prescriptive period during which the applicability of section 6(4) is proved is disregarded in calculating the total prescriptive period.[79]

6.114   The fraud or error must, however, occur before the claim is made, since it must induce the pursuer to refrain from making a claim, rather than—for example—refrain from pursuing the claim to final disposal. It follows that this subsection provides no remedy directly for the case that, owing to fraud or error induced by the defender, the pursuer abandons a claim which he has already raised. On the other hand, if the pursuer, disabused of the error or fraud, wished to raise a subsequent action, it would presumably be open to him to plead section 6(4) and seek to have disregarded for the purposes of computing the prescriptive period the period from abandonment until he discovered the error or fraud.

By whom must the fraud or error be induced?

6.115   The fraud or error must be induced by "the debtor or any person acting on his behalf". This is a broad expression, which appears to be capable of extending beyond duly appointed agents or other representatives. In England it has been held—on different statutory wording—that a property developer can be affected by the fraud of an independent building contractor employed by him; so in that case fraud or breach of contract by the builder prevented the limitation period running against a claim against the property developer himself.[80] It is at least arguable that, given the broad wording of section 6(4), the same result might be reached in Scotland.

Fraud

6.116   Fraud is not defined, so the ordinary meaning falls to be applied. Some of the modern textbook writers[81] take the view that the proper definition of fraud is essentially that of *Derry v. Peek*, namely that "fraud is proved when it is shown that a false representation has been made (1) knowingly, or (2) without belief in its truth, or (3) recklessly, careless whether it be true or false".[82] But it has been strongly argued that in Scots law "fraud" extends further than this[83]; that a better working definition is that of Erskine—"fraud is a machination or contrivance to deceive"—[84] and that this extends to representations, concealment, and other unfair acts.[85] This would accord with the broad interpretation of "fraud" applied for the purposes of the equivalent English legislation. There it is clear that no deceit is necessary, and that what matters is that, having regard to the relationship between the parties, the defendant's conduct is unconscionable, or such that it is inequitable for him to avail himself of the lapse of time.[86]

---

[79] *cf.* in England, *Sheldon v. R. H. M. Outhwaite (Underwriting Agencies) Ltd* [1996] A.C. 102.
[80] *Archer v. Moss* [1971] 1 All E.R. 747, CA.
[81] Gloag, *Contract*, p. 478; Walker, *Contract* (3rd ed), para. 14.85.
[82] *Derry v. Peek* (1887) 14 App. Cas. 337 at 374, *per* Lord Herschell.
[83] McBryde, *Contract*, paras 10.04 *et seq.*
[84] Erskine, III, i, 16.
[85] McBryde, *Contract*, paras 10.25 *et seq.*, 28 *et seq.*, and 53 *et seq.*
[86] Limitation Act 1980, s. 32; *Clark v. Woor* [1965] 1 W.L.R. 650; *Archer v. Moss*, above.

Much the same issues will arise for each type of fraudulent act, **6.117** whether representation, concealment or other unfair act. "Concealment" here can mean mere silence, but this can be relevant only where there is a duty of disclosure.[87] In *Fisher & Donaldson Ltd v. Steven*[88] it was held that there is fraud for the purposes of section 6(4) if a wrong has been committed knowingly or recklessly in circumstances in which it is unlikely that the sufferer from the wrong will find out about it for a considerable time. This is a concept of fraud which is very wide, and slightly curious inasmuch as it appears to make the ease with which the wrong can be discovered central to the question whether there actually is fraud.

It does, however, emphasise the fact that the courts are here faced **6.118** with a choice: to apply the ordinary meaning of fraud may make it difficult for a pursuer to succeed, since deliberate or even reckless deception will often be hard to prove. But the courts might take the view that in determining whether there has been fraud such as so suspend the running of prescription a broader approach is admissible, perhaps along the English lines that it is inequitable for the defender to avail herself of the lapse of time. In the absence of much Scottish authority on the point, it is not possible to be more definitive here.

An obvious instance of fraud is the concealment by builders of defects **6.119** in their work. The work is covered up and the defects become undiscoverable.[89] For this conduct to be "fraudulent" for the purposes of section 6(4), it must be either deliberate or perhaps reckless. It is unlikely that concealment of a defect owing to a careless or negligent failure to appreciate its significance would have any effect on suspending the prescriptive period.

It may be appropriate to interpret "fraud" as extending to recklessness **6.120** too. Take the case where representations are made which are entirely untrue. If proof of "fraud" requires the pursuer to prove that the defender had the specific intention of making false representations, this is a serious practical restraint on the scope of the section. But if proof of recklessness suffices, it becomes legitimate to approach the matter more broadly, drawing inferences from the defender's conduct in the circumstances. This will matter particularly where the fraud relied upon by the pursuer is fraud on the part of a person acting on behalf of the defender: the defender will not be able to defeat the section simply by turning a blind eye to the wrongful act.[90]

Standard of proof

Although fraud is a criminal offence, the normal rule is that in civil **6.121** proceedings it will be proved on a balance of probabilities.[91] There must, however, be a colourable basis for pleading it.

Error

It has already been noted that error will be relevant only where **6.122** induced by or on behalf of the debtor in the obligation.

---

[87] McBryde, *Contract*, paras 10.28 *et seq.*
[88] 1988 S.C.L.R. 337.
[89] See *Archer v. Moss*, above; *King v. Victor Parsons & Co.* [1973] 1 W.L.R. 29.
[90] *cf. King v. Victor Parsons & Co.*, above.
[91] *Fisher & Donaldson v. Steven*, 1988 S.C.L.R. 337; Walkers, *Evidence*, p. 80; Macphail, *Evidence*, paras 22.33–22.34.

6.123   There does not seem to be any reason why error should not extend both to error of fact and error of law. But since, to be relevant for these purposes, error has to be induced by the debtor in the obligation, an error of law could only be as to some feature of the particular transaction between the parties. General error of law would therefore not be relevant. This is a satisfactory conclusion. It may be noted that one alarming consequence of the recent abolition in England of the rule against recovery of payments made under mistake of law is that, since the limitation period does not begin to run until a plaintiff has discovered the mistake, a plaintiff can by pleading error of law open up transactions lying in the remote past.[92] In Scotland the wording of section 6(4) obviates this danger.

6.124   In one case, where the facts were within the defender's rather than the pursuer's knowledge, the defender adopted a new defence introducing facts which led the pursuer to amend and to advance an additional case based on breach of contract and on delict. The defender argued that that new case had prescribed. It was held that the new case was based on the same obligation, so the remarks on section 6(4) were *obiter dicta*, but the pursuer was held to be entitled to rely on that subsection: she was in error as to what had happened, her error was induced by the defender, and, had she refrained from making a relevant claim, that would have been why.[93]

6.125   Most of the cases in which section 6(4) has been pleaded have been professional negligence claims raised against solicitors for advising their client in such a way that he or she was in error about the proper defender to sue or about the possibility of claiming against an additional defender. For example, a pursuer pled that she was led to believe by the defenders, her solicitors, that she had a claim against two persons only and nobody else; she became aware of her claim against them only after seeing an opinion by counsel.[94] Her claim was therefore that prescription should run only from the date she received counsel's opinion.

6.126   In another case the pursuer pled that he had been induced by the advice of his solicitors not to pursue insurance brokers, so the prescriptive period should run only from the date when the old solicitors withdrew from acting and he obtained advice from new solicitors.[95] There were no specific averments supporting a case under section 6(4), so the matter was not considered very fully by the court. It was, however, pointed out that it was doubtful whether the remedy in this sort of case should be sought in section 6(4), and that the appropriate remedy might be found in the "discoverability" provisions of section 11(3). That point requires further attention.

Error and lack of awareness

6.127   Section 6(4) suspends the running of prescription (*inter alia*) where the pursuer is labouring under error which has induced him not to claim. Section 11(3), on the other hand, postpones the start of the prescriptive

---

[92] Limitation Act 1980, s. 32; *Kleinwort Benson Ltd v. Lincoln C.C.* [1998] 4 All E.R. 513 at 543–544. The reason is that, on the so-called declaratory theory of law, the law declared by the court is retrospectively applicable at the date of the events in question so that, even if there was at the time of payment a settled understanding of the law, it is still possible years later, when the courts declare that the law is in fact something else, to say that the payment was made under a mistake.

[93] *Safdar v. Devlin*, 1995 S.L.T. 530.

[94] *Robertson v. Watt & Co.*, 2nd Div., July 4, 1995, unreported.

[95] *Arif v. Levy & McRae*, Lord Coulsfield, December 17, 1991, unreported.

period where the pursuer is unaware of loss injury or damage caused by an act neglect or default. Clearly, there is a potential overlap here, since lack of awareness of a claim and error inducing the pursuer not to claim may often be much the same thing. There does not seem to be any reason why a pursuer should not rely on whichever of these sections is more advantageous to him: often it will be difficult to show how error was induced by the defender or someone acting on her behalf: in such cases section 11(3) will be preferable. On the other hand, if on the facts it is hopeless for the pursuer to claim that he did not know about the loss more than five years before raising an action, then section 6(4) will be his only resort.

One case in which section 11(3) may be the only way forward is where **6.128** what has induced the pursuer to refrain from making a relevant claim is a negligent omission by the defender.[96] Since the only error which is covered by section 6(4) is error induced by "words or conduct", it is not clear that the running of prescription would be suspended by an omission rather than a positive act; certainly, this would not be an ordinary construction of the word "conduct". For this reason, and owing to the relief available under section 11(3), it seems better to assume that omissions inducing error will not suspend the running of prescription but will be capable of supporting an argument for postponement of its starting date.

Reasonable diligence

What the creditor could have discovered with reasonable diligence **6.129** should, as with section 11(3), be tested by what an ordinary prudent person would do having regard to all the circumstances.[97]

Legal disability

"Legal disability" is defined in section 15(1) as meaning "legal **6.130** disability by reason of nonage or unsoundness of mind".

So far as age is concerned, the Age of Legal Capacity (Scotland) Act **6.131** 1991 provides that references in statutes to legal disability and to "incapacity by reason of nonage" arc to be construed as references to a person under 16 years.[98]

"Unsoundness of mind" is not defined. This is in striking contrast to **6.132** the elaborate definition given in the English legislation.[99] "Unsoundness of mind" would no doubt cover the cases in which a tutor-dative or guardian under the Mental Health (Scotland) Act 1984 might be appointed to a person. In the first of these cases the necessary degree of unsoundness of mind is not clear, although it has been suggested that it

---

[96] *e.g.* where the negligent failure of solicitors to notify the appointed executor of the existence or contents of the will prevented him from raising any proceedings until he was eventually informed of those facts: *Hawkins v. Clayton* (1988) 164 C.L.R. 539 at 590, *per* Deane J.

[97] Above, paras 6.101–104; *Peco Arts Inc. v. Hazlitt* [1983] 1 W.L.R. 1315 at 1323.

[98] s. 1(2); there are transitional provisions in s. 8 which apply to those aged between 16 and 18 immediately before the commencement of the Act; their effect, however, is that the five-year prescription terminates 20 years after commencement of the Act, namely on July 25, 1996.

[99] Limitation Act 1980, s. 38(3); see McGee, *Limitation Periods*, pp. 315 *et seq.*

would turn on whether the person has a level of understanding to take decisions about his life in relation to the powers which are sought for the tutor.[1] The 1984 Act, on the other hand, does define "mental disorder".[2] But it remains unclear how much broader the category of "unsoundness of mind" may be. The courts therefore have some flexibility in the application of this provision.

6.133   These grounds for suspending prescription are available only to "the original creditor (while he is the creditor)", a formulation which indicates two things. First, that the assignee of an obligation cannot seek to rely on the incapacity of the assignor in order to justify suspending the running of prescription: he is not the original creditor. Secondly, that the incapacity of the original creditor is relevant to justify suspension only while he remains the creditor. On the hypothesis that the original creditor assigned an obligation and subsequently took a reassignation of it, only the period during which he was the creditor would be relevant to the application of section 6(4).

Other reasons for suspending prescription?

6.134   Section 6(4) lists the reasons which Parliament thought to be good ones for suspending the operation of the five-year prescription. If Parliament had so intended, further mitigating circumstances could have been mentioned. The fact that none are mentioned suggests that none are relevant. There is therefore no reason to think that any other disability or equitable excuse for not having claimed will have any effect in suspending prescription. To give but one example: suppose a creditor thought the acknowledgment he had received from the debtor was adequate as a relevant acknowledgment and had therefore not raised an action. He was wrong. This reason too would require to be recognised by the Act as a good one before it was sufficient to prevent prescription running. As was noted in *Greater Glasgow Health Board v. Baxter Clark & Paul*,[3] section 6(4) appears to be designed to cover the situation where personal bar might be pleaded. It would therefore be curious if it was also competent to invoke a plea of bar outwith the statutory provisions.

6.135   Although this means that there will be situations in which it seems harsh or unfair that a creditor's claim should be cut off, that is prescription.

---

[1] *Stair Memorial Encyclopaedia*, Vol. 11, para. 1239.
[2] s. 1(2), with *Stair Memorial Encyclopaedia*, Vol. 11, paras 1240 *et seq.*, Vol. 14, paras 1401–1402.
[3] 1990 S.C. 237.

CHAPTER 7

TWENTY-YEAR PRESCRIPTION

Introduction

While the five-year prescription is a creation of the 1973 Act, what is **7.01**
now the 20-year prescription under section 7 of the Act has a much
better pedigree. It was introduced by two Acts of James III (1469, c. 4
and 1474, c. 9) and regulated further under James VI in 1617, c. 12.
Those Acts, like the civil law and the canon law, provided for a
prescriptive period of 40 years, and that remained the relevant period
until the Conveyancing (Scotland) Act 1924 substituted a period of 20
years in relation to the rights covered by the negative prescription of the
1617 Act. A uniform prescriptive period for all obligations was provided
only by the 1973 Act.

The 1973 Act deals with 20-year prescription in two sections, 7 and 8. **7.02**
Each of those sections provides for a negative prescription of 20 years.
This chapter is in four parts: it deals first with the main points specially
affecting prescription under section 7; then with section 8; next with the
question which rights are affected by which of those sections; and finally
with the question of suspension of the running of prescription.

The 20-year prescriptions of sections 7 and 8 run against the Crown.[1] **7.03**

I. PRESCRIPTION UNDER SECTION 7

"Extinction of obligations by prescriptive periods of twenty years **7.04**
7.—(1) If, after the date when any obligation to which this section
applies has become enforceable, the obligation has subsisted for a
continuous period of twenty years—

(a) without any relevant claim having been made in relation to
the obligation, and
(b) without the subsistence of the obligation having been relevantly acknowledged,

then as from the expiration of that period the obligation shall be
extinguished:
Provided that in its application to an obligation under a bill of
exchange or a promissory note this subsection shall have effect as if
paragraph (b) thereof were omitted.
(2) This section applies to an obligation of any kind (including an
obligation to which section 6 of this Act applies), not being
an obligation to which section 22A of this Act applies or an
obligation specified in Schedule 3 to this Act as an imprescriptible obligation or an obligation to make reparation in respect of

---

[1] s. 24.

167

personal injuries within the meaning of Part II of this Act or in respect of the death of any person as a result of such injuries."

Fundamental points about section 7

7.05   Many of the provisions of section 7 are precisely the same as those made for the five-year prescription of section 6 and have been discussed in earlier general chapters on negative prescription. There is therefore no need to say any more here about the nature of an obligation[2]; the notion of a continuous prescriptive period[3]; or the question of interruption of that period by a relevant claim[4] or relevant acknowledgment.[5]

(1) To which obligations does the 20-year prescription apply? The answer to this is clear: it applies to all obligations unless they are excluded from it. This is in stark contrast to the five-year prescription of section 6, which is applicable only to certain specified obligations. Section 7 applies to all obligations except (a) those which prescribe under the 10-year prescription for product liability cases[6]; (b) obligations to make reparation for personal injuries or death resulting from them[7]; and (c) a list of imprescriptible obligations set out in Schedule 3.[8]

Since all other obligations are subject to section 7 prescription, there is nothing to be gained by making a list of them here.

(2) It follows—and it is expressly stated in section 7(2)—that obligations which prescribe under five-year prescription also prescribe under section 7, unless they are imprescriptible. This matters because the start of the five-year prescription of section 6 can be postponed, and its running can be suspended, in certain circumstances.[9] In some instances the 20-year prescription will therefore extinguish an obligation before the five-year one does.[10]

(3) It also follows that the obligations excepted from the five-year prescription in paragraph 2 of Schedule 1 to the Act prescribe under section 7.

(4) The same statutory definition of "obligation" applies to section 7 as to section 6: where appropriate, the term "obligation" includes the right correlative to the obligation.[11]

(5) Obligations to make reparation are governed (as for the five-year prescription) by section 11: in the ordinary case the obligation becomes enforceable on the date when loss, injury or damage occurred (section 11(1)); and, in the case of continuing act, neglect or default, the appropriate date is the date on which the act, neglect or default ceased (section 11(2)). It should be noted that the Scottish Law Commission has proposed that, for these obligations only, the 20-year prescriptive period should be reduced to 15 years, but this proposal has not been enacted.[12]

---

[2] See above, paras 2.02 *et seq.*
[3] See above, paras 4.93 *et seq.*
[4] See above, paras 5.04 *et seq.*
[5] See above, paras 5.66 *et seq.*
[6] s. 22A; below, para. 9.05.
[7] ss. 17 and 18.
[8] See above, para. 3.01.
[9] ss. 11(3) and 6(4); above, paras 6.105 *et seq.*
[10] For an example see below para. 7.16.
[11] s. 15(2).
[12] SLC Report no. 122 (1989), paras 3.36 *et seq.* and rec. 16. Their reasoning turns essentially on a trend since 1973 towards shorter prescriptive periods: *e.g.* 10 years under the Consumer Protection Act 1987; 15 years in the equivalent English statute, Limitation Act 1980, s. 14B.

As with the five-year prescription, so here, for prescription to commence it is necessary that the loss, injury or damage be material[13]; and where there is more than one wrong it will be necessary to examine the question of causation to determine what loss follows from which wrong, and when the prescriptive period in respect of that obligation begins to run.[14]

The only difference is that the "discoverability" provisions of section 11(3) do not apply to 20-year prescription.[15] Accordingly, in all cases, whether or not the creditor knows or could have known of the loss, injury or damage, prescription begins to run from the date the obligation becomes enforceable.

This points up the fact that the word "enforceable" in this section has to be read in a restricted sense. Under the five-year prescription, given the existence of the "discoverability" provisions, it makes sense to speak of the date when an obligation becomes enforceable: where relevant this can be taken to mean the date when loss, injury or damage of which the creditor had actual or constructive knowledge flowed from the debtor's act, neglect or default. The obligation is clearly enforceable in the sense that the creditor could have raised an action in respect of it. Under the present section, by contrast, "enforceable" cannot be given its usual meaning, since to say that the obligation is "enforceable" when the creditor was quite unaware of its existence is to use the word in an unusual sense. But it is equally clear that this section must be read in this way since (a) the policy of the Act is to cut off stale claims; (b) to allow a period of 20 years from the discovery of the loss would seem absurdly generous; and (c) to read it otherwise would deprive it of any content with respect to section 6, section 7 being consciously designed as a long stop, to cut off claims irrespective of whether the creditor knew or could have known of their existence.

(6) Twenty-year prescription, unlike five-year prescription, does not allow for periods of time to be disregarded during which the creditor was under legal disability or was led to refrain from making a claim by induced error or by fraud.[16] The question whether any common law entitlement survives to have periods of time disregarded is considered below.

Recently the Scottish Law Commission has reviewed the question whether fraud or error inducing a pursuer not to claim should postpone or suspend the prescriptive period, whether a pursuer's legal disability should do so, and whether there should be a judicial discretion to extend the prescriptive period. No change in any of these matters has been recommended in relation to 20-year prescription, since all of them are regarded as having

---

[13] Above, paras 4.24–27. *Pirelli General Cable Works Ltd v. Oscar Faber & Ptrs Ltd* [1983] 2 A.C. 1; *Renfrew Golf Club v. Ravenstone Securities Ltd*, 1984 S.C. 22; *Ketteman v. Hansel Properties Ltd* [1987] 1 A.C. 189; *London Borough of Bromley v. Rush & Tompkins Ltd* (1985) 4 Con. L.R. 44, Q.B.D.

[14] *Dunlop v. McGowans*, 1979 S.C. 22; 1980 S.C. (H.L.) 73; *GA Estates Ltd v. Caviapen Trustees Ltd*, 1993 S.L.T. 1045 at 1051; *Sinclair v. MacDougall Estates*, 1994 S.L.T. 76; *Greater Glasgow Health Board v. Baxter Clark & Paul*, 1990 S.C. 237; *Stevenson v. Pontifex & Wood* (1887) 15 R. 125; *Strathclyde R.C. v. W. A. Fairhurst & Ptrs*, 1997 S.L.T. 658.

[15] s. 11(4).

[16] s. 14(1)(b); contrast for five-year prescription s. 6(4).

the potential to undermine the certainty which it is intended to achieve.[17]

(7) Paragraphs (5) and (6) above point up the fact that section 7 is expressly conceived as a long stop, a prescription which will in all circumstances, without regard to special factors, "discoverability" or equities, extinguish an obligation.

Many other legal systems have arrived at the same solution to problems of prescription: a short prescriptive period which may be extended, mostly on grounds of "discoverability", and a long period which disregards such considerations entirely.[18]

(8) The burden of proof is an important issue for section 7 and is discussed elsewhere.[19]

Obligations which prescribe only under section 7

7.06 The previous chapter discussed the cases to which the five-year prescription applies. This is a list of a few cases to which it does not apply and to which only the 20-year prescription applies. Prescription runs from the date mentioned.

(1) Legal rights prescribe from the date of death of the deceased.

(2) Prescriptible claims relating to trusts (for example an obligation to make reparation or restitution arising from a negligent breach of trust) will prescribe from the date of the negligent act. But this must be subject to the rider that, where the claimant's right vested only after the negligent act, prescription runs from that date. Prior to it, it cannot be said that the obligation was enforceable.

(3) Creditors' claims against executors are exigible, and therefore prescribe, from a date six months after the death of the deceased.[20]

(4) Claims under warrandice in dispositions. For those that depend on eviction (for example, warranty of absolutely good title) the date of eviction will be the date on which the obligation becomes enforceable, and this is therefore the date on which prescription begins to run.[21] For those which do not require eviction (for example, warranties that there are no subordinate real rights and no unusual real conditions) the starting date for prescription will be the date of delivery of the disposition.[22]

(5) Until the Prescription and Limitation (Scotland) Act 1984 came into force on September 26, 1984, obligations to make reparation for personal injuries prescribed under section 7. The same was true under the Act 1617. Accordingly, if the pursuer sustained injury more than 20 years before September 26, 1984, his right to seek reparation would have been extinguished by 20-year pre-scription.[23] Now obligations to make reparation for personal

---

[17] SLC Report no. 122 (1989), paras 3.17, 4.8, 4.30 and recs 14, 18 and 22.

[18] England: Limitation Act 1980, ss. 14A(4) and 14B(1): six years from accrual of cause of action or three years from discoverability (if later); 15 years long stop from date of act or omission; Germany: BGB, Art. 852 I: three years from discovery; 30 years long stop; Switzerland: OR 60: one year from date of knowledge; 10 years long stop from date of wrong.

[19] See above, para. 20.14.

[20] *Taylor & Ferguson Ltd v. Glass's Trs*, 1912 S.C. 165; Gloag and Henderson, para. 45.7.

[21] *cf.* in France *Code Civil*, Art. 2257 al. 2.

[22] Reid, *Property*, paras 707 and 714.

[23] For these purposes the pursuer's knowledge of his injury was not material; *cf. Paterson v. George Wimpey & Co. Ltd*, 1999 S.L.T. 577.

injuries do not prescribe but are only subject to a three-year limitation period.[24]

II. PRESCRIPTION UNDER SECTION 8

"Extinction of other rights relating to property by prescriptive 7.07
periods of twenty years
8.—(1) If, after the date when any right to which this section applies has become exercisable or enforceable, the right has subsisted for a continuous period of twenty years unexercised or unenforced, and without any relevant claim in relation to it having been made, then as from the expiration of that period the right shall be extinguished.
(2) This section applies to any right relating to property, whether heritable or moveable, not being a right specified in Schedule 3 to this Act as an imprescriptible right or falling within section 6 or 7 of this Act as being a right correlative to an obligation to which either of those sections applies."

Six fundamental points about section 8

"(1) *"Property"*. This section applies to "any right relating to prop- 7.08
erty, whether heritable or moveable". While it is not self-evident that "any right relating to property" includes ownership of that property, this seems likely to be so, since the Act (a) excludes from prescription any real right of ownership in land; (b) excludes from prescription the owner's right to recover stolen property from its thief (and certain others).[25] Neither of these exclusions would be necessary unless the right of ownership might in principle fall within the prescription of section 8.

The section says nothing to suggest that incorporeal and corporeal property are to be treated differently. On the face of it, it therefore appears that rights in intellectual property are capable of being extinguished by a 20-year prescription. It seems unlikely, however, that this can be so. The various forms of intellectual property are subject to specific statutory regulation, providing *inter alia* for the periods for which such property rights can subsist.[26] It would be most odd and unsatisfactory if such rights could be extinguished by the 20-year prescription rather than in accordance with the terms of the relevant Act. It therefore appears that, for the purpose of the 1973 Act, the term "property" in section 8 has to be construed to mean "corporeal property". This can be justified as (a) removing an antinomy with the other Acts of Parliament which cannot otherwise be explained satisfactorily[27]; (b) the terms of section 8, speaking of a right

---

[24] ss. 17, 18; below, and Chap. 10.
[25] Sched. 3(a) and (g).
[26] Trade marks: 1994 Act, ss. 42 and 43 (10 years, subject to renewal); patents: Patents Act 1977, ss. 2, 25 and 31(2) (20 years); copyrights: Copyright Designs and Patents Act 1988, ss. 1(2) and 12–15 (mostly 50 years); designs: 1988 Act, ss. 213(1), 216 and 222 (15 years).
[27] *e.g.* on the basis *lex posterior derogat priori*: this would have the odd effect that *e.g.* in the case of patents the general law of prescription applied from 1973 to 1977 (the 1973 Act being later than the Patents Act 1949) but the specific statutory regime on patents applied from the enactment of the 1977 Act. Such an arbitrary result is unacceptable. The difficulty discussed here is avoided in England by the existence of s. 39 of the Limitation Act 1980, whose effect is that the 1980 Act does not apply to any action where an alternative period of limitation is prescribed by any other enactment.

which is "exercisable", do not fit well with certain incorporeal
rights, such as patents. Patents consist essentially in the right to
prevent others making use of the patented product or process. It
therefore appears that the section was drafted without regard to
such rights.[28] This limitation might, however, usefully be clarified.

(2) *Relevant claim.* For the purposes of this section, the Act provides
a different definition of "relevant claim" from the one applicable
to prescription of obligations.[29] The definition for the sections
dealing with prescription of obligations makes reference to a
claim directed at implement or part-implement of an obligation.
It is obvious that that definition is unsuitable for property rights,
which are not "implemented". In this section, by contrast, the
claim is directed either at establishing the right or at contesting
any claim to a right inconsistent with it. This clearly includes (a)
an action of declarator of a right; (b) an action of reduction of a
title or other deed purporting to establish an adverse right; and
(c) an action of delivery.

It does not, however, appear to cover actions for payment. So,
for example, an action for payment of hire will operate as a
relevant claim which interrupts prescription of any claim based on
the personal obligation in contract. But such an action will not
necessarily be a relevant claim so far as the question of title to the
object of the hire is concerned: it does not necessarily raise any
question establishing property rights or challenging any adverse
right. It is of course conceivable that such issues might be raised
in the litigation, for example if the action were defended on the
basis that the object belonged to the defender, although this
would be likely to be the subject of a declaratory conclusion in a
counterclaim.

(3) *Relevant acknowledgment.* This is not mentioned in the section
and accordingly does not amount for its purposes to an interruption of prescription.

(4) This section speaks of a right being "exercisable or enforceable"
and of its prescription if it is "unexercised or unenforced" for the
prescriptive period. Here are two examples of how this works. In
the case of servitudes, the right is exercised by making use (for
example) of the right of way, or enforced by challenging any
obstruction of it. In the case of moveables, while the owner
possesses them the question of prescription can hardly arise, but
when he loses possession his right to recover them arises. It is true
that he cannot in practice exercise or enforce his right to recover
his property until he knows who has got it, but it appears that the
question of "enforceability" has to be read in a restricted sense.[30]
Just as there is no reason to postpone the commencement of the
20-year prescription until the creditor knows of the existence of
the obligation, so here there is no reason to postpone its
commencement until the creditor knows who to sue for delivery.
To allow the owner 20 years to sue after discovering the whereabouts of the object is clearly too generous.[31] Had that been the

---

[28] 1977 Act, s. 25(1).
[29] s. 9(2).
[30] As in the case of s. 7; above para. 7.05.
[31] *cf.* Carey Miller, "Title to art: developments in the USA" (1996) 1 S.L.P.Q. 115 at 123.
Note that in some U.S. jurisdictions time does start to run only when the owner knows
where the goods are.

intention of Parliament, it seems likely either that a "discoverability" provision would have been introduced or that the period of prescription would have been reduced.

(5) *Fraud, error and disability.* These do not suspend the running of time for the purposes of this section.[32]

(6) *Burden of proof.* Much the same considerations arise here as in the 20-year prescription of obligations; the issue is discussed elsewhere.[33] In the context of the present section this question may be important in such cases as the prescription of servitude rights (when did the servitude cease to be exercised?) or nuisance (when did the right to restrain the nuisance arise?).

III. PRESCRIPTION UNDER SECTION 7 OR SECTION 8?

The answer to this question is not always obvious. The reason it matters **7.09** is that the sections are worded differently: in particular, as already mentioned, the definition of "relevant claim" is different for each of the two sections; and there is no provision for "relevant acknowledgment" to interrupt prescription under section 8. There is common ground between the sections to the extent that neither applies to any imprescriptible rights or obligations.[34]

The headings of the two sections give at least some indication of what **7.10** to expect: section 7 is headed "Extinction of obligations by prescriptive periods of twenty years", and section 8 "Extinction of other rights relating to property by prescriptive periods of twenty years". The main concern of section 8 is therefore with property rights, whereas section 7 is concerned with obligations. The primary section is section 7,[35] and it is only where it does not apply that section 8 can.[36]

Since this is so, the first question is therefore: what falls outside the **7.11** scope of section 7? The answer is given in section 7 itself: (i) obligations arising under section 22A; (ii) imprescriptible obligations; (iii) obligations to make reparation in respect of personal injuries or death as a result of such injuries[37]; to which must be added (iv) rights which are not correlative to obligations falling within section 7.[38] It therefore appears that section 8 can apply only (1) where one of those section 7 exceptions is in question (but does not also extend to section 8) or (2) where there is no correlative obligation within section 7 or the context requires that section 7 should not be taken to include a reference to the particular correlative right in question.[39] In concrete terms, this seems to amount to the following instances:

---

[32] s. 14(1)(b).
[33] See below, para. 20.14.
[34] Sched. 3.
[35] s. 8(2).
[36] It may be noted that, since s. 7 itself applies to all obligations covered by s. 6, it would appear that the reference to s. 6 in s. 7(2) is redundant: s. 6 excludes product liability (Sched. 1, para. 2(ggg)); so does s. 7(2); s. 6 excludes personal injuries and deaths resulting from them (Sched. 1, para. 2(g)); so does s. 7(2); s. 6 excludes imprescriptible obligations (Sched. 1, para. 2(h)); so does s. 7(2).
[37] s. 7(2).
[38] s. 15(2).
[39] *ibid.*

(1) *Exceptions.* Section 8 itself excludes the imprescriptible rights of
     Schedule 3. From the obligations not covered by section 7, that
     appears to leave for the operation of section 8 only obligations
     arising under section 22A (*i.e.* under section 2 of the Consumer
     Protection Act 1987) so far as relating to property rights.
(2) *No correlative obligation.* This appears to be the real substance of
     the section. It has been suggested that section 8 might include in
     relation to heritable property, "any personal right against the
     owner relating to the particular heritable property, the right of a
     tenant, occupier or licensee, the right of a party in right of a
     servitude over the land and similar rights, the right of an adjacent
     proprietor to object to a use of land amounting to an actionable
     nuisance. In relation to moveable property it can include any
     personal right against the possessor, such as of a lessor, lender, or
     depositor to recover a thing let, lent or deposited, the right of a
     buyer to have delivery of goods bought, and similar rights, and
     rights in succession".[40]

7.12   This brief account cannot command wholehearted assent. No doubt
these relationships do fall within the broad expression "any right relating
to property".[41] But, so far as they amount to rights correlative to
obligations which fall within section 7, they must be covered by that
section and not by section 8. For example, the right of a licensee is no
more than the correlative of the obligation of the licensor; it has no
content which goes beyond a personal right against the licensor, and for
that reason must be dealt with as a right correlative to an obligation
falling within section 7.

7.13   Since personal rights relating to property will be correlative to
obligations, and therefore fall within section 7, and since real rights of
ownership in land are excluded from the operation of section 8,[42] it
follows that the scope of section 8 in relation to heritage is confined to
real rights less than ownership. Obligations in relation to land, on the
other hand, although excluded from the five-year prescription,[43] would
prescribe under section 7. This category would include such things as the
seller's obligation under missives to deliver a disposition of the subjects
of sale, and the obligations of landlord and tenant under a lease, so far
as they relate to land.[44]

7.14   It may be helpful to make a few further observations about cases
which have the potential to be awkward:

(1) *Leases.* The tenant under a lease has a real right in the subjects of
     lease provided he or she satisfies the terms of the Leases Act
     1449. But, viewed as a property right rather than as a personal
     right against the landlord, this right is not correlative to any
     obligation and can therefore prescribe under section 8 rather than
     section 7. The existence of the real right matters so far as insisting
     on rights in the property against persons other than the landlord
     is concerned.

---

[40] Walker, pp. 84–85.
[41] s. 8(2).
[42] See Sched. 3 (a); above para. 3.02.
[43] Sched. 1, para. 2(e).
[44] *Barratt Scotland Ltd v. Keith*, 1994 S.L.T. 1337 at 1343; *cf.* above, paras 6.55 *et seq.*

(2) *Nuisance.*[45] Here there are two aspects to consider: first, the victim's right to restrain it; secondly, the recoverability of damages. To take the second point first: recoverability of damages for nuisance rests on fault rather than on mere ownership of the property from which the nuisance emanates.[46] The obligation to pay damages is an obligation to make reparation which is covered by the principles set out in section 6 and 7 of the Act.[47] Prescription begins to run against that obligation from the date at which it becomes enforceable.[48]

So far as the question of restraining the nuisance is concerned, the right to restrain the wrong by interdict is independent of any fault on the part of the defender. It has been argued that this right prescribes under section 8.[49] But there is room for argument about that: if the right to restrain the nuisance is the correlative of an obligation in the defender to abate it, then it would fall within section 7 rather than section 8. This view is supported by authority to the effect that a person who commits a nuisance is under a continuing legal obligation to abate it.[50] It is also supported by the consideration that it is difficult to see why a failure on the part of one person to object to or seek abatement of a nuisance should debar his successors in title from objecting or seeking abatement.[51] If section 7 is the correct section, this would explain why it is a personal right to seek abatement which is lost rather than a right which affects successors too.

But the whole issue of prescription of the right to challenge a nuisance is problematic. If, as Lord President Inglis suggests in *Stevenson v. Pontifex and Wood,*[52] a fresh nuisance is committed every day, a fresh period of prescription of the right to restrain it commences on each day. In that event, however, it is hard to see how the prescriptive period will ever come to an end. That result might be thought quite satisfactory, since it is not immediately obvious why the author of a nuisance should after the passage of the prescriptive period become unchallengeable in his nuisance-making activities. Yet there is also authority to the effect that where a pursuer has the right to challenge a nuisance but fails to exercise it, by negative prescription he loses the right to do so.[53] It may therefore be necessary to restrict the scope of Lord President Inglis's remarks—their context was after all not prescription nor even restraining a nuisance but the recoverability of damages— and to say this: once the victim of the nuisance is exposed to harm or inconvenience which goes beyond what is tolerable (the cases often say what is *plus quam tolerabile*) he has a right of action to restrain the nuisance.[54] Prescription then runs on his right to seek abatement of that nuisance. But as soon as any fresh harm is

---

[45] See esp. *Stair Memorial Encyclopaedia*, Vol. 14, paras 2123–2126.
[46] *RHM v. Strathclyde R.C.*, 1985 S.C. (H.L.) 17; *Kennedy v. Glenbelle*, 1996 S.C. 95.
[47] See ss. 6, 7 and 11 and Sched. 1(d); above, paras 4.17 *et seq.*
[48] s. 11. On the question whether such an obligation falls under s. 6 or only under s. 7, see above paras 6.62–63.
[49] *Webster v. Lord Advocate*, 1985 S.C. 173.
[50] *Stevenson v. Pontifex and Wood* (1887) 15 R. 125 at 129, *per* L.P. Inglis.
[51] *cf. Stair Memorial Encyclopaedia*, Vol. 14, para. 2126.
[52] (1887) 15 R. 125.
[53] *Harvie v. Robertson* (1903) 5 F. 338; *Webster v. Lord Advocate*, 1985 S.C. 173 at 182.
[54] *Harvie v. Robertson*, above, at 345; *Watt v. Jamieson*, 1954 S.C. 56.

done, or the nuisance in any way increases, there is a new cause of action.[55] This preserves the pursuer's right of action where he is being exposed to increasing harm, but it protects the author of the nuisance where he is simply continuing an activity which he has begun long since. For example, in *Harvie v. Robertson*, one might say that after 40 years (as the prescriptive period then was) the lime burning should have ceased to go beyond what was tolerable.

If this explanation seems unconvincing, then the solution may perhaps be sought in *mora*. Even if the victim does not actually lose by negative prescription his right to object to the nuisance after it has continued for the prescriptive period, he might be barred by *mora*, taciturnity and acquiescence from exercising it.[56]

(3) *Servitudes*. Real rights in another's property (*jura in re aliena*), such as servitudes, are not imprescriptible.[57] They will prescribe, in the case of positive servitudes, from the date when they ceased to be exercised and, in the case of negative servitudes, from the date when the free exercise of the servitude was obstructed.[58] Equally, they are not properly regarded as rights correlative to any obligation. It is of course true that the right to cross someone's land involves that person in an obligation to allow the right to be exercised, but the legal construction of the right is not as one exercised by one individual against another but as a burden imposed on one property (the servient tenement) whereby its owner must submit to certain uses by, or restrictions of his own use in the interests of, the owner of the dominant tenement.[59] Since there is no correlative obligation owed by some other person, section 8 should apply.

But the Act itself appears to take a different view, since in the section dealing with constitution of positive servitudes by prescription it is provided that "this section is without prejudice to the operation of section 7 of this Act".[60] It has been suggested that the correct approach may be to take section 7 to apply to the extinction of a servitude so far as it relates to the servient tenement, and section 8 so far as it relates to the dominant tenement.[61] But this appears to overlook the fact that a servitude cannot be characterised from the perspective of either tenement as an obligation owed by one person to another.

It seems therefore that section 8 must be the relevant section in each case.[62] Support for this view is gained from the different definitions of "relevant claim" provided by sections 7 and 8 of the Act: section 7 speaks of claims for implement or part-implement of obligations as interrupting prescription, but the notion of implement of a servitude by the proprietor of a servient tenement, who is (mostly) under no obligation to do anything, is not very

---

[55] *cf.* for English law, Clerk and Lindsell, *Torts*, para. 30.21.

[56] *cf.* below, Chap. 19; for English law, *cf.* Clerk and Lindsell, *Torts*, para. 18.113.

[57] Sched. 3 para. (a) deals only with "any real right of ownership in land" and para. (c) with rights which are *merae facultatis*. See above, paras 3.02, 3.07 *et seq.*

[58] *Wilkie v. Scot* (1688) M. 11189; Reid, *Property*, para. 471.

[59] Reid, *op cit.*, paras 439 *et seq.*

[60] s. 3(5); also Sched. 1, para. 2(e) excludes from the five-year prescription of obligations "an obligation to recognize a servitude".

[61] *Stair Memorial Encyclopaedia*, Vol. 16, para. 2122.

[62] Halliday, *Conveyancing*, para. 35.28 and Cusine and Paisley, *Servitudes and Rights of Way*, para. 17.34 also favour extinction under s. 8. *Cf.* below, para. 17.05.

illuminating. By contrast, the definition in section 8(2) makes sense in this context: prescription of the servitude right can be interrupted by a claim "to establish the right or to contest any claim to a right inconsistent therewith". In servitude cases this can be taken to refer respectively to an action seeking to establish the right and one seeking to deny it.[63]

In any event, if a servitude is regarded as an obligation owed by one proprietor to another, and therefore extinguishable under section 7, what was extinguished could only be the obligation so far as those proprietors as individuals (or their universal successors) were concerned. The servitude would remain in force capable of affecting singular successors, such as purchasers of the respective properties. For them to be affected, it would be necessary for the servitude to be extinguished entirely, under section 8.

(4) *Real burdens*. Like servitudes, these are obligations imposed on the owner of a servient tenement for the benefit of the owner of a dominant tenement. Unlike servitudes, they give rise not to rights *in rem* but to rights *in personam* exigible against the proprietor for the time being of the servient tenement. Since they confer rights and impose correlative obligations, they will prescribe under section 7 rather than section 8 of the Act.[64] In a recent discussion paper, the Scottish Law Commission has suggested that real burdens should generally be subject to the five-year prescription,[65] except that a shorter period (two years) might be appropriate for burdens which restrict the use of land, and the 20-year prescription might be appropriate for those which closely resemble servitudes.[66] The question is also raised for discussion whether a "sunset rule" should apply, under which burdens would come to an end on the expiry of a period fixed by statute, subject to the possibility of renewal. It is suggested that this period ought not to be less than 100 years.[67]

(5) *Public rights of way*. These are capable of prescription, in the same way as servitudes. For the reasons given in connection with servitudes, it seems preferable to suppose that they prescribe under section 8 rather than section 7.[68]

(6) *Ownership of, and other rights in relation to, moveables*. The first question which arises here is whether the expression "right relating to property" used in section 8(2) is capable of covering ownership of moveables. (In other words: is a right of property a right relating to property?) There may be room for argument about that. The better view is that ownership of moveables is

---

[63] In civilian terminology, an *actio confessoria* and an *actio negatoria*. The same would seem to apply to the prescription of the right to object to a riparian proprietor's drawing excessive water: this would be lost by negative prescription under s. 8; it could also be argued that the right might by positive prescription become unchallengeable under s. 3 (below, para. 17.10): *Pirie & Sons Ltd v. Earl of Kintore* (1906) 8 F. (H.L.) 17; *J. White & Sons v. J.M. White* (1906) 8 F. (H.L.) 41.

[64] s. 15(2); Reid, *Property*, para. 431.

[65] Currently they are not, since "obligations relating to land" are excluded by Sched. 1, para. 2(e).

[66] SLC Discussion Paper no. 106, *Real Burdens* (1998), paras 5.41–5.47.

[67] paras 5.69–5.82.

[68] See Reid, *op cit.*, paras 472, n. 5 and 510 where, however, the view is taken that s. 7 is the relevant section.

covered by the section. The main support for this view is the consideration that Schedule 3 expressly excludes from the operation of section 8 rights of ownership in land, but makes no such provision for moveables.

As with land, so with moveables, the rights and obligations which arise often have to be seen from two different perspectives. A clear example is provided by the buyer's right to delivery of the thing following a contract of sale. Viewed from the perspective of the law of obligations, the right to delivery is correlative to the obligation of the seller to deliver. That right must fall within section 7 of the Act.[69] But the right can also be viewed from the perspective of the law of property. Under the Sale of Goods Act 1979 property will pass to the buyer when the parties intend it to pass.[70] Suppose, for example, that parties intend property to pass at the time of making the contract: the buyer then has a property right which he can exercise against the defaulting seller or anyone else in possession of the thing.[71] That right is not correlative to any obligation. Accordingly, it falls within section 8. The buyer's property right in the undelivered thing is extinguished 20 years after it could have been exercised or enforced.

The same distinction falls to be made in relation to other contracts having property consequences. The contractual right of a lender or depositor to recover the object of the contract from the borrower or depositee is correlative to the obligation of that party to return it, and that obligation will be extinguished under section 7 of the Act 20 years after it became enforceable.[72] Likewise, in the event of breach of contract, the obligation to make reparation for damages arising from the breach will be extinguished 20 years after it became enforceable. But the lender's or depositor's property right in the object of the contract cannot be extinguished under section 7 and will be extinguished by section 8.

(7) *Spuilzie*, as a possessory rather than proprietary remedy, may fall within section 7, on the basis that what is asserted is a right against a specific person—the dispossessor—rather than one good against the world, and so it correlates to an obligation to which section 7 applies.

(8) *Rectification and reduction.* The rights pursued by these actions may be susceptible of prescription under section 8, but it is important to stress that there are cases where the rights in question will be rights of ownership of land and therefore imprescriptible.

Where a document fails to give effect to the common intention of the parties to an agreement, or to the intention of its granter, application may be made to the court for rectification of the document.[73] It would be difficult to say that one party to a defective document was under any obligation to the other so far

---

[69] And also within s. 6 as an obligation arising in contract: Sched. 1, para. 1(g).

[70] Sale of Goods Act 1979, ss. 17 and 18.

[71] Subject to s. 24 of the Sale of Goods Act, and various other qualifications.

[72] It may be extinguished first under s. 6 and Sched. 1, para. 1(g). See, *e.g.*, *Macdonald v. North of Scotland Bank*, 1942 S.C. 369 at 373 for 20-year prescription applied to a bank deposit.

[73] Law Reform (Miscellaneous Provisions) (Scotland) Act 1985, s. 8.

as rectification is concerned. Prescription under section 7 will not therefore arise. But rectification could be viewed as a procedure whereby a right relating to property is asserted. If that is correct, the right to seek rectification may prescribe under section 8. But since ownership of land is an imprescriptible right,[74] no lapse of time will ever bar a petition for rectification where it is simply a procedure directed at asserting ownership.

The same will apply to actions of reduction: the right to pursue such an action can be lost, but not where it is simply a procedure for asserting ownership of land.

So, for example, it is under section 8 that the right at common law to challenge a fraudulent transaction in bankruptcy will be lost.[75] In such cases the trustee in sequestration raises an action of reduction of the disposition or other document by which the alienation was made. The alienation is voidable at the instance of the trustee. But an action of reduction is simply a procedure whereby the trustee asserts that ownership of the property remains with the bankrupt. It must follow that, where land is concerned, the right to bring such an action will never prescribe. It will, however, be excluded if the transferee completes a period of positive prescription and so acquires an unchallengeable title.

IV. SUSPENSION OF THE PRESCRIPTIVE PERIOD

In sections 7 and 8 there is no provision for disregarding periods during **7.15** which the creditor in the obligation was induced by fraud or error to refrain from advancing a claim, or else was under age or of unsound mind.[76] Under the general rules for computation of prescriptive periods, it is expressly stated that no regard is to be had to legal disability except where otherwise provided.[77] In its 1989 Report the Scottish Law Commission considered whether account should be taken of fraud or error or legal disability in the 20-year prescription and decided against it: the whole point of this prescription was to provide a reasonably ascertainable cut-off point and to protect defenders from stale claims.[78] That object would be prejudiced by relaxing the rules in these respects.

Two points arise. The first is that, owing to this difference between **7.16** sections 6 and 7, it is possible for the long-stop provisions of section 7 to cut off an obligation before it has been extinguished under section 6. This is clear if one takes the simple case of a person who is not of age, who under the Age of Legal Capacity (Scotland) Act 1991 will come of age at 16. If an obligation became enforceable at the instance of such a person at the age of six months, then the five-year prescription would not have finished running for 20 years and six months after that date, since the five-year period has to be added to the period of legal disability. But by then the 20-year prescription, which disregards questions

---

[74] Sched. 3(a).
[75] There are shorter time-limits on the statutory remedies: Bankruptcy (Scotland) Act 1985, ss. 34(3) and 36(1); *cf.* McBryde, *Bankruptcy* (2nd ed.), para. 12.51.
[76] "Legal disability" as defined in s. 15(1).
[77] s. 14(1)(b). The exception is provided in s. 6(4).
[78] SLC Report no. 122 (1989), recs 18 and 22. For the same reason, the suggestions that there should be judicial discretion to extend the prescriptive period was not supported: rec. 14.

of legal disability, would have been completed, so that the obligation would in fact cease to be enforceable after 20 years only.

7.17 Precisely because questions of "discoverability" may decisively affect the length of the prescriptive period under section 6, in some cases it will be appropriate to plead both prescriptions.[79]

7.18 Second, the question arises whether the common law plea that the pursuer was "unable to sue effectively" (*non valens agere cum effectu*) still survives.[80] This question is more interesting and important than it sounds. The 1973 Act does not mention this plea, either to preserve it or to abolish it. It is perhaps worth noting that the Scottish Law Commission prior to the 1973 Act took the view that the plea should be retained.[81] This plea could be advanced in opposition to the plea of long negative prescription under the previous legislation (Act 1617, c. 12). Its effect was to suspend the running of prescription during the period of inability to sue. The plea surfaces here and there in Roman law, is discussed by the Glossators and was formulated in its current terms already by Bartolus.[82] It is discussed by the institutional writers[83]; and Morison's *Dictionary* devotes a whole section to it,[84] in addition to recording various instances of it elsewhere. Broadly, it is fair to say that the reported cases illustrate two aspects to the plea, which are also put forward by Stair. First, the subjective aspect, that the particular pursuer was unable to advance his or her claim for a certain period. Secondly, the objective aspect, that as a matter of law no claim could be advanced, because it would have been premature, based on an obligation which was not yet enforceable.[85]

7.19 So far as the second of these aspects is concerned, it is clear that the plea has now disappeared. The reason for this is plain. The plea was necessary under the old statutes, which either did not say what the starting date for prescription was, or else mostly stated it to be the date of the deed in question. (An exception to this is the case of warrandice, for which the Act 1617 expressly provided that the starting date for prescription should be not the date of the deed containing the warrandice but the date of eviction.) It followed that, under statute, prescription against a bond started to run before the creditor's right under the

---

[79] See, *e.g.*, *Strathclyde R.C. v. W. A. Fairhurst & Ptrs*, 1997 S.L.T. 658.

[80] Yes: Halliday (1974) 19 J.L.S.S. 51; no: Walker, p. 87; perhaps: Gloag and Henderson, para. 15.10, n. 61. For discussion of the previous law, Napier, pp. 435–475 (in connection with positive prescription), 639–645; Millar, p. 102.

[81] SLC Memo. no. 9 (1968), para. 24; Report no. 15 (1970), para. 33. In its report the Scottish Law Commission referred to "considerable divergence of views" but concluded that "no sufficient case has been made out for amendment of the law and that the plea of *non valens agere cum effectu* should remain available as an equitable plea in appropriate circumstances".

[82] For a historical survey, see K. Spiro, "Zur neueren Geschichte des Satzes *agere non valenti non currit praescriptio*" in *Festschrift Hans Lewald* (1953), pp. 585–602; also Spiro, *Die Begrenzung* para. 70.

[83] Stair, II, xii, 27; Erskine, III, vii, 36–III, vii, 37.

[84] M. 11182–11223.

[85] In French law, although no provision of this sort is made in the *Code Civil*, the courts have developed a doctrine according to which the running of prescription is suspended for any period during which the creditor is under an absolute impossibility of bringing an action, whether as a result of any impediment of law, agreement, or *force majeure*: Cour de Cassation, 1ère chambre civile, December 22, 1959, J.C.P. 1960 II 11494.

bond even became enforceable; and that a contractual right, if subject to a suspensive condition, might be extinguished before it ever became enforceable on satisfaction of the condition. In these circumstances, common law adjustment to the terms of the statute, in order to disregard any period before the claim could be brought effectually, plainly made the best possible sense. Under the current legislation, however, the prescriptive period only begins to run on the date on which the obligation in question becomes enforceable. There is therefore no scope for equitable adjustment of the statutory terms.

But what about the "subjective" aspect of the plea? Given the clear **7.20** terms of the Act, making legal disability (as defined) a matter of irrelevance except where otherwise provided, the plea of *non valens* could not be sustained where advanced by a person on the basis of nonage or unsoundness of mind. This fits with the law under earlier statutes. Although Roman law and the writers in the civil law and canon law traditions took a different view,[86] the accepted view in Scots law appears to have been, as stated by Bankton, that time was reckoned as continuous and not according to whether the pursuer was in fact capable at that time of pursuing; and that "unless the years of minority are expressly excepted in statutes introducing prescription, they are not deducted".[87] It is correct therefore to note, as the Scottish Law Commission does, that the circumstances in which the plea is applicable have been much reduced by statute, but also that extraordinary cases may yet occur in which the failure to pursue a claim might be justified by extrinsic factors.[88]

Yet there are other circumstances, which have nothing to do with what **7.21** the 1973 Act means by "legal disability", in which a person may in fact be debarred from pursuing a claim. The question arises whether these ought to be assimilated to legal disability in order to bar the plea, or ought, on the contrary, to be regarded as unaffected by the 1973 Act. The question does not appear to have come before the courts.

Since the Act did not affect this plea, except to the extent just **7.22** described, it ought in principle to survive as a matter of common law.[89]

---

[86] C. 7.39.3.1a (A.D. 424), the constitution introducing the 30-year prescription, expressly excludes the period of pupillarity from the prescriptive period; the same rule is put forward by later writers, *e.g.* Donellus, *Commentarii*, 22.2; Grotius, *Inleiding*, 3.46.4 (among a number of other grounds for exclusion such as absence from the country; other impediments preventing a man from asserting his right); among the canonists, see Lessius, *de iustitia et iure*, 2.6.16 with further references; see also above, paras 1.38 *et seq.* Voet, *Commentarius*, 44.3.11 gives examples: creditors cannot sue the heir, and their rights against him therefore do not prescribe, until the heir has made an inventory of the estate (C. 6.30.22.11 (531)); fideicommissaries cannot sue for recovery of property subject to *fideicommissum* until the condition for their acquiring the property has been purified, and until then their rights do not prescribe (C. 6.43.3.3a (531)); wives, while their marriages subsist, cannot sue their husbands, and so their claims against them for alienation of dotal property arise only on termination of marriage (C. 5.12.30.2 (529)).

[87] Bankton, II, xii, 43. The years of minority were expressly excepted in the Act 1617, c. 12, but the exception was removed by the amendments made in the Conveyancing (Scotland) Acts of 1874 (s. 34) and 1924 (ss. 16 and 17).

[88] SLC Report no. 15 (1970), para. 33.

[89] *cf.* in connection with the Conveyancing (Scotland) Act 1924, s. 17, *Campbell's Trs v. Campbell's Trs*, 1950 S.C. 48 at 57, *per* L.P. Cooper to the effect that one "cannot hold that the whole of our common law and decisions designed to give effect to the expanded equitable plea of *non valens agere cum effectu* was swept away in 1924 by this reference to "any person . . . under a legal disability"".

Indeed, it is arguable that the lack of any reference to it in the 1973 Act is itself implement by Parliament of the Scottish Law Commission's recommendation that the availability of the plea should be unaffected by the new statute. This might be very important. In the civil law tradition there is authority for prescription not running during time of war or plague; in relation to church property when a church is without a rector; when the person against whom prescription is pleaded cannot sue, that is, the person is a minor or pupil or a wife during her marriage.[90] Clearly, as indicated already, the law is now different so far as minors and pupils are concerned; and in the case of wives, emancipation has brought it about that there is no impediment to their suing their husbands during the currency of their marriages.[91] But the status of the other interludes to prescription is less clear.

7.23   At the end of a lengthy discussion of the scope of the plea, Napier concluded that the position when he wrote (1854) was that "any personal restraint, or temporary impediment, which may create difficulties, however great, in the way of pursuit, but which are not expressly intended, nor understood, to deprive the party of his legal rights, will not constitute a plea of *non valens agere*, whatever hardship may be in the case. But if the nature of the impediment be to deny, in law, to the party the very right of pursuit in question, the fact of his not pursuing becomes altogether incapable to infer a presumption of dereliction, and so he may plead *non valens agere*".[92] While this would exclude temporary disabilities, such as imprisonment[93] and voluntary absence from the country, it might not exclude forfeiture, at least where it was illegal.[94] It is not necessary to pursue such questions here. But there are less exotic instances in which it may be said that a party has been denied the opportunity of pursuit of his rights. In those cases it must be arguable that the plea of *non valens agere* should apply.

7.24   Here is one example. Suppose a company has been struck off the Register of Companies, and it later turns out that it had a substantial claim. It is possible to petition for restoration of the company to the Register under section 653 of the Companies Act 1985. But what if the claim has in the meantime prescribed? Is it proper to disregard the period during which the company was unable to sue because it did not exist? The Companies Act does not say. There is authority for incorporating in the order restoring the company to the register an order that the time during which the company was not on the Register should not count against creditors whose claims had not prescribed at the date of striking-off.[95] But there does not appear to be a case in which that

---

[90] Lessius, *op. cit.*, Bk 2, Chap. 6, dub. 16; *cf.* Covarruvias, *op. cit.*, pt. 2 sect. 12; above, para. 1.38.

[91] It may, however, be noted that on grounds of public policy—the unattractiveness of requiring spouses to sue one another in order to keep their claims alive—prescription does not run on claims between spouses while they remain married in German law: BGB, Art. 204 (this applies also to parents and children in minority and to children and their guardians); the same is true in France under *Code Civil*, Arts 2252–2253; *cf.* in South Africa, Prescription Act, No. 68 of 1969, s. 13(c).

[92] Napier, p. 643.

[93] Suspension of prescription under the Limitation (Enemies and War Prisoners) Act 1945 does not apply to the 20-year prescription.

[94] *ibid. cf.* Kames, *Elucidations*, 237, with the example of someone who was a "slave in Algiers many years".

[95] *Re Donald Kenyon Ltd* [1956] 1 W.L.R. 1397; for discussion of the English provisions—Limitation Act 1980, s. 33—see McGee, *Limitation Periods*, pp. 293–294. The equivalent order has been granted in Scottish petition proceedings.

provision has been made in order to preserve the company's own claims. That might be possible, although it is less easy to see why it would be appropriate, in proceedings which concern principally the company itself, to make provisions and pronounce orders which have an adverse effect on the company's debtors, who might no doubt have destroyed receipts or other evidence of value to them. But, even if that is not possible, it would not seem to be unreasonable to raise the plea of *non valens agere* against a defender who pleaded that the company's claim had prescribed. As a matter of law the company had for a period been unable to sue, and its inability went beyond a purely temporary impediment. Presumably, since such a plea would have no basis in the 1973 Act, the common law rules would have to apply. That is, the period of non-existence of the company would be disregarded in calculating the prescriptive period.[96]

This is only one possible example. The point is simply this: there are **7.25** cases of inability to sue which the Act does not expressly require to be disregarded and which go beyond purely temporary impediments to action. If it is right, as our institutional writers suggest, to take the basis for prescription to be acquiescence or abandonment, then as a matter of common law it seems likely that the plea of *non valens agere* still survives,[97] to meet exceptional cases in which the pursuer was unable to sue and therefore cannot be said to have acquiesced in the loss of any right or to have abandoned anything.

---

[96] For that period, prescription would, to use Lessius's term, "sleep". *cf.* Erskine, III, vii, 37; Bell, *Prin.*, s. 627; Hume, *Lectures*, 3.76–3.77.
[97] Above, paras 1.49 *et seq.*

CHAPTER 8

TWO-YEAR PRESCRIPTION

A prescriptive period of two years applies to obligations to make **8.01** contribution between wrongdoers. This prescriptive regime was introduced by the Prescription and Limitation (Scotland) Act 1984, which inserted a new section 8A into the 1973 Act.[1] Prior to that, obligations of this sort were subject to a two-year period of limitation.[2] These obligations also prescribe under the 20-year prescription and may also prescribe under the five-year prescription.[3] The prescription runs against the Crown.[4]

"Extinction of obligations to make contributions between wrongdoers
8A.—(1) If any obligation to make a contribution by virtue of section 3(2) of the Law Reform (Miscellaneous Provisions) (Scotland) Act 1940 in respect of any damages or expenses has subsisted for a continuous period of two years after the date on which the right to recover the contribution became enforceable by the creditor in the obligation—

    (a) without any relevant claim having been made in relation to the obligation; and
    (b) without the subsistence of the obligation having been relevantly acknowledged;
    then as from the expiration of that period the obligation shall be extinguished.

(2) Subsections (4) and (5) of section 6 of this Act shall apply for the purposes of this section as they apply for the purposes of that section."

Obligations affected
The only obligations affected by this prescriptive regime are those **8.02** between wrongdoers to make contribution. Section 3(2) of the 1940 Act provides:

"Where any person has paid any damages or expenses in which he has been found liable in any such action as aforesaid, he shall be entitled to recover from any other person who, if sued, might also have been held liable in respect of the loss or damage on which the action was founded, such contribution, if any, as the court may deem just."

---

[1] s. 1.
[2] Under s. 20 of the 1973 Act, repealed by the 1984 Act.
[3] s. 7; prescription under the five-year prescription would turn on regarding this obligation as one to redress unjustified enrichment: s. 6 and Sched. 1, para. 1(b); see further below, para. 8.10.
[4] s. 24.

The reference to "such action as aforesaid" is a reference to "any action of damages in respect of loss or damage arising from any wrongful acts or negligent acts or omissions".[5] The scope of the section therefore extends beyond delict to breach of contract, at least where it is wrongful or can be said to amount to a negligent act or omission.[6]

8.03   Section 3(2) enables the court to determine the proportions in which two or more parties are liable to the pursuer in an action, and this is not restricted to the case where both or all of those parties are defenders in the action. That fact occasioned some difficulty in the past, since it seemed unfair that the question of the extent of a person's liability might be settled in proceedings to which he was not a party.[7] But the difficulty is now overcome by the use of third-party procedure.

8.04   It is now well established that the words "if sued" in section 3(2) mean "sued to judgment", and therefore refer only to persons in respect of whom there has been a judicial determination of liability.[8] This requires a judicial determination in Scottish proceedings.[9] But the decree need not follow on proceedings which are contested right up to the moment of decree: if (as often happens) the parties agree the terms of a settlement and the court pronounces a decree giving effect to them, this falls within the terms of the section.[10]

8.05   It is now also clear that the relevant time for testing the issue whether a person "if sued" might have been held liable to make contribution is the date at which the person seeking contribution was himself sued in the principal action. The question is whether the person could then have been sued by the pursuer in such an action relevantly, competently and timeously pursued.[11] An important consequence of this is that it makes no difference to the right of the relief between the joint wrongdoers that the pursuer may arrive at some arrangement with one of them or even abandon the action against him. While that necessarily affects the obligation between the pursuer and the particular defender, it is incapable of having any effect on the quite separate obligation between the defenders.[12] For the same reason it makes no difference to the obligation of relief that the pursuer may fail to sue both or all defenders timeously and, owing to time-bar, may therefore be forced to sue only some.[13]

---

[5] 1940 Act, s. 3(1). This includes product liability: Consumer Protection Act 1987, s. 6(1)(b).

[6] *cf. Engdiv Ltd v. G. Percy Trentham Ltd*, 1990 S.C. 53. It seems that, owing to the use of the term "damages", the section may not extend to unjustified enrichment; the decision of the Court of Appeal to the opposite effect in *Friends Provident Life Office v. Hillier Parker May & Rowden* [1997] Q.B. 85 turns on the fact that the English statute, the Civil Liability (Contribution) Act 1978, s. 6(1), speaks, more broadly, of "compensation".

[7] See, *e.g. NCB v. Thomson*, 1959 S.C. 353 at 365.

[8] *Singer v. Gray Tool Co. (Europe) Ltd*, 1984 S.L.T. 149, overruling *Travers v. Neilson*, 1967 S.C. 155; *cf. Widdowson v. Hunter*, 1989 S.L.T. 478. (Walker, p. 88 does not take account of the more recent cases or the overruling of *Travers v. Neilson*.)

[9] *Comex Houlder Diving Ltd v. Colne Fishing Co. Ltd*, 1987 S.C. (H.L.) 85.

[10] *ibid.*

[11] *Dormer v. Melville, Dundas & Whitson*, 1989 S.L.T. 310; 1990 S.L.T. 186; *cf. Taft v. Clyde Marine Motoring Co. Ltd*, 1990 S.L.T. 170.

[12] *Douglas v. Hogarth* (1901) 4 F. 148; *Corvi v. Ellis*, 1969 S.C. 312.

[13] *Dormer v. Melville, Dundas & Whitson*, above.

Running of prescription

Prescription runs from the date when the right to recover the **8.06** contribution became enforceable by the creditor in the obligation. In terms of section 3(2) of the 1940 Act, an obligation to make contribution appears to become enforceable when the person seeking contribution has paid the damages or expenses for which he has been found liable by the court. That is the date from which the two-year prescription will run.

Interruption of prescription

Prescription is interrupted by relevant claim or acknowledgment, the **8.07** definitions of which are the same as for the five- and 20-year periods. These are discussed more fully above.[14] Only a few words need be added about relevant claims.

Since the claim must be in relation to an obligation to make **8.08** contribution, clearly a claim can be relevant to interrupt prescription under section 8A only if it seeks relief in terms of the 1940 Act. For reasons discussed above,[15] it seems doubtful whether an action of declarator of liability to make contribution would amount to a relevant claim. Nonetheless, if such a declarator were obtained, it seems likely that the joint wrongdoer's liability would cease to be a liability founded on an obligation of relief and would become a liability founded on the terms of the declaratory decree.[16] Such an obligation would not itself be an obligation to make contribution and would not therefore fall under the two-year prescription. Nor would it fall under the five-year prescription, which does not apply to obligations constituted by decrees.[17] It would therefore prescribe only under the 20-year prescription.

Under the old law it was sometimes useful to raise declaratory **8.09** proceedings in order to establish the existence of a right to relief which might otherwise cease to be enforceable, for example under a special statutory regime, even before the court had made a determination of the parties' liabilities.[18] It is not clear that this problem can arise in the present state of the law, since (1) the court is concerned with the question whether a person from whom contribution is sought could have been liable to make contribution to the person who seeks it at the time that person was himself sued by the victim of the wrong, and (2) the obligation to make contribution becomes enforceable only once a determination of liability has been made by the court. Two years from that time to obtain relief from a joint wrongdoer may well be sufficient. But if there is any risk that a person may cease to be liable before the court is able to make a determination of liability, a declarator may serve the practical purpose of extending the prescriptive period to 20 years.

Suspension of prescription

The running of prescription is suspended where the creditor in the **8.10** obligation is affected by fraud or error induced by the debtor or any person acting on his behalf, or by legal disability.[19] Section 8A adopts the

---

[14] See above, paras 5.04 *et seq.*, 5.66 *et seq.*

[15] See above, para. 5.26.

[16] See above, para. 6.42.

[17] *i.e.* this will not fall within Sched. 1, para. 1(b) because excluded by para. 2(a); see above, paras 6.39 *et seq.*

[18] *cf. Central SMT Co. v. Lanarkshire County Council*, 1949 S.C. 450.

[19] It may also be suspended in accordance with s. 1 of the Limitation (Enemies and War Prisoners) Act 1945.

approach taken for the purposes of the five-year prescription, which is discussed above.[20] As already noted, both the five-year and 20-year prescriptions also apply to obligations to the obligations affected by section 8A. But nothing turns on this so far as the five-year prescription is concerned, since it and the two-year prescription adopt the same provisions on suspension of the prescriptive period, with the consequence that the two-year prescription will always finish first. For the reasons explained above,[21] however, the 20-year prescription may finish before either, since there is no provision in the Act for it to be suspended.

---

[20] See s. 6(4) and (5); paras 6.105 *et seq.*
[21] at para. 7.16.

CHAPTER 9

TEN-YEAR PRESCRIPTION

A 10-year prescriptive period applies to obligations arising from liability **9.01**
under the Consumer Protection Act 1987. The 1987 Act was enacted in
order to give effect to the product liability regime of Council Directive
85/374. In short—and subject to a large number of qualifications, some
of which are mentioned below—the essential point of this legislation is
to make the manufacturer of a product, and certain other persons, liable
for defects in the product which cause damage to people or to other
property, without the need to prove any negligence on their part. The
ordinary five- and 20-year periods of prescription do not apply to these
obligations.[1]

The provisions on prescription of these obligations are inserted into **9.02**
the 1973 Act as section 22A in a new Part IIA of the Act which also
contains limitation provisions.[2] It is expressly provided that these provisions are to be construed as if they were contained in Part I of the 1987
Act.[3] This means that not very much significance can be read into the
fact that these provisions differ in certain ways from those on the five-
and 20-year prescriptions: the 1973 Act is not to be interpreted as a
whole as it would be in the normal case.

Nonetheless there is sufficient common ground between the prescrip- **9.03**
tive regimes of the 1973 and 1987 Acts for it to be possible to confine
comments here to a minimum. There is another—unexpected—reason
for doing so, and that is that since 1987 not a single reported case has
arisen under these provisions. Various factors may have contributed to
this, among them the complexity of the defences available against claims
under the 1987 Act; and the fact that for many products a 10-year
prescriptive period may be extremely short, since defects may remain
latent for periods considerably in excess of that. Furthermore, ordinary
personal injuries claims are not subject to any period of prescription, but
only to a limitation period of three years,[4] whereas personal injuries
claims which are brought under the 1987 Act prescribe after 10 years.

The 10-year prescription runs against the Crown.[5]   **9.04**

"Ten years' prescription of obligations   **9.05**
22A.—(1) An obligation arising from liability under section 2 of the
1987 Act (to make reparation for damage caused wholly or partly by

---

[1] s. 6 and Sched. 1, para. 2(ggg); s. 7(2).
[2] These are discussed below, Chap. 13.
[3] s. 22D(2).
[4] 1973 Act, s. 7(2).
[5] s. 24.

a defect in a product) shall be extinguished if a period of 10 years has expired from the relevant time, unless a relevant claim was made within that period and has not been finally disposed of, and no such obligation shall come into existence after the expiration of the said period.

(2) If, at the expiration of the period of 10 years mentioned in subsection (1) above, a relevant claim has been made but has not been finally disposed of, the obligation to which the claim relates shall be extinguished when the claim is finally disposed of.

(3) In this section a claim is finally disposed of when—

(a) a decision disposing of the claim has been made against which no appeal is competent;

(b) an appeal against such a decision is competent with leave, and the time limit for leave has expired and no application has been made or leave has been refused;

(c) leave to appeal against such a decision is granted or is not required, and no appeal is made within the time limit for appeal; or

(d) the claim is abandoned;

'relevant claim' in relation to an obligation means a claim made by or on behalf of the creditor for implement or part implement of the obligation, being a claim made—

(a) in appropriate proceedings within the meaning of section 4(2) of this Act; or

(b) by the presentation of, or the concurring in, a petition for sequestration or by the submission of a claim under section 22 or 48 of the Bankruptcy (Scotland) Act 1985; or

(c) by the presentation of, or the concurring in, a petition for the winding up of a company or by the submission of a claim in a liquidation in accordance with the rules made under section 411 of the Insolvency Act 1986;

'relevant time' has the meaning given in section 4(2) of the 1987 Act.

(4) Where a relevant claim is made in an arbitration, and the nature of the claim has been stated in a preliminary notice (within the meaning of section 4(4) of this Act) relating to that arbitration, the date when the notice is served shall be taken for those purposes to be the date of the making of the claim.

Interpretation of this Part

22D.—(1) Expressions used in this Part and in Part I of the 1987 Act shall have the same meanings in this Part as in the said Part I.

(2) For the purposes of section 1(1) of the 1987 Act, this Part shall have effect and be construed as if it were contained in Part I of that Act.

(3) In this Part, 'the 1987 Act' means the Consumer Protection Act 1987.

Obligations affected

9.06   This section applies only to an obligation arising from liability under section 2 of the 1987 Act. Liability under that section arises where any damage is caused wholly or partly by a defect in a product. "Damage" is defined as "death or personal injury or any loss of or damage to any property (including land)".[6] Damage to the product itself is, however, excluded, so claims for pure economic loss cannot be made under the Act. Any claim for economic loss would have to result directly from personal injuries or damage to property other than the product.[7] To fall within the terms of the Act, any damage to property must be to property ordinarily intended for private use, occupation or consumption: the Act is, after all, concerned with the protection of consumers.[8] The combined effect of these provisions is to narrow down the scope of the Act considerably.

This is not the place for a detailed discussion of product liability.[9] **9.07** Here it is enough to draw attention to two points: (1) the term "defect" is defined in the Act in a rather complex manner, but the main emphasis in the definition is on the safety of the product[10]; (2) under the Act liability is in principle strict: no fault need be proved. But to speak of strict liability is something of an oversimplification, in particular because of the existence of a statutory defence based on the state of scientific and technical knowledge at the relevant time in relation to the question whether the defender knew of the defect.[11] The effect of this defence is that questions about reasonableness necessarily enter into considerations about the defender's liability. If there is to be such a development risks defence,[12] it certainly makes little sense to interpret it by reference to some supreme abstract standard which would impose liability on a defender because in theory, without regard to cost or opportunity, the defender might have been in a position to discover the defect. But in that case it cannot be said that this liability is in the normal sense "strict".[13] The combined effect of the provisions about what "persons generally are entitled to expect" and development risks is that liability under the 1987 Act may not be substantially different from a negligence-based liability. Its significance, with respect to ordinary claims for negligence, may instead lie in the fact that the burden of proving the development risks defence rests on the defender.[14] But, so far as

---

[6] s. 5(1).

[7] s. 5(2).

[8] s. 5(3).

[9] See, *e.g.*, J. Stapleton, *Product Liability* (London, 1994); Charlesworth and Percy, *Negligence*, paras 14.09 *et seq*.

[10] 1987 Act, s. 3(1) "Subject to the following provisions of this section, there is a defect in a product for the purposes of this Part if the safety of the product is not such as persons generally are entitled to expect; and for those purposes 'safety', in relation to a product, shall include safety with respect to products comprised in that product and safety in the context of risks of damage to property, as well as in the context of risks of death or personal injury." The remainder of s. 3 is concerned with the factors relevant to determining what "persons generally are entitled to expect".

[11] s. 4(1)(e): the defendant has a good defence if he proves "that the state of scientific and technical knowledge at the relevant time was not such that a producer of products of the same description as the product in question might be expected to have discovered the defect if it had existed in his products while they were under his control".

[12] Not all countries have adopted it: Finland and Luxembourg have not; Germany does not allow it in relation to medicine; and Spain excludes both medicine and food. There is some question that France, when it implements the Directive, may not introduce any such defence.

[13] *cf.* Stapleton, above, pp. 236–242. *Cf. European Commission v. UK* [1997] All E.R. (E.C.) 481, holding that it was implicit in the wording of the defence as set out in the Directive that the knowledge had to have been accessible at the time. For comments, see C. Hodges, (1998) 61 M.L.R. 560.

[14] s. 4 is clear on this: "it shall be a defence for him [the defender] to show"; *cf. European Commission v. UK*, above.

pursuers are concerned, liability under the 1987 Act suffers from the distinct drawback that an obligation to make reparation can prescribe before its existence is known or even discoverable.

9.08   Causation of the damage in whole or in part as a result of the defect must be proved in the normal manner, and this should therefore mean that similar considerations will arise here as in common law delictual (or other statutory) claims about relating the particular damage to the defect, especially where a pursuer suffers more than one occurrence of damage.[15] Essentially the same considerations will arise here as were discussed earlier on the need to identify the particular obligation which has or has not prescribed.[16]

9.09   This liability is imposed by section 2(2) on three classes of person: the producer of the product; a person who has held himself out to be the producer of the product, by putting his name, trade mark or other distinguishing mark on it; and a person who has imported the product into a Member State of the European communities from a place outside them, in order to supply it to another in the course of any business of his. This may be described as the primary liability under the Act.

9.10   The supplier of the product may, however, be secondarily liable, on certain conditions.[17] Read short, these are that, within a reasonable period after suffering the damage and when it is not reasonably practicable for him to identify the persons covered by section 2(2), the person who suffered the damage asks the supplier to identify any of the persons who fall within section 2(2), and the supplier does not within a reasonable period either do so or identify the person who supplied the product to him.[18] Since the supplier himself becomes liable under section 2 for the damage if he does not provide the necessary information, the same prescription provisions apply to him as to the producer, importer and "own-brander".

9.11   Two or more persons liable under these provisions are jointly and severally liable.[19]

Running of prescription
9.12   Prescription starts to run at the "relevant time", which is defined in section 4(2) of the 1987 Act:

> "In this section 'the relevant time', in relation to electricity, means the time at which it was generated, being a time before it was transmitted or distributed, and in relation to any other product, means—

---

[15] See above, paras 2.11, 2.24 and 4.24 *et seq.*
[16] Subject to what is said below in connection with the starting date for prescription: paras 9.14–16.
[17] s. 2(3).
[18] Where the person who suffered the damage has died from his injuries, his relatives may make the request to the supplier for information; in that case the supplier's liability is dependent on their making the request rather than on the deceased having done so: 1987 Act, s. 6(2).
[19] s. 2(5); it follows that the contribution provisions of s. 8A of the 1973 Act may become relevant: above, para. 8.02.

(a) if the person proceeded against is a person to whom subsection (2) of section 2 above applies in relation to the product, the time when he supplied the product to another;

(b) if that subsection does not apply to that person in relation to the product, the time when the product was last supplied by a person to whom that subsection does apply in relation to the product."

The prescriptive period is completed when a period of 10 years has **9.13** expired from the relevant time—without interruption by a relevant claim. On completion of the 10-year period (without interruption) the obligation is extinguished.

Prescription runs from the date of supply by a producer,[20] importer or **9.14** person who has branded the goods with his name or mark. The effect of section 4(2)(b) appears to be that if the defender is not a producer, importer or "own-brander" of the goods, time will run from the date when the goods were last supplied by such a person. Clearly, that date may be well before the date on which a consumer actually obtained the product from a supplier. This is particularly likely to be the case if the defender is a supplier of the goods rather than their producer, importer or an "own-brander".[21] Nonetheless, this is a "long-stop" prescription. It takes no account of latency of defects or the pursuer's knowledge or lack of knowledge of defects. It follows that obligations under section 2 of the 1987 Act may be extinguished before any defect has come to light.

"Relevant time" was defined in the 1987 Act in order to establish the **9.15** reference point at which the defectiveness of the product and the development risks defence were to be assessed. But the same definition is used to define the starting point for the running of prescription.[22] This has one important general consequence, which flows from the fact that time does not run—as under other prescriptive regimes—from a date when an obligation came into being or became enforceable. The "relevant time" is quite independent of those matters: the point from which time runs is the appropriate date of supply. Since that is so, time can start to run not merely before the pursuer knows of any obligation, but before there actually is an obligation at all.[23] In a sense, therefore, to describe this regime as prescription of obligations (as the Act does) is a misnomer. What it is is an absolute bar on pursuing a claim under section 2 of the 1987 Act once a period of 10 years has passed, regardless of the question whether an obligation existed for all or any of those 10 years.

The "relevant time" is defined in the 1987 Act by reference to the **9.16** particular defender in question: for the producer, the importer, and the "own-brander", time runs from the date of supplying the product to another; in the case of any other defender (in other words, a supplier),

---

[20] Defined in s. 1(2) of the 1987 Act.
[21] *i.e.* where s. 2(3) of the 1987 Act is relied upon.
[22] s. 22A(3).
[23] This is, by contrast, not possible for prescription under ss. 6, 7 and 8A, which require that an obligation subsist before it can begin to prescribe.

time runs from the date when the product was last supplied by a producer, "own-brander" or importer.[24] It will therefore be necessary to assess the 10-year prescriptive period separately for each of the people liable.

Interruption of prescription

9.17   Prescription under the 1987 Act is interrupted only by the making of a relevant claim during the running of the prescriptive period. There is no provision, as for example under sections 6 and 7 of the 1973 Act, for interruption by relevant acknowledgment.

9.18   The definition of "relevant claim" for the purposes of this prescriptive regime is very similar but not identical to the statutory definition given for the other forms of negative prescription.[25] In the following instances the similarity is sufficient simply to allow cross-reference to be made to the discussion in Chapter 5 above.[26] The claim must be made by or on behalf of the creditor for implement or part-implement of the obligation; it must be made in appropriate proceedings,[27] by the presentation of or concurring in a petition for sequestration or the submission of a claim in a sequestration,[28] or by the presentation of or concurring in a petition for winding up a company or the submission of a claim in a liquidation.[29] Provision is also made, as it is in the other forms of prescription of obligations, for a claim to be made in a preliminary notice relating to arbitration proceedings.[30]

9.19   The differences in the definition of relevant claim are that a claim made by a creditor to a trustee acting under a trust deed is not covered, and neither is diligence directed towards enforcement of the obligation.

9.20   A welcome difference between this section and section 9 is that it is explained what the effect is of the relevant claim being in dependence.[31] Section 22A(2) indicates that if a claim has been brought within the prescriptive period then the obligation on which it is based will not be extinguished during the dependence of the claim but only when it has been "finally disposed of". The expression "finally disposed of" is defined.[32] The provision requires little comment: its contents may be categorised under three headings. A final disposal is made by:

   (1) A decision which is unappealable. This extends to decisions against which no appeal is competent (such as decisions of the House of Lords) and decisions where leave to appeal is required and is not granted.[33]

---

[24] 1987 Act, s. 4(2).

[25] ss. 22A(3) and 9.

[26] Above, paras 5.05 *et seq.*, 5.21 *et seq.*, 5.46 *et seq.*

[27] Defined in s. 4(2) of the 1973 Act.

[28] Under s. 22 or s. 48 of the Bankruptcy (Scotland) Act 1985.

[29] In accordance with rules made under s. 411 of the Insolvency Act 1986.

[30] *cf.* s. 9.

[31] See above, paras 5.34 *et seq.* for the problems this causes in relation to the other forms of negative prescription.

[32] s. 22A(3). The terminology of the 1987 Act—"decision" and "appeal"—is not very Scottish, and needs to be translated into "interlocutor" and (for the Court of Session) "reclaiming motion".

[33] For the details on which interlocutors can be reclaimed or appealed against with or without leave, see RCS, r. 38.3; Sheriff Courts (Scotland) Act 1907 and OCR, rr. 31.1 and 31.2.

(2) A decision which is unappealed. This extends to decisions where no appeal is made within the time-limit for appeal, whether or not leave is required, or where leave to appeal is required but has not been sought within the time limit for seeking it.
(3) Abandonment of the claim.

Section 22A does not explain what happens after the prescriptive **9.21** period has been interrupted, except for the case that the claim continues in dependence at the expiry of the 10-year prescriptive period. Since the Act provides for extinction of the obligation only "if a period of 10 years has expired from the relevant time unless a relevant claim was made within that period and has not finally been disposed of", it would seem to follow that, provided the claim has been disposed of within the 10-year period, the obligation will be extinguished at latest after 10 years. The period of dependence of the claim would not be disregarded for the purpose of calculating the length of the prescriptive period. The 10-year period would continue to run against the obligation while the claim was in dependence.[34]

In essence what this means is that here the Act has departed from the **9.22** time-honoured notion of "interruption" of prescription and instead makes use of the notion of extending the prescriptive period, for the limited case that a relevant claim continues beyond the end of the normal 10 years.

Suspension of prescription

No provision is made for the prescriptive period to be suspended (for **9.23** example, for reasons such as nonage) and none is made for its commencement to be postponed, for reasons such as "discoverability". It is provided that no such obligation shall come into existence after the expiration of 10 years from the relevant time.[35]

---

[34] This may account for the fact that s. 22A does not speak of a "continuous period" of 10 years, unlike ss. 6, 7 and 8A; although it is true that not much weight can be placed on this, since s. 22A has to be construed as if it were contained not in the 1973 Act but in the 1987 Act.
[35] s. 22A(1).

PART II

LIMITATION OF ACTIONS

Part II and part of Part IIA of the 1973 Act deal with limitation of actions. Part II is concerned with actions of damages for personal injuries, actions where death has resulted from personal injuries, and actions of defamation. The limitation provisions in Part IIA of the Act deal with actions arising from product liability under the Consumer Protection Act 1987.[1]

Sections 17–19 of the 1973 Act as originally enacted were the subject of serious judicial criticism.[2] The sections were replaced by the present sections 17 and 18, and section 19 was repealed by the Prescription and Limitation (Scotland) Act 1984.[3] The Act in its present terms applies to rights of action arising both before and after the commencement of the 1984 Act.[4]

Prior to the 1984 redrafting, in order to deal with some of the difficulties which the sections in their original terms had created, the court was in 1980 given power to override the time-limits provided by sections 17–19.[5] Although the offending sections have now been redrafted, the power to override time-limits under section 19A remains.

It has therefore to be borne in mind that decisions up to 1984 are based on a wording of sections 17 and 18 which is different from the present one. Those decisions are not a safe guide to interpretation of the current provisions.

The legislative history of the limitation provisions of the Act is quite different from that of the prescription provisions. Unlike prescription, limitation is a concept derived in Scotland from English influences, and a recent import. It goes back only to the Law Reform (Limitation of Actions) Act 1954, which was followed by the Limitation Act 1963 and the Law Reform (Miscellaneous Provisions) Act 1971. Not only is the legislative history quite different from that of prescription, but so is the language employed by the Act in its limitation provisions. For that

---

[1] s. 16A.

[2] "[T]his Act has a strong claim to the distinction of being the worst drafted Act on the statute book": *Smith v. Central Asbestos Co. Ltd* [1973] A.C. 518 at 529, *per* Lord Reid (on the equivalent English provisions).

[3] See also SLC Report no. 74 (1983), *Prescription and Limitation: Report on Personal Injuries Actions and Private International Law Questions*; on the 1984 Act see also H.C. Deb., Vol. 49, cols 1108–1145; H.L. Deb., Vol. 453, cols 1089–1094.

[4] 1984 Act, s. 5(1). The fact that the redrafted sections apply even to pre-1984 cases might just be of importance today in a case where the right of action arose before 1984 but, owing to the pursuer's lack of knowledge or legal disability within s. 17(2)(b) or 17(3), the limitation period has not yet expired.

[5] Law Reform (Miscellaneous Provisions) Act 1980, s. 23(a), introducing a new s. 19A into the 1973 Act.

reason there is little mileage in trying to explain the meaning of a section in one Part of the Act by reference to sections in another.

All of these limitation periods run against the Crown.[6]

CHAPTER 10

ACTIONS FOR PERSONAL INJURIES

Section 17 of the 1973 Act deals with personal injuries and section 18 **10.01**
with death resulting from personal injuries. This chapter follows the
same division. The obligations to which these sections apply, unlike
other obligations to make reparation, are not subject to any period of
prescription but only to a three-year limitation period.[1] Much of what is
said here about section 17 is true of section 18 too, but it is convenient
to deal with that section as a whole at the end of this chapter.

I. ACTIONS FOR PERSONAL INJURIES

"Actions in respect of personal injuries not resulting in death **10.02**
17.—(1) This section applies to an action of damages where the
damages claimed consist of or include damages in respect of
personal injuries, being an action (other than an action to which
section 18 of this Act applies) brought by the person who sustained
the injuries or any other person.
(2) Subject to subsection (3) below and section 19A of this Act, no
action to which this section applies shall be brought unless it is
commenced within a period of three years after—

  (a) the date on which the injuries were sustained or, where the
      act or omission to which the injuries were attributable was a
      continuing one, that date or the date on which the act or
      omission ceased, whichever is the later; or
  (b) the date (if later than any date mentioned in paragraph (a)
      above) on which the pursuer in the action became, or on
      which, in the opinion of the court, it would have been
      reasonably practicable for him in all the circumstances to
      become, aware of all the following facts—
      (i) that the injuries in question were sufficiently serious to
          justify his bringing an action of damages on the assump-
          tion that the person against whom the action was
          brought did not dispute liability and was able to satisfy a
          decree;
      (ii) that the injuries were attributable in whole or in part to
           an act or omission; and
      (iii) that the defender was a person to whose act or omission
            the injuries were attributable in whole or in part or the
            employer or principal of such a person.

(3) In the computation of the period specified in subsection (2)
above there shall be disregarded any time during which the person

---

[1] s. 6(2) and Sched. 1, para. 2(g); s. 7(2).

199

who sustained the injuries was under legal disability by reason of nonage or unsoundness of mind."

Personal injuries

10.03   The actions which fall under section 17 are defined not according to the legal obligation from which they arise[2] but only by being actions for damages "in respect of personal injuries". Accordingly, section 17 applies not just to actions founded on delict (at common law or for breach of statutory duty) but also to actions founded (for example) on breach of contract, provided they are directed at damages for personal injuries. Nor is any distinction made between negligently and deliberately inflicted personal injuries.

10.04   Since section 17 applies where the damages sought "consist of or include" damages for personal injuries, it is not possible to avoid section 17 by pursuing claims for property damage and personal injuries arising from the same delict in the same action. A defender can still plead limitation where an action includes any element of damages for personal injury, even although the best part of the claim is directed (for example) at damage to property quite independent of the personal injury.[3] This conclusion follows from the fact that section 17 deals purely with the action in which claims are made, as opposed to the obligations on which the claims are founded. If the action is time-barred, it nonetheless remains possible for the claim for property damage to be pursued separately, since on its own it is unaffected by limitation.

The meaning of "personal injuries"

10.05   "Personal injuries" are defined in section 22(1): " 'personal injuries' includes any disease and any impairment of a person's physical or mental condition".[4]

10.06   The definition is not exhaustive, but apparently takes the trouble only to refer to matters which might otherwise have been doubtful. So, for example, it is plain that a broken leg is a personal injury. But it would not be plain that loss of one of the senses was a personal injury, if it were not for the express reference to "impairment" in this section. Similarly, it would not be obvious whether asbestos-related diseases were within the meaning of "personal injuries", were it not for the express reference in the section to "disease". It is true, however, that some asbestos-related disease is asymptomatic, so it is not clear that it would fall within the definition; in practice any difficulty this point might otherwise cause is resolved by the "discoverability" provisions of section 17(2)(b).[5]

10.07   The opinion has been expressed that injury to feelings is also included within the meaning of "personal injuries",[6] although it has also been doubted whether "upset to health" and "damage to personality" are

[2] As is the case with prescription.
[3] And so would be expected to prescribe under s. 6.
[4] This is the same as the definition employed in the English legislation: Limitation Act 1980, s. 38(1).
[5] See below, paras 10.29 *et seq.*
[6] *Barclay v. Chief Constable, Northern Constabulary*, 1986 S.L.T. 562 at 563 (*obiter*).

sufficiently specific to amount to personal injuries.[7] In practice this too may not cause much difficulty since, if the averments of injury to feelings are specific enough to be relevant, it may well be clear that they are within the scope of "personal injuries" and therefore section 17. In *Fleming v. Strathclyde Regional Council* the pursuer averred that she had sustained distress and inconvenience following on the flooding of her house.[8] The court held that this fell within the scope of "personal injuries". It also held that it was preferable to characterise distress as "personal injuries" rather than as an impairment of mental condition; and that personal injuries need not involve a medical condition, let alone the need for medical assistance. It was observed that the phrasing of section 22(1) seemed to be intended to cover various ensuing medical conditions.[9]

On this broad approach to the meaning of personal injuries, it must **10.08** follow that an action for breach of contract which includes a claim for damages for distress and inconvenience would be subject to limitation under section 17. This applies only to a small class of contract, such as those where expectations as to a holiday have been frustrated and caused distress and disappointment.[10]

Particular difficulty may be caused by so-called wrongful birth claims. **10.09** It is not obvious that a woman who gives birth following a failed sterilisation operation sustains personal injury.[11] In England the Court of Appeal has been prepared to hold that in such circumstances the woman has suffered an impairment of her physical condition, in the sense of physical change to her body which she did not want and had sought to avoid. On this basis, there is a personal injury and the limitation rules apply. But it was left open as to whether the same could be said where a failed male sterilisation resulted in the pregnancy of a willing woman.[12] In any event, if the woman claimed damages for suffering sustained during pregnancy or childbirth, the claim would appear to fall within the definition of "personal injuries". The main point is that what makes these cases problematic is not just the fact that the loss sustained may be purely economic but the much more fundamental question whether there is a personal injury at all. If there is no personal injury, section 17 does not apply; any claim for damages is therefore likely to fall under the general regime for prescription of obligations to make reparation.[13]

There will remain difficulties of categorisation. Three further exam- **10.10** ples will illustrate this:

(1) There is authority that a wrong consisting in allowing a right of action against employers for personal injuries to lapse is not itself

---

[7] *Smith v. City of Glasgow D.C.*, Lord Morton of Shuna, March 28, 1991, unreported.
[8] 1992 S.L.T. 161.
[9] at 163E.
[10] See McBryde, *Contract*, paras 20.98 and 20.99; *Jarvis v. Swan's Tours* [1973] 1 Q.B. 233.
[11] This was held not to be a personal injury in *McFarlane v. Tayside Health Board*, 1997 S.L.T. 211, reversed in the Inner House, 1998 S.C. 389 (under appeal to the House of Lords). For discussion, see J. Blaikie, (1997) 2 S.L.P.Q. 287–296.
[12] *Walkin v. South Manchester Health Authority* [1995] 1 W.L.R. 1543; *cf. Pattison v. Hobbs, The Times*, November 11, 1985.
[13] s. 6 and Sched. 1, para. 1(d).

a claim for personal injuries.[14] The claim is not founded upon the personal injuries but on the quite separate negligent act which meant that a claim was not made timeously. There is therefore a separate wrong which is the basis of the action.

(2) There is nothing in the section to confine the actions in question to those brought by a pursuer in respect of his own personal injuries. Accordingly, if the pursuer has a title to sue in respect of personal injuries sustained by someone else, that action would appear at least to be capable of falling within section 17. The current state of the law of delict may mean that there is no room for such a claim, since it would be purely for economic loss. But a claim for breach of contract would, for instance, be open to an employer who sustained loss as a result of a supply of dangerously defective goods to him, the use of which injured his employee. In such a case the supply of the defective goods to the employer is responsible for personal injury to the employee and also economic loss to the employer as a result of the personal injury to his employee. It is at least arguable—although there appears to be no authority on this question either way—that the employer's action for damages for breach of contract against the supplier is an action which includes damages "in respect of personal injuries".[15] The distinction between this case and the previous one is that here there is no independent wrong (such as professional negligence). The basis both of the employer's and the employee's claims is the same negligent act: supply of dangerously defective goods.

(3) Some actions which are, loosely speaking, in respect of personal injuries can be argued actually to be directed at the recovery of economic loss. One example is a claim by a child for injuries sustained ante-natally. This may be a claim for economic loss only, since the injury is sustained at a time before the child has legal personality, and the child's loss when born consists in the economic costs of disability.[16] Nonetheless, on the broad approach outlined above, it seems more likely that a claim of this sort would be treated as relating to "personal injuries".

Title to sue

10.11   Section 17 applies whether the pursuer is the person who sustained the injuries or somebody else. In practice this is likely to be a guardian in the case of a person under 16[17]; a *curator bonis* in the case of an *incapax*; a *curator ad litem* in either of those cases, where appropriate; or in certain cases a trustee in bankruptcy.[18] The case of an executor is dealt with under section 18.[19]

---

[14] *McGahie v. Union of Shop Distributive and Allied Workers*, 1966 S.L.T. 74 at 75; *cf. Mackenzie v. Digby Brown & Co.*, 1992 S.L.T. 891.

[15] *cf. Howe v. David Brown Tractors (Retail) Ltd* [1991] 4 All E.R. 30 at 36, 41 and 43, CA; the wording of the English Limitation Act 1980, s. 11(1) is slightly clearer: "damages in respect of personal injuries to the plaintiff or any other person".

[16] Kennedy and Grubb, *Medical Law* (2nd ed.), p. 936.

[17] Age of Legal Capacity (Scotland) Act 1991.

[18] *Grindall v. John Mitchell (Grangemouth) Ltd*, 1987 S.L.T. 137; *Watson v. Thompson*, 1990 S.C. 38; *cf.* McBryde, *Bankruptcy* (2nd ed.), para. 10.86. The trustee will only be able to raise an action for patrimonial loss, but is entitled to sist himself in place of the bankrupt even in proceedings (*e.g.* for solatium) which he could not himself have raised: see *Coutts's Tr. v. Coutts*, 1988 S.C.L.R. 729.

[19] See below, paras 10.89–93.

In section 17(2) reference is made to the pursuer's awareness of **10.12** certain facts. Where the action is pursued by a guardian or *curator bonis*, on the face of it this ought to mean that it is his awareness of facts, rather than that of the person under 16 or *incapax*, which is relevant. That interpretation could be supported on the grounds that (i) had it been the intention of Parliament, it would have been perfectly easy to state that it was the date of awareness of the injured person which mattered[20]; and (ii) the position of persons under legal disability is protected by other provisions in the section.[21] But this interpretation appears to lead to absurd results: section 17(3) provides that the limitation period is not to run while the injured person is under a legal disability. If that is so, it cannot make any sense to decide when the limitation period commences by reference to the awareness of some other person. The result would be that the period would start by reference to the state of mind of one person, and be suspended by reference to that of another. Confusion would result. Accordingly, the better view appears to be to take the "pursuer" whose awareness is in question in section 17(2) as being the injured person, even where a guardian or other person is suing on his behalf.[22]

Where the pursuer is an assignee of the injured person's claim, there **10.13** is no reason why the position of the defender should be prejudiced merely because of the assignation, and the assignee is therefore affected by the assignor's own date of awareness.[23] It is not clear but must at least be arguable that this applies not just to voluntary but also to statutory assignees, such as trustees in sequestration.

The running of the limitation period

Section 17(2) provides a range of possible starting points for the **10.14** limitation period: the pursuer's action is time-barred if, excluding any period during which the person who sustained the injuries was under legal disability,[24] three years have passed since:

(i) the date of the injuries; or
(ii) if later, the date of cessation of the act or omission which caused them; or
(iii) if later than (i) or (ii), the date on which the pursuer was aware of all the facts set out in section 17(2)(b); or
(iv) the date on which in the opinion of the court it was reasonably practicable for him to be aware of those facts.

Quite apart from these provisions, a pursuer may wish to invoke the **10.15** equitable discretion of the court to allow him to bring the action late.[25]

Little need be said about the first of these: it will be the starting date **10.16** unless a case is made for one of the later dates. There are two possible

---

[20] This is in effect what is done for the case of assignees in s. 22(2), on which see immediately below.
[21] s. 17(3); see below.
[22] *cf.* for s. 18(3), *Paton v. Loffland Brothers North Sea Inc.*, 1994 S.L.T. 784.
[23] s. 22(2).
[24] s. 17(3); below, paras 10.75–81.
[25] s. 19A: see below, Chap. 12; on the other hand, there is no need to invoke this jurisdiction if the pursuer's case is simply that the starting date in terms of s. 17(2) is in fact later than the date of the injury.

arguments for a later date, based respectively on continuance of the act or omission and on the pursuer's lack of awareness.

Continuing act or omission

10.17   If the act or omission continues, then the limitation period does not commence until the act or omission has ceased.[26] Although this is not spelled out in so many words, it seems that this must be intended to refer to the date when the act or omission ceased to affect the pursuer: the section is confined to the act or omission "to which the injuries were attributable". Suppose, for example, that in an industrial deafness case the pursuer left the employment in question, and the employers' business continued without change, the same excessive level of noise was generated and still no adequate ear protection was provided.[27] Clearly the only reasonable view is that the date on which the limitation period began was the date on which the pursuer ceased to be affected by the act or omission, that is, at latest the date on which he left the employment. Fixing this date is distinctly simpler than fixing the date on which the injuries were actually sustained, which in cases of insidious disease may be exceptionally difficult.[28]

10.18   It is of course possible (to use the same example) that the pursuer remains in the same employment, the excessive noise never ceases and adequate ear protection is never provided. On those facts, the period of limitation would never start to run. In an earlier chapter it was suggested that this might be an objectionable conclusion in the case of prescription.[29] It seems less objectionable in this context, where by definition the concern is with injuries sustained by individuals, which prompts both uneasiness about cutting off the claim while the act or omission continues and the reflection that the timescale cannot extend indefinitely into the future but must relate to the term of a pursuer's working life.

10.19   In England the courts have been prepared to attempt apportionment of the injury sustained in one period rather than another. This may be necessary (1) where the defendants' breach of duty does not extend over the whole period during which injury was sustained, for example because of their state of knowledge[30]; or (2) where the whole of the plaintiff's injuries do not arise within the limitation period, but some of them predate it. So, for example, in an industrial deafness case,[31] the court found that the pursuer had suffered from deafness since 1960 but that, owing to his knowledge, his claim was time-barred except for the period after 1967. Since the defendants' negligence continued after that date, the plaintiff's claim did not fail completely. The court proceeded to

---

[26] See, *e.g.*, *Kennedy v. Steinberg*, 1998 S.C. 379: here it was held that a doctor's failure to take a patient off a particular drug treatment was not negligent, but that, had it been a negligent omission, it was in any event a continuing one, so the limitation period had not been completed.

[27] Under the Noise at Work Regulations 1989 the first action level is 85 dB(A) and the second 90 dB(A); Munkman, *Employers' Liability* (12th ed.), pp. 268–269.

[28] See, *e.g.* *McGhee v. British Telecommunications plc*, Lord Hamilton, December 20, 1995, unreported.

[29] See above, paras 4.71–73. This applies especially to the 20-year prescription.

[30] *Thompson v. Smiths Shiprepairers Ltd* [1984] Q.B. 405 at 437–444, *per* Mustill J., on the principles of apportionment.

[31] *Berry v. Stone Manganese & Marine Ltd* [1972] 1 Lloyd's Rep. 182 at 193, QBD.

attempt to assess the deterioration which had occurred since 1967. Clearly, where the harm is incremental, this may be an extremely difficult exercise.[32]

In Scotland there is little evidence of this kind of apportionment. In **10.20** the first case mentioned above, there seems no reason why it should not in an appropriate instance be attempted.[33] In the second case, however, apportionment appears not to be admissible. This is because the date on which the pursuer became (actually or constructively) aware of the statutory facts is material only if it is later than the date on which a continuing act or omission ceased. Provided the act or omission continues, there is no warrant for asking when the pursuer knew the statutory facts.

Lack of awareness of facts

Two possible dates come into consideration here. The later of them is **10.21** the date on which the pursuer had actual awareness of the statutory facts. The court may, however, take an earlier date as the starting date if satisfied that on that date it was reasonably practicable for the pursuer to have been aware of those facts.

What is awareness?

There will be more to say about "awareness" in connection with the **10.22** specific facts referred to in section 17(2)(b), but some general considerations can be raised here. A preliminary point arises. There is very little Scottish authority on the meaning of the word "awareness" in this context. For that reason there is something to be gained from looking at the main issues which have arisen in relation to very similar English statutory provisions.

The equivalent provisions of the English legislation speak of **10.23** "knowledge" rather than "awareness".[34] For these purposes even "knowledge"—which seems to suggest a greater level of certainty—has been held not to mean "know for certain and beyond possibility of contradiction" but to know with sufficient confidence to submit a claim to the defendant, take legal and other advice and collect evidence.[35] Recently the Court of Appeal put it this way:

> "A plaintiff has the requisite knowledge when she knows enough to make it reasonable for her to begin to investigate whether or not she has a case against the defendant. Another way of putting this is to say that she will have such knowledge if she so firmly believes that her condition is capable of being attributed to an act or omission which she can identify (in broad terms) that she goes to a solicitor to seek advice about making a claim for compensation. . . .

---

[32] See, *e.g.*, *Clarkson v. Modern Foundries Ltd* [1957] 1 W.L.R. 1210, criticised in *Cartwright v. GKN Sankey Ltd* [1972] 2 Lloyd's Rep. 242 and *Cartledge v. E. Jopling & Sons Ltd* [1962] 1 Q.B. 189 at 207, CA; also McGee, *Limitation Periods*, pp. 150–151; Law Com. Consultation Paper no. 151 (1998), paras 3.24–3.28.

[33] *cf. Balfour and Begg v. Beardmore & Co.*, 1956 S.L.T. 205 (apportionment in a case of progressive disease, in order to determine the liability of one employer, earlier employers not being liable as the risk was not at that time foreseeable).

[34] Limitation Act 1980, ss. 11(4) and 14(1).

[35] *Halford v. Brookes* [1991] 1 W.L.R. 428 at 443.

On the other hand she will not have the requisite knowledge if she thinks she knows the acts or omissions she should investigate but in fact is barking up the wrong tree; or if her knowledge of what the defendant did or did not do is so vague or general that she cannot fairly be expected to know what she should investigate; or if her state of mind is such that she thinks her condition is capable of being attributed to the act or omission alleged to constitute negligence, but she is not sure about this, and would need to check with an expert before she could be properly said to know that it was."[36]

10.24   This is in line with Scottish authority on the pre-1984 section 18 of the 1973 Act, which referred to "knowledge" rather than "awareness": "whether a person 'knows' a fact seems to me to involve a question of degree. I do not consider it advisable to attempt to define it, but at least I think it involves something approximating more to certainty than mere suspicion or guess. Moreover . . . some information, suspicion or belief falling short of knowledge is not transformed into knowledge if it happens to be correct."[37]

10.25   It seems to make sense to take "awareness" in the same sort of way. The point of section 17(2)(b) is, after all, to fix the starting date for the limitation period, so it seems not unreasonable to require only a relatively modest level of awareness, given that from that point on there still remain three years to carry out necessary investigations, arrive at a clearer view of the cause or nature of the injuries, and raise an action. Equally, so far as awareness of the seriousness of injury and its causation is concerned, it makes no sense (except for an expert pursuer) to interpret a pursuer's "awareness" as connoting any detailed knowledge about the prognosis or aetiology of his injuries or disease.

10.26   There is a further question. What if the pursuer is so incapable, physically or mentally, or so inexperienced that he or she does not gain awareness of the statutory facts? Does this delay the running of time (because the test of awareness is subjective) or not (because it is objective)?

10.27   Here some of the cases are less helpful than they appear at first sight.[38] But such authority as there is in Scotland is in favour of a test which includes a subjective element. In *Carnegie v. Lord Advocate*,[39] it was held that "the appropriate test to be applied is not an objective one defined by reference to the ordinary reasonable man but one which takes into consideration the particular circumstances of the individual pursuer". In

---

[36] *Spargo v. North Essex District Health Authority* [1997] P.I.Q.R. P235 at P242, CA. This approach is favoured by the English Law Commission in its recent Consultation Paper no. 151, *Limitation of Actions* (1998), paras 12.46–12.47.

[37] *Comer v. James Scott & Co. (Electrical Engineers) Ltd*, 1978 S.L.T. 235 at 240, *per* Lord Maxwell.

[38] In *Comer*, above, which in any event was decided on the old wording of the section, it was conceded by the defenders that the test was subjective (at 238); in *Comber v. Greater Glasgow Health Board*, 1989 S.L.T. 639, the fact that the pursuer was naive and withdrawn was raised in relation not to the present section but to the equitable discretion under s. 19A.

[39] 1998 S.L.T. 872. *Cf. Blake v. Lothian Health Board*, 1993 S.L.T. 1248, which was followed in this case. See also below in connection with s. 17(2)(b)(i).

Kane v. Argyll and Clyde Health Board,[40] the pursuer averred that she was unaware that she had a legal remedy until a date which was less than three years before she raised the action. Preliminary proof before answer was allowed on this question. Clearly the court took the view that the pursuer might satisfy a test of subjective unawareness. In fact at the proof she failed to do so. It was held that any ignorance on her part did not justify her failure to seek advice.[41] This raises the question of constructive awareness, which is discussed immediately below.

So far as actual awareness is concerned, the approach should therefore **10.28** be to ask what this individual pursuer knows, and whether his or her awareness of the statutory facts goes beyond the vague and general and is sufficiently firm to make it reasonable for him or her to investigate whether there is a case against the defender.

Constructive awareness: subjective or objective?
The date on which the limitation period begins in terms of section **10.29** 17(2)(b) will be either the date on which the pursuer was aware of the statutory facts or the date on which in the opinion of the court it was "reasonably practicable for him in all the circumstances" to be aware of them.

Here too the question arises whether the test is subjective, objective or **10.30** includes elements of both. Taken to either extreme, the provision degenerates into meaninglessness. Suppose, for example, that the pursuer is of limited intelligence and therefore is not actually aware of one of the statutory facts. Apply a purely subjective test. If constructive and actual awareness are assessed according to precisely the same standard— a pursuer of limited intelligence—then the constructive awareness test adds nothing to the actual awareness test. The pursuer of limited intelligence is neither aware, nor is it reasonably practicable for him or her to become aware, of the statutory fact.[42]

Conversely, if a purely objective test is applied, which takes no account **10.31** of the pursuer's limited intelligence, then the constructive awareness test destroys the whole point of the actual awareness test. Lip service is paid to the fact that this pursuer of limited intelligence did not know the statutory fact. But on an objective test of what was reasonably practicable for a person of ordinary intelligence, it can be said that it was reasonably practicable for the pursuer to become aware of the statutory fact. An approach of this sort risks undermining the policy of the section, which is to prevent time starting to run before the actual pursuer knew the facts.[43]

On general principle, therefore, it appears that a test which combines **10.32** objective and subjective elements is likely to be fairest,[44] and this indeed

---

[40] Lord Marnoch, May 24, 1996, unreported.
[41] 1997 S.L.T. 965.
[42] *cf. Parry v. Clwyd Health Authority* [1997] P.I.Q.R. P1 at P10, QBD; *Forbes v. Wandsworth Health Authority* [1997] Q.B. 402 at 414 and 423–425, CA.
[43] *cf.* Law. Com. Consultation Paper no. 151 (1998), paras 12.52–12.54; *O'Driscoll v. Dudley Health Authority* [1996] 7 Med. L.R. 408 at 414, QBD.
[44] *cf.* Law. Com., *ibid.*; *Nash v. Eli Lilly & Co.* [1993] 1 W.L.R. 782, CA.

appears to fit best with the statutory wording. The test appears to be subjective, inasmuch as it is directed at what was reasonably practicable "for him",[45] the pursuer, "in all the circumstances"; but it appears to be objective inasmuch as it is directed at what was "reasonably practicable". This was, as it happens, the intention of the Scottish Law Commission in drafting this section: "The words 'reasonably practicable for him in all the circumstances' are designed to reflect the fact that the test of knowledge is mainly objective but not wholly so. This will allow the courts a certain degree of flexibility in order to take account of the different circumstances of individuals and the differing nature of their injuries."[46]

10.33   At the least, therefore, it appears that an objective test has to be applied having regard to all the circumstances in which the pursuer found himself. It is what was reasonably practicable in those circumstances which the court must assess.[47]

10.34   It is more difficult to be clear whether the section as worded goes a step further and allows the intelligence or capacity of the individual pursuer to be taken into account. What does at least seem plain is that not every characteristic of the pursuer can possibly be relevant. Otherwise lazy and careless pursuers would have a clear advantage.

10.35   In any event, the question is not whether the pursuer had a reasonable excuse for not asking questions or not uncovering information but whether it would have been reasonably practicable for him to do so. The opinion has been expressed that it would be reasonably practicable for a pursuer to become aware of necessary information if he would be able to do so without excessive expenditure of time, effort or money. The mere fact that he did not feel like asking questions could not make the acquisition of the information other than reasonably practicable.[48]

10.36   The section makes no reference to the question whether the pursuer ought to have obtained expert advice.[49] The Scottish Law Commission deliberately left this out of its draft, on the view that it was for the courts to develop the test of constructive knowledge.[50]

The awareness of agents
10.37   The question arises whether the actual or constructive knowledge of the pursuer's agents is to be imputed to him. There is little authority on this question under the current legislation,[51] although cases decided

---

[45] *cf.* the emphasis placed by Lord Reid on the words "for him" in the previous legislation (Limitation Act 1963, s. 7(5)) in *Smith v. Central Asbestos Co. Ltd* [1973] A.C. 518 at 530: "In order to avoid constructive knowledge the plaintiff must have taken all such action as it was reasonable for him to take to find out. I agree with the view expressed in the Court of Appeal that this test is subjective. We are not concerned with 'the reasonable man'. Less is expected of a stupid or uneducated man than of a man of intelligence and wide experience."

[46] SLC Report no. 74 (1983), explanatory note on draft cl. 17(2)(b).

[47] *cf. Nicol v. British Steel Corp. (General Steels)*, 1992 S.L.T. 141 at 144.

[48] *Elliot v. J. & C. Finney*, 1989 S.L.T. 208 at 210–211, OH; 605, IH.

[49] Contrast the English Limitation Act 1980, ss. 14(3)(b) and 14A(10) which both speak of "appropriate expert advice which it is reasonable for him to seek".

[50] SLC Report no. 74 (1983), para. 3.7.

[51] In *Dormer v. Melville, Dundas & Whitson*, 1987 S.C.L.R. 655 at 663 the pursuer was held to be affected by his agents' knowledge.

under the earlier limitation provisions decided that the actual or constructive knowledge of the pursuer did not include that of his or her legal advisers.[52]

There is a good deal, however, to be said for the opposite point of **10.38** view.[53] On normal principles of agency, the actual awareness of the pursuer's agent is imputed to him where the agent acquired the awareness within the scope of his authority to act for the pursuer.[54] This also seems reasonable for the purpose of applying limitation provisions, since, if the pursuer is not affected by his advisers' knowledge, (1) a pursuer who has instructed agents can wash his hands of the further progress of his claim[55]; and (2) in the event that the agent acquires but fails to make appropriate use of the relevant information, it seems fairer that the agent's failings in discovering or communicating information to the pursuer should prejudice not the defender but the pursuer, who can have recourse against his agent in contract.

This approach also squares with the considerations raised earlier **10.39** about what it is reasonably practicable for a pursuer to do. For instance, the very nature of the pursuer's injury might make it appropriate (and reasonably practicable) for him to seek advice, which would have made him aware of the relevant facts. Then it would seem reasonable that, if a pursuer sought no advice or information, yet it was reasonably practicable for him to have done so, he should be fixed with constructive awareness of the advice or information he would have acquired. On the other hand, if he sought advice or information but the person consulted failed to make appropriate inquiries or uncover the necessary information, it seems likely in most cases that it could not be said that it was reasonably practicable for the pursuer to become aware of the fact in question. There might, however, be cases in which the person consulted provided information or advice so manifestly incomplete or unconvincing that it could be said to be appropriate and reasonably practicable for the pursuer to make further inquiries or consult other people.

The three relevant facts

Section 17(2)(b) speaks of "facts", and that is to be taken literally. As **10.40** the Act spells out: "For the purposes of the said subsection (2)(b) knowledge that any act or omission was or was not, as a matter of law, actionable, is irrelevant."[56] What this means is that the court, in deciding at what date the pursuer has the necessary awareness, will be interested only in matters of fact. If the pursuer is aware of all the statutory facts, it does not make any difference that he is unaware that on those facts he has a legal remedy.[57] On the same basis, it should also make no

---

[52] *Hunter v. Glasgow Corporation*, 1971 S.C. 220; *cf. Pickles v. National Coal Board* [1968] 1 W.L.R. 997 on s. 7 of the Limitation Act 1963.

[53] SLC Report no. 74 (1983) notes in para. 3.7. that draft cl. 17(2)(b) would enable the court where appropriate to attribute to a pursuer his adviser's awareness of facts.

[54] Bowstead and Reynolds on *Agency* (16th ed., 1996), paras 8.204 *et seq.*

[55] Note the criticism of this consequence by Lord Fraser in *Hunter v. Glasgow Corporation*, above, at 232.

[56] s. 22(3).

[57] Accordingly it is a matter for consideration (if at all) under s. 19A: see, *e.g.*, *Comber v. Greater Glasgow Health Board*, 1989 S.L.T. 639; *McLaren v. Harland and Wolff Ltd*, 1991 S.L.T. 85.

difference that he may not appreciate the legal significance of a fact: for example, that 90 dB(A) is a level of noise which is as a matter of law excessive in workplace environments where employees are not furnished with such things as ear defenders.

10.41   Two cases seem to be particularly important here. First, where the pursuer is aware of significant injuries, which are capable of being attributed to something done or not done by the defender, and his reason for delaying in bringing an action is simply that he did not realise that there was any fault or actionable act or omission. Time runs against him in spite of this.[58] Secondly, where on the same facts the pursuer delays bringing the action because he has received incorrect legal advice. Here too time runs, provided the legal advice was about the actionability of the act or omission, rather than (for example) purely factual advice.

10.42   Awareness of all of the facts is required in order for time to begin running; it is enough for the pursuer to demonstrate that he or she was unaware of just one of the three. And it is awareness (actual or constructive) only of these facts which is critical in determining the date from which time runs against the pursuer. It is of no importance whatsoever that the pursuer may have been ignorant of other facts, however closely related to the question whether or not to raise an action.

10.43   The facts which are relevant under section 17(2)(b) are complex, and have to be discussed at some length.

The seriousness of the injuries
10.44   The fact which is relevant under this provision is not just that the pursuer has sustained injury but that he has sustained injury of a certain seriousness: sufficient seriousness to warrant raising an action (on certain assumptions). The court will therefore have to consider the nature of the injuries; for example, in one case a pursuer argued that the injuries he sustained in an accident were trivial, *de minimis*; his principal claim was for traumatic arthritis, of which he had become aware only later.[59] The initial injuries were very severe bruising and abrasions, and the pursuer had been unable to walk without assistance. The court disagreed with the pursuer, regarding his initial injuries as sufficiently serious to justify his raising an action. On the other hand, in another case nightmares and somnambulism were found not to be sufficiently serious to bar a pursuer who was later diagnosed as having post-traumatic stress disorder.[60] Similarly, in a progressive disease—such as dermatitis may be—the fact that the disease later becomes worse does not stop time running against a pursuer where his injuries were sufficiently serious that he ought to have claimed earlier.[61]

10.45   Similar difficulties arise in pharmaceuticals cases. Where the pursuer's complaint is about injury caused by drugs, clearly he will be expecting

---

[58] *Dobbie v. Medway Health Authority* [1994] 1 W.L.R. 1234, CA on the equivalent English provisions, ss. 11 and 14 of the Limitation Act 1980.
[59] *Mackie v. Currie*, 1991 S.L.T. 407.
[60] *Heathfield v. Elf Enterprise Caledonia Ltd*, Lord Milligan, February 15, 1995, unreported.
[61] *Miller v. London Electrical Manufacturing Co. Ltd* [1976] 2 Lloyd's Rep. 284, CA.

the drugs to have some effect on him, and probably he will be prepared to tolerate some side-effects. The injuries cannot be said to be sufficiently serious until the side effects go beyond what can be regarded as acceptable.[62]

Latent disease

Many or most diseases are in their initial stages latent. This causes **10.46** peculiar difficulty, since it is hard for medical evidence to pinpoint precisely when the disease occurs. The date of exposure to a risk such as asbestos may bear no clear relation to the date when scarring of the lung (asbestosis) or an asbestos-induced malignancy (mesothelioma) occurs, if at all, in any individual. In general, there is great difficulty in determining in cases of latent or insidious disease when the relevant injuries were sustained by the pursuer.

There is a range of possible starting dates for the limitation period: **10.47**

(1) the "first breath", that is, the date on which the plaintiff was first exposed to the risk; (2) the "last breath", that is the date when the plaintiff was last exposed to the risk; (3) the date on which the disease occurred, even if asymptomatic; (4) the date on which symptoms of the disease first appeared.

American courts have been much troubled by—and have now substan- **10.48** tially departed from the "first breath" rule.[63] Since, under the 1973 Act, the critical question is whether the injuries are "sufficiently serious" to justify the pursuer in bringing an action it is clear that the "first breath" rule does not apply. This formulation shifts the emphasis from the question of exposure to harm onto the question of sustaining injury. But it still leaves room for argument about the proper starting date for limitation.

It may be necessary in order to resolve this question (among others) to **10.49** decide whether the various changes in the pursuer's physical condition are separate diseases or features of a single disease. Accordingly, medical evidence will be critical. Examples may assist: in a pneumoconiosis case it was held that the pursuer merely had present in his lungs siliceous dust which might or might not cause loss in the future. There was therefore no injury at that stage.[64] In *Shuttleton v. Duncan Stewart & Co. Ltd*,[65] a case of asbestos-related disease, the evidence before the court was to the effect that pleural plaques, pleural thickening and asbestosis could each be caused by exposure to asbestos. The court found that each was a distinct consequence of exposure to asbestos; that none was a cause or initial stage of the others; and that pleural plaques were asymptomatic and not generally a disability. The presence of any of these conditions therefore pointed to the likelihood of exposure to asbestos. But it was held that, where two or more impairments could be caused by the same delict, relevant or imputed knowledge of one would

---

[62] *Nash v. Eli Lilly & Co.* [1993] 1 W.L.R. 782 at 791, CA.
[63] See M. D. Green (1988) 76 California Law Rev. 965–1014.
[64] *Brown v. North British Steel Foundry Ltd*, 1968 S.C. 51 at 64. A similar issue arose in a recent case about mesothelioma, *Paterson v. George Wimpey & Co. Ltd*, 1999 S.L.T. 577.
[65] Lord Prosser, August 2, 1995, unreported; reported in note form 1996 S.L.T. 517.

not bar the pursuer from pursuing a claim in respect of the other. In *Shuttleton* the three conditions identified were found to be independent, and pleural plaques (as to which most of the evidence was led) were held not to be of sufficient seriousness to give rise to damages, so that on those facts the pursuer's case was not time-barred. Whether or not medical evidence confirms this view of the interrelationship of these conditions, the critical point here is that there is a distinction between illnesses or diseases where the conditions from which the pursuer suffers are independent and those in which one condition is simply a continuation or natural exacerbation of what went before.

10.50   Where the various conditions are independent, to hold that knowledge of one does not bar a claim based on another seems unproblematic. It is more difficult where the first condition is no more than an early stage of the second one.[66] Here in principle it would appear that (1) knowledge of the first stage ought to be the relevant moment even for the second stage and so be capable of barring a claim based on it; but (2) that there would be a bar only if the first stage was itself sufficiently serious to justify bringing an action. Accordingly, where a pursuer is aware that he is suffering from the early stages of a disease which will become sufficiently serious to justify raising an action, time is not yet running against him, since he cannot be expected to raise an action for injuries which have yet to emerge when at present he suffers from nothing which would justify raising an action.

The statutory assumptions

10.51   The seriousness of the injuries has to be assessed in the light of the statutory assumptions that "the person against whom the action was brought did not dispute liability and was able to satisfy a decree".[67] These assumptions appear to be intended to focus attention purely on the seriousness of the injuries and to exclude pragmatic considerations such as the likelihood of recovery of damages and the expense involved in attempting to recover them.[68] The wording is no doubt intended to protect a pursuer to some extent, by preventing time running against him if his injuries are no more than trivial.

10.52   Nonetheless, on the assumption that liability is not in issue, an injury need not be very serious at all before it is worth raising an action. On a purely economic view, it would be worth doing so provided the anticipated damages exceeded the amount of the expenses which could not be recovered from the defender. But if this is intended to be the test, it provides for a starting date for limitation which is rather hard on the pursuer.

10.53   There is not much authority on what these assumptions mean: the cases tend simply to gloss the words "sufficiently serious" as meaning more than *de minimis* or "something more than trivial".[69] More detailed

---

[66] *cf. Shuttleton v. Duncan Stewart & Co. Ltd*, above, at 28–29.

[67] s. 17(2)(b)(i).

[68] *cf.* Law Reform Committee 24th Report, *Latent Damage*, Cmnd. 9390 (1984), paras 4.7–4.8.

[69] *Mackie v. Currie*, 1991 S.L.T. 407; *Ferla v. Secretary of State for Scotland*, 1995 S.L.T. 662; *Shuttleton v. Duncan Stewart & Co. Ltd*, above.

consideration was given to the assumptions in *Blake v. Lothian Health Board*.[70] There the court held that injuries which went beyond the minimal or trivial were not necessarily sufficiently serious to justify raising an action; the question was what the reasonable claimant would think and do. In this case, after a preliminary proof, it was found that the initial injuries would have attracted damages of less than £200 together with irrecoverable expenses and the general worries of litigation, and it was held that a reasonable claimant would not have raised an action in these circumstances. The pursuer had only had a "presentable" claim within three years before raising the present action, and it was therefore not time-barred.

Two points may be made about this. First, the section gives no warrant **10.54** for a general consideration of factors which might influence a pursuer in deciding whether to raise an action or not, such as the possibility that raising an action might imperil his future job prospects or make personal relations difficult.[71] Strictly speaking, the quantum of recoverable damages is not relevant under this section either, except in the obvious sense that it is connected with the seriousness of the injuries.[72] The only relevant factors are those which relate to the seriousness of the injuries.

Second, there is nothing in this section which expressly directs the **10.55** court to apply the statutory assumptions on an objective basis. The equivalent English provisions speak of the plaintiff "reasonably" considering the injury "sufficiently serious" to raise an action,[73] and so introduce a test that goes beyond the purely subjective. Although the Scottish provisions say nothing about reasonableness, it is virtually impossible to operate the section without employing that concept. Suppose that a rather seriously injured pursuer argued that he himself did not consider his injuries sufficiently serious to raise an action; as a question purely of subjective belief, it is impossible to argue with that. But it is equally impossible that this can be what the subsection means. It therefore becomes necessary to introduce an element of objectivity into the test.

There is another reason for this. Nothing is more likely than that the **10.56** ordinary pursuer will have given absolutely no thought to the question whether the prospective defender is solvent or will admit liability. But again this can hardly matter: it cannot prevent time starting to run, and nor can it be necessary for the court to hear evidence on whether the pursuer actually did consider these points[74]; what matters is the seriousness of the injuries and what conclusions they lead to.

---

[70] 1993 S.L.T. 1248.

[71] In *Carnegie v. Lord Advocate*, 1998 S.L.T. 872, the court took account of the fact that the pursuer was a young recruit anxious to remain in the army and therefore inhibited about complaining about bullying. But this does not appear to fall within the scope of the s. 17(2)(b)(i) test. It might, however, be arguable that such considerations would be relevant to the assessment of the pursuer's conduct for the purposes of s. 19A (on which see below, paras 12.10–11): *cf. McCafferty v. Metropolitan Police Receiver* [1977] 1 W.L.R. 1073, CA.

[72] By contrast under the old s. 22(3), repealed in 1984, it is expressly made a consideration that the action would result in "an award of damages sufficient to justify the bringing of the action".

[73] Limitation Act 1980, s. 14(2). *cf.* also *McCafferty v. Metropolitan Police Receiver*, above, at 1081, on Limitation Act 1939, s. 2A(7), the terms of which are for present purposes the same as those of the 1980 Act.

[74] The opposite is suggested by *Lowe v. Grampian Health Board*, 1998 S.L.T. 731.

10.57   Accordingly, it seems appropriate to adopt the approach taken in *Blake* and other cases[75] and to ask the question "what would the reasonable pursuer have done in the circumstances of this case?". On this basis it may on the facts be quite reasonable for an (eventual) pursuer to take the view that he has recovered from his injuries and only later, when serious consequences emerge, to address his mind to the question whether his injuries are serious enough to warrant raising an action.

Provisional damages

10.58   It is clearly the law that all damages arising from the same wrongful act must be recovered in one action.[76] This means that a pursuer may be tempted to wait, and to some extent is justified in waiting, to see what the consequences of his injury turn out to be. To sue too soon is to risk recovering less than full compensation. Nonetheless, time is running against the pursuer from the moment he is aware of all the statutory facts. To wait too long is to risk recovering nothing.

10.59   Here the pursuer's position is to some extent relieved by the availability since 1982 of awards of provisional damages. Where appropriate,[77] and where there is a risk that at some time in the future the injured person will, as a result of the act or omission, develop some serious disease or suffer some serious deterioration in his physical or mental condition, the court may award damages assessed on the assumption that he will not develop the disease or suffer the deterioration and may award further damages if in the future he does.[78]

Attribution of the injuries to an act or omission

10.60   For time to run against him, the pursuer must (actually or constructively) be aware that the injuries are attributable in whole or in part to an act or omission.[79] The difficulty in the individual case is to determine how much factual knowledge the pursuer can have before time begins to run against him.

10.61   It does not seem plausible that his awareness must extend to how precisely the injuries were caused by the act or omission. In cases of any complexity the pursuer is never likely to have any such knowledge, and proof of the causal connection between act or omission and injury will be supplied by expert evidence. The courts in any event take a common sense approach to questions of causation.[80] English authority has adopted the view that "attributable to" means "capable of being attributed to" rather than "caused by"[81]; and that this means attribution is "a real possibility and not a fanciful one, a possible cause as opposed to a probable cause of the injury".[82]

---

[75] *Lowe*, above.

[76] *Stevenson v. Pontifex & Wood* (1887) 15 R. 125.

[77] On the conditions which have to be satisfied for such an award, see Administration of Justice (Scotland) Act 1982, s. 12; RCS, rr. 43.11–43.13.

[78] 1982, Act, s. 12(2)–(4).

[79] It should be noted that the terms of the equivalent English provision are narrower: Limitation Act 1980, s. 14(1)(b) "the injury was attributable in whole or in part to the act or omission which is alleged to constitute negligence, nuisance or breach of duty".

[80] See H. L. A. Hart and A. M. Honoré, *Causation in the Law* (2nd ed., 1995).

[81] *Davis v. Ministry of Defence*, July 26, 1985, unreported, CA; *Dobbie v. Medway Health Authority* [1994] 1 W.L.R. 1234 at 1240, CA.

[82] *Nash v. Eli Lilly & Co.* [1993] 1 W.L.R. 782 at 797–798, CA.

It seems best to take this awareness requirement in the general sense **10.62** that the pursuer is conscious that his injuries are the result, wholly or partly, of a specific thing which was done or not done, as opposed to mere chance or an act of God. So for example it would demand an awareness that a respiratory disease was not the result of living in an unhealthy climate or smoking cigarettes but was connected—at least in part—with a particular act or omission of some person (such as generating fumes or failing to provide breathing apparatus) as opposed to another act or omission of the same or another person. Or, as it was put in *Nash v. Eli Lilly & Co.*,[83] a pharmaceutical case: "What is required is knowledge of the essence of the act or omission to which the injury is attributable". In that case, what was needed to satisfy that test was not the precise terms in which the defendants' conduct would be pleaded as amounting to negligence or breach of duty but, more generally, the defendants' "providing for the use of patients a drug which was unsafe in that it was capable of causing persistent photosensitivity in those patients and/or in failing to discover that such was the case so as properly to protect such patients".

It may in certain circumstances be enough if the pursuer is aware that **10.63** the system of work is unsafe.[84] But this does raise the question of knowing what the act or omission complained of actually is. It cannot be enough to have a vague suspicion that there is something less than perfectly safe about the working environment provided by the defender. The words "act or omission" in the section must go further than that, so that time does not run against the pursuer until he can identify at least in broad terms what act or omission is the cause of his injuries. In one case what was in issue was the pursuer's awareness, actual or constructive, of a causal connection between using a chainsaw and hand–arm vibration syndrome: the pursuer had to be able to attribute his injuries to a particular omission.[85] Of course, in order to establish negligence, the pursuer will anyway have to be specific about the particular precautions or protective measures which he alleges the employer ought to have taken. So, for example, in another case it was held that what was needed was awareness of working close to a source of asbestos dust in the absence, in general, of any protective measures for dust removal and inhalation prevention.[86]

In *Nicol v. British Steel Corporation (General Steels) Ltd*,[87] the pursuer **10.64** was injured in an explosion. He was aware that one possibility was that the accident was attributable to an act or omission of one of a particular group of people. This was held not to go far enough to start time running against him. It was observed more generally that it may sometimes be possible to say that injuries must have been caused by an act or omission, even though it is not possible to say precisely what it was or what precise mechanism connected it to the accident. If so, it may also be possible to say that the act or omission must have been the act or

---

[83] [1993] 1 W.L.R. 782, CA.
[84] *McLaren v. Harland and Wolff Ltd*, 1991 S.L.T. 85; *Wilkinson v. Ancliff (BLT) Ltd* [1986] 1 W.L.R. 1352.
[85] *Dickenson v. Lord Advocate*, Lord Osborne, June 8, 1995, unreported.
[86] *McLaren v. Harland and Wolff Ltd*, above, at 87 (*obiter*).
[87] 1992 S.L.T. 141.

omission of one of a class of persons, such as the employees of a
particular employer, without being able to specify the individual. But it
would not be enough that the pursuer was aware that his injury might be
attributable to an act or omission of one of a particular group of persons.
If that possibility is only one of a number of possibilities, and there is no
reason to choose between them, the pursuer cannot be said in any
meaningful sense to be aware that the injury is attributable to the act or
omission, and so this does not go far enough to start time running
against the pursuer.[88] As a matter of logic, this is clearly right, since an
awareness that something was caused by A or B does not amount to
an awareness that it was caused by A.

10.65   Omissions raise one further consideration. Take the case where a
pursuer's injuries are attributable to the fact that he has not had an
operation in hospital. In most cases he will be well aware that he has not
had an operation. But he cannot in any real sense be aware that his
injuries are attributable to an omission until he is aware that, had the
operation (or a different operation) taken place at or before a certain
time, he might not have sustained the injuries, or injuries as serious as
those, which he actually did sustain. In practice this may mean that the
pursuer cannot be aware that his injuries are attributable to an omission
until he is also aware that there was a specific failure to act and therefore
negligence. Although this may appear to infringe the statutory provision
that knowledge that any act or omission is actionable as a matter of law
is irrelevant,[89] the critical point is that awareness is being used in this
context not in relation to actionability but merely to make the causal
connection between the injury and the omission.[90]

Sexual abuse

10.66   This raises questions not dissimilar to those posed by latent disease.
There does not appear to be any Scottish authority on the matter. The
limitation period does not begin to run until the person injured reaches
age 16.[91] Much more difficult in practice, however, is the question of
postponing the start of the limitation period for reasons connected with
the injured person's lack of awareness of necessary facts. The experience
of other jurisdictions suggests that cases are likely to divide into two
categories: first, those where the pursuer knew of the abuse but was not
aware of the causal connection between it and the harm he or she later
suffered[92]; second, those where the pursuer had no memory of the abuse
until it was later triggered by some event.[93]

10.67   Although both of these clearly raise difficult questions, as a general
rule the pursuer in the second case will be in a somewhat stronger
position with respect to limitation. In the first case, a pursuer who is
aware of the injury done to him or her and of the identity of the

---

[88] 1992 S.L.T. 141 at 144.
[89] s. 22(3).
[90] *cf. Forbes v. Wandsworth Health Authority* [1997] Q.B. 402 at 411 and 421, CA.
[91] s. 17(3).
[92] *cf.* s. 17(2)(b)(ii).
[93] *cf.* s. 17(2)(b)(ii) and (iii). In *Johnson v. Johnson* (1988) 701 F. Supp. 363 these are
respectively described as type 1 and type 2 cases. For general discussion, see Law Com.
Consultation Paper no. 151 (1998), paras 10.118–10.122; *cf. Stubbings v. Webb* [1993] A.C.
498, noted by McGee in (1993) 109 L.Q.R. 356.

defender, will have to rely on arguing either that, until not more than three years before the raising of the action, the injuries were not sufficiently serious to justify bringing an action, or that it was not reasonably practicable for him or her to be aware that they were sufficiently serious. And this in turn raises the question how far the pursuer ought to have sought advice or treatment.

Actions brought many years after the events in question always raise **10.68** difficulties, and that is especially true owing to the sensitivity of allegations of sexual abuse, coupled with the devastating effects which such abuse can have. Many of these issues are canvassed in the opinions in a case of the Supreme Court of Washington,[94] in which the Court was divided 5–4. The majority was concerned about the potential effects on the system of justice of allowing a case to proceed at so late a date, uneasy about the plaintiff's alleged recovery of a memory after psychotherapy, and uncomfortable with the quality of psychiatric opinion as compared with what was described as objective evidence or medical diagnosis. The minority emphasised the need to protect those who had suffered from such abuse, the fact that allowing the case to proceed presupposed nothing but simply allowed the plaintiff an opportunity to prove the allegations, and was more impressed by the quality of the psychiatric evidence.

These are considerations with which the courts are bound to be faced **10.69** in a case of damages for sexual abuse.

Attribution of the injuries to an act or omission of the defender

The pursuer must also be aware (actually or constructively) that the **10.70** defender was a person to whose act or omission the injuries were attributable in whole or in part, or the employer or principal of such a person. This raises two issues.

First, the types of case in which this provision is likely to be relevant **10.71** are few.[95] The best examples are the hit-and-run driver; the case where the pursuer has been operated on by a surgeon whose name he does not know; and the case where the pursuer is employed by a company of whose precise identity he is unaware, usually because it is one of a number of interrelated companies with similar names or because it has been taken over.[96] This of course raises the question of reasonable practicability. The court may find that the pursuer did not actually identify the defender but still take the view that it was reasonably

---

[94] *Tyson v. Tyson*, 727 P. 2d 226 (1986). Note that since this case the limitation statute of the state of Washington has been amended so that, for the particular case of actions concerning sexual abuse, time now runs in three years from the date of the act of abuse or, if later, the date the plaintiff actually discovered the abuse, unless the plaintiff could reasonably have discovered the act of abuse at an earlier date.

[95] The provision has been held not to be relevant to the case where the pursuer knew the identity of the (legal) person responsible for his injuries, but that legal person ceased to exist and its obligations and liabilities were transferred to another legal person: *Stephen v. North of Scotland Water Authority*, 1999 S.L.T. 342. *Cf.* in relation to the Limitation Act 1980, s. 35, *Yorkshire Regional Health Authority v. Fairclough Building Ltd* [1996] 1 W.L.R. 216.

[96] *Comer v. James Scott & Co. (Electrical Engineers)*, 1978 S.L.T. 235; *Simpson v. Norwest Holst Southern Ltd* [1980] 1 W.L.R. 968.

practicable for him to do so.[97] A clear example of how he might proceed would be by means of a company search or an application under section 1(1A) of the Administration of Justice (Scotland) Act 1972.[98]

10.72   Second, this provision covers the case of vicarious liability. Time will start to run against an action directed at the employer or principal only from the date the pursuer has actual or constructive awareness of the fact that he is the employer or principal of the person to whose act or omission the injuries are attributable.

10.73   It follows that the limitation period for a claim based on the vicarious liability of the employer or principal may start at a later date than a claim based on the personal liability of the employee.

Computation of the limitation period

10.74   In terms of section 17(2) the action has to be commenced within a period of three years after the date ascertained according to the provisions of the section. Since no statutory definition of "commenced" is provided and nothing is said in this Part of the Act about computation of the limitation period,[99] it appears that the intention of Parliament must have been that the common law rules should apply. Under these rules an action commences on the date of citation of the defender.[1] So far as computation of periods of time is concerned,[2] the limitation period will begin at the beginning of the first complete day and be completed at the last instant of the last day three years later. So, where a pursuer was injured (or became aware of his injuries) in the course of June 1, 2000, the limitation period would begin to run at the first instant on June 2, 2000 and would be completed at the last instant on June 1, 2003.

Suspension of the limitation period

10.75   Section 17(3) provides that any period during which the person injured was under legal disability by reason of nonage or unsoundness of mind is disregarded in calculating the limitation period. Nonage ends at age 16.[3]

10.76   This applies only to the computation of a period after the date on which limitation starts to run,[4] so it does not operate to postpone the start but only to suspend the completion of the limitation period.

10.77   Although there is no express provision[5] that periods before and after a period of legal disability are to be regarded as continuous, the general

---

[97] *Dormer v. Melville, Dundas & Whitson*, 1987 S.C.L.R. 655: here the pursuer was not able to invoke this provision when a defender brought a third party into the action on averments of fact unknown to the pursuer and, after the limitation period had run, the pursuer sought to convene the third party as a defender: it was held that the pursuer must aver why it was not reasonably practicable for him to be aware of the new facts which pointed to the third party.

[98] *McDyer v. Celtic Football and Athletic Co. Ltd*, 1999 S.L.T. 2.

[99] Contrast s. 14, for Pt I of the Act.

[1] See above, para. 5.09.

[2] See above, para. 4.97.

[3] Age of Legal Capacity (Scotland) Act 1991.

[4] s. 17(2), (3).

[5] Such as in s. 6(5).

wording of section 17(3) seems to bear the implication that periods separated in this way should be regarded as continuous.

Section 17(3) is directed at the legal disability of the person who **10.78** sustained the injuries, and takes no account of the disability of the pursuer, if different.[6] It is now well settled that the pursuer need not establish a causal connection between his disability and any delay in proceeding with the action: this subsection gives him a blanket exemption for the period of his legal disability.[7]

It is worth emphasising that subsection (3) is the only provision in this **10.79** context which expressly takes account of the legal disability of the injured person (as opposed to the pursuer, if different). Suppose, for example, that a person sustains brain damage or immediately enters a coma as a result of an act or omission. If he can be said to be under legal disability owing to unsoundness of mind, then time will not run against him so long as that disability continues.

Nonetheless, section 17(2)(b) may also become relevant in this **10.80** context, so as to postpone the start of the limitation period until the pursuer is aware of certain facts. Although in such a case any action would be likely to be pursued by a *curator bonis* appointed to the injured person, and the provision is drafted in terms of the awareness of the pursuer, it has already been argued that the section can only be given a satisfactory meaning if it is interpreted as referring to the awareness of the injured person rather than his *curator bonis*.[8] In this example, the injured person is clearly not in a position to be aware of any facts. Accordingly, the limitation period will not begin to run.

This interpretation does not destroy the point of section 17(3), since **10.81** there remain circumstances (such as nonage) where there is no potential for overlap with section 17(2)(b).

Suspension of the limitation period may also arise under section 1 of **10.82** the Limitation (Enemies and War Prisoners) Act 1945. This provides for the suspension of the running of limitation during a period when the person in question was an enemy or detained in enemy territory, and also that the limitation period shall not expire less than 12 months from the date when the person in question ceased to be an enemy or to be detained. The 1945 Act is drafted in broad terms: what has so far been paraphrased as the "person in question" is in the Act "any person who would have been a necessary party to such an action or who was a party to such obligation". For limitation purposes this has no doubt to be read as referring only to the injured person; it could not be said that any particular representative of the pursuer was a necessary party to an action.

Procedure

Issues involving section 17(2) are likely to arise (1) when amendment **10.83** of the record is sought after the limitation period has passed (this is discussed in Chapter 20); (2) on procedure roll; (3) at preliminary proof

---

[6] Contrast s. 22B(4) for product liability actions.

[7] *Sellwood's C.B. v. Lord Advocate*, 1998 S.L.T. 1438; *Paton v. Loffland Brothers North Sea Inc.*, 1994 S.L.T. 784 (on s. 18(3)); *contra, Bogan's C.B. v. Graham*, 1992 S.C.L.R. 920.

[8] See above, para. 10.12.

on the question of time-bar; (4) at proof before answer on the whole case including the plea of limitation.

10.84   If it is clear on the pleadings that the pursuer cannot satisfy section 17(2), the court can dismiss the action at procedure roll. The same will apply if the admissions in the pleadings extend far enough to make proof unnecessary. But where there is any doubt about the facts which bear on the application of the statutory test—for example, which facts the pursuer knew when, or which it was reasonably practicable for him to know when,[9] or where the medical reports leave doubt about the sufficient seriousness of the pursuer's injuries[10]—clearly the case cannot be decided on the pleadings alone. Here a preliminary proof on the question of limitation is likely to be appropriate.[11] In many cases the issue of the court's equitable discretion under section 19A will be dealt with at the same time.

10.85   Where the pursuer relies on section 17(2)(b) to postpone the start of the limitation period, the action cannot go to a jury trial.[12]

II. ACTIONS WHERE DEATH HAS RESULTED FROM PERSONAL INJURIES

10.86 These actions fall under the provisions of section 18, which are sufficiently similar to those of section 17 that it will be enough simply to comment on the main points of difference.

> **"Actions where death has resulted from personal injuries**
> **18.**—(1) This section applies to any action in which, following the death of any person from personal injuries, damages are claimed in respect of the injuries or the death.
> (2) Subject to subsections (3) and (4) below and section 19A of this Act, no action to which this section applies shall be brought unless it is commenced within a period of three years after—
>
> (a) the date of death of the deceased; or
> (b) the date (if later than the date of death) on which the pursuer in the action became, or on which, in the opinion of the court, it would have been reasonably practicable for him in all the circumstances to become, aware of both of the following facts—
> > (i) that the injuries of the deceased were attributable in whole or in part to an act or omission; and
> > (ii) that the defender was a person to whose act or omission the injuries were attributable in whole or in part or the employer or principal of such a person.
>
> (3) Where the pursuer is a relative of the deceased, there shall be disregarded in the computation of the period specified in sub-

---

[9] *Heathfield v. Elf Enterprise Caledonia Ltd*, Lord Milligan, February 15, 1995, unreported.

[10] *Hooks v. White Horse Distillers Ltd*, Lord Gill, October 20, 1995, unreported.

[11] See, *e.g.*, *Kane v. Argyll and Clyde Health Board*, 1997 S.L.T. 965; *Blake v. Lothian Health Board*, 1993 S.L.T. 1248; *Shuttleton v. Duncan Stewart & Co. Ltd*, Lord Prosser, August 2, 1995, unreported.

[12] s. 22(4).

section (2) above any time during which the relative was under legal disability by reason of nonage or unsoundness of mind.

(4) Subject to section 19A of this Act, where an action of damages has not been brought by or on behalf of a person who has sustained personal injuries within the period specified in section 17(2) of this Act and that person subsequently dies in consequence of those injuries, no action to which this section applies shall be brought in respect of those injuries or the death from those injuries.

(5) In this section 'relative' has the same meaning as in Schedule 1 to the Damages (Scotland) Act 1976."

Scope of section 18

Where a person has suffered personal injuries and has died from **10.87** them, section 18 governs the question of limitation of actions both for damages for the injuries and damages for the death. The exception is that where such actions arise out of product liability under the Consumer Protection Act 1987 they are treated under separate limitation (and prescription) provisions.[13]

The definition of "personal injuries" is the same as for section 17.[14] **10.88** This section applies only where the death has been "from personal injuries". The section appears not to apply where the death has not been from personal injuries, but from some other cause: if the death has not been culpably caused, there would be no claim; if it has been culpably caused, but by some independent act, there will be a claim in relation to that independent culpable act.[15]

Title to sue

Two main possibilities arise following the death of an injured person.[16] **10.89** First, there may be a claim transmitted by the deceased to his executor. Second, claims by relatives of the deceased arise on his death. This section covers both of these cases. All that section 18(1) requires is that damages are claimed in respect of the injuries or the death of a deceased following upon his death from the injuries. That wording covers both a (transmitted) action for damages raised by an injured person who subsequently died and an action raised (in respect of the death) only after the death.

The foundation of the claims in each of these two cases is different. **10.90** The executor's title to sue is based on transmission of the deceased's own claim. This is regulated by the Damages (Scotland) Act 1976.[17] The effect is that the executor has the same rights as the deceased had, including the right to claim for patrimonial loss arising before the death, for services rendered to or by the deceased before death,[18] and for solatium, but excluding any claim to patrimonial loss in respect of a period after the death of the deceased.[19] It is important to note,

---

[13] s. 22C (limitation); s. 22A (prescription).
[14] s. 22(1).
[15] See further below on s. 18(4).
[16] The following paragraphs provide only the briefest of summaries: see further McEwan & Paton, *Damages*, Chap. 13.
[17] 1976 Act, s. 2.
[18] Administration of Justice (Scotland) Act 1982, ss. 7–9.
[19] 1976 Act, s. 2(1)–(3); the transmissibility of the claim to solatium was introduced only by the Damages (Scotland) Act 1993, amending these provisions of the 1976 Act.

however, that the executor has title to pursue such an action whether or not the deceased had raised an action during his lifetime.[20] What matters is that it is the right of action, rather than the action itself, which transmits.

10.91 Claims by relatives are founded on the Damages (Scotland) Act 1976,[21] whose definition of "relative" is employed in the 1973 Act.[22] Claims for loss of support provided by the deceased, and for loss of services,[23] can be made by all or any of a class of relatives including a surviving spouse (or person living with the deceased in that relationship immediately before the death), ascendants, descendants and collaterals.[24] Claims for distress in enduring the suffering of the deceased before death, grief caused by the death and for loss of society can be brought only by a narrower class of relatives, members of the deceased's "immediate family": a surviving spouse (or person living with the deceased in that relationship immediately before the death), parent, child (including a posthumous, adopted or illegitimate child, or one accepted by the deceased as a child of the family).[25]

10.92 Claims by the executor and by relatives are not mutually exclusive. It is perfectly possible for the deceased's own claim to transmit to his executor, while his relatives raise their own claims after his death.[26] The preferable course, however, is for all claims to be conjoined in a single action.[27] The Rules of Court require a pursuer in such cases to aver that there are no "connected persons" who could make a claim arising from the death, or seek warrant to intimate the action to them, or seek dispensation from intimation on the grounds that their whereabouts are unknown or the value of their claims is less than £200. A "connected person" who receives intimation but does not enter the process and later raises a separate action will recover expenses only on cause shown.

10.93 On the other hand, it is also possible for all claims to be barred if the deceased has discharged or compromised them during his lifetime.[28]

Running of the limitation period

10.94 Section 18(2) provides three possible starting points for the limitation period: the pursuer's action is time-barred if three years (excluding any period of legal disability if the pursuer is a relative of the deceased)[29] have passed since:

   (i) the date of death of the deceased; or
   (ii) if later than the date of death, the date on which the pursuer was aware of the facts set out in section 18(2)(b); or

---

[20] 1976 Act, s. 2A(1)(a). This must, however, be subject to the question whether the deceased's right of action had become time-barred: see below on s. 18(4).

[21] 1976 Act, s. 1. By s. 1A rights to damages vested in relatives under s. 1 transmit on their deaths to their executors.

[22] s. 18(5), referring to 1976 Act, Sched. 1.

[23] 1982 Act, s. 9(2).

[24] 1976 Act, ss. 1(1), (3) and Sched. 1, para. 2 (as amended).

[25] *ibid.* ss. 1(1), (3) and (4) and 10(2) and Sched. 1, para. 1.

[26] *cf.* 1976 Act, s. 4 (as amended).

[27] RCS, r. 43.

[28] 1976 Act, ss. 1(2), 1A and 2A.

[29] s. 18(3).

(iii) the date on which in the opinion of the court it was reasonably
practicable for him to be aware of those facts.

In addition, it is open to a pursuer to invoke the equitable discretion **10.95**
of the court to extend the time-limit within which the action must be
brought.[30]

Little needs to be said about the first of these possible dates, since in **10.96**
most cases the date of death will be ascertainable. The cases in section
18(2)(b) cause more difficulty. Here the later of the two possibilities is
the date on which the pursuer had actual awareness of the statutory
facts, but the court may take the view that it was reasonably practicable
for the pursuer to have been aware of those facts at an earlier date. In
that event, it is from that earlier date that the limitation period runs.

Awareness
Since there is no need here to repeat the points set out in connection **10.97**
with section 17(2)(b) about the meaning of actual and constructive
awareness of facts,[31] a few short points will suffice. One important
consideration is that in cases covered by section 18 there will often be
several pursuers. For each of them the issues raised in section 18(2)(b)
must be addressed separately, so there may be different starting dates for
limitation, for example because the evidence shows that one pursuer
knew the facts before another, or the court takes the view that it was
reasonably practicable for one pursuer but not for another to know them
on a particular date.

The statutory facts
The main difference between the statutory facts relevant under section **10.98**
18 and those under section 17 is that there is no need to consider the
sufficient seriousness of the injuries, it being enough that death has
followed from them. Accordingly, the pursuer need be aware only that
the injuries of the deceased were attributable to an act or omission, and
that the defender was a person (or the employer or principal of a
person) to whose act or omission the injuries were attributable. Both of
these facts also appear in section 17(2), and it is enough to refer to the
comments made on them there.[32]

A jury trial is not possible where a pursuer relies on section 18(2)(b) **10.99**
to postpone the start of the limitation period; the same is (of course)
true of section 17(2)(b) cases.[33]

Suspension of the limitation period
Section 18(3) provides that any period during which a pursuer who is a **10.100**
relative of the deceased was under legal disability by reason of nonage or
unsoundness of mind is disregarded in calculating the limitation period.
Nonage ends at age 16.[34]

---

[30] ss. 18(2) and 19A.
[31] See above, paras 10.21–36.
[32] See above, paras 10.60 *et seq.*, 10.70 *et seq.*
[33] s. 22(4).
[34] Age of Legal Capacity (Scotland) Act 1991. This supersedes the decisions in *Forbes v.
House of Clydesdale*, 1988 S.L.T. 594 and *Fyfe v. Croudace*, 1986 S.L.T. 528.

10.101   Just as in section 17 cases, so here section 18(2)(b) allows a pursuer to argue for the postponement of the starting date for limitation, on grounds of lack of awareness of the relevant statutory facts, while the scope of section 18(3) is confined to suspending a limitation period which has already started to run, during any period of legal disability.

10.102   Under section 17(3) suspension of the limitation period takes place when the injured person is affected by legal disability.[35] The difference under section 18 is that it is the legal disability of the pursuer (rather than the injured person) which is relevant, and that this is a consideration only for the case of pursuers who are relatives of the deceased. Again, it will be essential to consider the case of each pursuer separately. An obvious case would be when a widow and children sue in respect of the death of the husband and father. Here the limitation period for each child's claim will not commence until he or she reaches age 16[36]; and the period for any individual pursuer affected by unsoundness of mind will be subject to further adjustment. There is no need to plead a causal connection between the legal disability and the failure to raise the action within the limitation period. Provided disability is present, time is automatically at a standstill.[37]

10.103   Where an action is pursued on behalf of a child or an incapable person, the actual pursuer in the action will be the guardian of the child or a *curator bonis* or *curator ad litem*. An argument that such an action does not fall within section 18(3)—unless by chance the guardian or *curator* happens to be a relative of the deceased—has been rejected as producing a ludicrous construction of the subsection which would be apt to defeat one of its principal objects.[38]

10.104   There is a potential for overlap between sections 18(2)(b) and 18(3), since both the provisions about postponement on grounds of lack of awareness and those about suspension on grounds of legal disability are drafted so as to refer to the pursuer. It would seem to follow that a pursuer could argue either for postponement in terms of section 18(2)(b) or for suspension in terms of section 18(3), founding as appropriate on his own lack of awareness or legal disability.

10.105   The deceased's own disability is not a factor which is directly relevant to claims made by relatives. Their claims in any event arise at the date of death of the deceased, and they are affected only by certain events before the date of death, such as compromise, discharge or limitation of claims.

10.106   On the other hand, where a claim is made by the deceased's executor, the executor is unable to rely on any suspension of the limitation period owing to his own disability, but should take the benefit of any suspension of the limitation period as a result of the deceased's own legal disability.

---

[35] See above, paras 10.75–81.
[36] Age of Legal Capacity (Scotland) Act 1991.
[37] *Paton v. Loffland Brothers North Sea Inc.*, 1994 S.L.T. 784 (declining to follow *Bogan's C.B. v. Graham*, 1992 S.C.L.R. 920); *cf. Sellwood's C.B. v. Lord Advocate*, 1998 S.L.T. 1438 (on s. 17(3)).
[38] *Paton v. Loffland Brothers North Sea Inc.*, above. *Cf.* the comments made on the related provisions of s. 17: above, para. 10.78.

Section 18(4)

This provision deals with the case where no action for personal **10.107** injuries was brought by or on behalf of a person during his lifetime, within the limitation period specified by section 17(2), and he then died from the injuries. It provides that, subject to section 19A, no action shall subsequently be brought in respect of those injuries or that death.

The main point appears to be that if the deceased's own right of **10.108** action would have been time-barred, his death does not put his executor in any better position. That seems logical, and no more need be said about it.

This consequence is extended to the case of relatives too. The same **10.109** logic does not apply to them, since their own claims originate only on death of the deceased. But a different logic leads to the same result. The relatives' claims are independent and not derivative of the claim by the deceased, in the sense that they claim for their own loss rather than the deceased's. But their claims nonetheless arise from the same actionable wrong done to the deceased and they are not unaffected by it. A claim by a relative has been described as a "corollary or adjunct to the primary right of the deceased".[39] So, for example, the relatives' claims are affected by any defence of contributory negligence pleadable against the deceased[40]; the reason this is so is that their claims are not in every sense independent of the deceased's own claim. They are subject to the same defences which can be pleaded against his. More generally, there is authority for saying that the relatives' claims are actionable only if the deceased himself could, if alive, have claimed for his own injury.[41] Accordingly, if time has run against the deceased's claim, then (subject to section 19A) there is no claim which his relatives can now pursue.

It follows from the view that section 18(4) deals with cases where the **10.110** deceased's own right of action was time-barred, for example, that (i) if the deceased did not survive his injuries for as much as three years, his right of action cannot have become time-barred, and therefore section 18(4) does not affect it[42]; (ii) if the deceased's own right of action did not become time-barred because the limitation period did not run during a period of his legal incapacity,[43] section 18(4) should not bar a subsequent action by his executor.

This appears to be an instance in which the rule that the executor is **10.111** the same legal person as the deceased does not apply. If it did, it would mean (for example) that, if a man sustained injuries as a result of an accident and died of them just before three years had expired, his executor would have only the balance of the three-year limitation period in which to bring an action in respect of the injuries. But section 18 makes it clear that actions of this kind are limited at earliest three years after the date of death of the deceased, and it gives no warrant for excising parts of the claim on the basis that they relate to a transmitted claim which is more than three years old.

---

[39] *Horn v. North British Ry* (1878) 5 R. 1055 at 1061.
[40] Law Reform (Contributory Negligence) Act 1945, s. 1(4).
[41] *Horn v. North British Ry*, above; *McKay v. Scottish Airways*, 1948 S.C. 254 at 259.
[42] This view is supported by the word "subsequently" in s. 18(4).
[43] This consideration arises for s. 18(4) since s. 17(2) is expressly subject to s. 17(3).

10.112   Section 18(4) is subject to section 19A. Accordingly, it is open to the court to exercise an equitable discretion, in the light of an explanation by the relative why no action was timeously raised by or on behalf of the deceased.

10.113   Section 18(4) applies only to the case where the injured person has died from "those injuries". If he dies from some completely independent cause—say, in an earthquake—section 18(4) does not apply so as to bar the relatives' claims. This appears at first sight to have the rather odd consequence that, even if the deceased's right of action would have been barred, the relatives' right is not. The answer to this point, however, appears to be to rely on what was said above: the relatives' claims are actionable only if the deceased could, if still alive, have claimed.

Section 19A
10.114   The equitable discretion of the court to extend the time-limit within which an action may be brought applies in the same way to section 18 cases as to section 17.[44] Reliance on section 19A prevents the pursuer from seeking a jury trial.[45]

Procedure
10.115   There are no material differences, so far as procedure is concerned, between section 17 and section 18.

---

[44] See Chap. 12.
[45] s. 19A(4).

CHAPTER 11

ACTIONS OF DEFAMATION AND ACTIONS OF HARASSMENT

I. ACTIONS OF DEFAMATION

Until 1985 actions for defamation were not subject to limitation; they **11.01** simply prescribed under the 20-year negative prescription. The Law Reform (Miscellaneous Provisions) (Scotland) Act 1985 introduced a new section 18A into the 1973 Act[1]:

> **"Limitation of defamation and other actions**
> **18A.**—(1) Subject to subsections (2) and (3) below and section 19A of this Act, no action for defamation shall be brought unless it is commenced within a period of three years after the date when the right of action accrued.
> (2) In the computation of the period specified in subsection (1) above there shall be disregarded any time during which the person alleged to have been defamed was under legal disability by reason of nonage or unsoundness of mind.
> (3) Nothing in this section shall affect any right of action which accrued before the commencement of this section.
> (4) In this section—
>
> > (a) 'defamation' includes *convicium* and malicious falsehood, and 'defamed' shall be construed accordingly; and
> > (b) references to the date when a right of action accrued shall be construed as references to the date when the publication or communication in respect of which the action for defamation is to be brought first came to the notice of the pursuer."

Scope of section 18A

The partial definition offered by section 18A(4)(a) indicates that **11.02** defamation is not to be construed in the narrow sense of statements which are false and which, in themselves or by innuendo, amount to imputations on a person's morality, capacity or solvency. In this section, "defamation" extends also to *convicium* and to malicious falsehood. *Convicium* denotes insult or abuse; malicious falsehood (sometimes also known as verbal injury) covers statements which are actionable because they are false and malicious but which are not necessarily defamatory in the narrow sense.

Section 18A(3) makes it clear that the three-year limitation period **11.03** does not apply to a right of action which accrued before the commencement of section 18A. Accordingly, where the pursuer had notice of the defamatory publication or communication before December 30, 1985,[2]

---

[1] 1985 Act, s. 12(2).
[2] The commencement date of the 1985 Act.

no limitation period applies. It follows that the right of action will be
extinguished only by prescription. Prior to 1973, the long negative
prescription applied to such rights. The 20-year prescription of the 1973
Act still does apply to them. The point is discussed in more detail at the
end of this chapter.

Running of the limitation period

11.04   The limitation period begins on the date when the publication or
communication in question first came to the notice of the pursuer.[3] The
most fundamental point about limitation in this context is that the date
on which it begins is not the date of publication but the date on which
the publication came to the notice of the pursuer. The structure of
section 18A is therefore quite different from that of sections 17 and 18,
where the primary date for limitation turns on a matter of fact (date of
injury or date of death) but may be postponed to take account of the
pursuer's awareness of material information. Under section 18A,
however, the only date for limitation is the date when the pursuer had
notice of the publication. There is no way of fixing the date on which the
limitation period begins independently of the knowledge of the pursuer.
It one case it was argued that a statement constituted a continuing
defamatory publication while it remained in the minutes of a local
authority council. The argument was rejected.[4] It seems anyway to be
misconceived, since time does not begin to run until the pursuer has
notice of the publication, and it then runs from when the publication
"first came to the notice of the pursuer".

11.05   A straightforward example is that of an obscure magazine or local
newspaper, which does not come to the pursuer's notice for a significant
period after publication. The fact that it has already been published for a
significant period is irrelevant. Time does not start to run until the
pursuer has notice of it. This seems rather favourable to the pursuer, and
correspondingly harsh to the defender, but it is difficult to see how it
could be otherwise. In personal injuries cases it makes sense to say (in
effect) that the pursuer is put on notice that he had better think about
claiming, once he is aware that his injuries are of a certain seriousness,
and that they are attributable to the act or omission of a particular
person. If he then fails to do so, he may be defeated by the statutory
provisions on constructive notice. But in the case of defamation it can
hardly be said that the pursuer is under any duty to scour the press, on
the off-chance that he may have been defamed. Nor does it make much
sense to regard it as reasonably practicable for the pursuer to become
aware of the defamatory publication, because he could readily have
bought the offending newspaper. Nobody can be under any obligation to
read a newspaper.

Suspension of the limitation period

11.06   Section 18A(2) provides for suspension of the limitation period for
any period during which the person alleged to have been defamed was
under legal disability by reason of nonage or unsoundness of mind.
Nonage ends at age 16.[5]

---

[3] s. 18A(1) and (4)(b).
[4] *Smith v. Glasgow D.C.*, Lord Morton of Shuna, March 28, 1991, unreported.
[5] Age of Legal Capacity (Scotland) Act 1991.

Twenty-year prescription

Defamation actions are subject not just to a three-year limitation **11.07** period but also to the 20-year prescription.[6] This long stop may become relevant for any of three reasons: (1) that the publication did not come to the notice of the pursuer for many years; (2) that the pursuer was under legal disability; or (3) that the pursuer invoked the equitable discretion of the court to extend the limitation period.[7] This last possibility is not likely to be important in practice, since it is rarely likely to be equitable to allow an action for defamation to proceed so late that a 20-year cut-off point could become material. The other reasons are more substantial.

This is particularly true of the question when the publication first **11.08** came to the notice of the pursuer. It has just been observed that this rule may operate harshly so far as the defender is concerned. Matters are improved by the fact that the defender's liability is extinguished after a period of years, so balancing the interests of the parties somewhat better. Nonetheless, it is doubtful whether it is appropriate to let such claims expire only under the twenty-year prescription. That, however, was clearly the intention of Parliament in the Law Reform (Miscellaneous Provisions) (Scotland) Act 1985, which expressly excluded defamation actions from the five-year prescription.[8]

In England the current limitation period for defamation actions, **11.09** introduced by the Defamation Act 1996,[9] is one year, subject to the discretion of the court to extend the period. The Law Commission has, however, recently proposed that defamation actions should be subject to the same regime as other actions in tort, that is, a proposed uniform limitation period of three years and long-stop of 10 years, with no judicial discretion to extend either period.[10]

Whether or not these proposals are proceeded with in this form in **11.10** England, given the generosity to the pursuer of the wording of section 18A, it does appear that there is much to be said for considering a long-stop in Scotland of less than 20 years.

II. ACTIONS OF HARASSMENT

The Protection from Harassment Act 1997 introduced new provisions **11.11** concerning civil and criminal liability for harassment. The relevant provisions came into force on June 16, 1997.[11] Civil actions for harassment in which damages are sought are subject to a limitation period of three years, in accordance with provisions inserted into the 1973 Act as section 18B:

---

[6] s. 7(2).
[7] s. 19A.
[8] 1985 Act, s. 12(5).
[9] 1996 Act, s. 5.
[10] Law Com. Consultation Paper no. 151 (1998), paras 13.38–13.43, also paras 12.95, 12.113 and 12.187–12.196. The three-year period would run from the date of "discoverability", the 10 years from the date of the tort; a 30-year long-stop is proposed for personal injuries actions alone.
[11] S.I. 1997 No. 1418.

"Actions of harassment

11.12   **18B.**—(1) This section applies to actions of harassment (within the meaning of section 8 of the Protection from Harassment Act 1997) which include a claim for damages.

(2) Subject to subsection (3) below and to section 19A of this Act, no action to which this section applies shall be brought unless it is commenced within a period of three years after—

 (a) the date on which the alleged harassment ceased; or

 (b) the date (if later than the date mentioned in paragraph (a) above) on which the pursuer in the action became, or on which, in the opinion of the court, it would have been reasonably practicable for him in all the circumstances to have become, aware, that the defender was a person responsible for the alleged harassment or the employer or principal of such a person.

(3) In the computation of the period specified in subsection (2) above there shall be disregarded any time during which the person who is alleged to have suffered the harassment was under legal disability by reason of nonage or unsoundness of mind."

Scope of section 18B

11.13   Section 8 of the Protection from Harassment Act 1997 sets out the elements of harassment: "a person must not pursue a course of conduct which amounts to harassment of another and (a) is intended to amount to harassment of that person; or (b) occurs in circumstances where it would appear to a reasonable person that it would amount to harassment of that person".[12] "Conduct" is defined as including speech, "harassment" as including causing a person alarm or distress, and a course of conduct must involve conduct on at least two occasions.[13] The statute provides a defence in the event that the course of conduct complained of was authorised under any enactment or rule of law, was pursued for the purpose of preventing or detecting crime, or was in the particular circumstances reasonable.[14] The damages which may be awarded in an action of harassment include damages for any anxiety caused by the harassment and any financial loss resulting from it.[15]

Running of the limitation period

11.14   There is a range of possible starting points for the limitation period:

 (i) the date when the alleged harassment ceased; or

 (ii) if later, the date when the pursuer became aware that the defender was a person responsible for the harassment, or the employer or principal of such a person; or

 (iii) the date on which in the opinion of the court it was reasonably practicable for him to be aware of that fact.

11.15   Furthermore, the pursuer may wish to invoke the equitable discretion of the court to allow him to bring the action later than any of these dates.[16]

---

[12] 1997 Act, s. 8(1).
[13] 1997 Act, s. 8(3).
[14] 1997 Act, s. 8(4).
[15] 1997 Act. s. 8(6).
[16] s. 19A.

These provisions bear a certain resemblance to those on the limitation **11.16**
of actions for personal injuries under sections 17 and 18 of the 1973 Act.
They are, however, much simpler. First, there is only one "normal" date
for the start of the limitation period, namely the date when the
harassment ceased. This seems reasonable, since by definition what is
being complained of is a course of conduct. Second, it is awareness of
only one fact,[17] namely the identity of the defender (whether liable
personally or vicariously) which may be material in order to postpone
the start of the limitation period.

It is not necessary here to repeat the comments made earlier on the **11.17**
pursuer's awareness of the identity of the defender,[18] nor to reiterate
that the effect of a test of what awareness was "reasonably practicable
for him in all the circumstances" involves both subjective and objective
elements.[19]

Suspension of the limitation period
Section 18B(3) provides for suspension of the limitation period for **11.18**
any period during which the person alleged to have been harassed was
under legal disability by reason of nonage or unsoundness of mind.[20]
Nonage ends at age 16.[21]

Twenty-year prescription
Actions of harassment are subject not just to a three-year limitation **11.19**
period but also to the 20-year prescription.[22] This may at least in theory
become relevant if (i) the pursuer did not become aware and it was not
reasonably practicable for him in all the circumstances to become aware
that the defender was a person responsible for the harassment, or the
employer or principal of such a person; or (ii) the pursuer was under
legal disability; or (iii) the pursuer invoked the equitable discretion of
the court to extend the limitation period.[23] As with actions of defamation, the last of these possibilities is not likely to be important in
practice, since it is rarely likely to be equitable to allow an action of
harassment to proceed so late that a 20-year cut-off point could become
material. Given the definition of harassment, it must also be doubtful
whether the first of these possibilities could seriously be entertained as
late as 20 years after the cessation of the harassment.[24] Accordingly, it
seems that the real significance of the applicability of the 20-year
prescription to actions of harassment will be in cases of the pursuer's
legal disability.

The obligation against which prescription runs arises from breach of **11.20**
statutory duty consisting in harassment. This will become enforceable,
and therefore begin to prescribe, as soon as there is a course of conduct
such as satisfies the statutory requirements for "harassment".[25] So far as

---

[17] Rather than three, as in s. 17(2)(b), or two as in s. 18(2)(b).
[18] Above, paras 10.71–73.
[19] Above, paras 10.21–39.
[20] For further comment on this in relation to s. 17, see above paras 10.75–81.
[21] Age of Legal Capacity (Scotland) Act 1991.
[22] s. 7(2). Unless they are regarded as relating to "personal injuries": see above, paras 10.07–08.
[23] See ss. 18B(2)(b), and 18B(2) and 19A respectively.
[24] s. 18B(2)(a) and the Protection from Harassment Act 1997, s. 8.
[25] 1997 Act, s. 8(3).

claims for damages are concerned, however, the ordinary provisions will apply which postpone the start of prescription until a continuing act, neglect or default has ceased.[26]

---

[26] s. 11(2), (4).

CHAPTER 12

EQUITABLE DISCRETION TO EXTEND THE
LIMITATION PERIOD

"Power of court to override time-limits, etc.   **12.01**
19A.—(1) Where a person would be entitled, but for any of the provisions of sections 17, 18, 18A or 18B of this Act, to bring an action, the court may, if it seems to it equitable to do so, allow him to bring the action notwithstanding that provision.
(2) The provisions of subsection (1) above shall have effect not only as regards rights of action accruing after the commencement of this section but also as regards those, in respect of which a final judgment has not been pronounced, accruing before such commencement.
(3) In subsection (2) above, the expression 'final judgment' means an interlocutor of a court of first instance which, by itself, or taken along with previous interlocutors, disposes of the subject matter of a cause notwithstanding that judgment may not have been pronounced on every question raised or that the expenses found due may not have been modified, taxed or decerned for; but the expression does not include an interlocutor dismissing a cause by reason only of a provision mentioned in subsection (1) above.
(4) An action which could not be entertained but for this section shall not be tried by jury."

Scope of section 19A

This section gives the court power to override the normal limitation **12.02** periods. It was introduced into the 1973 Act by the Law Reform (Miscellaneous Provisions) (Scotland) Act 1980.[1] The effect of subsections (2) and (3) is that certain causes of action which arose before the commencement date in 1980 are also amenable to the court's jurisdiction under section 19A. Where final judgment has been pronounced, the issue cannot be reopened. Only causes of action which are still before the court are amenable to the exercise of this jurisdiction.[2] Where an action was dismissed "by reason only" of the limitation provisions of section 17, 18 or 18A, that interlocutor is not a final judgment of the court.[3] The effect is that it remains open to a pursuer to raise such an action again and to attempt to persuade the court to exercise its discretion in terms of section 19A to allow the action to proceed. This consequence was (of course) not an oversight on the part of Parliament: it was pointed out by Lord Fraser of Tullybelton that this was "a particularly gross example of restrospective legislation",[4] but Parliament proceeded with it nonetheless. The curious result is that any action

---

[1] 1980 Act, s. 23.
[2] s. 19A(2).
[3] s. 19A(3).
[4] H.L. Deb. Vol. 413, col. 1895.

dismissed on grounds of limitation before 1980 can be raised again. The only exception will be actions based on obligations which were extinguished by prescription before that possibility was removed in 1984.[5] Presumably the balancing exercise discussed below will prevent these floodgates from opening.

Relationship of this section with sections 17, 18 and 18A

12.03   The wording of the section appears to require the court first to decide that an action is time-barred,[6] and then to consider, notwithstanding that fact, whether the action should be allowed to proceed. It is accordingly very doubtful whether it is competent for the court to decide that it is equitable to allow an action to proceed in terms of section 19A and that the questions raised by section 17, 18 or 18A need not therefore be considered.[7] Where the court has decided that the action is not time-barred within one of those sections, strictly speaking it need not consider section 19A. In practice, however, it will be necessary to do so where the pursuer has relied on it and the case may be appealed or reclaimed. That then places the court in the curious position of having to balance the equities on the hypothetical assumption that the action actually was time-barred.[8]

Principles of the section 19A jurisdiction

12.04   Two preliminary points may be made, before the principles on which the court exercises its discretion are examined. First, it is clear that the overall burden of satisfying the court that it is equitable to allow the action to proceed lies on the pursuer.[9] Nonetheless, the burden of proving the individual facts relied upon by each party to influence the court in the exercise of its discretion must rest upon the party pleading the particular fact.

12.05   Second, where the pursuer relies on section 19A to overcome the limitation provisions, the case may not go to jury trial.[10]

12.06   No guidance is given in the section as to the principles on which this power is to be exercised. In the years immediately following the introduction of this power in 1980, an orthodoxy grew up, following the case of *Carson v. Howard Doris Ltd*,[11] that the power is to be exercised "sparingly and with restraint" since otherwise it would drive a "coach and six" through the limitation provisions.[12] But apart from the general notion underlying the Act, that stale claims should be barred, there

---

[5] See 1973 Act, s. 7(2), as amended by the Prescription and Limitation (Scotland) Act 1984, s. 5(3) and Sched. 1, para. 2. This came into force on September 26, 1984. See *Paterson v. George Wimpey & Co. Ltd*, 1999 S.L.T. 577.

[6] Under s. 17, 18 or 18A.

[7] For this approach, see *Kidd v. Grampian Health Board*, 1994 S.L.T. 267; *Docherty v. Argyll & Clyde Health Board*, Lord Morton of Shuna, March 10, 1993, unreported (1993 G.W.D. 1119); *Carnegie v. Lord Advocate*, 1998 S.L.T. 872.

[8] See the observations of Lord Prosser in *Shuttleton v. Duncan Stewart & Co. Ltd*, August 2, 1995, unreported (at 32 *et seq.*).

[9] *Clark v. McLean*, 1994 S.C. 410 at 413.

[10] s. 19A(4).

[11] 1981 S.C. 278, followed in *Munro v. Anderson-Grice Engineering Co. Ltd*, 1983 S.L.T. 295; *Whyte v. Walker*, 1983 S.L.T. 441.

[12] This view resurfaced in *Wilkinson v. Allseas Marine Contractors SA*, Lord Cameron, October 24, 1997, unreported.

is nothing to suggest anything of the sort: all the court is asked to do is determine whether it is equitable that the pursuer should be allowed to proceed, in spite of the fact that he or she falls foul of the normal limitation provisions.

Clearly, the general rule remains that an action to which these sections **12.07** apply is time-barred after three years, and the onus is on the pursuer to persuade the court that it should override the time-bar.[13] But the only question before the court in terms of the section is the balancing of the equities for and against allowing the pursuer to proceed, so it is not clear what it means to say, once that balancing exercise has been carried out, that the court should exercise its power sparingly and with restraint. This approach to the exercise of the court's discretionary power has been criticised.[14]

Similarly, the converse assertion in recent cases that the court should **12.08** generally find it equitable to allow an action to proceed if delay has not seriously affected the evidence available, distorts the balancing exercise envisaged by section 19A to the opposite effect.[15] There cannot be any advance presumption in an individual case for or against allowing it to proceed. The whole point of the balancing exercise is that the court approaches it afresh in the individual circumstances of each case. The proper approach was set out in the Inner House in *Donald v. Rutherford*: the court's discretion on whether or not to allow the action to proceed is unfettered, but must be exercised having regard to the interests and conduct of the parties and their advisers as well as the nature and circumstances and prospects of success in pursuit of the claim.[16] For this reason it is not particularly helpful to embark upon a catalogue of decided cases.[17] Nonetheless it may be worth setting out some of the factors which have been considered important in past cases. The most important decisions are the Inner House decisions noted below.[18] These set out no general rules which a court can be guaranteed to follow, but are simply factors relevant to the exercise of the discretion in the individual case.[19]

Relevant factors

Unlike the English legislation,[20] section 19A does not list the factors **12.09** the court is to consider in exercising its discretion. In *Carson v. Howard Doris Ltd* Lord Ross put forward three issues which the court should

---

[13] This is invariably conceded by pursuers and so rarely mentioned in the cases; see, *e.g.*, *Donald v. Rutherford*, 1983 S.L.T. 253, OH.

[14] *Donald v. Rutherford*, 1984 S.L.T. 70 at 75; *Firman v. Ellis* [1978] Q.B. 886.

[15] *Docherty v. Argyll & Clyde Health Board*, Lord Morton of Shuna, March 10, 1993, unreported (1993 G.W.D. 1119); *Kidd v. Grampian Health Board*, 1994 S.L.T. 267.

[16] 1984 S.L.T. 70 at 75.

[17] In case they may be of any assistance, however, here is a list of some of the more recent unreported cases: *Wrightson v. AOC International Ltd*, Lord Gill, October 20, 1995, unreported; *Caygill v. Stena Offshore SA*, Lord Macfadyen, March 20, 1996, unreported; *Ross v. Robertson*, J.F. Wheatley, Q.C., July 10, 1996, unreported; *Wilkinson v. Allseas Marine Contractors SA*, Lord Cameron, October 24, 1997, unreported. For some comments on some recent cases, E. Russell (1997) 2 S.L.P.Q. 328–334.

[18] *Donald v. Rutherford*, 1984 S.L.T. 70; *Forsyth v. A. F. Stoddard & Co.*, 1985 S.L.T. 51; *Elliot v. J. & C. Finney*, 1989 S.L.T. 605; *McCabe v. McLellan*, 1994 S.C. 87; *Anderson v. City of Glasgow D.C.*, 1987 S.L.T. 279; *Clark v. McLean*, 1994 S.C. 410.

[19] *cf. Anderson v. City of Glasgow D.C.*, above, at 287–288; *McFarlane v. Breen*, 1994 S.L.T. 1320 at 1322.

[20] Limitation Act 1980, s. 33(3).

consider in balancing the equities: (1) the conduct of the pursuer; (2) prejudice to the pursuer; and (3) prejudice to the defender, and these considerations have been raised in most of the cases since.

The conduct of the pursuer

12.10   The pursuer must provide a reasonable explanation of failure to take timeous action.[21] If the pursuer is not personally at fault but his agents are, he has to answer for his agents' fault, although this of course connects with the question of an alternative remedy against them.[22] In general it can be said that either the pursuer should have acted timeously himself and, in failing to do so, is at fault; or else his agents should have done so, in which case the pursuer is responsible for their fault while acting within the scope of their authority. The pursuer's remedy then lies against the agents in breach of contract for failure to exercise due skill and care.[23]

12.11   It is not enough that the pursuer's explanation should cover only part of the period of delay. So, for example, a pursuer who was advised in 1974 not to proceed on a cause of action which arose in 1973 needed (which he had not done) to aver circumstances between 1974 and 1980, when he raised the action, against which the reasonableness of his actions could be assessed.[24] The fact that he had at some point acted reasonably raised no presumption that it would be equitable to allow him to proceed. A pursuer who decided not to proceed but later changed his mind for reasons unconnected with any culpable conduct on the part of the defenders was found not to have satisfied section 19A.[25] A pursuer who was aware of her rights and had decided on taking advice not to proceed was held not to have provided a reasonable explanation, while the inaction of one who thought his industrial deafness was simply due to old age was thought excusable.[26] A pursuer's ignorance of the fact that he had a legal remedy has been held to be a relevant factor.[27] The explanation of the pursuer's failure to serve the summons timeously may also be relevant. Where an error had been made in the defender's Christian name in the summons and immediate steps had been taken to correct it, the court allowed the action to proceed[28]; but where service of the summons had been ineffectual and the pursuer's agents took six months to re-serve, the action was dismissed[29]; so too when the pursuers'

---

[21] *Whyte v. Walker*, 1983 S.L.T. 441; *cf. Millar v. Newalls Insulation Co. Ltd*, 1988 S.C.L.R. 359. If a pursuer's averments are inadequate on the question of reasonable practicability (s. 17(2)(b)), they may equally be insufficient to found a case under s. 19A: *Cowan v. Toffolo Jackson & Co. Ltd*, 1998 S.L.T. 1000.

[22] See below. *Donald v. Rutherford*, 1984 S.L.T. 70; *Forsyth v. A. F. Stoddard & Co. Ltd*, 1985 S.L.T. 51. Some more recent Outer House decisions have suggested that the fact that it was the pursuer's agents' fault rather than his own would be relevant: *Oliver v. KCA Drilling Ltd*, Lord Marnoch, December 16, 1994, unreported; *Caygill v. Stena Offshore AS*, Lord Macfadyen, March 20, 1996, unreported.

[23] *cf.* Bowstead and Reynolds on *Agency* (16th ed., 1996), paras 6.015 *et seq.*

[24] *Munro v. Anderson-Grice Engineering Co. Ltd*, 1983 S.L.T. 295.

[25] *Henshaw v. Carnie*, 1988 S.C.L.R. 305; *cf. Hamilton v. Fife Health Board*, T.G. Coutts, Q.C., January 27, 1995, unreported; *cf.* also *Pritchard v. Tayside Health Board*, Lord Milligan, March 23, 1989, unreported (1989 G.W.D. 643).

[26] *Williams v. Forth Valley Health Board*, 1983 S.L.T. 376; *Black v. British Railways Board*, 1983 S.L.T. 146.

[27] *McLaren v. Harland and Wolff Ltd*, 1991 S.L.T. 85.

[28] *Ferguson v. McFadyen*, 1992 S.L.T. 44.

[29] *Anderson v. John Cotton (Colne) Ltd*, 1991 S.L.T. 696.

averments did not disclose why it was not reasonably practicable to identify the defender in time and what efforts they had made to do so.[30]

The defender's conduct is also relevant, although this is less likely to **12.12** be a factor. In one case, it was the defenders, through their agents, who were responsible for the dismissal of an action by failing to arrange for it to table as they had agreed to do. In effect they had become entitled to found on section 17 only because of their breach of agreement. The Second Division allowed the action to proceed.[31] In general, questions such as fraud by the defender or error induced by the defender to prevent the pursuer claiming, which do not automatically suspend the running of the limitation period,[32] might be relevant to the exercise of the court's discretion under section 19A.

Prejudice to the pursuer
The availability of an alternative remedy to the pursuer in the form **12.13** (typically) of a claim against his professional advisers is a factor which points away from prejudice to the pursuer.[33] In recent years the courts appear to have moved away from regarding the existence of an alternative remedy as enough in itself and considered the practicalities of pursuing that remedy, giving weight to the costs, the delay and evidential difficulties or complications.[34] Clearly this factor has greater weight if the pursuer is particularly prejudiced by delay, for example by reason of a depressive condition exacerbated by the litigation.[35]

The availability of a claim against other defenders arising from the **12.14** same incident—for example, operators or occupiers as well as employers—is a further factor to be taken into account. Here too the court's decision depends substantially on the strength of the case against those other defenders.[36]

The facts that on dismissal the pursuer would face a substantial **12.15** interim liability for expenses and have to fund a further action against his solicitors, and that this liability might only be discharged in the event of his later succeeding against his solicitors, have been held relevant; so has the fact that the pursuer's union would not fund a further action, so the pursuer would have to fund it himself.[37]

Something will turn too on the strength of the pursuer's alternative **12.16** claim. Where it looks relatively insecure, the courts have not given this factor much weight, for instance where there may be problems in showing which of several professional advisers is the one to blame for

---

[30] *Bain v. Philip*, Lord Weir, March 11, 1992, unreported.
[31] *McCluskey v. Sir Robert McAlpine & Sons Ltd*, 1994 S.C.L.R. 650.
[32] Contrast, in the case of five-year prescription, s. 6(4); above, paras 6.112 *et seq*.
[33] *Forsyth v. A. F. Stoddard & Co. Ltd*, 1985 S.L.T. 51; *Beaton v. Strathclyde Buses Ltd*, 1992 S.L.T. 931.
[34] See *e.g. McFarlane v. Breen*, 1994 S.L.T. 1320.
[35] *Johnston v. Thomson*, 1995 S.C.L.R. 554; *McCluskey v. Sir Robert McAlpine & Sons Ltd*, 1994 S.C.L.R. 650.
[36] *Speedwell v. Allied Bakeries Ltd*, Lord MacLean, February 1, 1994, unreported; *Oliver v. KCA Drilling Ltd*, Lord Marnoch, December 16, 1994, unreported.
[37] *Elliot v. J. & C. Finney*, 1989 S.L.T. 208 (upheld in the Inner House 1989 S.L.T. 605); *Ross v. Robertson*, J.F. Wheatley, Q.C., July 10, 1996, unreported.

missing the time-bar,[38] or where there may be complications, such as the
need to restore the intended defender company to the Companies
Register,[39] or the need to pursue an action to its conclusion against other
defenders in order to know what loss if any flowed from the advisers'
breach of contract or duty.[40] The same is true where there would be
general difficulty in quantifying damages (for example, owing to the need
to take the possibility of extrajudicial settlement into account),[41] or it is
desirable to hear evidence about two related injuries in one action rather
than first in a personal injuries action and then in a professional
negligence action.[42] On the other hand, a solid case against professional
advisers may well strengthen the grounds for declining to let the
personal injuries action proceed,[43] although it is quite clear that there is
no need for the pursuer's prospects of success in an action against his
advisers to be almost certain before this factor becomes relevant.[44]
Clearly, if the pursuer is to proceed against his advisers, this will involve
the expense and delay associated with raising another action, and that
may sometimes be a factor in moving the court to allow the existing
action to proceed.

12.17   Presumably, if it were clear that the measure of damages in any
subsequent action would be significantly less favourable to the pursuer,
that would be likely to be relevant. But in the ordinary case of suing a
solicitor for failing to raise an action before expiry of the limitation
period, it is not clear that this is so. Suppose that the pursuer had had a
60 per cent chance of success in his personal injury action. The damages
in the professional negligence action would aim to put the pursuer in the
position he would have been in had his solicitor not been negligent, that
is, possessed of a claim for damages of a certain value, with 60 per cent
prospects of success. In both the personal injuries and the negligence
actions, the quantum of damages therefore involves discounting the full
value of the claim to take account of the appropriate probability that the
pursuer would not have been successful.[45] And since the valuation in
either case is made as at the same date, there would be no prejudice
in that respect either.[46]

Prejudice to the defender

12.18   Late intimation of the claim may make it difficult or impossible for the
defender to investigate the circumstances of the accident, since records
may not have been retained or, if the incident was never notified in the
first place, never compiled in the first place, or the pursuer's medical
condition from the time of the incident may not have been monitored.[47]

---

[38] *Henderson v. Singer (UK) Ltd*, 1983 S.L.T. 198.

[39] *Griffen v. George MacLellan Holdings Ltd*, 1994 S.L.T. 336. It does not seem obvious
that a petition of this sort (under s. 651 of the Companies Act 1985) is in fact particularly
difficult or burdensome.

[40] *Anderson v. City of Glasgow D.C.*, 1987 S.L.T. 279 at 289.

[41] *Clark v. McLean*, 1994 S.C. 410; *Mackenzie v. Middleton Ross & Arnot*, 1983 S.L.T. 286
at 289; *Donald v. Rutherford*, 1984 S.L.T. 70 at 78.

[42] *Tomkinson v. Broughton Brewery Ltd*, 1995 S.C.L.R. 570.

[43] *Donald v. Rutherford*, 1983 S.L.T. 253; *Williams v. Forth Valley Health Board*, 1983
S.L.T. 376; *Craw v. Gallagher*, 1988 S.L.T. 204.

[44] *Anderson v. City of Glasgow D.C.*, above.

[45] cf. *Caygill v. Stena Offshore AS*, Lord Macfadyen, March 20, 1996, unreported; *Kyle v.
P & J Stormonth Darling WS*, 1992 S.C. 533 at 548.

[46] *Whyte v. Walker*, 1983 S.L.T. 441.

[47] *Williams v. Forth Valley Health Board*, 1983 S.L.T. 376.

It is this sort of consideration—rather than any concept such as personal bar—which makes it reasonable to take into account the fact that a pursuer may have indicated to a defender that he did not intend to make a claim.[48] It may also be difficult to trace witnesses and, once traced, to obtain reliable testimony from them, memories of the incident having faded. But the fading of memories is of course something which will affect the pursuer's own ability to prove his case.[49] And the same must apply to the attempt to prove the state (for example) of medical knowledge or good practice many years in the past. Conversely, if the defender has, owing to timeous intimation of a claim (in spite of late service of the summons), had early notice of the case against her, prejudice is less likely since she will have had opportunity to carry out investigations in good time.[50] Similarly, the fact that a party has been in the action as a third party is likely to reduce the degree of prejudice when it is sought to convene him as a defender, since he will have had in any case to investigate the circumstances of the claim made (originally) by the defender against him.[51] The fact that a defender states no defence on the merits may be regarded as a point in favour of the pursuer.[52]

The weight of many of these factors is likely to increase, the greater **12.19** the delay.

The fact that a defender is entitled to an indemnity in respect of the **12.20** claim against another defender already in the action has also been regarded as a relevant factor.[53] And the fact that the pursuer is an assisted person from whom the defender will be unable to recover expenses has been held to be relevant in assessing prejudice to the defender.[54] This will be true in many personal injury actions if the pursuer is not assisted by a union.

The decisions conflict on the relevance of the fact that the defender is **12.21** or is not insured. The question has arisen in particular in relation to changes in arrangements between health authorities and their liability insurers, leading to health authorities having to satisfy larger proportions of claims from their own resources. The decisions appear to be equally balanced between regarding this as a relevant and an irrelevant factor.[55] The most cogent argument in favour of taking account of the defender's insurance arrangements appears to be this: "if it is, as it is, legitimate to take into account when considering prejudice to the plaintiff that he will have a claim aganst his solicitors, it must in my judgment follow that it is legitimate to take into account that the defendant is insured. If he is

---

[48] See *e.g. Lowe v. Grampian Health Board*, 1998 S.L.T. 731.

[49] *cf. Beaton v. Strathclyde Buses Ltd*, 1992 S.L.T. 931; *McLaren v. Harland and Wolff Ltd*, 1991 S.L.T. 85.

[50] *Donald v. Rutherford*, 1984 S.L.T. 70; *Henderson v. Singer (UK) Ltd*, 1983 S.L.T. 198.

[51] *Carson v. Howard Doris Ltd*, 1981 S.C. 278; *Harris v. Roberts*, 1983 S.L.T. 452; *Webb v. BP Petroleum Development Ltd*, 1988 S.L.T. 775.

[52] *Craw v. Gallagher*, 1988 S.L.T. 204 (inconclusive).

[53] *Oliver v. KCA Drilling Ltd*, Lord Marnoch, December 16, 1994, unreported.

[54] *Forsyth v. A. F. Stoddard & Co. Ltd*, 1985 S.L.T. 51; *Anderson v. John Cotton (Colne) Ltd*, 1991 S.L.T. 696.

[55] For: *Hamilton v. Fife Health Board*, T.G. Coutts, Q.C., January 27, 1995, unreported; *cf. Gascoigne v. Haringey Health Authority*, Tudor-Evans J., December 20, 1991, unreported; against: *Kane v. Argyll & Clyde Health Board*, 1997 S.L.T. 965; *cf. Antcliffe v. Gloucester Health Authority*, Schiemann J., July 31, 1991, unreported.

deprived of his fortuitous defence he will have a claim on his insurers."[56]
It is difficult to deny the force of this argument.

Factors not relevant

12.22 In an obvious sense the defender is disadvantaged by the fact that
section 19A will allow an action to go ahead where the normal limitation
rules would have halted it in its tracks. It is an intriguing question
whether this obvious disadvantage is a type of prejudice to the defenders
which ought to be weighed in the balance by the court. Some light is
thrown on the question by the case of *Bell v. Greenland*,[57] in which the
action was four months out of time owing to a failure on the part of
the pursuer's solicitors to serve the summons on the correct party. Lord
Jauncey regarded the pursuer's case against the defender as "cast iron".
But if it was not allowed to proceed, the pursuer's solicitors had
admitted their fault and accepted their liability to satisfy the pursuer's
claim. It was argued that the pursuer's solicitors would be prejudiced if
the action was not allowed to proceed, but Lord Jauncey held that this
was not a relevant consideration and that in any event a liability to make
reparation for an act amounting to negligence or breach of contract
could not be considered prejudice. He held that any prejudice there may
have been to the pursuer was far outweighed by the prejudice to the
defender in losing immunity under section 17, and therefore dismissed
the action.

12.23 It might be objected, however, that, by parity of reasoning, a liability
on the part of the defender to make reparation for personal injuries, at
least in a cast-iron case, should not be considered prejudice. It is not the
infliction of a loss but simply the deprivation of a potential gain, or, to
use the expression of some of the English cases, a windfall benefit. That
might imply—there being a general presumption against windfalls—that
in a clear case of liability the court should make every effort to allow the
action to proceed. But this again falls foul of the equitable demand to
approach each case on its own merits.

12.24 Instead, the defender's loss of immunity under the normal limitation
rules ought surely to be treated as irrelevant in weighing the equities in
favour of and against allowing the action to proceed. Equally irrelevant
is the fact that the pursuer will in an obvious sense be prejudiced if the
action is not allowed to proceed. It is true that many of the cases do not
support this view, but the following reasoning does:

(1) Section 19A gives the court the power, if it seems to it equitable
    to do so, to allow a pursuer to bring an action notwithstanding the
    normal limitation rules. That is, notwithstanding the fact that an
    action is barred by the passage of three years since the relevant
    date determined under the relevant section. The question the
    court has to decide is whether, notwithstanding the operation of
    time-bar, the action should proceed. It follows that the fact that
    the action is time-barred is not a relevant consideration in the
    exercise of the court's discretion under section 19A. It is not a
    factor material to the exercise of the court's discretion but the

---

[56] *Hartley v. Birmingham City D.C.* [1992] 1 W.L.R. 968 at 980, *per* Parker L.J.
[57] 1988 S.L.T. 215.

very subject-matter of the discretion itself. Put more simply, to take this factor into account in the balancing exercise amounts to double counting. (2) Equally—a related point—it is doubtful whether a factor which by definition applies in every case in which section 19A is invoked, namely loss of the protection of the normal limitation rules, can be relevant in balancing the equities in an individual case. (3) Essentially the same point is well put in an English case: "in all, or nearly all, cases the prejudice to the plaintiff by the operation of the relevant limitation provision and the prejudice which would result to the defendant if the relevant provision were disapplied will be equal and opposite. The stronger the plaintiff's case the greater is the prejudice to him from the operation of the provision and the greater will be the prejudice to the defendant if the provision is disapplied. Likewise the weaker the case of the plaintiff the less is he prejudiced by the operation of the provision and the less is the defendant preju-diced if it is disapplied".[58] For these reasons it seems appropriate to ignore the question of prejudice to either party arising purely from the operation of the limitation provisions.

On the whole the courts do not appear to have followed the line **12.25** advanced here.[59] In some cases the assertion that the defender is prejudiced by losing the protection of section 17 can probably just be taken to mean that in the circumstances she is prejudiced by some additional factor such as the loss of evidence in the face of an old claim.[60] But in others no such explanation seems convincing. In the Inner House in *Donald v. Rutherford*, Lord Dunpark maintained that the starting point in considering the equities was that the defenders would be prejudiced if ultimately found liable to pay a large sum of damages they would otherwise not have to pay.[61] Outer House decisions too many to mention repeat the same point.[62] Accordingly, it has to be conceded that there is authority, including Inner House authority,[63] for weighing in the balance the prejudice to the defender in losing the protection of section 17, however little sense this may seem to make.

The interests of insurers

Some of the cases suggest that it is legitimate to consider, among **12.26** the factors potentially prejudicial to the defender, the interests of the defender's insurers.[64] This seems odd. The reasons given tend to be that the insurer is the true *dominus litis* and that one of the objects of limitation is to allow the insurers to close their file.

---

[58] *Hartley v. Birmingham City D.C.*, above, at 979, *per* Parker L.J. *Cf.* recently *Cowan v. Toffolo Jackson & Co. Ltd*, 1998 S.L.T. 1000 at 1003: "The prejudice to the pursuer if the case does not proceed and to the defenders if it does are obvious and cancel each other out."

[59] The exception is *Cowan v. Toffolo Jackson & Co. Ltd*, above.

[60] *McCabe v. McLellan*, 1994 S.C. 87 at 98–99.

[61] 1984 S.L.T. 70 at 78.

[62] *e.g. Bell v. Greenland*, 1988 S.L.T. 215; *Craw v. Gallagher*, 1988 S.L.T. 204; *Whyte v. Walker*, 1983 S.L.T. 441; *Beaton v. Strathclyde Buses*, 1993 S.L.T. 931; *Kane v. Argyll and Clyde Health Board*, Lord Marnoch, May 24, 1996, unreported; *Wilson v. Telling (Northern) Ltd*, 1996 S.L.T. 380.

[63] *Forsyth v. A. F. Stoddard & Co. Ltd*, 1985 S.L.T. 51.

[64] *Bell v. Greenland*, 1988 S.L.T. 215; *Craw v. Gallagher*, 1988 S.L.T. 204 (concession); *Whyte v. Walker*, 1983 S.L.T. 441.

12.27   It is true, of course, that the assessment of the conduct of the pursuer may involve assessment of the conduct of his agents, for whom he is responsible. In the same way the conduct of the defender (where relevant) might extend to the conduct of her agents or insurers in responding to requests for information by the pursuer, and so forth.[65] But it is rather a different thing to extend this to saying that the interests of agents are also to be taken into account.

12.28   When the question arises whether the pursuer has an alternative remedy against his solicitors rather than against the defender, it is not suggested that the interests of the pursuer's solicitors are to be taken into account. Nor would this make any sense. It would simply be one more constant factor weighing against the defender. Neither, for the same reason—that this would be one more constant factor weighing against the pursuer—can it sensibly be suggested that the interests of the defender's insurers are to be taken into account when the question arises whether they will have to meet the pursuer's claim.[66] Agents and insurers are relevant only in so far as their acts fall to be imputed to the pursuer or to the defender.

Procedure

12.29   Questions involving section 19A typically arise (1) when amendment of the record is sought after the limitation period has passed (this is discussed in Chapter 20); (2) on procedure roll; (3) at preliminary proof on the question of time-bar; (4) at proof before answer on the whole case including the plea of limitation.

12.30   If it is clear on the pleadings that the pursuer cannot satisfy section 19A, the court can dismiss the action at procedure roll. The same will apply if the admissions in the pleadings extend far enough to make proof unnecessary. But where there is any doubt about the facts which bear on the exercise of the court's discretion, clearly the case cannot be decided on the pleadings alone. Here a preliminary proof on the question of limitation is likely to be appropriate.[67] The Inner House has held that the appropriate course is to allow a preliminary proof, and that it should rarely be necessary to allow a proof with pleas to both limitation and the merits standing.[68] So, for example, where it was not clear from the pleadings how much discussion there had been, before the limitation period expired, between the pursuer and the new defenders he sought to convene, the court was not prepared to dispose of the section 19A question at procedure roll and sent it to proof; in the circumstances, because other defenders were involved and had agreed proof before answer, the case went to proof before answer.[69] Equally, if there would be a significant duplication of the evidence required in a preliminary proof and that required on the merits, the court might take the view that proof before answer on the whole case would be appropriate.[70]

---

[65] *cf. Thompson v. Brown* [1981] 1 W.L.R. 744 at 751.

[66] Curiously enough, in *Bell v. Greenland*, above, it was suggested on the one hand that the interests of the pursuer's solicitors were not relevant and on the other that the interests of the defender's insurers were. This disequilibrium surely cannot be right.

[67] *Donald v. Rutherford*, 1984 S.L.T. 70; *Wrightson v. AOC International Ltd*, Lord Gill, October 20, 1995, unreported.

[68] *Clark v. McLean*, 1994 S.C. 410 at 413.

[69] *Faulkner v. Clyde Rigging & Boiler Scaling Co. Ltd*, Lord Johnston, February 22, 1994, unreported.

[70] *McGhee v. British Telecommunications plc*, Lord Hamilton, December 20, 1995, unreported.

Reform?

The question arises whether there is any need for the courts to have **12.31**
the discretion conferred by section 19A. As already mentioned,[71] it was
introduced into the 1973 Act at a time when the principal limitation
sections of the Act, sections 17–19, were widely regarded as unsatisfactory. The present sections have not attracted the same degree of
criticism.

On the other hand, criticism can readily be levelled at the discretion- **12.32**
ary power granted by section 19A. The Scottish Law Commission was
not in favour of the introduction of this judicial discretion.[72] Section 19A
surfaced by way of an amendment made in the House of Commons to
the Law Reform (Miscellaneous Provisions) (Scotland) Act 1980.[73] It is
worth noting that the Lord Advocate, Lord Mackay of Clashfern, in
commending the clause to the House said this: "I think no one is
satisfied with the basic structure underneath this [that is, sections 17–19
as originally enacted] . . . I hope that in the not too distant future basic
proposals for reforming the law in this area will come forward. Therefore, this is in the nature of an interim solution with this bad structure to
cope with. We have tried to modify its worst evils by a discretion."[74] It is
a reasonable question whether, the "bad structure" of sections 17–19
having been reformed in 1984, the interim solution represented by
section 19A may have outlived its usefulness.

The English Law Commission, in a fundamental review of the law of **12.33**
limitation, has recently suggested that the courts should not have any
discretionary power to extend the limitation period. The Commission's
principal concerns were the loss of certainty this power introduces about
when the limitation period ends; the additional uncertainty caused by the
fact that judges will reasonably differ in their exercise of this discretion;
and the great expense which is caused by plaintiffs quite reasonably
trying to reap the benefits of this situation.[75]

Any kind of discretion plainly reduces the certainty which it is one of **12.34**
the objects of limitation to achieve, and to some extent undermines the
benefits otherwise conferred on defenders, such as the possibility of
disposing of records.[76] Unfairness which might otherwise affect a pursuer
is much reduced by preventing the limitation period from beginning until
he is aware of the key elements of his claim. There is much to be said for
the view that a pursuer's interests are adequately protected by a
"discoverability" test, so that if a workable and satisfactory test is
provided by sections 17(2)(b) and 18(2)(b), the discretion given to the
courts under section 19A is substantially redundant. The same is surely
true of defamation, since section 18A already appears to err on the side
of generosity to the pursuer, by providing that time runs only from when
the pursuer first had notice of the offending publication.

---

[71] Above, Introduction to Part II.
[72] SLC Consultative Memorandum no. 45 (1980), paras 2.21–2.29.
[73] H.C. Deb., Vol. 989, cols 1660–1661.
[74] H.L. Deb., Vol. 413, col. 1898.
[75] Law Com. Consultation Paper no. 151 (1998), paras 12.187–12.196.
[76] On the other hand, this is a question which may be taken into account in the exercise
of the discretion.

12.35   It may therefore be that the most desirable course for the law to follow would be to reject the discretionary extension provided by section 19A in favour of improving the clarity and coherence of the "discoverability" test.

CHAPTER 13

LIMITATION OF ACTIONS UNDER THE CONSUMER PROTECTION ACT 1987

Specific statutory provision is made for limitation of actions to enforce **13.01** obligations arising from product liability, that is, liability under the Consumer Protection Act 1987. The main points arising are discussed in Chapter 9, in the context of the 10-year prescription of obligations introduced by the Act. The present chapter is confined to a few points specifically concerned with limitation of actions. Here too, in the same way as under the ordinary limitation regime, separate sections of the Act deal with personal injuries and with death resulting from personal injuries. The two sections are considered in turn.

I. ACTIONS OF PERSONAL INJURIES

"Three year limitation of actions   **13.02**
22B.—(1) This section shall apply to an action to enforce an obligation arising from liability under section 2 of the 1987 Act (to make reparation for damage caused wholly or partly by a defect in a product), except where section 22C of this Act applies.
(2) Subject to subsection (4) below, an action to which this section applies shall not be competent unless it is commenced within the period of three years after the earliest date on which the person seeking to bring (or a person who could at an earlier date have brought) the action was aware, or on which, in the opinion of the court, it was reasonably practicable for him in all the circumstances to become aware, of all the facts mentioned in subsection (3) below.
(3) The facts referred to in subsection (2) above are—

  (a) that there was a defect in a product;
  (b) that the damage was caused or partly caused by the defect;
  (c) that the damage was sufficiently serious to justify the pursuer (or other person referred to in subsection (2) above) in bringing an action to which this section applies on the assumption that the defender did not dispute liability and was able to satisfy a decree;
  (d) that the defender was a person liable for the damage under the said section 2.

(4) In the computation of the period of three years mentioned in subsection (2) above, there shall be disregarded any period during which the person seeking to bring the action was under legal disability by reason of nonage or unsoundness of mind.
(5) The facts mentioned in subsection (3) above do not include knowledge of whether particular facts and circumstances would or would not, as a matter of law, result in liability for damage under the said section 2.
(6) Where a person would be entitled, but for this section, to bring an action for reparation other than one in which the damages

245

claimed are confined to damages for loss of or damage to property, the court may, if it seems to it equitable to do so, allow him to bring the action notwithstanding this section."

13.03   The ordinary rules on limitation do not apply to actions based on product liability under the Consumer Protection Act 1987.[1] Instead, the 1987 Act introduced a special regime of limitation for those actions. There are many resemblances between this regime and the ordinary limitation rules for personal injuries actions, and so it is possible to confine comment here to the most important differences.

13.04   The substantive limitation provisions for these purposes are sections 22B and 22C of the 1973 Act. There are also provisions on interpretation specific to these cases.[2]

Comparison between the ordinary limitation rules and those in cases of product liability

13.05   (1) The ordinary limitation rules provide that "no action . . . shall be brought" after the limitation period has ended; the provisions for liability under the 1987 Act state that "no action shall be competent". The difference does not appear to be material.

(2) The ordinary limitation rules are concerned purely with personal injuries[3]; the rules under the 1987 Act are concerned not only with personal injuries (which are defined in the same way as in the 1973 Act)[4] but with property damage too.[5]

(3) Both limitation and prescription provisions apply to obligations under section 2 of the Consumer Protection Act 1987. An action will be limited after three years, subject to considerations of "discoverability", and the possibility of extension on equitable grounds or suspension on grounds of legal disability.[6] But the right of action will in any case be cut off by the long-stop of 10-year prescription.[7] This is different in ordinary personal injuries cases, where no prescription applies to obligations to make reparation for personal injuries.[8] The existence of this long-stop prescription may be a factor in explaining the very limited impact which this Part of the 1987 Act has had.[9] It is rather puzzling that within the period of three years from 1984 to 1987 Parliament should have both excluded ordinary personal injuries actions from the scope of the 20-year negative prescription and enacted legislation imposing an even shorter prescriptive period on personal injuries actions brought in product liability cases.[10]

---

[1] See s. 16A.

[2] s. 22D.

[3] ss. 17–18, apart of course from defamation (s. 18A), not relevant here.

[4] 1987 Act, s. 45(1); 1973 Act, s. 22(1): the only difference between the two formulations, the fact that in the expression "any disease and any other impairment of a person's physical or mental condition" the word "other" does not appear in the 1973 Act, does not seem to be material.

[5] 1987 Act, s. 5(1); see below.

[6] s. 22B(4) and 22C(3); see below.

[7] s. 22A, plus, where appropriate, any extension to the date of final disposal of the action in question; see above, para. 9.20.

[8] s. 6(2) and Sched. 1, para. 2(g); s. 7(2).

[9] *cf.* above, para. 9.03.

[10] Prescription and Limitation (Scotland) Act 1984, amending s. 7 of the 1973 Act; 1987 Act.

There is, however, no reason why a pursuer whose right under the 1987 Act has been cut off by prescription before he was aware of it should not proceed in an ordinary (non-1987 Act) action for reparation for personal injuries, which will not be subject to any such bar.[11]

(4) Both the ordinary and the product liability limitation regimes enable the court to allow an action for personal injuries to be brought out of time when this seems equitable to the court.[12] The ordinary limitation regime for personal injuries rules out jury trials both where postponement of the start of the limitation period is claimed on grounds of lack of awareness of material facts and where the equitable discretion of the court is invoked.[13] But there is no such provision under the product liability regime. This is the more surprising given the complexity of the statutory definitions and defences.

(5) Both regimes allow postponement or suspension of the running of the limitation period, but in ordinary cases this is determined by reference to the legal disability of the injured person, while in product liability cases it applies to the pursuer in the action.[14]

Scope of the section

Section 22B applies only to actions to enforce obligations arising from **13.06** liability under section 2 of the 1987 Act. Liability under section 2 of the 1987 Act arises where any damage is caused wholly or partly by a defect in a product; "damage" is defined as "death or personal injury or any loss of or damage to any property (including land)".[15] Further comment on these provisions, and on those who are liable under the 1987 Act, is made in connection with prescription.[16] Here it is enough simply to emphasise that the intention of the Act is to protect consumers, so damage to business or public property is excluded; and, since damage to the product itself is also excluded, there is no question of the Act's extending to the recovery of pure economic loss.[17]

Running of the limitation period

In terms of section 22B(2), the limitation period runs from the **13.07** "earliest date on which the person seeking to bring (or a person who could at an earlier date have brought) the action was aware" of the relevant statutory facts.

So far as damages for personal injury are concerned, the reference to **13.08** a person who could have brought the action at an earlier date seems to be capable of referring only to the case where the action is being brought by an assignee. In that case it is the knowledge of the injured person, the assignor, which is relevant. This result would anyway follow from the normal principles of assignation.[18] So far as property damage is

---

[11] Liability under the 1987 Act is without prejudice to liability arising otherwise: 1987 Act, s. 2(6).
[12] s. 19A; 1987 Act, ss. 22B(6) and 22C(5).
[13] s. 19A(4); 1987 Act, ss. 22B(4) and 22C(3).
[14] ss. 17(3) and 22B(4).
[15] 1987 Act, s. 5(1).
[16] Above, paras 9.09–10.
[17] 1987 Act, s. 5(2) and (3).
[18] The Latin tag *assignatus jure auctoris utitur* is regularly cited.

concerned, the same applies to assignation. In addition it is possible that, without assignation of any right of action, property is simply transferred by one person to another. Without a provision of the present sort, each transfer of property would postpone the limitation period.[19] As it is, that result is not arrived at because the limitation period is not assessed by reference to the date of "discoverability" of the new transferee but that of "a person who could at an earlier date have brought" the action. It is rather unsatisfactory that the section is drafted simply to refer to "a person", because it leaves it quite unclear which person that should be, if there have been more persons than one. All that can quite clearly be said is that, whichever person it is, it is not the last transferee of the property.

The statutory facts

13.09   There is a broad similarity between the facts material for these limitation provisions and those material under the ordinary limitation rules. Under the regime of the 1987 Act, knowledge of the following four facts is material:

(a) that there was a defect in a product; (b) that the damage was caused or partly caused by the defect; (c) that the damage was sufficiently serious to justify the bringing of an action on the assumptions that liability was not disputed and the defender was solvent; (d) that the defender was liable for the damage.

13.10   Facts (b) and (d) taken together are parallel to the requirement of knowledge under the ordinary limitation regime that the injuries in question should be attributable in whole or in part to an act or omission, and that the defender is a person (or the employer or principal of a person) to whose act or omission the injuries are in whole or part attributable.[20] Fact (c) is paralleled by the need for knowledge under the ordinary limitation regime that the injuries were sufficiently serious to justify bringing an action on the assumptions that liability was not disputed and the defender was solvent.[21] For these three facts it is therefore sufficient to refer to the points raised in connection with the parallel provision under the ordinary limitation rules.[22]

13.11   In the ordinary limitation rules, there is no equivalent to fact (a), the need for knowledge that there was a defect in the product. "Defect" is defined by section 3 of the 1987 Act, but since knowledge of whether facts or circumstances involve liability as a matter of law is expressly excluded,[23] and relevant knowledge is knowledge of facts alone, it cannot be the case that a pursuer needs to know that the defect of which he complains falls within the statutory definition. It must be enough that he is aware that as a matter of fact the product suffers from a defect.

13.12   It is possible for a person to become aware of the statutory facts at different times in relation to different claims arising from the same defective product. Suppose, for example, that a product causes physical harm and also generates a latent personal injury, knowledge of which

---

[19] This appears to be the law in England: Limitation Act 1980 s. 14(1A) proviso.
[20] s. 17(2)(b)(ii)–(iii).
[21] s. 17(2)(b)(i).
[22] See above, paras 10.44 *et seq.*, 10.60 *et seq.*, 10.70 *et seq.*
[23] s. 22B(5).

comes to the injured person only later. It seems that time should run against the claim for property damage from one date, and against that for personal injury from another.

Postponement or suspension of the limitation period

The running of the limitation period can be postponed or suspended **13.13** where the person seeking to bring the action was under legal disability by reason of nonage or unsoundness of mind.[24] So the start of the limitation period is postponed until that person reaches the age of legal capacity, 16. Equally, the running of the period may be suspended if in the course of it he or she is for some period of unsound mind. These provisions are to be taken alongside section 22(3) which, on grounds of the lack of knowledge of the person seeking to bring the action, postpones the starting date for the limitation period.[25]

Although these provisions mean that the limitation period may be **13.14** either very long or never completed at all, because the 10-year prescription of section 22A applies,[26] all claims will be cut off once that period has run.

Extension of the limitation period

The court has discretion to allow an action to proceed out of time **13.15** where it seems to it equitable to do so. But this discretion applies only to personal injuries and not to claims for loss or damage to property alone.[27] If an action includes heads of claim both for personal injuries and for property damage, it falls within the scope of the discretion. The only actions which do not are those "confined to damage for loss of or damage to property".

Presumably the discretion would be exercised in line with the **13.16** principles already developed by the courts in connection with section 19A of the 1973 Act.

II. CASES WHERE DEATH HAS RESULTED FROM PERSONAL INJURIES

Special provision is made in section 22C for cases in which death has **13.17** resulted from personal injuries.

> **"Actions under the 1987 Act where death has resulted from personal injuries**
> 22C.—(1) This section shall apply to an action to enforce an obligation arising from liability under section 2 of the 1987 Act (to make reparation for damage caused wholly or partly by a defect in a product) where a person has died from personal injuries and the damages claimed include damages for those personal injuries or that death.

---

[24] s. 22B(4).
[25] Note that s. 22B(2) and (4) are framed to refer to the same person, namely the person seeking to bring the action. This is different in the ordinary limitation rules of s. 17(2) and (3), the first of which refers to the pursuer and the second to the injured person; for comment, see above, paras 10.12, 78.
[26] See above, Chap. 9.
[27] s. 22B(6).

(2) Subject to subsection (4) below, an action to which this section applies shall not be competent unless it is commenced within the period of three years after the later of—

(a) the date of death of the injured person;
(b) the earliest date on which the person seeking to make (or a person who could at an earlier date have made) the claim was aware, or on which, in the opinion of the court, it was reasonably practicable for him in all the circumstances to become aware—
  (i) that there was a defect in the product;
  (ii) that the injuries of the deceased were caused (or partly caused) by the defect; and
  (iii) that the defender was a person liable for the damage under the said section 2.

(3) Where the person seeking to make the claim is a relative of the deceased, there shall be disregarded in the computation of the period mentioned in subsection (2) above any period during which that relative was under legal disability by reason of nonage or unsoundness of mind.

(4) Where an action to which section 22B of this Act applies has not been brought within the period mentioned in subsection (2) of that section and the person subsequently dies in consequence of his injuries, an action to which this section applies shall not be competent in respect of those injuries or that death.

(5) Where a person would be entitled, but for this section, to bring an action of reparation other than one in which the damages claimed are confined to damages for loss of or damage to property, the court may, if it seems to it equitable to do so, allow him to bring the action notwithstanding this section.

(6) In this section 'relative' has the same meaning as in the Damages (Scotland) Act 1976.

(7) For the purposes of subsection (2)(b) above there shall be disregarded knowledge of whether particular facts and circumstances would or would not, as a matter of law, result in liability for damage under the said section 2."

Scope of the section

13.18   The actions affected are those where a person has died from personal injuries and damages are claimed for those injuries or that death on the basis that the injuries were caused wholly or partly by a defect in a product. For the basics about the definitions of "defect" and "damage" and those who are liable under these provisions, it is enough to refer back to the discussions of section 22B and of prescription under the 1987 Act.[28] The only speciality here is that the person injured must have died.

13.19   Ordinarily it is a precondition of a supplier's liability that he has been requested by the injured person to identify the persons liable in terms of section 2(2) of the 1987 Act and has failed to do so within a reasonable time. It is expressly provided, for the purposes of claims made in respect of the death of the injured person by relatives under the Damages

---

[28] Above, paras 9.06–11, 13.06.

(Scotland) Act 1976, that that precondition shall not apply.[29] It is enough therefore if the relative makes the request.

Title to sue

When an injured person has died, two types of claim have to be **13.20** considered: the deceased's own claim, which is transmitted to his executor; and the claims of his relatives, which arise on his death. More is said about these claims in connection with section 18.[30] Here it is enough to note that the same definition of "relative" is employed here as in the ordinary limitation regime, and that the same claims for damages are available to those relatives by virtue of the provisions of the Damages (Scotland) Act 1976 and the Administration of Justice (Scotland) Act 1982.[31]

As in cases under the ordinary limitation provisions, so here, if the **13.21** deceased's right of action became time-barred before his death, an action cannot normally be raised after his death in terms of section 22C.[32] The reasons for this are discussed in connection with section 18.[33] This general rule is subject only to the equitable discretion of the court to allow an action to proceed in such circumstances.[34]

Section 22C(2) is expressly said to be "subject to subsection (4) **13.22** below". The cross-reference seems at first sight odd; the equivalent cross-reference in section 22B is to the subsection dealing with suspension of the limitation period on grounds of legal disability.[35] But both subsections (2) and (4) are concerned to provide for circumstances in which an action to which section 22C applies shall not be competent. It therefore seems perfectly appropriate that section 22C(2) should be subject to section 22C(4), since subsection (4) adds a further item to the list of circumstances in which the action may not be brought, namely that it was limited before the death of the deceased. It remains odd, nonetheless, that no reference is made to subsection (3).

Running of the limitation period

The limitation period begins to run on the later of (1) the date of **13.23** death of the deceased and (2) the date on which the person making the claim was actually or constructively aware of the statutory facts.

There is no more to say here about the statutory facts than was said in **13.24** connection with section 22B. The only difference is that, since death has already resulted, there is no need to consider the question whether the injuries are sufficiently serious. Knowledge of whether facts or circumstances involve liability as a matter of law is once again expressly excluded. Relevant knowledge here is knowledge of facts alone.[36]

Different dates may of course apply to different relatives, depending **13.25** on the dates on which they acquired the necessary knowledge of the facts.

---

[29] 1987 Act, s. 6(2).
[30] Above, paras 10.89–92.
[31] s. 22C(6); 1987 Act, s. 6(1)(c) and (d).
[32] s. 22C(4).
[33] s. 18(4); above, paras 10.107 *et seq.*
[34] s. 22C(5).
[35] That is, s. 22B(2) refers to s. 22B(4).
[36] s. 22C(7).

Postponement or suspension of the limitation period

13.26   For claims made by relatives of the deceased only, the Act allows the start of the limitation period to be postponed, or its running to be suspended, during any period for which they are below the age of legal capacity (16) or suffer from unsoundness of mind.[37] Precisely the same applies under the ordinary limitation rules applying where death has resulted from personal injuries.[38] Since the death of a person may give rise to the possibility of claims by several relatives, the limitation period applicable to each may be different according to whether he or she is or was at any relevant time under legal disability.

Extension of the limitation period

13.27   The court has discretion to allow an action to proceed out of time where it seems to it equitable to do so. This discretion is, however, confined to actions of damages for personal injuries only, or for personal injuries and property damage. It is not available for actions which seek damages for loss of or damage to property only.[39]

---

[37] s. 22C(3).
[38] s. 18(3); above, paras 10.100 *et seq.*
[39] s. 22C(5).

PART III

POSITIVE PRESCRIPTION

The first five sections of the 1973 Act deal with positive prescription. The provisions fall broadly into three categories: the normal prescriptive regime of section 1, which requires 10 years' possession proceeding upon a recorded or registered deed; the special regime of section 2, under which in certain cases 20 years' possession is required but the deed need not be recorded; and finally, the case of positive servitudes and public rights of way.

There is, however, a good deal of common ground between these different categories, so the following chapters treat them together where possible. Chapters 14, on the notion of positive prescription, and 16, on possession, are relevant to all forms of positive prescription. Chapter 15, on interests in land, deeds and titles, is relevant to both sections 1 and 2, although they require at certain points to be discussed separately. Chapter 17 deals with the specialities of prescription of positive servitudes and public rights of way. Chapter 18 touches on an issue not mentioned in the 1973 Act, the positive prescription of moveables.

CHAPTER 14

THE NOTION OF POSITIVE PRESCRIPTION

The purposes of positive prescription

The long title of the 1973 Act itself makes clear that positive **14.01**
prescription can serve more than one purpose: it refers to "the establishment and definition by positive prescription of title". The main purposes
are these:

(1) to render a defective title unchallengeable ("establishment" in the
    long title of the Act); (2) to fix the extent of a title, where
    the deed itself leaves the boundaries uncertain ("definition" in the
    long title of the Act); (3) to promote ease in conveyance by
    making it unnecessary to investigate titles which date from before
    the prescriptive period, since the title fortified by prescription is
    exempt from challenge.

On the functions of the law of positive prescription, the following **14.02**
remarks of Lord Justice-Clerk Moncreiff, about the effect of possession
following on a sufficient ("habile") title, are helpful:

"[T]he effect of forty years' possession on a habile title is not, in any
accurate sense, to construe the title. Its effect is to establish the
right. It is of no consequence what the true construction of the title
may be, as long as it is susceptible of a construction consistent with
the prescriptive possession, and when that has run, it is the
possession, not the words of the charter, which establishes
the right."[1]

These remarks are capable of applying both to the case where prescription fortifies an existing defective title and to that where it explains the
extent of the title which has been granted.

Although the main purpose of positive prescription may seem to be **14.03**
the curing of defective titles, explanation of the extent of existing titles is
equally important.[2] Since the purpose of prescription is to secure
property rights by rendering them exempt from challenge, the certainty
prescription provides about the extent or bounds of a title is as
important as its role in rendering defective rights unchallengeable. A
case where difficulties have often arisen is salmon fishings: here, if there
is no express grant, prescriptive possession on a sufficient title will be
necessary in order to make the right unchallengeable. But even if there is
an express grant, it may often be uncertain what exactly its bounds are.
The best method of establishing that is to rely on possession following
upon the grant. Here the possession explains the grant; for example, in a

---

[1] *Auld v. Hay* (1880) 7 R. 663 at 668.
[2] It is important to note that, where a title is ambiguous and has been followed by
undisputed possession, even possession which is short of the prescriptive period may be
capable of explaining the extent of the grant.

255

case in which salmon fishings had been granted over half of the River Ness, possession explained which half.[3]

Positive prescription and acquisitive prescription

14.04   Positive prescription is not the same as acquisitive prescription.[4] Acquisitive prescription is prescription by which the possessor acquires title to the thing possessed, by completing possession for the prescriptive period. This was the case, for example, with *usucapio* in Roman law, on completion of which the possessor was *dominus*, owner. *Usucapio* was therefore a means of acquiring original title, not dependent on the validity of any previous title to the thing. The corollary of the completion by one person of *usucapio* was that the ownership of any other person in the thing was extinguished. This regime still exists in some jurisdictions today.[5]

14.05   This, however, does not seem to be the sort of prescription which operates under the now-conventional term "positive prescription" in the 1973 Act. What the Act provides in all the operative sections on positive prescription is that, on satisfactory completion of the prescriptive period, "the validity of the title so far as relating to the said interest in the particular land"—or, in the case of section 3, "the servitude"—"shall be exempt from challenge".

14.06   It is possible to take the view that the words "exempt from challenge" fall short of the finest parliamentary draftsmanship and are intended to indicate that a person who has completed positive prescription has obtained ownership in the property in question. That view has distinguished support.[6] If it is correct, the law is certainly simpler. But what if—as in the old law—positive prescription does not lead to acquisition of ownership? The remainder of this chapter examines this possibility.

14.07   It would be nothing new if completing positive prescription did not involve the acquisition of a new title. The Act 1617, c. 12 took the same approach in providing that on completion of the prescriptive period "suche persounes thair heiris and successoures sall nevir be trublit persewed nor Inqueyted in the heretable right and propertie of thair saidis landis and heretages foirsaidis". The Act went on to set out the type of title—charter or instruments of sasine—on which this prescriptive possession must follow and provided: "whiche Rightis his Maiestie with aduyse and consent of the estaittis foirsaidis findis and declairis to be goode valide and sufficient Rightis (being cled with the said peciable and Continewall possessioun of fourty yearis) without any lauchfull interruptioun as said is for bruiking of the heretable right of the same landis and utheris foirsaidis". The critical word here is "bruiking": it

---

[3] *Warrand's Trs v. Mackintosh* (1890) 17 R. (H.L.) 13; *Fraser v. Grant* (1866) 4 M. 596; in general, Gordon, *Land Law*, paras. 8.66–8.67.

[4] In its Memo. no. 9 (1968), paras 2 and 12 and its Report no. 15 (1970), the Scottish Law Commission seems to have been confused on this point in speaking of "Positive prescription (acquisitive prescription or usucapion)".

[5] Germany: BGB, Art. 937 (10-year acquisitive prescription for moveables only); France: *Code Civil*, Art. 712; also Art. 2265 (acquisitive prescription of land after 10 or 20 years, when based on a title and acquisition in good faith); Arts 2262 and 2229 (thirty-year acquisitive prescription of land without need for good faith).

[6] Reid, *Property*, para. 674, classifying prescription as a means of original acquisition.

means "possession". Accordingly, this provision means that the deeds referred to are sufficient titles for the prescriptive possession, which is to follow, of the heritable right in question.

Since the Conveyancing (Scotland) Acts of 1874 and 1924 simply **14.08** extended the effect of the Act 1617 to apply after completion of a shorter prescriptive period (20 years), the prescription of which they speak is of precisely the same kind.[7]

None of these enactments says anything about completion of the **14.09** prescriptive period making the possessor owner.[8] It is worth quoting one (long) sentence from Erskine on this point:

"Positive prescription is generally defined by our lawyers, as the Romans did usucapion, the acquisition of property by the continued possession of the acquirer for such a time as is described by the law as sufficient for that purpose; but it ought rather to have been defined, the establishing or securing to the possessor his right against all future challenge; for both the Roman law and ours require an antecedent title in the possessor, capable of transferring property; and therefore it may be observed that our statute establishing the positive prescription (1617, c. 12) does not once mention the acquisition of property; but supposes the person whose right is secured by that prescription to have been formerly the proprietor."[9]

More succinct but equally accurate is what Lord Watson said of the **14.10** cases covered by the Act 1617: "The effect of prescription, in these cases, is not to constitute the right of the possessor, but to fortify it against all future challenge."[10]

Accordingly, an accurate account of what positive prescription **14.11** achieves, so far as sasine titles are concerned,[11] is not that it constitutes a new title. It creates an irrebuttable presumption (*praesumptio juris et de jure*) that the title on which the possessor holds is valid. The reason this approach is adequate is that prescription anyway runs only when there is a title sufficient to support it, so that there is necessarily an existing grant which comes to benefit from the irrebuttable presumption of validity.

The point is well put in the defender's argument in the case of **14.12** *Miller v. Dickson*[12] as reported by Kames:

"the argument for the pursuers has no better foundation than a misapprehension of our act of 1617, concerning the positive prescription, as if it were copied from the Roman *usucapio*, which is far from being the case. The Roman *usucapio* is defined '*modus*

---

[7] 1874 Act, s. 34, 1924 Act, s. 16; cf. Bell, *Prin.*, s. 2005.

[8] Bankton, II, xii, 1 is inaccurate in so describing the effect of the Act 1617. Kames, *Elucidations*, 257 and 259 is clear that positive prescription is different from usucapion.

[9] Erskine, III, vii, 2. When Erskine speaks of the requirement of a title in Roman law, he appears to be referring for the need for there to be a cause (*causa*) why the possessor should acquire ownership by *usucapio*. There was no need for any written title. cf. also Bell, *Prin.*, s. 606; Napier, pp. 51–57 and 119; Rankine, *Land Law*, p. 31.

[10] *Mann v. Brodie* (1885) 12 R. (H.L.) 52 at 57.

[11] On Land Register titles, see below, para. 14.15.

[12] (1766) M. 10937 at 10943.

adquirendi dominii per continuationem temporis' [*i.e.* "a means of
acquiring ownership through the passage of time"]; whence it
indeed follows that if the possessor be in the course of acquiring the
property, there must be another in the course of losing it. Our act
1617 rests upon a foundation more just and more expedient. It is no
part of its intendment to transfer property from one to another, nor
can it be defined *modus adquirendi dominii.* On the contrary, it
supposes the possessor to be the proprietor, and to have been so
from the date of his title downward."

14.13   The fact that the possessor does not acquire title produces curious
results, especially given that the right of ownership cannot be lost by
negative prescription.[13] Suppose that both A and B have titles sufficient
to include a strip of land between their neighbouring properties, but B's
title has been granted by a non-owner. B then possesses for 10 years. A
cannot be said to have lost his ownership by negative prescription. But
nor is it accurate to say that B has acquired a new title by positive
prescription: according to the Act, all that has happened is that B's
existing title has become unchallengeable.[14] But if B has not become
owner of the land and merely enjoys an unchallengeable title to it, it
must follow that B himself can never transfer ownership in it.[15] It is true
that this does not really matter as a question of conveyancing practice,
since all that is required is a valid progress of titles covering the
prescriptive period. But it does leave the rather inelegant situation that
B is not owner but has an unchallengeable title; while if A was ever
owner, he must still be, although he cannot challenge B or those deriving
title from B.[16]

14.14   The effect of completing prescription upon a sufficient title is therefore nothing to do with acquisition of ownership. The title simply
becomes exempt from challenge, and all inquiry into the title prior to the
prescriptive period is excluded.[17]

14.15   What has been said so far applies strictly to sasine titles only. But so
far as titles registered in the Land Register are concerned, the practical
consequences are essentially the same, if for different reasons. In cases
of registration of title, the very act of registration makes B, the person
registering, the owner of the registered interest in land.[18] A, the former
owner, is thereby divested of ownership.[19] The new title, however,
becomes exempt from challenge only after 10 years; until that time B,

---

[13] Sched. 3(a); above, para. 3.02.

[14] *cf.* Gordon, *op cit.*, para. 2.25.

[15] In this sort of case the dictum is sometimes cited that "nobody can transfer a greater
right to another than he has himself". The older cases prefer it in the original Latin: *nemo
plus iuris ad alium transferre potest quam ipse haberet* (D. 50.17.54, Ulpian 46 *ad edictum*).

[16] Given this outcome for the existing law of prescription relating to heritable property,
it is rather puzzling that the Scottish Law Commission, in discussing prescription in
relation to moveables, should say in SLC Memo. no. 30, *Corporeal Moveables: Usucapion
or Acquisitive Prescription* (1976), para. 3: "Merely to cut off a remedy without fortifying a
right of ownership in anyone would be to create a vacuum and uncertainty as to title—a
result which a sound law of prescription or usucapion should avoid."

[17] *Fraser v. Lord Lovat* (1898) 25 R. 603 at 616, *per* L.P. Robertson.

[18] *Registration of Title Practice Book* ("ROTPB"), para. C. 63.

[19] 1979 Act, s. 3. See the discussion by K. Reid, '*A non domino* conveyances and the
Land Register', 1979 J.R. 79–95.

the disponee (and new owner), is liable to be challenged by way of proceedings for rectification of the Land Register. In other words, he has a voidable title.[20] The result therefore is that an originally voidable title is fortified by prescription and becomes unchallengeable. In this case, however, the title in question is a title of ownership.

---

[20] On the question of negative prescription of the right to seek rectification, see above, para. 3.04.

CHAPTER 15

INTERESTS IN LAND, TITLES AND DEEDS

I. INTERESTS IN LAND

The 1973 Act provides two different regimes for prescription of titles to **15.01** interests in land (as defined in the Act). The first of these (section 1) requires the deed which is the foundation of the title to be recorded or the interest in land registered. This is the normal rule, and most of this chapter is concerned with it. The second regime (section 2) applies only to what the Act calls "special cases": in these the deed need only be executed. It need not be recorded. Nothing is said in either section about prescription based on no deed at all.

The Act is drafted in terms of positive prescription of "interests in **15.02** land". The use of that expression has been criticised. Its meaning is discussed below.[1] The Scottish Law Commission has recently proposed amendments to the 1973 Act, the main purport of which is to remove the expression "interest in land" from the 1973 Act and replace it with the term "real right in land".[2] These proposals are contained in the draft Abolition of Feudal Tenure etc. (Scotland) Bill which is intended to come before the Scottish Parliament at an early date. If this Bill is enacted as proposed, the effect on the 1973 Act will be to substitute new sections 1 and 2, drafted in terms of real rights in land.[3] The text of those draft sections is set out below. The effect on this and the following chapters is that discussion of the term "interest in land" will become redundant.

The 1973 Act binds the Crown; in some instances, noted below, the **15.03** applicable prescriptive period is longer than the normal one.[4]

Section 2 applies only to a few special cases of interests in land, which **15.04** are listed. For section 1, however, the question arises what the interests in land are to which it applies.

Existing section 1

"**Interests in land: general** **15.05**
1.—(1) If in the case of an interest in particular land, being an interest to which this section applies,—

(a) the interest has been possessed by any person, or by any person and his successors, for a continuous period of ten

---

[1] paras 15.07 *et seq.*
[2] SLC Report no. 168 (1999), *Abolition of the Feudal System*, paras 9.5–9.6.
[3] Draft Bill, cl. 70(1) and Sched. 8, Pt I, paras 35 and 36.
[4] s. 24; see s. 1(4). The Act 1617 also bound the Crown: *H.M. Advocate v. Graham* (1844) 7 D. 183 at 190 and 204. See also Dirleton's *Doubts and Questions in the Law, s.v. "Prescription against the King".*

years openly, peaceably and without any judicial interruption, and
(b) the possession was founded on, and followed
  (i) the recording of a deed which is sufficient in respect of its terms to constitute in favour of that person a title to that interest in the particular land, or in land of a description habile to include the particular land, or
  (ii) registration of that interest in favour of that person in the Land Register of Scotland, subject to an exclusion of indemnity under section 12(2) of the Land Registration (Scotland) Act 1979,
then, as from the expiration of the said period, the validity of the title so far as relating to the said interest in the particular land shall be exempt from challenge.

(1A) Subsection (1) above shall not apply where—

(a) possession was founded on the recording of a deed which is invalid *ex facie* or was forged; or
(b) possession was founded on registration in respect of an interest in land in the Land Register of Scotland proceeding on a forged deed and the person appearing from the Register to be entitled to the interest was aware of the forgery at the time of registration in his favour.

(2) This section applies to any interest in land the title to which can competently be recorded or which is registrable in the Land Register of Scotland.
(3) In the computation of a prescriptive period for the purposes of this section in a case where the deed in question is a decree of adjudication for debt, any period before the expiry of the legal shall be disregarded.
(4) Where in any question involving an interest in any foreshore or in any salmon fishings this section is pled against the Crown as owner of the regalia, subsection (1) above shall have effect as if for the words 'ten years' there were substituted the words 'twenty years'.
(5) This section is without prejudice to the operation of section 2 of this Act."

Proposed new section 1

15.06   "**1.**—(1) If land has been possessed by any person, or by any person and his successors, for a continuous period of ten years openly, peaceably and without any judicial interruption, and the possession was founded on, and followed—

(a) the recording of a deed which is sufficient in respect of its terms to constitute in favour of that person a real right in
  (i) that land; or
  (ii) land of a description *habile* to include that land; or
(b) registration of a real right in that land, in favour of that person, in the Land Register of Scotland, subject to an exclusion of indemnity under section 12(2) of the Land Registration (Scotland) Act 1979,

then, as from the expiry of that period, the real right so far as relating to that land shall be exempt from challenge.
(2) Subsection (1) above shall not apply where—

(a) possession was founded on the recording of a deed which is invalid *ex facie* or was forged; or

(b) possession was founded on registration in the Land Register of Scotland proceeding on a forged deed and the person appearing from the Register to have the real right in question was aware of the forgery at the time of registration in his favour.

(3) In subsection (1) above, the reference to a real right is to a real right which is registrable in the Land Register of Scotland or a deed relating to which can competently be recorded; but this section does not apply to servitudes or public rights of way.

(4) In the computation of a prescriptive period for the purposes of this section in a case where the deed in question is a decree of adjudication for debt, any period before the expiry of the legal shall be disregarded.

(5) Where, in any question involving any foreshore or any salmon fishings, this section is pled against the Crown as owner of the *regalia*, subsection (1) above shall have effect as if for the words 'ten years' there were substituted 'twenty years'.

(6) This section is without prejudice to the operation of section 2 of this Act."

The interests to which section 1 applies

This prescriptive regime extends to any interest in land the title to **15.07** which can competently be recorded[5] or is registrable in the Land Register of Scotland.[6] The definition of "interest in land" provided in the Act says no more than that "'interest in land' does not include a servitude".[7] "Land" is defined as including "heritable property of any description".[8] For that reason "land" includes legal separate tenements in land such as salmon fishings,[9] the right to gather mussels or oysters, and other rights of less importance now, such as the right to hold fairs and markets or operate a port or ferry.[10] Also included are tenements such as minerals: these can be held separately from the land below which they lie.[11]

The expression "interest in land" is not very clear. In the official guide **15.08** to land registration it is even noted that the term "interest in land" can lead to some confusion, since it can mean the *dominium utile* or *dominium directum* of land, or the interest of one person or another in the *dominium utile*, or an interest in land over another interest in land, such as a standard security.[12]

The notion with which Scottish land law has always worked is that of **15.09** the real right in land; it therefore seems odd that the Act should prefer a

---

[5] "Recording" refers in the Act to recording in the General Register of Sasines: s. 15(1).

[6] s. 1(2).

[7] s. 15(1). Servitudes are dealt with in s. 3. The definition of "interest in land" will cease to have effect on amendment of the 1973 Act in terms of the Abolition of Feudal Tenure etc. (Scotland) Bill, Sched. 8, Pt I, para. 33(4).

[8] s. 15(1).

[9] *Ogston v. Stewart* (1896) 23 R. (H.L.) 16.

[10] Reid, *Property*, paras 210–211.

[11] *Lord Advocate v. Wemyss* (1899) 2 F. (H.L.) 1.

[12] ROTPB, para. C. 113.

different and more obscure expression. This causes some difficulty especially in relation to the question of possession, which is discussed in the next chapter.[13] For present purposes, however, there can be no real doubt that what is intended is that the expression "interest in land" should refer to real rights in land, title to which can competently be recorded or registered.

15.10   The main interests to which title can competently be recorded in the General Register of Sasines are: *dominium directum, dominium utile,* long leases,[14] standard securities[15] and proper liferents. So far as land registration is concerned, the Land Registration (Scotland) Act 1979 sets out the "interests in land" which are registrable in the Land Register. It defines "interest in land" as follows: "any estate, interest, servitude or other heritable right in or over land, including a heritable security but excluding a lease which is not a long lease".[16] A definition of "heritable security" is incorporated into the Act: "any security capable of being constituted over any interest in land by disposition or assignation of that interest in security of any debt and of being recorded in the Register of Sasines".[17]

15.11   The creation over a registered interest in land of a heritable security, liferent or incorporeal heritable right is registrable. Once registered, these themselves become registered interests in land.[18] All that the 1979 Act says about "incorporeal heritable right" is that it does not include a right to salmon fishing.[19] An obvious example of such an incorporeal heritable right is a servitude[20]: this is registrable by the proprietor of the dominant tenement.[21]

Effect of the proposed amendment of section 1

15.12   As already mentioned, the expression "interest in land" has to be construed so as to refer to real rights in land. The consequence of the proposed amendment of the Act to speak in terms of real rights, instead of interests, in land does not therefore appear to affect the scope of section 1. The section will apply to any real right which is registrable in the Land Register or a deed relating to which can competently recorded in the General Register of Sasines.[22] But section 1 will not apply to servitudes or public rights of way.[23]

---

[13] See paras 16.09 *et seq.*

[14] Registration of Leases (Scotland) Act 1857.

[15] Other forms of heritable security were abolished for the future by the Conveyancing and Feudal Reform (Scotland) Act 1970, s. 9(3); Halliday, *Conveyancing*, Chap. 47.

[16] s. 28(1).

[17] Conveyancing and Feudal Reform (Scotland) Act 1970, s. 9(8).

[18] s. 2(3).

[19] s. 28(1).

[20] But, owing to the definition of "interest in land" in the 1973 Act, the provisions of s. 1 of the Act do not apply to servitudes; instead s. 3 applies: see below, para. 17.03.

[21] So far as the servient tenement is concerned, however, a servitude is an overriding interest: 1979 Act, s. 28(1).

[22] SLC Report no. 168 (1999), *Abolition of the Feudal System*, paras 9.5–9.6; draft Bill, cl. 70(1) and Sched. 8, Pt I, para. 35(2).

[23] Curiously enough under the existing wording of s. 1 it is not made clear that the section is not intended to apply to public rights of way. This is because it is stated only that the section does not apply to "interests in land", but they are defined in s. 15(1) only so as to exclude servitudes.

II. TITLES AND DEEDS

Earlier legislation

The Act 1617 required a "heritable infeftment" on which prescription **15.13** might run; in the Conveyancing (Scotland) Acts of 1874 and 1924 this became an "*ex facie* valid irredeemable title ... recorded in the appropriate Register of Sasines".[24] Before the 1973 Act came into force, prescription could therefore proceed on a redeemable title only under the Act 1617, and the prescriptive period was 40 years. Only irredeemable titles benefited from the reduction of the prescriptive period to 20 years in the 1874 Act.[25]

Redeemable titles

So long as legislation permitted prescription only upon an "*ex facie* **15.14** valid irredeemable title to an estate in land",[26] it followed that (for example) a creditor could not prescribe any right upon a title which *ex facie* was granted in security. That restriction no longer applies, so prescription will run where the necessary possession follows upon the recording or registration of such a title. Fortification of the title in this way will not of course convert it from a redeemable into an irredeemable title.

The 1973 Act draws no distinction between redeemable and irredeem- **15.15** able titles. But it does provide for the case of a decree of adjudication for debt.[27] Here, for the purposes of computing the prescriptive period, any period before expiry of the legal is to be disregarded. The legal expires 10 years after the date of the adjudication, and during those 10 years the debtor is entitled to redeem. On expiry of the legal, the creditor can either seek declarator of expiry of the legal, which has the effect of vesting an absolute and irredeemable title to the land in him, or, without seeking declarator, he can await the running of the prescriptive period.

What is unclear is whether it is positive or negative prescription which **15.16** runs from the expiry of the legal; whether the creditor must achieve an irredeemable right by positive prescription, by possession for the prescriptive period, or whether the debtor's right to redeem is cut off by negative prescription. In the old law the answer to the question was both unclear and unimportant, because the prescriptive period was the same for each kind of prescription. But now the answer to this question makes a practical difference, since positive prescription is completed in 10 years, while the relevant negative prescription takes 20. There is something to be said on each side.[28]

In favour of negative prescription, the following can be said: **15.17**

---

[24] 1874 Act, s. 34; 1924 Act, s. 16.
[25] *Hinton v. Connell's Trs* (1883) 10 R. 1110, holding that s. 34 of the 1874 Act did not apply to a decree of adjudication with infeftment thereon duly recorded and charter of confirmation bearing to be in security for debt and redeemable.
[26] 1874 Act, s. 34, 1924 Act, s. 16.
[27] s. 1(3).
[28] The arguments are fully set out in G. L. Gretton, "Prescription and the foreclosure of adjudications", 1983 J.R. 177–187, and Gretton, *Inhibition and Adjudication*, p. 212. His conclusion is that what the adjudger gets is two titles, a heritable security and conditional ownership.

(1) Prescription runs not against the debtor's right of ownership (which is imprescriptible)[29] but against his right to redeem;

(2) although the right to redeem is a *res merae facultatis* and so itself imprescriptible,[30] once the adjudication has been recorded or registered, this can no longer be the case, since an adverse interest has been insisted upon against the debtor;

(3) since the effect of positive prescription is not to confer a right of property but to render a title unchallengeable, it is difficult to see how it can make a redeemable title into an irredeemable one.[31]

It must be conceded, however, that argument (1) depends on regarding the expiry of the legal as vesting the title to the land in the creditor. Otherwise there is no way round the objection that ownership is not subject to negative prescription. But this concession itself raises a further puzzle: if the title is vested in the creditor, on what basis can the debtor be entitled to redeem at any time during the 20 years following expiry of the legal?

15.18 In favour of positive prescription, on the other hand, it may be said that the 1973 Act itself is evidently drafted with this in mind. This is suggested not least by the fact that the present provision appears in section 1 of the Act. Time therefore runs from expiry of the legal. But this simple statement leaves unexplored the difficulties referred to above. In particular, in order to escape from argument (3) above, it will be necessary to say that on expiry of the legal the creditor acquires a title to the land. Without this, there is nothing on which positive prescription can run. Since it is not obvious how prescription could turn a redeemable into an irredeemable title, it also seems necessary to conclude that the title acquired on expiry of the legal is an irredeemable one.

General Register of Sasines and Land Register of Scotland

15.19 The Act deals separately with the two systems of registering ownership of land in Scotland, namely, the General Register of Sasines, a register of deeds, and the Land Register of Scotland, a register of defined "interests in land". The provisions regarding prescription are quite different in these two cases. The main reason for this is that, because the General Register of Sasines is a register of deeds, a critical question is the construction of the deed on which prescriptive possession is claimed to follow. That question does not arise when an "interest in land" has been registered in the Land Register. For these reasons the two systems are treated separately here. The first requires a much more detailed discussion.

15.20 Positive prescription has a relatively modest part to play under the system of land registration, for reasons discussed later. With the projected extension of registration of title throughout Scotland by 2003,[32] the role of positive prescription will in due course be much reduced.

---

[29] Sched. 3(a); above, paras 3.02 *et seq.*
[30] Sched. 3(c); above, paras 3.07 *et seq.*
[31] *cf.* perhaps *Robertson v. Duke of Athol* (1815) 3 Dow 108 at 114.
[32] See 1997 S.L.T. (News) 218.

1. General Register of Sasines
What deeds? The question arises what sort of deeds are relevant to **15.21**
section 1. It is clear that they must be deeds which are capable of
constituting in their grantee title to an "interest in land". This would
extend to dispositions, feu dispositions and charters.[33] It would not
extend to purely contractual deeds such as missives, or to maps and plans
which are not annexed to deeds, or to such things as resolutions to grant
titles.[34]

The term "deed" is partially defined in section 5(1).[35] **15.22**

"Further provisions supplementary to sections 1, 2 and 3
5.—(1) In sections 1, 2 and 3 of this Act 'deed' includes a judicial
decree; and for the purposes of the said sections any of the
following, namely an instrument of sasine, a notarial instrument and
a notice of title, which narrates or declares that a person has a title
to an interest in land shall be treated as a deed sufficient to
constitute that title in favour of that person.
(2) [Repealed by the Requirements of Writing (Scotland) Act 1995
(c. 7), Sched. 5 (effective August 1, 1995).]"

The term "deed" includes a judicial decree, provided that it can **15.23**
competently be recorded in the General Register of Sasines. The main
type of decree relied upon for the purpose of constituting a title is a
decree of adjudication, whether for debt, in implement, declaratory,[36] or
following upon an action of division and sale.[37] Decree of service as heir
is another (now obsolete) example.[38]

Any of these deeds is therefore capable of operating as what **15.24**
conveyancers call the "foundation writ",[39] the writ upon which possession follows, and beyond which it is unnecessary to investigate the
circumstances of the title.

The deed—questions about validity. Several well-known dicta make the **15.25**
obvious point that good titles stand in no need of prescription. Prescription is a doctrine which makes good defects. "If the title be in itself
perfectly good, and derived from the true proprietor, there can be no
need of prescription, which is only necessary to cure bad titles."[40] "I hold
that it is the purpose of prescription to exclude all enquiry as to whether
titles, habile in their form, on which prescriptive possession has followed,
were in their original nature and constitution good or bad—and specially

---

[33] For example, Crown charters: *Walker v. Miln* (1871) 9 M. 823.
[34] *Lord Sempill v. Hay* (1903) 5 F. 868; *Caledonian Ry v. Jamieson* (1899) 2 F. 100; *Scot v. Ramsay* (1827) 5 S. 340 (NE 367); *Bain v. Grant* (1884) 22 S.L.R. 132.
[35] In s. 5(1) the words "title to an interest . . constitute that title" will be replaced by "right in land shall be treated as a deed sufficient to constitute that right" on amendment of the 1973 Act in terms of the Abolition of Feudal Tenure etc. (Scotland) Bill, Sched. 8, Pt I, para. 33(3).
[36] Gretton, *Inhibition and Adjudication*, pp. 211–212 at 225.
[37] *Hilson v. Scott* (1895) 23 R. 241 (although in this case the superior anyway granted a charter in the terms set out in the decree of sale adjudging the property).
[38] The Succession (Scotland) Act 1964 abolished this procedure for deaths on or after September 10, 1964.
[39] Halliday, *Conveyancing*, paras 36.06–36.09; Gretton and Reid, *Conveyancing*, pp. 110–112.
[40] *Duke of Buccleuch v. Cunynghame* (1826) 5 S. 53 at 57, *per* L.P. Hope.

the enquiry, whether the author from whom they have proceeded had power to grant them or not. When prescription has run, there is an absolute presumption that they are good."[41]

15.26 The effect of prescription is to raise an irrebuttable presumption that a title is good, and to exclude all inquiry into the validity of the prior title, or the terms on which it was granted.[42] As Lord McLaren put it, "all inquiry into antecedent titles is excluded, whether for the purpose of giving a more limited construction to the grant, or for any other purpose inimical to the prescriptive title which is set up".[43] In spite of a clear line of authority in favour of this proposition, there are two cases in which it has been held to be admissible to examine prior titles. In *Duke of Argyll v. Campbell* the court allowed this in order to determine whether the possessor's possession was actually to be ascribed to a title habile for prescription, or (as it held) was merely as keeper for a superior.[44] In *Lord Advocate v. Hunt* the court examined prior titles for the purpose of determining whether lands were held as pertinents.[45]

15.27 Even if this approach was legitimate then (which seems doubtful),[46] there is no reason to believe that it is now. In terms of section 1 of the 1973 Act (read short) the validity of the title so far as relating to the interest in land shall be exempt from challenge if: the interest has been possessed openly, peaceably and without judicial interruption for 10 years; and the possession was founded on and followed a deed sufficient in respect of its terms to constitute a title to that interest in land. So if there is a sufficient deed and adequate possession, the title to the interest constituted by the deed is exempt from challenge. If questions arise about what the interest in land is, they are to be answered by reference to the deed upon which possession has followed (the "foundation writ") and not earlier deeds. If questions arise about the deed, they are to be directed at the foundation writ and no earlier deed; accordingly, whether the right is, for instance, that of a feuar or a superior (terms which will not of course survive the proposed abolition of the feudal system), a tenant or a creditor in a standard security is a question which has to be answered by looking to the terms of the foundation writ alone, for it is it that constitutes title to the right in question. And if questions arise about possession, they are to be answered by looking at the quality of possession itself, and not by recourse to events which took place before the start of the prescriptive possession. Cases such as that of the *Duke of Argyll* can be satisfactorily and fairly resolved, without breaking the rule that earlier deeds are not to be examined, by asking whether the possession was adequate, in the sense of being an assertion of right adverse to the Duke.[47]

---

[41] *H.M. Advocate v. Graham* (1844) 7 D. 183 at 205 *per* Lord Moncreiff; also 196, *per* L. J.-C. Hope.

[42] In addition to the cases referred in the preceding paragraph, see *Macdonald v. Lockhart* (1842) 5 D. 372 at 376; *Ramsey v. Spence*, 1909 S.C. 1441 at 1444; *Troup v. Aberdeen Heritable Securities Co.*, 1916 S.C. 918 at 924.

[43] *Cooper's Trs v. Stark's Trs* (1898) 25 R. 1160 at 1167.

[44] 1912 S.C. 458 at 501; this is the passage that the statements in Walker, pp. 18, 25 and 27 rely upon.

[45] (1867) 5 M. (H.L.) 1.

[46] See Reid, *Property*, para. 205, n. 6.

[47] See below, para. 16.26.

The importance of excluding recourse to prior deeds is obvious: if **15.28** exceptions to this rule are opened up, one of the principal benefits of prescription, the fact that it streamlines conveyancing transactions by making it unnecessary to examine titles earlier than the foundation writ, will be lost.

Cases in which prescription does not run. Positive prescription does not **15.29** operate where possession was founded on a deed which is (1) invalid *ex facie* or (2) was forged.[48]

Ex facie invalidity. For prescription to operate, a deed need not be valid **15.30** but it must not be *ex facie* invalid. "Prescription does not cure *ex facie* nullities, but only excludes grounds of challenge not disclosed on the face of the title."[49] In practice only serious defects have had the effect of making a deed *ex facie* invalid. This is because (1) the test for *ex facie* invalidity was set very high—"the deed must *per se* afford complete and exclusive proof of its nullity. It must be, in short, a self-destructive title".[50] If extrinsic evidence was needed to demonstrate that a deed was invalid, then it was not regarded as being *ex facie* invalid within the terms of the legislation.[51] (2) Until 1995 so-called "informalities of execution" were curable under a procedure provided by the Conveyancing (Scotland) Act 1874,[52] whereby the court declared that the deed had been subscribed by the granter and the witnesses. Section 5(2) of the 1973 Act provided that a deed which had been rectified in this manner was to be regarded as not having been at any time *ex facie* invalid. The result was that only where the court was unable to find that the deed had been subscribed by the granter and the witnesses would the deed fail. This would be the case, for example, if the granter had not signed, or only one witness had attested, or if the signatures were not "subscriptions" in the strict sense, or the witnesses had not witnessed.[53]

The procedure under the 1874 Act and the references to it in the 1973 **15.31** Act have now been repealed by the Requirements of Writing (Scotland) Act 1995 with respect to deeds made on or after August 1, 1995.[54] A deed which creates, transfers, varies or extinguishes an interest in land is now valid if it is simply subscribed by the granter.[55] If it is also attested by a witness, then there is a presumption that the deed was subscribed by the granter.[56] Where the deed does not satisfy the requirements of the Act so as to become "self-proving", it is not necessarily invalid and may nonetheless be set up by an application to the court.[57] Invalidity attaches only to deeds which are not subscribed by the granter. *Ex facie* invalidity will therefore remain extremely rare.

---

[48] s. 1(1A)(a).
[49] *Glen v. Scales' Trs* (1881) 9 R. 317 at 325; Erskine, III, vii, 9; Bell, *Prin.* s. 2015; Napier, pp. 153–162.
[50] *Cooper Scott v. Gill Scott*, 1924 S.C. 309 at 323 and 344; *cf. Fleeming v. Howden* (1868) 6 M. 782; *Watson v. Shields*, 1994 S.C.L.R. 819; 1996 S.C.L.R. 81.
[51] Napier, p. 162; see, *e.g.*, *Abbey v. Atholl Properties Ltd*, 1936 S.N. 97.
[52] s. 39.
[53] See Halliday, *Conveyancing*, paras 3.44–3.45 for a summary; most recently, *Williamson v. Williamson*, 1996 S.L.T. 92; 1997 S.L.T. 1044.
[54] For discussion, see Halliday, *Conveyancing*, paras 3.92–3.171.
[55] 1995 Act, ss. 1(2) and 2.
[56] s. 3; to raise this presumption, wills have to be signed on every page: s. 3(2). Subscription and signature are defined in s. 7.
[57] 1995 Act, s. 4.

15.32 *Rectification of the deed.* Suppose that a deed is rectified under the provisions of section 8 of the Law Reform (Miscellaneous Provisions) (Scotland) Act 1985, on the basis that it "fails to express accurately the intention of the granter". It is possible that rectification might cure a defect in a deed or otherwise transform it into a sufficient title for the purposes of prescription. Rectification is in the ordinary case retroactive, so the deed once rectified would be treated as having always been executed in its rectified form, and always recorded in that form.[58] This is subject only to the discretion of the court to order that rectification take effect from a later date, so as to protect the interests of persons who had reasonably relied on the terms of the deed, and had not known that it failed to express the granter's intention.[59]

15.33 In principle, therefore, any possession which followed upon the recording of the unrectified deed[60] would count towards the prescriptive period, even though much of it may have ante-dated the rectification. But it seems likely that, where recorded deeds are concerned, the court might often find reason why it should exercise its discretion in the interests of third parties to defer the date of rectification, and with it the running of prescription upon a sufficient title.

15.34 *Reduction.* The right to reduce a deed is excluded once positive prescription has run, except in the case of deeds which do not benefit from the protection of prescription since they are *ex facie* invalid or forged. If before the prescriptive period has run the deed upon which possession is founded is reduced, it is clear that there is now no foundation for prescriptive possession.[61]

15.35 *Forgery.* The 1617 Act provided that a title upon which 40 years' possession had followed should not be challengeable "except for falsehood", which was interpreted as forgery. The grant of a disposition by someone who was not the owner was therefore not automatically regarded as falsehood.[62]

15.36 The 1973 Act follows the same line: prescription will not run upon a forged deed, but apart from that prescriptive possession following upon the recording of the deed will fortify the title. In particular, there is no requirement that the disponee should be in good faith. He need not believe either that the disponer is the owner of the property conveyed or that the foundation writ is valid.[63]

15.37 **Recording of the deed must precede possession.** For prescription to operate there has to be possession which was "founded on and followed" the recording of a deed. "Recording" means recording in the General Register of Sasines.[64] Only under the rather different prescriptive regime

---

[58] 1985 Act, s. 8(4) and (5).

[59] ss. 9(4) and (5).

[60] Or simply its execution in cases covered by s. 2 of the 1973 Act.

[61] *Duke of Buccleuch v. Mags of Edinburgh* (1843) 5 D. 846.

[62] *Duke of Buccleuch v. Cunynghame* (1826) 5 S. 53, 56 (N.E.); *Auld v. Hay* (1880) 7 R. 663 at 673.

[63] Bell's, *Prin.*, s. 2004 was alone in stating the opposite (later editions take a different line).

[64] s. 15(1).

of section 2 is there no need for recording.[65] These words make clear a fundamental requirement: there must be not merely a title but possession following upon it. Neither title nor possession on its own will achieve prescription.[66] The possession relied upon must relate to the title relied upon and not proceed on some other basis which might not be adequate for prescription.[67] There is no need for the possession to begin the moment recording has taken place. The point is simply that any period of possession which preceded the recording of the deed is irrelevant so far as prescription is concerned.[68]

The words "founded on" immediately raise a more intricate question: **15.38** whether the possession asserted is consistent with the deed on which it purportedly proceeds. The possession must be consistent with the grant.[69] Only then can it be said that the possession is founded on the deed. The terms of the deed therefore need to be examined.

The terms of the deed. The Act requires that the deed be "sufficient in **15.39** respect of its terms to constitute in favour of that person a title to that interest in the particular land, or in land of a description habile to include the particular land".

There are several questions here which construction of the deed must **15.40** answer. Are the terms of the deed sufficient to constitute a title to an interest in land? If so, what interest? And what land?

Sufficiency of terms. An obvious case where the terms of a deed were **15.41** insufficient to constitute a title to the land was where the deed in fact conveyed no title to the land at all but only a right to build on it.[70] In another case the proprietor of an upper storey laid claim to ownership of an access stairway, which he had used exclusively for the prescriptive period.[71] But his claim failed, because the terms of the deed were insufficient. He had been granted a right of access. It followed that the right must have been granted over someone else's land, and it was found to be a right in the nature of a servitude rather than a property right. There was therefore no basis in the terms of the deed on which prescriptive possession could follow so as to constitute a title. As Lord Kyllachy observed in that case, where the construction of the title is clear, there is no room for drawing inferences about it from evidence of possession.[72] So too a right of access to a loch is not a sufficient basis to found a claim to a right to fishings in it.[73] Similarly, if a feu grant or

---

[65] See below, paras 15.70 *et seq.*

[66] *Andersons v. Low* (1863) 2 M. 100 at 103; *Johnston v. Fairfowl* (1901) 8 S.L.T. 480.

[67] Gordon, *Land Law*, para. 12.48; *Earl of Fife's Trs v. Cuming* (1831) 9 S. 336 (use consistent with a servitude); *Officers of State v. Earl of Haddington* (1830) 8 S. 867 (possession as keeper); *Leck v. Chalmers* (1859) 21 D. 408 (use consistent with servitude); *Houstoun v. Barr*, 1911 S.C. 134 (use consistent with lease).

[68] This was not so in the older law, in which possession prior to infeftment could be relied upon if connected with the infeftment, so to this extent the old cases are not to be relied upon: *Crawford v. Durham*, Dec. 20, 1822, F.C.; Gordon, *Land Law*, para. 12.52.

[69] *cf.*, *e.g.*, *Officers of State*, above, at 872.

[70] *Ross v. Milne* (1843) 5 D. 648.

[71] *Robertson's Trs v. Bruce* (1905) 7 F. 580; the terms of the right of access were "access thereto by a street door from Wellington Street".

[72] at 588.

[73] *Montgomery v. Watson* (1861) 23 D. 635; *cf.* also *Fergusson v. Shirreff* (1844) 6 D. 1363.

disposition is expressly under reservation of minerals, possession of minerals on that title could not support prescription.[74] This is simply because the title is not sufficient to support the prescriptive possession. But if the reservation of minerals comes to be omitted from titles to the land, then it will be possible for a person who has such a title and who possesses the minerals by working them to acquire an unchallengeable right to them.[75]

15.42 **"Interest".** It may be a question of construction to what "interest" (or what real right) in land the deed constitutes a title. For example, the question may arise whether the interest in land is the *dominium utile* or a superiority.

15.43   While the feudal system remains, it is indeed possible for a person to have a title to more than one right in the same land, for instance to the *dominium utile* and a superiority. There might also be title to the *dominium utile* and a long lease. Where this is the case, it will be necessary to establish to which of the titles possession is to attributed, in order to determine which, if either of the titles, has been fortified by prescription. If that cannot be established, the presumption is that possession followed upon the more favourable and less restricted title, generally speaking the superiority title rather than the feuar's title, or the feuar's title rather than the lessee's.[76]

15.44   If a superior possesses the lands on a recorded title for the prescriptive period, the feu can be extinguished, and the *dominium utile* consolidated with the superiority.[77] For this to occur, the superior's title requires to be sufficient to constitute a title to the *dominium utile*, which will not be the case where it is expressly confined to the superiority or the *dominium directum* in the land.[78] It is no objection to this that the superior may himself have disponed the land. Provided he has then possessed it or part of it for the prescriptive period, he can prescribe title to it and so in a sense derogate from his own grant.[79]

---

[74] *Fleeming v. Howden* (1868) 6 M. 782. It is a difficult question whether a title may be sufficient to support prescriptive possession of minerals when it does not expressly exclude them but merely makes reference to earlier deeds which exclude them.

[75] *Millar v. Marquess of Lansdowne*, 1910 S.C. 618.

[76] Gordon, *op cit.* paras 12.49–12.51; for details, Napier, pp. 199–288. See, *e.g.*, *Earl of Glasgow v. Boyle* (1887) 14 R. 419; *Earl of Fife v. Innes* (1809) Hume 468. In the case of holding under a lease and under a feu grant, there would be no reason in the modern law to insist that prescription could run on the feu grant only once the lease had terminated (the contrary decision in *Duke of Roxburgh v. Wauchope* (1734) 1 Pat. 126 evidently turned upon the now irrelevant consideration that the pursuers had not been in a position effectively to raise an action challenging the disputed possession until the lease had terminated: on the old common-law plea *non valens agere cum effectu* see above, paras 7.18–25).

The same presumption for possession on the more favourable title also applies where two titles are held to precisely the same interest in land: see, *e.g.*, *Smith & Bogle v. Gray* (1752) M. 10803; *Duke of Hamilton v. Westenra* (1827) 6 S. 44; *Robertson v. Duke of Athol* (1808) Hume 463; *Maule v. Earl of Dalhousie & Maule* (1782) M. 10963 and 2 Hailes 899 at 900; *Auld v. Hay* (1880) 7 R. 663 at 671. The consequence is that, once prescription has followed on the more favourable title, the restrictions in the less favourable title cease to be of any effect.

[77] *Lord Elibank v. Campbell* (1833) 12 S. 74; *Love-Lee v. Cameron*, 1991 S.C.L.R. 61; Halliday, *Conveyancing*, para. 32.114.

[78] *cf.* Halliday, *Opinions*, no. 176.

[79] The same applies in other contexts: see below on break-off dispositions; and, for a case where the Crown reacquired by prescriptive possession a right of patronage which it had granted, *Mags of Peebles v. Officers of State* (1800) Hume 457.

Land. In the nature of things, prescription is likely to be relied upon by a **15.45**
possessor where there is ambiguity or uncertainty about the extent of his
title. Entitlement to the area of land in controversy need not appear on
the face of the title. What matters is that the title is capable of being
construed so as to include that land.[80] Again the question is of ensuring
that what is claimed under prescription is consistent with the grant. So,
for example, in *Auld v. Hay*,[81] the description given in a charter could be
construed as covering either the whole of some lands or only part of
them. There was therefore a title which, in the language of the 1973 Act,
was "sufficient in respect of its terms" to constitute a title to the whole.
Whether prescription had run on that title so as to make it unchallengeable depended on the extent of the possession which had followed upon
it.

Bounding titles. The general principle is that the owner cannot prescribe **15.46**
in a sense inconsistent with his title of possession.[82] A clear illustration of
this principle lies in the critical distinction between titles which are and
those which are not bounding. Where the boundaries of a title are
delimited, for example by measurements, description, specification, a
plan, or some combination of these, there is no scope for relying on
prescriptive possession to acquire title to an interest in land lying beyond
these boundaries.[83] The same result follows if the title contains a
description which refers to lands lying within a parish or county. It is
then no basis for prescribing title to areas lying beyond the parish or
county boundary. The reason is simple: the terms of the deed are not
then sufficient to constitute a title beyond the boundaries contained in
the deed.[84] Similarly, it will not be possible to prescribe title to an area of
land which is expressly excepted from a grant as the title is a bounding
title so far as the excepted areas of land are concerned.[85]

The same principle applies to salmon fishings. Where a grant names **15.47**
the river pools in which the fishings are granted, the title is not habile for
prescription of fishings in the river beyond them.[86] The same is true
where the grant is limited by the mid-channel of a river. It is not then
habile for the prescription of fishings on the far side of the river.[87]

Deciding whether a title is bounding is a matter of construing the **15.48**
dispositive clause in the title in question.[88] The short point is that,

---

[80] See, *e.g.*, *Mead v. Melville* (1915) 1 S.L.T. 107.

[81] (1880) 7 R. 663; *cf.* also *Duke of Argyll v. Campbell*, 1912 S.C. 458 at 490.

[82] *Cooper's Trs v. Stark's Trs* (1898) 25 R. 1160 at 1168–1169; *North British Ry v. Hutton*
(1896) 23 R. 522 at 525–526.

[83] Erskine, II, vi, 3; Napier, pp. 166–168; *Brown v. North British Ry* (1906) 8 F. 534;
Gordon v. Grant (1850) 13 D. 1 (application to a barony title within a particular parish).
The general rule is that the boundary of a subject does not itself form part of the subject:
Houstoun v. Barr, 1911 S.C. 134; *Mags and Town Council of St. Monans v. Mackie* (1845)
7 D. 582.

[84] Stair II, iii, 26; *Suttie v. Gordon* (1837) 15 S. 1037; *Nisbet v. Hogg*, 1950 S.L.T. 289;
Luss Estates Co. v. BP Oil Grangemouth Refinery Ltd, 1987 S.L.T. 201 at 205; *Suttie v.
Baird*, 1992 S.L.T. 133.

[85] *North British Ry v. Hutton* (1896) 23 R. 522.

[86] *Duke of Argyll v. Campbell* (1891) 18 R. 1094.

[87] *Milne v. Smith* (1850) 13 D. 112; note however (1) that the meaning of a right to
fishings which is bounded by the mid-channel (*medium filum*) of a river is that from the
mid-channel each proprietor is entitled to fish as far out into the stream as he can by any
lawful method: *Fothringham v. Passmore*, 1984 S.C. (H.L.) 96; and (2) that a bounding
description may be held to apply only to the land and not to an incorporeal right such as
fishing attached to it: *Earl of Zetland v. Tennent's Trs* (1873) 11 M. 469.

[88] *Luss Estates Co. v. BP Oil Grangemouth Refinery Ltd*, 1987 S.L.T. 201 at 205.

provided the boundaries are both specified and identifiable, they must receive effect and the proprietor cannot prescribe beyond them. But not all titles are bounding titles. In such cases, provided the deed is capable of being construed so as to carry title to the interest claimed, the extent of possession may be able to fix the boundaries.

15.49   A problematic case is where the property of one person is described as bounded by that of another. Here it may often be the case that the boundaries, although specified, cannot be identified and must therefore be proved by the extent of possession. It follows that the boundary may advance or recede, according to the possession of the proprietors on either side.[89]

15.50 *Break-off dispositions.* In the case of a so-called "break-off disposition", a disponing proprietor dispones not all but only part of his property to his disponee. This raises one new point worth comment. As a result of the disposition, a boundary comes into existence between the property of the disponee and that of the disponer. It is possible for the disponing proprietor to prescribe against his disponee. This is because the title he has, which extends to the whole subjects, continues to be sufficient to include the areas disponed. If he has disponed such that the disponee has a bounding title, then the consequence must be that the disponee cannot prescribe against him, being confined within the bounds of the title. But no such consequence affects the disponer. If he possesses part of the disponed property for the prescriptive period, he can reacquire it by prescription. It may seem odd that a person can in this way derogate from his own grant, but it is a necessary consequence of the fact that prescription looks only for possession on a sufficient, non-bounding title.[90] It is only after a further disposition of the retained lands, which ought to except the parts already disponed, that it would be likely or at least possible that the title to the (once) retained lands would itself be bounding with respect to the areas first disponed.

15.51 Parts and pertinents.[91] The ordinary rules of prescription apply to the case of "parts and pertinents", that is, heritable rights which are automatically, and without the need for express conveyance, transferred together with a particular piece of heritable property. The expression "parts and pertinents" includes, for example, buildings which have become part of the land by accession. It may also extend to areas of land which are held together with the land and are subsidiary to it. This subsidiary relationship may arise either by express grant—where for example a disposition of a house declares that a garage is carried by the conveyance as a pertinent of the house—or by prescription.

15.52   In the case of prescription, the subsidiary property may become a pertinent of a principal property by possession following upon a sufficient

---

[89] *Reid v. McColl* (1879) 7 R. 84; *Education Trust Governors v. Macalister* (1893) 30 S.L.R. 818 at 820; *Troup v. Aberdeen Heritable Securities Co.*, 1916 S.C. 918 at 927; *Suttie v. Baird*, above.

[90] *cf.* above, para. 15.44 for cases on this point in connection with consolidation of *dominium utile* and superiority; Gretton and Reid, *Conveyancing*, pp. 114–115.

[91] Reid, *Property*, paras 199–206; Napier, pp. 163–166; Gordon, *Land Law*, paras 4.13–16; Erskine, II, vi, 4; Bell, *Prin.*, s. 739.

title; equally, it may cease to be a pertinent of that property where a possessor of other property has possessed the subsidiary property on a sufficient title for the prescriptive period. Where there is dispute, each of two proprietors claiming the same land as part and pertinent on a sufficient title, it is possession alone which can determine the question of its ownership.[92] What is necessary is that the subsidiary property should be capable of being a pertinent of the principal, and that means, as ever, that this must not be inconsistent with the terms of the grant of the principal property. So far as possession of the pertinent is concerned, what is necessary is that it should be possessed not merely along with but actually as pertinent of the principal property.[93] This is essentially the corollary of the requirement that there should be a title as the basis of the possession.

The fact that subjects are expressly included in the title of one person **15.53** (A) does not prevent another (B) from prescribing title to them, provided that B's title is sufficient for this purpose, and one situation in which this can occur is where it is argued that the subjects are parts and pertinents in relation to B's title. If the necessary possession has followed, B's title is unchallengeable.[94] In short, a general title followed by prescriptive possession of subjects as parts and pertinents is stronger than a title expressly including the subjects but without possession.

Usually pertinents will be small areas of land, but there is no **15.54** established limit on size, nor indeed need they be land in any strict sense.[95] Usually, too, pertinent property will adjoin its principal,[96] but this is not essential, and there are cases of prescriptive acquisition of pertinents which do not adjoin. Indeed, since the grant of pertinents does not add anything to the principal grant,[97] it is perhaps in the context of prescriptive acquisition of discontinuous lands that pertinents have their main significance. Although it has been said that there is a presumption against one of two discontiguous properties being a pertinent of another, the relationship can be established by proof of express grant or possession in connection with the principal subject.[98] An extreme case is one which concerned an island in a river: while the island appeared expressly in the title of a third party and the fishings between the island and the claimant's land also belonged to the third party, it was held that the claimant's title was sufficient to allow prescription of title to the island as a pertinent of his land facing the island.[99] In another case it was held that "the pertinents" of a property "bounded on the south by the sea" might include the foreshore.[1]

---

[92] *Carnegie v. MacTier* (1844) 6 D. 1381 at 1408.

[93] *Lord Advocate v. Hunt* (1867) 5 M. (H.L.) 1; also *Young*, above, at 56; *Duke of Argyll v. Campbell*, 1912 S.C. 458 at 501.

[94] *Mags of Perth v. Earl of Wemyss* (1829) 8 S. 82; *Earl of Fife's Trs v. Cuming* (1830) 8 S. 326; also *Young v. Carmichael* (1671) M. 9636; *Countess of Moray v. Wemyss* (1675) M. 9636.

[95] In *McArly v. French's Trs* (1883) 10 R. 574 a shop sign which extended up beyond the mid-line between the ground and first floors of a building was possessed as part and pertinent.

[96] *e.g.* an adjoining moor: *Earl of Fife's Trs v. Cuming* (1830) 8 S. 326; the foreshore of a navigable river: *Buchanan and Geils v. Lord Advocate* (1882) 9 R. 1218.

[97] A "grant of the lands of A . . . is as extensive as a grant of A with parts and pertinents": *Gordon v. Grant* (1850) 13 D. 1 at 7, *per* L. J.-C. Hope.

[98] *Scott v. Lord Napier* (1869) 7 M. (H.L.) 35 at 81, *per* Lord Chelmsford.

[99] *Mags of Perth v. Earl of Wemyss* (1829) 8 S. 82.

[1] *Young v. North British Ry* (1887) 14 R. (H.L.) 53.

15.55   The main limitations on prescriptive acquisition of parts and pertinents are two:

(1) It is settled that a bounding title is inconsistent with acquisition as
a pertinent of property lying beyond the boundary.[2] Although this
may be rational where the bounds are broadly stated—"the lands
of X with parts and pertinents in the county of Y"—,[3] for more
narrowly bounded titles the good sense of this rule has been
rightly doubted, since the bounding title can surely be taken to
bound only the principal property, a pertinent often lying beyond
its bounds.[4] Even on a bounding title, however, it is possible to
acquire a servitude right beyond the bounds of the property. In a
sense this is obvious, since one can only have a servitude over
another's property, and one thing a bounding title does make
clear is that beyond the bounds lies the property of another.[5]

(2) In general, parts and pertinents clauses do not extend to legal
separate tenements, such as salmon fishings. The rule is that
(except for barony titles) the word "fishings" must appear in the
dispositive clause of a disposition. There are, however, instances
in which the word "pertinents" in the dispositive clause of a
disposition has been interpreted as meaning fishings, where the
fishings are themselves mentioned in the tenendas clause.[6]

15.56 *Special cases*

(1) *Barony title.* A barony title is one created by direct grant from the
Crown. It is the highest form of feudal tenure. The title is
regarded as a whole, a *universitas*, and this has certain consequences for prescription.[7] The main ones are these: (a) the title
will carry all parcels of land connected with the barony without
their being specially mentioned or covered by a clause of parts
and pertinents; (b) the title is capable of carrying even *regalia
minora* such as salmon fishings without mention of them (provided that possession has followed upon the title)[8]; (c) possession
of part of an established barony can be treated as possession of
the whole.[9]

(2) *The foreshore.* The foreshore is defined as the part of the shore
which is wholly covered by the sea at high tide and wholly
uncovered at low tide, the relevant tides being ordinary spring
tides.[10] The principle on which property in the foreshore could be

---

[2] Stair, II, iii, 73; Erskine, II, vi, 3; Bell, *Prin.*, s. 739.

[3] *e.g.* in *Lord Advocate v. Wemyss* (1899) 2 F. (H.L.) 1.

[4] Reid, *Property*, para. 205.

[5] *Beaumont v. Lord Glenlyon* (1843) 5 D. 1337; *Troup v. Aberdeen Heritable Securities
Co.*, 1916 S.C. 918 at 929; *McDonald v. Dempster* (1871) 10 M. 94 at 98. If the servitude
were argued for on the basis of possession following upon a deed, clearly the terms of the
deed would remain relevant: s. 3(1) discussed below, paras 17.06 *et seq.* Napier, pp. 352–
357.

[6] Gordon, *Land Law*, paras 8.58–8.62; Reid, *Property*, para. 322; *Lord Advocate v.
Sinclair* (1875) 5 M. (H.L.) 97 at 106; *Lord Advocate v. McCulloch* (1874) 2 R. 27 at 35.

[7] A useful account of barony title is given by Lord Wood in *Duke of Montrose v.
Macintyre* (1848) 10 D. 896 at 914. See also Stair, II, iii, 60–61.

[8] See below, para. 15.56(3).

[9] See below, para. 16.34.

[10] *Bowie v. Marquis of Ailsa* (1887) 14 R. 649 at 661. Areas not covered by ordinary tides
are not included: *Aitken's Trs v. Caledonian Ry and Lord Advocate* (1904) 6 F. 465.

acquired was disputed until *Agnew v. Lord Advocate*,[11] so earlier authorities are not a safe guide. The modern law is that the foreshore may be acquired either by grant from the Crown or other owner or by prescriptive possession on a title habile to include the foreshore.[12] Where a person seeks to prescribe title to the foreshore against the Crown, the prescriptive period is 20 years. In all other cases it is ten years.[13]

The question arises which titles are bounding and so exclude the foreshore, and which are sufficient to include it. The cases establish that where subjects are bounded by the sea,[14] that is taken to refer to the low-water mark and so is capable of including the foreshore. The same applies where the boundary is the seashore. But a reference which clearly relates to the high-water mark, such as the "flood mark", excludes the foreshore.[15] While the Crown may alienate property in the foreshore to a private proprietor, there is no presumption that it has done so just because the title is sufficient to include the foreshore; whether prescription has been completed turns on the extent of possession.[16] A recent example where the title was found not to be sufficient to include the foreshore, because the boundary was evidently the high-water mark is provided by *Luss Estates Company v. BP Oil Grangemouth Refinery Ltd.*[17] There the view that that was the boundary was supported by measurements of distance and area, a plan, and the fact that the boundary was described as having been "staked out", a procedure much drier and therefore more probable for the high-water than for the low-water mark.

(3) *Salmon fishings*.[18] The right to salmon fishings is quite separate from the question of ownership of the water in which the right is exercised. The fishings are a legally separate tenement. The right is classified *inter regalia minora*, as a right which is vested in the Crown but which is capable of alienation.[19] Many such rights have been alienated and are therefore conveyed in ordinary dispositions rather than by Crown charters. The right may be acquired by the express grant of "salmon fishings" in the dispositive clause of a disposition. Alternatively, it may be acquired by prescriptive possession following upon a sufficient title.[20] In the ordinary case, in order to be sufficient, a title must include the word "fishings"[21]; in the case of a barony title, however, that is not necessary.[22] It has been observed that, since an express grant has to be of

---

[11] (1873) 11 M. 309.

[12] Reid, *Property*, para. 314.

[13] s. 1(4).

[14] A line which may move: *Campbell v. Brown*, Nov. 18, 1813, F.C. (at 447, *per* Lord Glenlee).

[15] *Berry v. Holden* (1840) 3 D. 205 at 212.

[16] *Agnew v. Lord Advocate* (1873) 11 M. 309; *Lord Advocate & Clyde Trs v. Lord Blantyre* (1879) 6 R. (H.L.) 72.

[17] 1987 S.L.T. 201.

[18] See generally Reid, *op cit.*, paras 320–330; Gordon, *op cit.*, paras 3.52–3.74; Stair, II, iii, 69; Erskine, II, vi, 15.

[19] See, *e.g.*, Erskine, II, vi, 13 and II, vi, 15.

[20] *Lord Advocate v. Cathcart* (1871) 9 M. 744 at 752.

[21] *ibid.*

[22] *Nicol v. Lord Advocate* (1868) 6 M. 972.

"salmon fishings", it might in theory be argued that a mention in a writ only of "fishings" would not constitute a title sufficient for prescription of salmon fishings. There is no authority on the point under the present legislation.[23] Where a person seeks to prescribe title to salmon fishings against the Crown, the prescriptive period is 20 years. In all other cases it is 10 years.[24]

2. Land Register of Scotland[25]

15.57 There are some significant differences between the prescriptive regimes applicable to sasine and to Land Register titles. Most of them rest on the fact that it is not the deed but the interest in land which is registered in the Land Register. For this reason, once a title has been registered, there is no need to construe the terms of the deed in order to determine whether they are sufficient to support the ensuing possession. The question is whether the registered interest in land supports the possession. And it is upon registration of the interest in land that possession must follow.

15.58 Registration of an interest in particular land subject to an exclusion of indemnity. The 1973 Act allows prescription to run on a registered title only where the Keeper has excluded indemnity,[26] that is, he has refused make State compensation available in the event that the registered proprietor suffers loss in certain circumstances. For present purposes, the most important circumstances are loss arising from rectification of the register, or refusal to rectify it, or from an error or omission in a land certificate or charge certificate.[27] Exclusion of indemnity is relatively uncommon. A clear instance in which the Keeper would normally exclude indemnity is that of a disposition granted by a non-owner (*a non domino* disposition). Here, in the course of examination of the title by the Keeper, it would no doubt normally appear that there was a competing claim to the title to the land. Even if it did not, the applicant for registration of such a disposition would be unable to provide a progress of titles and this alone might induce the Keeper to refuse indemnity. It would be open to the Keeper to refuse registration altogether, but the normal procedure is to register it under exclusion of indemnity.[28]

15.59 Uninterrupted possession for 10 years on a registered title fortifies the registered proprietor's title against challenge.[29] Once that time has run, a registered proprietor can apply to the Keeper with evidence of his prescriptive possession in order to have the title sheet rectified. Rectification will involve the removal of the name of the earlier proprietor, and at the same time the withdrawal of the exclusion of indemnity.[30]

---

[23] Reid, *op cit.*, para. 324.

[24] s. 1(4).

[25] Gordon, *Land Law*, paras 12.08–12.18; Reid, "*A non domino* conveyances and the Land Register", 1991 J.R. 79–95, as well as Reid's earlier articles in (1984) 29 J.L.S.S. 171–177, 212–217, 260–263; R. Rennie, "Prescriptive possession in the Sasine and Land Registers" (1997) 2 S.L.P.Q. 309–315.

[26] 1973 Act, s. 1(1)(b)(ii); 1979 Act, s. 12(2).

[27] 1979 Act, s. 12(1).

[28] ROTPB, para. H. 1.08. For a recent case confirming this approach, *Hamilton v. Ready Mixed Concrete (Scotland) Ltd*, 1999 S.L.T. 524.

[29] In short, for the purposes of land registration, the expression "exempt from challenge" means "not rectifiable".

[30] ROTPB, para. C. 71.

Challenges to entries in the Land Register are made by application to **15.60** have the Register rectified.[31] It is true that a person can bring an action of reduction against a deed which has led to the registration of an interest in the Land Register. But it is important to note that, although reduction will nullify the deed, it has no effect on the validity of the registered title. For the title to be affected, it is necessary to seek rectification of the Register.[32]

The purpose of rectification is to correct inaccuracies in the Register, **15.61** but the circumstances in which this can be done are restricted, in the interests of the registered proprietor, to the following: where the registered proprietor is not in possession or, where he is, the rectification is for the purpose of noting an overriding interest, has been consented to by all persons likely to be affected, or is necessary to correct an inaccuracy caused wholly or substantially by the fraud or carelessness of the proprietor in possession.[33]

The effect of completion of positive prescription is therefore to make **15.62** it impossible for rectification to succeed against the registered proprietor. It is convenient to emphasise here again that positive prescription does not create a new title; indeed, that is obvious, since the very act of registration of title makes the registered proprietor the owner of the registered interest. All that prescription does is to render the title unchallengeable. At that point the Keeper can safely withdraw the exclusion of indemnity.

Where the Keeper has not excluded indemnity, prescription cannot **15.63** run. It is true that in most doubtful cases indemnity is likely to have been excluded, so that prescription will run and will resolve the doubts and defects in title. But rectification is possible even where indemnity has not been excluded, in the situations already mentioned. The difficulty here is that the title will not become exempt from challenge after 10 years, because positive prescription does not run. In these cases, a person who suffers loss as a result of rectification of the Register will have to rely on redress from the indemnity.[34] The title will cease to be challengeable after 20 years because the right to seek rectification would be extinguished by negative prescription.[35] Until then, the title will remain voidable, and the Keeper of the Registers will remain vulnerable to a demand for indemnity. It is improbable, however, that this situation could often arise, both because in doubtful cases indemnity is likely to have been excluded, and because in most instances the registered proprietor will be in possession and therefore not normally capable of being affected by rectification of the Register.

---

[31] 1979 Act, s. 9; *Short's Tr v. Keeper of the Registers of Scotland*, 1996 S.C. (H.L.) 14.

[32] *Short's Tr*, above. The consequence is that the Keeper will not register a decree of reduction; and the only effect of an action of reduction is to constitute judicial interruption of the possessor's possession; see below, para. 16.20 para. (4). For discussion of the (complex) details, K. Reid, "Void and voidable titles and the Land Register", (1996) 1 S.L.P.Q. 265–276.

[33] 1979 Act, s. 9(3)(a)(i), (ii) and (iii).

[34] s. 12.

[35] Reid, *Property*, para. 674; *Short's Tr v. Keeper of the Registers of Scotland*, 1996 S.C. (H.L.) 14 at 24. The right to seek rectification is not itself a procedure for asserting a right of ownership (which would be imprescriptible within Sched. 3(a)), since until rectification the owner is the person in whose name the title is registered. See above, para. 3.04.

15.64 Invalid and forged deeds. Since registration is of the interest in land rather than the deed, and registration follows an examination of the title by the Keeper, there will generally be no cause subsequently to investigate the validity of the deed. In particular, if there is *ex facie* invalidity, this should presumably be noticed by the Keeper and lead to rejection of the deed. There is therefore no need for specific provision in the Act excluding prescription upon an *ex facie* invalid deed where registration is concerned.

15.65 In the case of forgery, however, the 1973 Act makes special provision. Prescription will not run where possession is founded on registration of an interest which proceeded upon a forged deed, and the person appearing from the Register to be entitled to the interest was aware of the forgery at the time of registration.[36] The effect of this provision is that the title will remain voidable, in the sense of being vulnerable to rectification. The circumstances in which this applies are very narrow. It will not be often that it can be shown that the entitled person was aware of the forgery at all, let alone at the time of registration. In any event, provided that the entitled person is in good faith, there will be no question of his or her title being impugned by this provision. This protection of titles against all but forgery in which the entitled person is complicit is justified by the consideration that the purpose of land registration is so far as possible to introduce certainty about the validity of titles to land.

15.66 *Land Register titles.* There are several points to note about Land Register titles, all of which have the effect of reducing the possible scope of positive prescription:

(1) Most Land Register titles, apart from titles to flats, are bounding. This is because they incorporate a title plan, a detailed plan of the horizontal area which they cover.[37] For this reason, apart from the fact that prescription can operate only if indemnity is excluded, there is no scope for prescribing title to property lying beyond the bounds registered on the title plan.

(2) The same point applies to prescription of title to property as part and pertinent of another property.[38] It seems that, only where a deed contains a grant of a pertinent which the Keeper has included on the title plan with exclusion of indemnity, will there be scope for prescribing title to the pertinent.[39]

(3) *Consolidation.* In operational areas for registration of title, if title to a superiority is registered in the Land Register, it will be registered expressly as such and will therefore not be sufficient for acquisition of title to the *dominium utile.* Consolidation of the *dominium utile* and a superiority in the same land could therefore not take place by prescription. This would, however, be possible if the title to the superiority were recorded in the General Register of Sasines, regardless whether title to the *dominium utile* was recorded or registered. In this case, possession on a sufficient

---

[36] s. 1(1A)(b).

[37] ROTPB, para. E. 14.

[38] As with sasine titles, so here a title to the lands of X carries with it all parts and pertinents express or implied: 1979 Act, s. 3(1)(a).

[39] Reid, *Property*, para. 205.

sasine title would at the end of the prescriptive period enable the superior to apply to the Keeper for cancellation of the title sheet of the *dominium utile*.[40]

(4) *The foreshore*. There is one speciality to note here, the purpose of which is to allow the Crown to challenge a title to the foreshore or an interest in it before it has been fortified by prescriptive possession. This provision applies where a title to the foreshore or a right in it has been registered, or an application for registration has been made, and (a) it appears to the Keeper that the title will be fortified against the Crown only once prescription has run and (b) the Keeper excludes or proposes to exclude indemnity in respect of the foreshore or right in it. If the person who has registered or applied for registration has requested the Keeper not to exclude indemnity, the 1979 Act requires the Keeper to intimate that request to the Crown.[41] If the Crown notifies its interest within one month and informs him within three months that it is taking steps to challenge the title, the Keeper is obliged to exclude indemnity until the prescriptive period has run or, if earlier, until the Crown has either ceased to challenge the title or its challenge has been unsuccessful.[42]

(5) In operative areas for registration of title, the interests of lessees under long leases, those holding under udal tenure, and kindly tenants[43] cease to be capable of being constituted as real rights by prescription alone. Prescription will be relevant to them only so far as it fortifies a registered title to such an interest.

3. Effect of completion of the prescriptive period

Once the requisite period of uninterrupted prescriptive possession has **15.67** followed upon the recording or registration, the title becomes "exempt from challenge". This means, so far as sasine titles are concerned, only that the title cannot be challenged on the basis of the deficiencies of the prescriptive progress of deeds which is relied upon. It does not, of course, prevent another person from attempting to obtain an unchallengeable title to the land by means of his or her own prescriptive progress of titles. For that to occur, there would necessarily have to be a title (granted by a non-owner) followed by possession for the prescriptive period. The effect of that would be to make the second title unchallengeable and so exclude the first title.

The same principle applies to Land Register titles, the only additional **15.68** requirement for them being that prescription can run only if indemnity has been excluded. If the Keeper was aware of a competing sasine title, he would routinely exclude indemnity, so prescription could run on the second title. If he was not aware of it, the second grantee would become owner at the moment of registration, although his title would remain challengeable. So long, however, as he remained in possession the Land Register could not be rectified against him against his will.[44]

---

[40] Gordon, *Land Law*, para. 12.51; Halliday, *Conveyancing*, paras 32.122–32.123; ROTPB, paras D. 4.30–4.31.

[41] 1979 Act, s. 14; ROTPB, paras C. 91–92.

[42] 1979 Act, s. 14(2).

[43] *ibid.* s. 3(3).

[44] *ibid.* s. 9(3)(a)(iv).

15.69   Where there are two competing Land Register titles, if indemnity has
not been excluded, a registered proprietor need not rely on prescription
but can seek to have the register rectified against the competing title
simply by producing evidence that he is in possession. Where indemnity
has been excluded, the proprietor can seek rectification of the Land
Register against his competitor only by producing evidence of prescriptive possession. Rectification in favour of the proprietor will be possible
provided that he rather than his competitor is in possession.[45]

4. Section 2: special cases
15.70   Section 2 of the Act deals with what it describes as "special cases".
Two things are special about them. First, in these cases possession need
not be founded upon a recorded or registered deed. Secondly, the
prescriptive period is 20 years. Apart from this, the terms of section 2
are identical to those of section 1.

15.71   The Scottish Law Commission has proposed the substitution of a new
section 2 for the existing one. The purpose is to rid the section of
references to interests in land and to rephrase it in terms of real rights in
land.[46]

15.72   Each of sections 1 and 2 is expressly stated to be without prejudice to
the provisions of the other.[47] This seems to be primarily for the
avoidance of doubt: some of the interests in land covered by section 2
also fall within the category of interests in land title to which can
competently be recorded or registered, so it is important to indicate that
this fact does not affect the operation of the section 2 prescriptive
regime.

Existing section 2
15.73   **"Interests in land: special cases**
2.—(1) If in the case of an interest in particular land, being an
interest to which this section applies,—

> (a) the interest has been possessed by any person, or by any
> person and his successors, for a continuous period of twenty
> years openly, peaceably and without any judicial interrup-
> tion, and
> (b) the possession was founded on, and followed the execution
> of, a deed (whether recorded or not) which is sufficient in
> respect of its terms to constitute in favour of that person a
> title to that interest in the particular land, or in land of a
> description habile to include the particular land,

then, as from the expiration of the said period, the validity of the
title so far as relating to the said interest in the particular land shall
be exempt from challenge except on the ground that the deed is
invalid *ex facie* or was forged.
(2) This section applies—

> (a) to the interest in land of the lessee under a lease;

---

[45] 1979 Act, s. 9(3)(a)(iv); ROTPB, paras H. 1.04–1.07.
[46] SLC Report no. 168 (1999), *Abolition of the Feudal System*, with draft Bill, cl. 70(1)
and Sched. 8, Pt I, para 35.
[47] ss. 1(5) and 2(3).

  (b) to any interest in allodial land;
  (c) to any other interest in land the title to which is of a kind
      which, under the law in force immediately before the
      commencement of this Part of this Act, was sufficient to
      form a foundation for positive prescription without the deed
      constituting the title having been recorded.

  (3) This section is without prejudice to the operation of section 1 of
  this Act."

Proposed new section 2

  "2.—(1) If—   **15.74**

  (a) land has been possessed by any person, or by any person and
      his successors, for a continuous period of twenty years
      openly, peaceably and without any judicial interruption; and
  (b) the possession was founded on, and followed the execution
      of, a deed (whether recorded or not) which is sufficient in
      respect of its terms to constitute in favour of that person a
      real right in that land, or in land of a description *habile* to
      include that land,

  then, as from the expiry of that period, the real right so far as
  relating to that land shall be exempt from challenge except on the
  ground that the deed is invalid *ex facie* or was forged.
  (2) This section applies—

  (a) to the real right of the lessee under a lease; and
  (b) to any other real right in land, being a real right of a kind
      which, under the law in force immediately before the
      commencement of this Part of this Act, was sufficient to
      form a foundation for positive prescription without the deed
      constituting the title to the real right having been recorded,

  but does not apply to servitudes or public rights of way.
  (3) This section is without prejudice to section 1 of this Act or to
  section 3(3) of the Land Registration (Scotland) Act 1979."

  On the length of the prescriptive period it is necessary to say only this: **15.75**
prescription runs from the date of execution.[48] This is the case whether
or not the deed is ultimately recorded. Since the Conveyancing
(Scotland) Act of 1874, which reduced the prescriptive period from 40 to
20 years, confined itself to titles "recorded in the appropriate register of
sasines", it appears that the prescriptive period for these interests in land
was until the enactment of the 1973 Act still 40 years.[49]

  The main point which it is necessary to discuss here is the interests in **15.76**
land which, in terms of section 2(2), can be fortified by prescription
without the need for a recorded deed. There are three categories, two
specific and one general:

  (1) *The interest in land of the lessee under a lease.* In operational areas
      for registration of title, a real right in the land can be obtained

---

  [48] In relation to a deed executed on several dates, this means the last of those dates:
s. 15(1).
  [49] 1874 Act, s. 34; *cf.* Conveyancing (Scotland) Act 1924 s. 16; *Wallace v. University Court
of St Andrews* (1904) 6 F. 1093 at 1111.

only by registration.[50] Elsewhere, prescription may run on an unregistered lease so that, if the lessee possesses for 20 years following the execution of the lease, his interest in the land—that is, the lease—is exempt from challenge. That in turn means that the lessee would prevail over a person who had a registered lease to the land but had not possessed it. This is therefore a qualification to the rule that registered leases rank according to their date of registration, but it is consistent with the fact that the Registration of Leases (Scotland) Act 1857 introduced registration of leases as an alternative to (not a substitute for) possession, for the purposes of perfecting a real right in the lessee.[51]

There is no need for the lease to be of any particular duration in order for this provision to apply to it. So there seems to be no reason why, if possession continued under a short lease by tacit relocation for a period of 20 years, the lessee's interest in the lease should not be fortified by prescription. But since tacit relocation takes place only from year to year, the effect could only be to fortify the right from year to year.

(2) *Any interest in allodial land.*[52] Allodial land is land which, unlike feudal land, is held without any recognition of a superior. The land to which this properly applies is:

(a) Crown land which has either never been feued out or which has reverted to the Crown such that any subordinate estates are consolidated with the Crown's ultimate superiority.[53]

Naturally enough, if the Scottish Law Commission proposals on abolition of the feudal system are adopted, there will be no distinction between feudal and allodial land, and the proposed new section 2 therefore includes no equivalent of section 2(2)(b).[54]

(b) Udal land in Orkney and Shetland. This is a form of tenure under Norse law which survives in Orkney and Shetland, under which land was held allodially and without any need for written title or conveyance. Under this provision, title to such land can be fortified by the necessary prescriptive possession—but there will have to be a deed, even though it is not recorded. There is, however, land in Orkney and Shetland which is held feudally, either under Crown grant or by grant from the Bishop of Orkney or Earl of Orkney and Shetland. This land does not fall within the present provision, and is subject to the normal prescriptive regime of section 1. The effect of the Land Registration (Scotland) Act 1979 is that, once Orkney and Shetland become operative areas for land registration,[55] both writing and registration will be mandatory.

---

[50] s. 2(2)(a). Land Registration (Scotland) Act 1979, s. 3(3).

[51] 1857 Act, s. 16; Halliday, *Conveyancing*, para. 41.06.

[52] In general, see Gordon, *Land Law*, Chap. 3, also paras 10.49 and 19.15; Reid, *Property*, paras 47 and 646; *Stair Memorial Encyclopaedia*, Vol. 24, "Udal land".

[53] The Crown's ultimate superiority is itself necessarily allodial, since it acknowledges no superior.

[54] SLC Report no. 168 (1999), *Abolition of the Feudal System*, with draft Bill, cl. 70(1) and Sched. 8, Pt I, para. 33(2).

[55] This is projected for 2003: 1997 S.L.T. (News) 218.

(c) *Parish churches and churchyards*

Although land acquired by compulsory purchase under statutory powers has sometimes been spoken of as allodial, the better view appears to be that the Crown's ultimate superiority over such land is unaffected, so that it remains a feudal holding.[56]

It is also not quite clear whether the tenure of the kindly tenants of Lochmaben is feudal or allodial. It is in any event very close to a feudal right. The question is discussed in the Scottish Law Commission's report on abolition of the feudal system, where the abolition of this form of tenure is also recommended.[57]

(3) *Any other interest in land, title to which was immediately before July 25, 1976 sufficient to form a foundation for positive prescription without the deed constituting the title having been recorded.*[58] The class of cases which fall into this category appears to be a small one. Titles which, immediately before the commencement of these provisions of the 1973 Act on July 25, 1976, clearly did not require recording in order to form a foundation for prescription were (a) an unfeudalised right to teinds[59] and (b) an unfeudalised right of patronage.[60] To provide any other instances is difficult.[61] It may be that this provision is capable of applying to wayleaves in favour of public utilities which are constituted over land in writing but without recording. There is, however, no authority on this point.[62] It has been suggested that this provision is also apt to cover agricultural charges and floating charges, which do not require to be recorded in the General Register of Sasines, as well as charging orders made under the Housing (Scotland) Act 1987.[63] But the section cannot apply to agricultural charges, since they are not constituted over interests in land.[64] Nor is it applicable to charging orders under the housing legislation: under the statute in force immediately before the commencement of the present provision, charging orders required to be recorded in the General Register of Sasines. They now require to be either recorded or else registered in the Land Register.[65] Nor can it apply to floating charges: the creditor does not take possession, and the receiver does not have a title, so prescription cannot run.

---

[56] Gordon, *Land Law*, para. 3.21; Reid, *Property*, para. 47.

[57] SLC Report no. 168 (1999), paras 8.4–8.9.

[58] s. 2(2)(c).

[59] Erskine, III, vii, 3; Bell, *Prin.*, s. 2013; Gordon, *Land Law*, para. 10.62; *Solicitor of Teinds v. Budge* (1797) Hume 455; *Gordon v. Kennedy* (1758) M. 10925; *Irvine v. Burnet* (1764) M. 10830.

[60] Stair, II, xii, 23; *H.M. Advocate v. Graham* (1844) 7 D. 183 at 189 and 194, *per* L. J.-C. Hope.

[61] Walker, p. 37 provides a lengthy list but some of these cases are obsolete (as he notes, terce and courtesy; and adjudication under a jedge and warrant; so too is adjudication in security) and some do not properly belong here at all (see below).

[62] Such rights are overriding interests for the purposes of the Land Registration (Scotland) Act 1979, s. 28(1) items (e)–(eg).

[63] Walker, p. 37.

[64] Agricultural Credits (Scotland) Act 1929, s. 5(2): a charge can be constituted only over "stocks of merchandise".

[65] Housing (Scotland) Act 1969, s. 25(4) and Sched. 2, para. 3; Housing (Scotland) Act 1987, s. 109(5) and Sched. 9, para. 3.

CHAPTER 16

POSSESSION

Sections 1, 2 and 3 all require possession for a continuous period openly, **16.01**
peaceably and without judicial interruption. The question arises how far
these requirements restate the law before the 1973 Act.

Several of the requirements of the old law are reflected in the use of **16.02**
the term "possession" itself (which is not defined in the Act, other than
to the effect that it includes civil possession). So, for instance, it is clear
that possession is to some extent a question of fact. But it involves more
than mere physical control: the control must be accompanied by the
intention to hold for oneself or on one's own account. It is of the essence
of possession that it be exclusive and that it be held for oneself, as an
assertion of right, not a matter of tolerance by another.[1] That possession
should be an assertion of right is therefore implicit in the word
"possession" itself, and does not depend on any of the qualifications
"openly, peaceably and without any judicial interruption". Uses which do
not come up to this standard, of asserting a right, are simply not
possession.[2]

A glance at section 1 of the Act shows that possession is relevant for **16.03**
prescriptive purposes only if it meets a number of conditions: it must be
of an interest in particular land, for a continuous period of 10 years,
openly, peaceably and without judicial interruption. And it must be
founded on and follow either the recording of a deed sufficient in its
terms to constitute a title to that interest, or the registration of that
interest in the Land Register with exclusion of indemnity. So far as
section 2 is concerned, the only material difference is that the deed need
not be recorded or registered. And so far as section 3 is concerned, the
difference is only that it is a positive servitude or public right of way
which is being possessed.

Possession on a sufficient title

The notion of a title sufficient for prescription was discussed in the **16.04**
last chapter.

Possession need not be begun or completed in good faith

Although this was not the rule of Roman law,[3] nor that set out by Bell **16.05**
in his *Principles*,[4] there is clear authority that possession for the purposes
of prescription need not be in good faith. Not only is nothing said in
the Act about this but (with the exception of Bell and Kames[5]) the

---

[1] Reid, *Property*, paras 114 and 118; Gordon, *Land Law*, para. 14.03; Stair, II, i, 17;
Erskine, II, i, 20.
[2] See, *e.g.*, *Wallace v. Police Commrs of Dundee* (1875) 2 R. 565 at 586.
[3] At least so far as *usucapio* was concerned; above, para. 1.14.
[4] *Prin.*, s. 2004.
[5] Kames, *Essay on Prescription* (1722), p. 113.

institutional and other authoritative writers are clear on the point.[6] Furthermore, the Scottish Law Commission consulted on this issue before the 1973 Act was enacted, and a majority favoured the view that bad faith should not affect the operation of prescription.[7] The matter is straightforward: good faith, as Stair says, is not required "because our prescription is so long".[8] Its rules therefore reasonably differ from those of Roman *usucapio*, which was completed in classical times in two years at most.

Possession by a person and his successors

16.06　　　Possession, to be relevant, can be by a "person and his successors". There is nothing here to suggest that the successors must be universal, and the pre-1973 law allowed singular successors to continue a prescriptive possession. This therefore remains the law.

16.07　　　Because the possession must be founded on the recording of a deed or the registration of an interest in land, it is essential that a successor who pleads prescription can demonstrate his own connection with the foundation writ, by proving that he is the successor of the person who first possessed following upon and founding on the deed.[9]

16.08　　　It does not seem that such a successor need actually be infeft: there is nothing in the section to suggest so. What matters is the continuity of possession following upon the foundation writ. It therefore appears that, provided that the original possessor possessed upon an adequate deed, it is open to any successor simply to continue possession without ever recording the disposition which gave him his own right to the land.[10] This is, however, a somewhat precarious position since, although the *jus ad rem* of such an uninfeft proprietor is not subject to negative prescription, it is vulnerable to supersession if another party acquires an unchallengeable title to the land through positive prescription.[11]

Possession of an interest in land

16.09　　　The notion of possession of an interest in land is difficult.[12] As Stair pointed out, once possession came to be divided among the several interests in land, "then did the difficulties arise".[13] Happily, these difficulties will disappear if the Scottish Law Commission's proposals for amendment to the 1973 Act are enacted, since the expression "interest in land" will vanish from the text of the Act.[14] Much of the following discussion will also cease to matter.

16.10　　　The reason for the difficulty is that, in its original signification, possession involves the physical detention of a thing with an intention of

---

[6] Stair, II, xii, 11 and II, xii, 19; Erskine, III, vii, 15; Napier, pp. 51–57; *cf. Duke of Buccleuch v. Cunynghame* (1826) 5 S. 53.

[7] SLC Report no. 15 (1970), para. 13.

[8] II, xii, 11.

[9] *cf.* Napier, pp. 189–198 (on the Act 1617); *H.M. Advocate v. Graham* (1844) 7 D. 183 at 198 on the need to make a connection with the title recorded.

[10] *Earl of Glasgow v. Bryce* (1887) 14 R. 419 at 423; *Crawford v. Durham*, Dec. 20, 1822, F.C.; *Earl of Marchmont v. Earl of Home* (1724) M. 10797; *Caitcheon v. Ramsay* (1791) M. 10810; *Middleton v. Earl of Dunmore* (1774) M. 10944.

[11] See above, para. 3.55; 1973 Act, Sched. 3(h).

[12] *cf. Hamilton v. McIntosh Donald Ltd*, 1994 S.L.T. 212 at 218–219, *per* Lord Prosser. *cf. Kaur v. Singh* 1999 S.L.T. 412 at 420, I.H.

[13] Stair, II, i, 1.

[14] SLC Report no. 168 (1999) with draft Bill, cl. 70(1) and Sched. 8, Pt I, paras 35–36.

holding it for oneself.[15] Nonetheless, it is possible to possess even without personally having the physical detention of the thing: a person can possess through those who hold possession for him in his own name.[16] In Scots law this is known as "civil possession", and it is discussed further in the next section. But the original (Roman) idea of civil possession is that there is possession only on the part of the person in whose name the possession is held, not that there is concurrent possession by both the natural and civil possessors. For instance, a lender or depositor never gives up possession but continues to exercise it civilly through the borrower or depositee, who has mere detention of the thing.

This doctrine, however, suffers some variation when applied in **16.11** modern law:

(1) *Leases*. As soon as a lease comes to be regarded as constituting more than a personal right and as being capable of supporting a real right, which can be fortifed against singular successors of the landlord by possession or by registration,[17] it becomes necessary to say that the tenant has possession for the purposes of the lease which is quite independent of the landlord's own possession. Although the tenant possesses on his own account—and his possession, if it is being asserted against a reluctant singular successor, may even be adverse to the landlord—the landlord is still regarded as retaining civil possession. Stair and Bankton explain that the tenant holds for the landlord to the extent of the rent, but beyond that possesses for himself.[18]

(2) *Standard securities*. According to Erskine, the debtor and the pledge creditor possess upon their own rights at the same time: "as in the case of a pledge, where the proprietor is considered as possessing the subject by the creditor to whom it was impignorated [*i.e.* pledged], insofar as is necessary for supporting his right of property, notwithstanding which the creditor possesses in his own name the right of impignoration or security which he has in it".[19] What has to be envisaged here is that the creditor is in actual possession of the thing, which has been pledged to him; but, through the creditor, the debtor has civil possession in his own right, although not of course such that he can assert his own possession against the creditor.

The converse case, where the debtor remains in possession of the property pledged, cannot normally arise with moveables, over which there is in general no security without possession. It can, however, arise in the case of land. It is not obvious that here the creditor has any possession at all, although it has been suggested that he nonetheless enjoys possession of his interest in the land by insisting on the debtor's compliance with its terms.[20] Whether this issue much matters may be doubted, since all that really concerns the creditor is being able to enforce the security against the

---

[15] Erskine, II, i, 20.
[16] Erskine, II, i, 22; D. 41.2.9, Gaius 25 *ad edictum provinciale*.
[17] Bell, *Prin.*, ss. 1190 and 1209–1211; Leases Act 1449; Registration of Leases (Scotland) Act 1857; Land Registration (Scotland) Act 1979.
[18] Stair, II, i, 14; Bankton, II, i, 27.
[19] Erskine, II, i, 22.
[20] Reid, *Property*, para. 120.

debtor or any successor he may have as owner of the land. But the enforcement of the security does not turn on whether the creditor can be described as having possession.

(3) *Servitudes*. Erskine indicates that the dominant proprietor in the servitude and the possessor of the servient land may each possess upon their different rights at the same time.[21] But, as he notes elsewhere, few servitudes are capable of proper possession: "The lands indeed which are charged with the servitude may be possessed, but it is the owner of the servient tenement who possesses these, and not he who claims the servitude"; the use or exercise of the servitude right, which is what makes it good against singular successors, is therefore improperly called "possession".[22] Some of the Roman legal sources speak of "quasi possession" in this context.[23]

(4) *Incorporeal things in general*. By analogy with the case of servitudes, Bankton extends the notion of possession to incorporeal things generally. As he notes, possession is properly of things corporeal "but there is likewise a kind of possession of incorporeal things, as of servitudes".[24]

16.12   The upshot is that the Scottish authorities, quite apart from the question of natural and civil possession, vouch the proposition that two people can concurrently possess the same thing for their own interests, whether it be landlord and tenant, fiar and liferenter, creditor and debtor, or servient and dominant proprietor. The consequence is that determining how many people are in possession of an interest in land for the purposes of prescription may be a complex matter.

Civil possession[25]

16.13   "'Possession' includes civil possession and 'possessed' shall be construed accordingly", says the 1973 Act.[26] This issue is closely connected with the points just discussed. It is clear, accordingly, that a possessor can continue in possession through others, who have the physical (or "natural") possession of the thing. Landlords have civil possession through the natural possession of their tenants; pledge debtors through pledge creditors[27]; fiars through liferenters; superiors through vassals.[28] Corporations possess through the natural possession or detention of natural persons.[29]

16.14   In terms of sections 1 and 2 the only possession which is relevant is the natural or civil possession of a person in whose favour a title to the land

---

[21] Erskine, II, i, 22.

[22] Erskine, II, ix, 3.

[23] D. 8.5.10, pr., Ulpian 53 *ad edictum*; Gaius, Inst. 4.139.

[24] Bankton, II, i, 28; as authority he cites D. 8.1.20, Iavolenus 5 *ex post*. Labeonis and C. 3.34.14, but these are mainly just concerned with protection by means of possessory remedies.

[25] Napier, pp. 174–182.

[26] s. 15(1).

[27] That is, the debtor can rely upon the creditor's possession as against third parties, although not against the creditor himself: Erskine, III, vii, 5; *Burgy v. Strachan* (1667) M. 1305; Rankine, *Land Law*, p. 42.

[28] Napier, pp. 181–185; Reid, *Property*, para. 121; Stair, II, xii, 16; *Nielson v. Erskine* (1823) 2 S. 216; *Lord Advocate v. McCulloch* (1874) 2 R. 27; *Duke of Argyll v. Campbell*, 1912 S.C. 458; *Love-Lee v. Cameron*, 1991 S.C.L.R. 61.

[29] *Birrell Ltd v. City of Edinburgh D.C.*, 1982 S.L.T. 111 at 114.

may be constituted by prescription. It follows that natural possession by any third parties cannot be relevant for the purposes of prescriptive possession by a person unless it amounts to civil possession in that person. It is a question of some difficulty what the limits on this principle are.

(1) *Employees*. Where an employee possesses property of his employer for the purposes of his employment—or even simply in the course of it—it will be possible to say that through this possession the employer maintains civil possession. So, for instance, a farm manager or grieve, if he has possession at all, must possess for his employer.[30]

It is not obvious that this is so, however, when the possession by the employee and the employer–employee relationship really have nothing to do with one another, for example if, on his own initiative, the farm employee shoots on land or cuts peat there or carries out some other act purely for his own benefit. So in one case salmon fishing carried on by the tenants of cottages on a landowner's estate for their own benefit was held not to amount to possession of the fishings by him, because they paid him no rent for it.[31]

The question arose in the case of *Hamilton v. McIntosh Donald Ltd*,[32] where the principal evidence of possession by the defenders was that their farm manager and his son were authorised by them to shoot on the land in question and also had authority to permit others to shoot there. This was regarded by both the Lord Ordinary and a majority of the Second Division as sufficient possession by the defenders. So far as authority to allow others to shoot there is concerned, this is certainly a very broad interpretation of the civil possession of the defenders, since there was no relationship between them and those who did the shooting, and the defenders may have had no knowledge that the shooting was taking place. How can it be possible to maintain possession through someone you do not even know is there?

The notion that civil possession is exercised through those to whom authority has been given to carry out shooting or other acts of possession is also rather wide. It is necessary that it should be known which acts by which third parties are to be ascribed to a person claiming civil possession, and which are not. The natural possession of one person will amount to civil possession in another only where it acknowledges or is derived from the right of the civil possessor: "wherever one possesses in the right of another, his possession will profit that other person".[33] But, while on this principle it is self-evident that tenants possess for their landlords and that squatters do not, it is not clear that an informal grant of permission always amounts to the necessary relationship between the parties so that the natural possession of one can be construed as the civil possession of the other. The mere fact that permission has been given does not always mean that the person

---

[30] Erskine, II, i, 22.
[31] *Lord Advocate v. Hall* (1873) 11 M. 967.
[32] 1994 S.L.T. 212, O.H.; 793, I.H.
[33] *Clerk v. Earl of Home* (1746–47) M. 10661 at 10665 (also in Kilkerran no. 16 at 14); Napier, p. 175.

permitting retains possession and the person permitted has only custody; there are plenty of contractual relationships in which this is not the case.[34] It is therefore arguable that, at least in some cases of informal permission, possession is merely by licence. The general rule in that case is that the licensee possesses for himself, even though he is unable to set up his possession against the licensor.[35] If that is so, possession by the licensee would not constitute possession in the licensor, and acts carried out by the licensee would have no significance for the question whether the licensor was in possession.

Whether or not this argument is correct, the conclusion must be that, unless there is an insistence on a clear relationship between civil and natural possessor, considerable difficulty may arise in determining whose possessory acts are relevant for purposes of prescription. Since the operation of prescription excludes challenges to the title which it fortifies, it is essential that it should be clear who can be said to possess during the prescriptive period, and for whom.

(2) The civil possessor ceases to possess when the natural possessor ceases to possess for him. So a tenant who ceases to pay rent ceases to hold for his landlord.[36] (It follows that the tenant could prescribe title against the landlord once he began to possess for himself, so long as his possession followed upon the recording of a sufficient title—necessarily granted by a non-owner in this case.)

(3) There may be room for argument as to who the civil possessor is who enjoys possession through the natural possessor. It is likely that civil possession is attributable to the person from whom the natural possessor derives his right or whose claim he acknowledges in some way such as the payment of rent.[37]

Possession openly, peaceably and without any judicial interruption

16.15   It is critical to positive prescription that the possessor relying on it should assert his or her claim openly. Prescription does not allow the acquisition of rights by stealth but protects only rights which have been openly asserted. The reason is obvious. Only if the possessor openly possesses can a party whose interest is affected by the adverse possession be said to have had a fair chance to challenge the right asserted; only then, if he fails to challenge, can that party be said to have slept on his rights. For example, what seem at first sight to be obscure concerns about the manner of fishing necessary for prescriptive possession actually reflect the important requirement that it be sufficiently public and open. For that reason fishing with a rod used to be regarded as insufficient to support prescription, although this is not the case now.[38] Similarly, where rough shooting is relied upon as an element in prescriptive possession, it is necessary that it should be carried on openly, so as to amount to an assertion of right, not a trespass.[39]

---

[34] *Hamilton v. Western Bank of Scotland* (1856) 19 D. 152 at 161, *per* Lord Ivory; Reid, *Property*, paras 123–125.

[35] Erskine, II, i, 23; Reid, *Property*, para. 128.

[36] Napier, p. 184.

[37] Reid, *Property*, para. 121.

[38] *Ramsay v. Duke of Roxburghe* (1848) 10 D. 661 at 665; see now *Warrand's Trs v. Mackintosh* (1890) 17 R. (H.L.) 13; Reid, *Property*, para. 325, n. 6; Gordon, *Land Law*, paras 8.71–8.72.

[39] *Bain v. Carrick*, 1983 S.L.T. 675.

But it is not necessary that a party whose interest is challenged by the **16.16** possession should know of the possessor's assertion of right. Clearly, if it were, and the possessor had to prove the other's knowledge, that would amount to a major obstacle to the running of prescription. And it would conflict with the very policy grounds which justify the running of prescription: that titles should not remain uncertain for too long; and that those who do not protect their rights should lose them.

A clear example is provided by *Wemyss's Trs v. Lord Advocate*,[40] where **16.17** the possession was of submarine coal workings. It was held to be unnecessary to show that the Crown had been advised of or knew of the coal workings. What mattered is that they were not carried out clandestinely. In fact, they were well known in the district, had been discussed publicly by scientists and had been inspected in the normal way by government inspectors of mines.

Peaceable
Possession which was open but maintained forcibly would fall foul of **16.18** the requirement of peaceable possession.[41] Similarly, possession which was exercised openly but challenged by another party might not amount to peaceable possession.[42]

Without any judicial interruption
The expression "judicial interruption" is defined in section 4 of the **16.19** Act:

> **"Judicial interruption of periods of possession for purposes of sections 1, 2 and 3**
> 4.—(1) In sections 1, 2 and 3 of this Act references to a judicial interruption, in relation to possession, are references to the making in appropriate proceedings, by any person having a proper interest to do so, of a claim which challenges the possession in question.
> (2) In this section 'appropriate proceedings' means—
>
> (a) any proceedings in a court of competent jurisdiction in Scotland or elsewhere, except proceedings in the Court of Session initiated by a summons which is not subsequently called;
> (b) any arbitration in Scotland;
> (c) any arbitration in a country other than Scotland, being an arbitration an award in which would be enforceable in Scotland.
>
> (3) The date of a judicial interruption shall be taken to be—
>
> (a) where the claim has been made in an arbitration and the nature of the claim has been stated in a preliminary notice relating to that arbitration, the date when the preliminary notice was served;
> (b) in any other case, the date when the claim was made.
>
> (4) In the foregoing subsection 'preliminary notice' in relation to an arbitration means a notice served by one party to the arbitration on

---

[40] (1896) 24 R. 216 at 229, *per* L.P. Robertson.
[41] *cf.* Gordon, *Land Law*, para. 12.45.
[42] *e.g.* in a servitude case deliberate obstruction by the servient owner: *Stevenson v. Donald*, 1935 S.C. 51.

the other party or parties requiring him or them to appoint an arbiter or to agree to the appointment of an arbiter, or, where the arbitration agreement or any relevant enactment provides that the reference shall be to a person therein named or designated, a notice requiring him or them to submit the dispute to the person so named or designated."

16.20   (1) *"Judicial" interruption.* The definition of "judicial" interruption is of fundamental importance. Under the 1973 Act, interruption is relevant only if it is made in appropriate proceedings, that is, in a court of competent jurisdiction or in an arbitration. This is a change from the earlier law. The Act 1617 used the expression "peaceably without any lawful interruption"; the Conveyancing (Scotland) Acts of 1874 and 1924 spoke of the possessor possessing "and that peaceably, without any lawful interruption".[43] In the old law interruption could be made (a) by citation in an action, which had to be renewed every seven years[44]; (b) by calling and persisting in an action; (c) by presenting or concurring in a petition for sequestration or liquidation. But "lawful interruptions" also included extrajudicial interruptions, such as adverse possession or notarial protest.[45] Before 1973 it was therefore possible to interrupt prescriptive possession without resort to court or to arbitration. This is not now the case.[46] Extrajudicial interruptions would be relevant now only if they meant that the possessor's possession could not be described as "peaceable". Similarly, the exercise of diligence formerly amounted to interruption. Now it does not, since it is clearly excluded by the Act's definition of "judicial interruption".[47]

The main discussion of judicial interruption is to be found above, in the context in which it has generated most litigation, negative prescription.[48] Here it is enough to deal with a few points relevant specifically to judicial interruption in relation to possession.

(2) The claim must be made in a court of competent jurisdiction in Scotland or elsewhere, in an arbitration in Scotland, or in an arbitration elsewhere an award in which would be enforceable in Scotland.

Examples of limits on the jurisdiction of Scottish courts are the fact that the sheriff court has a privative jurisdiction in relation to actions whose value is below a certain monetary sum,[49] while the Court of Session has exclusive jurisdiction in relation to actions of reduction (other than *ope exceptionis*). Further details may be found in the textbooks on procedure. Here it is enough to say that (as explained further below) an action would be capable of constituting a judicial interruption only if brought in the court

---

[43] 1874 Act, s. 34; 1924 Act, s. 16.

[44] To affect singular successors, the citation also had to be recorded.

[45] Erskine, III, vii, 39–III, vii, 40; to affect singular successors protest also had to be recorded.

[46] In general, the Act restricts the role of extrajudicial interruption of prescription, whether positive or negative (on which see above, para. 5.65).

[47] Contrast the case of negative prescription: see s. 9.

[48] Above, paras 5.09 *et seq.*

[49] Sheriff Courts (Scotland) Act 1971, s. 31; the sum in question is increased from time to time.

which is competent to hear it. Otherwise the claim will have no effect on the running of prescription.

Foreign courts too can competently found jurisdiction over a person who is in course of prescriptive possession of land in Scotland. Under the Brussels and Lugano Conventions, the primary ground of jurisdiction is the domicile of the defender, but there are many other special grounds on which jurisdiction can be founded against a defender.[50] So, in appropriate circumstances, the establishment of jurisdiction over a defender in another state is unproblematic in principle.

The question arises whether a claim of the sort contemplated in section 4 of the 1973 Act which "challenges the possession in question" might be made in those foreign proceedings. Under the Brussels Convention actions concerning rights *in rem* in immoveable property are subject to the exclusive jurisdiction of the courts of the jurisdiction in which the property is situated.[51] This, however, has been interpreted to apply only to actions within the scope of the Convention "which seek to determine the extent, content, ownership or possession of immovable property or the existence of other rights *in rem* therein and to provide the holders of those rights with the protection of the powers which attach to their interest".[52] This does not appear to exhaust all claims which could be regarded as judicial interruptions. For example, a claim for rent for occupation of disputed land might in some circumstances amount to a challenge to its possession, and such a claim need not be brought in Scotland.

So far as arbitration is concerned, there is judicial interruption where a claim is made in an arbitration in Scotland or another country where the arbitration is one "an award in which would be enforceable in Scotland". Detailed discussion of this provision is to be found elsewhere.[53]

(3) What has to be made in the appropriate proceedings is "a claim which challenges the possession in question". This would seem to include a challenge of part rather than the whole extent of the possession.[54]

(4) What amounts to a "challenge" of the necessary kind? There are two aspects to this: the identity of the pursuer and the nature of the action.

So far as the pursuer is concerned, it seems likely that a claim challenging possession which was brought by a person who had no title or interest to bring it could not be effective to interrupt prescription. This does not mean that, in order to interrupt prescription, an action would have to be successful. But, as explained elsewhere,[55] a claim which was so incompetent that it was beyond redemption by amendment could not be described as a judicial interruption at all, and this must be true of one made by a person

---

[50] Brussels Convention, Arts 2 and 5: see Civil Jurisdiction and Judgments Act 1982, Sched. 1.

[51] Art. 16(1).

[52] *Reichert v. Dresdner Bank* [1990] E.C.R. I-27 at I-42; Anton and Beaumont, *Civil Jurisdiction in Scotland* (2nd ed.), paras 7.07–7.11.

[53] See above, paras 5.07 *et seq.*

[54] Stair, II, xii, 26.

[55] Above, paras. 5.17 *et seq.*

who had no interest to pursue the claim. It has been observed that
in order to constitute judicial interruption the challenger must not
just assert that the possessor has no title to possess but must also
put forward a competing right and show that he or someone else
has a title better than the possessor.[56] But this involves a rather
narrow construction of the sorts of actions which amount to
challenges of the required sort, and it may be that this should not
be treated as a universal requirement.

There is nothing in the section to say that it matters who
challenges possession. There is therefore no reason why someone
should not be able to rely on the fact that a challenge to
possession was made by a third party. That would amount to a
disruption of the continuous uninterrupted possession which the
Act requires. To be relevant as a judicial interruption, however,
such an action would have (as section 4(1) requires) to be pursued
by a person having a proper interest to do so, and it would have
to amount to a challenge to possession of a particular interest in
land.

What is the necessary content of a challenge to possession?
Although the expression "challenge to possession" is not very
precise, it seems likely that it should be construed broadly. At any
rate it cannot be confined to reduction of the possessor's title.
The Act treats arbitrations on the same footing as actions, and it
is clear that whatever else may be possible within a deed of
submission to arbitration, reduction (for example) of a title to
land is not. For that reason, it seems preferable to interpret
section 4 as covering any challenge to the possessor's possession
as of right.

This is very much the line favoured by Hume, when he says that
"any action shall be sufficient which substantially, plainly, and in
effect implies a denial or challenge of the possessor's heritable
ground of right; though the process be not in the shape of a
formal and direct (technical and reductive) impeachment of that
right".[57] The reason is that such an action will both assert the
pursuer's intentions and interrupt the possessor's tranquillity.
More recently, the point has been put in this way: "any form of
claim which, brought in an appropriate forum by a person having
a proper interest to do so, competently puts in issue the validity of
the defender's possession of the interest in the particular land is
apt to constitute judicial interruption".[58]

Within this class of case there would therefore fall an action of
ejection or removing; an action of reduction of the title upon
which the possessor founds; an action of declarator that the
possessor has no title; and an action or petition to interdict
the possessor from possessing.

Less clear would be cases such as an action for payment,
seeking payment for occupation of land which the defender had
occupied in the knowledge that the pursuer did not intend her
occupation to be gratuitous.[59] It might be thought that this would

---

[56] *Scammell v. Scottish Sports Council*, 1983 S.L.T. 462 at 467.
[57] Hume, *Lectures*, 4.518.
[58] *MRS Hamilton Ltd v. Baxter*, 1998 S.L.T. 1075.
[59] *Shetland Islands Council v. BP Petroleum Development Ltd*, 1990 S.L.T. 82.

ratify the possessor's remaining in possession, no attempt being made to challenge her. On the other hand, such an action could be said to be a challenge to the possessor's possession as of right, since it would seek to establish that possession was actually on the basis of tolerance by the true proprietor. For that reason it seems plausible to treat it as as claim which challenges possession.

There is no need for judicial interruption actually to impact on the possessor's real right. It has been held that an action of reduction of a Land Register title did amount to a judicial interruption, even though the title itself was unaffected by the reduction and would be affected only by rectification of the Land Register.[60]

To constitute judicial interruption, challenge must be made to possession of an interest in land. So far as interests in land other than *dominium utile* are concerned, some care is needed in determining exactly which interest in the land has been the subject of judicial interruption. Take the example of a lease: the purpose of fortification of a lease by prescription is to secure the position of the tenant against others claiming a tenancy of the same land as well as against singular successors of the landlord. It therefore seems that only an action of removing or declarator of irritancy would amount to a challenge to the tenant's possession. A mere claim for rent or arrears of rent would be an affirmation of, rather than a challenge to, the landlord–tenant relationship.

A claim for rent would, however, be an assertion that the possessor was in possession not as of right but by tolerance of the landlord. Accordingly, a claim for payment—or one of the various more exotic actions in which rent can be sued for, such as multiplepoinding, maills and duties, or count, reckoning and payment—would appear to amount to a challenge to any possession the tenant sought to set up against the landlord. The short point is therefore that the question whether an action amounts to a judicial interruption has to be assessed according to the particular interest in land which is in question.

(5) When is a judicial interruption made, and how long does it last? The Act says nothing about this, and there are several questions here of some difficulty. These are discussed in connection with negative prescription.[61] The fundamental point is that in Court of Session proceedings there is no judicial interruption unless the summons has called.[62] Section 4(3)(b) provides that the date of commencement is the date "when the claim was made". The date of commencement of an action is the date of citation of the defender.[63] That is true of Court of Session proceedings, except that a summons which is served but not called will not interrupt prescription. Provided it is called, the date of interruption will be

---

[60] *MRS Hamilton Ltd v. Baxter*, above.

[61] Above, paras 5.34 *et seq.*

[62] The old cases need to be used here with some caution, *e.g. Lord Leslie* (1630) M. 11320, *McKie v. Lag* (1637) M. 11320. But even in the old law it was not enough to interrupt prescription simply to raise a summons; it must be "brought to some judicial act": Hope, *Major Practicks*, 6.43.6.

[63] *Miller v. NCB*, 1960 S.C. 376 at 383; *Barclay v. Chief Constable Northern Constabulary*, 1986 S.L.T. 562.

the date of citation. In arbitration proceedings the date of a judicial interruption is in certain circumstances the date of the preliminary notice.[64]

It is an awkward question whether interruption is a single event or a continuing process. If it is a single interrupting event, then prescription would begin to run again immediately afterwards, presumably the following day.[65] Matters are much more complicated if it is a continuing process.[66]

(6) After an interruption, prescription must begin to run again.[67] No credit can be given for any time that ran before the interruption, since it is not continuous with time running after that.

Possession means possession of the character of which the thing is capable[68]

16.21   It is of the essence of possession that it is exclusive. But for the purposes of prescriptive possession this needs to be qualified. What matters is that the possessor asserts a right. There are two aspects to this. There must, on the one hand, be sufficient acts indicating that possession is being asserted. On the other hand, where rival assertions of possession are made by others, there must be evidence of their being resisted.[69] Take the case that what is being asserted is ownership of a field which is also used by an adjoining landowner. Prescription will require that there be sufficient acts indicating possession. But in a case of this sort extensive use by the adjoining landowner will cast doubt on the quality of the possession which has to be relied upon: whether it actually is an assertion of right and unequivocally referable to ownership. In a case of this sort, it may therefore in practice be necessary to exclude such an adjoining landowner in order that one's own acts of possession are seen to have the right quality.[70] Similarly, if each of two people claims to have prescribed title to salmon fishings by possessing on a title sufficient to include them, the quality of the possession has to be tested both positively (did it amount to the positive assertion of a right?) and negatively (were any incursions which were made by one into the possession of the other intentionally adverse and sufficient to neutralise the other's possession?).[71]

16.22   This, however, would not be true in other cases—such as possession of the foreshore—in which exclusive possession would be impossible to obtain or to demonstrate. Accordingly, exclusivity is essentially a factor which arises in considering the extent of the claimant's acts of possession and whether they are truly referable to the assertion of a right adverse to the other party.

16.23   In a leading case it was pointed out that "possession of the foreshore in its natural state can never be, in the strict sense of the term, exclusive. The proprietor cannot exclude the public from it at any time, and it is

---

[64] s. 4(3).
[65] s. 14(1)(c).
[66] Above, paras 5.34 *et seq.*, 5.96.
[67] Erskine, III, vii, 42.
[68] *Young v. North British Ry* (1887) 14 R. (H.L.) 53 at 56, *per* Lord Fitzgerald.
[69] *ibid.* at 55; Erskine, III, vii, 3.
[70] *Houstoun v. Barr*, 1911 S.C. 134 at 143.
[71] *Ogston v. Stewart* (1896) 23 R. (H.L.) 16 at 19.

practically impossible to prevent occasional encroachments on his right".[72] The sorts of acts which, in that case, were found relevant to support the claim to the foreshore were appropriation of part of the shore by a retaining wall, taking stones and gravel, taking drift seaware for manure,[73] building and using a private bathing house. Similarly, the fact that people walked on the foreshore or shot or took reeds or sand was found in *Buchanan and Geils v. Lord Advocate*[74] not to be adverse to a claim of prescriptive possession, while the sort of evidence which supported the prescriptive claim was using the foreshore as pastureland, reclaiming land from the river, granting part of the land for shipbuilding, being asked for permission to take reeds and sand, and receiving compensation from the river trustees. The same practical considerations about how much resistance the proprietor can be expected to show arose in a case concerning prescription of a right of common property in a remote area of the highlands: as Lord Redesdale noted, "In these vast wilds trespasses were very easily committed, and with great difficulty restrained".[75]

Possession of minerals also involves the same requirement. It is not **16.24** enough to possess the surface, even on a title habile to carry the minerals. There must also be possession of the mineral workings themselves. But it is not practicable to work the minerals across the whole workings at the same time. Accordingly possession of parts must suffice.[76]

In short, as Lord Moncreiff put it, "in judging of the sufficiency of the **16.25** possession, regard will be had to the nature of the subject and the uses to which it can be put".[77]

Possession must be unequivocally referable to an assertion of right

What is necessary on the part of the person prescribing title is an **16.26** assertion of right. Acts which do not go this far are irrelevant as a matter of prescriptive possession. A mere trespass on land would be an obvious example. Accordingly, it is not enough that possession is exercised by tolerance of some other person. If that is the case, no prescriptive right adverse to that person can be set up against him. So, for example, in *Duke of Argyll v. Campbell*,[78] the vassal who asserted title to Dunstaffnage Castle was found to hold it not as possessor for himself but as keeper under a title granted by his superior. In those circumstances there was no room for the argument that he had prescribed a right against his superior. In any event, a vassal's possession acknowledges the superior's right.[79] Put simply, if a vassal holds property, the superior cannot tell whether a right is being asserted against him or not. He has no reason to defend his own interests since he has no reason to suppose that they are being challenged. A true challenge by a vassal to a superior's title would

---

[72] *Young v. North British Ry* above, at 54, *per* Lord Watson.
[73] *cf. Marquess of Ailsa v. Monteforte*, 1937 S.C. 805.
[74] (1882) 9 R. 1218.
[75] *Fraser v. Chisholm* (1814) 2 Dow 561.
[76] *Forbes v. Livingstone* (1827) 6 S. 167; see below for qualifications as to continuity and the notion *tantum praescriptum quantum possessum.*
[77] *Aitken's Trs v. Caledonian Ry and Lord Advocate* (1904) 6 F. 465 at 470.
[78] 1912 S.C. 458.
[79] Stair, II, xii, 16.

necessarily have to be made as superior, that is at least at the same rather than at a subordinate level in the feudal hierarchy.

16.27 Equally, it is not enough if the possession can be referred to some other right than ownership, for example, if the possessor is also entitled to hold the land under a lease or if he is entitled to use a right of way over a road. In that case, his possession can just as easily be ascribed to the lease or the servitude, rather than to any assertion of ownership.[80] This therefore does not amount to prescriptive possession against another. The explanation for this requirement is obvious: where the acts are referable just as easily to a lease as to an assertion of ownership, there is no reason why the landlord should attempt to defend his own interests, since he has no ground to suppose that they are being challenged. That will change only if the tenant ceases to pay rent. But suppose that he does that, and also obtains a title to the land in his favour granted by a non-owner. Prescriptive possession on that title will fortify the (former) tenant's right, and his failure to pay rent throughout the prescriptive period will prevent his possession from being referred to the lease.[81] Where salmon fishings are concerned, it is settled that what is required is possession by a method recognised by the law and commonly known to be lawful. Again, this is connected with the notion of asserting a right, rather than mere poaching.[82]

Possession must be over a continuous period

16.28 The basic requirement under section 1 is that possession must extend over a continuous period of 10 years; prior to the 1973 Act the periods were much longer.[83] "Continuous" is a term which requires to be interpreted according to the sort of possession of which the subjects in question are capable. To take an obvious case, salmon fishings are hardly likely to be possessed every day, first, because there is a limited season for salmon fishing and, secondly, because even within that season it does not make much sense to insist that the rights must be exercised at every available moment.

16.29 Stair points out that, even if possession is not proved to have continued every quarter, month or year, ordinary possession will be sufficient, as, if the beginning and end of the possession are proved, the period between them is presumed, as long as it is not too great.[84] As that last qualification recognises, this doctrine is not to be taken too literally. The following is a useful summary of what is required: "What must be shown, with the aid of presumptions if need be, is a continuous series of acts, in which the gaps are explicable as normal or natural. For example,

---

[80] *Houstoun v. Barr*, 1911 S.C. 134 at 143 (lease); *Hamilton v. Ready Mixed Concrete (Scotland) Ltd*, 1999 S.L.T. 524 (lease); *Robertson's Trs v. Bruce* (1905) 7 F. 580 (servitude of access not property right); *French v. Pinkstan* (1835) 13 S. 743 (entail); *Montgomery v. Watson* (1861) 23 D. 635 (right of access not fishing); *Fothringham v. Passmore*, 1984 S.C. (H.L.) 96 at 99 (agreement).
[81] *Grant v. Grant* (1677) M. 10876 (I am grateful to Dr A. J. Ewen for the reference to this case); Millar, p. 41.
[82] *Maxwell v. Lamont* (1903) 6 F. 245 at 260.
[83] 20 years under the Conveyancing (Scotland) Act 1874, s. 34; 40 under the Act 1617, c. 12.
[84] Stair, IV, xl, 20: "*quia probatis extremis praesumuntur media*; if the distance be not too great"; also IV, xlv, 17, presumption XVII.

if the party in possession spends a lengthy holiday away from the subjects, but resumes acts of possession on his return, it will be possible to link the former acts with the latter and count the whole period. However, it will always be a matter of degree whether acts are considered to form a continuous series, or whether they are considered as occasional intrusions, tolerated by the true owner or not objected to because unknown."[85] Accordingly, the continuity of possession necessary must be judged according to the interest in land in question and must take account of the fact that gaps in the assertion of possession may be normal and in no way suggest that possession is no longer being asserted.

Mineral workings raise a similar issue: possession for every day or **16.30** even every year cannot be required but, as it was put in *Forbes v. Livingstone*, "there must be such a possession by working the coal, as must, or in reason ought, to have kept up in both parties all along during the prescriptive period the impression that the coal was in the possession of the party pleading prescription".[86] In that instance, minings began in 1756 for a few months and were discontinued for 29 years. "It is impossible to hold that, during so long an interval, the effect of the possession, so very transient in itself, could continue, or that the true proprietor could have doubted, during the latter part of the period, that the intruder had given up all claim to the coal".[87] So in this case the possession could not be held to be continuous between 1756 and 1789, because there was a gap in possession which could not be accounted for.

There is a difficulty with subjects which are actually incapable of **16.31** continuous possession.[88] Must it follow that they are incapable of prescription? Or ought the Act to be interpreted with some latitude? Erskine deals in particular with presentation to benefices. Here the question of exercising the right to present a minister to a particular church arises only irregularly, when there is a vacancy in the office.[89] The patron has no control over how frequently he exercises his rights of patronage, since he has none over how frequently a vacancy occurs. It has been held that a single act of presentation under a title to patronage is not sufficient to constitute prescriptive possession.[90] It would seem contrary to principle to hold that possession had been continuous although attested by only one act. Even if it seems slightly arbitrary, it is nonetheless more principled to insist on a minimum of two acts to span a continuous period of possession. The alternative would simply be to say that prescription cannot run on such rights, but the rationale for excluding them is not strong, and the public interest in prescription in general speaks against this.

The amount possessed is the amount prescribed

It is a general rule that the extent of the right which has been acquired **16.32** by prescription is measured by the extent of the possession. This rule is regularly referred to, especially in the old cases, by the Latin tag *tantum*

---

[85] Gordon, *Land Law*, para. 12.48.
[86] (1827) 6 S. 167 at 175.
[87] at 175.
[88] Napier, pp. 409–416.
[89] Erskine, III, vii, 3.
[90] *Macdonell v. Duke of Gordon* (1828) 6 S. 600 at 603, *per* Lord Corehouse.

praescriptum quantum possessum ("the amount possessed is the amount prescribed"). The broad rule requires some qualification.

16.33   First, there is a distinction between "the prescriptive possession which establishes a new and adverse right in the possessor, and the prescriptive possession which the law admits, for the purpose of construing or explaining, in a question with its author, the limits of an antecedent grant or conveyance".[91] So if A makes a grant of the lands of X to B, a much more liberal effect is given to partial acts of possession by B as evidence of proprietary possession of the whole of the lands of X.[92] The purpose of the distinction is plain: where the subjects are already constituted as a separate tenement, possession of part can reasonably be regarded as demonstrating possession of the whole. But where there is no separate tenement already in existence, there is no reason to treat anything as possessed which has not itself actually been possessed. The proper place of the rule *tantum praescriptum quantum possessum* is therefore in cases where prescription is used to set up a new right in the possessor.

16.34   Second, where prescription is used to set up a new right in the possessor, the rule applies as much to barony titles as to any others. It is true that possession of part of an existing barony is treated as possession of the whole. But it is not possible to acquire additional lands for the barony by prescription without actually possessing them.

16.35   Third, although possession is the measure of the right prescribed, it may nonetheless be possible on the facts to treat acts of possession each of which is over less than the whole subjects as justifying, taken together, an assertion of right with respect to the subjects as a whole.[93]

16.36   The rule *tantum praescriptum quantum possessum* has been applied to:

(1) *Servitudes*. Here the right acquired by prescriptive possession is the right as actually possessed.[94]

(2) *Salmon fishings*.[95] Here the effect of the maxim is that fishing in one area will not generally amount to possession of fishings in another, so rights will only be acquired over parts of the water which were actually fished.[96] Even in the case of barony titles, fishing in one area can only amount to possession of other fishings if they are already established as being part of the barony title; it cannot extend the title into separate areas which have not been possessed and have no existing connection with the title.[97]

(3) *Minerals*. Working minerals in one area of land does not amount to possession of the minerals in another area.[98] Beyond that, the

---

[91] *Lord Advocate v. Wemyss* (1899) 2 F. (H.L.) 1 at 9, *per* Lord Watson.
[92] *ibid.* at 10.
[93] *Hamilton v. McIntosh Donald*, 1994 S.L.T. 212, OH; 793, IH; comment: 1994 S.L.T. (News) 261.
[94] See below, para. 17.09.
[95] Gordon, *Land Law*, paras 8.73–8.74.
[96] *Richardson v. Hay* (1862) 24 D. 775.
[97] *Lord Advocate v. Cathcart* (1871) 9 M. 744; *Lord Advocate v. Lovat* (1880) 7 R. (H.L.) 122.
[98] *Forbes v. Livingstone* (1827) 6 S. 167.

position is somewhat less clear. It is not obvious to what extent the working of a coal seam ought to be taken to assert possession over the whole of a coal field. It has been held that possession of minerals at one point does not amount to possession of them at all further points which can be reached from that point.[99] It may be that the possession should be taken to extend to what lies within the same mineral field or deposit, although it could equally be argued that the possession should be taken to extend only to the strata actually being worked.[1]

Proof of possession

It is not possible to lay down an exhaustive classification of acts which **16.37** are and acts which are not relevant to the question of possession. But the following examples may give some sense of the acts which may be considered.[2] It has been held that all the various acts of possession and all the circumstances can be taken together to build up a case of possession.[3] From this it follows that acts are relevant, if they go to possession of the necessary quality, even if they were not carried out repeatedly or over the subjects as a whole.

Some acts, indeed, are most unlikely to be carried out either repeat- **16.38** edly or over the whole subjects, so that they will only be capable of contributing together with other evidence to a case of prescriptive possession. This applies, for example, to such things as survey activity and drilling of boreholes,[4] reclaiming land from a river, and receiving compensation from river trustees,[5] entering into leases or dispositions of part of the land.[6] On the other hand, some acts are not likely to be regarded as significant as a matter of possession unless performed with some regularity. This is likely to be true of shooting,[7] taking reeds or sea ware from the foreshore or using it as pastureland.[8] But there is a continuum rather than a clear division between these two categories, so it seems likely that such things as extracting peat, gravel or stones, or carrying out dumping might fall on either side of the divide, and their precise weight would depend on what other evidence of possession there was.

A further category is that of acts which would not be expected to be **16.39** repeated but which themselves demonstrate the intention to possess or not to possess. The prime example here is fencing. Fences may indicate an assertion of possession of the land enclosed. Conversely, they may indicate a lack of possession of land lying beyond them, especially where the fence contains no gates for access to that land.[9]

---

[99] *Wemyss's Tr. v. Lord Advocate* (1899) 2 F. (H.L.) 1 at 10, *per* Lord Watson.

[1] Gordon, *Land Law*, para. 6.42.

[2] See recently *Hamilton v. McIntosh Donald Ltd*, 1994 S.L.T. 212 at 220, OH; 793, IH with R. Rennie, "Possession: nine tenths of the law", 1994 S.L.T. (News) 261; also *Young v. North British Ry* (1887) 14 R. (H.L.) 53 at 54.

[3] *Hamilton*, above, at 800–801.

[4] *ibid.* at 798.

[5] *Buchanan and Geils v. Lord Advocate* (1882) 9 R. 1218.

[6] *Luss Estates Co v. B.P. Oil Grangemouth Refinery Ltd*, 1982 S.L.T. 457.

[7] *Hamilton*, above; *Bain v. Carrick*, 1983 S.L.T. 675.

[8] *Buchanan and Geils v. Lord Advocate*, above.

[9] *Bain v. Carrick*, above.

Onus on party relying on prescription to establish possession

16.40   It is clear that in general the party who relies on prescription bears the onus of proving the facts necessary to support it. In the context of possession, this means proof that possession of the necessary quality has followed upon a sufficient title for the requisite period.[10] Although some of the old cases doubted whether this rule applied to barony titles, it appears now to be settled that it does. There is no presumption in favour of such a title.[11]

16.41   On the other hand, if the pleadings disclose the necessary possession following upon a sufficient title, it will be for the party who challenges the assertion that prescription has been completed to show, for example, that the title is not in fact sufficient to fortify the right claimed.[12]

Computation of the prescriptive period

16.42   "**Computation of prescriptive periods**

14.—(1) In the computation of a prescriptive period for the purposes of any provision of this Part of this Act—

(a) time occurring before the commencement of this Part of this Act shall be reckonable towards the prescriptive period in like manner as time occurring thereafter, but subject to the restriction that any time reckoned under this paragraph shall be less than the prescriptive period;

(b) any time during which any person against whom the provision is pled was under legal disability shall (except so far as otherwise provided by subsection (4) of section 6 of this Act including that subsection as applied by section 8A of this Act) be reckoned as if the person were free from that disability;

(c) if the commencement of the prescriptive period would, apart from this paragraph, fall at a time in any day other than the beginning of the day, the period shall be deemed to have commenced at the beginning of the next following day;

(d) if the last day of the prescriptive period would, apart from this paragraph, be a holiday, the period shall, notwithstanding anything in the said provision, be extended to include any immediately succeeding day which is a holiday, any further immediately succeeding days which are holidays, and the next succeeding day which is not a holiday;

(e) save as otherwise provided in this Part of this Act regard shall be had to the like principles as immediately before the commencement of this Part of this Act were applicable to the computation of periods of prescription for the purposes of the Prescription Act 1617.

(2) In this section 'holiday' means a day of any of the following descriptions, namely, a Saturday, a Sunday and a day which, in Scotland, is a bank holiday under the Banking and Financial Dealings Act 1971."

---

[10] See, *e.g.*, *Lord Advocate v. Hunt* (1867) 5 M. (H.L.) 1 at 10.

[11] *Luss Estates Co. v. B.P. Oil Grangemouth Refinery Ltd*, 1981 S.L.T. 97 at 99 referring to *Agnew v. Lord Advocate* (1873) 11 M. 309.

[12] *Luss Estates Co. v. B.P. Oil Grangemouth Refinery Ltd*, 1982 S.L.T. 457.

Possession must be continuous for a period of 10 years or, in some **16.43** instances, 20 years.[13]

The whole prescriptive period cannot lie before the commencement of **16.44** the 1973 Act on July 25, 1976.[14] This is simply a transitional provision, which seems unlikely now to have any practical significance. Since the Act does not demand that prescriptive possession must continue right up to the date of any eventual challenge, but only that the right has at some time in the past been fortified by prescription,[15] it was necessary for it to insist that its provisions should not apply to any period which lay entirely in the past but only to periods which continued beyond July 25, 1976.[16]

Time is reckoned from the first moment in the day. So possession **16.45** which began during Monday will be reckoned to have begun at the first instant after midnight, that is at the very beginning of Tuesday.[17] The corollary is that time runs until the last moment of the day. Although this is not stated expressly in the Act, it was the rule under the previous legislation, whose principles are stated to apply except so far as is otherwise provided.[18]

It follows from this that, in order to enjoy the shortened prescriptive **16.46** period, the possession relied upon must end not earlier than the commencement of the relevant Part of the Act, that is not earlier than July 25, 1976.[19] So, for example, a right of way must be acquired by 40 years' prescriptive possession if the possession terminated before July 25, 1976, but only by 20 years' possession if it continues thereafter. It does not matter that 19 years and 364 days may lie before the change in the law on July 25, 1976.

In all cases prescription will start to run not earlier than the date **16.47** possession began. In section 1 cases, however, the only possession which is relevant is that which follows upon the recording or registration of the deed which is the foundation for prescription. In cases based on unrecorded deeds,[20] the possession will similarly have to begin after execution of the deed.

For completeness, the following points should be noted: **16.48**

(1) There is no suspension of the running of positive prescription against a person who is under a legal disability, which is defined in the Act as nonage (that is, age less than 16) or unsoundness of mind.[21]

---

[13] ss. 1(4), 2 and 3.

[14] s. 14(1)(a).

[15] For an example, concerning a right of way, see *Mann v. Brodie* (1885) 12 R. (H.L.) 53.

[16] *cf.* on the reduction of the prescriptive period from 20 to 10 years by the Conveyancing and Feudal Reform (Scotland) Act 1970, s. 8, *Lock v. Taylor*, 1976 S.L.T. 238 at 241.

[17] s. 14(1)(c).

[18] s. 14(1)(e); *Simpson v. Melville* (1899) 6 S.L.T. 355; *Simpson v. Marshall* (1900) 2 F. 447.

[19] See s. 25(2). Under s. 4(a) of the Interpretation Act 1978 an Act comes into force at the beginning of the day in question; accordingly, it seems right to assume that the divide here lies between July 24 and 25, 1976, three years having passed (as required by s. 25(2)(b)) from the date on which the Act was passed at the end of July 24, 1976.

[20] ss. 2 and 3(1).

[21] s. 14(1)(b); for further discussion, see above, paras 6.105 *et seq.*

(2) The prescriptive period cannot end on a holiday,[22] so if the 10 or 20 years do end then, the period is extended to include any succeeding days which are holidays and the next succeeding day which is not a holiday.[23] It follows that it remains possible to interrupt the prescriptive period on the very last day, and that is evidently the purpose of this provision.

---

[22] As defined in s. 14(2).
[23] s. 14(1)(d).

CHAPTER 17

SERVITUDES AND PUBLIC RIGHTS OF WAY

"Positive servitudes and public rights of way   **17.01**
3.—(1) If in the case of a positive servitude over land—

  (a) the servitude has been possessed for a continuous period of twenty years openly, peaceably and without any judicial interruption, and

  (b) the possession was founded on, and followed the execution of, a deed which is sufficient in respect of its terms (whether expressly or by implication) to constitute the servitude,

then, as from the expiration of the said period, the validity of the servitude as so constituted shall be exempt from challenge except on the ground that the deed is invalid *ex facie* or was forged.
(2) If a positive servitude over land has been possessed for a continuous period of twenty years openly, peaceably and without judicial interruption, then, as from the expiration of that period, the existence of the servitude as so possessed shall be exempt from challenge.
(3) If a public right of way over land has been possessed by the public for a continuous period of twenty years openly, peaceably and without judicial interruption, then, as from the expiration of that period, the existence of the right of way as so possessed shall be exempt from challenge.
(4) References in subsections (1) and (2) of this section to possession of a servitude are references to possession of the servitude by any person in possession of the relative dominant tenement.
(5) This section is without prejudice to the operation of section 7 of this Act."

I. SERVITUDES[1]

Section 3 sets out a special prescriptive regime for servitudes and public **17.02** rights of way. Both the Conveyancing (Scotland) Acts 1874 and 1924 expressly excluded servitudes, public rights of way and other public rights from their provisions, so until the 1973 Act the law in force was the Act 1617.[2]

Since sections 1 and 2 of the 1973 Act are concerned only with **17.03** "interests in land", and the term "interest in land" is defined in the Act so as to exclude servitudes, those sections have no application here. The

---

[1] In general, see Reid, *Property*, paras 458–460; Gordon, *Land Law*, paras 24.42–24.53; for a detailed discussion, Cusine and Paisley, *Servitudes and Rights of Way* (1998), Chap. 10.
[2] 1874 Act, s. 34; 1924 Act, s. 16(2), also s. 17(2) (rule on extinction by disuse also not affected).

same will be true under the proposed new drafting of sections 1 and 2.[3] Nonetheless, much of the language used in section 3 is common to sections 1 and 2 and requires no further comment here.

17.04   Section 3 deals only with the prescription of positive servitudes. Nothing is said about negative servitudes. As Bell explains, "Negative servitudes can be constituted only by grant; being incapable of possession, and so of prescription".[4]

17.05   Positive servitudes may be constituted by grant, express or implied, or they may be constituted by prescriptive possession. Section 3 deals with these two cases separately. Common to both of these regimes are the following points:

(1) The prescriptive period is 20 years.
(2) Possession must be open, peaceable and without judicial interruption. To what is said elsewhere on this subject there is no need to add very much. For example, the possession must be open in the sense of taking place with the knowledge of the proprietor of the alleged servient tenement, so putting him on notice that he must object to the possession in order to preserve his own right.[5] Measures of obstruction by the alleged servient owner would prevent the possession being peaceable.

Since a judicial interruption must "challenge the possession in question" but can be made only by a person having a "proper interest" to do so, the class of those who can interrupt prescription of a servitude right is likely to be limited to those who have a right in the servient tenement. This would clearly cover not just the owner but those with lesser real rights in the servient tenement, presumably such as the tenant, proper liferenter or creditor in a standard security. It is not clear, however, that a "proper interest" necessarily involves a real right in the subjects. It is at least conceivable that a person with a personal licence over the alleged servient tenement might qualify.

(3) Prescriptive possession of servitudes must, as with other forms of positive prescription, be as of right, and not attributable to tolerance by the proprietor of the servient tenement.[6] So, for example, where the alleged servient proprietor maintained padlocked gates on a track and gave the alleged dominant proprietor keys to the padlock, access by the alleged dominant proprietor took place only on the basis of tolerance and could not therefore amount to prescriptive possession.[7]

(4) Possession is, as section 3(4) makes clear, possession by any person in possession of the relevant dominant tenement. There is therefore no need for the possessor to have a recorded or registered title to the dominant tenement. The law in force before the 1973 Act did require infeftment.[8]

---

[3] SLC Report no. 168 (1999), cl. 70(1) and Sched. 8, Pt I, para. 35: each of the proposed new sections expressly states that it does not apply to servitudes or public rights of way (the reference to the exclusion of public rights of way is new).

[4] Bell, *Prin.*, s. 994; *cf.* Erskine, II, ix, 35.

[5] See above, para. 16.26; *Macnab v. Munro Ferguson* (1890) 17 R. 397 at 400.

[6] *McInroy v. Duke of Athole* (1891) 18 R. (H.L.) 46 at 48, *per* Lord Watson; *Macnab v. Munro Ferguson*, above.

[7] *Middletweed v. Murray*, 1989 S.L.T. 11.

[8] Stair, II, vii, 2 ("ordinarily"); Erskine, II, ix, 3; Bell, *Prin.*, s. 993; Rankine, *Land Law*, p. 429. Halliday, *Conveyancing*, para. 35.19 still says that there is a requirement of infeftment, but the Act is clear that this is not so.

Since a servitude, by definition, runs with the land, it must be relevant to prove possession of the servitude for the prescriptive period by any person or persons during their possession of the dominant tenement.[9] This is so because it is not their possession of the servitude as individuals which is material, but their possession of it in their capacity as possessors of the dominant tenement, this demonstrating an assertion of right by the possessor of that tenement against the servient tenement. But acts of possession which are not attributable to the possessor of the dominant tenement have no significance for the question whether the servitude has been acquired by positive prescription.[10]

(5) Civil possession is sufficient: a person may therefore rely on natural possession of the servitude by others on his behalf.[11]

(6) The necessary continuity and extent of possession raise issues similar to those discussed in connection with section 1. The sort of possession which is appropriate obviously varies with the type of servitude: a servitude of way is possessed by going along the way; and a servitude of pasturage by pasturing animals in the pasture. Clearly, there is no requirement that possession of a servitude be exercised constantly. It is in the nature of positive servitudes that they are asserted by discrete rather than continuous acts. "So in the case of servitudes, acts which are consistent with the general right of servitude claimed are sufficient to establish the right, and it is not necessary that the full use of which the servitude claimed is capable should have been made throughout the prescriptive period."[12] It follows that the right need not be exercised very often, as long as it is exercised sufficiently regularly to establish a pattern of continuous possession. On this basis, deliveries of garden materials once or twice a year have been found to amount to sufficiently continuous possession.[13]

Furthermore, "the prescriptive use of a private way not merely establishes the *existence* of the right but, in some most important ways, defines the *extent* of the right".[14] So prescriptive possession will determine, for example, how burdensome a right of way is, whether it is for pedestrian traffic only or goes beyond that. (This is subject, however, so far as servitudes founded on a grant are concerned, to consistency with the terms of the grant.[15]) This is quite different from the question what the purpose is for which the right is exercised. Except in special cases, that is not a relevant consideration.[16]

Conversely, the continuity of possession may be broken by interruption. The modern law requires that the interruption be judicial: accordingly, older cases which deal with extrajudicial

---

[9] *Drummond v. Milligan* (1890) 17 R. 316; *cf. Maitland v. Lees* (1899) 6 S.L.T. 296.
[10] *Earl of Morton v. Stuart* (1813) 5 Pat. 720, HL.
[11] s. 15(1). See above, para. 16.11: the term "possession" is in any case used loosely so far as servitudes are concerned.
[12] *Carstairs v. Spence*, 1924 S.C. 380 at 394, *per* Lord Blackburn. *cf.* Napier, p. 586.
[13] *Scotland v. Wallace*, 1964 S.L.T. (Sh.Ct) 9.
[14] *Carstairs v. Spence* at 385, *per* LP Clyde.
[15] See below on s. 3(1) and (2).
[16] *Carstairs v. Spence*, above, at 388; Reid, *Property*, para. 487; Cusine and Paisley, *Servitudes and Rights of Way* (1998), para. 10.04.

interruption, for example by obstructing rights of way,[17] are not relevant to the question of interruption. They may, however, be relevant to the question whether the possession has been peaceable. A deliberate attempt to obstruct the servient owner's right might well render his possession non-peaceable.

(7) The onus lies on the person claiming to be dominant proprietor to prove the existence of the servitude and the prescriptive possession necessary to support it. It would be surprising if the rule were otherwise, since the law does not readily presume any inhibition or diminution of an owner's right in his own property; and in general the presumption is for the least burden or restriction on an owner's right.[18]

(8) Non-use and extinction of the servitude. Completion of the prescriptive period means that the right is exempt from challenge, except of course that it may be lost again by non-use for the relevant prescriptive period. This is in conformity with the previous law.[19]

Since servitudes and public rights of way are not among the property rights excluded from negative prescription, they can be extinguished when negative prescription runs against them.[20] This requires, in the case of positive servitudes, non-use for a period of 20 years, and, in the case of negative servitudes, obstruction for 20 years.

It seems reasonably clear that the intention of the Act is that servitude rights be extinguished under section 7, which deals with the 20-year prescription of obligations.[21] There are, however, good reasons for thinking that section 8 of the Act, the 20-year prescription of rights relating to property, should be the operative section. This question is discussed further in connection with negative prescription.[22] If this is correct, it is not at all clear what meaning can be ascribed to section 3(5), although the general intention is no doubt to clarify that the rules on positive and negative prescription of servitudes and public rights of way operate independently.

Cases where there is a deed[23]

17.06   Section 3(1) applies to cases where there is a deed.[24] In these cases possession must be founded on and follow execution of the deed, and the deed must be sufficient in respect of its terms, whether expressly or by implication, to constitute the servitude. If those conditions are met, then on expiry of the prescriptive period the validity of the servitude so constituted is exempt from challenge, except on the ground that the deed is invalid *ex facie* or forged.

---

[17] *Stevenson v. Donald*, 1935 S.C. 51.

[18] Hume, *Lectures*, 3.267. *Cf. Clark & Sons v. School Board of Perth* (1898) 25 R. 919 at 921; *Cronin v. Sutherland* (1899) 2 F. 217.

[19] See *Mann v. Brodie* (1885) 12 R. (H.L.) 52.

[20] Sched. 3(a), (c); Napier, p. 585.

[21] s. 3(5).

[22] Above, para. 7.14. Halliday, *Conveyancing*, para. 35.28 and Cusine and Paisley, *op. cit.*, para. 17.34 also favour extinction under s. 8.

[23] Cusine and Paisley, *op cit.*, paras 10.06 *et seq.*

[24] "Deed" is defined in s. 5(1) and includes a judicial decree. For an example of a servitude constituted in that way, *School Board of Edinburgh v. Simpson* (1906) 13 S.L.T. 910.

The following points require some comment: **17.07**

(1) The relevant date which prescriptive possession must follow is the date of execution of the deed. There is no requirement for the deed ever to be recorded or registered. Even if it is, the relevant date remains the date of execution of the deed.

(2) The "'date of execution' in relation to a deed executed on several dates, means the last of those dates".[25]

(3) When a servitude is granted by deed, and the granter of the deed is infeft in the servient tenement, the servitude will generally be valid without need for prescription.[26] But there will be circumstances where prescription is needed to fortify a defective grant, for instance if the grant is made by a non-owner. Then a grant in sufficient terms could be fortified by prescriptive possession founded on and following upon it.[27] Clearly, the possession needed to fortify such a grant would have to be possession for the prescriptive period by or on behalf of the grantee or his successors (singular or universal) in the dominant tenement.

(4) Prescription in relation to interests in land under sections 1 and 2 must proceed upon a sufficient title. Similarly, in the case of servitudes, there arises the question whether the deed is sufficient to support the right claimed. There is the difference only that the deed is capable of doing this either expressly or by implication.

So far as express constitution of a servitude is concerned, the position is essentially the same as for the "interests in land" dealt with in section 1. The extent of, or the location of, the servitude as granted may be explained by prescriptive possession, which will fortify the right as possessed. This necessarily requires that the possession be consistent with the grant. For instance, a grant of a servitude of pedestrian access could not—under section 3(1)[28]—through possession for the prescriptive period be transformed into a servitude of vehicular access.

The cases in which servitudes are constituted by implication are few. The main one is where an owner dispones part of his lands, and the effect of the disposition is that there is now no access to the part disponed or to the part retained by the owner. In such cases a servitude of an appropriate right of way is, as a matter of law, implied in the grant to the disponee or in the title reserved by the disponer.[29] Here the law implies that there must be a means of access, but the precise route which this access follows can be determined only by possession. Other recognised servitudes may also be constituted by implication where they are necessary for the comfortable enjoyment of the property disponed.[30]

---

[25] s. 15(1).

[26] For a recent discussion, G. Gretton, "Servitudes and uninfeft proprietors", (1997) 2 S.L.P.Q. 90–92. Absence of infeftment could be cured by accretion: Halliday, *Conveyancing*, para. 35.05; *Stephen v. Brown's Trs*, 1922 S.C. 136.

[27] *Contra*, Walker, pp. 39–40.

[28] But see s. 3(2).

[29] Bell, *Prin.*, ss. 992–993; *cf. Walton Bros v. Glasgow Mags* (1876) 3 R. 1130; *McLaren v. City of Glasgow Union Ry* (1878) 5 R. 1042.

[30] *Ewart v. Cochrane* (1861) 4 Macq. 117; *Alexander v. Butchart* (1875) 3 R. 156.

Cases where there is no deed[31]

17.08   Section 3(2) deals with cases where there is no deed expressly or impliedly granting the servitude, and the claim to the servitude is therefore founded on prescriptive possession alone. Here, after undisturbed possession for 20 years, the existence of the servitude as possessed is exempt from challenge.

17.09   This section is capable of covering both the case of a new servitude right on the one hand and that of the extent of a recognised right on the other. In the case of establishing a new and adverse right in the dominant proprietor against the servient proprietor, the rule that the amount possessed is the amount prescribed (*tantum praescriptum quantum possessum*) evidently applies: the measure of possession is the measure of what has been prescribed.[32]

17.10   One case in which this provision may be relevant is that of water rights. Generally speaking, a riparian proprietor can take only a reasonable quantity of water from a river for secondary uses and is obliged to leave enough for the uses of proprietors below. But the right to take a greater quantity of water may be capable of being acquired as a servitude of *aquaehaustus* if possessed for 20 years. The measure of the right possessed would be the measure of the right prescribed.[33] The alternative interpretation of this situation is that the other proprietor loses his right to object, by the running of negative prescription: this is discussed elsewhere.[34]

17.11   So far as the extent of a servitude is concerned, where there is no deed, plainly there is no other evidence of the extent of the right claimed than the possession enjoyed. But the same may apply even where there is a deed. Take the case that a deed grants a pedestrian right of access. In terms of section 3(1) prescription will run as soon as possession follows upon the date of execution of the deed. But suppose that, since that date, what has actually been exercised for the prescriptive period is a right of vehicular access. That falls within section 3(2). There is nothing in the Act to suggest that section 3(2) cannot apply when there is a deed. It therefore appears that in this case it is possible for a person to prescribe a right which is inconsistent with the terms of the grant.

17.12   In short, prescriptive possession supersedes the necessity of producing a title to the servitude. There is, however, nothing new about this. As Napier explains, if possession continues for the prescriptive period uninterrupted, there is no need to produce any evidence of the original grant. The title to a servitude is in quite a different position from that necessary for prescription of titles to land, where no length of possession is allowed to supersede production of an infeftment in support of the right to possess as feudal proprietor.[35]

---

[31] Cusine and Paisley, *Servitudes and Rights of Way*, paras 10.11 *et seq.*; Napier, pp. 374–398 discusses the cases where prescription in the absence of a deed was possible in the earlier law.

[32] Erskine, II, ix, 4; *Lord Advocate v. Wemyss* (1899) 2 F. (H.L.) 1 at 9; *cf. Kerr v. Brown*, 1909 S.C. 140 at 147 for application of this rule in the case of servitudes.

[33] J. *White & Sons v. J. & M. White* (1906) 8 F. (H.L.) 41 at 47; *Earl of Kintore v. Pirie & Sons Ltd* (1906) 8 F. (H.L.) 1; Gordon, *Land Law*, paras 7.32 and 7.52.

[34] Above, para. 7.14.

[35] Napier, p. 345.

Given the terms of section 3(2), the precise basis upon which a **17.13** servitude not constituted by grant rests does not greatly matter now. In the earlier law there was some controversy about its legal basis: was long continued use presumed to be in exercise of a grant? Or did there require to be a grant, although the grant might be implied from usage?[36]

II. PUBLIC RIGHTS OF WAY[37]

Public rights of way are dealt with in section 3(3). The terms of the **17.14** subsection are almost the same as those of section 3(2), and comments here can therefore be restricted to an outline of the basic requirements for a right of way to come into being, and the notion of possession by the public.

Public rights of way differ from servitudes in that they exist for the **17.15** benefit of the public at large, rather than for that of the proprietor of a particular dominant tenement. They can accordingly be vindicated by any member of the public for the public, and decree in such an action will generally be *res judicata* against the public at large.[38]

In general it is through prescriptive possession that rights of way come **17.16** into being. The precise basis of the possession is, or at least was, disputed: did it rest on a presumed grant, or presumed acquiescence by the landowner, or was the title to the right of way the Crown's own right?[39] In a leading case it was held that none of these was the case and that according to the law of Scotland "the constitution of such a right does not depend upon any legal fiction, but upon the fact of user by the public, as matter of right, continuously and without interruption, for the full period of the long prescription".[40] It has since been observed that "[t]he origin of the right the law is content to leave in obscurity".[41] In any event, section 3(3) says nothing about a grant or title and focuses entirely on the question whether there has been possession for the prescriptive period of 20 years.

This being the modern approach, some decisions made under the **17.17** previous law could not now stand. For example, in one case it was held that a road originally made by a proprietor for his own use, and used by the public as a footpath for the prescriptive period, did not become a public right of way on foot. The reason was that the proprietor's motivation in constructing the road excluded any presumption that it was intended to be a grant of a right of way to the public.[42] But this reasoning (which even then seemed wrong to one of the judges, Lord

---

[36] *Grierson v. School Board of Sandsting and Aithsting* (1882) 9 R. 437 at 441 and 442; Bell, *Prin.*, s. 993; Reid, *Property*, para. 459; Gordon, *Land Law*, para. 24.42.

[37] See generally Napier, pp. 370–371; Gordon, *Land Law*, paras 24.111–24.133; Reid, *Property*, paras 499–501; Cusine and Paisley, *op cit.*, para. 19.14 and Chap. 20.

[38] For this reason, the courts will be particularly concerned that the declaratory conclusion for any right of way is appropriately framed: *Ayr B.C. v. British Transport Commission*, 1955 S.L.T. 219.

[39] The last was suggested by Napier, p. 370.

[40] *Mann v. Brodie* (1885) 12 R. (H.L.) 52 at 57, *per* Lord Watson.

[41] *Rhins District Committee of Wigtownshire C.C. v. Cuninghame*, 1917 2 S.L.T. 169 at 170.

[42] *Napier's Trs v. Morrison* (1851) 13 D. 1404.

Cockburn)[43] is plainly inconsistent with the terms of the 1973 Act, according to which possession, provided it is sufficient in quality and continuity, renders the right of way unchallengeable.

17.18 The relevant possession under the old law has been summarised as follows: "(1) The termini must be public places. (2) There must be user from end to end on a continuous journey. (3) The route must follow a definite line. (4) There must be continuous user for forty years as of right."[44] Apart from the reduction of the prescriptive period to 20 years, these propositions remain accurate in the modern law.

17.19 So far as the first proposition is concerned, it is essential to a right of way (but not, of course, to a servitude) that it forms a route between public places, although the definition of what constitutes a public place is uncertain.[45] To give just two examples, cases indicate that a churchyard counts as a public place, and that a sub-post office on private property does not.[46]

17.20 Second, use of the whole route must be made. In one case the evidence was principally of acts which did not make full use of the way, such as learner drivers practising, children playing, tradesmen and visitors calling, and rubbish being collected. That did not go far enough to establish the right of way claimed.[47] By contrast, use of a walkway in a town centre by the public for the purposes of access to church, the railway station, town hall, school, health centre, swimming pool, places for entertainment, banks, and so on was sufficient use of the whole route.[48] Once the route is established as a right of way, its use is not restricted only to those who make use of the full route; this would be an unwarranted restriction on the notion of a "public" right of way.[49]

17.21 Third, a right of way must follow a defined route. It is not a general licence to wander about on the land through which it passes.[50] But a defined route does not necessarily have to be visibly marked,[51] nor is it necessary that it follow precisely the same route throughout the course of the prescriptive period.[52] Here something may turn on the nature of the land: different considerations might reasonably apply to farmland

---

[43] It was also doubted by Lord Kinnear in *Mags of Edinburgh v. North British Ry* (1904) 6 F. 620 at 633.

[44] *Rhins District Committee*, above, at 170, *per* Lord Sands; approved in *Marquis of Bute v. McKirdy & McMillan*, 1937 S.C. 93 at 120–121; applied in *Renfrew v. Russell*, 1994 G.W.D. 2032.

[45] For a detailed discussion, see Cusine and Paisley, *Servitudes and Rights of Way*, paras 20.03–20.22.

[46] *Smith v. Saxton*, 1927 S.N. 98; *Love-Lee v. Cameron*, 1991 S.C.L.R. 61; Reid, *Property*, para. 496. It has also been held that use of a route to get to a market which is open only on certain days is a doubtful case, although this seems to turn less on the nature of the place than on whether it is possible to say that such restricted use is as of right rather than by tolerance: *Ayr B.C. v. British Transport Commission*, above, at 222.

[47] *Strathclyde (Hyndland) Housing Society Ltd v. Cowie*, 1983 S.L.T. (Sh.Ct) 61.

[48] *Cumbernauld and Kilsyth D.C. v. Dollar Land (Cumbernauld) Ltd*, 1993 S.L.T. 1318.

[49] *McRobert v. Reid*, 1914 S.C. 633 at 639, *per* L.P. Strathclyde.

[50] *Mackintosh v. Moir* (1871) 9 M. 574 at 578–579 (the reference to *jus spatiandi* appears to derive from D. 8.1.8 pr., Paul 15 *ad Plautium*).

[51] *Wills' Trs v. Cairngorm Canoeing and Sailing School Ltd*, 1976 S.C. (H.L.) 30 at 168, *per* Lord Fraser.

[52] *Hozier v. Hawthorne* (1884) 11 R. 766; *Jenkins v. Murray* (1866) 4 M. 1046.

and to moors respectively. Proof of a right of way to some public places such as the foreshore may run into difficulties on the question of following a defined route, if for example there are several ways of reaching the same place.[53]

Fourth, continuous use as of right for the prescriptive period is **17.22** required, as it was under the previous law.[54] There is little to add here to what has already been said about this. In general, the use made of the alleged right of way will determine, for instance, whether it is a pedestrian or vehicular route which has been established. Some of the old cases show a more liberal approach to this question in connection with public rights of way than with servitudes. Now the question must turn on whether the 1973 Act in stating that "the existence of the right of way as so possessed shall be exempt from challenge" refers only to the route which has been possessed or also to the nature of the acts of possession of the route by the public.[55]

Trespass is not enough. Evidence is needed of how the public came to **17.23** be on the road, what they were doing there, and whether the circumstances in which they were there indicated a right.[56] What is essential is that the possession is by the public,[57] and not ascribable, for instance, to servitude rights or to occupiers' impliedly permitting or licensing tradesmen or other visitors to visit them[58]; "the user must be of the whole road, as a means of passage from the one terminus to the other, and must not be such user as can be reasonably ascribed either to private servitude rights or to the license of the proprietor. Then, as regards the amount of user, that must just be such as might have been reasonably expected if the road in dispute had been an undoubted public highway".[59]

Clear indications by the owner that use of the alleged right of way is **17.24** by tolerance will prevent it from being the necessary assertion of right. But the fact that the use is not adverse to the owner's own interests does not mean that the courts will ascribe it to the owner's tolerance.[60] In general, once the use is established, an owner who wishes to argue that it has been only by his tolerance rather than as of right will bear the burden of demonstrating that. There are two aspects to this. First, occasional use by a few people may readily be ascribed to a landowner's tolerance, but there may come a point when the use is so extensive and persistent that it cannot be accounted for otherwise than as an assertion of public right.[61] It is then that the landowner must take steps to prevent the right arising. Second, at this stage at the latest the landowner must give some indication that the use is by tolerance only, whether this is by

---

[53] *Richardson v. Cromarty Petroleum Co. Ltd*, 1982 S.L.T. 237.
[54] Computation of the prescriptive period is discussed above, paras 16.42–48.
[55] Gordon, *Land Law*, para. 24.121.
[56] *Jenkins v. Murray*, above.
[57] Cusine and Paisley, *Servitudes and Rights of Way*, paras 20.24–20.27 consider the meaning of "the public" in detail.
[58] *cf. Strathclyde (Hyndland) Housing Society*, above.
[59] *Mann v. Brodie*, above, at 57–58; *Marquis of Bute v. McKirdy & McMillan*, 1936 S.C. 97 at 119–120, *per* L.P. Normand.
[60] *Cumbernauld and Kilsyth D.C.*, above; *Marquis of Bute*, above.
[61] *Mags of Edinburgh*, above, at 634.

placing signs or by at least occasional restrictions on use of the way. How extensive these restrictions need to be in order to prevent or interrupt prescriptive possession is presumably, like other issues about possession, a question of fact, as to which general rules may not be very helpful.[62] The question has been raised (but not answered) whether locking a gate across the right of way once a year would be sufficient to prevent prescriptive possession.[63] It is clear that under the 1973 Act the locking of a gate has no effect as an "interruption", since only judicial interruptions now serve to interrupt prescriptive possession. But it might none the less be relevant either as demonstrating that the possession was not peaceable (as required by section 3(3)) or that it was not an assertion of right.[64]

17.25   As with prescriptive possession in other contexts, it is the continuity of the period rather than the use which matters: there may be gaps in use provided that they can be accounted for, so a substantially continuous use will support a claim that there has been possession for a continuous period. The continuity of possession required must also take account of the circumstances. It is obvious that more use will be expected in a densely populated urban area than in a remote rural one.[65]

17.26   One speciality should be mentioned. Questions have arisen about rights of way across land acquired under statutory powers. It is clear that, if the right of way is inconsistent with the exercise of those powers, the acquiring body has no authority to grant a public right of way. That would be *ultra vires*. It has been held that on the same principle the acquiring body is not capable of acquiescing in the prescriptive acquisition by the public of such a right: "a landowner who has no power to grant has no power to acquiesce".[66] But acquiescence is not really the point. A person without legal capacity cannot grant a servitude, yet positive prescription can run against him. The same ought to be true of legal persons. Accordingly, it seems that public rights of way can be established in the normal way over lands acquired under statutory powers.

---

[62] *Mann v. Brodie*, above, at 57.

[63] *Lauder v. McColl*, 1993 S.C.L.R. 753. Compare *Wallace v. Police Commissioners of Dundee* (1875) 2 R. 565, where gates were locked frequently and systematically, particularly at night: no right of way came into being.

[64] *cf.* above, paras 16.01–02, for discussion of how the terms of the 1973 Act relate to the earlier law.

[65] *Macpherson v. Scottish Rights of Way and Recreation Society Ltd* (1888) 15 R. (H.L.) 68 at 71, *per* Lord Watson; *Strathclyde (Hyndland) Housing Society*, above.

[66] *Mags of Edinburgh*, above, at 637; *Kinrossshire C.C. v. Archibald* (1899) 7 S.L.T. 305; *cf. Ellice's Trs v. Commrs of Caledonian Canal* (1904) 6 F. 325.

CHAPTER 18

MOVEABLES

It is uncertain whether there exists a regime of acquisitive prescription of **18.01**
moveable property in Scotland.[1] References to such an institution are
found in some of the institutional writers, but they are mainly directed at
the application of the Act 1617 to moveables, by analogy with its
application to heritage.[2] But, since the Act 1617 was repealed by the
1973 Act, the question whether it properly extended to acquisitive
prescription of moveable property is empty of practical content.

It remains possible, however, that acquisitive prescription of move- **18.02**
ables is recognised at common law. The need for any such thing is,
however, much diminished by the fact that it has long been recognised
that possession carries the presumption that the possessor is owner. A
person challenging the possessor must prove not only that he formerly
owned the object but also how he came to lose possession of it.[3]

There will, however, be cases in which this presumption provides **18.03**
insufficient protection. There will be cases in which after a very lengthy
period it is still possible for a person to prove that he formerly owned an
object and how he came to lose it. Works of art which disappeared for
extended periods after the Second World War provide an obvious
example. The issue of prescription is particularly acute here, since works
of art may be durable, are likely to be unusually identifiable, and often
appreciate greatly in value.

It is true that a possessor in these circumstances may be protected by **18.04**
negative prescription. Ownership of corporeal property prescribes in 20
years.[4] After that time, the possessor can therefore no longer be
dispossessed by the original owner. But neither, unless there is an
acquisitive prescription which can run in his favour, can the possessor be
said to be the owner. The consequence, if the original owner is no longer
the owner and the possessor is not the owner either, must be that
ownership vests in the Crown, as it does for all property which becomes
ownerless.[5]

This result will not follow if there is a common law doctrine of **18.05**
acquisitive prescription of moveables. But is there? The evidence is

---

[1] See generally Carey Miller, *Corporeal Moveables*, paras 7.01–7.04 and the same author
in 1989 S.L.T. (News) 285 and (1996) 1 S.L.P.Q. 115; Reid, *Property*, paras 565–567.
[2] Stair, II, xii, 11; Bankton. II, xii, 2.
[3] *cf.* Stair, III, ii, 7; Erskine, III, vii, 7; Bankton. II, i, 34; Hume, *Lectures*, 3.229–3.231;
Reid, *Property*, para. 130.
[4] s. 8; it does not fall within Sched. 3, unless the possessor stole the property or was privy
to the theft: Sched. 3(g); above, para. 3.51.
[5] Reid, *Property*, para. 540: *quod nullius est fit domini regis.*

extremely thin.[6] Among the writers, Hume is clearly in favour of a 40-year acquisitive prescription.[7] Stair appears to be, although there may be room for interpreting his remarks as dealing with negative prescription.[8] Of the cases which are sometimes mentioned in this context,[9] only one appears even possibly to be concerned with acquisitive rather than negative prescription.[10] In a dispute over the ownership of some valuable jewels which had been in the possession of the defender for 10 to 12 years, the defender apparently took the points that a presumption of ownership arose from his possession of the jewels and that he had in any event completed *usucapio*, acquisitive prescription. The court found that the pursuer had proved enough to rebut the presumption and, in Stair's report of the case, held "that there is no usucapion in Scotland, by possession, in less than forty years". But in referring to this case in his *Institutions*,[11] Stair does not even mention the question of usucapion and deals with the case purely as one where the presumption arising from possession was rebutted, because jewels of such value could not be purchased in good faith from the sort of person from whom the defender had purchased them. The weight of the usucapion argument is therefore uncertain. It is obvious too that to say that there is no usucapion in less than 40 years does not necessarily say, imply or determine that there is usucapion in 40 years or more.

18.06   For these reasons it is quite uncertain whether there is any common law regime for the acquisitive prescription of moveables. Other countries have such a regime, just as Roman law did.[12] In the interests of clarity, and of doing justice in cases which might involve highly valuable and significant cultural property, it may well be desirable to legislate, in order to dispel the murky obscurity of the common law.

18.07   The Scottish Law Commission proposed in a consultative memorandum that there should be a five-year acquisitive prescription of moveables where possession is founded on apparent title and taken in good faith; and a 10-year prescription where it is based purely on open, peaceable and uninterrupted possession which is adverse to the owner.[13] This consultation took place more than 20 years ago, and no report has yet followed upon it.

---

[6] Napier, pp. 38–39 and 72–77.

[7] Hume, *Lectures*, 3.228.

[8] Stair, II, xii, 11.

[9] *Parishioners of Aberscherder v. Parish of Gemrie* (1633) M. 10972; *Sands v. Bell & Balfour*, May 22, 1810, F.C.; both with Carey Miller, *Corporeal Moveables*, para. 7.03.

[10] *Ramsay v. Wilson* (1666) M. 9113 at 9115. This ground of decision appears in only one of the three reports, that of Stair.

[11] III, ii, 7.

[12] Germany: BGB, Art. 937 (10 years); France: Arts 2219 and 2262 (30 years), although of limited significance in practice owing to Art. 2279 "*En fait de meubles, la possession vaut titre*".

[13] SLC Consultation Memorandum no. 30, *Corporeal Moveables: Usucapion or Acquisitive Prescription* (1976), paras 9–14.

PART IV

PRESCRIPTION AND LIMITATION

This part deals with issues which are common to prescription and limitation. Chapter 19 deals with the place of the common law plea of delay against the background of a statutory system of prescription and limitation. Chapter 20 is concerned with the burden of proof and with procedural points. Chapter 21 discusses international private law.

COMMON LAW DELAY (*MORA*)[1]

The statutory rules of prescription and limitation are rigid. The periods **19.01** are fixed. It is true that they can in certain cases be extended to take account of questions such as fraud or error, the legal incapacity of the creditor, or the fact that the existence of a right or claim was not discoverable.[2] But the primary position is that (for example) after precisely 10 years it is in the public interest that questions of property right should be definitively clarified; and that after precisely the prescriptive number of years a person can be deemed to have acquiesced in the loss of his right or property.

What of the common law? There does remain the doctrine of delay, or **19.02** more precisely "*mora*, taciturnity and acquiescence". This can bar a pursuer from enforcing his rights. There is an obvious difficulty about common law delay: if there already exist clear and rigid statutory rules on the loss of rights by prescription or limitation, how can it be justifiable to introduce other, different, more flexible rules? The point was once put like this: "We are not to rear up new kinds of prescription under different names."[3] It is true, nonetheless, that the statutory provisions do not guarantee that a right or obligation will remain enforceable until the statutory period has run. All they postulate is that, once that period has run, it shall not be. It is therefore consistent with the statutory rules that there should be some common law doctrine of delay.[4] But what is essential is that this should not undermine the statutory provisions. What this means is that it is not the mere passage of some period of time short of the prescriptive period which gives rise to a plea of delay. Instead it is the passage of time combined with other factors, namely taciturnity or acquiescence.

The requirements of the plea of *mora*, taciturnity and acquiescence **19.03** were set out in Maclaren's *Court of Session Practice* and have been approved in the Inner House[5]:

"*Mora*, or delay, is not of itself a defence, unless the delay has been for such a period, and the circumstances are such, that prescription

---

[1] See generally J. Rankine, *A Treatise on the Law of Personal Bar in Scotland* (Edinburgh, 1921); Walker, pp. 139–143; *Stair Memorial Encyclopaedia*, Vol. 16, paras 2206–2207; Gloag and Henderson, paras 14.26–14.27.

[2] See above, paras 6.87 *et seq.*, 6.105 *et seq.* on ss. 6(4) and 11(3).

[3] *Mackenzie v. Catton's Trs* (1877) 5 R. 313 at 317, *per* Lord Deas.

[4] The same is true elsewhere: in England the equitable doctrine of laches subsists alongside the Limitation Act; in Germany under BGB, Art. 242, a creditor may be debarred from enforcing a right which has yet to prescribe if this would be unfair and inconsistent with good faith: BGHZ (=*Entscheidungen des Bundesgerichtshofes in Zivilsachen*) 25 (1958) 47, 51; 43 (1965) 289, 292. But see now *Richardson v. Quercus Ltd* 1999 S.C. 278, 290, I.H.

[5] Maclaren, p. 403; *Halley v. Watt*, 1950 S.C. 370 at 374.

applies. It is, therefore, not a proper separate plea in law, the proper expression of the plea being 'the action is barred by *mora*, taciturnity and acquiescence'. The latter must be supported by an averment of facts and circumstances inferring prejudice or acquiescence, and it is a plea to the merits and not a dilatory plea."

This passage makes clear the main principle which keeps the plea of common law delay in bounds: there is a critical distinction between prescription (or limitation), where all that is required is that time should have run, and common law delay, where that is not enough. It is essentially this difference which justifies the continuing existence of the common law plea in apposition to a statutory scheme of prescription and limitation.[6]

19.04   Although the early cases do not present a very clear or consistent picture,[7] the requirements the plea must meet are two: (1) that, since the date on which the pursuer was able to advance his claim, he has delayed in doing so; (2) that the pursuer's inaction warrants the inference that he has no right or has abandoned it; or else that the defender, as a result of the pursuer's inaction, has materially altered or prejudiced her position.

19.05   On the first of these requirements, there is clear authority that the lapse of time does not amount to delay unless the pursuer was capable of bringing an action during it; for instance, a policeman who sued for slander after three years had passed had not delayed, because for most of that period he had remained in employment as a police officer, with the consequence that he could not bring an action without permission of the chief constable, and this had been sought but refused.[8] The same would be true if a pursuer was excusably ignorant of his or her legal rights.[9]

19.06   The length of the delay which would be regarded as material will vary from case to case. Although one of the cases refers to "excessive and unreasonable delay",[10] it is still a question for each case when the delay has reached those proportions. Many years may be too short and several weeks too long. This question therefore has to be addressed in conjunction with the second requirement, of acquiescence or prejudice. The length of time which is material to support the plea must to some extent depend on the proper inference to be drawn from the pursuer's inaction or else on the reliance the defender has come to place on it.

19.07   Acquiescence does not mean simply that the pursuer has allowed the delay to occur. Two different factors crop up in the cases: some emphasise that the delay should be such as to warrant the inference that the pursuer either never had a right or has abandoned it; most

---

[6] Similarly in English law laches and acquiescence exist alongside the Limitation Act: for a recent summary, Law Com. Consultation Paper no. 151, *Limitation of Actions* (1998), paras 9.12–9.20.
[7] For discussion, Rankine, pp. 117–139; for an example, see the divergent opinions of Lords Shand and Deas in *Mackenzie v. Catton's Trs*, above, at 316–317.
[8] *Cassidy v. Connochie*, 1907 S.C. 1112.
[9] *Countess-Dowager of Kintore v. Earl of Kintore* (1886) 13 R. (H.L.) 93.
[10] *Assets Co. v. Bain's Trs* (1904) 6 F. 692 at 705.

emphasise reliance by, or prejudice to, the defender.[11] These factors must be considered as a matter of the merits of the claim, since the plea of delay does not bar the action as such: it goes to the merits.

The two factors, however, are not really so separate as this may imply. **19.08** Delay such as to warrant the inference of abandonment requires a further word of explanation. If it is interpreted simply to mean that the pursuer has delayed sufficiently long that it is not expected that he will now assert his right, it surely does not go far enough. For then it amounts to no more than saying that after a time which is shorter than the prescriptive period, he has lost his right; but it cannot be said, given the statutory scheme of prescription and limitation, that there can be any general expectation that pursuers will sue in any less than the three or five or 20 years which the Act allows them. Nobody really expects that an employee will raise his personal injuries claim more than 15 years after the event, but that does not mean that any claim can be presumed to have been abandoned.[12] For example, in the rather strange case of *Moncrieff v. Waugh*,[13] the defender, who was being sued for aliment for an illegitimate child born nearly 40 years earlier, argued both the plea of *mora* and that the pursuer had previously raised an action for aliment, about which he led no evidence. The court had little difficulty in saying that these inconsistent pleas hardly pointed to a presumption that the pursuer had abandoned her claim. It is against this background that the remarks in the case about the presumption of abandonment, and the lack of any comment on prejudice or reliance, have to be read. Accordingly, even where the cases speak of the plea of delay being supported on grounds of the pursuer's acquiescence, this will generally be coupled with considerations about the reliance the defender or third parties have placed on the pursuer's inaction, and the prejudice which would be caused to them if he were only now to spring into action.

The following examples may help to clarify the nature of the plea: **19.09**

(1) In one case, the right to object more than 30 years later to encroachment on land was held to have been lost.[14] But it is important to note that the question of acquiescence in encroachment can arise without any issue of delay[15]; and the same is true of cases of acquiescence in infringement of a servitude right or of feuing conditions.[16] All that can really be said of the lapse of time is that it shows a greater amount of acquiescence and so may provide the defender with a stronger case.

---

[11] See the cases referred to in the following notes; also *Cullen v. Wemyss* (1838) 1 D. 32; *Cook v. North British Ry* (1872) 10 M. 513 at 516; *Lees' Trs v. Dun*, 1912 S.C. 50 at 64–65. In *Stewart v. North* (1893) 20 R. 260 at 268 and 272, an action for a partnership accounting, there is no mention of acquiescence or prejudice as such, but the notion seems to be that claims based on partnership should be brought within a reasonable time; and that a pursuer who has allowed a claim to slumber for many years needs to give an explanation why.

[12] *Bethune v. A. Stevenson & Co. Ltd*, 1969 S.L.T. (Notes) 12 (the action was based on the law before the current limitation regime was in force).

[13] (1859) 21 D. 216.

[14] *Duke of Buccleuch v. Mags of Edinburgh* (1865) 3 M. 528. The same seems likely to apply in the case of failure to object to a nuisance: see above, para. 7.14.

[15] *Wilson v. Pottinger*, 1908 S.C. 580.

[16] *Muirhead v. Glasgow Highland Society* (1864) 2 M. 420; *Howard de Walden Estates Ltd v. Bowmaker Ltd*, 1965 S.C. 163.

(2) In many cases the principal result of delay will be the loss of
evidence, and there is no need to hold that the action is barred
where the only result of this loss is that the pursuer will bear a
very heavy burden of proof, which may indeed be so heavy as to
be incapable of being discharged. So, for instance, an action of
declarator of heirship was found not to be barred by *mora*,
taciturnity and acquiescence many years after the events, the
difficulty of proof being one for the pursuer. Similarly, a claim
against executors (who had never given in accounts or obtained a
discharge) which was made after a delay of 18 years was not
barred, the prejudice arising from the delay resting on the
pursuer.[17] The result was the same when (before the current
limitation regime existed) an employee raised an action for
personal injuries against his employer more than 15 years after
sustaining the injury.[18] It is essentially in connection with these
difficulties of proof long after the event that it can be said that
there may be a presumption of satisfaction, or discharge or
abandonment; in these circumstances, "every fact thereby left
doubtful will be presumed in favour of the defender".[19] This
appears to extend to the court's making presumptions about what
the pursuer must have known, and not concerning itself as much
as ordinarily it would with the state of the pursuer's actual
knowledge.[20]

(3) On the other hand, where a transaction has been formally closed
and third parties acting in good faith would be prejudiced by its
being opened up again, the plea of *mora*, taciturnity and acquiescence may be good.[21] It is difficult, however, to say that delay in
these instances does any more than amplify a degree of prejudice
which would anyway be present, whether or not much time had
passed.

(4) There are certain actions which generally have to be brought
expeditiously.[22] An example is an action of reduction, where the
pursuer may have to explain any delay in raising proceedings, and
the court may where appropriate exercise its discretion to refuse
to allow a case to proceed. Another example is an action
complaining of slander. In general it would not be reasonable to
do nothing about the slander for some years and then decide
to pursue it.[23] Nonetheless, since a three-year limitation period
applies to actions of defamation,[24] there cannot be any general
rule that the action has to be commenced within any shorter
period than that.[25] Again, therefore, it is considerations of

---

[17] *Bosville v. Lord Macdonald*, 1910 S.C. 597 at 608; *Miller's Exrx v. Miller's Trs*, 1922 S.C.
150.

[18] *Bethune v. A. Stevens & Co. Ltd*, above.

[19] Gloag, *Contract*, p. 543; *cf.* Erskine, III, vii, 29. See also *McKenzie's Exrx v. Morrison's
Trs*, 1930 S.C. 830 at 835.

[20] Rankine, p. 128.

[21] *Assets Co v. Bain's Tr* (1904) 6 F. 692; *Bell's Tr v. Bell's Tr*, 1907 S.C. 872; *Mackenzie v.
Catton's Trs* (1877) 5 R. 313 at 317.

[22] Similarly, in order to avoid being faced with the plea of "competent and omitted", a
defender has to take a point in defence when it arises, rather than reserving it for future
litigation.

[23] *Cassidy v. Connochie*, above.

[24] s. 18A.

[25] Some statutes do, of course, impose shorter periods: *e.g.* a right of rejection of
defective goods under the Sale of Goods Act 1979, ss. 35(4) and 59 must be exercised
"within a reasonable time".

acquiescence or prejudice which would, if appropriate, warrant giving effect to a plea of *mora*, taciturnity and acquiescence.

By far the most important area in which delay may be of significance **19.10** in modern practice is judicial review. This is intended to be a swift remedy, and, in the interests of the public bodies whose decisions may be challenged by it, it is essential that the right to seek review be exercised within a reasonable time of the decision.[26] No limitation period applies to a petition for review as such.[27] But a petition for judicial review has been dismissed on grounds of *mora*, taciturnity and acquiescence when brought two years after the decision complained of[28]; the result was the same in another case in which only three weeks had been allowed to elapse since the decision was made.[29] In these cases the principal ground of the judgment was that the pursuer had acquiesced in the decision.[30] Acquiescence was all the more telling because of the public interest in the matter. Here it can be said that delay is a factor in the determination whether there has been acquiescence of any substantial sort and particularly in forming a view about whether it would or would not be appropriate to allow the decision to be reviewed. But the element of time on its own is never decisive.[31] That conclusion is supported by a case in which the plea of delay was not upheld, because the court found that the petition did not come so late as to be detrimental to good administration.[32] In that case the court distinguished the *Hanlon* case (in which the petition was dismissed as coming too late after a delay of only three weeks). In *Hanlon* the petitioners' acquiescence in the decision had led to a material change of circumstances, while in the present instance that was not so.[33]

The approach taken by the European Court of Justice is not dissimi- **19.11** lar. In one case it was argued that a delay of more than three years in raising proceedings under Article 85 of the Treaty of Rome for breach of competition law exceeded any reasonable limitation period.[34] Since the Treaty provided no limitation period for such proceedings,[35] this was effectively a plea in the nature of *mora*. The court held that "the fundamental requirement of legal certainty has the effect of preventing

---

[26] See in general C. Reid, 1981 S.L.T. (News) 253.

[27] Although to the extent that damages, for example, are sought, the ordinary five-year prescriptive period of s. 6 would apply; and the 20-year prescription would apply to a prayer for reduction: see above, paras 6.25–29.

[28] *Atherton v. Strathclyde R.C.*, 1995 S.L.T. 557.

[29] *Hanlon v. Traffic Commissioner*, 1988 S.L.T. 802; *cf.* N. Collar, 1989 S.L.T. (News) 309.

[30] Conversely, in *Swan v. Secretary of State for Scotland*, 1st Div., February 24, 1998, unreported, the court appears to have been influenced by the fact that the petitioner's delay had caused no prejudice.

[31] On the same basis, it seems possible that a plea of *mora*, taciturnity and acquiescence might be opposed to a petition under s. 459 of the Companies Act 1985, where there had been prejudice or acquiescence: see in England *Re a Company* [1989] D.C.L.C. 383 at 397–398.

[32] *Perfect Swivel Ltd v. City of Dundee District Licensing Board (No. 2)*, 1993 S.L.T. 112.

[33] *Perfect Swivel Ltd*, distinguishing *Hanlon*, above. For relevant considerations, *cf.* the English case of *R. v. Dairy Produce Quota Tribunal for England and Wales, ex p. Caswell* [1990] 2 A.C. 738 at 748–750, *per* Lord Goff of Chieveley.

[34] (Case 48/69) *ICI v. Commission* [1972] E.C.R. 619.

[35] Note that EEC Regulation 2988/74 does set limitation periods for recovery of fines and penalties for infringement of transport and competition law.

the Commission from indefinitely delaying the exercise of its powers to impose fines".[36] On the facts of that case there had been no such delay.[37]

19.12   The conclusion which seems to follow from these considerations is that the plea of *mora*, taciturnity and acquiescence is not well named. Although some of the old cases seem to favour such a doctrine, and it was perhaps of greater importance when the prescriptive period was as long as 40 years, it is difficult on principle to say that delay or *mora* on its own should be of any significance, or that mere silence should be. That would, as Lord Jeffrey once put it, be a "vague and alarming" doctrine.[38] The correct view therefore appears to be that of the three elements of the plea it is acquiescence which is significant,[39] but as a rule only when coupled with reliance by or prejudice to others. This simply emphasises that the plea of *mora*, taciturnity and acquiescence is just one aspect of personal bar. That detrimental reliance is at its core is therefore unsurprising.

---

[36] at 653.
[37] See the opinion of the Advocate General at 702–703, drawing attention to: the fact that this was a continuing wrong; interruption of the limitation period; the lack of acquiescence; and the fact that in the circumstances the delay had not been long enough to have the effect contended for.
[38] *Seath v. Taylor* (1848) 10. D. 377 at 379.
[39] Rankine treats *mora* and taciturnity as a sub-species of acquiescence.

CHAPTER 20

PROCEDURAL QUESTIONS

This chapter deals with two topics relevant both to prescription and **20.01** limitation. The first is the burden of proof. The second is procedure.

I. THE BURDEN OF PROOF

A distinction has to be drawn here between prescription and limitation. **20.02** But the issues are similar enough for it to be convenient to deal with both in the same chapter.

Limitation

There is little authority in Scotland on where the burden of proof lies **20.03** in the defence of limitation. The Act as originally enacted was clear at least on this point, since it was expressly provided that the time-bar section[1] would afford no defence "if it is proved that the material facts relating to that right of action were or included facts of a decisive character which were outside the knowledge (actual or constructive) of the pursuer until a date which was not earlier than three years before the date on which the action was brought".[2] The burden of proof was therefore placed squarely on the pursuer. On the present wording of the relevant section,[3] matters are less clear.

It is clear that the plea of limitation is a defender's plea. So it is up to **20.04** the defender to bring the matter into issue. This is quite different from the case of prescription: in a case of limitation, the right on which the pursuer's action is founded still exists, and there is merely a procedural bar to his bringing the action. The defender can therefore waive her defence of limitation, and the court cannot insist that she plead it. Accordingly, the onus is on the defender to plead limitation if she wishes to do so. The question arises whether she need go any further.

There is a large number of cases which at least touch on this point in **20.05** other legal systems, but no unanimity about the proper approach. The prevailing view in England appears to be that it is for the plaintiff to show that his cause of action accrued within the limitation period.[4] Sometimes it is also said that it is not enough for him to show generally that there was damage within the period: the burden on the plaintiff is to show that the cause of action came into existence on a day within the period of limitation.[5] In either event, if the plaintiff discharges this

---

[1] What was then s. 17(1).
[2] s. 18(3); *cf.* s. 19(3); see *Provan v. Glynwed Ltd*, 1975 S.L.T. 192.
[3] s. 17(2).
[4] *Cartledge v. E. Jopling & Sons Ltd* [1963] A.C. 758 at 784; *Crocker v. British Coal Corp.*, Times L.R., July 5, 1995. It may be that the issue where the burden of proof lies is more important in English than Scottish practice: Walkers, *Evidence*, p. 65.
[5] *London Congregational Union, Ltd v. Harriss & Harriss* [1988] 1 All E.R. 15 at 30, CA.

burden, the burden passes to the defendant to show that in fact the cause of action accrued earlier. This view has been followed often.[6]

20.06   On the other hand, it is sometimes asserted that the burden is always on the defendant to show that the plaintiff's cause of action accrued before the limitation period.[7] The defence of limitation simply puts in issue the defendant's allegation that damage was sustained outside the limitation period but it does not shift the burden to the plaintiff.[8] This is what such Scottish authority as there is appears to suggest.[9]

20.07   The preferable view appears to be that the burden of proving limitation rests on the defenders. There are two main reasons for this. The first is that a limitation period does not extinguish a pursuer's right but simply bars his remedy. If the defender chooses not to plead limitation the action can proceed. There is no need for the pursuer to plead at the outset that his claim is within time. The second reason is that it seems fairer to say that in doubtful cases the defender should lose her defence of limitation (leaving her, of course, with any defence she may have on the merits) rather than that, without the merits being in any way investigated, the pursuer should forfeit his right of action.[10]

Prescription

20.08   Matters are rather less clear in the case of prescription. That the burden rests on the defender has regularly been conceded.[11] It would follow that the pursuer need not make specific averments placing the arising of the claim within the prescriptive period, except of course so far as this is needed to overcome the inferences to be drawn from the defender's own pleadings. There is little relevant authority: most of the old cases deal with one of the forms of limitation which existed prior to 1973 and are not therefore directly in point.[12]

20.09   For prescription proper the question appears to have been mentioned only in three cases. In the first it was held in the Outer House that it was for the defenders to show that the pursuer's loss occurred prior to the prescriptive period.[13] In the second it was held that the burden was on

---

[6] *The Pendrecht* [1980] 2 Lloyd's Rep. 56 at 59–60, QBD; *London Congregational Union Ltd v. Harriss & Harriss*, above; *London Borough of Bromley v. Rush & Tompkins Ltd* (1985) 4 Con. L.R. 44, QBD; *Driscoll-Varley v. Parkside Health Authority* [1991] 2 Med. L.R. 346.

[7] *Crump v. Torfaen Borough Council* [1982] 1 E.G.L.R. 143; *EDAC v. Wm Moss Group Ltd* (1984) 2 Con. L.R. 1 at 41. For discussion of the position in the USA see (1950) Harvard L.R. 1177 at 1199.

[8] *Pullen v. Gutteridge Haskins & Davey Pty Ltd* [1993] 1 V.R. 27 at 77; noted in (1993) 109 L.Q.R. 215.

[9] *Hamill v. Newalls Insulation Co. Ltd*, 1987 S.L.T. 478; *McArthur v. Strathclyde R.C.*, 1995 S.L.T. 1129 at 1134.

[10] *Humphrey v. Fairweather* [1993] N.Z.L.R. 91 at 101.

[11] *Strathclyde R.C. v. Border Engineering Contractors Ltd*, 1997 S.C.L.R. 100; *Sinclair v. MacDougall Estates Ltd*, 1994 S.L.T. 76 at 81D.

[12] *Caledonian Ry v. Chisholm* (1886) 13 R. 773; *Alcock v. Easson* (1842) 5 D. 356; *Neilson v. Mags of Falkirk* (1899) 2 F. 118, all dealing with the Triennial Prescription Act 1579 (in spite of the name actually a provision for limiting proof to writ or oath once a limitation period had been completed); *Shaw v. Renton & Fisher Ltd*, 1977 S.L.T. (Notes) 60 (limitation under s. 17 of the 1973 Act but under its old pre-1984 wording).

[13] *Dunlop v. McGowans*, 1979 S.C. 22 at 27 (the point was not raised in the Inner House or House of Lords).

the party alleging the affirmative, in this case the defenders.[14] In the third it was remarked (*obiter*) that once the question of prescription has been raised it is for the pursuer to prove that his title to sue has been preserved.[15] So the score on the question who bears the burden is: Defenders 2, Pursuers 1. This uncertainty is itself burdensome.

Sometimes it is said that the burden rests on the party who asserts the **20.10** affirmative proposition; so a defender who asserts that an obligation has prescribed will bear the burden of proving that.[16] But this seems too simple. In the first place, it places excessive weight on precisely how the pleadings are formulated: it is not difficult to advance the same proposition in positive form and in negative form, and it would be odd if the precise phrasing made all the difference for the question of prescription. It is therefore more satisfactory to say that this rule is not to be taken literally but should be regarded as indicating that where an allegation, either positive or negative, is essential to a party's case the proof of it rests on him.[17]

In the second place, prescription means that the right itself has ceased **20.11** to exist. It therefore seems reasonable to suppose that the court is able to take notice of the prescription of an obligation, whether or not it is pled by the defender.[18] From that in turn it follows that it is not a complete answer to the question—on whom does the burden of proof lie?—to say that it must lie on the party who pleads prescription.

The burden of proof will generally come to matter only where there is **20.12** genuine doubt about the date on which loss occurred.

For the five-year negative prescription,[19] because the start of the **20.13** prescriptive period can be postponed until the date when the pursuer knew or ought to have known that he had sustained loss,[20] the problem is not particularly acute. Real doubt about when an obligation became enforceable is most likely to occur when it arises in relation to a latent defect. The main question for the court will then be when the pursuer actually did know, or ought to have known, of the loss. Nonetheless, if the pursuer fails to make a case for postponing the starting date,[21] the court will still have to decide who must prove when, viewed objectively, the loss occurred. Since the five-year prescription is not conceived as a long stop, it may be that in general the burden of proving that it has

---

[14] *Strathclyde R.C. v. W. A. Fairhurst & Ptrs*, 1997 S.L.T. 658.

[15] *Richardson v. Quercus Ltd*, J. F. Wheatley, Q.C., March 25, 1997, unreported. In a fourth case, *Paterson v. George Wimpey & Co. Ltd*, 1999 S.L.T. 577, it was ultimately accepted by the defenders that, so far as the 20-year prescription was concerned, the onus lay on them to aver the date on or by which the loss had been sustained.

[16] Walkers, *Evidence*, p. 67.

[17] *Pullen v. Gutteridge Haskins & Davey Pty Ltd*, above, at 76.

[18] Macphail, *Sheriff Court Practice* (2nd ed.), para. 2.114; Walker, p. 5; *cf.* McGee, *Limitation Periods*, p. 116 on prescription under s. 2 of the Consumer Protection Act 1987. This proposition seems to be correct unless it is, as for example in South Africa, expressly stated that the court shall not of its own motion take notice of prescription: Prescription Act 68 of 1969, s. 17.

[19] s. 6.

[20] s. 11(3); see above, paras 6.87 *et seq.* for fuller discussion.

[21] The burden of doing so rests on him: see below.

been completed should rest on the defender. But this general rule must be subject to exceptions in cases where it would involve the defender in proving a negative or proving facts peculiarly within the pursuer's knowledge.

20.14   The question on whom the burden of proof rests is particularly acute in the case of the 20-year prescription,[22] owing to the fact that it takes no account of when the pursuer discovered his claim (sometimes now known as the question of "discoverability"). For example, if a defect occurs in a structure which is buried underground, there may be little basis for determining the date on which loss occurred. Is it for the defender to show that the defect in fact arose more than 20 years before the action was raised, so that the obligation arising from it has prescribed? Or is it incumbent on the pursuer to show that the obligation which he is bringing into court is still valid and subsisting?[23] At this point the law is faced with a genuine dilemma: on the one hand, the notion underlying the long-stop prescription is that it should bring a defender's liability to a definite end. On the other, as with limitation, so here it seems in principle fairer to say that in doubtful cases the defender should lose her defence of prescription (leaving her with any defence she may have on the merits) rather than that, without the merits being in any way investigated, the pursuer should forfeit his right.

20.15   The following considerations seem relevant:

(1) Something may turn on whether proof of prescription would place a burden on one party of proving a negative, or of proving facts peculiarly within the other party's knowledge. For example, where a defender is under a duty not to do a particular act, the prescriptive period will run from the date when she breaches that duty. If the date of her breach is within her own knowledge, it would be odd to insist that the pursuer should prove it, or prove the negative proposition that the defender did not infringe until a particular date within the prescriptive period. Here the onus should be on the defender. But this does not advance matters very far for cases such as the fracturing of the underground pipe.

(2) Something may turn on the procedural stage. At procedure roll, for example, just as with any other ground for dismissal or (occasionally) absolvitor, so with prescription it will be for the defender to persuade the court that the pursuer's case is bound to fail. This seems reasonable, since only in the clearest cases will it be desirable to determine the question of prescription without evidence. The courts generally prefer to hear evidence on the question, and this can conveniently be done at a preliminary proof restricted to the question of prescription.

(3) Something may be gained from considering presumptions. For example, if the underlying principle of the 20-year prescription is that the pursuer is deemed to have abandoned his right, then there is little reason in the case of latent defects to say that in fact he has. But a more powerful presumption is that the purpose of the 1973 Act is to cut off all but imprescriptible rights and

---

[22] s. 7.
[23] *Strathclyde R.C. v. W. A. Fairhurst & Ptrs*, above.

obligations after 20 years, without regard to whether the person enjoying the benefit of the right or obligation knew of their existence or not.

The acid test will remain this: what happens if the evidence discloses that loss occurred at some point between 19 and 21 years earlier? Perhaps some loss could be separated out as clearly before or clearly after the prescriptive period.[24] But so far as any other loss is concerned, there is no room for presumptions, and here the judge will have had the benefit of hearing the evidence. It might seem reasonable to say that, if he is not satisfied that the obligation has ceased to exist, then he must proceed on the basis that it does and go on to consider defences on the merits. The conclusion may seem lame. But it is impossible to be more definitive. There would be something to be said for statutory provision as to the burden of proof of prescription.[25]

Matters which the pursuer must prove[26]

Limitation

So far as provisions postponing the start of the limitation period are concerned,[27] a general principle of statutory interpretation is relevant: a party who wishes to rely on a statutory provision in his favour must bring himself within it.[28] The provisions of sections 17(2)(b) and 18(2)(b) of the 1973 Act favour the pursuer by providing a date for the commencement of the limitation period which is later than any date ascertained objectively (in accordance with paragraph (a) of the subsection), namely the date when the pursuer became aware of various facts. It is true that paragraph (b) is concerned not just with the pursuer's actual awareness of facts but also with his constructive awareness, that is, the date on which in the opinion of the court he ought to have been aware of the facts, but this date itself can only be ascertained by reference to the pursuer's individual circumstances. To require the pursuer to undertake the burden of bringing himself within these provisions makes sense, since it is he who will know when he became aware of certain facts; and, even where it is a question of constructive awareness, the pursuer is likely to know more than the defender about the circumstances from which the court will reach a view on the operative date for limitation. It has sometimes been accepted that the burden of proof lies on the defender,[29] but it is suggested in view of what has just been said that defenders should not hurry to assume any such burden.

20.16

---

[24] *cf. Berry v. Stone Manganese and Marine Ltd* [1972] 1 Lloyd's Rep. 182 (a limitation case).

[25] Some Canadian provinces have this. It might, for instance, be appropriate to consider a rule such as that of the Alberta Limitations Act 1996, s. 3(5) to the effect that the pursuer should bear the burden when issues of discoverability arise and that the defender should when a long-stop prescription is in question. In its recent Consultation Paper no. 151, the English Law Commission provisionally proposes that the burden of proof in limitation should be on the plaintiff and asks whether those consulted might favour a long-stop limitation period in which the burden of proof would be on the defendant (paras 14.28–14.32).

[26] For all of these points in the USA, see (1950) Harvard L.R. 1177 at 1200.

[27] ss. 17(2)(b) and 18(2)(b).

[28] Walkers, *Evidence*, p. 68; Bennion, *Statutory Interpretation* (3rd ed., 1997), p. 850.

[29] *Dickenson v. Lord Advocate*, Lord Osborne, June 8, 1995, unreported.

20.17   If this approach is correct, then it is clear from the terms of section 17(2)(b) that it is not enough for a pursuer simply to aver that he was not aware of one or more of the facts set out in this section; he must go further, and aver why it was not reasonably practicable for him to be aware of one or more of them. If he fails to do this, he fails to bring himself within the statutory provision as a whole and therefore cannot rely on it.[30] This approach makes sense, since only the pursuer can really be expected to know what was reasonably practicable for him; and it would make no sense to require the pursuer to bring himself within some of the statutory provisions and require the defender to exclude him from others.[31] The corollary of this approach is that time begins to run against the pursuer from the date on which, in the opinion of the court, it was reasonably practicable for him to be aware of all of those facts.

Prescription

20.18   It is generally accepted that a pursuer bears the burden of proving: (1) factors which delay the start of prescription[32]; and (2) factors which suspend its running.[33] This accords with the general principle that exceptions must be set up by those who rely upon them.[34] (3) On the same basis, it seems reasonable that a pursuer who relies on interruption of prescription by a relevant claim or relevant acknowledgment should prove that; admittedly, in the case of acknowledgment in particular, this will be a matter which is also within the defender's own knowledge.

II.   PROCEDURE

20.19 The 1973 Act contains separate provisions on when positive prescription is subject to judicial interruption and when negative prescription is interrupted by a relevant claim.[35] But for the purposes of both it is important to know when, as a matter of procedure, a judicial interruption or relevant claim is taken to be made. Equally, for the purposes of limitation periods, it is important to know when an action is taken to be raised or a particular claim in it made. These different regimes of prescription and limitation therefore have to deal with similar procedural considerations, such as what the effect is of amending an action to bring in a new case or defender, or sisting a new pursuer, or serving a third party notice. It is therefore convenient to deal with these common procedural issues in the same chapter.

---

[30] *Webb v. BP Petroleum Development Ltd*, 1988 S.L.T. 775; *Hamill v. Newalls Insulation Co. Ltd*, above, at 479; *McArthur v. Strathclyde R.C.*, above, at 1134; *Cowan v. Toffolo Jackson & Co. Ltd*, 1998 S.L.T. 1000; *McDyer v. Celtic Football and Athletic Co. Ltd*, 1999 S.L.T. 2.

[31] *McArthur v. Strathclyde R.C.*, above.

[32] s. 11(3). *Kirk Care Housing Association Ltd v. Crerar & Ptrs*, 1996 S.L.T. 150; *Greater Glasgow Health Board v. Baxter Clark & Paul*, 1990 S.C. 237; *Glasper v. Rodger*, 1996 S.L.T. 44; *Strathclyde R.C. v. W. A. Fairhurst & Ptrs*, above; *cf. Peco Arts Inc. v. Hazlitt Gallery Ltd* [1983] 1 W.L.R. 1315; Spiro, *Die Begrenzung*, para. 359. The same should apply to the special case of Sched. 2, para. 1; above, paras 6.67–73.

[33] s. 6(4) and, paras 6.105 *et seq.* above; this is implicit in *Robertson v. Watt*, 2nd Div., July 4, 1995, unreported, where the pursuer was held to have averred enough to warrant inquiry on the issue of prescription. (If the plea *non valens agere cum effectu* were still to exist and were pleaded, the burden would lie on the pursuer.) *Cf. Humphrey v. Fairweather* [1993] N.Z.L.R. 91; Spiro, *op cit.*, para. 359.

[34] *Nimmo v. Alexander Cowan & Sons Ltd*, 1967 S.C. (H.L.) 79 at 109

[35] More is said about each of these questions above, paras 5.04 *et seq.*, 16.19 *et seq.*

Nonetheless, it is appropriate to deal with prescription and limitation **20.20**
cases separately. This is for two reasons. First, the fact that the one
regime extinguishes a claim whereas the other does not makes significant
procedural differences. Second, for prescription what matters is that
there should be a continuous prescriptive period, whereas for limitation
all that matters is that an action should be brought before the period has
expired. This means that in limitation the fact that the action was
brought is an end of the matter, whereas for prescription the continuing
fate of a claim after it has been made is relevant.[36]

Prescription cases

(1) *Adjustment*. It is well established that the court has no discretion **20.21**
   to regulate the adjustment of pleadings: short of adding scan-
   dalous matter, it is open to a pursuer to adjust pleadings even if
   they amount to fundamental alterations of his original case after
   the expiry of the prescriptive period. So in *Sellars v. IMI Yorkshire
   Imperial Ltd*[37] the averments added by the pursuer related to a
   different accident at a different locus, with a different cause for
   the accident and different grounds of fault. It was held that the
   court had no power to refuse the adjustments. For the issue of
   prescription it follows that, even if the obligation in question is
   not pleaded in the summons, it will still be open to a pursuer as of
   right to introduce a case at adjustment which does make a claim
   with respect to that obligation, and the fact that this adjustment is
   made after the expiry of the prescriptive period is immaterial.

   This, however, should not be the end of the matter. If the
   averments added at adjustment relate to an obligation which
   prescribed before they were added, it must be open to a defender
   to argue that they should be excluded from probation as being
   founded on a non-existent obligation or else to seek absolvitor so
   far as that obligation is concerned.[38] For these purposes, it seems
   likely that the date of the claim will be the date on which the
   adjustments were made to the open record and intimated to
   the defender.[39]

(2) *Amendment to delete averments*. Here a claim ceases to be made
   from the date the record is amended to exclude it.[40] Presumably,
   the same must apply where averments are struck out following on
   a procedure roll discussion: the claim ceases to be made as at the
   date the court orders the averments to be deleted.

   It would seem to make sense for the same to apply to
   adjustments, although this may need to be qualified, since the
   conclusions of a summons cannot be removed by adjustment.
   Nonetheless, if all supporting averments and pleas-in-law were
   deleted, and a conclusion for payment of money could be

---

[36] For prescription, so long as a relevant claim is viewed as an event which takes place in
the instant the claim is raised and which interrupts prescription on that date, there is little
need to consider many of the finer points about adjustment and amendment of pleadings.
But, on the currently prevailing view that a claim is being made continuously so long as an
action founded on the relevant obligation is before the court, these matters assume critical
importance; see above, paras 5.34 *et seq.*

[37] 1986 S.L.T. 629 at 634.

[38] *cf.*, in the context of limitation, *NCB v. Thomson*, 1959 S.C. 353 at 379–380.

[39] RCS, r. 22.2(3).

[40] *GA Estates Ltd v. Caviapen Trustees Ltd (No. 2)*, 1993 S.L.T. 1045 at 1049H.

understood perfectly well as relating (for example) to a contractual rather than a restitutionary claim, then it seems reasonable to suppose that the restitutionary claim ceased to be advanced once the adjustments were made.

(3) *Amendment to add a case or a new defender.* There is an important preliminary point. At the stage of amendment the court has a discretion to allow or to refuse the receipt of the minute of amendment or (more usually) amendment of the record in terms of the minute of amendment. In the case of prescription,[41] whether a right or obligation still exists is the substantive question. There is no need for this to be disposed of at the stage the amendment is moved. This is because the question whether the right on which the pursuer sues still subsists necessarily remains before the court throughout the proceedings. And this has an impact on the question of discretion. While it is true that the court has a wholly unfettered discretion on whether or not to allow the amendment of the record, where it is a question of prescription that is not the end of the matter. After all, allowing pleadings relating to a non-existent (because prescribed) obligation to enter the record does not affect the fact that there is still no obligation. In clear cases, therefore, it seems that the court should refuse such amendments at the time the motion is made either for receipt of the minute of amendment or for amendment of the record in terms of the minute of amendment.[42] But there will be cases in which it is not possible to determine the issue on the pleadings alone and inquiry will be necessary in order to determine whether the plea of prescription is made out. In many cases what will be in issue is whether the minute of amendment actually does introduce a new defender, or a new claim which is alleged to have prescribed, or whether it is simply an elaboration of a claim which was raised in time.[43]

In general, proceedings based on one obligation will not save from prescription a claim based on a different obligation. The introduction in a minute of amendment of a claim based on another obligation will be the introduction of a claim based on an obligation which may well have prescribed.[44] But where the amendment concerns what might be called a more formal matter, such as to indicate that the pursuer is suing not personally but in a representative capacity, it is not clear that the fact that this comes after the expiry of the prescriptive period is necessarily fatal; it will, however, be a material factor in the exercise of the court's discretion.[45] On the other hand, where the minute of amendment merely adds to or substitutes grounds for making a claim in relation to the original obligation, it will raise no new issue about prescription.

---

[41] The case of limitation is entirely different: see below, para. 20.22.

[42] *cf. Stewart v. Highland and Islands Development Board*, 1991 S.L.T. 787.

[43] So, *e.g.*, in *Classic House Developments Ltd v. G. D. Lodge & Ptrs*, Lord Macfadyen, January 20, 1998, unreported, it was held that a claim based on defects in design due to failure to carry out proper investigations was founded on a different obligation from one based on failure to design properly: amendment was refused.

[44] *Macleod v. Sinclair*, 1981 S.L.T. (Notes) 38; *Lawrence v. McIntosh & Hamilton*, 1981 S.L.T. (Sh.Ct) 73; *J. G. Martin Plant Hire Ltd v. Bannatyne Kirkwood France & Co.*, 1996 S.C. 105.

[45] *Herries v. Heath (Scotland) Ltd*, Extra Div., May 15, 1998, unreported.

A claim raised outside the prescriptive period against a new defender will in most cases, simply because the obligation owed by the new defender will by definition be a different obligation, be a claim on an obligation which has prescribed. This tends to happen in particular if, after the prescriptive period has run, the defender convenes a third party whom the pursuer may wish to join as a defender, or the pursuer only then learns the true identity of the defender.

What is the date of the claim when a pursuer seeks to introduce a new claim against an existing defender or convene a new defender? The answer to the question matters in order to determine whether the obligation which is the foundation of the new claim has prescribed. In principle the appropriate date might be any of: the date of lodging the minute of amendment; the date of intimating the motion to have the minute of amendment received; the date the motion for it to be received was granted; or the date on which amendment of the record was allowed.

Unfortunately, cases on prescription have supported most of these views: the date of intimation of the motion to allow the minute of amendment to be received[46]; the date of lodging the minute of amendment[47]; and the date when the minute of amendment was allowed to be received.[48] The prevailing view is that the correct date is that of intimation of the motion to allow the minute of amendment to be received. This view goes back to a limitation case, *Boyle v. Glasgow Corporation*,[49] where it was held in the Inner House that the critical issue was that the defender should receive fair notice of the claim before the expiry of the limitation period. It was held that lodging a minute of amendment brought it within the judicial process, much as did the signeting of a summons; and that the date of intimation of the motion for the minute of amendment to be received was the date at which the claim made in the minute of amendment was made against the defenders. It was not necessary for the record actually to have been amended in terms of the minute of amendment before the claim could be said to have been made. This line has been followed in other limitation cases.[50]

Clearly, on the view that the allowance of receipt of the minute, or the date of intimation of a motion to that effect, is the critical date, the question arises what happens if the record is not in fact amended in terms of the minute. This might be either because the court refuses the amendment or because no motion for amendment is ultimately made. By analogy with abandonment of an action, it would seem logical to say that a relevant claim has been made even if no amendment proceeds.[51]

There is, however, something to be said against the *Boyle* line. In another limitation case,[52] the Lord Ordinary was bound to (and

---

[46] *Stewart v. Highlands and Islands Development Board*, above; *Kinnaird v. Donaldson*, 1992 S.C.L.R. 694, IH.

[47] *Arif v. Levy & McRae*, Lord Coulsfield, December 17, 1991, unreported (noting that this was when the action commenced "at the earliest").

[48] *Stewart v. J. M. Hodge & Sons*, Lord Coulsfield, February 17, 1995, unreported.

[49] 1975 S.C. 238; 1978 S.L.T. (Notes) 77.

[50] *Robertson v. Crane Hire (Paisley) Ltd*, 1982 S.L.T. 505; *Eunson v. Braer Corp.*, Lord Gill, July 30, 1998, unreported.

[51] *cf. Kinnaird v. Donaldson*, above.

[52] *Morrison v. Scotstoun Marine*, 1979 S.L.T. (Notes) 76.

did) follow *Boyle*. In that case third parties, who were convened as second defenders by the minute, argued that at the very least it was necessary that the court should have ordered intimation to them of the fact that decree was sought against them, so that it was a prerequisite that the court should at least have allowed the minute to be received. Lord Ross found there to be much force in that, and much to be said for the view that actual amendment of the record might be necessary in order to interrupt the running of the limitation period.

At any rate, there is nothing in the language of the 1973 Act[53] to suggest that a relevant claim can be made against a new defender simply by giving fair notice within the prescriptive period that a claim is intended or imminent. Section 4 of the Act speaks against this by requiring that the "appropriate proceedings" in which the claim is made be "any proceedings in a court of competent jurisdiction in Scotland or elsewhere, except proceedings in the Court of Session initiated by a summons which is not subsequently called". A summons is called after it has been served on the defenders[54]; accordingly a defender may well have fair notice of a claim owing to service of the summons but that will still not interrupt prescription if the summons does not call. If this is so, it is difficult to see why giving fair notice of a minute of amendment should be sufficient to interrupt prescription.

(4) *Sisting a new pursuer.* This raises essentially the same issues discussed in connection with amendment to introduce a claim founded on a different obligation.[55] All that need be added here is that the cases fall into two groups, according to whether the new pursuer is conceived as raising a new claim (which may have prescribed) or simply as sisting himself as a party to an existing claim, in which event no new issue of prescription is raised.

No new issue of prescription will arise if the obligation in question is single and indivisible, since a relevant claim is made on it even by one party, although properly it ought to be pursued by another party too.[56] But where each party sues in a separate right, clearly the claim of each must be tested separately on the question of prescription.[57] So, for example, the addition of a firm as a pursuer in addition to one of its partners was held to be the commencement of an action by a new, different pursuer.[58] The addition of a claim by a pursuer in a new capacity, for example as an individual rather than as executor, will raise similar questions.[59] In each of these cases the claim by the new pursuer, if made after the expiry of the prescriptive period, is founded on an obligation which has prescribed and should therefore not be allowed to proceed.[60]

---

[53] s. 9 on relevant claims; s. 4 on judicial interruptions.

[54] RCS, r. 13.13.

[55] A minute of sist is not needed: *Stewart v. Highlands and Islands Development Board*, 1991 S.L.T. 787 at 790.

[56] *Grindall v. John Mitchell (Grangemouth) Ltd*, 1987 S.L.T. 137; *cf. Cole-Hamilton v. Boyd*, 1963 S.C. (H.L.) 1 at 12.

[57] *Maclean v. British Railways Board*, 1966 S.L.T. 39.

[58] *Arif v. Levy & McRae*, above. The motion was refused.

[59] *Robertson v. Watt & Co.*, 2nd Div., July 4, 1995, unreported.

[60] *ibid.*: the action was raised timeously by the pursuer as executor, but the pursuer's claim as an individual was introduced by minute of amendment more than five years after the appropriate date. Inquiry was allowed on the pursuer's averments under s. 6(4) about error having induced her not to pursue her personal claim.

(5) *Third party notice.* Where a defender seeks contribution, indemnity or relief from a third party, the date of the defender's claim against the third party will presumably be the date of service of the third party notice; this will be the first intimation the third party necessarily has of the defender's claim.[61] Where the pursuer seeks to convene the third party as an additional defender, the date of the pursuer's claim against the third party and new defender would turn on the considerations discussed above in connection with minutes of amendment. On the prevailing view outlined above, the date would be that on which the pursuer intimated to the third party the motion to have received the minute of amendment in which the third party was convened as a defender.[62]

(6) *Counterclaims.* On this approach, it seems correct to say that the date of making a relevant claim in the form of a counterclaim is the date on which the counterclaim was intimated to the party claimed against. If the Rules of Court are complied with, this will in any event be the date of lodging the counterclaim.[63] There is no provision in Scotland equivalent to section 35 of the Limitation Act 1980 in England, which deems a counterclaim to have been made at the same date as the principal action was raised.

(7) *Abandonment or dismissal on grounds of relevancy or competency.* A claim ceases to be made when it is abandoned or dismissed.[64] The effect will be that a new period of prescription begins to run again the next day.[65] Abandonment mostly indicates that the pursuer was unpersuaded of the merits of his case; dismissal that the court was. Is there any reason why the fact that a claim was not a good claim should make a difference, so that the period for which it interrupted prescription should be disregarded?[66] Although this does seem very generous to the pursuer, and is not the law in some other jurisdictions,[67] it is difficult in principle to see why the period of interruption by the abandoned action should be disregarded, unless the action was actually null. As long as it was not a nullity, it should have the normal effect of interrupting prescription for the period during which it was being insisted in.[68]

(8) *Final disposal.* Where the case proceeds to a final judgment, the claim will cease (subject to any appeal). It seems probable that the claim ceases to be made on the date of the final interlocutor.

It might, however, be argued (a) that the relevant date is the date not of the interlocutor but of extract; or (b) that, provided

---

[61] RCS, r. 26.4. A claim for contribution under s. 3 of the Law Reform (Miscellaneous Provisions) (Scotland) Act 1940 could, however, be made only once there was a judicial determination of the extent of contribution due: see above, para. 8.04.

[62] *Aitken v. Norrie*, 1966 S.C. 168 at 174; *Morrison v. Scotstoun Marine*, above; *Robertson v. Crane Hire (Paisley) Ltd*, 1982 S.L.T. 505.

[63] RCS, r. 25.1; at the time of lodging a copy must be sent to the other parties to the action: RCS, r. 4.6.

[64] *GA Estates Ltd v. Caviapen Trustees Ltd*, 1993 S.L.T. 1051 at 1059I and 1065J.

[65] See above, para. 5.36.

[66] *cf. GA Estates Ltd v. Caviapen Trustees Ltd*, above, at 1065K. In *Gobbi v. Lazzaroni* (1859) 21 D. 801 it was held that an abandoned action did not constitute an interruption of prescription, but this is generally regarded as wrongly decided (*cf. Caviapen* at 1047).

[67] In France (*Code Civil*, Art. 2247) and Italy (*Codice Civile*, Art. 2945) an abandoned action is disregarded and prescription is regarded as uninterrupted.

[68] *cf.* above, paras 5.17–20 for a fuller comment on this point.

that appeal or reclaiming is competent, the relevant claim is being made until the days for appealing or reclaiming have expired without any appeal or reclaiming motion being made, or leave to appeal or reclaim has been refused; or (c) that until an interlocutor has disposed of the question of expenses, a claim is still being made. Which of these views is preferable is hard to determine on any clear principle. View (a) may be thought improbable, since extract is a matter which goes essentially to execution of the judgment, and it is not obvious why it should have any bearing on whether the claim is regarded as being made or not. View (c) also seems improbable, since the court pronounces separate interlocutors dealing with expenses, and there is therefore no obvious reason why the subsistence of the principal claim should be measured by them rather than by the final interlocutor on the merits. View (b) is the position applicable to the prescription of obligations arising from product liability under the Consumer Protection Act 1987.[69] There would be something to be said for interpreting the ordinary prescription rules consistently with section 22A of the 1973 Act, which deals with the product liability cases.[70]

(9) *Reclaiming or appeal.* Where the interlocutor is appealed or reclaimed, this too may be a relevant claim, provided it is made in a court of competent jurisdiction and is directed at implement or part-implement of the obligation in question, for example by seeking review of an interlocutor dismissing the claim.

Limitation cases

20.22   Here it is sufficient to note only differences from the position outlined already:

(1) *Adjustment.* Since the court has no discretion to regulate adjustment of the pleadings, it follows that it cannot refuse adjustments which add a new case; provided that they are added to an action which was commenced before the limitation period had run, they are as much part of the action as any case on which it was originally founded.

(2) *Amendment.* The courts are frequently faced with applications by a pursuer to add a new case after the limitation period has already expired and when this can no longer be done by adjustment. The issues which arise here are different from those where prescription is concerned. In limitation cases there is no question of an obligation having been extinguished.[71] For that reason it is essential that the introduction of the new case by amendment should be opposed (at latest) when the motion is made to amend the closed record (or summons). Once amendment of the record has been allowed, the court has no further discretion, at least on the ground of time-bar, to eliminate the averments introduced by amendment.[72] For by that stage the procedural barrier—which is all that limitation is—has been surmounted.

---

[69] 1973, Act s. 22A(3); see above, para. 9.20.

[70] The fact that the wordings of ss. 9 and 22A differ is of no significance for construction of the 1973 Act, since they derive from different sources and s. 22A was inserted into the 1973 Act only in 1987.

[71] See above, para. 20.20.

[72] *Jones v. Lanarkshire Health Board*, 1991 S.L.T. 714.

It follows from this that, if the court disposes of the plea of limitation and allows the record to be amended, no pleadings about limitation should enter the closed record. Limitation has ceased to be an issue. The parties should therefore ensure that the plea of limitation does not enter the record.[73]

Presumably there might be exceptional cases in which the court would be unwilling to determine the question of limitation without evidence. The difficulty is that there could not be a proof unless the pleadings were closed, but closing them would involve disposing of the issue about amendment. In any case, a proof would not be appropriate where the decision for the court was not whether to sustain or repel a plea-in-law but only whether to grant a motion. The solution in these exceptional cases might be to deal with the question on the motion roll, but to make use of productions or affidavits. An alternative would be to continue the motion to a procedure roll hearing; essentially the same procedure would have to be followed there, although with the unusual feature that the pleadings had not yet been closed.

When faced with the assertion that new averments are time-barred by section 17, 18 or 18A, the court has its usual discretion to allow amendment or to refuse it. In the case of actions which are not time-barred but in which a new (time-barred) case is added to an existing action, on the face of it the court's discretion to allow an out-of-time action to proceed under section 19A does not apply; the discretion which the court exercises in such cases is its ordinary one rather than that special statutory discretion. But the court may nonetheless find that the statutory principles are relevant background to the exercise of its ordinary discretion.[74]

There is no need to set out any detailed comments on amendment; those can be found in the works on procedure. The following is the briefest summary.

The test applied by the courts remains that set out by Lord Justice-Clerk Cooper in *Pompa's Trustees v. Edinburgh Magistrates*: "the court will not in general allow a pursuer by amendment to substitute the right defender for the wrong defender, or cure a radical incompetence in his action, or to change the basis of his case if he seeks to make such amendments only after the expiry of a time limit which would have prevented him at that stage from raising proceedings afresh."[75] It is appropriate to deal separately with two categories of amendment after the limitation period has expired: (a) a new case against an existing defender; (b) a case against a new defender in an existing action.

(a) So far as making a new case against an existing defender is concerned, the test has been further elaborated in later cases. The dividing line falls between changing "not the basis of the action so much as the method of formulating the ground of action", so that the pursuer can claim "not to have offered a new front but only to have presented the old front from a new angle, not to have changed the foundation of his action, but only to have made certain alterations in the

---

[73] *Gibson v. Droopy & Browns*, 1989 S.L.T. 172.
[74] *Hendrie v. Gray & Dick Ltd*, Lord Hamilton, July 10, 1997, unreported.
[75] 1942 S.C. 119 at 125; *cf. McPhail v. Lanarkshire County Council*, 1951 S.C. 301 at 309.

superstructure".[76] There is no shortage of subsequent cases which apply the same test[77]: does the amendment amount to a fundamental change in the pursuer's case?[78] Application of this test is necessarily a matter of degree, and what the court seeks to do is establish on which side of a fine line the case falls. If it is simply a reformulation of existing grounds of action, the amendment will be allowed; but if it is a radical alteration and amounts virtually to a new action, the amendment is likely to be refused.[79] Otherwise, the court's exercise of its discretion to permit amendment would amount simply to a means of defeating the limitation rules.[80]

Where the amendment introduces an additional ground on which the defenders failed in the exercise of a duty of reasonable care, but the accident and the danger complained of remain the same, the amendment is likely to be on the right side of the line.[81] This has been held to apply, for example, to the addition to a case of personal liability of a new case of vicarious liability, or vice versa[82] or to the addition to a common law case of a statutory case, or vice versa[83] or to the introduction of a new common law case.[84] The Second Division recently put it in this way: "What is important is that no material change has been made to the factual averments regarding the way in which the accident occurred nor as to the danger against which it is said the defenders were required to take precautions for the safety of the pursuer."[85] But where the cases of fact and fault would be altered almost out of recognition, the line has been crossed.[86] This has, for example, been held to apply where a new *locus* for the accident is averred, and no prior report of that accident had been made, or where the *locus* of the accident was now said to be different, its alleged cause different, and the sole ground of fault pleaded was radically altered.[87]

Since each case is a matter for the court's discretion, it is not possible to lay down any rules which go much further

---

[76] *McPhail v. Lanarkshire County Council*, above; *Black v. John Williams and Co.*, 1924 S.C. (H.L.) 22.

[77] For a recent review of the cases, *Evans v. Northern Coasters Ltd t/a Stena Offshore*, 2nd Div., January 20, 1995, unreported.

[78] *McCluskie v. National Coal Board*, 1961 S.C. 87; *Mackenzie v. Fairfields Shipbuilding and Engineering Co. Ltd*, 1964 S.C. 90; *Anderson v. British Railways Board*, 1973 S.L.T. (Notes) 20; *Cork v. Greater Glasgow Health Board*, 1994 S.L.T. 404.

[79] *Greenhorn v. J. Smart & Co. (Contractors) Ltd*, 1979 S.C. 427 at 431, *per* L.P. Emslie.

[80] *Hynd v. West Fife Co-operative Ltd*, 1980 S.L.T. 41 at 43.

[81] *ibid.*

[82] *Mackenzie v. Fairfields Shipbuilding and Engineering Co. Ltd*, above; *Evans v. Northern Coasters Ltd*, above.

[83] *Evans v. Northern Coasters Ltd*, above.

[84] *McGrattan v. Renfrew D.C.*, 1983 S.L.T. 678 (failure to devise a safe system of work added to case of failure to provide equipment).

[85] *Evans v. Northern Coasters Ltd*, above, at 15.

[86] *Dryburgh v. National Coal Board*, 1962 S.C. 485.

[87] *Grimason v. National Coal Board*, 1986 S.L.T. 286 (I.H.: 1987 S.L.T. 714); *Rollo v. British Railways Board*, 1980 S.L.T. (Notes) 103. A less extreme case where the amendment was refused is *Davies v. BICC Ltd*, 1980 S.L.T. (Sh.Ct) 17 (the facts pleaded were slightly changed and vicarious liability was substituted for personal liability).

than this. Perhaps all that can usefully be added is that prejudice is a vital consideration. Within this framework, where there is no obvious prejudice to the defender, the court may be more inclined to allow the motion; and where the pursuer's conduct of the action has been exceptionally dilatory, it may be more inclined to refuse.[88] Something will also turn on the stage at which amendment is sought: if only a few days before proof, the pursuer's prospects are less good.[89]

(b) The second type of amendment is to bring a case against a new defender. Most commonly this issue arises when the defences have brought in a third party, and the pursuer seeks to convene the third party as an additional defender. It is of course also possible for the pursuer to seek to convene a new defender without any such prompting. Where third parties are concerned, the pursuer's hand is generally stronger, since the third party may already have been in the action for some period of time and, after service of the third party notice by the defender, will have had reason to investigate the circumstances of the accident. Consequently, convening the third party as a defender will amount only to making him subject to a direct claim, of which indirectly he already had notice. For that reason it may be relatively difficult for the third party to mount a convincing case of prejudice such as would incline the court to refuse the proposed amendment.[90] Often the only (supposed)[91] prejudice will be the loss of the time-bar defence. Here, however, the court may be tempted to approach the question by applying the tests relevant to the exercise of its discretion to allow actions to proceed out of time.[92] In this sort of case the attraction is particularly clear, since there is an obvious similarity between raising a new action out of time and introducing a new defender into an existing action out of time. If these principles are adopted, it follows that where (for example) the pursuer has a clear case against existing defenders and no good reason for not having proceeded timeously against the third party, the motion might be refused.[93]

The separate category of substituting the right defender for the wrong defender also belongs here, since it amounts in essence to the introduction of a new defender or defenders. This has been allowed, under reference to section 19A, in order to substitute for the company which had been sued but did not exist the joint venture and its partners who were the proper defenders.[94]

---

[88] See, *e.g.*, *Brady v. Clydeport Stevedoring Services Ltd*, 1987 S.L.T. 645; *Little v. East Ayrshire Council*, Lord Abernethy, April 21, 1998, unreported.

[89] *Dryburgh v. National Coal Board*, above.

[90] *Carson v. Howard Doris Ltd*, 1981 S.L.T. 273; *Harris v. Roberts*, 1983 S.L.T. 452; *Webb v. BP Petroleum Development Ltd*, 1988 S.L.T. 775.

[91] See above, para. 12.24.

[92] s. 19A.

[93] *Speedwell v. Allied Bakeries Ltd*, Lord MacLean, February 1, 1994, unreported; *cf. Boslem v. Paterson*, 1982 S.L.T. 216.

[94] *McCullough v. Norwest Socea Ltd*, 1981 S.L.T. 201; *cf.* also *McHardy v. Bawden International Ltd*, 1993 S.C.L.R. 893; *Farmer v. James Keiller & Sons Ltd*, 1995 S.C.L.R. 589.

(3) So far as sisting a new pursuer, third party notices, and counterclaims are concerned, there is nothing to add here to what was said in connection with prescription.

CHAPTER 21

INTERNATIONAL PRIVATE LAW

Prior to September 26, 1984, when faced with a case which was governed **21.01** by a foreign legal system, a Scottish court was obliged to characterise provisions on time limits in that system as rules of either prescription or limitation. If they were the first, they were regarded as matters of substantive law and were applied by the Scottish court; if they were the second, they were regarded as rules of foreign procedure and were disregarded. Establishing where the borderline lay between substantive and procedural time-limits was not always straightforward.

Where obligations are concerned, it is now mostly unnecessary to do **21.02** this. The Prescription and Limitation (Scotland) Act 1984 introduced a major change in the law.[1] This is inserted into the 1973 Act as section 23A:

"**Private international law application**
23A.—(1) Where the substantive law of a country other than Scotland falls to be applied by a Scottish court as the law governing an obligation, the court shall apply any relevant rules of law of that country relating to the extinction of the obligation or the limitation of time within which proceedings may be brought to enforce the obligation to the exclusion of any corresponding rule of Scots law.
(2) This section shall not apply where it appears to the court that the application of the relevant foreign rule of law would be incompatible with the principles of public policy applied by the court.
(3) This section shall not apply in any case where the application of the corresponding rule of Scots law has extinguished the obligation, or barred the bringing of proceedings prior to the coming into force of the Prescription and Limitation (Scotland) Act 1984."

The force of section 23A is that, when the substantive law of another **21.03** country governs an obligation, a Scottish court will apply the rules of that system regardless whether they extinguish an obligation (prescription) or only restrict the time within which it may be enforced (limitation). This is subject only to the proviso that the court may decline to apply the foreign rule of prescription or limitation if it would be incompatible with public policy.

Although this is nowhere stated, it seems likely that the Scottish court **21.04** would also have to decline to apply the foreign rules if there was no evidence about what they were. The ordinary rule is that foreign law must be proved as a matter of fact; if that is not done, the courts cannot apply it.[2]

---

[1] 1984 Act, s. 7(2).
[2] Anton, *Private International Law*, pp. 774 *et seq.*

21.05 Section 23A also provides for the exclusion of the Scottish rules of prescription or limitation when an obligation is governed by a foreign system of law.[3]

21.06 What the Scottish court will apply is "any relevant rules of that country relating to the extinction of the obligation or the limitation of time within which proceedings may be brought". This means that the court may have to concern itself with such questions under the foreign system of law as when an obligation or right of action comes into being; whether the running of time is postponed for reasons connected with "discoverability" or lack of legal capacity; whether it is suspended for reasons such as lack of legal capacity, disability, fraud or error; whether it has been interrupted; and what effect completion of the prescription or limitation period has on the obligation or right of action. All these are matters which have to be resolved under the foreign system of law and to the exclusion of Scots law.[4]

21.07 This section is concerned only with obligations. Nothing is said about prescription, positive or negative, in relation to property rights. So far as land is concerned, it is clear that the law which governs questions of prescription will be, as with virtually all issues relating to land, the law of the country where the land is situated (*lex situs*).[5] Probably the same applies to prescription of corporeal moveable property.[6] A Scottish court will have to resort to the common law approach of characterising the rules of the *lex situs* as procedural or substantive and giving effect to those that are substantive.

21.08 For obligations, with which section 23A is actually concerned, it may be useful to set out the briefest summary of the circumstances in which an obligation is governed by the substantive law of a particular country:

(1) *Contract*.[7] Under the Rome Convention, applied in the United Kingdom by the Contracts (Applicable Law) Act 1990, the law which applies to a contract is—subject to a number of exceptions—the law chosen by the parties and, in the absence of any choice, the law of the country with which the contract is most closely connected.[8] It is this law which determines what prescription or limitation rules apply to the contract in question; the same provision is indeed made in the Rome Convention itself.[9] In terms of section 23A, a Scottish court must apply those provisions, apart from any issue of public policy that may militate against doing so.[10]

---

[3] s. 23A(3) makes transitional provisions. The effect is that the Scottish rules are not excluded where they would have extinguished a foreign obligation or limited a foreign right of action before this section came into force. If the obligation or right of action would have prescribed or been limited before that date, that remains the case.

[4] *cf.* for a case in which the French courts applied English limitation rules as those proper to the contract in question, *Société Mobil v. Compagnie Française d'Entreprises Métalliques*, Cour d'Appel Paris, March 3, 1994, J.C.P. 1995 II 22367; Cour de Cassation (1st Civil Chamber), March 11, 1997, (1997) 86 *Revue critique de droit int. privé* 702.

[5] Anton, *Private International Law*, pp. 602–611.

[6] *ibid.* pp. 611–620.

[7] Dicey and Morris, *Conflict of Laws*, pp. 1211–1239; Anton, *op cit.* Chap. 11.

[8] This is determined under Art. 4 of the Rome Convention.

[9] Art. 10(1)(d).

[10] A public policy exception is also found in Art. 16 of the Rome Convention.

(2) *Delict*.[11] For most delicts, the question what substantive law applies is now determined under the Private International Law (Miscellaneous Provisions) Act 1995. There is a general rule and an exception. In general, the applicable law is the law of the country in which the events constituting the delict occur[12]; where elements of those events occur in different countries, the applicable law is (a) in cases of personal injury (or death resulting from it), the law of the country where the individual sustained the injury; (b) in cases of damage to property, the law of the country where the property was when it was damaged; (c) in any other case, the law of the country in which the most significant element or elements of those events occurred.[13] The exception is that, if it appears in all the circumstances that it is substantially more appropriate for the applicable law to be the law of a country other than that determined by the general rule, then the law of that country is the applicable law.[14] Once it is clear what the applicable law is, the way is clear in terms of section 23A for the Scottish court to apply the limitation or prescription provisions stipulated by that law.

It used to be doubted whether section 23A could apply to obligations arising in delict: the reason was that the section in terms applies only to cases where a substantive foreign law is to be applied to the exclusion of Scots law. This was not so under the old double actionability rule, which required that, for a delict committed abroad to be actionable in Scotland, it must be actionable both according to Scots law and according to the law of the place where it occurred.[15] This doubt, however, has now been laid to rest, together with the double actionability rule, so far as actions within the scope of the 1995 Act are concerned.

The 1995 Act, however, does not apply to defamation,[16] and so the ordinary common law delictual regime continues to apply. That requires that the defamation be actionable both under Scots law and under the law of the place where it occurred. It is arguable, for the reasons just given, that section 23A may not apply to this case. If that is so, the court would have to determine whether the time-limit under foreign law was procedural or substantive; if the view was taken that it was substantive, then presumably the time-limit would be applied.

(3) *Unjustified enrichment*.[17] Unjustified enrichment is governed by its own rules. It has recently been settled that, so far as jurisdiction is concerned, unjustified enrichment is not assimilated either to the rules on delict or quasi-delict or to those on contract.[18] It seems not unlikely that the same independent approach may be adopted to questions of determining the applicable law. But at present the law is unclear.

---

[11] Dicey and Morris, *Conflict of Laws* (4th suppl. to 12th ed.), pp. 216–288; B. Rodger (1996) 1 S.L.P.Q. 397.

[12] 1995 Act, s. 11(1).

[13] *ibid.* s. 11(2).

[14] *ibid.* s. 12.

[15] Anton, *op cit.* p. 406.

[16] 1995 Act, s. 13.

[17] Dicey and Morris, *op cit.*, pp. 1471–1479; Anton, *op cit.*, pp. 309–311; J. Blaikie, 1994 J.R. 112; H. Gutteridge and K. Lipstein (1939) 7 C.L.J. 80.

[18] *Kleinwort Benson Ltd v. Glasgow D.C.* [1997] 4 All E.R. 641 on Art. 5(1) and (3) of the Brussels Convention: Civil Jurisdiction and Judgments Act 1982, Sched. 1.

21.09   It has been suggested, so far as English law is concerned, that the common law rules are that (1) where enrichment arises in connection with a contract (although not under a contract), the applicable law is the law applicable to the contract; (2) where enrichment arises in connection with land, the applicable law is that of the country where the land is situated; and (3) that otherwise the obligation to restore enrichment is governed by the law of the country where the enrichment has occurred.[19]

21.10   There is very little authority on the question. On the last of these propositions, an old case does indeed appear to apply an English limitation period in a case where the enrichment occurred in England.[20] On the first proposition, the critical case is when a contract turns out to be void. It is clear that there is no need to conclude that this is governed by the law applicable to the contract, since there is no contract, and the consequences of nullity of the contract are not determined by the law applicable to the contract.[21] Recently, it has been suggested that the appropriate law is the one with which the critical events (that is, the void transactions generating the enrichment) have their closest and most real connection.[22] Presumably, this might turn out to be the law which governed the (void) contract, or the law of the country where the enrichment occurred, or neither of them.

21.11   A further difficulty may be caused by the obligation of relief: it is true that, if it is contractual, the contractual scheme will apply to determine the applicable law. But if there is no contract and the obligation is regarded as being based on unjustified enrichment,[23] then the question what law applies is more problematic. It would seem in principle preferable to apply a rule related to unjustified enrichment rather than, for example, automatically to assimilate a case of contribution in respect of liability in delict to the choice of law rules which apply to delicts.[24] Which law applies might of course be crucial, since (for instance) in Scotland there is a statutory right to contribution in respect of delictual liability only for liability established in Scottish proceedings,[25] and the prescription period is very short: two years.[26]

21.12   In short, it is not possible to state with any confidence when a foreign law is likely to be held to govern a question of unjustified enrichment and when therefore foreign prescription or limitation provisions will have to be applied by a Scottish court.

---

[19] Dicey and Morris, *op cit.*, p. 1471.

[20] *Rae v. Wright* (1717) M. 4506.

[21] The Contracts (Applicable Law) Act 1990, s. 2(2) expressly provides that the applicable law does not govern the consequences of nullity of the contract (Art. 10(1)(e) of the Convention), presumably for the precise purpose of having this determined not by the law applicable to the contract but by whatever system of law is appropriate as a matter of the law of unjustified enrichment.

[22] *Baring Bros & Co. Ltd v. Cunninghame D.C.*, Times L.R., September 30, 1996.

[23] *Moss v. Penman*, 1994 S.L.T. 19.

[24] For further discussion of this uncertain area, see Anton, *Private International Law*, p. 408; SLC Report no. 115, *Report on Civil Liability—Contribution* (1988), paras 3.100–3.104; *cf.* Dicey and Morris, *Conflict of Laws* 1533–1534.

[25] *Comex Houlder Diving Ltd v. Colne Fishing Co. Ltd.*, 1987 S.C. (H.L.) 85 at 123–124 on s. 3(2) of the Law Reform (Miscellaneous Provisions) (Scotland) Act 1940.

[26] s. 8A.

Effect of choice of law rules on prescription and limitation

The determination of the substantive law governing the contract can **21.13** be of the greatest significance in matters of prescription and limitation for three main reasons: first, one system of law may apply a more generous prescription or limitation period than another; second, even if the periods are of the same length, one system of law may provide for time to start running before the other does, or for it to be interrupted or suspended more readily than the other permits; third, the decision on which law applies may determine whether an obligation is extinguished by prescription or whether an action to enforce it is subject to limitation. This makes a difference if, for instance, a question of set-off might arise: for, if the action to enforce an obligation has merely been subject to limitation, it may be possible for it to be set off in defence to another action; whereas, if the obligation has been extinguished, no question of set-off is capable of arising.

Here are some examples: **21.14**

(1) *An obligation arising in delict.* In Scotland, the obligation prescribes in five years from the date of the loss or, if later, the date the pursuer became, or could with reasonable diligence have become, aware of the loss; there is, however, no need for the pursuer to be aware of the identity of the defender before time starts to run.[27] In Germany, the obligation is subject to limitation three years after the pursuer knew of the loss and the identity of the defender, but in any event 30 years after the date the loss occurred.[28] It is clear from this example that which system of law applies will determine not merely the length of the prescriptive period but also, if a provision about "discoverability" is relevant, which facts must be known before time starts to run.

(2) *An obligation arising from breach of contract.* In Scotland, time runs from the date loss follows on the breach; in England, it runs from the date of the breach.[29] Even although the limitation period in England (six years) is longer than the prescription period in Scotland (five years), it is possible that the English limitation period may expire first, since it will have begun first. Whether it actually does will depend not just on the time interval between the breach and the loss but also on what rules each system recognises for the postponement or suspension of the running of the prescription or limitation period.[30]

(3) *An obligation to redress unjustified enrichment.* In Scotland, this obligation is extinguished in five years; in England, it is limited in six. (This difference—together with the issue of postponement of the running of the prescription or limitation period—was the reason jurisdiction was so keenly contested in the recent case of *Kleinwort Benson v. Glasgow City Council*.[31]) But quite apart from that, the fact that one system applies a principle of limitation and

---

[27] s. 6, Sched. 1(d) and s. 11(3): the proper interpretation of s. 11(3) is a complex question (see above, paras 6.87–104), and the above statement is only a paraphrase.

[28] BGB, Art. 852 I.

[29] 1973 Act, s. 6 and Sched. 1(g); Limitation Act 1980, s. 5 (the cause of action in contract cases accrues at the date of breach).

[30] cf. *Kleinwort Benson Ltd v. Glasgow D.C.*, above.

[31] [1997] 4 All E.R. 641 at 644.

the other a principle of prescription means that such things as set-off or the enforceability or otherwise of accessory obligations might be vitally affected by the determination which system of law applied to the obligation.[32]

---

[32] How this question would turn out in practice would depend on whether the rules of set-off of the obligation in question were, under the law applicable to it, to be characterized as substantive or procedural: Dicey and Morris, *Conflict of Laws*, pp. 181–182.

PRESCRIPTION AND LIMITATION (SCOTLAND) ACT 1973

(1973 c. 52)

An Act to replace the Prescription Acts of 1469, 1474 and 1617 and make new provision in the law of Scotland with respect to the establishment and definition by positive prescription of title to interests in land and of positive servitudes and public rights of way, and with respect to the extinction of rights and obligations by negative prescription; to repeal certain enactments relating to limitation of proof; to re-enact with modifications certain enactments relating to the time-limits for bringing legal proceedings where damages are claimed which consist of or include damages or solatium in respect of personal injuries or in respect of a person's death and the time-limit for claiming contribution between wrongdoers; and for purposes connected with the matters aforesaid.

[25th July 1973]

PART I

PRESCRIPTION

Positive prescription

Interests in land: general

[1] **1.**—(1) If in the case of an interest in particular land, being an interest to which this section applies—

   (a) the interest has been possessed by any person, or by any person and his successors, for a continuous period of ten years openly, peaccably and without any judicial interruption, and

   (b) the possession was founded on, and followed (i) the recording of a deed which is sufficient in respect of its terms to constitute in favour of that person a title to that interest in the particular land, or in land of a description habile to include the particular land, or (ii) registration of that interest in favour of that person in the Land Register of Scotland, subject to an exclusion of indemnity under section 12(2) of the Land Registration (Scotland) Act 1979,

then, as from the expiration of the said period, the validity of the title so far as relating to the said interest in the particular land shall be exempt from challenge.

(1A) Subsection (1) above shall not apply where—

   (a) possession was founded on the recording of a deed which is invalid *ex facie* or was forged; or

   (b) possession was founded on registration in respect of an interest in land in the Land Register of Scotland proceeding on a forged deed and the person appearing from the Register to be entitled to the interest was aware of the forgery at the time of registration in his favour.

(2) This section applies to any interest in land the title to which can competently be recorded or which is registrable in the Land Register of Scotland.

(3) In the computation of a prescriptive period for the purposes of this section in a case where the deed in question is a decree of adjudication for debt, any period before the expiry of the legal shall be disregarded.

(4) Where in any question involving an interest in any foreshore or in any salmon fishings this section is pled against the Crown as owner of the regalia, subsection (1) above shall have effect as if for the words "ten years" there were substituted the words "twenty years".

(5) This section is without prejudice to the operation of section 2 of this Act.

NOTE
[1] As amended by the Land Registration (Scotland) Act 1979 (c. 33), s. 10. Excluded by the Coal Industry Act 1994 (c. 21). s. 10(2)(b) (effective 31st October 1994: s. 68(2) and S.I. 1994 No. 2553).

Interests in land: special cases
[1] **2.**—(1) If in the case of an interest in particular land, being an interest to which this section applies—
  (a) the interest has been possessed by any person, or by any person and his successors, for a continuous period of twenty years openly, peaceably and without any judicial interruption, and
  (b) the possession was founded on, and followed the execution of, a deed (whether recorded or not) which is sufficient in respect of its terms to constitute in favour of that person a title to that interest in the particular land, or in land of a description habile to include the particular land,
then, as from the expiration of the said period, the validity of the title so far as relating to the said interest in the particular land shall be exempt from challenge except on the ground that the deed is invalid *ex facie* or was forged.

(2) This section applies—
  (a) to the interest in land of the lessee under a lease;
  (b) to any interest in allodial land;
  (c) to any other interest in land the title to which is of a kind which, under the law in force immediately before the commencement of this Part of this Act, was sufficient to form a foundation for positive prescription without the deed constituting the title having been recorded.

(3) This section is without prejudice to the operation of section 1 of this Act.

NOTE
[1] See the Registration of Leases (Scotland) Act 1857 (c. 26), s. 16(2), and the Land Tenure Reform (Scotland) Act 1974 (c. 38). s. 18 and Sched. 6, para. 3. Excluded by the Coal Industry Act 1994 (c. 21), s. 10(2)(b) (effective October 31, 1994, s. 68(2) and S.I. 1994 No. 2553).

Positive servitudes and public rights of way
  3.—(1) lf in the case of a positive servitude over land—

    (a) the servitude has been possessed for a continuous period of twenty years openly, peaceably and without any judicial interruption, and

    (b) the possession was founded on, and followed the execution of, a deed which is sufficient in respect of its terms (whether expressly or by implication) to constitute the servitude,

then, as from the expiration of the said period, the validity of the servitude as so constituted, shall be exempt from challenge except on the ground that the deed is invalid *ex facie* or was forged.

(2) If a positive servitude over land has been possessed for a continuous period of twenty years openly, peaceably and without judicial interruption, then, as from the expiration of that period, the existence of the servitude as so possessed shall be exempt from challenge.

(3) If a public right of way over land has been possessed by the public for a continuous period of twenty years openly, peaceably and without judicial interruption, then, as from the expiration of that period, the existence of the right of way as so possessed shall be exempt from challenge.

(4) References in subsections (1) and (2) of this section to possession of a servitude are references to possession of the servitude by any person in possession of the relative dominant tenement.

(5) This section is without prejudice to the operation of section 7 of this Act.

Judicial interruption of periods of possession for purposes of sections 1, 2 and 3

4.—(1) In sections 1, 2 and 3 of this Act references to a judicial interruption, in relation to possession, are references to the making in appropriate proceedings, by any person having a proper interest to do so, of a claim which challenges the possession in question.

(2) In this section "appropriate proceedings" means—

    (a) any proceedings in a court of competent jurisdiction in Scotland or elsewhere, except proceedings in the Court of Session initiated by a summons which is not subsequently called;

    (b) any arbitration in Scotland;

    (c) any arbitration in a country other than Scotland, being an arbitration an award in which would be enforceable in Scotland.

(3) The date of a judicial interruption shall be taken to be—

    (a) where the claim has been made in an arbitration and the nature of the claim has been stated in a preliminary notice relating to that arbitration, the date when the preliminary notice was served;

    (b) in any other case, the date when the claim was made.

(4) In the foregoing subsection "preliminary notice" in relation to an arbitration means a notice served by one party to the arbitration on the other party or parties requiring him or them to appoint an arbiter or to agree to the appointment of an arbiter, or, where the arbitration agreement or any relevant enactment provides that the reference shall be to a person therein named or designated, a notice requiring him or them to submit the dispute to the person so named or designated.

Further provisions supplementary to sections 1, 2 and 3

5.—(1) In sections 1, 2 and 3 of this Act "deed" includes a judicial decree; and for the purposes of the said sections any of the following, namely an instrument of sasine, a notarial instrument and a notice of title, which narrates or declares that a person has a title to an interest in land shall be treated as a deed sufficient to constitute that title in favour of that person.

(2) [Repealed by the Requirements of Writing (Scotland) Act 1995 (c. 7), Sched. 5 (effective August 1, 1995).]

Extinction of obligations by prescriptive periods of five years

6.—(1) If, after the appropriate date, an obligation to which this section applies has subsisted for a continuous period of five years—

(a) without any relevant claim having been made in relation to the obligation, and

(b) without the subsistence of the obligation having been relevantly acknowledged,

then as from the expiration of that period the obligation shall be extinguished:

Provided that in its application to an obligation under a bill of exchange or a promissory note this subsection shall have effect as if paragraph (b) thereof were omitted.

(2) Schedule 1 to this Act shall have effect for defining the obligations to which this section applies.

(3) In subsection (1) above the reference to the appropriate date, in relation to an obligation of any kind specified in Schedule 2 to this Act is a reference to the date specified in that Schedule in relation to obligations of that kind, and in relation to an obligation of any other kind is a reference to the date when the obligation became enforceable.

[1] (4) In the computation of a prescriptive period in relation to any obligation for the purposes of this section—

(a) any period during which by reason of—

(i) fraud on the part of the debtor or any person acting on his behalf, or

(ii) error induced by words or conduct of the debtor or any person acting on his behalf,

the creditor was induced to refrain from making a relevant claim in relation to the obligation, and

[2] (b) any period during which the original creditor (while he is the creditor) was under legal disability,

shall not be reckoned as, or as part of, the prescriptive period:

Provided that any period such as is mentioned in paragraph (a) of this subsection shall not include any time occurring after the creditor could with reasonable diligence have discovered the fraud or error, as the case may be, referred to in that paragraph.

(5) Any period such as is mentioned in paragraph (a) or (b) of subsection (4) of this section shall not be regarded as separating the time immediately before it from the time immediately after it.

NOTES

[1] Applied by the Merchant Shipping (Liner Conferences) Act 1982 (c. 37), s. 8(3).
[2] See the Age of Legal Capacity (Scotland) Act 1991 (c. 50), s. 8.

Extinction of obligations by prescriptive periods of twenty years

7.—(1) If, after the date when any obligation to which this section applies has become enforceable, the obligation has subsisted for a continuous period of twenty years—

(a) without any relevant claim having been made in relation to the obligation, and

(b) without the subsistence of the obligation having been relevantly acknowledged, then as from the expiration of that period the obligation shall be extinguished:

Provided that in its application to an obligation under a bill of exchange or a promissory note this subsection shall have effect as if paragraph (b) thereof were omitted.

[1] (2) This section applies to an obligation of any kind (including an obligation to which section 6 of this Act applies), not being an obligation to which section 22A of this Act applies or an obligation specified in Schedule 3 to this Act as an imprescriptible obligation or an obligation to make reparation in respect of personal injuries within the meaning of Part II of this Act or in respect of the death of any person as a result of such injuries.

NOTE
[1] As amended by the Prescription and Limitation Act 1984 (c. 45), Sched. 1, para. 2, as regards any obligation not extinguished before September 26, 1984: *ibid.* s. 5(3), and by the Consumer Protection Act 1987 (c. 41), Sched. 1, para. 8.

Extinction of other rights relating to property by prescriptive periods of twenty years

8.—(1) If, after the date when any right to which this section applies has become exercisable or enforceable, the right has subsisted for a continuous period of twenty years unexercised or unenforced, and without any relevant claim in relation to it having been made, then as from the expiration of that period the right shall be extinguished.

(2) This section applies to any right relating to property, whether heritable or moveable, not being a right specified in Schedule 3 to this Act as an imprescriptible right or falling within section 6 or 7 of this Act as being a right correlative to an obligation to which either of those sections applies.

Extinction of obligations to make contributions between wrongdoers

[1] **8A.**—(1) If any obligation to make a contribution by virtue of section 3(2) of the Law Reform (Miscellaneous Provisions) (Scotland) Act 1940 in respect of any damages or expenses has subsisted for a continuous period of two years after the date on which the right to recover the contribution became enforceable by the creditor in the obligation—

  (a) without any relevant claim having been made in relation to the obligation; and
  (b) without the subsistence of the obligation having been relevantly acknowledged;

then as from the expiration of that period the obligation shall be extinguished.

(2) Subsections (4) and (5) of section 6 of this Act shall apply for the purposes of this section as they apply for the purposes of that section.

NOTE
[1] Inserted by the Prescription and Limitation (Scotland) Act 1984, s. 1.

Definition of "relevant claim" for purposes of sections 6, 7 and 8

[1] **9.**—[2] (1) In sections 6, 7 and 8A of this Act the expression "relevant claim," in relation to an obligation, means a claim made by or on behalf of the creditor for implement or part-implement of the obligation, being a claim made—

(a) in appropriate proceedings; or

³ (b) by the presentation of, or the concurring in, a petition for sequestration or by the submission of a claim under section 22 or 48 of the Bankruptcy (Scotland) Act 1985; or

(c) by a creditor to the trustee acting under a trust deed as defined in section 5(2)(c) of the Bankruptcy (Scotland) Act 1985;

⁴ (d) by the presentation of, or the concurring in, a petition for the winding up of a company or by the submission of a claim in a liquidation in accordance with rules made under section 411 of the Insolvency Act 1986;

and for the purposes of the said sections 6, 7 and 8A the execution by or on behalf of the creditor in an obligation of any form of diligence directed to the enforcement of the obligation shall be deemed to be a relevant claim in relation to the obligation.

(2) In section 8 of this Act the expression "relevant claim," in relation to a right, means a claim made in appropriate proceedings by or on behalf of the creditor to establish the right or to contest any claim to a right inconsistent therewith.

(3) Where a claim which, in accordance with the foregoing provisions of this section, is a relevant claim for the purposes of section 6, 7, 8 or 8A of this Act is made in an arbitration, and the nature of the claim has been stated in a preliminary notice relating to that arbitration, the date when the notice was served shall be taken for those purposes to be the date of the making of the claim.

(4) In this section the expression "appropriate proceedings" and, in relation to an arbitration, the expression "preliminary notice" have the same meanings as in section 4 of this Act.

NOTES

¹ As amended by the Prescription and Limitation (Scotland Act 1984, Sched. 1, para. 3.

² As amended by the Bankruptcy (Scotland) Act 1985, Sched. 7, para. 11, with effect from April 1, 1986.

³ As amended by the Prescription (Scotland) Act 1987. s. 1(2).

⁴ Inserted by the Prescription (Scotland) Act 1987, s. 1(1). By section 1(3) of the same Act:

"The said section 9 as amended by subsection (1) above shall have effect as regards any claim (whenever submitted) in a liquidation in respect of which the winding up commenced on or after 29th December 1986."

Relevant acknowledgment for purposes of sections 6, 7 and 8A

¹ **10.**—(1) The subsistence of an obligation shall be regarded for the purposes of sections 6, 7 and 8A of this Act as having been relevantly acknowledged if, and only if, either of the following conditions is satisfied, namely—

(a) that there has been such performance by or on behalf of the debtor towards implement of the obligation as clearly indicates that the obligation still subsists;

(b) that there has been made by or on behalf of the debtor to the creditor or his agent an unequivocal written admission clearly acknowledging that the obligation still subsists.

(2) Subject to subsection (3) below, where two or more persons are bound jointly by an obligation so that each is liable for the whole, and the subsistence of the obligation has been relevantly acknowledged by or on behalf of one of those persons then—

(a) if the acknowledgment is made in the manner specified in paragraph (a) of the foregoing subsection it shall have effect for the purposes of the said sections 6, 7 and 8A as respects the liability of each of those persons, and

(b) if it is made in the manner specified in paragraph (b) of that subsection it shall have effect for those purposes only as respects the liability of the person who makes it.

(3) Where the subsistence of an obligation affecting a trust estate has been relevantly acknowledged by or on behalf of one of two or more co-trustees in the manner specified in paragraph (a) or (b) of subsection (1) of this section, the acknowledgment shall have effect for the purposes of the said sections 6, 7 and 8A as respects the liability of the trust estate and any liability of each of the trustees.

(4) In this section references to performance in relation to an obligation include, where the nature of the obligation so requires, references to refraining from doing something and to permitting or suffering something to be done or maintained.

NOTE
[1] As amended by the Prescription and Limitation (Scotland) Act 1984, Sched. 1, para. 4.

Obligations to make reparation

11.—(1) Subject to subsections (2) and (3) below, any obligation (whether arising from any enactment, or from any rule of law or from, or by reason of any breach of, a contract or promise) to make reparation for loss, injury or damage caused by an act, neglect or default shall be regarded for the purposes of section 6 of this Act as having become enforceable on the date when the loss, injury or damage occurred.

(2) Where as a result of a continuing act, neglect or default loss, injury or damage has occurred before the cessation of the act, neglect or default the loss, injury or damage shall be deemed for the purposes of subsection (1) above to have occurred on the date when the act, neglect or default ceased.

(3) In relation to a case where on the date referred to in subsection (1) above (or, as the case may be, that subsection as modified by subsection (2) above) the creditor was not aware, and could not with reasonable diligence have been aware, that loss, injury or damage caused as aforesaid had occurred, the said subsection (1) shall have effect as if for the reference therein to that date there were substituted a reference to the date when the creditor first became, or could with reasonable diligence have become, so aware.

[1] (4) Subsections (1) and (2) above (with the omission of any reference therein to subsection (3) above) shall have effect for the purposes of section 7 of this Act as they have effect for the purposes of section 6 of this Act.

NOTE
[1] As amended by the Prescription and Limitation (Scotland) Act 1984, Sched. 2.

Savings

12.—(1) Where by virtue of any enactment passed or made before the passing of this Act a claim to establish a right or enforce implement of an obligation may be made only within a period of limitation specified in or determined under the enactment, and, by the expiration of a prescriptive period determined under section 6, 7 or 8 of this Act the right or obligation would, apart from this subsection, be extinguished before the expiration of the period of limitation, the said section shall

have effect as if the relevant prescriptive period were extended so that it
expires—

(a) on the date when the period of limitation expires, or
(b) if on that date any such claim made within that period has not
been finally disposed of, on the date when the claim is so
disposed of.

(2) Nothing in section 6, 7 or 8 of this Act shall be construed so as to
exempt any deed from challenge at any time on the ground that it is
invalid *ex facie* or was forged.

Prohibition of contracting out
   [1] **13.**—(1) Any provision in any agreement purporting to provide in
relation to any right or obligation that section 6, 7, 8 or 8A of this Act
shall not have effect shall be null.

NOTE
   [1] As amended by the Prescription and Limitation (Scotland) Act 1984, Sched. 1, para. 5.

General

Computation of prescriptive periods
   14.—(1) In the computation of a prescriptive period for the purposes
of any provision of this Part of this Act—

(a) time occurring before the commencement of this Part of this Act
shall be reckonable towards the prescriptive period in like
manner as time occurring thereafter, but subject to the restriction that any time reckoned under this paragraph shall be less
than the prescriptive period;
   [1] (b) any time during which any person against whom the provision is
pled was under legal disability shall (except so far as otherwise
provided by subsection (4) of section 6 of this Act including that
subsection as applied by section 8A of this Act) be reckoned as if
the person were free from that disability;
(c) if the commencement of the prescriptive period would, apart
from this paragraph, fall at a time in any day other than the
beginning of the day, the period shall be deemed to have
commenced at the beginning of the next following day;
(d) if the last day of the prescriptive period would, apart from
this paragraph, be a holiday, the period shall, notwithstanding
anything in the said provision, be extended to include
any immediately succeeding day which is a holiday, any further
immediately succeeding days which are holidays, and the next
succeeding day which is not a holiday;
(e) save as otherwise provided in this Part of this Act regard shall be
had to the like principles as immediately before the commencement of this Part of this Act were applicable to the computation
of periods of prescription for the purposes of the Prescription
Act 1617.

(2) In this section "holiday" means a day of any of the following
descriptions, namely, a Saturday, a Sunday and a day which, in Scotland,
is a bank holiday under the Banking and Financial Dealings Act 1971.

NOTE
   [1] As amended by the Prescription and Limitation (Scotland) Act 1984, Sched. 1, para. 6.

Interpretation of Part I

15.—(1) In this Part of this Act, unless the context otherwise requires, the following expressions have the meanings hereby assigned to them, namely—

"bill of exchange" has the same meaning as it has for the purposes of the Bills of Exchange Act 1882;

"date of execution," in relation to a deed executed on several dates, means the last of those dates;

"enactment" includes an order, regulation, rule or other instrument having effect by virtue of an Act;

"holiday" has the meaning assigned to it by section 14 of this Act;

"interest in land" does not include a servitude;

"land" includes heritable property of any description;

"lease" includes a sub-lease;

"legal disability" means legal disability by reason of nonage or unsoundness of mind;

"possession" includes civil possession, and "possessed" shall be construed accordingly;

[1] "prescriptive period" means a period required for the operation of section 1, 2, 3, 6, 7, 8 or 8A of this Act;

"promissory note" has the same meaning as it has for the purposes of the Bills of Exchange Act 1882;

"trustee" includes any person holding property in a fiduciary capacity for another and, without prejudice to that generality, includes a trustee within the meaning of the Trusts (Scotland) Act 1921; and "trust" shall be construed accordingly;

and references to the recording of a deed are references to the recording thereof in the General Register of Sasines.

(2) In this Part of this Act, unless the context otherwise requires, any reference to an obligation or to a right includes a reference to the right or, as the case may be, to the obligation (if any), correlative thereto.

(3) In this Part of this Act any reference to an enactment shall, unless the context otherwise requires, be construed as a reference to that enactment as amended or extended, and as including a reference thereto as applied, by or under any other enactment.

NOTE
[1] As amended by the Prescription and Limitation (Scotland) Act 1984, Sched. 1, para. 7.

Amendments and repeals related to Part I

16.—(1) The enactment specified in Part I of Schedule 4 to this Act shall have effect subject to the amendment there specified, being an amendment related to this Part of this Act.

(2) Subject to the next following subsection, the enactments specified in Part I of Schedule 5 to this Act (which includes certain enactments relating to the limitation of proof) are hereby repealed to the extent specified in column 3 of that Schedule.

[1] (3) Where by virtue of any Act repealed by this section the subsistence of an obligation in force at the date of the commencement of this Part of this Act was immediately before that date, by reason of the passage of time, provable only by the writ or oath of the debtor the subsistence of the obligation shall (notwithstanding anything in sections 16(1) and 17(2)(a) of the Interpretation Act 1978, which relates to the effect of repeals) as from that date be provable as if the said repealed Act had not passed.

NOTE
[1] As amended by the Interpretation Act 1978, s. 25(2).

[1] PART II

LIMITATION OF ACTIONS

NOTE
[1] Saved by the Administration of Justice Act 1982 (c. 53), s. 73(5).

Part II not to extend to product liability
[1] **16A.** This Part of this Act does not apply to any action to which section 22B or 22C of this Act applies.

NOTE
[1] Inserted by the Consumer Protection Act 1987 (c. 43), Sched. 1, para. 9.

Actions in respect of personal injuries not resulting in death
[1] **17.**—(1) This section applies to an action of damages where the damages claimed consist of or include damages in respect of personal injuries, being an action (other than an action to which section 18 of this Act applies) brought by the person who sustained the injures or any other person.

(2) Subject to subsection (3) below and section 19A of this Act, no action to which this section applies shall be brought unless it is commenced within a period of three years after—

  (a) the date on which the injuries were sustained or, where the act or omission to which the injuries were attributable was a continuing one, that date or the date on which the act or omission ceased, whichever is the later; or

  (b) the date (if later than any date mentioned in paragraph (a) above) on which the pursuer in the action became, or on which, in the opinion of the court, it would have been reasonably practicable for him in all the circumstances to become, aware of all the following facts—

    (i) that the injuries in question were sufficiently serious to justify his bringing an action of damages on the assumption that the person against whom the action was brought did not dispute liability and was able to satisfy a decree;

    (ii) that the injuries were attributable in whole or in part to an act or omission; and

    (iii) that the defender was a person to whose act or omission the injuries were attributable in whole or in part or the employer or principal of such a person.

[2] (3) In the computation of the period specified in subsection (2) above there shall be disregarded any time during which the person who sustained the injuries was under legal disability by reason of nonage or unsoundness of mind.

NOTES
[1] Substituted by the Prescription and Limitation (Scotland) Act 1984 (c. 45), s. 2, as regards rights of action accruing both before and after the commencement of that Act: *ibid.* s. 5(1).
[2] See the Age of Legal Capacity (Scotland) Act 1991 (c. 50), s. 8.

Actions where death has resulted from personal injuries

[1] **18.**—(1) This section applies to any action in which, following the death of any person from personal injuries, damages are claimed in respect of the injuries or the death.

(2) Subject to subsections (3) and (4) below and section 19A of this Act, no action to which this section applies shall be brought unless it is commenced, within a period of three years after—

(a) the date of death of the deceased; or

(b) the date (if later than the date of death) on which the pursuer in the action became, or on which, in the opinion of the court, it would have been reasonably practicable for him in all the circumstances to become, aware of both of the following facts—

  (i) that the injuries of the deceased were attributable in whole or in part to an act or omission; and

  (ii) that the defender was a person to whose act or omission the injuries were attributable in whole or in part or the employer or principal of such a person.

[2] (3) Where the pursuer is a relative of the deceased, there shall be disregarded in the computation of the period specified in subsection (2) above any time during which the relative was under legal disability by reason of nonage or unsoundness of mind.

(4) Subject to section 19A of this Act, where an action of damages has not been brought by or on behalf of a person who has sustained personal injuries within the period specified in section 17(2) of this Act and that person subsequently dies in consequence of those injuries, no action to which this section applies shall be brought in respect of those injuries or the death from those injuries.

(5) In this section "relative" has the same meaning as in Schedule 1 to the Damages (Scotland) Act 1976.

NOTES

[1] Substituted by the Prescription and Limitation (Scotland) Act 1984 (c. 45), s. 2, as regards rights of action accruing both before and after the commencement of that Act: *ibid.* s. 5(1).

[2] See the Age of Legal Capacity (Scotland) Act 1991 (c. 50), s. 8.

Limitation of defamation and other actions

[1] **18A.**—(1) Subject to subsections (2) and (3) below and section 19A of this Act, no action for defamation shall be brought unless it is commenced within a period of three years after the date when the right of action accrued.

[2] (2) In the computation of the period specified in subsection (1) above there shall be disregarded any time during which the person alleged to have been defamed was under legal disability by reason of nonage or unsoundness of mind.

(3) Nothing in this section shall affect any right of action which accrued before the commencement of this section.

(4) In this section—

(a) "defamation" includes *convicium* and malicious falsehood, and "defamed" shall be construed accordingly; and

(b) references to the date when a right of action accrued shall be construed as references to the date when the publication or communication in respect of which the action for defamation is to be brought first came to the notice of the pursuer.

NOTES
  [1] Inserted by the Law Reform (Miscellaneous Provisions) (Scotland) Act 1985 (c. 73), s. 12(2).
  [2] See the Age of Legal Capacity (Scotland) Act 1991 (c. 50), s. 8.

Actions of harassment
  [1] **18B.**—(1) This section applies to actions of harassment (within the meaning of section 8 of the Protection from Harassment Act 1997) which include a claim for damages.

(2) Subject to subsection (3) below and to section 19A of this Act, no action to which this section applies shall be brought unless it is commenced within a period of 3 years after—

  (a) the date on which the alleged harassment ceased; or
  (b) the date, (if later than the date mentioned in paragraph (a) above) on which the pursuer in the action became, or on which, in the opinion of the court, it would have been reasonably practicable for him in all the circumstances to have become, aware, that the defender was a person responsible for the alleged harassment or the employer or principal of such a person.

(3) In the computation of the period specified in subsection (2) above there shall be disregarded any time during which the person who is alleged to have suffered the harassment was under legal disability by reason of nonage or unsoundness of mind.

NOTE
  [1] Inserted by the Protection from Harassment Act 1997 (c. 40), s. 10(1).

19.—(1) [Repealed by the Prescription and Limitation (Scotland) Act 1984 (c. 45), s. 2.]

Power of court to override time-limits, etc.
  [1] **19A.**—[2] (1) Where a person would be entitled, but for any of the provisions of section 17, 18, 18A or 18B of this Act, to bring an action, the court may, if it seems to it equitable to do so, allow him to bring the action notwithstanding that provision.

(2) The provisions of subsection (1) above shall have effect not only as regards rights of action accruing after the commencement of this section but also as regards those, in respect of which a final judgment has not been pronounced, accruing before such commencement.

(3) In subsection (2) above, the expression "final judgment" means an interlocutor of a court of first instance which, by itself, or taken along with previous interlocutors, disposes of the subject matter of a cause notwithstanding that judgment may not have been pronounced on every question raised or that the expenses found due may not have been modified, taxed or decerned for; but the expression does not include an interlocutor dismissing a cause by reason only of a provision mentioned in subsection (1) above.

  [3] (4) An action which could not be entertained but for this section shall not be tried by jury.

NOTES
  [1] Inserted by the Law Reform (Miscellaneous Provisions) (Scotland) Act 1980 (c. 55), s. 23(a).
  [2] As amended by the Prescription and Limitation (Scotland) Act 1984 (c. 45), Sched. 1, para. 8(a), the Law Reform (Miscellaneous Provisions) (Scotland) Act 1985 (c. 73), s. 12(3) and the Protection from Harassment Act 1997 (c. 40), s. 10(2).

[3] Added by the Prescription and Limitation (Scotland) Act 1984 (c. 45), Sched. 1, para. 8(b).

20, 21. [Repealed by the Prescription and Limitation (Scotland) Act 1984 (c. 45), Sched. 2.]

Interpretation of Part II and supplementary provisions

[1] **22.**—(1) In this Part of this Act—

"the court" means the Court of Session or the sheriff court; and

"personal injuries" includes any disease and any impairment of a person's physical or mental condition.

[2] (2) Where the pursuer in an action to which section 17, 18 or 18A of this Act applies is pursuing the action by virtue of the assignation of a right of action, the reference in subsection (2)(b) of the said section 17 or of the said section 18 or, as the case may be, subsection (4)(b) of the said section 18A to the pursuer in the action shall be construed as a reference to the assignor of the right of action.

(3) For the purposes of the said subsection (2)(b) knowledge that any act or omission was or was not, as a matter of law, actionable, is irrelevant.

(4) An action which would not be entertained but for the said subsection (2)(b) shall not be tried by jury.

NOTES

[1] Substituted by the Prescription and Limitation (Scotland) Act 1984 (c. 45), s. 3.

[2] As amended by the Law Reform (Miscellaneous Provisions) (Scotland) Act 1985 (c. 73), s. 12(4).

[1] PART IIA

PRESCRIPTION OF OBLIGATIONS AND LIMITATION OF ACTIONS UNDER PART I OF THE CONSUMER PROTECTION ACT 1987

NOTE

[1] Inserted by the Consumer Protection Act 1987 (c. 43), Sched. 1, para. 10.

Prescription of Obligations

Ten years' prescription of obligations

22A.—(1) An obligation arising from liability under section 2 of the 1987 Act (to make reparation for damage caused wholly or partly by a defect in a product) shall be extinguished if a period of 10 years has expired from the relevant time, unless a relevant claim was made within that period and has not been finally disposed of, and no such obligation shall come into existence after the expiration of the said period.

(2) If, at the expiration of the period of 10 years mentioned in subsection (1) above, a relevant claim has been made but has not been finally disposed of, the obligation to which the claim relates shall be extinguished when the claim is finally disposed of.

(3) In this section a claim is finally disposed of when—

(a) a decision disposing of the claim has been made against which no appeal is competent;

(b) an appeal against such a decision is competent with leave, and the time limit for leave has expired and no application has been made or leave has been refused;

    (c) leave to appeal against such a decision is granted or is not required, and no appeal is made within the time limit for appeal; or

    (d) the claim is abandoned;

"relevant claim" in relation to an obligation means a claim made by or on behalf of the creditor for implement or part implement of the obligation, being a claim made—

    (a) in appropriate proceedings within the meaning of section 4(2) of this Act; or

    (b) by the presentation of, or the concurring in, a petition for sequestration or by the submission of a claim under section 22 or 48 of the Bankruptcy (Scotland) Act 1985; or

    (c) by the presentation of, or the concurring in, a petition for the winding up of a company or by the submission of a claim in a liquidation in accordance with the rules made under section 411 of the Insolvency Act 1986;

"relevant time" has the meaning given in section 4(2) of the 1987 Act.

    (4) Where a relevant claim is made in an arbitration, and the nature of the claim has been stated in a preliminary notice (within the meaning of section 4(4) of this Act) relating to that arbitration, the date when the notice is served shall be taken for those purposes to be the date of the making of the claim.

Limitation of actions

Three year limitation of actions

    22B.—(1) This section shall apply to an action to enforce an obligation arising from liability under section 2 of the 1987 Act (to make reparation for damage caused wholly or partly by a defect in a product), except where section 22C of this Act applies.

    (2) Subject to subsection (4) below, an action to which this section applies shall not be competent unless it is commenced within the period of three years after the earliest date on which the person seeking to bring (or a person who could at an earlier date have brought) the action was aware, or on which, in the opinion of the court, it was reasonably practicable for him in all the circumstances to become aware, of all the facts mentioned in subsection (3) below.

    (3) The facts referred to in subsection (2) above are—

    (a) that there was a defect in a product;

    (b) that the damage was caused or partly caused by the defect;

    (c) that the damage was sufficiently serious to justify the pursuer (or other person referred to in subsection (2) above) in bringing an action to which this section applies on the assumption that the defender did not dispute liability and was able to satisfy a decree;

    (d) that the defender was a person liable for the damage under the said section 2.

    (4) In the computation of the period of three years mentioned in subsection (2) above, there shall be disregarded any period during which the person seeking to bring the action was under legal disability by reason of nonage or unsoundness of mind.

    (5) The facts mentioned in subsection (3) above do not include knowledge of whether particular facts and circumstances would or would not, as a matter of law, result in liability for damage under the said section 2.

(6) Where a person would be entitled, but for this section, to bring an action for reparation other than one in which the damages claimed are confined to damages for loss of or damage to property, the court may, if it seems to it equitable to do so, allow him to bring the action notwithstanding this section.

Actions under the 1987 Act where death has resulted from personal injuries
22C.—(1) This section shall apply to an action to enforce an obligation arising from liability under section 2 of the 1987 Act (to make reparation for damage caused wholly or partly by a defect in a product) where a person has died from personal injuries and the damages claimed include damages for those personal injuries or that death.

(2) Subject to subsection (4) below, an action to which this section applies shall not be competent unless it is commenced within the period of three years after the later of—
  (a) the date of death of the injured person;
  (b) the earliest date on which the person seeking to make (or a person who could at an earlier date have made) the claim was aware, or on which, in the opinion of the court, it was reasonably practicable for him in all the circumstances to become aware—
      (i) that there was a defect in the product;
      (ii) that the injuries of the deceased were caused (or partly caused) by the defect; and
      (iii) that the defender was a person liable for the damage under the said section 2.

(3) Where the person seeking to make the claim is a relative of the deceased, there shall be disregarded in the computation of the period mentioned in subsection (2) above any period during which that relative was under legal disability by reason of nonage or unsoundness of mind.

(4) Where an action to which section 22B of this Act applies has not been brought within the period mentioned in subsection (2) of that section and the person subsequently dies in consequence of his injuries, an action to which this section applies shall not be competent in respect of those injuries or that death.

(5) Where a person would be entitled, but for this section, to bring an action for reparation other than one in which the damages claimed are confined to damages for loss of or damage to property, the court may, if it seems to it equitable to do so, allow him to bring the action notwithstanding this section.

(6) In this section "relative" has the same meaning as in the Damages (Scotland) Act 1976.

(7) For the purposes of subsection (2)(b) above there shall be disregarded knowledge of whether particular facts and circumstances would or would not, as a matter of law, result in liability for damage under the said section 2.

Supplementary

Interpretation of this Part
22D.—(1) Expressions used in this Part and in Part I of the 1987 Act shall have the same meanings in this Part as in the said Part I.

(2) For the purposes of section 1(1) of the 1987 Act, this Part shall have effect and be construed as if it were contained in Part I of that Act.

(3) In this Part, "the 1987 Act" means the Consumer Protection Act 1987.

Amendments and repeals related to Part II
23. [Repealed by the Consumer Protection Act 1987 (c. 43), Sched. 1, para. 11.]

[1] PART III

SUPPLEMENTAL

NOTE
[1] Saved by the Administration of Justice Act 1982 (c. 53), s. 73(5).

Private international law application
[1] 23A.—(1) Where the substantive law of a country other than Scotland falls to be applied by a Scottish court as the law governing an obligation, the court shall apply any relevant rules of law of that country relating to the extinction of the obligation or the limitation of time within which proceedings may be brought to enforce the obligation to the exclusion of any corresponding rule of Scots law.

(2) This section shall not apply where it appears to the court that the application of the relevant foreign rule of law would be incompatible with the principles of public policy applied by the court.

(3) This section shall not apply in any case where the application of the corresponding rule of Scots law has extinguished the obligation, or barred the bringing of proceedings prior to the coming into force of the Prescription and Limitation (Scotland) Act 1984.

NOTE
[1] Inserted by the Prescription and Limitation (Scotland) Act 1984 (c. 45), s. 4, as regards proceedings commenced on or after 26th September 1984; *ibid.* s. 5(2).

The Crown
24. This Act binds the Crown.

Short title, commencement and extent
25.—(1) This Act may be cited as the Prescription and Limitation (Scotland) Act 1973.

[1](2) This Act shall come into operation, as follows:—
  (a) Parts II and III of this Act, Part II of Schedule 4 to this Act and Part II of Schedule 5 to this Act shall come into operation on the date on which this Act is passed;
  (b) except as aforesaid this Act shall come into operation on the expiration of three years from the said date.

(3) [Repealed by the Prescription and Limitation (Scotland) Act 1984, Sched. 2.]

(4) This Act extends to Scotland only.

NOTE
[1] As amended by the Prescription and Limitation (Scotland) Act 1984 (c. 45), Sched. 2.

SCHEDULES

SCHEDULE 1

OBLIGATIONS AFFECTED BY PRESCRIPTIVE PERIODS OF FIVE YEARS UNDER
SECTION 6

1. Subject to paragraph 2 below, section 6 of this Act applies—
   (a) to any obligation to pay a sum of money due in respect of a
       particular period—
       (i) by way of interest;
       (ii) by way of an instalment of an annuity;
       (iii) by way of feuduty or other periodical payment under a feu
             grant;
       (iv) by way of ground annual or other periodical payment under
            a contract of ground annual;
       (v) by way of rent or other periodical payment under a lease;
       (vi) by way of a periodical payment in respect of the occupancy
            or use of land, not being an obligation falling within any
            other provision of this sub-paragraph;
       (vii) by way of a periodical payment under a land obligation, not
             being an obligation falling within any other provision of this
             sub-paragraph;
   (b) to any obligation based on redress of unjustified enrichment,
       including without prejudice to that generality any obligation of
       restitution, repetition or recompense;
   (c) to any obligation arising from *negotiorum gestio*;
   (d) to any obligation arising from liability (whether arising from any
       enactment or from any rule of law) to make reparation;
   (e) to any obligation under a bill of exchange or a promissory note;
   (f) to any obligation of accounting, other than accounting for trust
       funds;
   (g) to any obligation arising from, or by reason of any breach of, a
       contract or promise, not being an obligation falling within any
       other provision of this paragraph.

2. Notwithstanding anything in the foregoing paragraph, section 6 of
this Act does not apply—
   (a) to any obligation to recognise or obtemper a decree of
       court, an arbitration award or an order of a tribunal or
       authority exercising jurisdiction under any enactment;
   (b) to any obligation a rising from the issue of a bank note;
   (c) [Repealed by the Requirements of Writing (Scotland) Act
       1995 (c. 7), Sched. 5 (effective August 1, 1995).]
   (d) to any obligation under a contract of partnership or of
       agency, not being an obligation remaining, or becoming,
       prestable on or after the termination of the relationship
       between the parties under the contract;
   (e) except as provided in paragraph 1(a) of this Schedule, to
       any obligation relating to land (including an obligation
       to recognise a servitude);
   (f) to any obligation to satisfy any claim to terce, courtesy,
       legitim, *jus relicti* or *jus relictae*, or to any prior right of a
       surviving spouse under section 8 or 9 of the Succession
       (Scotland) Act 1964;

(g) to any obligation to make reparation in respect of personal injuries within the meaning of Part II of this Act or in respect of the death of any person as a result of such injuries;

[1] (gg) to any obligation to make reparation or otherwise make good in respect of defamation within the meaning of section 18A of this Act;

[2] (ggg) to any obligation arising from liability under section 2 of the Consumer Protection Act 1987 (to make reparation for damage caused wholly or partly by a defect in a product);

(h) to any obligation specified in Schedule 3 to this Act as an imprescriptible obligation.

NOTES
[1] Inserted by the Law Reform (Miscellaneous Provisions) (Scotland) Act 1985 (c. 73), s. 12(5).
[2] Inserted by the Consumer Protection Act 1987 (c. 43), Sched. 1, para. 12.

3. [Repealed by the Requirements of Writing (Scotland) Act 1995 (c. 7), Sched. 5 (effective August 1, 1995).]

4. In this Schedule—
(a) "land obligation" has the same meaning as it has for the purposes of the Conveyancing and Feudal Reform (Scotland) Act 1970;
(b) [Repealed by the Requirements of Writing (Scotland) Act 1995 (c. 7), Sched. 5 (effective August 1, 1995).]

SCHEDULE 2

APPROPRIATE DATES FOR CERTAIN OBLIGATIONS FOR PURPOSES OF SECTION 6

1.—(1) This paragraph applies to any obligation, not being part of a banking transaction, to pay money in respect of—
(a) goods supplied on sale or hire, or
(b) services rendered,
in a series of transactions between the same parties (whether under a single contract or under several contracts) and charged on continuing account.

(2) In the foregoing sub-paragraph—
(a) any reference to the supply of goods on sale includes a reference to the supply of goods under a hire-purchase agreement, a credit-sale agreement or a conditional sale agreement as defined (in each case) by section 1 of the Hire-Purchase (Scotland) Act 1965; and
(b) any reference to services rendered does not include the work of keeping the account in question.

(3) Where there is a series of transactions between a partnership and another party, the series shall be regarded for the purposes of this

paragraph as terminated (without prejudice to any other mode of termination) if the partnership or any partner therein becomes bankrupt; but, subject to that, if the partnership (in the further provisions of this sub-paragraph referred to as "the old partnership") is dissolved and is replaced by a single new partnership having among its partners any person who was a partner in the old partnership, then, for the purposes of this paragraph, the new partnership shall be regarded as if it were identical with the old partnership.

(4) The appropriate date in relation to an obligation to which this paragraph applies is the date on which payment for the goods last supplied, or, as the case may be, the services last rendered, became due.

2.—(1) This paragraph applies to any obligation to repay the whole, or any part of, a sum of money lent to, or deposited with, the debtor under a contract of loan or, as the case may be, deposit.

(2) The appropriate date in relation to an obligation to which this paragraph applies is—

(a) if the contract contains a stipulation which makes provision with respect to the date on or before which repayment of the sum or, as the case may be, the part thereof is to be made, the date on or before which, in terms of that stipulation, the sum or part thereof is to be repaid; and

(b) if the contract contains no such stipulation, but a written demand for repayment of the sum, or, as the case may be, the part thereof, is made by or on behalf of the creditor to the debtor, the date when such demand is made or first made.

3.—(1) This paragraph applies to any obligation under a contract of partnership or of agency, being an obligation remaining, or becoming, prestable on or after the termination of the relationship between the parties under the contract.

(2) The appropriate date in relation to an obligation to which this paragraph applies is—

(a) if the contract contains a stipulation which makes provision with respect to the date on or before which performance of the obligation is to be due, the date on or before which, in terms of that stipulation, the obligation is to be performed; and

(b) in any other case the date when the said relationship terminated.

4.—(1) This paragraph applies to any obligation—

(a) to pay an instalment of a sum of money payable by instalments, or

(b) to execute any instalment of work due to be executed by instalments,

not being an obligation to which any of the foregoing paragraphs applies.

(2) The appropriate date in relation to an obligation to which this paragraph applies is the date on which the last of the instalments is due to be paid or, as the case may be, to be executed.

SCHEDULE 3

RIGHTS AND OBLIGATIONS WHICH ARE IMPRESCRIPTIBLE FOR THE PURPOSES OF SECTIONS 7 AND 8 AND SCHEDULE 1

The following are imprescriptible rights and obligations for the purposes of sections 7(2) and 8(2) of, and paragraph 2(h) of Schedule 1 to, this Act, namely—

(a) any real right of ownership in land:
(b) the right in land of the lessee under a recorded lease;
(c) any right exercisable as a *res merae facultatis*;
(d) any right to recover property *extra commercium*;
(e) any obligation of a trustee—
    (i) to produce accounts of the trustee's intromissions with any property of the trust;
    (ii) to make reparation or restitution in respect of any fraudulent breach of trust to which the trustee was a party or was privy;
    (iii) to make furthcoming to any person entitled thereto any trust property, or the proceeds of any such property, in the possession of the trustee, or to make good the value of any such property previously received by the trustee and appropriated to his own use;
(f) any obligation of a third party to make furthcoming to any person entitled thereto any trust property received by the third party otherwise than in good faith and in his possession;
(g) any right to recover stolen property from the person by whom it was stolen or from any person privy to the stealing thereof;
(h) any right to be served as heir to an ancestor or to take any steps necessary for making up or completing title to any interest in land.

SCHEDULE 4

Enactments Amended

Part I

Amendment Taking Effect on Expiration of three years from Passing of this Act

The Limitation (Enemies and War Prisoners) Act 1945

In subsection (1) of section 1, as substituted for Scotland by paragraph (a) of section 4, in the list of enactments appended to the subsection for the entries relating to the Acts of the Parliament of Scotland 1579 cap. 21, 1669 cap. 14 and 1695 cap. 7, and to section 37 of the Bills of Exchange (Scotland) Act 1772, there shall be substituted the words "section 6 of the Prescription and Limitation (Scotland) Act 1973".

[1] Part II

Amendments Taking Effect on Passing of this Act

NOTE
[1] As amended by the Prescription and Limitation (Scotland) Act 1984, Sched. 2.

The Carriage by Air Act 1961

In section 11(c), for the words "section six of the Law Reform (Limitation of Actions, &c.) Act 1954" there shall be substituted the words "section 17 of the Prescription and Limitation (Scotland) Act 1973".

The Law Reform (Miscellaneous Provisions) Act 1971

In section 4(2), for the words "section 6 of the Law Reform (Limitation of Actions, &c.) Act 1954" there shall be substituted the words "section 22(1) of the Prescription and Limitation (Scotland) Act 1973".

SCHEDULE 5

REPEALS

PART I

REPEALS COMING INTO FORCE ON EXPIRATION OF THREE YEARS FROM
PASSING OF THIS ACT

Chapter	Short title	Extent of Repeal
1469 c. 4.	The Prescription Act 1469.	The whole Act.
1474 c. 9.	The Prescription Act 1474.	The whole Act.
1579 c. 19.	The Prescription (Ejections) Act 1579.	The whole Act.
1579 c. 21.	The Prescription Act 1579.	The whole Act.
1594 c. 24.	The Prescription Act 1594.	The whole Act.
1617 c. 12.	The Prescription Act 1617.	The whole Act.
1617 c. 13.	The Reduction Act 1617.	The whole Act.
1669 c. 14.	The Prescription Act 1669.	The whole Act.
1669 c. 15.	The Interruptions Act 1669.	The whole Act.
1685 c. 14.	The Prescriptions Act 1685.	The whole Act.
1695 c. 7.	The Cautioners Act 1695.	The whole Act.
1696 c. 9.	The Prescription Act 1696.	The whole Act.
1696 c. 19.	The Interruptions Act 1696.	The whole Act.
12 Geo. 3. c. 72.	The Bills of Exchange (Scotland) Act 1772.	Sections 37, 39, 40.
31 & 32 Vict. c. 64.	The Land Writs Registration (Scotland) Act 1868.	Section 15.
45 & 46 Vict. c. 61.	The Bills of Exchange Act 1882.	In section 100, the words from "this section shall not apply" to the end of the section.
14 & 15 Geo. 5. c. 27.	The Conveyancing (Scotland) Act 1924.	Sections 16, 17.
1 & 2 Geo. 6. c. 24.	The Conveyancing Amendment (Scotland) Act 1938.	Section 4.
1969 c. 39.	The Age of Majority (Scotland) Act 1969.	In Schedule 1, the entry relating to the Prescription Act 1617.
1970 c. 35.	The Conveyancing and Feudal Reform (Scotland) Act	Section 8.

TABLE OF PRESCRIPTION OR LIMITATION PERIODS PROVIDED BY STATUTES OTHER THAN THE PRESCRIPTION AND LIMITATION (SCOTLAND) ACT 1973

The list of enactments which follows is not exhaustive, but the attempt has been made to include most provisions which are encountered reasonably frequently.

It is not stated anywhere in the 1973 Act that it is not to apply where other enactments establish a prescriptive or limitation period for specific rights or remedies. (By contrast, this is stated expressly in the English legislation, the Limitation Act 1980, s. 39.) Nonetheless, as a matter of general principles of statutory construction, it can be assumed that an enactment of a special nature takes precedence over an enactment of a general nature: the 1973 Act is therefore displaced by more specific provision in other enactments.

The list which follows is grouped loosely according to subject-matter, except that groups 3 and 7 are miscellaneous. The groups are:

1. Companies;
2. Carriage;
3. Miscellaneous breaches of statutory duty;
4. Employment and discrimination;
5. Taxation and social security;
6. Planning;
7. Miscellaneous statutory procedures; and
8. European Community law.

Act	Type of action	Start of limitation period	Limitation period
1. Companies			
Companies Act 1985			
s. 5(3)	Application to cancel alteration to memorandum	Date resolution to alter memorandum was passed	21 days
s. 54(3)	Application to cancel resolution to reregister a public company as a private company	Date resolution for re-registration was passed	28 days
s. 92	Action to recover loss caused by breach of pre-emption rights	Date of delivery to registrar of companies of return of allotment (or date of grant for non-equities)	2 years
s. 157(3)	Application to cancel resolution authorising financial assistance for purchasing of shares	Date resolution authorising financial assistance was passed	28 days
s. 176	Application to cancel resolution approving payment out of capital for redemption or purchase of company's shares	Date resolution was passed	5 weeks
s. 651	Application to declare a dissolution of a company void	Date of dissolution	2 years
s. 653	Application to restore to register a company struck off the register as defunct	Date of publication in *Gazette* of s. 652 notice	20 years

Companies (Tables A to F) Regulations 1985, Table A, Art. 108	Action to recover dividends declared but not paid	Date payment was due	12 years
Company Directors Disqualification Act 1986 s. 7	Application for a disqualification order	Date company became insolvent	2 years (except with leave of the court)

2. Carriage

Carriage by Air Act 1961 Sched. 1, Art. 29	Damages for loss of life, personal injury, loss of baggage or cargo	Date of arrival at destination or date aircraft should have arrived, or date carriage stopped	2 years
Carriage of Goods by Road Act 1965 Sched., Art. 32	Action under Convention on Contract for the International Carriage of Goods by Road	In case of partial loss, damage or delay: date of delivery. In case of total loss: 30 days after expiry of agreed time-limit or 60 days after goods were taken over by carrier. In all other cases: 3 months after making of contract	1 year (3 years in case of wilful misconduct)
Carriage of Goods by Sea Act 1971 Sched. 1, Art. III, para. 6	Loss of or damage to goods	Date of delivery or date when goods should have been delivered	1 year
Carriage of Passengers by Road Act 1974 Sched., Art. 22	Death of or personal injury to passenger	Date person sustaining injury had or should have had knowledge if it	3 years (subject to limitation of 5 years from date of accident); period may be extended by court
	Other action arising out of carriage	Date vehicle arrived at destination or, in case of non-arrival, date it ought to have arrived	1 year

Act	Type of action	Start of limitation period	Limitation period
International Transport Conventions Act 1983	Death of or personal injury to passenger	Day after accident or, if injured person has died, day after death	3 years (subject to limitation of 5 years from date of accident); period may be extended by the court
Merchant Shipping Act 1995 s. 190(3)	Loss or damage to property, cargo or other ship, or loss of life or personal injury, caused by fault of ship	Date of loss or injury	2 years
s. 224 and Sched. 11, Pt I, Art. 23	Claim under International Convention on Salvage 1989	Date salvage operations terminate	2 years (not applicable to claim for indemnity)
ss. 183 and 184 and Sched. 6, Pt I, Art. 16	Death or personal injury of passenger or loss of or damage to luggage	Date of disembarkation or date disembarkation should have taken place (for personal injuries or death); whichever is later of date disembarkation was due or took place (for loss of or damage to luggage)	2 years (for death after disembarkation, a maximum of 3 years)

3. Miscellaneous breaches of statutory duty

Act	Type of action	Start of limitation period	Limitation period
Game (Scotland) Act 1832 s. 17	Action arising from trespass on land for game	Date of trespass	6 months
Limitation of Actions and Costs Act 1842 s. 5	Action for anything done under a local or personal Act of Parliament	Date of act complained of	2 years (or, where damage continues, 1 year from its cessation)

Foreign Jurisdiction Act 1890 s. 13	Action against any person for anything done under the Act or an order made under it	Date of act complained of, or date continuing act ceased, or date parties came within the jurisdiction of the court	6 months
Nuclear Installations Act 1965 s. 15	Claim for compensation for breach of statutory duty	Date of occurrence or last in series of occurrences	30 years
	Claim for loss injury or damage caused by an occurrence involving nuclear matter stolen from or lost or abandoned by a person under statutory duty	Date of theft, loss or abandonment	20 years
Forestry Act 1967 s. 11(3)	Claim for compensation for deterioration owing to refusal of felling licence	If trees not felled, date claim for compensation arose; otherwise date of felling	10 years if trees not felled; 1 year if trees felled
Sewerage (Scotland) Act 1968 s. 20(3)	Claim for compensation for loss injury or damage sustained by reason of exercise of statutory powers	Date loss injury or damage occurred	12 months (to be increased to 24 months when Local Government etc. (Scotland) Act 1994, Sched. 13, para. 75(17)(b) comes into force)
Post Office Act 1969 s. 30	Claim for loss of or damage to registered inland packet	Date of postage	12 months
Merchant Shipping (Oil Pollution) Act 1971 s. 9	Damage caused by discharge from ship of persistent oil	Date claim for damage caused by discharge of oil arose	3 years (subject to limit of 6 years after the occurrence or first occurrence resulting in the discharge)

Act	Type of action	Start of limitation period	Limitation period
Licensing (Scotland) Act 1976 s. 130	Claim against sheriffs and other officials on account of anything done in execution of the Act	Date the claim arose	2 months
4. Employment and discrimination			
Equal Pay Act 1970 s. 2	Claim for equal pay for work of equal value	Termination of employment in question	6 months
Employment Rights Act 1996 s. 111	Complaint of unfair dismissal	Effective date of termination	3 months (may be extended)
Sex Discrimination Act 1975 s. 76	Complaint of discrimination in employment (s. 63);	Date act complained of was done	3 months (may be extended)
	in other cases		6 months (8 months in education-related cases)
	Enforcement action by Equal Opportunities Commission in relation to breach of ss. 38–40 (discriminatory advertising, etc.)		6 months
	Interdict against further breach of ss. 38–40		5 years
	Application to Equal Opportunities Commission for preliminary finding of discrimination (s. 73)	Date act complained of was done	6 months (may be extended)

Race Relations Act 1976 s. 68	Complaint of discrimination in employment	Date act complained of was done	3 months (may be extended)
	in other cases		6 months (8 months in education-related cases)
	Enforcement action by Commission for Racial Equality in relation to breach of ss. 29–31 (discriminatory advertising, etc.)		6 months
	Interdict against further breach of ss. 29–31		5 years
	Application by Commission for Racial Equality for preliminary finding of discrimination		6 months
Disability Discrimination Act 1995 s. 8 and Sched. 3 para. 3	Complaint of discrimination in employment	Date act complained of was done	3 months (may be extended)
	in other areas		6 months
5. Taxation and social security			
Taxes Management Act 1970 s. 33(1)	Claim for relief on grounds of error against excessive assessment to income or capital gains tax	January 31 next following the year of assessment to which the return relates	5 years
s. 33A	Claim for relief by partners for excessive tax paid due to error in partnership statement	Filing date	5 years
s. 34(1)	Assessment to income and capital gains tax	January 31 next following the year of assessment to which the return relates	5 years

Act	Type of action	Start of limitation period	Limitation period
s. 40	Assessment to tax on personal representatives	January 31 next following the year of assessment in which the deceased died	3 years
s. 43	Claim for relief against income or capital gains tax	January 31 next following the end of the accounting period to which it relates	5 years, where no longer or shorter period is provided elsewhere in the Taxes Acts
Social Security (Claims and Payments) Regulations 1987 reg. 19 and Sched. 4, para. 1	Claim for jobseekers' allowance	Day in respect of which claim is made	That day
Sched. 4, para. 2	Claim for sickness or invalidity benefit or severe disablement allowance	Day in respect of which claim is made	1 month (for original claim); otherwise 6 days for first claim or 10 days for continuing claim
reg. 19(6)(a)	Claim for guardian's allowance, child benefit, increase in benefit in respect of dependant	Day on which claimant is entitled	6 months
reg. 19(6)(b)	Claim for retirement pension, widow's benefit, maternity allowance, invalid care allowance	Day on which claimant is entitled	12 months
Sched. 4, para. 3	Claim for disablement benefit	Day on which claimant is entitled	3 months
Sched. 4, para. 6	Claim for income support or family credit	Day in respect of which claim is made	That day
Sched. 4, para. 8	Claim for social fund payments for maternity expenses	Date of confinement	3 months

Sched. 4, para. 9	Claim for social fund payments for funeral expenses	Date of funeral	3 months
Sched. 4, para. 11	Claim for disability working allowance	Day in respect of which claim is made	That day

6. Planning

Town and Country Planning (Scotland) Act 1997, s. 124(1) and (2)	Enforcement notice by planning authority in relation to (a) operations on land or (b) change of use to a dwelling-house	In (a) date of substantial completion of operation; in (b) date of breach of planning control	4 years
s. 124(3)	Enforcement notice by planning authority for any other breach of planning control	Date of breach of planning control	10 years

7. Miscellaneous statutory procedures

Acquisition of Land (Authorisation Procedure)(Scotland) Act 1947 Sched. 1, paras 15 and 16	Challenge to validity of compulsory purchase order or any provision in it	Date on which notice of the confirmation or making of the order or giving of the certificate is published	6 weeks
Uniform Laws on International Sales Act 1967 Arts 39 and 40	Notice of non-conformity of goods to contract description	Date of handover of goods	2 years (but notice must in any event be given promptly)
Parliamentary Commissioner Act 1967 s. 6(3)	Complaint made to member of parliament of maladministration by government department	Date on which complainer first had notice of matter complained of	12 months (may be extended in special circumstances)
Presumption of Death (Scotland) Act 1977 s. 5	Order varying the effect on property of a declarator of death	Date of declarator	5 years

Act	Type of action	Start of limitation period	Limitation period
Matrimonial Homes (Family Protection) (Scotland) Act 1981 s. 6(3)(f)	Enforcement of occupancy rights in a matrimonial home	Where the entitled spouse has permanently ceased to be entitled to occupy the home, the date on which the non-entitled spouse ceased to occupy it	5 years
Representation of the People Act 1983 s. 78	Claim against candidate or election agent in respect of election expenses	Date result of election is declared	14 days
s. 129	Petition questioning an election under the Local Government Acts	Date election held	21 days
Law Reform (Miscellaneous Provisions)(Scotland) Act 1985 s. 9	Action to reduce an order rectifying a defectively expressed document, or for compensation	Date of order rectifying the document	5 years, or 2 years from the date the order came to the pursuer's notice, whichever is earlier
Bankruptcy (Scotland) Act 1985 s. 8	Petition for sequestration	Date of apparent insolvency	4 months (except for debtor or trustee under trust deed)
Copyright, Designs and Patents Act 1988 ss. 113 and 203	Action for delivery up of material infringing copyright or performance rights	Date the infringing copy or recording was made	6 years (subject to extension on grounds of fraud or disability)

8. European Community law

[Note: for details such as extensions of time on account of distance (10 days in the case of the U.K.; and official holidays, see *Butterworths European Court Practice* (1993), Chap. 13.]

Treaty of Rome Art. 173	Annulment of Community measure	Date of publication of measure, or of its notification to pursuer, or on which it came to pursuer's notice	2 months
Art. 175	Failure by Community institution to act in accordance with Treaty obligation	The last day of a 2-month period starting with the date on which the Community institution was called upon to act and ending without the Community institution having defined its position	2 months
Art. 215; Protocol on the Statute of the Court of Justice of the European Economic Community, Art. 43	Non-contractual claim against Community	Date of event giving rise to the liability	5 years
E.C. reg. 2988/74, Art. 1	Power of Commission to impose fine or penalty for infringement of E.C. rules on transport or competition	Date the infringement was committed or, if it was a continuing infringement, date it ceased	3 years in the case of applications, notifications of undertakings or associations, requests for information or carrying out of investigations; 5 years in all other cases

INDEX